Guidebook for
MARINES

Eighteenth Revised Edition
Third Printing, June 2006

Published by the Marine Corps Association
Quantico, VA

Guidebook for
MARINES

Eighteenth Revised Edition

Published by the Marine Corps Association
Quantico, VA

PREFACE AND ACKNOWLEDGEMENTS

Once again the Marine Corps Association is proud to publish a revised edition of the *Guidebook for Marines*. This, the eighteenth edition, contains the most current information available at the time of printing on those subjects considered essential for Marines to sustain their professional skills.

A text such as the *Guidebook* cannot have validity without input from the experts. The assistance received from those of The Basic School, The Staff N.C.O. Academy and Marksmanship Training Unit of the Marine Corps Combat Development Command (MCCDC) was invaluable. So also was the excellent cooperation of the many Marines at Quantico who on short notice posed for many of the still photos contained herein. Special thanks to Majors Mike Ettore and Jim Desy, and Colonel J. Greenwood, Colonel Bill White, and Colonel Lou Piantadosi of the MCA staff. Lastly, were the many hours of detailed work by members of the MCA Graphics Department: Jon Dodd, Charli Jackson, Isabella Wade, and Pamela Ward. Ron Lunn did the new photography and scanning, typing was performed by Betty Allen and editing was done by Sharla Desy. Special thanks, also, to the production coordinator on the printing end, Don Beville.

A Marine Corps Association service, one dedicated to all Marines, past, present and future.

Quantico, Virginia
November 2001

Les Palm
MajGen, US Marine Corps (Ret)
President and CEO
Marine Corps Association

Copyright 2001, by the Marine Corps Association
Printed in the United States of America
ISBN 0-940328-07-0

All readers, particularly training officers and NCOs, are encouraged to report discrepancies which may occur as a result of major policy changes, new weapons being adopted or new concepts of military operation. Address your correspondence to:

The Guidebook Editor
Marine Corps Association
Box 1775
Quantico, VA 22134

Table of Contents

Chapter One

What is the Corps?

The United States Marine Corps is America's amphibious force-in-readiness. This role stems from the country's position as a maritime nation with worldwide interests.

Marines and the Marine mission have long been associated with the sea and with amphibious capability. The word "marine" itself comes from the Latin marinus, meaning "related to the sea." The "amphibious" comes from the Greek amphibion – literally, "living a double life."

Marines today have a dual responsibility. To serve on land, sea and in the air; and to develop and exploit the advantages of readiness and amphibious capability.

The capability to project seapower ashore is an essential element of national strategy. In the words of the military historian, B.H. Liddel Hart, "Amphibious flexibility is the greatest strategic asset that a seabased power possesses." This strategic flexibility is based upon the ability to conduct amphibious operations, a task the Marine Corps is expressly charged with by the Congress.

Marine amphibious forces, operating with the fleet, provide the nation's only major capability to forcibly enter any hostile area from the sea. They can proceed without interruption from a naval to land campaign with the ability to build up a strong fighting force. They are a combined force having all the elements of combat power.

Their versatility and responsiveness lend a significant dimension to the options available to the National Command Authority in time of crisis.

Today's Marine Corps emphasizes three fundamentals: readiness, versatility and the totally integrated capabilities of the Marine air-ground team. Operational readiness is the Marines' top priority. It is the cornerstone of the Marine Corps' existence as a fighting military organization.

Versatility refers to the Marines' method of tailoring air-ground teams in size, structure and striking power to meet worldwide needs. It ensures, too, that Marine forces will remain flexible enough at all times "to perform such other duties as the President may direct…" a mission deliberately expressed in general terms to permit the Marines to respond swiftly, when needed, as a general purpose force.

The air-ground team demonstrates a concept pioneered by the Marine Corps. Marine air power is included not as a supplement to the organic firepower of the ground combat elements, but as a fully integrated component of the Marine air-ground team.

This capability greatly enhances the combat effectiveness of Marine air-ground task forces and their total response to any situation. It is consistent with the Marines' primary mission as stated in the National Security Act: "…to provide fleet marine forces of combined arms together with supporting air components, for service with the fleet…"

The great majority of Marines still come from the sea and return by way of the sea in training and deployments, in amphibious landings, in crisis situations and in combat.

So, today, as in the past, Marines must and do cast a constant eye seaward…and beyond.

Mission

Like the other Armed Services within the Department of Defense, the Marine Corps has specific roles and missions authorized by statute.

The present structure, missions and functions of the Marine Corps are set forth in the National Security Act of 1947 as amended. This act states that the Marine Corps' minimum peacetime structure shall consist of "…not less than three combat divisions and three aircraft wings, and such other land combat, aviation and other services as may be organic therein…" In addition, the Marine Corps maintains a fourth Marine division and aircraft wing in reserve.

To carry out its missions, the Marine Corps is periodically authorized personnel strength levels which will permit it to maintain the forces stipulated by the National Security Act. During peacetime, these strength levels have remained essentially the same since 1953, providing an active duty strength of around 175,000 Marines. In addition, the Marine Corps Reserve maintains a strength of approximately 103,000.

Beginning with their primary mission, the following specified missions have been assigned the Marines.

The first mission is to provide Marine air and ground forces for service with the fleet as landing forces in the conduct of amphibious assault operations. This mission reflects the Marine Corps' statutory role as America's force-in-readiness and calls into play the full resources of the Navy and the Marine Corps operating together.

Using Navy combat power and Marine air and surface landing forces, a fully integrated amphibious assault can be carried out. This type of operation is considered the most powerful conventional option that can be used against a well-organized enemy coastal defense.

As demonstrated by the Marines, amphibious assault is a combined surface and helicopter operation, capitalizing on the best features of the surface landing craft and the helicopter. It is totally compatible with the amphibious assault shipping organic to the fleet.

The amphibious assault also remains one of the most difficult and dangerous forms of warfare. Critics have suggested that no amphibious assault could succeed in the face of modern weaponry and, specifically, in the event of a nuclear attack. Any assault, however – whether land, sea, air or amphibious – is difficult in a high-threat environment.

"That the marine corps,... shall, any time, be liable to do duty in the forts and garrisons of the United States, on the seacoast, or any other duty on shore, as the President, at his discretion, shall direct."

It is for this reason that amphibious operations must be conducted where they are possible – not where they are impossible. The Navy-Marine partnership gives Marine forces aboard amphibious ships the geographic flexibility they need to be selective.

To execute an assault landing successfully requires extreme skill, intensive training and the highest possible measure of coordination among the many different elements of the amphibious task force. It is costly, but in addition to its major objectives, it produces a range of other capabilities – to conduct rescue missions or show of force in a situation that could otherwise escalate into a major crisis.

The second mission is the oldest Marine Corps mission – duty afloat aboard armed vessels of the Navy.

The third mission is to develop in coordination with other services, the tactics, techniques and equipment for landing forces in amphibious operations. It is a logical extension of the primary mission and establishes the Marine Corps' distinct responsibility toward the other Armed Services.

The fourth mission is to be prepared for wartime expansion in accordance with Joint Mobilization Plans. It is common to all the Armed Services. Simply stated, mobilization plans require the activation of Marine reserve forces.

The fifth mission is to perform such other duties as the President may direct. As noted earlier, this mission was deliberately expressed in general terms in the National Security Act. It permits the President to call upon Marines as a ready force in times of crisis. The Marine Corps is the only one of the Armed Services assigned such a mission by law.

Before passage of the Act of 1947, the statutory basis for Marine Corps missions had been expressed only in very general terms in the Act of 1798. That earlier law established the Marine Corps as a separate service with these duties: "That the detachments of the corps of marines... shall be made in lieu of the respective quotas of marines, which have been established or authorized for the frigates, and other armed vessels and gallies, which shall be employed in the service of the United States; and the President of the United States may detach and appoint such of the officers of the marine corps, to act on board the frigates, and any of the armed vessels of the United States, respectively, as he shall, from time to time, judge necessary."

"That the marine corps,... shall, any time, be liable to do duty in the forts and garrisons of the United States, on the seacoast, or any other duty on shore, as the President, at his discretion, shall direct."

Justification for assigning Marines to duty on both land and sea was based on the desire of Congress to usefully employ the Marines when they were "occasionally" on shore.

This law, with minor changes, remained the only legal authority for Marine Corps missions for 149 years. Under its broad provisions, Marine Corps roles and missions evolved through necessity.

But for those first Marines, service afloat, amphibious operations and land warfare in support of the Army were the primary missions. Each of these missions was performed with great credit for the fledgling United States. Each set a precedent. Each took its place in American history and tradition; and each, even at present, is still a mission of the Marine Corps.

Organization and Function

The overall organization of the Marine Corps falls into two broad categories: the operating forces and the supporting establishment. Together they comprise more than 90 percent of the total strength of the Marine Corps.

Operating Forces

Marine Security Forces. Marines provide approximately 3,400 Marines to the Marine Corps Security Forces (MCSF) who protect key naval installations and facilities worldwide. Although not assigned to combatant commands, they are part of the operating forces of the Marine Corps. These security forces include Marine barracks and Marine security force companies in the continental United States (CONUS) and abroad.

Marine Security Guard Detachments. Additionally, The Marine Security Guard battalion provides forces to the Department of State for embassy security. These Marines are currently assigned to more than 120 diplomatic posts in 115 countries throughout the world.

Fleet Marine Forces. In 1992 Marine Corps componency was established and Marine Corps component commanders, who are referred to as the Commander, Marine Corps Forces (COMMARFOR), were assigned or designated for each of the five geographic combatant commands. Fleet Marine Forces Atlantic (FMFLANT) and Fleet Marine Forces Pacific (FMFPAC) were redesignated Marine Corps Forces Atlantic (MARFORLANT) and Marine Corps Forces Pacific (MARFORPAC), respectively, and assumed the missions and responsibilities of Service component commands. Headquarters, Fleet Marine Forces Europe (FMFEUR), was redesignated Headquarters, Marine Corps Forces Europe (MARFOREUR). Marine Corps component planning liaison cells were established in Central Command (CENTCOM) and Southern Command (SOUTHCOM).

In addition to providing Marine Corps representation to each combatant command, these Marine Corps components have assumed many of the administrative and logistic requirements previously performed by Marine Corps forces. This change allowed the Marine Corps component's assigned MAGTF to concentrate on combat operations. The new joint force organization, supported by the activation of Marine Corps components, significantly changed the operational environment in which Marine Corps forces deployed and operated. Marine Corps forces are also provided to naval commands by the Marine Corps component commander who may also perform the duties of a Fleet Marine Forces commanding general with the status of a naval type commander. Assignments as a commander, Marine Corps forces, and commanding general, Fleet Marine Forces, have separate, distinct command relationships and missions. For example, Commander, MARFORPAC—the Marine Corps component commander—provides Marine Corps forces to the Commander in Chief, U.S. Pacific Command. As the Commanding General, Fleet Marine Forces Pacific—naval type commander status—Commander, MARFORPAC, provides Marine air-ground task forces to the Commander, U.S. Pacific Fleet. The Marine Forces contain both ground and aviation combat elements, and combat service support elements. These elements are the Marine Division, the Marine Aircraft Wing (MAW), and the Force Service Support Group (FSSG).

Marine Division: The mission of the Marine division is to execute amphibious assault operations and such other operations as may be directed. The Marine division must be able to provide the ground amphibious forcible-entry capability to an amphibious task force (ATF) and conduct subsequent land operations in any operational environment. The division commander fights by using combined-arms tactics and tailors the force to the demands of each mission. The division is composed of a headquarters, infantry and artillery regiments; and tank, amphibious assault vehicle, light armored infantry, and combat engineer battalions; with approximately 18,000 personnel and over 1,000 combat vehicles.

Marine Aircraft Wing: The MAW is task organized to provide a flexible and balanced aviation organization that is capable of providing the full range of aviation operations in a variety of areas without the requirement for prepositioned support, control, and logistical facilities. The MAW is the smallest unit with the inherent capability of performing all six functions of Marine aviation. The wing is composed of a headquarters, a control group, a support group, and fixed- and rotary-wing aviation groups, with approximately 18,000 personnel and 350 aircraft. Aviation organizations smaller than a wing can provide the capabilities to accomplish any or all of the six aviation functions by using task organization.

Force Service Support Group. The FSSG is a composite grouping of functional components that provides CSS above the organic capability of supported units to all elements of the MEF. In this respect, it is structured to support, in garrison or deployed, a one-division/one-wing-configured MEF. All elements of the FSSG are structured to provide permanently organized sub elements to support independently deployed battalions, regiments, MEUs (i.e., task-organized groups to provide support, as required and preplanned), or geographically separated units in garrison. The FSSG CE provides general and direct support and sustained CSS above the organic capabilities of supported elements of MAGTFs in the functional areas of CSS during deployment and employment of the MEF and smaller, geographically separated MAGTFs in all levels of conflict. The FSSG includes approximately 9,000 personnel and thousands of pieces of support equipment.

Supporting establishment

This includes recruiting, training, research and development, administration, and the logistical support required for Marines to perform their mission.

Marine Air-Ground Task Forces

The MAGTF is the Marine Corps' principle organization for the conduct of all missions across the range of military operations. MAGTFs are balanced, combined-arms forces with organic ground, aviation, and sustainment elements. They are flexible, task-organized forces that can respond rapidly to a contingency anywhere in the world and are able to conduct a variety of missions.

Although organized and equipped to participate as part of naval expeditionary forces, MAGTFs also have the capability to conduct sustained operations ashore. The MAGTF provides a combatant commander or other operational commander with a versatile expeditionary force that is capable of responding to a broad range of crisis and conflict situations. MAGTFs are organized, trained, and equipped to perform missions ranging from humanitarian assistance to peacekeeping to intense combat and can operate in permissive, uncertain, and hostile environments. They may be shore- or sea-based in support of joint and multinational major operations and/or campaigns. MAGTFs deploy as amphibious, air-contingency, or maritime prepositioning forces (MPFs),

either as part of a naval expeditionary force or via strategic lift. They can present a minimal or a highly visible presence and are able to project combat power ashore in measured degrees or can provide secure staging areas ashore for follow-on forces. MAGTFs are prepared for immediate deployment overseas into austere operating environments, bringing all means necessary to accomplish the mission. When deployed aboard amphibious shipping, MAGTFs maintain a continuous presence at strategic locations around the globe and can be rapidly moved to and indefinitely stationed at the scene of potential trouble. The MAGTF provides the JFC with the capability of reconstitution, which is the ability of an expeditionary force to regenerate, reorganize, replenish, and reorient itself for a new mission without having to return to its home base. MAGTF operations are built on a foundation of six special core competencies: expeditionary readiness, combined-arms operations, expeditionary operations, sea based operations, forcible entry from the sea, and Reserve integration. To carry out their mission, MARFOR must be—

- Organized, trained, and equipped for combat essential to the prosecution of a naval campaign to seize objectives against the best and most modern equipped enemy.
- A balanced force of combined arms and services.
- Primarily trained, organized, and equipped for offensive employment.
- Adaptable to the active defense of advanced naval bases.
- Trained, equipped, and ready for prompt and effective employment in any climate or terrain.
- Trained and equipped for airborne operations as required, in accordance with policies and doctrines of the JCS.
- Provided with sufficient organic CSS capability to establish and sustain combat power in the execution of normal missions and capable of supporting—
  o Supply.
  o Maintenance.
  o Transportation.
  o Deliberate engineering.
  o Services.
  o Health services.
  o Provided with organic aviation units primarily organized, trained, and equipped to operate in conjunction with ground units in amphibious operations and capable of performing—

4

- Offensive air support (OAS).
- Antiair warfare (AW).
- Assault support.
- Air reconnaissance.
- Electronic warfare (EW).
- Control of aircraft and missiles.

Although MAGTFs are task organized, each MAGTF, regardless of its size or mission, has the same basic structure. Each MAGTF has four core elements: a CE, a ground combat element (GCE), an aviation combat element (ACE), and a CSS element (CSSE). The CE is the MAGTF headquarters. It is task organized to provide command and control capabilities (including intelligence and communications) necessary for effective planning, direction, and execution of all operations. The GCE is task organized to conduct ground operations in support of the MAGTF mission. It is normally formed around an infantry organization reinforced with requisite artillery, reconnaissance, armor, and engineer forces and can vary in size and composition from a rifle platoon to one or more Marine divisions.

The ACE is task-organized to support the MAGTF mission by performing some or all of the six functions of Marine aviation. The ACE is normally built around an aviation organization that is augmented with appropriate air command and control, combat, combat support, and CSS units. The ACE can operate effectively from ships, expeditionary airfields, or austere forward operating sites and can readily and routinely transition between sea bases and expeditionary airfields without loss of capability. The ACE can vary in size and composition from an aviation detachment with specific capabilities to one or more MAWs.

The CSSE is task organized to provide the full range of CSS functions and capabilities needed to support the continued readiness and sustainability of the MAGTF as a whole. It is formed around a CSS headquarters and may vary in size and composition from a support detachment to one or more Marine FSSGs.

Marine Expeditionary Force

The MEF is the principal Marine Corps warfighting organization. It is capable of missions across the range of military operations, through amphibious assault and sustained operations ashore in any environment. With appropriate augmentation, the MEF CE is capable of performing as a JTF headquarters. There are three standing MEFs: I Marine Expeditionary Force (I MEF), based in southern California and Arizona; II Marine Expeditionary Force (II MEF), based in North and South Carolina; and III Marine Expeditionary Force (III MEF), based in Japan and Hawaii. Each standing MEF consists of a permanent CE and one Marine division, MAW, and FSSG.

Marine Expeditionary Unit
(Special Operations Capable)

The Marine expeditionary unit (special operations capable (MEU (SOC)) is the standard forward deployed Marine expeditionary organization. Marine Corps Forces Atlantic and Pacific maintain forward-deployed MEUs (SOC) in the Mediterranean Sea, the western Pacific, and the Indian Ocean or Arabian Gulf region. The MEU (SOC) can be thought of both as a self-contained operating force capable of missions of limited scope and duration and as a forward-deployed extension of the Marine Expeditionary Force. MEUs routinely receive special training before deploying that results in their being designated as "special operations capable." To receive the certification, the MEU undergoes an intensive 26-week, standardized predeployment training program that includes an exercise and a final evaluation. The MEU must demonstrate competence across the entire spectrum of required capabilities, be able to plan and execute any assigned mission within six hours of notification, and conduct multiple missions simultaneously. These MEUs are augmented with selected personnel and equipment to provide enhanced conventional and selected maritime special operations capabilities. There are seven standing MEU (SOC) CEs. Residing within I MEF are the 11th, 13th, and 15th MEUs (SOC); residing within II MEF are the 22nd, 24th, and 26th MEUs (SOC); residing within III MEF is the 31st MEU (SOC). Although each MEU (SOC) is task organized, a typical MEU (SOC) includes—

- A standing CE.
- An infantry battalion reinforced with artillery, reconnaissance, engineer, armor, assault amphibian units, and other detachments as required.
- A reinforced helicopter squadron with transport, utility, and attack helicopters, a detachment of vertical/short takeoff and landing (V/STOL) fixed-wing attack aircraft, and other detachments as required.
- A task-organized CSSE.

Special Purpose
Marine Air-Ground Task Force

A special-purpose MAGTF (SPMAGTF) is a non-standing MAGTF temporarily formed to conduct a specific mission. It is normally formed when a standing MAGTF is either inappropriate or unavailable. SPMAGTFs are organized, trained, and equipped to conduct a wide variety of missions ranging from crisis response, to regionally focused training exercises, to peacetime missions. Their SPMAGTF designation derives from the mission they are assigned, the location in which they will operate, or the name of the exercise in which they will participate (e.g., "SPMAGTF (X)," "SPMAGTF Somalia," "SPMAGTF UNITAS," "SPMAGTF Andrew," etc.). A SPMAGTF may be any size, but normally it is the size of a MEU (or smaller) with narrowly focused capabilities chosen to accomplish a particular mission. It may be task organized deliberately from the assets of a standing MEF, or may be formed on a contingency basis from an already-deployed MAGTF to perform an independent, rapid-response mission of limited scope and duration. By definition, SPMAGTFs include all four of the basic elements of a MAGTF.

Marine Expeditionary Brigade

The Marine Expeditionary Brigade (MEB) bridges the gap between the MEU at the tip of the spear and the MEF, our principal warfighter. These three MAGTFs provide the JFC a seamless scalability of combat power through the range of military operations. The MEB is not a new concept. For part of Marine Corps history, Marine Air-Ground Task Forces, organized as Brigades, have been employed from Korea through Desert Storm. Nonetheless, standing MEB Command Elements were eliminated in the early 1990s as part of a force structure reduction. Certain personnel and assets within each MEF were designated to deploy as a MEF Forward and assume the role of our traditional MEB command element. While a viable concept, the MEF forward did not fully define or place adequate emphasis on this mid-size organization. Over the past few years, the USMC has lost visibility and identity of this warfighting organization.

Though personnel constraints still prevent the USMC from having a full time stand-alone MEB command element, the Commandant has directed each MEF Commander to form a MEB command element that will be embedded within the MEF.

1st, 2d and 3d MEB have been activated in I, II and III MEF, respectively. The MEB is an inherently expeditionary combined arms team that provides the JTF commander robust command and control and the full range of military operational capabilities.

Operating literally in "every climate and place," Marines take part in cold-weather training in Europe and Korea, as well as a variety of multination exercises in other parts of the world.

Task organized the MEB is capable of rapid deployment and employment via a variety of means. It is important to note, since the MEB is tactically tailored, the need for strategic lift is minimized as it only brings into theater the required capabilities to accomplish the mission. The mission of the MEB is to plan, coordinate, and conduct sustainable combined arms combat and other expeditionary operations across the spectrum of conflict, including such tasks as: forcible entry; deploy to CINC' s Area of Responsibility (AOR) as part of Joint or Combined Force; provide a nucleus JTF HQ; enable follow-on forces; be prepared to act as the Marine Corps Service Component; be prepared to serve as the lead echelon of a MEF.

The MEB provides combatant commanders with an extremely flexible force, which is normally built around a ground combat element of a reinforced infantry regiment, supported by aviation and combat service support elements. The MEB Command Element is the MAGTF headquarters. As with all other elements of the MAGTF, it is task organized to provide command, control and coordination essential for effective planning and execution of operations by the other elements of the MEB. The Command Element contains detachments of the MEF Headquarters Group, Marine Liaison Element, Radio Battalion, and Force Reconnaissance Company.

The MEB GCE is task organized to conduct ground operations to support the MEB mission. It is normally formed around an infantry regiment reinforced with requisite artillery, reconnaissance, armor and engineer forces. The MEB's ACE is task organized to perform those functions of Marine Corps Aviation required to support the MAGTF mission. It is composed of a composite Marine Aircraft Group which can consist of Fixed and Rotary Wing Squadrons, Marine Air Control Groups, Unmanned Aerial Vehicle squadron, and a Tactical Air Control Center and supporting agencies.

The MEB's Brigade Service Support Group is task organized to provide the full range of combat service support functions and capabilities necessary to support the MAGTF mission, such as enabling the flow of follow-on forces through ports and airfields. It is important to note that the MEB comes into theater with 30 days organic sustainment. Service functions include such things as security (military police), messing, postal, disbursing, and legal, etc. The MEB is commanded by a general officer, and brings increased command and control capabilities, for operations in the joint environment, over that of a typically deployed MEU and significantly expanded battlespace functions and capabilities. The MEB brings into theater Contingency Theaters Aviation Planning Software, (CTAPS) and the Global Command and Control System (GCCS.) The MEB fulfills the gap between our existing MEUs and our warfighting MEF. Versatile MAGTFs will allow JFC to shape the strategic environment and respond to regional challenges with a scalable, inherently flexible, combined arms force that is capable of operating across the spectrum of conflict. Additionally, the MEB can be paired with Maritime Prepositioned Force (MPF) shipping assets. This combination provides the CINC a power projection capability that minimizes global response time. MPF Squadrons are strategically based around deployed MEU/MEB operating areas in the Med, Persian Gulf, and the Indian and Pacific Oceans. MPF combines the capability and flexibility of prepositioned sealift with the speed of strategic airlift. Additionally, MPF greatly reduces strategic lift requirements.

Disposition and Readiness

Headquarters, Marine Forces Atlantic (MARFORLANT) is located in Norfolk, Virginia. Its major units consist of the II Marine Expeditionary Force (II MEF), headquartered at Camp Lejeune, North Carolina. The MEF has three major subordinate commands (MSCs); Second Marine Division (MarDiv), 2d Force Service Support Group (FSSG), both headquartered at Camp Lejeune; and 2d Marine Aircraft Wing (MAW) headquartered at Marine Corps Air Station Cherry Point, North Carolina.

Headquarters, Marine Forces Pacific (MARFORPAC) is located in Hawaii. Its major units are the I Marine Expeditionary Force, headquartered at Camp Pendleton, CA, and the III Marine Expeditionary Force, headquartered in Okinawa, Japan. I MEF in California has three MSCs; 1st MarDiv, 1st FSSG, and 3d MAW, all located at Camp Pendleton. III MEF is comprised of forward-deployed forces from I MEF and II MEF, and has 3d MarDiv, 3d FSSG, and 1st MAW as its MSCs, all located in Okinawa.

These air-ground teams are kept in an advanced state of combat readiness. The division-wing team maintained on the East Coast is ready to respond in the Atlantic hemisphere and has a primary commitment to the defense of NATO. The division-wing team based on the West Coast can be deployed rapidly to meet commitments world-wide, or to reinforce forward-deployed forces anywhere in the world. The division-wing team in the Western Pacific is prepared to move quickly in support of U.S. policy in the Pacific hemisphere and the Indian Ocean area.

In addition, units of the reserve division-wing team - and 4th Marine Division and 4th Marine Aircraft Wing, headquartered in New Orleans - train alongside regular Marine units and maintain the same high standards of readiness as the active forces. This side-by-side training supports overall readiness, the team concept and the "Total Force" policy.

The Marine Corps' global perspective is evidenced also in more than 40 major exercises conducted annually around the globe. Operating literally in "every climate and place," Marines take part in cold-weather training in Europe and Korea, as well as a variety of multi-nation exercises in other parts of the world.

About ten Combined Arms Exercises (CAX) are also conducted each year at the Marine Corps' unique air-ground combat training center located at Twentynine Palms, California. Here, in the open, unrestricted environment of the Mojave Desert, the readiness and combined arms capabilities of all elements of the Marine air-ground team are exercised and evaluated. Using live firing, each exercise is built around an infantry unit, ranging in size from a battalion to a brigade. Exercises are supported by fixed and rotary wing aircraft, artillery, light armored vehicles, amphibious assault vehicles and tanks.

The exercises provide realistic training to prepare today's Marines for tomorrow's battlefields.

New Developments

To carry the Marine Corps into the 21st century, the Marines are looking into several new areas. Some of those areas are: The incorporation of 21st century operational-level amphibious, maritime prepositioning, aviation, and land mobility, maneuver, and sustainment capabilities into the operating forces; ensuring access to the littorals through evolving expeditionary operations (to include mine and obstacle countermeasures, naval surface fires, etc.), maritime prepositioning, national sealift, high-speed troop lift, and naval aviation capabilities; and lastly, networking operational communications, information, and intelligence systems with joint and allied forces to provide a global access capability to domestic and international information resources. The major technological developments are the Advanced Amphibious Assault Vehicle (AAAV), the tilt-rotor MV22 Osprey, and the enhancements to the Landing

Craft Air Cushion (LCAC) vehicle fleet. These, and many other developments, such as Non-Lethal Weapons Programs, will enhance the Corps' ability to project power from the sea in support of the National Command Authority.

Summary

The total effort of the Marine Corps is oriented toward readiness for instant combat and for combat on the battlefields of the future.

The Marines have long held the expectation of being "first to fight." The close relationship between the Fleet Marine Forces and the U.S. Navy Fleet ensures that ready Marine forces will be on or near the scene when a crisis erupts.

Marine forces are prepared to carry out their primary mission with the fleet without sacrificing their capability to fulfill a broad range of general purpose missions. Equally important during peacetime, they serve as essential elements of U.S. deterrence. They project U.S. influence abroad by assisting diplomatic efforts, providing humanitarian relief, and protecting U.S. nationals, embassy personnel and American interests abroad. In times of impending crisis, they provide a stabilizing influence or an on-the-scene initial response with a balanced combat capability within the air-ground task force framework. They are capable of being rapidly deployed and rapidly reinforced; and they arrive combat-equipped and fully ready for action.

With this range of commitments, the Marines' global perspective remains unchanged. The Marine emphasis on operational readiness, versatility, and the integrated role of the air-ground team brings a vital capability to their task in the national defense.

By any standards, Marine training has always been – and will remain – tough, realistic and extremely demanding. A level of training which, experience has proven, is essential to survival in combat. Among the Corps' unchanging priorities is the team concept – Marines train and fight as a team.

The fully integrated air-ground team is the core of the Marine battle ethic, using all the weapons and firepower assets available to the combat Marine, in a coordinated, skillful combination of infantry, armor, anti-armor, artillery and air power.

In the amphibious role, the Marines' primary mission, the team concept includes a solid partnership with the Navy.

The overall mission of the Marine Corps has been defined by tradition and statute. Its organization and functions are keyed to its constant task as a force-in-readiness.

The historic resolution of 1775 charged the Marines "...to serve to advantage by sea when required..." That Marines HAVE served "to advantage by sea" – and land and air – is a matter of history.

Chapter Two

History and Tradition

During its many years of experience in peace and war, the Marine Corps has developed many traditions: traditions of devotion to duty, self-sacrifice, versatility and dependability; traditions of loyalty to country and to Corps; traditions of uniform, insignia and equipment. Since the American Revolution, generations of Marines have maintained and perpetuated these traditions.

Marines learn that their traditions are as much a part of their equipment as a pack, rifle or ammunition. Pride of person is instilled in every Marine. But the making of Marines is not alone a matter of smart appearance, drill and discipline. Of greater importance, Marines learn to know their equipment and how to use it so that they are ready to meet any emergency that may arise and to report: "The Marines have landed and the situation is well in hand."

Symbols of Tradition

The familiar emblem of globe and anchor, adopted in 1868, embodies the tradition of worldwide service and sea traditions. The spread eagle, symbol of the nation itself, holds in its beak a streamer upon which is inscribed the famous motto of the United States Marines: "Semper Fidelis," which means in Latin "always faithful."

The term "Leatherneck" as applied to Marines is widely used but few people associate it with the uniform. The fact that the United States Marines wore a black leather stock, or collar, from 1798 to 1880 may have given rise to the name. According to tradition, the stock was originally worn to protect the jugular vein from the slash of a saber or cutlass. However, official records fail to bear this out.

The sword with a Mameluke hilt, presented to Lieutenant Presley N. O'Bannon of the Marine Corps by a former Pasha of Tripoli, became the symbol of authority of Marine Corps officers for more than 100 years. It symbolized the exploits of O'Bannon and his Marines on the shores of Tripoli in 1805, an episode climaxed by the raising of the American flag for the first time in the Old World.

Marine Origins

The use of fighting men as part of the regular complement of ships of war was common to the Phoenicians and to all maritime states of Greece at least five centuries before the Christian Era. The Marines of that day had definite tactical missions: first, to fight in naval engagements, defending the bulwarks of their own ships, and conducting boarding parties against the ships of the enemy; second, to capture and hold the land approaches to a harbor when it was necessary for the fleet to put into port in some strange country; and third, to enable the fleet to strike a blow on land by means of a raiding party or a small, compact offensive force.

British Marines

The custom of using fighting soldiers aboard ships, coming down from the Greeks and Romans, was continued in the British Fleet. But not until the year 1664, during the reign of Charles II, was there any military organization placed under authority of the British Admiralty. This was accomplished by an Order in Council (October 28, 1664), which directed the organization of "The Admiral's Maritime Regiment," in deference to the Duke of York and Albany, whose title was Lord High Admiral of England. The regiment was designated later as "Regiment of Marines," and in case of war was first to embark with the fleet for service afloat.

Colonial Marines

The American Colonial Marines came into existence early in the year 1740, when three regiments of Marines were raised in the American Colonies, concurrently with the reestablishment of the British Marines, for service in naval operations in the West Indies with the fleet under command of Admiral Edward Vernon of the Royal Navy. Native Americans were supposedly better fitted for service in this climate than Europeans, and their uniforms of "camlet coats, brown linen waistcoats, and canvas trousers" were considered well adapted for their duties. On April 2, 1740, the King commissioned Alexander Spotswood, former Governor of the Colony of Virginia, a colonel, to be commandant of the entire organization of American Marines.

After the death of Colonel Spotswood (June 7, 1740), the force of Marines was formed into a single regiment of four battalions under the command of Colonel William Gooch of Virginia, generally referred to as Gooch's Marines. It ranked in the British Army list as the 43d Regiment. One of the officers of the American Marines was Lawrence Washington, the half-brother of George. The reestablishment of the British Marines, the creation of the first American Marines and their joint Caribbean service more than two centuries ago is commemorated by both services in their mutual use of the colors scarlet and gold.

Continental Marines

An organization of Marines, as a regular branch of our country's service, was formed by an act of the Continental Congress passed on November 10, 1775. (Now observed throughout the world as the Marine

The Bon Homme Richard encounters the Serapis.

Corps' birthday.) The American Marines, though few in number, performed notable service during the American Revolution. With the naval forces, they made several expeditions to the Bahamas, served with the lake fleets of the Continental Navy in the operations on Lake Champlain, with John Paul Jones, with the navies of the several states and with Washington's Army in the Battle of Princeton and Assanpink Creek. Following the close of that war, they, like the Navy, went out of existence.

Beginnings of the Corps

The Marine Corps, as it exists today, was formed by the Act of July 11, 1798, at the beginning of the Naval War with France. The Marines took part in that war from 1798 to 1801, and in the war with the Barbary corsairs from 1801 to 1805. They took an active part in the War of 1812, serving aboard practically all American warships which engaged the enemy; with the Army in the Battle of Bladensburg, August, 1814; and with Jackson at New Orleans.

In 1824, Marines formed part of a landing force which operated against a nest of pirates in Cuba. In 1832, Marines again saw action against pirates as part of a combined landing force from the U.S. frigate *Potomac*. Their mission was to punish the Malay pirates at Quallah Batto, Island of Sumatra, for the capture and plunder of the USS *Friendship*.

In 1833, Marines from the Boston Navy Yard suppressed a mutiny in the Massachusetts State Prison which was beyond the control of the civil authorities. During 1836 and 1837, they helped the Army fight the Creek and Seminole Indians in Georgia and Florida, where they served under their Commandant, Colonel Archibald Henderson.

The Mexican War

During the war with Mexico and in the conquest of California, the Marines took an important part both on the Atlantic and Pacific Coasts, assisting in the capture of Monterey, Yerba Buena (San Francisco), Mazatlan, Vera Cruz, Tampico and Tobasco. One battalion of Marines marched with General Scott to Mexico City, participating in the final attack on the Castle of Chapultepec and the march to the National Palace, the Halls of the Montezumas. This explains the words for many years inscribed on the colors of the Corps: "From Tripoli to the Halls of the Montezumas." The words are commemorated today in the first two lines of "The Marines' Hymn" – although the unknown author of

Assault on Chapultepec Castle.

Storming of fortification at Derne.

the words of the first verse shifted the chronology when he wrote: "From the Halls of Montezuma to the shores of Tripoli."

Marine Corps Mottos

Shortly after the Mexican War, the Marines carried the so-called "Tripoli-Montezuma" flag, which had the motto, "By Land, by Sea." When the current Marine Corps emblem was adopted in 1868, the Navy Department authorized the use of the words on the flag of the United States Marine Corps. The current motto, "Semper Fidelis," replaced "By Land, by Sea," on streamers above the eagle soon after the Civil War, and was officially adopted as the motto in 1880.

The march "Semper Fidelis," was composed by the late John Phillip Sousa, in the year 1888, during the time when he was leader of the U.S. Marine Band.

The Uniform

In the famous blue uniform of the Marine Corps, which was first authorized by Secretary of War James McHenry, August 24, 1797, just prior to the formal reestablishment of the Marine Corps on July 11, 1798, are incorporated many of the traditions of the Corps. Blue or "Navy Blue," an inconspicuous color of sea and employed generally by the naval forces of all countries, was selected by the U.S. Marines for their uniforms, while the pattern and trimmings of red and gold served at the same time to make them distinctive. Although the red edging or piping on the coat was used primarily for its decorative effect, it will be remembered that John Paul Jones dressed his Marines in red uniforms, and it is quite possible that sentiment played its part. In view of the fact that the early organization, duties and regulations of the American Marines were patterned somewhat after ways and customs of their forerunners, the British Marines, it is possible that the traditional red of the British uniform had its effect in the adoption of red for the uniform of the United States Marines.

The blue uniform with red trimmings was used from 1797 until July 4, 1834, when it was replaced by a grass green uniform with buff trimmings. This uniform lasted only six years until July 4, 1840, when the blue uniform trimmed with red was again prescribed.

From Civil War to World War I

During the Civil War, Marines served afloat and ashore. They took an active part in all the more important naval operations: those of the Gulf and the Mississippi Valley, the operation leading to the capture of New Orleans and also against the coastal defenses on the Atlantic seaboard, culminating in the last big amphibious operation of the war – the capture of Fort Fisher.

They also took part in a number of land engagements, including the fight on July 21, 1861, which was known in the North as "Bull Run" and in the South as "Manassas."

A noteworthy incident at the beginning of the Civil War period (1859) was the participation of Marines in the capture of John Brown at Harpers Ferry.

Scattered Actions

The "peacetime" activities of the Marine Corps from the close of the Civil War until the War with Spain, were in accordance with the Marines' tradition of versatility. They aided the civil authorities in suppressing labor riots in Baltimore and Philadelphia and enforcing the revenue laws in New York.

At the same time, they sent expeditions to the Caribbean area, Korea, China and other foreign countries for the purpose of protecting American lives and property.

During the years 1867 and 1870, they formed part of the Formosa expedition. A year later, in what was then termed the most important action since the Civil War, a battalion of Marines, as part of a naval brigade, led the advance against the Korean forts in reprisal for serious offenses against Americans.

In 1882, a detachment of Marines landed at Alexandria, Egypt, to assist in restoring order.

Spanish War

During the War with Spain, at Guantanamo Bay, Cuba, the Marines again were first to land in enemy territory. They served on the larger ships with Admirals Dewey and Sampson in the battles of Manila Bay and the naval battle off Santiago de Cuba.

Following the spectacular naval victory in Manila Bay, the Marines of the cruiser *Baltimore*, under the command of First Lieutenant Dion Williams, USMC, landed to take the Spanish Naval Arsenal at Cavite, and from then on Marines garrisoned this station.

Capture of Salee River Forts.

Marines land at Guantanamo Bay.

Philippine Insurrection

Not long after the War with Spain, a Marine brigade was sent to the Far East, where it helped to suppress the Philippine Insurrection. Notable among Marine Corps activities in the Philippines was their participation in the Battle of Novaleta and the ill-fated expedition across the Island of Samar.

Boxer Rebellion

During the Boxer Rebellion in China, in the summer of 1900, Marines from ships on the Asiatic station took part in the defense of the Legation Quarter at Peking, and a regiment of Marines formed part of the allied relief expedition from Taku to Peking, as well as participating in the Battle of Tientsin.

A very interesting and unique tradition of friendship between the Royal Welsh Fusiliers and the United States Marine Corps had its inception in this campaign. During the course of the desperate fighting at the walls of Tientsin, each of these two famous organizations was supported by or came to the assistance of the other on a number of occasions. The conspicuous service rendered by each organization resulted in mutual admiration. Saint David's Day (March 1) is marked annually by cabled greetings to each other, messages which contain the ancient Welsh password, "And Saint David."

The Lost Battalion of Samar.

In 1903, Marines were landed in Santo Domingo and Korea, while a detail of Marines served as guards for a diplomatic mission to Abyssinia by camel caravan across the desert to negotiate a treaty with King Menelik.

From 1906 to 1908, the Marines participated in the army of occupation in the Cuban Pacification, a number of expeditions to Panama and Nicaragua from 1909 to 1912 and the 1914 expedition to Vera Cruz, Mexico.

Marines in World War I

In World War I, the Marines participated in the fiercest fighting they had ever known. The 4th Brigade of Marines (Composed of the famous 5th and 6th Regiments and the 6th Machine Gun Battalion) served as one of the infantry brigades of the Second American Division, participating with distinction in the important battles of Belleau Wood, Soissons, St. Mihiel, Blanc Mont Ridge and the Argonne.

At Belleau Wood in June 1918, the Marines of the 4th Brigade fought with such ferocity that the Germans in their official reports referred to them as "teufel-hunden" ("devil-dogs"), a fighting name that increased in popularity with the passing of time.

The 5th Brigade of Marines (11th and 13th Regiments and the 5th Brigade Machine Gun Battalion) also took part in the war in France, mostly on guard duty.

Marine aviation units under command of Major Alfred A. Cunningham (who became the Marine Corps' first aviator in 1912) rendered conspicuous service as the Day Wing of the Northern Bombing Group in Northern France and Belgium.

The Marine pilots flew 57 bombing missions, dropping 52,000 pounds of bombs and shooting down at least a dozen German planes.

The 1st Marine Aeronautic Company under command of Major Francis T. Evans operated an anti-submarine patrol station in the Azores from January 1918 to January 1919.

Women Marines

Opha M. Johnson was the first woman Marine, enlisting on August 13, 1918, the day after the Secretary of the Navy granted the authority to enroll women in the Marine Corps Reserve for clerical duty at Headquarters Marine Corps and at other Marine offices in the U.S.

A total of 305 women enlisted during World War I, to "free a man to fight."

During World War II, the Women's Reserve was activated, and by June 1944, there were 1,000 officers and 18,000 enlisted women led by Colonel Ruth C. Streeter. This was roughly the equivalent of one division of men free to fight.

In 1948, women Marines were totally integrated into the regular Corps.

Between Two Wars

For more than a decade after World War I, the Marines were continually engaged in efforts to restore peace in the countries of the Caribbean area – always acting as the strong arm for carrying out the nation's foreign policy.

In three Caribbean countries they carried on extensive campaigns against disorderly elements, assisting the governments of those countries to put down armed insurrection, to organize efficient native constabularies to maintain order after they withdrew and to restore peace.

In Haiti from 1915 to 1934, they fought two wars with the Cacos; in the Dominican Republic, it took them six years to suppress banditry; and in Nicaragua, they fought the bandit elements from 1927 to 1932. The fighting in Nicaragua was the first evidence of the development of the famous Marine "air-ground team" concept known as the Marine Air-Ground Task Force (MAGTF). Cargo resupply by aircraft was also used for the first time.

Duty in China

For almost a century, the Marines have felt at home in China. As early as 1854, internal upheaval which endangered the lives of Americans required the presence of a landing force of Marines. From that time to the Boxer Rebellion of 1900, Marines and sailors landed on a number of occasions for the protection of our national interests.

The decade from 1901 was a comparatively peaceful one, but in 1911 and 1912, Marines operated in China to protect Americans during the overthrow of the Manchu Dynasty.

Beginning in 1924, conditions in China again became troublesome and contingents of Marines and sailors landed from time to time to protect American citizens and American interests.

In 1927, owing to the upheaval in that country and the attending danger to Americans, a force of about 5,000 Marines was dispatched and stationed at vari-

Marine occupation in defense of Shanghai.

ous trouble points, principally at Shanghai and Tientsin. Three squadrons, VF-6M, VO-10M and VS-1M, formed the aviation component. During the next two years, more than 3,000 sorties, mostly reconnaissance, were flown by Marine aviators.

By January 1929, the situation having improved, the force, which had been formed into the 3d Marine Brigade, returned to the United States after order had been restored, with the exception of the 4th Marines, which remained in Shanghai.

This two-battalion regiment, with occasional reinforcements in 1932 and 1933, was engaged in preventing the belligerents from entering the international settlement. In 1937, the 6th Marines, with a battery of anti-aircraft guns, contributed to the formation of the brigade at Shanghai, nearly 3,000 officers and men. After a few months, the 6th Marines returned to the United States, but the 4th Regiment remained on duty in China until withdrawn just before the attack on Pearl Harbor in December 1941.

Fleet Marine Force

In 1933, the Fleet Marine Force came into being as an integral part of the United States Fleet. The

14

troops regularly assigned to this organization were mostly stationed at San Diego, California, and Quantico, Virginia, and were constantly trained for their specialized duties by participation in the annual maneuvers of the Fleet.

At each of these stations there was maintained a reinforced brigade of reduced strength consisting of an infantry regiment, a battalion of light field artillery (pack howitzers), a battalion of antiaircraft artillery, an aviation group, a light tank company and small contingents of engineer and chemical troops. The aviation unit at each of these posts was composed of two fighting squadrons, two bombing squadrons, one observation squadron and one general utility squadron.

Marines in World War II

In 1941, Marine units were stationed halfway around the world, and approximately 2,000 Marines were serving in China and the Philippines under the command of the Commander in Chief of the Asiatic Fleet.

The 4th Regiment was stationed in Shanghai, with detachments in Peiping and Tientsin, North China and two detachments at Olongapo and Cavite in the Philippines.

In addition, several thousand Marines were serving at naval stations in the Hawaiian Islands, Guam, Wake, Midway, American Samoa, the Panama Canal Zone and Cuba.

The 1st Provisional Marine Brigade, taken largely from the Second Marine Division at San Diego, was on duty in Iceland, and provisional Marine companies were stationed on various islands in the Atlantic Ocean and the Caribbean area.

The Japanese Attack

When the Japanese struck in the Pacific, the Marines from the stations in China had been successfully withdrawn to the Philippines with the exception of the Marine detachments at Peiping and Tientsin in North China. The Marine garrisons at Cavite and Olongapo in the Philippines participated in the defense of Bataan and Corregidor, until the American forces were finally overpowered and captured by the Japanese.

The handful of Marines on Guam put up a heroic but futile defense. Marines on Wake Island made a gallant stand, the details of which are familiar to the American people.

In Hawaii, an aviation group consisting of one fighter and two dive bomber squadrons was almost completely put out of action by the Japanese raid.

Marines to the Defense

Immediately after the Japanese attack on December 7, 1941, additional Marines with defense battalion equipment were sent out from the United States to reinforce the Hawaiian Islands and the smaller islands (Midway, Johnston and Palmyra) lying to the westward.

At the same time, measures were taken to strengthen the chain of islands across the South Pacific which protected the line of communication to Australia. The 7th Defense Battalion of Marines had been stationed at Tutuila, American Samoa, since March 15, 1941, and had taken some steps toward fortifying the harbor at Pago Pago.

As further reinforcements for this important position, a brigade of Marines, the 2d, taken mostly from the Second Marine Division at San Diego, was formed and together with Marine Aircraft Group 13 (MAG-13) proceeded early in January of 1942 to American Samoa and set up defenses and air facilities on Tutuila.

An additional brigade of Marines, the 3d, was organized from units of the First Marine Division at New River, North Carolina, and sent to Western Samoa, where they arrived on May 8, 1942. This brigade took up and organized positions on Upolu and Savaii Islands and, with naval units, established important air and naval facilities.

A few weeks after the arrival of the 3d Brigade, one of its units, the 8th Defense Battalion (reinforced) was sent 400 miles farther west to occupy Wallis Island, which was turned over to the control of the Marines by the Free French.

The westward thrust of the Marines was resumed early the following October when a part of a Marine defense battalion occupied the island of Funafuti in the Ellice Islands. Several months later they again proceeded farther to the northwest and occupied the islands of Nanumea and Nukufetau.

Guadalcanal

In order to secure our line of communication to the southwest Pacific, the First Marine Division was sent to New Zealand in June of 1942. Even before the rear echelon arrived in New Zealand, Major General Alexander A. Vandegrift was notified that his division (reinforced by the 2d Marines of the Second

Marine Division, the 1st Raider Battalion and the 3d Defense Battalion) was to carry out a landing attack in the Tulagi-Guadalcanal area.

On August 7, 1942, the First Marine Division (reinforced) effected landings on the north coast of the islands of Guadalcanal, Tulagi and Florida. This amphibious assault marked the beginning of the United States' offensive operation against the Japanese empire. By August 10, the Marines had destroyed the Japanese garrison at Tulagi, Gavutu and Tanambogo, and had secured the airfield on Guadalcanal.

For the next four months, the First Marine Division, later reinforced by Army troops and additional elements of the Second Marine Division, supported by the ships and aircraft of the Navy and planes of the Army and the Marine Corps, successfully repulsed numerous Japanese attacks made by land, sea and air. This bitterly fought and grueling campaign was highlighted by the battles of the Tenaru River, Bloody Ridge and the Matanikau River. Pilots and enlisted men of the First Marine Aircraft Wing performed almost legendary feats in fighting off Japanese air attacks at Guadalcanal and carrying the fight to enemy ships and bases.

Up the Solomons

After winning Guadalcanal, which was used as the first stepping stone to Tokyo, our forces moved up the Solomons ladder and seized bases in the New Georgia Islands. Army and Marine Corps units had landed on the Russell Islands in February of 1943, which gave us an air base for operations against enemy bases in the New Georgia group.

In June and July 1943, Marine Corps and Army troops landed on New Georgia and Rendova Islands, followed by landings on Vella Lavella, Arundel and Kolombangara Islands.

On November 1, 1943, the Third Marine Division made a landing at Empress Augusta Bay, Bougainville. The Bougainville campaign marked the beginning of close air support in the modern sense. For the first time pilots (forward air controllers) and enlisted men (radiomen) from the wing reported to the division for duty, where they helped company and battalion commanders obtain and direct air attacks on specific enemy emplacements holding up the advance of the Marine ground units.

During the next 45 days, the Third Marine Division defeated the Japanese in the battles of Koromokina Lagoon and Piva Fork.

The Marines stormed Tarawa killing more than 4,700 in less than four days.

The Gilberts

After the seizure of Bougainville, the allied offensive against Japan was intensified. Army forces accelerated their leapfrog tactics up the north coast of New Guinea, and our Central Pacific forces breached the Japanese outer line of defense when on November 20, 1943, the Second Marine Division landed on Tarawa and elements of the Army 27th Division went ashore on Makin Island, both in the Gilberts Group.

Within four days, the Marines had wiped out all enemy resistance on Tarawa, but had suffered very heavy casualties. The Japanese had boasted that a million Americans could not take the triangular coral atoll of islands consisting of Tarawa, Makin, and Betio… not in a hundred years. It took the Marines 76 hours.

Robert Sherrod wrote: "The Marines fought almost solely on *espirit de corps*, I was certain. It was inconceivable to most Marines that they should let another Marine down, or that they could be responsible for dimming the bright reputation of their Corps. The Marines simply assumed that they were the world's best fighting men."

Of the 4,836 Japanese soldiers and Korean laborers on Betio, only 146 were taken prisoner."

In the meanwhile, American and Australian forces cleared New Guinea's north coast, and on December 15, 1943, crossed to Arawe, New Britain, in a drive aimed at cutting the Japanese southern line of communications to Rabaul.

On December 26, 1943, the First Marine Division went ashore on Cape Gloucester on the northern coast of New Britain, cutting the enemy northern line of communications and forcing the enemy to withdraw to the vicinity of Rabaul. In a series of bloody battles, Marines secured the Cape Gloucester airdrome and captured a number of strategic hills in the Borgan Bay area.

By March of the following year, the Japanese were fleeing eastward toward Rabaul. On April 28, 1944, the Commanding General of the First Marine Division turned over command of the Cape Gloucester-Talasea area to the Army.

The First Division's operations in the western New Britain campaign breached the enemy's defense arc from Java to Rabaul by cutting both northern and southern barge lines and creating a gap through which the Allied forces could drive northward.

The Marshalls

Meanwhile, to the north, our Central Pacific forces were smashing through the Japanese defensive

Heat and varied terrain proved as tough as the enemy that was dug in on Saipan. When the fighting was over, 6,050 Japanese defenders had been killed and American bombers had runways from which to bomb Tokyo.

line by seizing a number of islands in the Marshalls group.

The Fourth Marine Division captured Roi and Namur Islands at the northern end of Kwajalein Atoll, while the Army's 7th Infantry Division seized Kwajalein Island at the southern end. Organized enemy resistance ceased on Kwajalein Atoll February 7, 1944.

A landing on the St. Matthias Island by the 4th Marines on March 20, 1944, for all strategic military purposes, completed the campaign for the Solomon Islands and forged another link in the chain of encirclement of Rabaul, New Britain. The occupation of the St. Matthias Group, together with the concurrent Army operations in the Admiralty Islands, tightened the noose around the Bismark Archipelago and left approximately 70,000 Japanese troops to surrender or die by starvation and disease.

The Marianas

After the conquest of the Marshall Islands, our Central Pacific forces shifted their offensive to the north. On June 15, 1944, the Second and Fourth Marine Divisions with the 27th Army Division in reserve landed abreast on the western side of Saipan. The most bitterly defended of the group, the battle for Saipan evolved into three distinct stages: first, there was the fight for the beachhead, a bitter struggle in which the enemy offered the heaviest resistance; second, there was the fight for the Mount Tapotchau line; and third, there was the seizure of the northern part of the island, in which a desperate enemy counterattack of July 7 was the outstanding feature.

Within 10 days, the American forces had captured the Aslito Airfield and were blasting the enemy out of caves on Mount Tapotchau, the key terrain feature of the island. By June 26, the Second Marine Division had mopped up the Mount Tapotchau fortress and had established positions at the summit.

Meanwhile, the Fourth Marine Division had captured Kagman Peninsula on the eastern side of the island. On July 9, after 25 days of heavy fighting, all organized enemy resistance had ceased and the island was officially secured.

Eleven days later, July 21, 1944, the III Amphibious Corps, composed of the Third Marine Division, the 1st Provisional Marine Brigade and the 77th Infantry Division, began landing on the west coast of Guam. In spite of the rugged terrain and a number of strong enemy counterattacks, the American forces had by July 25, gained control of the southern half of Guam. Organized resistance ceased on Guam August 10, 1944.

Three days after the landing on Guam, the Second and Fourth Marine Divisions went ashore on Tinian and moved inland against light resistance under strong cover. The two divisions advanced across the northern part of the island, then wheeled to drive southward. Within two days, they had captured the Ushi Point Airfield and on July 31, smashed through the last Japanese defenses along the southern plateau of Tinian Island. By the afternoon of August 1, the two Marine divisions had smashed organized resistance in the difficult terrain on the southern part of the island and Tinian was secured.

No time was lost in taking advantage of our strategic position in the Marianas. Bombing runs on the Bonin Islands got underway almost at once. While Army land-based *Liberator* bombers continued the attacks on enemy-held Bonin Islands, the construction of air bases in the Marianas for B-29 *Superfortress* bombers was rushed to completion.

On November 23, 1944, Marianas-based B-29's made the first raid on Tokyo since April 18, 1942, when General Doolittle's 16 carrier-based B-25's had made their daring attack.

While these important breaches in the Japanese island defenses were being made, Marines of the ship's detachments had served with the Navy in support of the Allied landing in Normandy. On August 24, 1944, during the invasion of Southern France, Marine units from two United States cruisers landed on three small islands near Marseilles, captured Nazi installations and disarmed the enemy troops.

Palaus

In the Pacific, the shifting tide of the Allied offensive moved southward. On September 15, the First Marine Division landed on the southwest coast of Peleliu, a small but rugged island near the southern end of the Palau Islands chain. In spite of difficult reef conditions and heavy enemy opposition, a substantial beachhead was established and the attack pushed inland, although the Marines had to fight their way step by step over exceptionally rugged terrain and against strong enemy opposition from caves and pillboxes.

The Marines of the First Division had secured the major portion of the island by October 16.

Though the island and garrisoning Japanese forces were devastated, historians have argued whether the Battle of Peleliu was needed. It cost the 1st Marine Division 1,241 Marine lives. The Japanese garrison was destroyed, losing 10,695.

The Philippines

The capture of Peleliu neutralized the remaining islands of the Palau group and opened the way for an invasion of the Philippines by General Douglas MacArthur's South Pacific forces.

Within eight days after Peleliu had been secured, General MacArthur sent his forces ashore on the east coast of Leyte Island in the Central Philippines. Marine divisions were not committed in the Philippines, although the headquarters battery and two battalions of V Corps artillery and air liaison personnel participated.

But in Marine aviation annals, the Luzon campaign provides a notable milestone. Here the Marines set out to perform a distinct mission and they trained hard to achieve it – the assistance of ground troops advancing against the enemy. In this case the ground troops were U.S. Army divisions. Small detachments of Marine aviators with the Army units provided the necessary coordination between ground and air. Lessons learned on the paddy fields of Luzon paid off six years later in Korea.

When strong units of the Imperial Navy moved into the Philippines theater a few days after the Leyte landing to counter our latest move westward, a great naval and air action resulted. In this "Battle for Leyte Gulf" Marines aboard the battleships, carriers and cruisers of the mighty 3rd and 7th Fleets participated in the decisive victory, which not only gave the Allies control of the waters east of the Philippines but eliminated the Japanese Navy as a serious factor in future attacks upon enemy-held islands.

Marine aviators under the command of Colonel Clayton C. Jerome earned the gratitude of the Army's 24th, 31st and 41st Infantry Divisions. Marines flew a total of 1,964 sorties in support of the Army units. Major General Roscoe B. Woodruff, commander of the 24th Division wrote: "It is believed that no other division in the Pacific area has had such complete and cooperative air coverage." Marine pilots were credited with blasting enemy targets only a few hundred yards ahead of the American doughboys. The Marines were represented by Marine Aircraft Groups (MAG) 12, 14, 24 and 32, as well as Fighter Squadrons 541, 124 and 213. An even 100 Marines were killed in action; 129 were wounded in the skies over the Philippines while flying their *Corsair* fighters, *Mitchell* bombers, *Dauntless* dive bombers, *Helldiver* diverbombers, *Hellcat* fighters and *Skytrain* transports.

Iwo Jima

In order to provide fighter protection for the B-29 bombers based in the Marianas and at the same time eliminate the enemy's air base for attacks on the *Superforts*, it was necessary to secure Iwo Jima in the Volcano Islands.

The rugged, natural terrain of this bit of volcanic bleakness had been supplemented by extensive man-made fortifications.

On the morning of February 19, 1945, hundreds of landing boats roared through the pounding surf to spill thousands of Fourth and Fifth Division Marines onto Iwo's southeastern beaches. The Third Marine Division was held in reserve.

During the second day, the 28th Marines moved forward to the slope of Mount Suribachi, while the remainder of the Fifth Division and the Fourth Division, wheeling to the north, captured Airfield No. 1 and began the assault on the heavily fortified enemy positions between Airfields 1 and 2.

On the morning of February 23, members of the 2d Battalion, 28th Marines were ordered to the top of the Mount Suribachi crater. A 40-man patrol of Company "E" crawled to the lip of the crater and raised the first flag, photographed by *Leatherneck* Magazine photographer Technical Sergeant Louis Lowery. Meanwhile a larger flag was procured, and a

Members of the Fourth and Fifth Marine Divisions assaulted Iwo Jima using the island's black volcanic sands as cover. Marines would later advance and eventually take Mount Suribachi, in the background, pounded by naval gunfire and Marine air.

second flag raising was held which was photographed by Associated Press photographer Joe Rosenthal. The second flag raising photograph was to become the outstanding symbol of America's war effort. Six men were depicted in the Pulitzer Prize-winning photo: five Marines and a Navy corpsman. Three of the Marines were later killed on Iwo Jima and the corpsman was wounded in later action.

The 21st Regiment of the Third Marine Division landed during the afternoon of February 21 and the 9th Marines landed the afternoon of February 24. Meanwhile, on February 23, units of the 28th Marines captured Mount Suribachi, which eliminated enemy fire on the landing beaches and gave the Marines an excellent observation point.

On February 25, the three Marine divisions, spearheaded by tanks and supported by heavy bombardment from Marine Corps artillery, gunfire of 5th Fleet warships, and carrier-based planes, captured Airfield No. 2, thereby breaching the main Japanese defensive position.

By February 28, the Third Marine Division had captured Motoyama village, and was at the southern edge of Airfield No. 3. By nightfall on March 3, the three airfields and the Motoyama plateau had been seized by Marines.

On March 10, after extremely bitter fighting, the Third and Fourth Divisions reached the eastern beaches at several points, which split the Japanese force into small pockets.

Organized resistance ended on Iwo Jima at 1800, March 16, 1945, when the Third and Fifth Marine Divisions smashed through the enemy's lines to reach Kitano Point at the extreme northern tip of the island.

Okinawa

In the final great land battle of the Pacific area, the invasion of Okinawa, the Marine Corps was represented by the First, Second and Sixth Marine Divisions, which formed the III Amphibious Corps. Air support came from the Second Marine Aircraft Wing and a Task Unit including Marine Aircraft Groups 14, 22, 31 and 33. Carrier planes of the U.S. Navy also gave close support early in the campaign.

The III Corps, with the First and Sixth Marine Divisions in assault and the Second in reserve, began landing on the western beaches of Okinawa on April 1, 1945, as had the left corps of the Tenth Army. Enemy opposition was light and by the end of the second day, the American forces had reached the opposite coast, cutting the island in two.

By April 8, while the Army troops were making slight gains in their drive southward toward Naha, the Sixth Marine Division was fanning out onto Motobu Peninsula, while the First Marine Division was mopping up in its sector.

On April 10, the Sixth Division encountered the first major organized enemy resistance near the center of Motobu Peninsula in the northern part of the island.

By April 17, elements of the Sixth Marine Division had advanced under the protective support of Marine fighter-bombers to the northern coast of Okinawa, and had captured Mount Yae Take, key terrain feature on Motobu Peninsula. With the Mount Yae Take victory, the final pocket of Okinawa's enemy resistance in the northern part of the island was eliminated.

On May 1, the First Marine Division, attached to the XXIV Corps, relieved the 27th Infantry Division on the right (west) flank of the line above the city of Naha. On May 7, the First Division reverted to control of the III Amphibious Corps, and May 9 found

the Sixth Marine Division in the line on the right of the First Marine Division.

Increased pressure was brought against the enemy line of defense which stretched across the island from Naha on the west coast eastward to Yonabaru.

On May 13, units of the Sixth Marine Division entered the ruins of Naha, and on this and the following day, the capture of high ground to the east of Shuri by the 96th and 77th Infantry Divisions and the seizure of high ground to the west of the fortress by the First Marine Division, placed the jaws of a pincer around this position.

By nightfall of May 31, the First Marine Division had captured Shuri Castle, and on June 1, the capture of Shuri was completed and the Marine Corps and Army units continued their drive southward against diminishing resistance.

The First Marine Division plunged across the Naha-Yonabaru highway in a 1,000-yard advance on June 2, and the next day, the 7th Infantry Division, on the left flank, drove across the Chinen Peninsula. The Sixth Marine Division landed strong forces on Oroku Peninsula on June 4 and captured half of the Naha Airfield.

By June 7, the First Marine Division had advanced its lines to within 1,200 yards of the west coast, north of the town of Itoman, a move which cut

Okinawa was one of the most difficult campaigns of World War II. Fought at Japan's doorstep, it was also the last campaign of the war.

off escape for the enemy forces in the vicinity of Oroku Peninsula.

During the night of June 17-18, units of the 8th Marines, Second Marine Division, relieved the 7th Marines on Mezado and Kunishi Ridges.

More than 14,000 close air support sorties were flown during the Okinawa campaign, over half of them in support of Army troops. Marine nightfighters also recorded a highly increased effectiveness as they held off desperate Japanese attacks on this island of the Japanese homeland.

Meanwhile, other Marine aviators were fulfilling the U.S. Marine tradition of being ready for any emergency. Japanese Kamikaze planes threatened to overcome the air superiority of U.S. aircraft carriers.

During the first six months of 1945, the Marine fighter squadrons moved from land bases in the southwest Pacific to aircraft carriers to increase defensive capabilities of the fleet.

Japan Capitulates

The successful conquest of Okinawa enabled our ships, planes and submarines to tighten the blockade around Japan's home islands and sever her vital sea links to the Asiatic mainland and the areas to the south. With the end of the Okinawa campaign, the bombing attacks upon Japan were stepped up, which together with our submarines and ships further weakened Japan's ability to wage war.

In mid-July, 1945, while the U.S. 3rd Fleet was in the midst of its sustained assault on their homeland, the Japanese made a bid for peace, but they asked for terms more favorable than unconditional surrender. The Potsdam Declaration, however, killed any hope of a compromise.

On September 2, 1945, in a brief but solemn ceremony aboard the battleship *Missouri*, representatives of Japan signed the surrender documents. Thereafter, Allied occupation of Japan and the territory under Japanese control went steadily ahead, with Marines playing an important role.

Demobilization and Peacetime Posture

When the war with Japan ended in 1945, the Marine Corps numbered six divisions and five air wings. The Second and Fifth Divisions were assigned occupation duty in Japan. The Third and Fourth Divisions were deactivated. The First Marine Aircraft

Wing supported the ground troops in China and the Second Wing returned to Cherry Point, North Carolina. The Third, Fourth and Ninth Wings were decommissioned.

During the year following the end of the war, the Marine Corps accomplished a demobilization which cut its size from six to two divisions, from five to two wings, and from almost 500,000 men to about 100,000 by the end of 1946.

At this time, the Second Division and Second Wing were based in North Carolina and the First Division and First Wing in China. It was not until late in 1949 that the last Marine units left China and returned to the United States.

The First Division and First Wing were based in Southern California until the outbreak of the Korean War.

Amphibious Training

During World War II, the tactics and techniques of amphibious operations were greatly improved by the Navy and Marine Corps. A Troop Training Unit (TTU) under Marine command was established at San Diego, California, as part of the Navy's Amphibious Training Command. After the war this TTU was retained as TTU Pacific, and TTU Atlantic was organized at Norfolk, Virginia. In addition to these training units, the operating forces continued to emphasize amphibious training in individual and unit exercises. Marine air-ground team tactics were further evaluated and developed. Annual maneuvers by the combined ground and air units on each coast emphasized the coordinated combat-ready condition of the fighting forces of the Marine Corps even in the atmosphere of headlong demobilization which characterized the military picture in this country between 1945 and 1950.

National Security Act of 1947

This act specified the functions to be carried out by the Marine Corps for the first time in history. Now the role of the Marine Corps as a force in readiness was more than just a matter of tradition.

Women in the Regular Marine Corps

Before 1948 women served in the Marine Corps only as a special, wartime expediency. During World War I a total of 305 women served as Marines, performing clerical duties and holding ranks from private through sergeant. In World War II a Marine

Corps Women's Reserve was established in 1943 with Major (later Colonel) Ruth Cheney Streeter as its first Director. With the recruiting slogan "Free a Marine to Fight", the Women's Reserve rapidly expanded, reaching a peak strength of over 19,000. Women filled more than 200 type assignments in the continental United States and Hawaii, but at the end of the war the Women's Reserve was rapidly demobilized. Barely 100 women remained on active duty during 1946-48, serving at Headquarters Marine Corps, major posts and stations, and in the recruiting districts. They participated in the planning for the postwar Reserve and provided a nucleus for future expansion.

With passage of the Women's Armed Services Integration Act on June 12, 1948 (Public Law 625) the basis was provided for women to be accepted into the Regular component of the Marine Corps. These regulars were authorized to hold permanent rank of Lieutenant Colonel and to provide up to two percent of the total strength of the Marine Corps. Colonel Katherine A. Towle, who had succeeded Colonel Streeter as Director, Women's Reserve in December, 1945, was assigned as the first Director of Women Marines.

At the beginning of the Korean War there were fewer than 600 women Marines on active duty, but as part of the wartime expansion they reached a peak of 2,787. In the 50's and early 60's strength stabilized at about 1,500 women on active duty; the Vietnam expansion raised numbers again to about 2,700 and more professional opportunities such as career schools and overseas assignments became available for women in the Marine Corps. In the post-Vietnam era women were increasingly integrated into the full range of jobs, including assignment to the Fleet Marine Forces and to all occupational fields except combat arms. The special administration of women was discontinued in 1977 with the disestablishment of the Office of the Director of Women Marines. The last Director, Colonel Margaret A. Brewer, was assigned as the Deputy Director of Information, an assignment not previously available to a woman officer. The following year she was promoted to brigadier general and appointed Director Of Information. Today women continue to provide a significant part of the Marine Corps' personnel resources.

Marines In Europe

During 1948, the Marine Corps averaged about 80,000 enlisted men and 7,000 officers. Continuing the 177-year-old tradition of safeguarding American rights in war and peace, Marine units were regularly assigned to the Sixth Fleet operating in the Mediterranean area. Every four months a reinforced infantry battalion and one or two fighter squadrons reported aboard naval vessels of our European Fleet to keep them in a state of readiness for any emergency. In the performance of their duties, the Marines on the four month tour traveled throughout the Mediterranean, visiting such places as North Africa, Malta, Spain, France and Italy.

Continued Development of Amphibious Techniques

Intensive effort was made in the Marine Corps after World War II to develop and perfect the techniques and equipment associated with amphibious warfare. New concepts emerged in transport submarine operations; air transport, and especially helicopter transport of troops; cold weather operations; and improvement of amphibious vehicles and weapons. Marine personnel of the troop training units on both coasts continued their heavy schedules of training troops of all services for amphibious operations. In support of this growing program, the Marine Corps Schools at Quantico were reorganized in 1950 into two major subdivisions, the Marine Corps Education Center and the Landing Force Development Center.

Black Marines

By the end of World War II, the Marine Corps boasted 485,833 men and women, of whom 242,043 were overseas. Of this number, 19,168 were blacks who served in the 51st and 52d Defense Battalions or in one of the 51 depot companies or 12 ammunition companies. Segregated units served overseas in all major campaigns from Saipan on.

Alfred Masters and George Thompson were the first two black Marines, enlisting on June 1, 1942. Nine black Marines were killed in action or died of wounds in World War II and 78 others were wounded in action.

Frederick C. Branch, who had served as an enlisted Marine, became the first black officer.

By June 1949, blacks were fully integrated into the Marine Corps. They served bravely in Korea and during the long Vietnam struggle.

Marines in Korea

On June 25, 1950, the Communist North Korean Army invaded the Republic of South Korea. The move was immediately denounced by the Security Council of the United Nations. Supporting the decision of that body, the United States came to the defense of South Korea, first sending in what had been Army occupation troops in Japan, and then calling on U.S. Marines.

On July 7, the 1st Provisional Marine Brigade was activated, consisting of the 5th Marines (reinforced) and supported by Marine Aircraft Group 33. Embarkation followed five days later.

First offensive action against the enemy was made by MAG-33's fighter-bombers on August 2, and the Brigade first clashed with the enemy on August 7, exactly one month after it had been alerted for the move.

The Pusan Perimeter

The 1st Provisional Marine Brigade was attached to the Eighth U.S. Army in the Pusan Perimeter at the time when the North Korean advance had come within 35 miles of Pusan. The problem was one of holding against numerically superior enemy troops, and the Marines were used as "firemen" – a hard-hitting mobile reserve to be shifted from one threatened area to another for counterattacks. Three times the Brigade helped stop the enemy cold in such operations. The famous Marine "air-ground team" immediately began to prove the soundness of the post-war developments in close air support.

The Inchon Landing

September 15, 1950, was D-Day for the First Marine Division, less the 7th Marines, as X Corps landing force at Inchon, a daring amphibious landing which led to the capture of Seoul and the seizure of Kimpo airfield as a base of operations for the First Marine Air Wing units and the outflanking of the entire North Korean Army.

On the morning of the 15th, the 3d Battalion, 5th Marines, supported by tanks, air and naval gunfire, landed and seized the two harbor islands of Wolmi-do and Sowolmi-do. Late that afternoon the 1st and 5th Marine Regiments hit the beach at Inchon. Within 24 hours they had secured this west coast Korean seaport and swept on, under the *Corsairs* of Marine Fighter Squadrons 214 and 323 which alternately attacked, screened with smoke, observed and kept the sky free of enemy aircraft.

Cut off by eight Chinese divisions, the 1st Marine Division leathernecks fought their way out of the Chosin Reservoir and on to the sea, taking their dead and wounded with them.

The Capture of Seoul

The enemy resisted stubbornly along the approaches to Seoul and three days of street fighting were necessary to secure this city of a million and a half prewar population. The finish of the war seemed in sight as the 7th Marines, after landing on D plus 7, pushed north of Seoul to seize Uijongbu and the main road to the North Korean capital of Pyongyang. On October 7, the First Marine Division was relieved by Eighth Army elements and sent by sea around the peninsula.

Chosin Reservoir

After an administrative landing at Wonsan on October 25, the 1st and 5th Marines were assigned by X Corps to patrolling and blocking missions while the 7th Marines advanced from Hamhung toward the Chosin Reservoir.

On November 3, this regiment met and began battle with a Chinese Communist (CCF) division. It was the first large-scale battle between the Americans and the CCF. The 7th Marines, in a four-day battle, crippled this CCF division so badly that it never saw service on that front again.

On November 24, an offensive was launched by the Eighth Army in western Korea and by X Corps in the northeast. The next day, massed CCF forces struck back in overwhelming numbers, sending the Eighth Army into retreat and driving between it and X Corps. On the night of the 27th, the 5th and 7th Marines, which had advanced to Yudam-ni, west of the Chosin Reservoir, were attacked. Other CCF divisions cut the main supply route. From November 28 to December 2, the First Marine Division held its own against eight CCF divisions, including two in reserve.

In addition to fanatical enemy attacks which resulted in the temporary isolation of certain elements of the division, the Marines had to fight bitter sub-zero cold and howling snowstorms. Then began the fighting withdrawal over 70 miles of tortuous road through mountain passes and canyons dominated by CCF forces.

The long, twisting convoy battled through to Hagaru-ri with fighting units sweeping the foe from the nearby slopes. The reverse slopes and flanks became the responsibility of the supporting aircraft of the Marine air-ground team.

New chapters of heroism were written as cooks and bakers fought with rifles and bayonets on the ground while fliers braved tremendous difficulties and dangers in the air to support the withdrawal.

At Hagaru-ri, the reunited division was supplied by air drop and casualties were evacuated by aircraft from an improvised strip. The column began its breakout on the 6th, cutting a path through enemy forces to Koto-ri where more casualties were evacuated by air. Bitter resistance had to be overcome along the main supply route to Chinhung-ni and Marine engineers installed a 24-ton Treadway bridge, dropped by Air Force C-119's, to replace a vital span blown by the enemy. Marine close air support was reinforced by Marine Air Group 12 at Yonpo and Navy planes from carriers.

The First Marine Division reached Hamhung on December 11, having brought out its wounded, most of its dead and vehicles and equipment. The main body was evacuated on the 15th to South Korea by Task Force 90, which pulled out the remaining units of X Corps and 91,000 civilian refugees to complete its "amphibious landing in reverse."

Stopping the CCF Advance

Upon arrival at Pusan, the First Marine Division again passed into Eighth Army reserve. Its first mission was to neutralize a North Korean guerrilla division in the Pohang-Yongdok-Andong area. By February 6, 1951, the enemy had been reduced an estimated 60 percent in strength. The Marines then participated in Operation KILLER and Operation RIPPER, limited offensives in east central Korea designed to keep the enemy off balance.

Meanwhile, operating under 5th Air Force control, First Marine Aircraft Wing planes were shifted to interdiction missions, seeking enemy military targets far into North Korea.

On April 22, the Communists struck back in a large-scale counterattack. The First Marine Division in the Hwachon Reservoir area, exposed to CCF pressure from the flank as well as the front, beat off all enemy attacks and inflicted heavy losses. A second enemy offensive was stopped the following month. This was followed by attacks in which the Marines pursued and severely punished the enemy.

Truce Talks

Marines ended their first year in Korea in the "punchbowl" area just north of the 38th parallel, former dividing line of North Korea and South Korea. Early in July 1951, United Nations and Communist representatives met for the first peace talks which created a lull in the activities at the front. At first, action was limited on both sides to patrolling. After the first few months of unsuccessful negotiations, limited fighting broke out on many sections of the front.

During 1952, Marines continued experimenting with troop and supply lifts, using helicopters to bypass Korean hills. Beginning on Saint Patrick's Day, the Marine division was shifted to the extreme west side of the Korean Peninsula. Instead of facing North Koreans, the Marines were confronted by the 63rd and 65th Chinese armies.

The Marines fought a number of engagements; some, such as "The Battle of Bunker Hill," were large and costly. Others were named "Yoke" or "Warsaw" and "Reno," which were code references to outposts.

The truce was signed on July 27, 1953, and the First Marine Division returned to the United States in the Spring of 1955, after almost five years of outstanding service in Korea.

Marine Corps Expansion

The year 1952 was highlighted by legislation approved by Congress and the President which gave the Marine Corps a minimum strength of three combat divisions and three air wings with supporting troops. The Commandant of the Marine Corps was also authorized full status with the members of the Joint Chiefs of Staff in matters directly concerning the Corps.

The 3d Marine Brigade was activated at Camp Pendleton, California, on June 20, 1951. On January 7, 1952, it became the Third Division, composed of the 3d, 4th, 9th and 12th Marine Regiments and separate battalions. It deployed to Japan the following year. The Third Marine Aircraft Wing was activated at Miami, Florida, on February 1, 1952, composed of MAGs 31,32 and 45.

Force in Readiness

In the decades following the Korean War, the Marine Corps resumed the role of the nation's force in readiness.

To fulfill this mission, two regiments of the Third Marine Division deployed to Okinawa in mid-1955, and one regiment to Hawaii as the nucleus of the 1st Marine Brigade. The First Marine Division which had already departed Korea, moved to Camp Pendleton, California.

Camp Pendleton, is "home" for the First Marine Division. The huge Marine base was named in honor of Joseph H. Pendleton who served the Corps for 40 years. He was a veteran of the Spanish-American War and the "Banana Wars" of Nicaragua and the Dominican Republic. He died in February 1942 after retiring as a major general of Marines.

Meanwhile, the Second Marine Division, at Camp Lejeune, North Carolina, continued to provide landing forces for the amphibious ships of the U.S. Sixth Fleet on duty in the Mediterranean and also stood ready to move an expeditionary force into the Caribbean should the need arise.

Camp Lejeune was named in honor of John Archer Lejeune, the 13th Commandant of the Marine Corps, who served as a Marine officer for nearly 40 years. During World War I, he became the first Marine officer to command an Army division. He was appointed Commandant of the Marine Corps in June 1920, and is credited with establishing the Marine Corps Schools at Quantico, Va., and directing the Marine Corps in its role as an amphibious-prepared force in readiness. He retired in 1929, and died in November 1942. Camp Lejeune is the "home" of the Second Marine Division.

In the years after the cessation of hostilities in Korea, the Corps' activities were as varied as they were scattered. In August 1953, Marines of the Sixth Fleet assisted in relief activities following an earthquake in Greece. Elements of the Second Marine Division cruised off the coast of riot-torn Guatemala during July 1954, prepared to land security forces if necessary.

Lebanon Intervention 1958

The U.S. policy of maintaining forces for immediate deployment to potential trouble spots proved sound during the summer of 1958. Following the overthrow of a Western-aligned government in Iraq on July 14, President Camille Chamoun of Lebanon immediately requested U.S. troops to bolster his army against a growing rebel threat.

The following day, the first of four Marine battalions, under the command of Brigadier General Sidney S. Wade, landed at Beirut. In a highly sensitive situation, the discipline of the Marines was superb and there were no casualties. Later, additional American forces reinforced the Marines who, after the crisis had subsided, withdrew on October 4.

Developments

During the post-Korean years, the Marine Corps also developed concepts, tactics and equipment to continually update its readiness.

In 1948, Marine planners began work on the development of an integrated amphibious and heliborne force designed for a rapid assault from the sea. Eventually, this concept gave birth to the Navy's amphibious assault ship (LPH), a combat vessel capable of carrying a Marine battalion landing team (BLT) and a medium helicopter squadron (HMM). The early LPH's were converted aircraft carriers, but the first ship specifically designed to support such a force, the USS *Iwo Jima*, was commissioned in 1961. Before the end of the decade, the *Iwo Jima* and her sister ships participated in over 65 amphibious assaults which were conducted by Marine Special Landing Forces in Vietnam.

To provide close air support for an expeditionary force, the Marine Corps developed the Short Airfield for Tactical Support (SATS). Rapidly installed at the beachhead, this land-based carrier deck consisted of 4,000 feet of aluminum matting, a catapult, an arresting cable and portable control units to keep Marine attack aircraft in proximity of the landing force.

The 1960's

During the 1960s, there were two main areas of conflict which most affected the Marine Corps – Southeast Asia and the Caribbean.

Following the Communist invasion of Laos in late 1960, BLT's on board Seventh Fleet ships in the South China Sea remained on alert for possible deployment and, the following year, Marine helicopters provided logistical support for the Laotian government. In May 1962, the 3d Marine Expeditionary Unit, a BLT with helicopter and fixed-wing squadrons, was committed to Thailand because of external Communist pressure.

Meanwhile, HMM-362 of the First Marine Aircraft Wing, deployed to Vietnam where the helicopter squadron flew combat missions in support of the South Vietnamese armed forces. Under the code name SHU-FLY, these crews operated in the Mekong Delta and later deployed to Da Nang in I Corps. The initial Marine commitment to South Vietnam was approximately 600 men, including advisors to ground units.

In October 1962, there was a crisis in the Caribbean when U.S. Intelligence reported the installation of Soviet-built offensive missiles at several bases in Communist-controlled Cuba.

The long war in Vietnam saw the Marines operating less from landing tracked vehicles such as these and using helicopters to operate against communist aggressors along Vietnam's demilitarized zone.

President John F. Kennedy issued an ultimatum to the Russian and Cuban governments, demanding the removal of these weapons, and simultaneously mobilized the American Armed Forces.

In response to this alert, the Marine garrison at Guantanamo Bay, Cuba, received reinforcements and combat elements of the Second Marine Division, and the Second Marine Aircraft Wing deployed to forward positions for an immediate reaction.

An expeditionary brigade from the First Marine Division arrived shortly off the coast of Cuba. This show of American force led to delicate negotiations which eventually resulted in the removal of Russian missiles from Cuban soil.

Landing in South Vietnam

Early in 1965, Marines conducted two important landings, one of which would commit the Corps to the longest war in its history.

As the result of North Vietnamese torpedo boat attacks on U.S. ships in the Tonkin Gulf during August 1964, President Lyndon B. Johnson ordered air strikes against selected military targets in the north.

The following February, the Viet Cong attacked two U.S. installations in South Vietnam, killing several Americans, and again U.S. planes bombed North Vietnam. To guard against Communist retaliatory air strikes, the 1st Light Anti-Aircraft Missile Battalion deployed from Okinawa to Da Nang for air defense.

On March 8, 1965, the 9th Marine Expeditionary Brigade, commanded by Brigadier General Frederick C. Karch, began landing at Da Nang for additional security of the base, and by March 12, some 5,000 Marines were ashore. All of the Marines were formerly members of the III Marine Expeditionary Force stationed on Okinawa or other parts of Japan.

Two days later, an additional battalion from the 1st Marine Brigade in Hawaii arrived at Phu Bai, seven miles south of Hue. The Marines took up defensive positions at both enclaves, but conducted no major offensive operations against insurgents. They did, however, bolster the South Vietnamese forces who were losing an average of one battalion a week to the Viet Cong.

Dominican Republic

Halfway around the world, the 6th Marine Expeditionary Unit was moving into another trouble spot.

On April 24, 1965, the Commander Caribbean Task Group 44.9, with BLT 3/6 and HMM-264 embarked, was ordered to proceed to a position off the coast of the Dominican Republic, which was being rocked by internal disorder. The American Embassy in Santo Domingo reported that a coup was in progress against the existing government of President Donald Reid Cabral and the Marines were to stand by for possible evacuation of Americans and other foreign nationals.

With the rebels in control of the city, 500 Marines landed on April 28, 1965, to protect the refugees, since the local police could no longer handle the situation. As conditions continued to deteriorate, additional elements of the 6th MEU were committed to protect civilians and the U.S. Embassy. By the 29th, some 1,500 Marines were ashore. The next day, U.S. Army airborne units arrived, and on May 1, the 4th Marine Expeditionary Brigade, commanded by Brigadier General John G. Bouker, was activated. Marine and Army troops engaged rebel bands in sporadic fire fights and there were numerous sniping incidents.

On May 6, the Organization of American States voted to send an Inter-American Peace Force to help restore peace and constitutional government in the Dominican Republic. The first contingent of Brazilian troops arrived on May 25, and the Marines began their withdrawal the next day.

Eventually, units from Paraguay, Honduras, Nicaragua and Costa Rica reinforced the Brazilians, and on June 6, the last elements of the 4th MEB departed Santo Domingo. At one point, there were 8,000 Marines either ashore or afloat off the coast of the Dominican Republic. Final USMC casualties were 9 killed and 30 wounded.

Establishment of III MAF

While the 4th MEB departed Santo Domingo, the Marine Corps accelerated its commitment to the Republic of Vietnam (RVN). On May 3, 1965, Major General William R. Collins arrived at Da Nang with an advance party of the Third Marine Division. The 9th MEB was deactivated and the III Marine Expeditionary Force was established along with the Third Marine Division (Forward). At that time, ground elements consisted primarily of the 3d Marine Regiment, and all aviation units were under the control of MAG-16.

On May 11, Major General Paul J. Fontana brought the First Marine Aircraft Wing (Advance) to Da Nang and assumed operational control of all

Marine helicopter and fixed-wing assets in the country.

The designation of III MEF was changed to III Marine Amphibious Force on May 7. General Collins assumed the role as both division and force commander.

The same day, the 3d MAB, commanded by Brigadier General Marion E. Carl, made an unopposed landing at Chu Lai, 55 miles south of Da Nang and established the third Marine enclave in I Corps. Two days after this landing, Marine engineers and U.S. Navy Seabees began construction of a SATS field at Chu Lai.

Laboring under extremely adverse conditions, the working parties completed an operational strip by June 1, when the first A-4 *Skyhawks* of MAG-12 arrived from Cubi Pt., P.I.

Another important arrival was that of Major General Lewis W. Walt, who took command of III MAF and the Third Marine Division on June 5. General Walt assumed operational control of all U.S. Forces in I Corps and, in turn, was under the overall control of the U.S. Military Assistance Command, Vietnam (MACV), commanded by General William C. Westmoreland, U.S. Army. The Marines still maintained a defensive posture with orders to conduct only those limited offensive operations necessary to ensure the security of their perimeters.

Large Unit Operations

On July 1, 1965, Viet Cong demolition squads launched their first attack on the Da Nang airbase, and it became apparent that the Marines would have to expand their areas of responsibility and conduct deep patrolling to prevent further attacks.

In early August, General Westmoreland granted permission for General Walt to undertake major offensive operations in I Corps. This decision coincided with the arrival of the 7th Marines at Chu Lai.

Within four days of landing, Regimental Landing Team (RLT)-7 took part in the first major American battle of the war – Operation STARLITE. On August 18, RLT-7 moved quickly against the 1st VC Regiment, which was massing on the Van Tuong Peninsula, 15 miles south of Chu Lai. In a classic maneuver, one Marine force moved in from the north by amphibian tractor; a second conducted a helicopter assault to the west of the enemy regiment; a third launched an amphibious landing along the southern flank.

RLT-7 then compressed the 1st VC Regiment against the sea and in six days of heavy fighting,

killed over 600 enemy soldiers. On September 7, the 7th Marines attacked the remnants of the 1st VC Regiment in Operation PIRANHA and killed another 189 Communist troops.

The last major operation of the year took place near the Quang Tin Provincial capital of Tam Ky. In December, Brigadier General Jonas M. Platt's Task Force DELTA, along with South Vietnamese units participated in Operation HARVEST MOON, killing 300 Viet Cong and capturing a large quantity of enemy supplies and equipment.

By the end of 1965, there were 38,000 Marines in I Corps, with more on the way. In January 1966, the President authorized the deployment of the First Marine Division to Vietnam.

One regiment, the 7th Marines, along with two battalions of the 1st Marines, were already in Vietnam. By June, the 5th Marines had joined its parent unit. The division headquarters, with Major General Lewis Fields in command, was established at Chu Lai on March 29, 1966, and was assigned responsibility for the two southern provinces.

With its headquarters at Da Nang, the Third Marine Division, then commanded by Major General Wood B. Kyle, took over the central and northern provinces. In the first half of 1966, most of the action centered in southern provinces.

Task Force DELTA conducted a number of productive operations, including DOUBLE EAGLE, UTAH and TEXAS. These three efforts resulted in over 1,000 enemy dead, as well as tons of captured supplies.

Pacification

The Marines learned early that the war in Vietnam was not entirely a military struggle. In a counterinsurgency environment, the people were the key to success, and the III MAF initiated several programs to win the support of the populace.

In late 1965, the 9th Marines initiated GOLDEN FLEECE operations whereby Marine units protected the villagers' rice crop from the guerillas during harvest time. This effort was so successful in denying the VC logistical support that General Walt expanded the program throughout I Corps.

COUNTY FAIR, another 9th Marines innovation, was a combined US/ARVN cordon and search process aimed at the local guerillas. Moving into position before dawn, the Marines threw a cordon around a target hamlet to prevent the VC from escaping or receiving reinforcements. At last light, South Vietnamese troops entered the hamlet, where they took a census, fed the people, provided medical attention and entertainment, and searched the area. Those VC who were not killed or captured were disposed of by the Marines when they fled the hamlet.

The Combined Action Program, which was initiated by the 3d Battalion, 4th Marines, at Phu Bai, was designed to provide prolonged security for the villagers by preparing the militia-like Popular Forces (PF) for local defense. The basic operating unit was a 14-man Marine squad, with a Navy corpsman, which was integrated into a 35-man PF platoon, forming a Combined Action Platoon (CAP).

The Marines lived in the village, assisting in the military training of the PFs and initiating self-help projects for the peasants. These local defense groups were soon able to deny the Viet Cong access to rice and recruits from the hamlets and provided the villagers with a life free of Communist terror and intimidation.

By late 1966, the various pacification and civic action programs, shielded by Allied military operations, had extended government influence over 1,690 square miles and 1,000,000 people in I Corps.

War in the DMZ

As a result of Allied military and pacification successes along the coastal plain, the communists were forced to open a new front along the northern border of I Corps. In July 1966, the 324th NVA Division moved south across the DMZ in its first major invasion attempt. Besides seizing Quang Tri Province, the enemy hoped to draw the Marines away from the populated areas, thin out their forces and take pressure off the guerillas in the south.

General Walt responded quickly with Operation HASTINGS, which eventually pitted 8,000 Marines and 3,000 South Vietnamese troops against the enemy division. Heavy fighting continued until August 3, when the 324th retreated to the north, leaving over 1,000 dead behind.

To counter the continuing threat from the north, the Third Marine Division displaced to Phu Bai in October and established an advanced CP at Dong Ha. The First Marine Division then shifted to Da Nang as U.S. Army troops moved into the Chu Lai area, thus freeing Marines for duty farther north. Meanwhile, the Third Marine Division initiated a series of operations named PRAIRIE to apply steady pressure on enemy elements operating along the DMZ.

In the spring of 1967, the 325C NVA Division made a thrust into the south, this time against the isolated outpost at Khe Sanh. Two battalions of the 3d

Marines responded and, behind pinpoint bombing of Marine attack aircraft as well as massive artillery fire, drove two enemy regiments from the hills overlooking the base. In two weeks of bitter, uphill fighting, the Marines killed 940 NVA at a cost of 125 dead.

In July 1967, the action shifted farther to the east, where the 9th Marines blocked another invasion attempt with Operation BUFFALO. The North Vietnamese scored an early success when five NVA battalions surrounded and badly mauled one Marine company, but six Marine battalions, including both Special Landing Forces (SLFs), were committed to the action, and the enemy retreated after losing almost 1,300 men.

The direct assaults across the DMZ had resulted in heavy enemy losses. As a result, the NVA shifted to heavy artillery, rocket and mortar attacks along the northern border. The focal point for much of this fire was Con Thien. The Marines there endured heavy shelling throughout the late summer and the fall of 1967.

Meanwhile, the First Marine Division, U.S. Army units of Task Force OREGON, and South Vietnamese troops repeatedly attacked the 2nd NVA Division south of Da Nang and by the year's end had rendered it ineffective as a fighting unit.

The Tet Offensive

On January 31, 1968, the Communists unleashed their biggest offensive of the war. Taking advantage of the TET (Vietnamese Lunar New Year) holiday season and the poor weather associated with the northeast monsoons, the National Liberation Front infiltrated some 68,000 troops into the major population centers of South Vietnam.

They struck with amazing speed and secrecy. The enemy hoped to seize the cities, cause mass defections in the South Vietnamese armed forces and take control of the government.

While the Communists met with initial success, the Allies responded quickly, drove the invaders from the cities and in three weeks killed 32,000 enemy troops. Prolonged fighting continued in Saigon and Hue, where die-hard remnants held out for several weeks.

In Hue, a near division-size NVA force occupied the city and the Citadel, which encompassed the old imperial grounds. Marine, Army, and South Vietnamese troops conducted Operation HUE CITY to drive out the NVA. The 1st and 5th Marines, under Brigadier General Foster LaHue's Task Force X-RAY, cleared the southern half of the city in savage street fighting and then turned to the walled Citadel. This was the Marines' first combat in a built-up area since fighting in Seoul during the Korean War.

To minimize civilian casualties, the Marines had to forego their usually heavy application of supporting arms, and the fighting was house-to-house, with progress measured in yards. On February 24, the enemy flag, which had flown over the Citadel for 24 days, was ripped down and the last enemy pockets of resistance collapsed the next day. The battle cost the NVA 5,000 men.

While the fighting raged in Hue, the men of the 26th Marines were engaged in a different type of struggle at Khe Sanh.

Beginning in late 1967, two NVA divisions, the 325C and the 304th, had invested that garrison and on January 21, 1968, unleashed their first attack. General Westmoreland and Lieutenant General Robert E. Cushman, who had relieved General Walt in May 1967, reinforced the three organic battalions of the 26th Marines with the 1st Battalion, 9th Marines, and the 37th ARVN Ranger Battalion, setting the stage for one of the most dramatic battles of the war – Operation SCOTLAND.

For two and a half months, the Khe Sanh defenders fought off enemy ground attacks and weathered daily artillery, rocket and mortar attacks. During the siege, U.S. aircraft dropped over 100,000 tons of bombs on the hills surrounding Khe Sanh, while Marine and U.S. Army batteries fired in excess of 150,000 artillery rounds. Literally blown from their positions, the NVA withdrew in the face of a combined Marine, Army, and South Vietnamese Task Force (Operation PEGASUS), advancing toward Khe Sanh from the east.

All told, the NVA lost about 3,000 men during the two operations, although some estimates of enemy dead ran as high as 12,000.

Peace Talks

On March 31, 1968, President Johnson made a television address to the nation, during which he announced that he was limiting the U.S. air strikes against North Vietnam. This action eventually led to peace talks in Paris, which began on May 13, 1968. Even with talks underway, the fighting continued in South Vietnam.

Along the DMZ, the 3d Marine Division frustrated repeated enemy attempts for a major victory with Operations SCOTLAND II, LANCASTER, KENTUCKY, and NAPOLEON/SALINE. In the area south of Da Nang, the 1st Marine Division partici-

pated in such major operations as ALLEN BROOK, MAMELUKE THRUST, and MEADE RIVER. Additional reinforcements also arrived in I Corps when the 1st Air Cavalry Division, elements of the 101st Airborne Division and the temporarily assigned 27th Marines came under III MAF control. By the end of the year, General Cushman commanded 163,000 American troops, more than any Marine general in history.

Withdrawals

During early 1969, President Richard M. Nixon initiated efforts to end the war, achieve an honorable peace and withdraw American fighting forces from Vietnam. In June, he met with President Thieu of South Vietnam on Midway Island and announced that 25,000 U.S. troops would depart South Vietnam, beginning in July 1969.

In the first phase, the 9th Marines began their redeployment on July 14 and by mid-November, the remainder of the Third Marine Division had displaced to Okinawa. This withdrawal movement continued into the new year when, in March 1970, the 26th Marines departed Vietnam. Marine strength in I Corps had been up to 86,700 at one time, but by March 1970, there were only 42,000 remaining in Vietnam.

The U.S. Army took over the command responsibility for I Corps when the XXIV Corps replaced III MAF in March 1970, and assumed operational control of the remaining American troops in I Corps.

Slightly more than a year later, most Marine units had returned to their permanent bases and a small residual force remained to complete the final administrative and logistical tasks.

The Marine Corps began again to concentrate on preparations for its future assignments by resuming the role of our nation's amphibious force in readiness.

Force in Readiness

MAYAGUEZ Incident

On May 12, 1975, just two weeks after the evacuation of Saigon at the end of the Vietnam War, an unarmed American container ship *Mayaguez* was seized by a Cambodian gunboat and taken to the Cambodian offshore island of Koh Tang. Since no amphibious units were near the area, Marine units from Okinawa were airlifted to Utapao airbase in nearby Thailand for an assault on the ship and island using U.S. Air Force helicopters. Recapture of the ship proceeded smoothly with 69 Marines from Company D, 1st Battalion, 4th Marines landed on the destroyer escort *Harold E. Holt* for the final approach to the ship. The *Holt* came alongside *Mayaguez*, and the Marines boarded and seized the ship, which they found had been recently abandoned.

At the same time an assault was launched by a 210-man raiding force of Marines from Company G, 2nd Battalion, 9th Marines on the island of Koh Tang, where it was believed the American crew was being held. Landing from Air Force CH-53 and HH-

Marines were familiar with Beirut, Lebanon, in the last half of the 19th century, having been sent there twice to handle crisis situations. The first time was 1958 and the second was from 1982 to 1984.

53 helicopters, the assault encountered devastating ground fire. The Marines were in heavy combat on the island until their evacuation on the night of May 16.

Shortly after the assault landing, the crew members of the *Mayaguez* were picked up by a U.S. Navy ship from the same boat that the Cambodians were using in an effort to return them. The *Mayaguez* crew members were returned to their ship and were able to sail away while the fighting on the Koh Tang Island was still going on. Casualties in this operation were heavy, with 15 Marines, Navy men, and airmen killed, three Marines missing, and 50 other servicemen wounded. Three of the fifteen helicopters used in the operation were shot down and ten others received battle damage.

Marines in Lebanon – 1982-84

Marines returned to Lebanon on August 25, 1982, with the landing of roughly 800 men of the 32d MAU to form part of a multinational peacekeeping force. The other troops participating were 400 French and 800 Italians, and the mission of the force was evacuation of PLO guerrillas who were under siege in Beirut by Israeli forces. The evacuation was completed on September 10 and 32nd MAU departed aboard amphibious ships, however, on September 29 the MAU returned to Beirut to rejoin the French-Italian force which by then numbered 2,200 men. On October 30 the 32d MAU was relieved by the 24th MAU, and for the next sixteen months a MAU was maintained in Beirut with 22d MAU relieving in February 1982, the 24th MAU returning in May, and 22d MAU in November after participating in operations in Grenada.

During more than a year ashore in Lebanon, Marines experienced a variety of both combat and non-combat situations. These included rocket, mortar, artillery, automatic weapons and sniper attacks starting in March 1983 and continuing sporadically until the Marines departed 11 months later. These attacks were met by counter fire that included all weapons from sharpshooting riflemen and tanks to 155mm artillery and the 16-inch guns of the USS *New Jersey*. A suicide truck packed with 12,000 pounds of explosives, attacked the BLT 1/8 headquarters building at the Beirut International Airport killing 241 Americans and wounding 70 others on October 23, 1983.

Marines also participated in training of the Lebanese Army and later conducted combined patrolling and occupied combined positions with Lebanese Army units. After the worst winter storm in memory struck Lebanon in February 1983, Marines with helicopters, trucks, and amphibian tractors conducted relief operations in the Syrian-held central mountains and town of Quartaba.

Sectarian strife among the Lebanese developed and in February 1984 heavy fighting broke out between the Lebanese Army and Shiite militia units, with Druze and other Moslem militia seizing much of Beirut. The decision was made to redeploy Marines from Beirut International Airport to ships offshore. American civilians and other foreign nationals were evacuated by helicopter on February 10-11, and, leaving a residual force behind to protect the U.S. Embassy, the 22d MAU completed its redeployment to the amphibious ships on February 26, 1984.

Grenada – 1983

Following assassination of the Prime Minister and violent overthrow of the government of Grenada, U.S. intervention was requested by neighboring Caribbean nations. On October 21, 1983, the Naval task force which was transporting the Marines of the 22nd MAU to Lebanon was redirected to Grenada. On October 25 the Marines made helicopter and surface landings in the northern part of the island; their mission included seizure of Pearls Airport and the rescue of several hundred American students attending the local medical college. Simultaneous landings by U.S. Army airborne troops were aimed at seizure of a second large airfield in the south of the island. 22nd MAU accomplished its mission, capturing large quantities of weapons and ammunition as well as large numbers of Cuban and Grenadian insurgents. Hundreds of American students were evacuated by helicopter. On November 1 the MAU conducted assault landings on the island of Carriacou, 15 miles north of Grenada, capturing more weapons, ammunition and military personnel. On November 2 the MAU reembarked and sailed for its original destination of Lebanon.

Panama – 1989

Instability in Panama threatened the safety of Americans there as well as international use of the Panama Canal. Further complicating the issue were American criminal charges of narcotics smuggling against the Panamanian dictator, General Manuel Noriega. On December 20, 1989, five days after a Panamanian gunman killed a Marine officer, the U.S.

Army inserted a combat force to preserve the Panama Canal Treaty and apprehend Noriega. Marines from Company K, 3d Battalion 6th Marines, and Company D, 2d Light Armored Infantry Battalion (LAV mounted), who were stationed in the country to provide security for defense installations, supported the Army attack on the Panamanian Defense Force (PDF). Marines were tasked with protecting the Pacific entrance to the canal, establishing roadblocks and apprehending PDF members. A light armored infantry section also supported action against Noriega's headquarters. By the end of the first day, Marines had seized several PDF compounds, apprehended 1,200 Panamanians, and confiscated more than 550 weapons.

Operation Desert Shield

On August 2, 1990, Iraq invaded neighboring Kuwait. Saddam Hussein's army, which quickly gained control of the small but oil-rich Persian Gulf nation, poised units along the Kuwaiti border with Saudi Arabia. The American government anticipated a possible Iraqi attack on Saudi Arabia, which led President George Bush to order U.S. forces to the region. This began one of the most rapid overseas buildups of the American force in history. Much of the 1st Marine Division was in the Saudi desert by the end of the month. Other elements of the I and II Marine Expeditionary Forces followed through the fall of 1990. In addition, the President authorized the first large-scale activation of reserve units since the early 1950s.

When Iraq invaded neighboring Kuwait, Marine forces were among the first ashore in Saudi Arabia to hold the line against further Iraqi aggression in the Middle East.

Operation Desert Storm

With forces in place to defend Saudi Arabia, Kuwait became the focus of the United States and an American-led coalition of nations. President Bush, acting with the approval of the United Nations, established January 15, 1991, as the deadline for Iraqi forces to withdraw from Kuwait. Hussein, in turn, indicated an intent on retaining Kuwait and threatened the United States with the "mother of all wars" should the Americans and their allies attack the Iraqi army.

On January 16, the allies launched a massive airstrike against strategic targets in Iraq, beginning a five-week strategic and tactical air campaign. Allied air forces quickly achieved and maintained air supremacy throughout the theater. Marine F/A-18 *Hornets*, A-6E *Intruders*, AV-8B *Harriers*, and EA-6B *Prowlers* participated in the campaign. In the fourth week, even Marine C-130s took an offensive role, dropping several fuel-air-explosive bombs on tactical targets.

Marine ground forces – two divisions and service support within an expanded expeditionary force structure under the command of Lieutenant General Walter Boomer – were positioned south of Kuwait during the air campaign. The 1st Marine Division held positions near the Persian Gulf, while the 2d Marine Division was further inland. The 4th and 5th Marine Expeditionary Brigades and the 13th Marine Expeditionary Unit were embarked aboard amphibious shipping in the gulf. For the first two weeks of the war, ground forces did little more than maintain their equipment, with the exception of several battery-size artillery raids against Iraqi defensive positions along the Kuwaiti border.

On January 29, combat elements of an Iraqi corps attacked south into the Saudi town of Khafji. The attack was quickly repulsed by air and ground action, but it produced the first Marine ground casualties. Eleven Marines were killed while supporting a Saudi counterattack. Seven of those casualties resulted from friendly fire.

In the third week of February, light armored infantry units crossed the Kuwaiti border in a feint to the northwest of the Al Wafra oil fields. The action was a prelude to the corps-size attack that began on the morning of February 24. Both Marine divisions quickly breached the mined defensive lines and engaged the Iraqis in ground combat. A planned amphibious assault on Kuwait City was canceled out

Two Marine divisions attacked through Iraqi-mined defense lines to liberate Kuwait. Their maneuver is considered a classic in modern warfare and is still studied today.

of concern for shallow water mines, but the presence of embarked forces in the gulf, and the resulting Iraqi defensive posture along the coast, probably detracted from the Iraqi ability to respond to the Marine attack from the south.

The two-division attack actually was itself a diversion, an attempt at fixing the Iraqis in place in support of the campaign's main effort. As the Marines fixed the Iraqis with their headfirst plunge, U.S. Army and allied forces were to move into Iraq west of Kuwait to isolate and surround the Iraqi invasion force. The Iraqis crumbled, however, in the face of the Marine offensive, allowing both divisions to reach Kuwait City within 100 hours. President Bush ordered a ceasefire on February 28 with the 2d Marine Division pursuing Iraqi units near the city's western suburbs and the 1st Marine Division consolidating its gains near the international airport to the south of the city. A formal surrender was received by the allies shortly after. In four days of combat, the Marines destroyed 11 Iraqi divisions. Twenty-three Marines were killed in action during the four-day ground war.

Military Operations Other Than War

On April 7, 1991, a little more than a month after the Gulf War, the 24th Marine Expeditionary Unit was deployed in northern Iraq to assist refugee Kurds, a minority group in Iraq and Turkey. The Kurds, who were seeking a secession from Iraq, were being threatened by and fleeing from Iraqi troops. The Marines were part of a 10-nation force that, under the auspices of the Gulf War allies, and later the United Nations, was in place to provide humanitarian relief. It was one of several such military operations other than war (MOOTW) that, in addition to successes against the Iraqis, characterized the use of American forces in the 1990s.

Several MOOTW occurred in the months prior to the Gulf War. In April 1989, Marines from Company A, 1st Battalion, 4th Marines; HMM-166; and Company B, 1st Landing Support Battalion assisted with the cleanup effort after the Exxon Valdez oilspill in Alaska. In August 1990, Marines from Marine Air-Ground Task Force 4-90 helped search for survivors after a massive earthquake in the Philippines. In August 1990, as Marines were preparing to deploy to Southwest Asia, the 22d Marine Expeditionary Unit landed in the African nation of Liberia, where political instability was threatening the security of

Peacekeeping missions in the 1990s were exemplified by the 1992-93 mission to Somalia when Marines went in that famine-swept country to provide humanitarian relief to starving civilians.

foreign nationals. The 2d Battalion, 4th Marines and attachments; HMM-262; and MSSG-22 established a security zone at the U.S. embassy in Monrovia, from where they evacuated 1,705 foreign nationals. The 22d Marine Expeditionary Unit was relieved by the 26th Marine Expeditionary Unit later in August. That unit, made up of the 3d Battalion, 8th Marines and attachments; HMM-162; and MSSG-26, acted as a peace-keeping force and helped transport relief workers until reembarking on amphibious shipping in January 1991. Also in January, the 4th Marine Expeditionary Brigade landed in Somalia. Again reacting to political instability, Marines evacuated more than 400 foreign nationals from that nation's capital, Mogadishu.

Marines participated in numerous MOOTW since, including the following summary of major deployments. On May 15-19, 1991, the 5th Marine Expeditionary Brigade provided humanitarian relief after a major typhoon decimated much of Bangladesh in south Asia. In June of that year, the 15th Marine Expeditionary Unit and Contingency Marine Air-Ground Task Force 2-91 joined Marine Air-Ground Task Force 4-90 in the Philippines to help provide relief following the volcanic eruption of Mt. Pinatubo. In another volcano-related relief effort, the 24th Marine Expeditionary Unit in April 1992 attempted to stop or divert a lava flow from Mt. Etna in Sicily by airdropping cement. That effort, though innovative, failed to prevent lava from engulfing an evacuated Sicilian town.

In May 1992, the 3d Battalion, 1st Marines and the 3d Light Armored Infantry Battalion provided support to civilian law enforcement agencies during riots in Los Angeles. The Marines, as well as national guardsmen, provided security but did not directly participate in police activities, in accordance with American law. In another domestic support operation, Marines continue to participate in Joint Task Force 6, which has provided drug-interdiction support to patrol agencies along the American border with Mexico since 1989. A small number of Marines also continue to participate in drug eradication operations in South America.

In June 1992, the 9th Engineer Support Battalion and the 3d Recon Battalion helped provide drought relief to the Micronesian island of Chuuk. Two months later, the 1st Marine Expeditionary Brigade supported typhoon victims in Guam. The action was followed shortly by domestic hurricane disasters in Dade County, Florida, and Kauai, Hawaii. The I Marine Expeditionary Brigade supported victims in Kauai from August to October 1992, while about 1,000 Marines from various commands supported victims in Florida.

The Marines played a key role in one of the largest humanitarian operations in history. Responding to a war-induced famine in eastern Africa, Marines provided support during the insertion of Pakistani peacekeepers in Somalia in September 1992. In October, Marine operations expanded to include support in Kenya. Then, on December 9, the 15th Marine Expeditionary Unit landed in Mogadishu to take control of the massive famine relief effort. The Marines and Lieutenant General Robert B. Johnston, who commanded the joint task force that was built around assets from I Marine Expeditionary Force, were credited with a successful performance when they turned over control of the operation to the United Nations five months later.

Though immediate relief needs were met in Somalia, the political situation there slowly deteriorated during the rest of 1993 and 1994. Marines played a minor role in the U.N. operation during those months, but in March 1995 they were called back to center stage by President Clinton. The 13th Marine Expeditionary Unit, with elements of 3d Battalion, 1st Marines and 3d Battalion, 7th Marines, was tasked with supporting the extraction of multinational peacekeepers and recovering U.S. equipment and weaponry. Marines engaged Somalis in light fighting during the 73-hour operation. The most significant aspect of the encounter was the Marine use of nonlethal weapons, including sticky foam and stun grenades. It was the Corps' first employment ever of such weapons.

Throughout 1994, Marines participated in joint Caribbean Sea operations to prevent Haitian and Cuban boat people from reaching the United States illegally. Marines also maintained separate refugee camps for Haitian and Cubans at the U.S. naval base at Guantanamo Bay, Cuba. As political debate raged as to whether these people were economic or political refugees – an important distinction for those seeking immigration to the United States – President Clinton demanded that the Haitian military leaders return governmental control to that nation's democratically elected officials. American forces, including Marines, poised for offensive operations against the Haitian army. Last minute diplomacy defused the situation, however, and Americans instead were deployed as peacekeepers during the transfer of power. Americans faced little resistance after Marines from the 2d Battalion, 2d Marines encountered Haitians in a short firefight in Cap-Haitien.

On April 20, 1996, a reinforced rifle company from the 22d Marine Expeditionary Unit was airlifted into Monrovia, Liberia, to assist with the evacuation of American and designated foreign citizens because of decreasing stability in that country. Ten days later, Marines returned small arms fire near the American embassy, killing three gunmen and wounding several more. It was the second time in the 1990s the Marines would land in Monrovia because of an internal conflict that had been raging on and off since 1989. While off the coast of Liberia, Marines from the 22d Marine Expeditionary Unit also participated in an evacuation of Americans and others from the Central African Republic. The deployment also was significant for its demonstration of split-MEU operations, wherein a Marine expeditionary unit and its amphibious shipping deploy simultaneously to different areas of operation. In June, BLT 3/8 was back in the news as part of a SPMAGTF along with detachments from HMM-264, HMLA-167, and 2d FSSG that sailed on the USS *Ponce* to relieve the 22d Marine Expeditionary Unit (Special Operations Capable) off the coast of Monrovia, Liberia.

In August 1996, 22d Marine Expeditionary Unit (Special Operations Capable) deployed across western and central Africa to conduct Noncombatant Evacuation Operations (NEOs) in Liberia and Embassy Reinforcement in the Central African Republic. From March to July 1997, 26th Marine Expeditionary Unit (Special Operations Capable) conducted a NEO in Tirana, Albania during Operation SILVER WAKE, evacuating more than 800 civilians. Additionally, the Marine Expeditionary Unit assumed the role as Commander, Joint Task Force GUARDIAN RETRIEVAL for the planned NEO of Kinshasa, Democratic Republic of Congo. In July 1997, 22d Marine Expeditionary Unit (Special Operations Capable) evacuated more than 2500 civilians from Freetown, Sierra Leone, as part of Operation NOBLE OBELISK. Domestically, forest fires in the Midwest and West kept units from Camp Lejeune and Camp Pendleton busy for several summers. Additionally, numerous detachments deployed to the Caribbean and Central America in support of humanitarian missions.

Marines in the Persian Gulf

In Southwest Asia, forward deployed forces supported the enforcement of the No Fly Zones over Iraq, as part of Operations SOUTHERN WATCH and NORTHERN WATCH. Additionally, Marine Expeditionary Unit forces and elements of I Marine Expeditionary Force at Camp Pendleton deployed to the region as part of Operations VIGILANT WARRIOR (Fall 1994), VIGILANT SENTINEL (August 1995-February 1996) and DESERT THUNDER (February-July 1998 and again in November 1998), where the 31st Marine Expeditionary Unit (Special Operations Capable) went ashore in Kuwait.

Conflict in the Balkans

With United Nations peacekeepers unable to stabilize a war between the newly independent states of the former Yugoslavia, NATO established a no-fly zone in 1993 with the intention of preventing Serb aircraft from attacking or supporting attacks in Bosnia. Marine F/A-18 *Hornets* and EA-6B *Prowlers* participated in patrols to enforce that no-fly zone.

Under NATO command, Marine pilots also participated in airstrikes during 1994 and 1995. On April 11, 1994, two *Hornets* from VMFA-251 struck Serb targets near Gorazde. On November 21 of that year, *Hornets* from VMFA-533 hit targets at a Serb-controlled airfield. The following day, *Prowlers* from VMAQ-4 provided electronic support for a NATO strike against a Serb surface-to-air missile site in Croatia.

On June 8, 1995, a recovery team from the 24th Marine Expeditionary Unit extracted Captain Scott F. O'Grady, a downed U.S. Air Force pilot, from the Bosnian countryside. The team, mostly comprised of Marines from Weapons Company, 3d Battalion, 8th Marines, took Serb small arms and missile fire during the helicopter extraction but suffered no casualties.

On August 29, NATO responded to continuing Serb attacks into declared safe havens with a large-scale air attack. Marines from VMFA(AW)-533, VMFA(AW)-224, and VMFA-312 participated in the strikes, which continued around the clock for several days.

In June 1996, VMU-1, a Marine unmanned aerial vehicle squadron, deployed to Bosnia to provide reconnaissance support for the American elements of the NATO peacekeeping force. VMU-1 was the first (and currently only) Marine unit to deploy to Bosnia. As of the publishing of this edition, NATO continues to monitor the situation in the Balkans.

Marine units continued to support the NATO forces in the Republic of Bosnia-Hercegovina, flying combat aircraft in Operation DETERMINED FALCON, and providing presence during Operations JOINT ENDEAVOR, JOINT GUARD, and JOINT FORGE. In June 1999, 26th Marine Expeditionary Unit (Special Operations Capable) went ashore as the first American forces into Kosovo, for peacekeeping duty with NATO's KFOR (Kosovo FORces). The Marine Expeditionary Unit remained in Kosovo for six weeks, before handing the mission off to Army forces, and redeploying to amphibious shipping.

Chapter Three

Code of Conduct

The Code of Conduct was prescribed by the President of the United States in 1955 as a simple, written creed applying to all American fighting men. The words of the Code, presented in six articles, state principles that Americans have honored in all the wars this country has fought since 1776.

The Code is not intended to provide guidance on every aspect of military life. For that purpose there are military regulations, rules of military courtesy, and established customs and traditions. The Code of Conduct is in no way connected with the Uniform Code of Military Justice (UCMJ). The UCMJ has punitive powers; the Code of Conduct does not.

The six articles of the Code can be divided into three categories. Articles I and VI are general statements of dedication to country and freedom. Conduct on the battlefield is the subject of Article II. Articles III, IV, and V concern conduct as a prisoner of war.

Article I

I am an American, fighting in the armed forces which guard my country and our way of life. I am prepared to give my life in their defense.

It is a longstanding tradition of American citizens to willingly answer the call to arms when the peace

Corporal L.E. Smedley

and security of this nation are threatened. Patrick Henry stated it best in the early days of our country when he said, "Give me liberty or give me death." Nathan Hale, captured by the British during the Revolutionary War and charged with spying, personified the spirit of the American fighting person when he spoke the immortal words, "I only regret that I have but one life to lose for my country," just before his execution by hanging.

More recently, the threat to America has been less obvious as small countries such as South Korea, South Vietnam and Kuwait have borne the brunt of our enemies' attacks. Nevertheless, Americans have risen to the challenge and have proven their dedication and willingness to make the supreme sacrifice as much as in any of the wars in our history.

In December 1967, Marine Corporal Larry E. Smedley led his squad of six men into an ambush site west of the vital military complex at Da Nang in South Vietnam. When an estimated 100 enemy soldiers were observed carrying 122mm rocket launchers and mortars into position to launch an attack on Da Nang, Corporal Smedley courageously led his men in a bold attack on the enemy force which outnumbered them by more than 15 to 1.

Corporal Smedley fell mortally wounded in this engagement and was later awarded the Medal of Honor for his courageous actions. His bold initiative and fearless devotion to duty are perfect examples of the meaning of the words of Article I of the Code of Conduct.

Article II

I will never surrender of my own free will. If in command I will never surrender the members of my command while they still have the means to resist.

Nathan Hale - "I only regret that I have but one life to lose for my country."

John Paul Jones

This is an American tradition that dates back to the Revolutionary War. An individual may never voluntarily surrender. If isolated and unable to fight the enemy, a Marine is obligated to evade capture and rejoin friendly forces at the earliest possible time.

John Paul Jones always comes to mind when one reads Article II of the Code. It was in 1779 that the captain of the *Bonhomme Richard* challenged two British ships of war, the *Serapis* and *Countess of Scarborough*. Old, slow and hopelessly outclassed, the *Richard* was being badly battered, repeatedly set on fire, and rapidly filling with water when the captain of the *Serapis* called, "Do you ask for quarter?"

"I have have not yet begun to fight," said John Paul Jones. Hours later, the *Serapis* struck her flag and Jones and his crew boarded and captured the British ship as they watched their own ship sink.

Private M.E. Newlin

Where a unit is involved, the Marine in command may never surrender that unit to the enemy while it has the power to resist or evade. A unit that is cut off or surrounded must continue to fight until it is relieved by, or able to rejoin friendly forces.

Private First Class Melvin E. Newlin was manning a key machine gun post with four other Marines in July 1967 when a savage enemy attack nearly overran their position. Critically wounded, his comrades killed, Private Newlin propped himself against his machine gun and twice repelled the enemy attempts to overrun his position. During a third assault, he was knocked unconscious by a grenade, and the enemy, believing him dead, bypassed him and continued their attack on the main force. When he regained consciousness, he crawled back to his weapon and brought it to bear on the enemy rear, inflicting heavy casualties and causing the enemy to stop their assault on the main positions and again attack his machine gun post. Repelling two more enemy assaults, Private Newlin was awarded the Medal of Honor for his courageous refusal to surrender his position or to cease fighting because of his wounds.

In June 1966, Staff Sergeant Jimmie E. Howard and his reconnaissance platoon of 18 men were occupying an observation post deep within enemy-controlled territory in South Vietnam when they were attacked by a battalion-size force of enemy soldiers. During repeated assaults on the Marine position and despite severe wounds, Staff Sergeant Howard

Staff Sergeant J.E. Howard

encouraged his men and directed their fire, distributed ammunition, and directed repeated air strikes on the enemy. After a night of intense fighting which resulted in five men killed and all but one man wounded, the beleaguered platoon still held its position. Later, when evacuation helicopters approached the platoon's position, Staff Sergeant Howard warned them away and continued to direct air strikes and small arms fire on the enemy to ensure a secure landing zone. For his valiant leadership, courageous fighting spirit, and refusal to let his unit be beaten despite the overwhelming odds, Staff Sergeant Howard was awarded the Medal of Honor.

Article III

If I am captured, I will continue to resist by all means available. I will make every effort to escape and aid others to escape. I will accept neither parole nor special favors from the enemy.

Article IV

If I become a prisoner of war, I will keep faith with my fellow prisoners. I will give no information nor take part in any action which might be harmful to my comrades. If I am senior, I will take command. If not, I will obey the lawful orders of those appointed over me and will back them up in every way.

Article V

When questioned, should I become a prisoner of war, I am required to give name, rank, service number and date of birth. I will evade answering further questions to the utmost of my ability. I will make no oral or written statements disloyal to my country and its allies or harmful to their cause.

The misfortune of being captured by the enemy does not end a Marine's usefulness to the country. It is the Marine's duty to continue to resist the enemy by all possible means, and to escape and assist others to escape. A Marine may not accept parole from the enemy or special favors such as more food, warm clothes, less physical restrictions, etc., in return for promises not to escape, or informing, or providing information to the enemy.

Informing, or any other action endangering the well-being of a fellow prisoner is forbidden. Prisoners of war will not help the enemy by identifying fellow prisoners who may have knowledge of particular value to the enemy, and who may, therefore, be made to suffer brutal means of interrogation.

Strong leadership is essential to discipline. Without discipline, organization, resistance, and even survival may be extremely difficult. Personal hygiene, sanitation, and care of sick and wounded prisoners of war are absolute musts. All United States officers and noncommissioned officers will continue to carry out their responsibilities and exercise their authority if captured.

The senior line officer or noncommissioned officer within the prisoner of war camp or group of prisoners will assume command according to rank or date of rank, without regard to service. They are the lawful superior of all lower ranking personnel, regardless of branch of service.

The responsibility to assume command if senior cannot be avoided. If the senior officer or noncommissioned officer is incapacitated or unable to command for any reason, command will be assumed by the next senior person.

Article VI

I will never forget that I am an American, responsible for my actions, and dedicated to the principles which made my country free. I will trust in my God and in the United States of America.

Article VI and Article I of the Code are quite similar. The repeated words "I am an American" are perhaps the most important words in the Code, because they signify each American's faith and confidence in God, country, and service. Since John Paul Jones made his defiant reply, "I have not yet begun to fight," to the present, Americans have traditionally fought the enemy wherever found and with whatever weapons were available. When captured, the American fighting force has continued the battle in a new arena. When facing a Communist interrogator, they have been under fire just as though bullets and shell fragments were flying about them. Disarmed, the POW has fought back with mind and spirit, remaining faithful to fellow POW's, yielding no military information, and resisting every attempt of indoctrination. It is the responsibility of each Marine to honor these traditions by carefully adhering to the meaning of each article of the Code of Conduct. The many Americans who have accepted this responsibility are heroes in the finest sense of the word.

In February 1966, Lieutenant (jg) Dieter Dengler, USNR, was on a bombing mission over North Vietnam when his aircraft was badly damaged by ground fire. Lieutenant Dengler crash-landed his aircraft in nearby Laos and attempted to evade capture. After successfully evading for one day, he was captured and led to a village where he was interrogated and told to sign a Communist propaganda statement condemning the United States. Lieutenant Dengler's repeated refusal to give more than his name, rank, service number and date of birth, or to sign any statements, resulted in severe beatings. When he continued to refuse to answer questions, he was tied behind a water buffalo which dragged him through the bush. The interrogations and beatings continued for three days, but Lieutenant Dengler refused to give in. Later, he escaped from his guards but was recaptured and again severely beaten. After six months in captivity, Lieutenant Dengler successfully escaped, killing several enemy guards in the process. On the 17th day, a pilot who escaped with him was killed, and Lieutenant Dengler had to continue alone. Although suffering from malnutrition, jaundice, fatigue, and badly cut and swollen feet, Lieutenant Dengler refused to give up. Finally, on the 22nd day after his escape, he managed to lay out a crude SOS on a bed of rocks and attract the attention of a United States Air Force aircraft. Later a rescue helicopter plucked him to safety and ended his ordeal.

The stories of those who have steadfastly followed both the spirit and letter of Articles III, IV and V of the Code of Conduct are numerous.

Chapter Four

Law of War

The laws of armed conflict are the concern of every Marine from the Commandant to the newest private. Because of the terminology, "laws of armed conflict," you may think that only the Commandant, Secretary of the Navy, Secretary of Defense, Secretary of State, the Congress and the President concern themselves with the rules of war. While individuals at this high level of government from many countries have, over the years, drafted the basic legal documents governing man's treatment of his fellow man in wartime, the laws of armed conflict remain the direct concern of *everyone* who is ever engaged in war activities.

The laws of armed conflict can really be defined simply: how should you, an individual Marine, conduct yourself in wartime operations to accomplish your mission while still respecting the rights of civilians, your enemies and allies. This chapter of your guidebook provides you with some basic information on what to do and, just as important, what not to do in wartime situations.

Why We Need Laws in War

Unfortunately war is as old as man himself. People cause wars. Weapons don't. Man creates the weapons, which are merely the instruments that a nation uses to carry out its war objectives. Genghis Khan, the ancient Asian warlord, killed or maimed a greater percentage of people than any other leader in history. He did it with bows and arrows and other similarly primitive weapons. During Genghis Khan's era, there were no rules of war. Although man continues today to be the force behind the weapons, there exists now a certain orderliness to which people of most countries who find themselves on a battlefield subscribe.

The positive side of mankind has managed to improve the conditions under which war is conducted since the era of Genghis Khan. As newer weapons of warfare have made it easier for man to kill his fellow man, nations have sensed a need to eliminate unnecessary death, destruction and suffering. This need has been reflected in the moral values of civilized man and also of his military policies.

Binding customs and formal laws of war, presented in the Geneva conventions and Hague regulations, have evolved. They legally bind most nations to the practices set down at Geneva and The Hague. The United States has agreed to these rules. Any violation to them is the same as violation of the laws of the United States itself. The United States has led the world in adopting rules for its military forces which recognized that enemies are also human beings and that captured or detained people are entitled to retain their fundamental rights as humans regardless of their past conduct or beliefs. It is every Marine's duty, therefore, to know and obey the laws of armed conflict.

History shows that discipline and moral courage led our military forces to victory in battle after battle. These same characteristics apply to obedience to the laws of armed conflict. Although you will be in uniform and be an instrument of a nation state (the United States) in an armed conflict, this does not give you license to do anything you wish to do. There are limits on what you can do when waging war, and those limits are established by the laws of armed conflict. This chapter explains what you can and cannot do.

General Precepts of the Laws of Armed Conflict

When you enter into an armed conflict in another country, you should be aware of many of the characteristics of the country. Knowledge of these characteristics will better prepare you to follow the tenets of the laws of armed conflict.

Geography

A general understanding of a nation's geography will permit you to know where the country's population is concentrated. That knowledge should prepare you to deal with civilians and the enemy as you encounter them. In addition, you should know the general area of the country in which you are operating and the nations which border it, so that you may understand any trends that may impact on the implementation of the laws of armed conflict. You should know the capital city and the other major cities, the characteristics of the land (mountains, deserts, plains, etc.) and the climate. Knowledge of all these features will help you to better confront rules of war situations that might arise during your time in the country. You should receive information about the general characteristics of a nation's geography as part of instructional briefings given in connection with operational deployments.

People

Knowledge of the country's people can be invaluable to you in how you conduct yourself under the rules of war. Since nearly all offenses under the laws of armed conflict involve people, the more you know about the civilian populace of a country and of your enemy, the better off you will be. Know their ethnic backgrounds, their language, the educational level of the people, the very important cultural characteristics (particularly if they are different than the culture of the United States), the religions of the country and the social customs of the people.

Knowledge of the people is probably the most important thing for you to know about the country. Without it you cannot begin to understand the way the people think and act. Accordingly the chances of doing something in violation of the rules of war increase. If the enemy and the people are one and the same, then the questions posed above will serve for both. If not, you will need to ask the same questions about your enemy. You must know the military and nonmilitary characteristics of your enemy. Again, listen carefully to briefings which tell you important facts about the country's people.

History

There is no need for you to know the long and detailed history of a country except as it relates to why you are there. Historical circumstances involving politics, religion, or cultural values may have led you to being in the country. You need to have knowledge of and be sensitive to the historical circumstances dictating U.S. Marine Corps involvement in the country. Pay attention when you receive briefings on these matters. Read what you can find on the

subject (newspapers, periodicals, etc.). Knowing the country's history as it relates to your involvement can serve you well in a situation where you might have to decide what to do in a wartime situation under the laws of armed conflict.

Economy

Is the country poor or wealthy? Does it have wealth concentrated in a few people and enormous pockets of poverty among the general populace? You need answers to these questions, because such conditions may contribute to how you deal with the country's people and enemy. Current economic conditions are also important. (These include the conditions of growth, inflation, deflation, unemployment, poverty, etc.) Knowledge of the economic condition of a country can lead you to understand better how a country's people and the enemy might behave toward you and might assist in preventing a violation of the rules of war.

Foreign Relations

Knowing the country's alliances, allies, traditional enemies (if any) and the country's role in international organizations (e.g., the United Nations) can provide you with an understanding of what to expect. Will the country comply with the laws of armed conflict that you fight under, or can you expect behavior contrary to your training?

Government

Knowing something about the nature of the national government in a country may better prepare you to understand the nature and conduct of your enemy as well as the civilian populace. Is the country's government bound by the Geneva conventions and Hague resolutions? More importantly, will the government prosecute you for a crime against civilians or against the enemy for a violation of the rules of war? Even if the government does not comply with the rules of war in any way, it is your obligation as a Marine to conduct yourself under the laws of armed conflict which you are taught.

U.S. Relations with the Country

The United States' relations with the country that you are entering may be good, bad, or somewhere between these two extremes. The country's government may want the U.S. Marines to be there, but some of its people may not. You may encounter situations or actions from the enemy, from the government or from the general population that will try your patience. They may treat you as "Yankee, Go Home." If so, you must maintain your self-control and not violate the principles you have learned under the laws of armed conflict. You should be familiar with our relations with the country you are entering, because it can serve you well in precluding the creation of a situation where you might violate the rules of war.

Basically, what you have just read can be summed up in eight words: *Know the country in which you are going*. That's as important as knowing terrain features and enemy tactics.

Along with knowledge of the country in which you are operating, make sure you understand your mission fully. It is while you are conducting your mission that you will encounter situations when you will have the opportunity to succeed or fail in your practice of the laws of armed conflict.

When you complete this chapter, you should have sufficient knowledge of what to do and what not to do under most combat situations which will protect you from violating the laws of armed conflict. If you encounter a situation where you are not sure what action to take to accomplish your mission, get clearance from the next higher authority before continuing. For example, if some military action by you might endanger the lives of some local civilians and you are not sure how to proceed, be certain to get approval of your next action from the next higher authority.

Your Conduct Under the Laws of Armed Conflict

The laws of armed conflict tell you what you can and cannot do in combat situations. With the training you will receive, you will have the necessary discipline to do the right thing. But if you do not learn how you should conduct yourself in combat, you can be punished for mistakes.

All persons in uniform, carrying a weapon or participating in any way in military operations or activities are are known as combatants. Under the laws of armed conflict, only combatants are considered proper targets and may be fired upon. All others are called noncombatants. Noncombatants include civilians, medical personnel and chaplains. Knowing the difference between combatants and noncombatants

in guerrilla war situations may sometimes be difficult and requires great care. Humane treatment of noncombatants may also assist you in obtaining valuable intelligence to allow you to better pursue your mission. If you are in doubt in differentiating between combatants and noncombatants, consult your superior before pursuing any course of action.

Enemy Combatants

Never attack enemy soldiers who surrender or enemy soldiers who are captured, sick or wounded. When you have EPW's you should follow the five S's: *search, segregate, silence, speed (tag) and safeguard* the prisoners to the rear. You must never kill, torture or mistreat a prisoner, because such actions are a violation of the law and because prisoners may provide you vital information about the enemy. Treating a prisoner badly will also discourage other enemy soldiers from surrendering and harden the enemy's will to resist. But if we treat our prisoners well, this will encourage the enemy to treat his prisoners (our buddies) well. Humane treatment of EPW's is right, honorable and required under the laws of armed conflict. Improper treatment of prisoners by us is punishable by court-martial.

Let enemy soldiers surrender. The enemy may use different signals to convey to you that he is surrendering, but all of the signals should be noticeable. It is illegal to fire on an enemy who has thrown down his weapon and offered to surrender.

You should also provide medical care to the wounded whether friend or foe. You are required under the laws of armed conflict to provide the same kind of medical care to the sick and wounded as you would provide for your own.

When you capture someone, you may not be certain if the person is an enemy. That determination is made by specifically trained personnel at a higher headquarters. You may question your captives about military information of immediate value to your mission, but you may never use threats, torture, or other forms of coercion to obtain information.

You may not take personal property from a prisoner, except those items that are clearly of a military or intelligence value (weapons, maps or military documents). You do this only after the prisoner has been secured, silenced, and segregated. You take nothing that is not of military value. Only an officer may take money from a prisoner.

Captives may perform some types of work, but the work must not relate to assisting your war effort. The acceptable work performed must be limited to allowing captives to dig foxholes or build bunkers only for their own protection. Under the laws of armed conflict, you may never use captives as a shield for your attack or defense against the enemy; to search for, clear or place mines or booby traps; or to carry your ammunition or heavy gear.

Under the rules of armed conflict, you are not permitted to attack villages, towns or cities. But you are allowed to engage the enemy that is in a village, town or city and destroy any equipment or supplies that the enemy has there when your mission requires it. In all cases, you must not create more destruction than is necessary to accomplish your mission. When you use firepower in a populated area, you must attack only the military targets.

You may not attack protected property. While some protected property may mean little to you, the property in question may be of cultural importance to the people of the country. Examples of protected property include buildings dedicated to religion, art, science or charitable purposes; historical monuments; hospitals and places where the sick and wounded are collected and cared for; and schools and orphanages for children. If the enemy uses these places for refuge or for offensive purposes, your commander may order an attack. It is common sense to destroy no more than the minimum amount of protected property consistent with the accomplishment of your mission. To do more may undermine your mission.

Civilians

Earlier in this chapter, we discussed why you should know as much as possible about the country in which you are operating. Once there, you need to treat civilians humanely and private property as if it were your own.

Do not violate civilians' rights in war zones. If you know something about the people's culture and practices, you will have little trouble recognizing civilians' rights. Make sure civilians are protected from acts of violence, threats, and insults both from the enemy and from any of your fellow Marines.

On occasion it may be necessary to move or resettle civilians, because such action is urgently required for military activities. Under no circumstance do you burn civilian property without approval of higher authority. Similarly you do not steal from civilians. Failure to obey these rules is a violation of the laws of armed conflict and punishable by court-martial.

Under no circumstances should you fire upon any medical personnel or equipment used for the medical welfare of the people or the enemy. Most medical personnel and facilities are marked with a red cross on a white background. However, a few countries use a different symbol. This is one reason why it is important to be familiar with the customs of the country in which you are operating. Similarly, never pose as a Red Cross person when you are not one. Your life may depend on the proper use of the Red Cross symbol.

Parachutists are considered helpless until they reach the ground. Under the rules of war, you are not allowed to fire at them until they reach the ground. If they then resist with weapons or do not surrender, you may fire on them. *Paratroopers*, on the other hand, are always considered combatants and may be fired at while they are still in the air.

Under the law of armed conflict, you may not use poison or poisoned weapons. However you may use nonpoisoning weapons to destroy the enemy's food and water in order to prevent them from using them.

You may not alter your weapons in order to cause unnecessary suffering to the enemy. You cannot use altered rounds to inflict greater destruction on the enemy. These alterations are forbidden under the laws of armed conflict.

What Happens When Rules Are Violated

We have given you some basic rules showing what you can and cannot do in a wartime situation as it relates to the laws of armed conflict. This section instructs you on what to do if one of the rules is violated.

You must do your best to prevent violations of the laws of armed conflict, because those are criminal acts. If you see a criminal act about to be committed, you should try to prevent it by arguing against it, threatening to report the criminal act, repeating the orders of your superiors, stating your personal disagreement or asking a senior individual present to intervene. You will be able to do this if you are totally familiar with the country in which you are operating and are knowledgeable about the rules of war. In the event the criminal act immediately endangers your life or the lives of others, you may use the exact amount of force needed to prevent the crime, but only as a last resort. You should immediately report the criminal act through your chain of command. If the criminal act is committed or about to be committed by your immediate superior, report the act to his immediate superior. You are required to do this by the laws of armed conflict. Conversely, you are not required to commit a crime under the laws of armed conflict. If you are ordered to commit a crime under the rules of war, you must refuse to follow the order and report your refusal to the next higher authority. You can be prosecuted for carrying out an unlawful act under the laws of war, so you must know what is legal and act in accordance with the rules of armed conflict.

Conclusion

We all recognize that full compliance with the laws of armed conflict is not always easy, especially in the confusion and passion of battle. For instance, you might be extremely angry and upset because your unit has taken a lot of casualties from enemy booby traps or hit-and-run tactics. But you must never engage in reprisals or acts of revenge that violate the laws of armed conflict.

Chapter Five

Leadership

Every private in the Marine Corps is a potential squad leader. Every squad leader can become a sergeant major. The truth in these simple statements is obvious. It has provided the Corps with the world's finest body of small-unit leaders since 1775. As sure as a Marine's best friend is the rifle, the backbone of the Marine Corps is its noncommissioned officers. Every one of them started as a private.

All Marine noncommissioned officers are proud of their rank. They have a right to be. Some mighty good men have worn those same chevrons. Marines like Dan Daly, John Quick, Herman H. Hanneken and John Basilone have left today's NCOs a strong tradition of outstanding leadership.

War has changed a lot since Hanneken led Marines against bandits in Haiti. It is much faster and far more complex than when John Basilone's men held the line at Bloody Ridge. But wars are still fought by men, and fighting men must have good leadership to win.

No better example could be given than Vietnam, where the Marine Corps' efforts centered around the small-unit leader. Young corporals and sergeants were the backbone of our programs, both on the civic action side of the war and the battlefield. An entirely new group of "classroom examples" in the art of leadership came forward. Included in the group are names like Robert O'Malley, Jimmie Howard, Roy Wheat, Melvin Newlin, Rodney Davis, Paul Forster, William Perkins, Larry Smedley and Gary Martin – all Medal of Honor winners, and with the exception of Howard, all on their first enlistment when the action they were cited for took place.

The Marine Corps' sergeants and corporals provide the most direct and personal leadership found anywhere. They do it in peacetime as well as in war. And like their forerunners of the "old Corps," none of them was a "born leader." They were all born, true. But they became leaders through hard work, skill and a stern sense of duty.

This chapter deals with traits of character and the principles used to develop skills in leadership. When you develop them, you will have acquired that all-important sense of duty. The hard work part is up to you.

If you are now a private, the material here will tell you what is expected of NCO leaders in the Marine Corps. Study it and be ready to take on the responsibilities of higher rank when they come your way. If you are already a noncommissioned officer, a periodic review of this material and uncompromising practice of what it preaches will make you a better one.

Daly

Basilone

Davis

Martin

Leadership Traits

You don't inherit the ability to lead Marines. Neither is it issued. You acquire that ability by taking an honest look at yourself. You see how you stack up against 14 well-known character traits of a Marine NCO. These are:

1. **Integrity**
2. **Knowledge**
3. **Courage**
4. **Decisiveness**
5. **Dependability**
6. **Initiative**
7. **Tact**
8. **Justice**
9. **Enthusiasm**
10. **Bearing**
11. **Endurance**
12. **Unselfishness**
13. **Loyalty**
14. **Judgment**

Then you set out to acquire those traits which you might lack. You improve those you already have, and you make the most of those in which you are strong. Work at them. Balance them off, and you're well on the road to leading Marines in war or peace. Marines expect the best in leadership and they rate it. Give them the best and you'll find that you (1) accomplish your mission and (2) have the willing obedience, confidence, loyalty and respect of your charges. In fact, you will have lived up to the official definition of a military leader.

Now, let's take a closer look at each one of the traits of character which a leader must have.

1. Integrity. The stakes of combat are too high to gamble leadership on a dishonest person. Would you accept a report from a patrol leader who had been known to lie? Of course you wouldn't. All your statements, official or unofficial, are considered by your Marines to be plain, unadorned *fact*. Make sure they are. When you give your word, keep it. There are people depending on you to come through with the goods.

2. Knowledge. Know your job, weapons, equipment and techniques to be used. Master this GUIDEBOOK and your other training material. Be able to pass that knowledge on to your Marines. You can't bluff them. They are expert at spotting a fake. If you don't know the answer to a question, admit it. Then find out. Most important, *know your Marines.* Learn what caliber of performance to expect from each of them. Put confidence in those who you can. Give close supervision to those who need it.

3. Courage. This comes in two kinds: physical and moral. If you are in a tight place and feel fear, recognize it. Then get control over it and make it work for you. Fear stimulates the body processes.

You can actually fight harder, and for a long time, when you are scared. So don't let a little fear make you panic inside. Keep busy when under fire. *Fix your mind on your mission and your Marines.* Courage grows with action. When things are really tough, take some action, even though it might be wrong. Positive action on a poor decision is better than a half-hearted attempt on the best possible one.

As for moral courage, know what's right and stand up for it. Marines are not plaster saints by any means. But they serve God, Country, and Corps – in that order. The Ten Commandments are still a pretty good set of regulations, and they haven't had a change published for almost two thousand years. A Marine with the morals of an alley cat will never command the loyalty and respect of other Marines. A combat leader must also be a moral leader.

When you're wrong, say so. Don't try to weasel out of your mistake. Everybody makes a mistake now and then. The trick is not to make the same one twice. When a job is left undone, true leaders don't harp, "Sir/Ma'am, I told those people…" They fix the breakdown, not the blame.

Fix your mind on your mission and your Marines. Courage grows with action.

4. Decisiveness. Get the facts, all of them. Make your mind up when you've weighed them. Then issue your order in clear, confident terms. Don't confuse your Marines by debating with yourself out loud. *Say what you mean and mean what you say.* Make up your mind in time to prevent the problem from becoming bigger, but don't go off while still at the "half-cock" position. If the decision is beyond the scope of your authority, take the problem up the chain of command to the person who gets paid to make that decision. But if the decision is yours, make it. Don't pass the buck.

5. Dependability. If only one word could be used to describe Marine noncommissioned officers over the years, that one word would have to be "dependable." They get the job done, regardless of obstacles. At first they might not have agreed with the ideas and plans of their seniors. Being dependable, if they thought they had a better plan, they tactfully said so. But once the decision was made, the job was done to the best of their ability, whether or not it was their own plan which went into effect. Orders were followed to the letter, in spirit, and in fact. The mission came first, then the welfare of their Marines, then their own requirements.

Dependable noncommissioned officers are solid citizens. They're always on time, never make excuses and stay hot on the job until it's done. They're aboard when needed and out of the way when not needed. Duty demands that they often make personal sacrifices. They sense what has to be done, where duty lies. Country, Corps, and their Marines need and get dependability.

6. Initiative. Think ahead. Stay mentally alert and physically awake. Look around. If you see a job that needs to be done, don't wait to be told. If the squad bay is full of newspapers and food wrappers on a Sunday morning, organize a detail and get the place squared away. Don't wait for the Duty NCO to come around. If you spot an enemy OP, get some effective fire on it. By the time someone else finds that OP, it may have fire on you. Your situation and the lot of your Marines can always be improved. Do what you can. Use the means at hand. Think ahead, and you'll stay ahead.

7. Tact. The right thing at the right time, that's what we mean by tact. It embraces courtesy, but it goes much further. It's the Golden Rule; consideration for others, be they senior or subordinate. Courtesy is more than saluting and saying, "Sir/Ma'am." It doesn't mean you meekly "ask" your Marines to do a job, either. You can give orders in a courteous manner which, because it is courteous, leaves no doubt that you expect to be obeyed. The tactful leader is *fair, firm* and *friendly*. You always respect another's property. Learn to respect feelings as well. If an individual needs "reading off," then do it – but in private. Don't make a spectacle of them and yourself by doing it in public. On the other hand, when they do a good job, let their friends hear about it. They will be a bigger person in their eyes and you will too.

There are times, particularly in combat, when a severe "dressing down" of one person or a group of people may be required. Even so, this is tactful, for it is the right thing at the right time.

In dealing with seniors, the Golden Rule again applies. *Approach them in the manner you'd want to be approached were you in their position with their responsibilities.*

Use tact with juniors, but remember, a Marine NCO coddles nobody. Use tact with your seniors, but remember, nobody likes an "ear banger."

When you join a new outfit, just keep quiet and watch for a while. Don't noise it around that your old outfit was a better one just because it happened to do things differently. Make a few mental notes when you find something that is wrong. When you've got your feet on the ground, then make those changes *that you have the authority to make.* You might be surprised at how little really needs changing. Besides, you'll have learned another way of getting the job done.

8. Justice. Marines rate a square-shooting leader. Be one. Don't play favorites. Spread the liberty and the working parties around equally. Keep anger and emotion out of your decisions. Get rid of any narrow views which you may have about a particular race, creed, or section of the country. *Judge individuals by what kind of Marines they are; nothing else.*

Give your Marines a chance to prove themselves. Help those who fall short of your standards, but keep your standards high.

9. Enthusiasm. It's a fact that the more you know about something, the greater your interest and enthusiasm. Show it. Others will follow your lead. Enthusiasm is more contagious than the measles. Set a goal for your unit, then put out all you've got in the achievement of that goal. This is particularly applicable in training. Marines are at their best when in the field. After all, they joined the Corps to learn how to fight. They'll learn, all right, but only when their instructor is enthused about what is being taught. Show knowledge and enthusiasm about a subject and your troops will want that same knowledge. Show your dislikes and gripe about what's going on and you'll still be leading – but in the wrong direction. The choice is yours. Make the right one.

Don't get stale. "Take your pack off," can sometimes be good advice. Do it once in a while. Then come back strong with something new. When you find yourself forced to run problems over the same old terrain, run them from the other direction.

10. Bearing. Remember the DIs? They were lean, leather-lunged, and tanned to a bone-deep brown. They had drilled shoulders and knife-edge creases that sliced down their shirt and trousers all the way to a pair of shoes that looked back at you. Their brass glittered at every move and they didn't walk, they *marched*! And they taught you to do the same. They knew that when they inspected a platoon of 70 Marines just once, they had been inspected 70 times by 70 different pairs of eyes. Consequently, they had bearing. You learned from them that a uniform is more than a mere "suit of clothes." You wear a suit – but you believe in a uniform. Therefore, you maintained it – all the time. People often ask why Marines don't wear shoulder patches, cords, decals, loops, discs, brass crests, and so on. Marines don't need such trinkets. The eagle, globe and anchor – set against an immaculate blue or well-pressed forest green background – is enough identification. Besides, every stripe, every ribbon, every piece of of metal, that you see on a Marine was *earned*. It wasn't handed out like an early chow pass. You earned your uniform and everything on it. Wear it with pride.

That's part of what is meant by bearing. The rest of it is how you conduct yourself, in or out of formation, ashore or on board, verbally and emotionally. Learn control of your voice and gestures. A calm voice and a steady hand are confidence builders in combat. Don't ever show your concern over a dangerous situation, even if you feel it.

Speak plainly and simply. You're more interested in being understood than in showing off your vocabulary. If you ever rant and rave, losing control of your tongue and your emotions, you'll also lose control of your Marines. Swearing at subordinates is unfair. They can't swear back. It's also stupid, since you admit lack of ability to express displeasure in any other way. Don't lose your temper. Master yourself before you try to master others. There may be one exception to this rule. The time might come, in battle, when tough talk, a few oaths, and the right amount of anger is all that will pull your outfit together. But save your display of temper until it is absolutely needed. Otherwise it won't pay off, because you'll already have shot your bolt.

Sarcasm seldom gets results. Wisecrack to Marines – they've been around – they'll wisecrack back. Make a joke out of giving orders and they'll think you don't mean what you say. This doesn't mean to avoid joking at all times. A good joke, at the right time, is like good medicine, especially if the chips are down. As a matter of fact, it is often the Marine Corps way of expressing sympathy and understanding without getting sticky about it. Many a wounded Marine has been sent to the rear with a smile and a remark about, "What some people won't do to get outta' work!"

Dignity, without being unapproachable – that's what bearing is. Work at it.

11. Endurance. A five-foot Marine sergeant once led his squad through 10 days of field training in Japan. He topped it off with a two-day hike, climbing Mt. Fuji on the 36 miles back to camp. When asked how a man of his size developed such endurance, he said "It was easy. I had 12 guys pushing me all the way." What he meant, of course, was that 12 other Marines were depending on *endurance* to pull them through. He couldn't think about quitting. Leaders must have endurance beyond that of their troops. Squad leaders must check every position, then go build their own. On the march they will often carry part of another's load in addition to their own. They also have the burden of command upon them. An unfit body or an undisciplined mind could never make it.

Keep yourself fit, physically and mentally. Learn to stand punishment by undertaking hard physical tasks. Force yourself to study and think when tired. Get plenty of rest before a field problem. Don't stay on liberty until the last place is closed. The town will still be there when you get back. You'll enjoy it more then anyhow.

A favorite saying of Marines is that you don't have to be trained to be miserable. That's true. But you do have to train to *endure misery.*

12. Unselfishness. Marines NCOs don't pull the best rations from the case and leave the rest to their Marines. They get the best they can for all unit members, all the time.

Leaders get their own comforts, pleasures, and recreation after troops have been provided with theirs. Look at any chow line in the field. You'll see squad leaders at the end of their squads. You'll find staff noncommissioned officers at the end of the company. This is more than a tradition. It is leadership in action. It is unselfishness.

Share your Marines' hardships. Then the privleges that go with your rank will have been earned. Don't hesitate to accept them when the time is right, but until it is, let them be. When your unit is wet, cold and hungry – you'd better be too. That's the price you pay for leadership. What it buys is well worth the cost. The dry clothes, warm bunk and full belly can come later.

Give credit where credit is due. Don't grab the glory for yourself. Recognize the hard work and good ideas of your subordinates and be grateful you have such Marines. Your leader will look after you in the same way. They know the score, too.

13. Loyalty. This is a two-way street. It goes all the way up and all the way down the chain of command. Marines live by it. They even quote Latin for it – *"Semper Fidelis."* As a leader of Marines, every word, every action, must reflect your loyalty – up and down. Back your Marines when they're right. Correct them when they're wrong. You're being loyal either way. Pass on orders as if they were your own idea, even when they are distasteful. To rely on the rank of the person who told you to do the job is to weaken your own position. Keep your personal problems and the private lives of your seniors to yourself. But help your Marines in their difficulties, when it is proper to do so. Never criticize your unit, your seniors, or your fellow NCOs in the presence of subordinates. Make sure they don't do it either. If deserving persons get into trouble, go to bat for them. They'll work harder when it's all over.

When it comes to spreading corruption, the proverbial rotten apple couldn't hold a candle to the damage that can be done by a disloyal noncommissioned officer.

14. Judgment. This comes with experience. It is simply weighing all the facts in any situation, application of the other 13 traits you have just read about, then making the best move. But until you acquire experience you may not know the best move. What, then, do you use for *experienced judgment* in the meantime? Well, there are over two hundred years' worth of experienced judgment on tap in the Marine Corps. Some of it is available to you at the next link in the chain of command. Ask and you'll receive. Seek and you'll find.

Principles of Leadership

Now that you've had a look at the character traits required in a leader, let's see how these are fitted into what we call the *principles of leadership*. Eleven are set forth just for the sake of discussion. You may want to add or delete some. That's OK. We're not concerned as much about the words and phrases as we are about their application. They're all common sense items, anyway. When you get right down to it, a discussion of leadership is only *common sense with a vocabulary*. You've got the common sense. Let's put some of that vocabulary to work.

1. Take responsibility for your actions and the actions of your Marines. The leader, alone, is responsible for all that the unit does or fails to do. That sounds like a big order, but take a look at the authority that is given you to handle that responsibility. You are expected to use that authority. Use it with *judgment, tact and initiative*. Have the courage to be loyal to your unit, your Marines, and yourself. As long as you are being held responsible, be responsible for success, not failure. *Be dependable.*

2. Know yourself and seek self-improvement. Evaluate yourself from time to time. Do you measure up? If you don't, *admit it to yourself*. On the other hand, don't sell yourself short. If you think you're the best NCO in your platoon, admit that also to yourself. Then set out to be the best NCO in the company. Learn how to speak effectively, how to instruct, and how to be an expert with all the equipment that your unit might be expected to use.

3. Set the example. As an NCO, you are in an ideal spot to do this. Marines are already looking to you for a pattern and a standard to follow. No amount of instruction and no form of discipline can have the effect of your personal example. Make it a good one.

4. Develop your subordinates. Tell your Marines what you want done and by when. Then leave it at that. If you have junior leaders, leave the detail up to them. In this way, kill two birds with one stone. You will have more time to devote to other jobs and you are training another leader. An NCO with confidence will have confidence in subordinates. Supervise and check on the results. But leave the details to the person on the spot. After all, there's more than one way to skin a cat. And it's the whole fur you're after, not the individual hairs.

5. Ensure that a job is understood, then supervise it and carry it through to completion. *Make up your mind what to do, who is to do it, where it is to be done, when it is to be done, and tell your Marines why, when they need to be told why.* Continue supervising the job until it has been done better than the person who wanted it done in the first place ever thought it could be.

6. Know your Marines and look after their welfare. Loyal NCOs will never permit themselves to rest until their unit is bedded down. They always get the best they can for their Marines by honest means. With judgment, you'll know which of your troops is capable of doing the best job in a particular assignment. Leaders share the problems of their Marines, but they don't pry when an individual wants privacy.

7. Everyone should be kept informed. Make sure your Marines get the word. Be known as the person with the straight dope. Don't let one of your group be part of the so-called "10 percent." Certain information is classified. Let your Marines have only that portion that they need to know, but make certain they have it. Squelch rumors. They can create disappointment when they're good, but untrue. They can sap morale when they exaggerate enemy capabilities. Have the *integrity, the dependability* to keep your unit correctly posted on what's going on in the world, the country, the Corps and your unit. Never forget that the more your Marines know about the mission that has been assigned the better they will be able to accomplish it.

8. Set goals you can reach. Don't send two Marines on a working party that calls for five. Your Marines may be good, but don't ask the impossible. Know the limitations of your outfit and bite off what you can chew. In combat, a "boy sent to do a man's job" can lead to disaster. In peacetime, it leads to a feeling of futility. Conversely, those who have a reasonable goal and then achieve it, are a proud lot. They've done something and done it well. Next time, they'll be able to tackle a little more. Don't set your sights clear over the butts; keep them on the target.

9. Make sound and timely decisions. *Knowledge* and *judgment* are required to produce a sound decision. Include some *initiative* and the decision will be a timely one. Use your initiative and make your decisions in time to meet the problems that are coming. If you find you've made a bum decision, have the courage to change it before the damage is done. But don't change the word any more than you absolutely have to. Nothing confuses an outfit more than the eternal routine of "brown side out…green side out."

10. Know your job. This requires no elaborations. It does require hard work on your part. Stay abreast of changes. War moves fast nowadays. Look up the dope on the latest weapons and equipment. Read up on recent developments. Don't be the type who can only say, Well, that ain't the way we did it in the old Fifth Marines."

11. Teamwork. Train your unit as a *unit*. Keep that *unit integrity* every chance you get. If a working party comes up for three, take your whole fire team. The job will be easier with an extra hand, and your unit will be working as a team. Get your outfit on liberty together now and then. They work as a team; get 'em to play as one. Put your Marines in the jobs they do best, then rotate them from time to time. They'll learn to appreciate the other person's task as well. When one member of your team is missing, others can do that share. But don't ever permit several Marines to do another person's job when they're around. Everybody pulls their load in the Marine Corps.

When you and your unit have done something well, talk it up. This builds esprit de corps. Every Marine knows enough French to tell you what that means. You can't see it but you can feel it. An outfit with a lot of esprit holds itself in very high regard while sort of tolerating others. There's nothing wrong with that. All Marines have a right to figure their outfit is the best in the entire Corps. After all, they're in it!

What You Can Expect

We've spent some time on what the Corps expects of you as a junior leader. It's not all one way. There are certain things which you have a right to expect in return. First of all, since you are the link in the chain of command that lies squarely between your senior and your subordinates, you can expect the same leadership from above that you've just read about.

Then there's the additional pay you'll be getting along with every promotion – and promotion comes to real leaders, regularly. Also with promotion comes additional authority. It's granted to you on a piece of paper known as a Certificate of Appointment, commonly called a warrant. Take a look at it.

You'll see more there than simply a piece of paper – much more. First, there's an expression of "special trust and confidence" in your "fidelity and abilities." That is recognition of the highest order. It's appreciation for your hard work thus far. But look further. You don't rest on your laurels in the Marine Corps. There's a charge to "carefully and diligently discharge the duties of the grade to which appointed by doing and performing all manner of things thereunto pertaining." That means additional responsibility, which, when you think about it, is also a reward.

Next, you'll find that additional authority we mentioned a while back. It's in the words, "and I do strictly charge and require all personnel of lesser grade to render obedience to appropriate orders." Commanding officers who sign that Certificate are delegating a part of their authority to you. They get their authority from the President of the United States and have chosen you to help them in the execution of their responsibility. Notice, however, that they haven't delegated responsiblity by you, or by anybody.

When it comes to leadership, there is no truer statement. Only the noncommissioned officer is in a position to give the close, constant, personal type of leadership that we've been discussing. When you, as a Marine NCO, have provided your unit with that type of leadership, then you already will have reaped the greatest return. By definition you'll (1) have accomplished your mission and (2) command the willing obedience, confidence, loyalty and respect of the United States Marines under you. *There is no more satisfactory reward, anywhere.*

Chapter Six

Courtesy and Discipline

Courtesy is the accepted form of politeness among civilized people. Courtesy smooths the personal relationship among individuals in all walks of life. A good rule of thumb might be the golden rule: "Do unto others as you would have others do unto you."

The Salute

The most important of all military courtesies is the salute. This is an honored tradition of the military profession throughout the world. The saluting custom goes back to earliest recorded history.

It is believed to have originated in the days when all men bore arms. In those days, warriors raised their weapons in such a manner as to show friendly intentions. They sometimes would shift their weapons from the right hand to the left and raise their right hand to show that they did not mean to attack.

Just as you show marks of respect to your seniors in civilian life, military courtesy demands that you show respect to your seniors in the military profession. Your military seniors are the officers and noncommissioned officers senior to you. Regulations require that all officers be saluted by their juniors and that they return such salutes. In saluting an officer, a junior Marine is formally recognizing the officer as a military superior and is reaffirming the oath to obey the order of all officers appointed over the Marine. By returning the salute the senior officer greets the junior as a fellow Marine and expresses the appreciation of the junior's support. Enlisted personnel do not ordinarily exchange salutes.

The Hand Salute

Today, the salute has several forms. The hand salute is the most common. When a salute is executed, the right hand is raised smartly until the tip of the forefinger touches the lower part of the headgear. Thumb and fingers are extended and joined. The palm is turned slightly inward until the person saluting can just see its surface from the corner of the right eye. The upper arm is parallel to the ground with the elbow slightly in front of the body. The forearm is inclined at a 45-degree angle; hand and wrist in a straight line. Completion of the salute is executed by dropping the arm to its normal position in one sharp, clean motion. (See Fig. 6-1.)

Fig. 6-1. Hand Salute

Some General Rules

- When meeting an officer who is either riding or walking, salute when six paces away in order to give time for a return of your salute before you are abreast of the officer.
- Hold the salute until it is returned.
- Accompany the salute with "Good morning, sir/ma'am," or some other appropriate greeting.
- Render the salute but once if the senior remains in the immediate vicinity. If conversation takes place, however, salute again when the senior leaves or when you depart.
- When passing an officer who is going in the same direction, as you come abreast of the officer, on the left side if possible, salute and say, "By your leave, sir/ma'am." The officer will return the salute and say, "Carry on" or "Granted." You then finish your salute and pass ahead of the officer.

- Members of the naval service are required to render a salute to officers, regular and reserve, of the Navy, Army, Air Force, Marine Corps, Coast Guard, and to foreign military and naval officers whose governments are formally recognized by the government of the United States.
- Upon the approach of an officer superior in rank, individuals of a group not in formation are called to attention by the first person noticing the officer, and all come smartly to attention and salute.

Do Not Salute:

- if you are engaged in work or play unless spoken to directly.
- if you are a prisoner. Prisoners are denied the privilege.
- while guarding prisoners.
- under battlefield conditions.
- when not wearing a cover.
- with any item in your right hand.
- with a pipe or cigarette or other items in your mouth.
- when in formation, EXCEPT at the command "Present, Arms."
- when moving at "double time" – ALWAYS slow to a normal walk before saluting.
- when carrying articles in both hands, or otherwise so occupied as to make saluting impractical. (It would be appropriate, however, to render a proper greeting, e.g., "Good evening, sir/ma'am.")
- in public places where obviously inappropriate (theaters, restaurants, etc.).
- when a member of the guard engaged in performance of duty which prevents saluting. (See Chapter 9 for saluting procedures for sentries.)

Saluting Officers Wearing Civilian Clothing. A junior in uniform who recognizes a senior in civilian clothing is required to render the proper greeting and salute.

Saluting Civilians. Civilians entitled by reason of their position to gun salutes or other honors, such as the President of the United States or the Secretary of the Navy, rate a hand salute.

Saluting While Walking in a Group. When a group of junior personnel approaches a senior, the senior in the group initiates a salute by calling out, "Attention," and all in the group face and salute the approaching officer.

Saluting a Group of Officers. When several officers in company are saluted, all return the salute. For example: As a lieutenant, you approach a colonel accompanied by a captain. You salute the officers.

The colonel returns your salute, and at that point, the captain also salutes. If you, as an enlisted Marine are accompanying a captain and a lieutenant approaches, you would not salute until the lieutenant renders the proper salute to the captain you are with. When the captain returns the salute, you then render the proper salute.

Saluting indoors. Persons in the naval service never salute "uncovered," that is, not wearing a hat. If indoors, you are required to remove headgear and would not salute except under the following conditions:
- when under arms, that is, carrying or having attached to you by sling or holster, a weapon. A person wearing a "duty belt" is considered "under arms" if the belt is worn in the performance of their duties. (Wearing a belt for the sole purpose of carrying canteens is not considered "under arms.")
- when attached to or visiting a military service which does execute hand saluting indoors (i.e., entering an Army officer's office on a base where naval customs may not be known).

Saluting Officers in a Vehicle. Salute all officers riding in motor vehicles. Those in the vehicle render and return salutes. The driver of the vehicle is obligated to salute only if the vehicle is stopped. To do so while moving might endanger the safety of the occupants and, therefore, may be omitted.

Personal Honors Being Rendered. When personal honors are being rendered to individuals of high rank and you are NOT IN FORMATION, salute at the the first note of music, and hold the salute until the completion of the ruffles, flourishes and march.

Military Funerals. During funerals, officers and enlisted personnel remain covered while in the open. During religious services when you are attending officially, a salute would be appropriate whenever honors are rendered: when the body is removed from the hearse to the chapel, from the chapel to the caisson, from the caisson to the grave and when volleys are fired and taps is sounded.

As a participant in a nonmilitary funeral or burial service, an individual may follow the civilian custom and uncover (rather than salute) when such honors are called for, as during the procession to the grave and the lowering of the body.

Other Forms of Military Courtesy

- When ordered to report to an officer, either outdoors, or indoors if under arms, approach the officer at attention and halt about two paces away, render the appropriate salute and say,

"Sir/Ma'am, Private Jones reporting as ordered," using proper names and grades. Hold the salute until it is acknowledged. When the business is completed, take one step backward, salute, and after your salute has been returned, execute about face and depart at attention.

- When reporting to an officer indoors when not under arms, follow the same procedure except remove the headgear before approaching the officer and do not salute.
- When accompanying a senior, walk on their left.
- When entering an automobile or small boat, the junior goes first, and the others follow in inverse order of rank. In leaving an automobile or a small boat, the senior goes first, and the others follow in order of rank.

Honors to Colors and Anthem

- Honors to the National Anthem or to the colors are rendered as follows:
- Whenever the National Anthem or To The Colors is played to accompany raising or lowering the colors, and you are not in formation or not in a vehicle: Come to attention and face the colors when Attention is sounded. Render the prescribed salute at the first note of the National Anthem or To The Colors. Hold the salute until the last note of the National Anthem or To The Colors. Remain standing at attention until Carry On is sounded.
- If no flag is near, face the music and salute.
- If in formation, salute only on the order "Present Arms."
- Vehicles in motion are brought to a halt. Troop formations riding in vehicles do not disembark. They and the driver remain seated at attention and do not salute. Drivers and passengers riding in either military or private vehicles remain seated at attention and do not salute.
- If outdoors and uncovered, stand at attention and face the direction of the flag or music. When the National Anthem is played indoors, officers and enlisted persons will stand at attention and face the music or the flag if one is present.
- When passing or being passed by an uncased color which is being paraded, presented or is on formal display, salute at six paces distance, and hold the salute until six paces beyond it or until it has passed you by six paces.
- If uncovered, stand or march at attention when passing or being passed by an uncased color.

- The marks of respect shown above are also rendered to the National Anthem of any friendly country when played upon official occasions.

Boarding Naval Vessels

When boarding a naval ship, upon reaching the top of the gangway face aft and salute the national ensign. After completing this salute, salute the officer of the deck who will be positioned on the quarterdeck at the head of the gangway, and request permission to come aboard. When leaving the ship, render the same salutes in reverse order, requesting permission from the officer of the deck to leave the ship as you salute him.

Miscellaneous

When "under arms," uncover only when seated in attendance at a court or board (but sentries guarding prisoners do not uncover), when entering places of divine worship or when indoors not on duty, e.g., eating, etc.

The term "outdoors" is construed to include such buildings as drill halls, gymnasiums and other roofed enclosures used for drill or exercise of troops, theater marquees, covered walks and other shelters open on the sides to the weather. "Indoors" includes offices, hallways, kitchens, guard rooms, washrooms, squadrooms, etc.

The Rifle Salute

When armed with the rifle, and not in formation, salutes are rendered in accordance with the rules outlined previously, except, instead of the hand salute, the rifle salute is rendered. (EXCEPTION: When carrying the rifle at sling arms, the hand salute is used.)

Let's suppose you are returning to your barracks from the armory and have your rifle at "port arms" and are moving at "double time." You are approaching an officer. Your actions would be: First, come to "quick time," and then either (1) come to "Order Arms" and render the rifle salute, or (2) go to "Right Shoulder Arms" and render the rifle salute. (See Figs. 6-2 and 6-3.) In addition there is a third position in which you may render a proper rifle salute: Rifle Salute at Trail Arms, as discussed in Chapter 10.

Fig. 6-2. Rifle Salute (right shoulder arms).

Fig. 6-3. Rifle Salute (order arms).

Military Discipline

Military discipline is the state of order and obedience among military personnel resulting from training. When we speak of discipline in the Marine Corps we do not refer to regulations, punishments or a state of subservience. What we mean is the exact execution of orders resulting from an intelligent, willing obedience rather than one based solely upon habit or fear. Habit plays its part, however, and for this reason the Marine benefits from such things as gun drill, close order drill or bayonet drill. Punishment of individuals for breaches of discipline is sometimes necessary, but only to reform or eliminate those who are unfit to serve on the team.

Discipline is necessary to secure orderly action which alone can triumph over the seemingly impossible conditions of battle. The individual must be able to recognize and face fear, because fear is the enemy of discipline. Fear unchecked will lead to panic, and a unit that panics is no longer a disciplined unit but a mob. There is no sane person who is without fear, but with good discipline and high morale, all can face danger.

Some Marines do not appreciate the necessity for discipline until they have undergone the experience of battle. However, when a Marine learns to be a disciplined Marine, the individual has learned a sense of obligation to one's self and to one's comrades, commander and to the Marine Corps. The Marines have learned that they are members of a team which is organized, trained and equipped for the purpose of engaging and defeating enemies of their country. The final object of military discipline is effectiveness in combat – to make sure that a unit performs correctly in battle, that it reaches its objectives, performs its assigned mission and helps others to accomplish their missions.

A military commander is vested with a high degree of authority. This authority extends to matters which would normally be considered of personal concern to the individual alone. These include such things as the eating of food, the care and manner of wearing clothing, health habits and morale factors, all of which directly or indirectly affect the lives of the individuals under their command. It is important that a Marine promptly obey the orders of the commander even in matters which might, at first thought, appear to be of an individual or personal nature. The commander is genuinely interested in the welfare of the individuals within their unit, and developing the habit of prompt obedience to all orders will improve the discipline of each individual and the unit.

It is too late to learn discipline on the battlefield. It must be learned in training. A Marine trains together with other Marines so that as a team they can accomplish increasingly difficult tasks in a manner in which they can take pride. You must not forget that you carry the badge of your Corps and your country, and that those who see you regard you not as individuals but as representatives of the Corps whose insignia you wear. If you appear smart, alert and efficient, others will not only say, "that is a good Marine," but also "that is a good outfit."

The word "discipline" is frequently combined with other words to refer to specific phases of living and fighting. For example: we speak of "fire discipline" which means obedience to fire orders and the observance of all instructions pertaining to the use of weapons during firing or in combat. When a platoon first goes into action, its fire discipline may be poor. Even after an outfit has been through several actions, there may be one or two "trigger happy" Marines in it. A "trigger happy" Marine is one who wastes ammunition in battle and shoots at every sound heard at night. An entire platoon may pay with their lives for one person's lack of fire discipline. "Water discipline" means the proper use of water during marches, field exercises or battle. "March discipline" means prompt obedience to march orders, and alert, orderly conduct when on the march.

Naval Justice

Military Jurisdiction

As stated in the *Manual for Courts-Martial* the sources of military jurisdiction include the Constitution of the United States and international law. International law includes the law of war. The specific provisions of the Constitution relating to military jurisdiction are found in the powers granted to the Congress, in the authority vested in the President, and in the provisions of the 5th Amendment.

Uniform Code of Military Justice

In keeping with the powers granted to the Congress and by the authority vested in the President of the United States and the provisions of the 5th Amendment, all of the armed services were brought under a unified system of justice. That system was enacted by the Congress and signed into law by the President on May 31, 1951, and from that day on has been known as the Uniform Code of Military Justice (UCMJ).

The Code is of great importance to all members of the armed forces, because it not only explains the legal responsibilities of the members of the armed forces, but also clearly states legal requirements for the protection and guarantees of the rights of all members of the armed forces. It is imperative, therefore, that extensive instruction, training, and guidance be given. Accordingly, Article 137, UCMJ, requires that important articles of the Code be carefully explained to every enlisted person at the time of entrance on active duty, or within six days thereafter, and explained again after the enlisted person has completed six months of active duty, and upon reenlistment.

It should be also be noted that a complete text of the Uniform Code of Military Justice and of the regulations prescribed by the President thereunder must be made available to all persons on active duty upon their request, for their personal examination. For this reason, you will find copies of the Uniform Code of Military Justice posted in conspicuous places throughout the various commands of the Marine Corps and Navy.

The Code has been amended on a few occasions, and all of the amendments have been designed to ensure even greater protection of the individual rights of each service member than were stated in the original Code provisions. The intent and purpose of the Uniform Code of Military Justice is to provide uniform application of such substantive and procedural due process as relates to these rights and to assure safeguards in a system of justice for all members of the armed forces.

Agencies

These agencies through which military jurisdiction is exercised include military commissions; provost courts; courts-martial for the trial of offenders against military law; and in the case of general courts-martial, trial of persons who by the laws of war are subject to trial by military tribunals; commanding officers and officers in charge for nonjudicial punishment under Article 15, UCMJ; and courts of inquiry for the investigation of any matter referred to such court by competent authority.

Of these agencies, those with which the members of the armed forces are most familiar are those relating to commanding officers' nonjudicial punishment, which in the Marine Corps is known as "office hours," and courts-martial which in order of ascendancy in power and jurisdiction are the summary court (which is the lowest court), the special court-martial (which is an intermediate court of limited jurisdiction) and the general court-martial (which is the highest trial court in the military). A review of the function of these more familiar agencies for the exercise of military jurisdiction is as follows:

Commanding Officers' Nonjudicial Punishment – Nowhere in any legal system are persons given more protection of their rights and more procedural due process than in the military under the UCMJ. The procedural due process generally begins when it is alleged that someone has committed an offense. Preliminary inquiry is then ordered into the alleged offense, and if there is some indication that the individual may have been involved as alleged, the Marine is brought before the commanding officer for a hearing pursuant to the Uniform Code of Military Justice. This hearing is commonly called "office hours."

Among other things, the commanding officer informs the alleged offender of the offense of which accused and explains rights under Article 31, UCMJ. This is advice concerning self-incrimination. The commanding officer also explains to the accused the rights concerning consultation with lawyer counsel as required by cases handed down by the Supreme Court of the United States and the United States Court of Appeals for the Armed Forces. If the alleged offense is a serious offense, the commanding officer will either refer the charges to trial by court-martial if the officer is a convening authority of an appropriate court or, if one lacks such powers, forward the charges to an appropriate convening authority recommending trial by court-martial. The type of case will determine what additional pretrial procedures are followed at this point.

If, on the other hand, the alleged offense is a minor offense, the commanding officer may administer nonjudicial punishment under Article 15, UCMJ, pursuant to the procedural requirements and punitive limitations outlined in Part V, *Manual for Courts-Martial.*

The rank of the commanding officer dictates what punishments may be imposed. For example, if the officer is a captain or below, as the commanding officer, seven days of correctional custody may be imposed; reduction of one grade, provided the officer has the authority to promote to that grade; 14 days extra duty; 14 days restriction; and forfeiture of seven days pay. If the commanding officer is a major or higher, 30 days of correctional custody may be imposed; reduction of one grade, provided the officer has the authority to promote to that grade; 45 days extra duty; 60 days restriction; and forfeiture of one-half of one month's pay per month for two months. Note that these punishments are limitations as to the maximum punishment that can be administered. In no way is the commanding officer bound to administer the maximum in any given circumstance. It is rare that the maximum punishment is awarded for a minor offense when it is the first offense of the individual.

In addition to the individual punishments outlined above, certain combinations of punishments are permitted under the Code. These combinations are limited by the precise language of the law. A military person has the right to refuse nonjudicial punishment and demand trial by court-martial except aboard ship.

It should be noted that not only may the individual refuse nonjudicial punishment but one may also refuse a summary court-martial in the event that one is ordered upon refusal to accept nonjudicial punishment under Article 15 of the Code. The only exception to the rule that the accused may refuse punishment under Article 15 is in the case of a member attached to or embarked in a vessel. Personnel attached to or embarked in a vessel may receive nonjudicial punishment under Article 15 of the Code despite the fact that they do not desire the imposition of such punishment.

Any person punished under Article 15 of the Code who considers the punishment unjust or disproportionate to the offense may, through the proper channels, appeal to the next superior authority, and the appeal must be promptly forwarded and decided. In the meantime, while the appeal is pending, the individual may be required to undergo the punishment imposed.

However, if the appeal is later granted by the next superior authority, all rights, property and privleges of which the person has been deprived by virtue of the imposition of nonjudicial punishment will be restored. The appeal from nonjudicial punishment must be taken within a reasonable time, and this period has been determined to be a five-day period.

Nonjudicial punishments are recorded in the service record book of each Marine. They reflect in the conduct markings or fitness reports of each Marine and are considered at promotion time. In addition, more than one Article 15 punishment during any good conduct medal marking period changes the commencement date for the Good Conduct Medal period. Obviously, it is to the advantage of all Marines not to involve themselves in disciplinary matters wherein they are referred to their commanding officers for nonjudicial punishment or to a court-martial for trial. The essence of Marine Corps professionalism is discipline.

The word discipline in this sense does not mean punishment, but rather over-all adherence to the rules, regulations, laws, traditions, and customs of the Marine Corps. Discipline makes the individual Marine the finest military person in the world. Punishment is only a small aspect of discipline which is administered when there has been a breach of proper conduct. The idea is not to make discipline a thing to be feared, but rather something to be appreciated as that which unites the Corps into a military service without equal.

Kinds of Courts-Martial

There are three kinds of courts-martial in each of the armed forces. They are:

General Court-Martial – The general court-martial consists of a military judge and not less than five active-duty armed services members OR only a military judge, if before the court is assembled, the accused, knowing the identity of the military judge and after consultation with defense counsel, requests in writing a court composed only of a military judge, and the military judge approves this request.

Special Court-Martial – This court-martial consists of a military judge and not less than three active-duty armed services members; OR only a military judge, if the accused so requests under the same conditions prescribed in the general court-martial section above.

Summary Court-Martial – The summary court-martial consists of one commissioned officer with the rank of captain or higher, whenever practicable.

Let's discuss each type of court-martial in more detail.

Summary Court-Martial

Only enlisteds can be tried by summary court-martial. Before being tried, a Marine must be charged with an offense under the Code by someone who is subject to the Code and who has either personal knowledge of the offense or has investigated the offense. This person, who prefers (swears) the charge against the Marine, is known as the accuser.

Normally, the person accused is ordered to trial by court-martial by a commanding officer who is in the chain of command. If the officer who would normally order the trial is the accuser, i.e., the person who either prefers the charges against the accused or has ordered someone to do so in a case in which there is a personal interest, then that officer cannot order the trial, but must refer the entire matter to the next superior in the chain of command.

The reason for ordering ("referring") charges to trial by court-martial is that many offenses are too serious in nature to be disposed of by the commanding officer at office hours. However, some offenses are not grave enough to warrant trial by a special or general court-martial, and, thus, these offenses are referred to trial by summary court-martial.

The law provides, however, that no person may be brought to trial before a summary court-martial if objected thereto, and as stated above, the accused may object to the summary court-martial even though there was also objection to Article 15 nonjudicial punishment. If objection to trial by summary court-martial is made by an accused, trial may be ordered by a special or general court-martial. A summary court-martial is conducted by one officer. This officer must, according to law, impartially bring out the evidence on both sides, i.e., protecting the rights of the accused as well as prosecuting the case for the government. The officer then must decide whether the accused is guilty or not guilty, and one always starts with the presumption of innocence.

In the case of a verdict of guilty, the summary court-martial officer also imposes the sentence. The Uniform Code of Military Justice provides that the summary court officer may, under such limitation as the President may prescribe, adjudge any punishment not forbidden by the Code "except death, dismissal, dishonorable or bad conduct discharge, confinement for more than one month, hard labor without confinement for more than 45 days, restriction to specified limits for more than two months, or forfeiture of more than two-thirds of one month's pay."

Special Court-Martial

The next higher court is the special court-martial. As stated above, the special court-martial consists of a military judge and not less than three members together, or only a military judge sitting alone if the accused requests that the case be heard by the judge alone and the judge approves the request.

The members and the judge, or the judge when sitting alone, assure that the trial is conducted fairly and the members when they are present, or the judge when sitting alone, determine the guilt or innocence of the accused, and in the case of guilt, impose the sentence.

In the special court-martial, the accused is acquitted unless two-thirds or more of the members sitting in judgment find the accused guilty or in the case of the judge sitting alone, unless the judge finds the accused guilty. Any sentence imposed must have the vote of at least two-thirds of the members sitting, or in the case of the judge sitting alone, the judge imposes the sentence.

If the accused so requests, and is an enlisted person, one-third of the membership of the court may be enlisted personnel, unless it is wished that the military judge sit alone. The military judge is always a commissioned officer under the law. The enlisted members of the court cannot be detailed from the accused's company or from the crew of the accused's ship if they are members of a ship's detachment.

Normally, enlisted members assigned to courts are mature staff noncommissioned officers. For the special court-martial, the authority convening the court must detail a trial counsel and a defense counsel and such assistants as appropriate. Certain persons are disqualified from acting as trial and defense counsel, depending upon how much they were involved prior to the trial itself. Examples are the investigating officer or a military judge or a court member who acted in the same or related cases. The trial counsel in a special court-martial does not have to be a lawyer. However, the accused person shall be represented by defense counsel who is a lawyer.

The accused may also ask to be represented by lawyer counsel of their own choice and may decide whether the appointed counsel and counsel of their choosing should work together or whether or not the counsel of their choosing is to conduct the defense alone.

Under no circumstances will military personnel accept a fee for defending an accused before a court-martial, and no expenses are incurred by an accused for representation by an appointed lawyer before a court-martial, except in those cases where the accused chooses to hire a civilian lawyer. All other counsel furnished by the military are furnished without cost, and the entire trial is free from any expense to the accused. If a civilian lawyer is hired, the accused must pay whatever fees and expenses the civilian counsel may charge.

The military judge in a special court-martial will be a commissioned officer of the armed forces who is a member of the bar of a federal court or a member of the bar of the highest court of a state and who is certified as qualified for duty as a military judge by the Judge Advocate General of the Navy. No person is eligible to act as a military judge in a case if the individual is in fact the accuser or is a witness for the prosecution or has acted as an investigating officer or a counsel in the same case.

The military judge of a court-martial may not consult with the members of the court except in the presence of the accused, trial counsel and defense counsel, nor may the judge vote with the members of the court on either the guilt or innocence of the accused or on the sentence, unless the judge is sitting in trial of the case alone and there are no members present.

Only in cases in which the accused asks to be tried by the judge alone and waives the presence of other members, does the judge then act as the trier of the facts and as determiner of the law and in the event of a guilty finding does the judge impose sentence.

Special courts-martial are empowered by the UCMJ to "adjudge any punishment not forbidden by the Code except death, dishonorable discharge, dismissal, confinement in excess of six months, hard labor without confinement in excess of six months, forfeiture of pay exceeding two-thirds pay per month, or forfeiture of pay for a period exceeding six months." Thus, it can be seen that the special court-martial, although it tries more serious offenses, is limited by law as to the jurisdictional amount of punishment which it can impose. The maximum is a bad conduct discharge, confinement at hard labor for six months, forfeiture of two-thirds pay per month for six months, and reduction to private, along with such reprimands, censures or admonitions as may also be deemed appropriate.

In addition, it is important to note that a bad conduct discharge may not be adjudged unless a complete record of the proceedings and testimony at the trial has been made.

Note carefully that a special court-martial sentence, when the court is properly constituted, can include a bad conduct discharge. This is a very serious type of discharge which can genuinely handicap the future of anyone who receives it. The bad conduct discharge is only slightly less grave than a dishonorable discharge, and is a serious blot on one's record and future.

General Court-Martial

As mentioned above, the general court-martial must consist of a military judge and not less than five members OR, if the accused requests trial by judge alone and the judge grants it, then the case can be heard by the judge without the presence of the members.

A general court-martial is convened for the most serious offenses, such as, but not limited to, desertion, homicides, seriously aggravated assaults, most sex offenses and the like. When the general court-martial convenes with the members present, then the function of the members is to hear and weigh the evidence in order to determine the guilt or innocence of the accused and to impose a sentence if found guilty.

If the accused is permitted to be tried by the judge alone, then the judge is the trier of the guilt or innocence of the accused and also imposes the sentence.

In all cases where members are present, the judge only sits as the ruling officer on the law and does not take part in the deliberations on either the findings or the sentence. The military judge must be approved by the Judge Advocate General of the Navy as meeting rigorous professional requirements as a lawyer and as a judge. The judge decides the legal technicalities and ensures that the trial is conducted fairly. The military judge is very closely akin to a federal district judge who presides over a United States District Court.

An example of the functions performed by the judge are the ruling on objections by counsel, giving detailed instruction to the court members on all matters of law and on the correlation between matters of law and fact which must be considered by the members in their deliberations on both the guilt or innocence of the accused and also upon the imposition of sentence.

In all general courts-martial, counsel for both the accused and the government must be duly qualified lawyers. This ensures the full protection of all the rights of the accused. This is in keeping with the emphasis contained in the law, i.e., the full protection of the individual standing before the bar of justice.

The only limit to sentences which may be imposed by a general court-martial is the maximum punishment provided for each offense either in the articles of the Uniform Code of Military Justice itself or in the Table of Maximum Punishments which is determined by the President of the United States as a matter of executive decree.

There are, for example, some offenses for which the maximum punishment is death and others for which the maximum punishment is life imprisonment. The remainder of punishments vary down to those that have maximum punishments of only a few months confinement. These maximum punishments are directly proportionate to the gravity of the offense of which the individual is accused.

Court Procedures

No person who is subject to the UCMJ may be tried by a general court-martial until a formal investigation pursuant to Article 32 of the Code has been made of all charges and specifications which have been preferred against the individual and upon which the accused is to be tried. The investigation corresponds to the grand jury and other indictment proceedings as found in civil jurisdictions.

The investigation, however, is far more protective of the rights of the individual than any grand jury proceeding, since it does allow the individual to be present during all of the proceedings, to be represented by lawyer counsel, to confront and cross-examine witnesses against the accused, to present witnesses on behalf of the accused and to present any other evidence and make such argument as the accused may deem appropriate to bring out full consideration in the hearing.

The accused in the pretrial investigation enjoys the same rights that one does at office hours or before a court-martial, which, among other things, are the right to remain silent, the right to make no statement either written or oral, the right to be represented by counsel before and during any period of interrogation and the right to submit whatever evidence may be desired. The investigation results in either a recommendation for trial by general or lesser court-martial on some or all of the charges or it may, in fact, result in a recommendation that the accused not be tried and that the charges be either dismissed or reduced to lesser offenses and be handled on a level appropriate to the reduced offenses.

Rights of the Accused

The accused has certain basic rights before a court-martial, and before any judicial or nonjudicial proceedings in which the accused is subject to charges or in which conduct is subject to inquiry. The most significant of these rights are those guaranteed by Article 31 of the Uniform Code of Military Justice and the 5th Amendment to the Constitution, which basically is a right against self-incrimination.

In addition, an accused is entitled to confer with lawyer counsel prior to any interrogation and to have lawyer counsel present during any interrogation which is consented to by the accused. Military counsel will be provided to an accused without expense by the appropriate military authority. Civilian counsel may be retained at the accused's own expense.

In addition to the rights against self-incrimination and the right to confer with lawyer counsel and have counsel present during the proceedings, some of the more important safeguards are: that the accused is presumed innocent until proven guilty beyond a reasonable doubt. The burden of proof is always on the prosecution. If the evidence presented in court by the prosecution should leave a reasonable doubt in the minds of the required majority of the court, or in the mind of the judge if the judge is sitting alone as requested by the accused, then the accused is acquitted, even though the defense may not have presented one shred of evidence.

The accused does not have to take the witness stand, and no inference may be drawn from the fact that the accused chooses to remain silent and does not present any evidence either personally or through other witnesses or documentary type evidence. Witnesses who can present evidence favorable to the accused can be compelled to appear and testify before courts-martial, both by subpoena, for which their fees and travel expenses are paid by the government, or by military orders issued to the witnesses if they are in the military.

An accused who has been tried and acquitted by a legally constituted court-martial having jurisdiction in the case, cannot be tried again by a court-martial for the same offense. This is known as the Doctrine of Former Jeopardy or Double Jeopardy. If the accused is convicted by court-martial, but granted a rehearing because of some error in the record and is once again convicted at the rehearing, the accused is guaranteed the right to not receive a harsher sentence than the sentence imposed at the original trial. In other words, the new court-martial that is holding a rehearing in the case cannot impose a greater sentence than that which was imposed at the original trial, even though the Table of Maximum Punishments provides for a greater sentence.

Every conviction and sentence is subject to review. In every case there is more than one agency which must study the record of trial to see that no error was committed which might have been prejudicial to the substantial rights of the accused. In the case of a court-martial involving a punitive discharge, there will be not less than two and often there

will be three or four subsequent reviews of the case before any such sentence is approved. In addition, the accused has a right to present new evidence at any time within two years of a conviction, asking for a new trial and reconsideration of the former findings and sentence, when it is discovered that there is some new evidence available that might change the outcome of the case or that there has been some fraud committed on the court.

The accused also has the right to appeal to the Judge Advocate General of the Navy in any case which has not required review by the Court of Criminal Appeals, in cases of newly discovered evidence, fraud on the court, lack of jurisdiction or error prejudicial to the substantial rights of the accused. This review can be requested at any time and there is no time limitation.

Finally, although the UCMJ does not provide for a system of bail, either pending trial or subsequent thereto, pretrial confinement of an accused is limited to those cases in which the cognizant commander determines such to be necessary to ensure the presence of an accused at trial, or it is foreseeable that the accused will engage in serious criminal misconduct.

After trial, it is possible for the convening authority to permit the accused to remain unconfined pending the reviews of the case. In this event, the sentence does not commence to run until all reviews are final and the accused is ultimately confined if the sentence to confinement is approved.

Thus, it can be seen from a review of this entire area, that emphasis is absolutely placed on the protection of the rights of each of us as citizens of the United States and members of the military. Safeguards provided under the Code are the finest to be found in any judicial system in the world, and these rights are zealously protected so as to assure the complete fairness of the system for all of us.

The best course of conduct is, without question, to know and understand the law, and to live within its framework. This will not only assure each Marine of a fine record and the opportunity for promotion, but at the end of service, the Marine will be released, retired or discharged under the finest of conditions, by means of an honorable discharge representing excellence of character and performance of duty.

Chapter Seven

Insignia of Grade

One of the first things you will need to know upon entering the service is how to recognize the grades and ratings of the Marines and Navy personnel with whom you serve. To help you do this, the charts on the following pages outline Marine enlisted and officers grades and give corresponding Navy, Army and Air Force ratings. But if you are to fully understand these grades and ratings, you must do more than simply distinguish among the various insignia which are worn or the grade by which the various individuals are addressed. You must recognize at the same time everything which is represented by these grades and insignia.

You must recognize at the same time everything which is represented by these grades and insignia.

Specifically, you must understand that in the Marine Corps insignia of grade are worn only by those who have demonstrated ability and a willingness to accept responsibility. If these individuals are to discharge the responsibilities with which they are charged, it is necessary that they be equipped with a degree of authority as well. Remember that grade, insignia, ability, responsibility and authority all go together.

Enlisted Grades and Ratings

Marine enlisted persons wear insignia of grade on both sleeves.

Grade chevrons of the Marine Corps are forest green on the service uniform, with a background of red. On shirts, the background is khaki. For the dress blue uniform, chevrons are gold on scarlet. Marines wear one slanting service stripe, "hash mark," near the cuff of the sleeve on the service or dress blue uniform for each four years' enlistment completed.

All rating badges of Navy enlisted personnel are worn on the left sleeve between the shoulder and elbow.

All distinguishing marks (gun captain, range finder operator, etc.) are worn on the right sleeve between the shoulder and elbow, except that aviation and submarine qualification awards continue to be worn on the left breast as prescribed. (Other awards are naval aviation pilot, combat aircrewman, parachutists, submarine combat patrols.)

The pay grade and rating group of non-rated persons are indicated by diagonal stripes worn on the upper part of the left sleeve in the same position prescribed for rating badges.

Officer Grades

Marine Corps officers wear gold or silver insignia of grade on the shoulder straps of their coats or overcoats. They also wear small replicas of this insignia on their shirt collars. Navy officers' ranks can be determined by gold stripes on shoulder boards (epaulettes) of their white coats.

The stripes are either one-half or one-fourth inch wide, depending upon the grade indicated. On blue uniforms, the rank of the officer is shown by gold stripes around the bottom part of both coat sleeves. In addition to the stripes which designate rank, Navy officers may also wear on their shirt collars insignia like that of the corresponding Marine Corps ranks – bars, leaves, eagles and stars.

Marine Corps officers, in addition to their insignia of rank, can be identified by the quatrefoil (twisted braid) on top of their service caps.

Army and Air Force ranks are like those of Marine officers. Coast Guard ranks are like those of the Navy.

Enlisted

	E-1	E-2	E-3	E-4	E-5	E-6	E-7	E-8	E-9
NAVY *	Seaman Recruit	Seaman Apprentice	Seaman	Petty Officer Third Class	Petty Officer Second Class	Petty Officer First Class	Chief Petty Officer	Senior Chief Petty Officer	Master Chief Petty Officer
MARINES	Private	Private First Class	Lance Corporal	Corporal	Sergeant	Staff Sergeant	Gunnery Sergeant	First Sergeant / Master Sergeant	Sergeant Major / Master Gunnery Sergeant
ARMY	Private	Private	Private First Class	Corporal / Specialist 4	Sergeant / Specialist 5	Staff Sergeant / Specialist 6	Sergeant First Class or Platoon Sergeant	First Sergeant / Master Sergeant 8	Command Sergeant Major / Sergeant Major 9
AIR FORCE	Airman Basic	Airman	Airman First Class	Sergeant / Senior Airman	Staff Sergeant	Technical Sergeant	Master Sergeant / First Sergeant	Senior Master Sergeant / First Sergeant	Chief Master Sergeant / First Sergeant

*Includes Navy and Coast Guard.

63

Marine Corps		Navy	
Insignia	Grade	Grade	Insignia
Please see the Marine Corps and Navy Warrant Officer insignias and grades on the next page.			
	Second Lieutenant (Gold Bar)	Ensign	
	First Lieutenant (Silver Bar)	Lieutenant (Junior Grade)	
	Captain	Lieutenant	
	Major (Gold Leaf)	Lieutenant Commander	
	Lieutenant Colonel (Silver Leaf)	Commander	
	Colonel	Captain	
	Brigadier General	Rear Admiral (Lower Half)	
	Major General	Rear Admiral (Upper Half)	
	Lieutenant General	Vice Admiral	
	General	Admiral	
	No Corresponding Grade	Fleet Admiral	

MARINE CORPS
Warrant Officer/Chief Warrant Officer

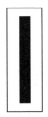

WO-1
red stripes on gold bar

CWO-2
red stripes on gold bar

CWO-3
red stripes on silver bar

CWO-4
red stripes on silver bar

CWO-5
red stripe on silver bar

NAVY
Warrant Officer/Chief Warrant Officer

WO-1
blue stripes on gold bar

CWO-2
blue stripes on gold bar

CWO-3
blue stripes on silver bar

CWO-4
blue stripes on silver bar

Chapter Eight

General Administration

The term "administration," as used in the armed services, means the management of all phases of military operations not directly involved in tactics and strategy. The administration of your unit means the interior management of the unit. It includes feeding, clothing, equipping, sheltering, paying, transporting and maintaining the health and welfare of the unit as a whole and of its individual members. A large portion of the Marine Corps is engaged in administration, but the three people who are directly responsible for administration as it concerns you as an individual are your platoon commander, your company or detachment commander and your first sergeant.

When you have a problem, if your unit leader or chief cannot help you, see the first sergeant. You are not allowed to go directly to the company or detachment commander without the first sergeant's permission. This job is held because the first sergeant has the training and experience to perform all duties as senior enlisted Marine of the unit. The first sergeant can handle most of your problems without either of you having to consult the company commander. If, after having talked to the first sergeant, you still want to see the company commander, you may then ask permission.

The first concern of the Marine Corps is that every Marine be employed in the manner which does most to maintain a force in readiness for our nation's defense.

You may at some time have an important problem which you want to present to no one but your company commander. In that situation, you may tell the first sergeant that you have a problem which you would rather discuss directly with the company commander and ask permission to see the company commander. Bear in mind, though, that this is not the normal procedure and is not usually the best procedure.

The concern with your welfare does not stop with your company or detachment commander. Your battalion commander, or whatever commanding officer you may have on the level above the company or detachment, is also available on occasion to hear your problems. The time and place and manner of arranging to see the commanding officer will be made known to you. You may have a private audience if you wish. The period which the commanding officer sets aside for this purpose is known as "request mast." If you go to request mast in good faith you need have no fear of prejudice to your interests.

It is the duty of every Marine to assist in the smooth administration of the unit. The way that you can do this is to keep yourself informed. Effective administration requires obedience to regulations and orders. To obey a regulation or order, you must know it and understand it. If you do not understand it, ask for an explanation. Most of the orders and regulations which you will have to comply with will either be announced at unit formations or posted on your unit's bulletin board. Keep your ears open at formations. When you join an organization, familiarize yourself with all of the material on the official bulletin board. Thereafter, read twice daily the new material which has appeared on the bulletin board since you last read it. Ignorance of what is on the bulletin board is no excuse for failing to comply with regulations or orders.

The first concern of the Marine Corps is that every Marine be employed in the manner which does most to maintain a force in readiness for our nation's defense. Unit administration is conducted with the objective of doing everything for your welfare which does not interfere with the primary objective of maintaining combat readiness. By looking out for its men and women, the Marine Corps has maintained its enviable *esprit de corps*. Insofar as it does not conflict with the effectiveness of your unit or of the Marine Corps as a whole, you are given considerable choice in your duty station, the type of work you do, they type of specialist training you get and the time you go on leave. Also, the Marine Corps will assist you when you are faced with serious financial or other emergencies, either directly or by securing the help of specialized agencies. The remainder of this chapter will go briefly into some of the features of personnel administration with which you should be familiar. For more complete information consult your first sergeant.

Military Specialty Structure

Marines are trained in the basic techniques of infantry ground combat and are taught how to take care of themselves in the field. In addition, each Marine learns a special job and, when they master it and progress in experience and grade, goes on to learn a more difficult and responsible job along the same line of work. Your qualifications for your specialty appear in your service record and in all personnel records all the way to Headquarters Marine Corps. The qualifications are classed as your Military Occupational Specialty (MOS). An MOS is described by both a title and a code number – for example, Machine Gunner 0331. Your primary MOS is the important one, because it is the basis for your assignment and promotion. Every Marine has a primary MOS. Some Marines have one or more additional MOS's. The machine gunner might, for example, have the additional MOS of 8541, Scout-Sniper.

Marine Corps units are organized in accordance with Tables of Organization (T/O) approved by the Commandant of the Marine Corps. The T/O for a unit shows a number of billets equal to the authorized number of officers and enlisted personnel in the unit. Each billet is shown by grade, duty in the unit and MOS code number of the individual who is supposed to fill it. You can see that "billet" and "MOS" do not mean the same thing. The title of a billet may differ from the title of the MOS which is required to fill that billet. For example, a T/O for a rifle company has in each rifle platoon billets for four sergeants, MOS 0311. Three of these billets are in the three rifle squads and appear in the T/O as "Squad Leader," MOS 0311. The remaining one is in the rifle platoon headquarters and appears as "Platoon Guide." Thus, if a sergeant with MOS 0311 is assigned to a rifle company, they might be assigned to any one of the billets where their MOS is required.

Classification is that part of personnel administration which entails interviewing individuals, testing them, preparing and maintaining their qualification records and classifying their military qualifications. The objective of our classification system is the assignment of a suitable MOS to every Marine. The *Marine Corps Manual* says of assigning a primary MOS: "That MOS will normally identify billets for which the Marine is best qualified, with due consideration given to such factors as:

a. The needs of the Marine Corps as a whole which will be determined by the Commandant of the Marine Corps.
b. The duty assignment policy for enlisted personnel.
c. The technical skills required.
d. The Marine's education, experience, aptitudes and capabilities.
e. The duty preference of the Marine."

The military specialty structure is divided into occupational fields. The first two digits of an MOS identify the occupational field and are often used in conversation in place of the name of that field. Thus, if one Marine tells another of an occupational field of 03, the Marine is in the infantry. If one says it is 04, the Marine is in logistics.

Normally, a Marine is not assigned to an occupational field until one has finished recruit training. The Marine is then assigned the basic MOS of an occupational field. The basic MOS for an occupational field is a four digit number. The first two digits identify the occupational field; the second two are a double zero.

Upon completion of either basic specialist training, on-the-job training or a formal school, Marines are assigned a primary MOS to identify the particular skill learned. Thus a Marine joins the Fleet Marine Force or reports to a new duty station fully trained to occupy a specific T/O billet.

The Marine Corps' military specialty structure is designed for career planning for the individual. The assignment of the right person to the right job is made in accordance with a plan. The plan is designed to advance your professional value as a Marine in the type of duty which is suited to your experience, ability, and interest. The plan will benefit you and the Marine Corps.

Promotion

As a general rule, Marines are never promoted more than one grade at a time. Promotion to private first class is achieved in accordance with policies established by the Commandant of the Marine Corps. In general, such promotion is based upon completion of a given period of time in grade, satisfactory personal conduct, certain standards of proficiency in duty performance and other factors of this nature. Promotion to lance corporal and to each of the non-commissioned officer grades comes to Marines who meet the specified requirements of service in grade,

MARK	CORRESPONDING ADJECTIVE RATING	STANDARDS OF CONDUCT
0 to 1.9	Unsatisfactory	Habitual offender. Conviction by general, special, or more than one summary court-martial. Give a mark of "0" upon declaration of desertion. Ordered to confinement pursuant to sentence of court-martial. Two or more punitive reductions in grade.
2 to 2.9	Poor	No special court-martial. Not more than one summary court-martial. Not more than two nonjudicial punishments. Punitive reduction in grade.
3 to 3.9	Fair	No court-martial. Not more than one nonjudicial punishment. No unfavorable impressions of the qualities listed in paragraph 4007.5a. Failure to make satisfactory progress while assigned to the weight control or military appearance program. Conduct such as not to impair appreciably one's usefulness or the efficiency of the command, but conduct not sufficient to merit an honorable discharge.
4 to 4.4	Good	No offenses. No unfavorable impressions as to attitude, interests, cooperation, obedience, after-effects of intemperance, courtesy and consideration, and observance of regulations.
4.5 to 4.8.	Excellent	No offenses Positive favorable impressions of the qualities listed in paragraph 4007.6a. Demonstrated reliability, good influence, sobriety, obedience, and industry.
4.9 to 5	Outstanding	No offenses. Exhibits to an outstanding degree the qualities listed in paragraph 4007.6a. Observes spirit as well as letter of orders and regulations. Demonstrated positive effect on others by example and persuasion.

Fig. 8-1. Standards of Conduct.

conduct, performance of duty, and the specialist knowledge required to hold the MOS of the next higher grade. The Marines selected throughout the Corps are those who are best qualified. The number chosen within each occupational field or MOS depends upon the vacancies at the time. When they are chosen, their commanding officers are then authorized to promote them. However, a commanding officer is not required to promote a Marine unless satisfied that the Marine has the necessary leadership, personality and moral character for the next higher grade.

The Commandant of the Marine Corps sends the promotion certificate of those staff sergeants through first sergeants/master sergeants who have been selected for promotion by a promotion board to their commanding officer as vacancies occur. Promotion is made immediately, unless the commanding officer determines the noncommissioned officer should not be promoted. In that event, the case is referred back to the Commandant of the Marine Corps.

It is a Marine Corps policy to maintain a personnel evaluation system in order to establish a record of marking for grading an individual Marine's performance and conduct. In the case of sergeants and above, a fitness report form is used, which provides an in-depth evaluation. Marines with a rank of private through corporal receive periodic proficiency and conduct marks by the commanding officer. These marks are then entered in the Marine's Official Military Personnel File (OMPF) in the Marine Corps Total Force System (MCTFS), which automatically

MARK	CORRESPONDING ADJECTIVE RATING	STANDARDS OF PERFORMANCE
0 to 1.9	Unsatisfactory	Does unacceptable work in most of duties, generally undependable; needs considerable assistance and close supervision on even the simplest assignment.
2 to 2.9	Poor	Does acceptable work in some duties but cannot be depended upon. Needs assistance and close supervision on all but the simplest assignments.
3 to 3.9	Fair	Handles routine matters acceptably but needs close supervision when performing duties not of a routine nature.
4 to 4.4	Good	Can be depended upon to discharge regular duties thoroughly and competently but usually needs assistance in dealing with problems not of a routine nature.
4.5 to 4.8.	Excellent	Can be depended upon to discharge regular duties, but needs assistance in dealing with extremely difficult or unusual assignments.
4.9 to 5	Outstanding	Does superior work in all duties. Even extremely difficult or unusual assignments can be given with full confidence that they will be handled in a thoroughly competent manner.

Fig. 8-2. Standards of Performance

computes the composite score and compares it to the cutting score for the appropriate promotion period. If the Marine's score meets or exceeds the cutting score, the MCTFS will automatically issue an advisory remark to the Marine's organization.

The standards shown in Figure 8-1 will be used as a guide in assigning conduct marks, however full discretion is left to commanders to deviate from them for good and sufficient reasons.

The standards shown in Figure 8-2 will be used as a guide in assigning duty proficiency marks, however, full discretion is left to the commanders to deviate from them for good and sufficient reasons.

Eligibility for promotion is determined from a composite score which includes such elements as service in grade, total active duty service, past performance of duty, physical fitness, off-duty education, etc. All elements are included in the score according to a mathematical formula established by the Commandant of the Marine Corps. Figure 8-3 is an example of a composite score sheet and an explanation of how the composite scores are computed.

The ratings for lines 1-3 are derived from rating tables in Marine Corps Order P1400.29B.

The GMP score (line 4) is obtained by dividing line 3 by the number of lines above line 3 which have a rating other than "not considered." This number is then multiplied by 100 and entered on line 5.

Lines 6 and 7 are the average of all duty proficiency marks assigned prior to the cut-off date designated in the appropriate HQMC directive but on or after the date of last promotion, reduction or enlistment (whichever is latest).

Line 8 is the total months in current grade from date of rank to the designated cut-off date.

Line 9 is the total months in service the Marine will have accrued on the designated cut-off date.

Line 10 applies to drill instructors, recruiters and graduates of the Marine Security Guard Battalion. The Commanding Officer, Marine Security Guard Battalion, is authorized to add 100 points to the composite score of Marine Security Guards upon completion of the Marine Security Guard School. This award will be valid for a period of one year.

Line 11 is the number of approved self-education courses completed since promotion to the current grade. A maximum of five courses may be included.

Bonus points are obtained from the following:

Courses	Bonus Points
MCI	1
Extension School subcourse	1
GED Test	1
High school course (semester)	2
College course (semester)	2
Vocational course (semester)	2

Composite Score Sheet

2501. <u>COMPUTATION (USMC/USMCR)</u>. The following format is used in the computation of composite scores for LCpl and Cpls. It is also used to <u>manually</u> compute the composite score prior to the submission of a remedial promotion request for any LCpl or Cpl (USMC or USMCR).

<u>Line No.</u>		<u>Rating</u>		

1.   Rifle marksmanship score   _____ = _____   _____ (Date of qual YYMMDD)
                                                 SCORE

2.   PFT _____ = _____   _____ (Date of test YYMMDD)
            SCORE

3.   Subtotal (line 1 + 2)   = _____

4.   GMP score (line 3 divided by 2)   = _____   <u>Score</u>

5.   GMP score (from line 4)   _____   x 100   = _____

6.   Average duty proficiency   _____   x 100   = _____
2501   MARCORPROMMAN, VOL 2, ENLPROM

7.   Average conduct   _____   x 100   = _____

8.   TIG (months)   _____   x 5   = _____

9.   TIS (months)   _____   x 2   = _____
         (computed from AFADBD for USMC and Active Reserve;
         and from PEBD for Drilling Reserve)

10.   DI/Recruiter/MSG bonus   _____   x 1   = _____

11.   Self-Education bonus: (a maximum of 75 points)

         a. MCI/Extension School   _____   x1.5   = _____

         b. College/CLEP/Vocational   _____   x 1.0   = _____

12.   Command Recruiting Bonus   _____   x 20   = _____
         (a maximum of 100 points may be earned)

13.   <u>Composite Score</u> (sum of lines 5 through 12)   = _____

Fig. 8-3. *Composite Score Sheet.*

At the discretion of your commanding officer, credit may be given for other courses having equivalent self-improvement value.

The scores for lines 5-11 are obtained by multiplying each element by the number indicated in the above example.

The Command Recruiting Bonus (line 12) is earned while on permissive TAD. If you assist a recruiter, for every person you get to join the Marine Corps, you earn 20 points. A maximum of 100 points can be earned.

Line 13, the Marine's composite score, is the sum of the values under the "Score" column for lines 5-12.

At Headquarters Marine Corps a cutting score is established so that the number of those Marines whose composite score is above the cutting score is equal to the number of vacancies in the rank and occupational field being considered.

Leave and Liberty

Leave is authorized vacation or absence from duty, as distinguished from liberty. Liberty is the authorized absence of a Marine from a place of duty for short periods and not chargeable to the leave account. In a civilian job, your annual vacation would be the counterpart of leave. Weekends, periods between the end of one work day and the beginning of work the next, and occasional days or afternoons off not counting against your annual vacation would correspond to liberty.

Marines may be granted annual leave at any time the absence would not be inconsistent with operational readiness requirements or the accomplishment of the mission of the command. You may not always be able to get your annual leave at the particular period or periods you would like. CO's are restricted as to the number of Marines they may allow to be on leave at one time. They must grant leave so that there is the least interference with duty and training schedules. You need not take all of your annual leave during one continuous period. You may make portions of it at different times during the year.

Leave is earned at the rate of two and one-half days a month. In twelve months you earn 30 days leave. No leave is earned during periods of unauthorized absence or during periods of confinement serving sentence of a court-martial. Your monthly Leave and Earnings Statement (LES) will keep you advised of your leave status.

A Marine may not be authorized more than 60 days annual leave during any fiscal year, nor may a Marine be authorized annual leave for a continuous period of more than 60 days unless specifically authorized by the Commandant of the Marine Corps.

Advance leave is leave granted to a Marine, with pay and allowances, prior to its accrual based on the reasonable expectation that the amount advanced will be earned before a Marine's separation, or in the case of a Marine who has executed a first extension of enlistment, before the effective date of that extension.

Excess leave is leave granted in excess of accrued and advance leave and is the term used to describe a minus leave balance on the effective date of separation. A minus balance on the date of discharge for the purpose of immediate reenlistment is excess leave only to the extent that it exceeds the leave accrual potential of the unserved period of enlistment terminated by the discharge.

Emergency leave will be authorized under the following circumstances as verified by such means as the leave granting authority considers sufficient. Verification may be by letter, telegram or telephone call from a family member, minister, physician, American Red Cross, etc.

- Upon the death of a member of a Marine's immediate family, i.e., father, mother, person standing in for a parent, spouse, son, daughter, brother, sister, or any only living relative.
- When the return of a Marine will contribute to the welfare of a dying member of his or her immediate family as defined above.
- When due to any serious illness or injury of a member of a Marine's immediate family as defined above, important responsibilities are placed upon a Marine which cannot be accomplished from the duty station.
- When failure to return home would create a serious and unusual hardship on a Marine or the family.

You may not go on leave without a written leave authorization which will prescribe the date and time your leave is effective and the date and time it ends. Keep your leave authorization with you while you are on leave and return it to your unit office when you get back. The most common written leave authorization is prepared on a form. Following are the instructions which appear on the back of the form:

1. "Leave is granted subject to immediate recall; therefore, maintain communications with your leave address. KEEP THESE LEAVE PAPERS IN YOUR POSSESSION AT ALL TIMES.
2. It is understood you have sufficient funds to defray your expenses on leave, including round-trip transportation. Each case of transportation obtained from recruiting stations, or other Marine Corps activities, by personnel on leave, will be investigated and where no urgent necessity was apparent in applying for transportation request, disciplinary action may be taken.
3. You are cautioned against the disclosure of any classified information. While it is desirable to tell the public about the Marine Corps, do not discuss any subject unless you are certain it is unclassified. In case you are asked to participate in a press conference, talk to reporters or speak through any other media on matters pertaining to the Naval Service, you should express a desire to cooperate, but should first consult with and obtain clearance from the nearest Marine Corps public information officer if at all practicable.
4. Inform yourself of transportation schedules, and make allowances for delays. Missing connections is not an excuse for UNAUTHORIZED ABSENCE. Train, bus and plane schedules and connections are frequently unreliable.

5. Cooperate with shore patrol and military police at all times. Military police, shore patrols, air police, officers, petty officers, and noncommissioned officers of the Armed Forces are authorized to take preventive measures, including apprehension, if necessary in the case of any member of the Armed Forces who is guilty of committing a breach of the peace, disorderly conduct, or any other offense which reflects discredit upon the services. Personnel on leave and liberty are subject to this authority. Misconduct will be cause for disciplinary action. You are subject to orders of your superior officers in all branches of the Armed Services.

6. If necessary to request an extension of leave, communicate with your commanding officer by telegram, telephone or letter. IF NO REPLY IS RECEIVED YOU WILL CONSIDER YOUR REQUEST NOT GRANTED.

7. In the event you encounter problems while on leave, it is recommended that you contact the nearest military unit for assistance.

8. In case of serious illness or injury incurred while on leave which requires medical attention or hospitalization, report facts to your commanding officer by telegram and request instructions. You are advised that costs incident to hospitalization or medical treatment received at other than Navy, Army, Air Force, or Public Health Service facilities, may be defrayed by the Marine Corps in emergency cases only. No charge against your leave, or reduction in total period of leave granted will be made for any period of hospitalization. Unless otherwise ordered, you will revert to a leave status upon release from a hospital, and will immediately notify your commanding officer that you have been released and have reentered leave status, giving leave address, preferably by telegram. Proof of hospitalization must be provided upon return from leave. (NOTE: IF MARINE IS UNABLE TO CONTACT COMMANDING OFFICER DUE TO ILLNESS, ACCIDENT OR DEATH, NOTIFICATION OF THIS FACT SHOULD BE MADE TO THE NEAREST MARINE CORPS ACTIVITY BY PERSON FAMILIAR WITH THE SITUATION (Parents, spouse, physician, etc.)).

9. It is understood that this leave commences at your duty station and that it expires at your duty station. Also it is clearly understood that you are required to report for duty at your duty station upon expiration of leave and that failure to do so may make you subject to disciplinary action under the Uniform Code of Military Justice, 10 U.S.C. 801-940. If you are authorized to check out and check in by telephone you are cautioned that commencement and termination of leave must be made in the immediate vicinity of your duty station (place from which you normally commute daily to and from work). You are directed to deliver your leave authorization to your commanding officer or the designated representative, at the commencement of the next regular working day subsequent to termination of your leave."

You may wish to visit your home while traveling to a new duty station. Unless orders from higher authority to your commanding officer directing your transfer to another station prevent them, your commanding officer is authorized to grant you delay en route to your new station. This delay will count as annual leave. The authorized number of days required to travel between your old and new stations is additional and does not count as leave. Your travel orders will tell you the date you are to report to your new station. If you are granted delay and report to your new station before the date specified, the unused portion of your delay is not counted as leave. You gain nothing, however, if the time you spend between stations is less than the travel time you are allowed. Be sure to keep your travel orders in your possession until you report to your new duty station.

Liberty is a privilege which is granted only when it does not interfere with the duty and training of the command or with its prescribed state of readiness. Your commanding officer will prescribe liberty limits beyond which members of the command may not go without written permission.

The instructions quoted which appear on the back of the leave authorization form for the most part apply to liberty and leave alike. Become familiar with them.

Off-Duty Education and Training

At almost every Marine Corps installation within the United States and overseas, off-duty education and training opportunities are available to help individuals improve and expand their abilities and skills as a Marine and, at the same time, reap personal benefit. There are several hundred colleges and universities that offer off-duty classroom study on or near Marine Corps installations. These civilian school courses serve as a sound basis for improvement in your Marine career and can frequently become part of a program leading to a college degree.

Financial assistance is available to qualified Marines through the Marine Corps Tuition Assistance Program which will pay 75 percent of the tuition costs for college courses. The Montgomery GI Bill is a voluntary contributory-matching program for service members initially entering active service after July 1, 1985. Each Marine entering military service after that date has the right to enroll in and make contributions to the program at any time during a tour of extended active duty.

In addition to the training received at service schools and on-the-job training, you may enroll in correspondence courses offered free through the Marine Corps Institute (MCI), and correspondence schools of the other armed services. These latter courses are specifically designed to help you advance in rank (by accruing more earned points and achieving a higher composite score) and to assume additional responsibilities as a United States Marine.

Your education officer will provide you with more information on the off-duty educational opportunities that are available and the current GI Bill and VA benefits. The education officer will also help you select courses of study and establish a program which will meet your individual needs.

Dependents

An enlisted Marine is entitled to basic allowance for housing for legal dependents when the government does not provide adequate quarters for the Marine and the dependents at a duty station. All enlisted Marines with legal dependents are required to make an application for basic allowance for housing in behalf of their dependents. Although a Marine is not required to allot a prescribed amount of pay to dependents, a government allotment is a sure and convenient means of ensuring that dependents receive continuous support. An enlisted Marine may receive basic allowance for housing for a spouse, legitimate or illegitimate minor child and for certain other dependents who rely upon the Marine for support. The regulations governing basic allowance for housing are complex and change frequently. If there is anyone for whom you have not claimed a dependent's allowance who is dependent upon you for support, you should immediately inform your first sergeant. Likewise, you should immediately inform your first sergeant of any change in the status of your dependents. This is particularly important since your pay will be checked and all payments made in behalf of your dependents after their entitlement ceases will be deducted. A Marine may submit a request for

waiver of recovery of the overpayment to the commanding officer. This request will then be forwarded to the Commandant of the Marine Corps for a final determination.

A married Marine may, subject to the approval of his or her commanding officer, be permitted to mess separately from an organization's general mess and be reimbursed a prescribed amount approximately equal to the cost to the government of the food consumed if eaten in the mess.

A dependent spouse and children are not normally entitled to government quarters, although low-cost government housing is sometimes available. Such housing is not normally available except at the base where the Marine is stationed.

Dependents are entitled to medical and dental benefits through the TRICARE medical plan, a health benefits plan which shares most of the costs of care from civilian doctors and hospitals when care is not provided through a military hospital or clinic. Dependents are enrolled in the program through the Defense Eligibility Enrollment Reporting System (DEERS), which is accomplished by notifying the administrative section whenever there is a change in the number or status of dependents. Dental benefits are also provided for dependents by TRICARE – Active Duty Family Member Dental Plan.

A Marine who is married and has to support a family on pay and allowance must forgo many of the luxuries and pleasures which could be afforded as a single person. The Marine is expected to practice the economy necessary to provide adequate support for dependents. If the dependents are subject to real privation and hardship because of sickness or other emergency, the American Red Cross or the Navy-Marine Corps Relief Society may provide financial assistance. It must be understood that these organizations do not have enough money to help those who are capable of meeting their emergencies without assistance. For instance, they could not be expected to lend money to a Marine who could raise the money by selling an automobile which was bought only for pleasure and convenience and not for essential transportation.

Legal Assistance

Most commands have legal assistance officers who are qualified to answer your questions about legal problems and advise and assist you in their solution. A legal assistance officer is prohibited by regulations from revealing confidences of personnel obtaining legal assistance to the same extent that a civilian lawyer is prohibited by legal ethics from revealing confidences of their clients. Throughout the United States, there are agencies set up within the legal profession to assist servicepeople with their legal affairs. The Department of the Navy maintains liaison with these agencies. If you have a legal problem which requires the services of such an agency, your commanding officer or legal assistance officer can advise you of the procedure to follow.

Medals and Decorations

MEDAL OF HONOR. The highest military award given by our country was first authorized in 1861 and is given for acts of bravery above and beyond the call of duty.

PURPLE HEART. This was the first medal awarded by our country. It was first awarded in 1782 and was given for acts of bravery. Later it was given for wounds only.

Other medals awarded for bravery in combat are:
Navy Cross
Silver Star

Distinguished Flying Cross
Navy and Marine Corps Medal (peacetime or combat not involving actual conflict with the enemy)
Bronze Star
Air Medal
Navy Commendation Medal

Ribbons were authorized in 1905 for wear on certain uniforms in lieu of medals. In addition to decorations, they represent service medals awarded for service performed in certain geographic areas during specified time periods. Stars and other devices worn on service medals and ribbons represent battles or campaigns in which the individual Marine participated. Stars, leaves or numerals on personal or unit decorations denote additional awards of the appropriate decoration to the individual Marine.

Marksmanship badges are awarded for degrees of proficiency with small arms.

Personal Finances

The Marine Corps recognizes that it is sometimes necessary to go into debt in order to provide the ordi-

Medal of Honor

Purple Heart

Navy Cross

Silver Star

Distinguished Flying Cross

Navy and Marine Corps Medal

Bronze Star

Navy Commendation Medal

nary essentials in life, but prompt settlement of indebtedness is expected.

Charge cards and time payment plans offered through commercial businesses and finance companies have become a popular method of acquiring personal items of service or merchandise. However, they are often misused and can be costly to the consumer because of the higher rates of interest to be paid back. When it becomes necessary to borrow money to purchase the essentials of life, it is wiser to go to a bank or your local credit union to take advantage of the lower interest rates and personal savings plans that are available to each member.

The need for a personal savings plan is important to every Marine. It will reduce the needs or amounts to borrow. Also, that money that you have saved will earn interest for you. You should save money for the less costly things that you may later wish to purchase or just to have money available for those unforeseen "emergencies" that may arise.

One of the most effective methods of saving money is by means of an allotment. An allotment is a regular sum of money automatically deducted from your pay monthly and paid by the government to a payee whom you designate. Allotments are made only upon your written request and only for purposes allowed by regulations. Information pertaining to allotments to dependents who are authorized dependency allowances may be obtained through your unit administrative supervisor or the local disbursing officer. Allotments may also be registered for relatives not authorized to receive dependency allowances. An allotment to a bank may be for the support of family or relatives. A savings allotment may be sent directly to a savings institution such as a bank (savings or checking account) or credit union (savings or loan account). U.S. Savings Bonds may be purchased in a regular amount each month and paid for by an allotment. So may monthly life insurance premiums, including premiums on commercial insurance, when the insurance is on the life of the grantor.

The Navy- Marine Corps Relief Society and the American Red Cross provide interest-free loans to qualified servicemen and women and often require payment through an allotment.

Leave and Earnings

A Leave and Earnings Statement (LES) is a monthly computerized printout based upon an individual Marine's pay information contained in the Marine Corps Total Force System (MCTFS). Direct deposit of pay is now mandatory, except in special cases.

The LES is prepared at the Marine Corps Finance Center in Kansas City, Mo., and distributed each month to your disbursing office and to your commanding officer. Your commanding officer will receive two copies of the LES. One will be audited and filed in your Service Record Book, and a copy will be provided to you. Upon receipt of the LES, you should review the information contained therein to determine whether or not it is accurate.

Each Marine should become familiar with the LES in order to use it effectively. Your copy will provide information concerning your identification and service, the total amounts of pay that you are entitled to each month, the total amount of allotments you have, your total amount of deductions such as Serviceman's Group Life Insurance (SGLI), income tax, social security payments, etc., a record of your past pay amounts, monthly and annual tax information, a record of your leave used and accrued and a remarks section that will show information pertinent to your pay. The reverse of the LES contains a generalized legend to explain information appearing on the face of the form.

If you should discover an error on your LES, bring it to the attention of your first sergeant in order to ensure that the error is corrected.

Chapter Nine

Military Security

Military security is achieved by Marines through special organizational measures such as establishment of an Interior Guard. It is achieved by individual Marines through being aware of security threats such as the possibility of terrorist attack and taking action to counter those threats. Both formal Interior Guard organization and the individual awareness of and counteraction to terrorist threats are tailored to the specific situation and location. The general rules to be followed are the same everywhere and are used as the basis for maintaining military security wherever Marines are located.

Interior Guard

Wherever you are stationed as a Marine, ashore or afloat, your commanding officer generally establishes and maintains an interior guard. This guard is charged with the preservation of order, protection of property, and the enforcement of orders and regulations. Guard duty is a function of special importance to Marines, because they are assigned to protect naval installations ashore. Such naval establishments as shipyards, ammunition dumps, proving grounds, administration buildings, airfields, and the like are guarded by Marines.

The functions of interior guards vary with the desires of the commanding officers of individual posts and with the nature of the particular posts and stations. For example, sentries at a naval ammunition depot generally have challenging posts, while stations like Quantico have few if any challenging posts.

When you are on duty with an interior guard, you are one member of a distinct organization with definite orders to carry out. The persons with authority over an interior guard are the commanding officer, the field officer of the day, when assigned, and the officer of the day. The field officer of the day or the officer of the day when no field officer of the day has been assigned, is the commanding officer's direct representative and is in charge of the security of the post, station, installation, or unit during the tour of duty.

There are four classes of personnel in an interior guard. These classes are: (1) the commander of the guard, (2) the sergeant of the guard, (3) the corporals of the guard, (4) the privates, PFC's and lance corporals of the guard.*

Usually there are three reliefs in each interior guard. Since a corporal is assigned to each relief, there are three corporals of the guard. There are enough privates and PFC's to provide three reliefs for each post the interior guard is assigned, plus a certain number of supernumeraries depending on the size of the guard. These supernumeraries are held in reserve in case of emergency.

Duties of Guard Personnel

When you are assigned to interior guard duty, you will find that there are certain set duties which must be performed. The following discussion outlines the principal duties and responsibilities of the commander, sergeant, corporals and privates of the guard.

Commander of the Guard

- Ensures proper instruction, discipline, and performance of duty of the main guard and, when directed, the brig guard.
- Obeys the orders of the commanding officer, field officer of the day (when assigned), officer of the day and, in emergencies, the senior line officer present only. The commander of the guard reports to the officer of the day any additional orders which the commander or other authorized persons have issued.
- Ensures that all members of the guard are correctly instructed in their orders and duties and that they understand and properly perform them. The commander of the guard questions the noncommissioned officers of the guard and sentries about the instructions they may have received from the old guard.

These titles address specific billets and do not necessarily denote rank.

76

- Inspects the guard when directed by the officer of the day, but must inspect each relief at least once while on post. The commander ensures that the Marines, their arms, and their equipment are in proper condition, and that the special orders for each post are posted in their proper location.
- Keeps the sergeant of the guard informed of one's location at all times.
- When an alarm is sounded, the commander expeditiously forms the reserve, if necessary. If the situation is serious, the commander causes the proper call to be sounded and notifies the officer of the day immediately. Should a sentry call, "GUARD," or discharge their piece three times in rapid succession, the commander will send a strong patrol to that post.
- Details Marines to raise and lower the national flag at morning and evening colors. The commander ensures that the national flag is kept in good condition and never handled except in the performance of duty. The commander reports to the officer of the day when the flag is not in serviceable condition.
- Ensures that reliefs are posted on schedule.
- Unless otherwise ordered, the commander may permit members of the guard not on post to leave the guardhouse for short periods of time.
- The commander informs the officer of the day immediately of any dangerous, suspicious, or unusual occurrence.
- The commander notifies the officer of the day when any person is apprehended by the guard and will detain such person at the guardhouse for appropriate action by the officer of the day.
- The commander ensures the security of prisoners under charge of the guard. Before each relief is posted, the commander causes the corporals of the guard of the old and new reliefs to verify together the number of prisoners. The commander will be guided in the performance of duties in connection with the brig by the brig manual.
- When formal relief is prescribed, the commander effects the relief of the sergeants of the guard before being relieved. The commander examines the guard report before being relieved, causes any errors therein to be corrected, enters a report of their tour of duty thereon under the heading, "Report of the Commander of the Guard," and signs one's name and grade under the last entry. The commander then reports to the old officer of the day with the new commander of the guard for relief.

Sergeant of the Guard

The sergeant of the guard assists the commander of the guard in ensuring proper instruction, discipline and performance of duty of the guard. If there is no commander of the guard, the sergeant will perform the duties prescribed for the commander of the guard. The sergeant of the guard performs the following tasks:

- The sergeant of the guard has general supervision over the corporals of the guard and other subordinate members of the guard. The sergeant will be thoroughly familiar with their orders and duties.
- The sergeant of the guard is responsible for the property under charge of the guard and will see that it is cared for properly. The sergeant will report any discrepancies to the commander of the guard.
- The sergeant of the guard will assign members of the guard to reliefs, unless this has been done by higher authority. The sergeant of the guard will prepare duplicate lists of the names of the noncommissioned officers and other members of the guard, showing reliefs and posts or duties of each. One list is given to the commander of the guard, and the other is retained by the sergeant.
- The sergeant of the guard will see that all reliefs are turned out at the proper time and that the corporals of the guard thoroughly understand and are prompt and efficient in the discharge of their duties. The sergeant will designate bunks in the same vicinity for each relief so that the members may be quickly found and turned out.
- The sergeant of the guard will make such inspections and see that the other noncommissioned officers of the guard make such inspections and patrols as may be prescribed by higher authority.
- The sergeant of the guard will turn over duties to the next ranking noncommissioned officer on duty before absenting from the guardhouse.
- The sergeant of the guard will take the place of the corporal of the guard whose relief is on post or designate another noncommissioned officer to do so, should the corporal of the guard be called away from the guardhouse.
- The sergeant of the guard will be responsible for the proper police of the guardhouse, including the area around it.
- The sergeant of the guard will report the following to the commander of the guard or, if none is assigned, to the officer of the day:
  - Any suspicions or unusual occurrence that comes to attention.

- All persons apprehended by the guard.
- The approach of an armed party.
- Any orders or instructions received from persons other than the commander of the guard or the officer of the day.

- When the brig guard is included in the interior guard, the sergeant of the guard may be assigned the duties of brig warden. When so assigned, the sergeant will administer the brig in accordance with the orders of the officer of the day, the commander of the guard, and other applicable instructions.

Corporal of the Guard

An enlisted Marine assigned duty in charge of a relief of the guard will be officially known as the corporal of the guard. The corporal of the guard performs the following tasks:

- If members of the guard are not assigned to reliefs and posts by higher authority, the corporal of the guard assigns the members of the relief to posts by numbers immediately after the guard is divided into reliefs. These assignments are not changed during the same tour of guard except by direction of higher authority.
- Makes a list of the members of the relief, including oneself. The list shows the number of the relief, the post to which each Marine is assigned, and the name and organization. The list is made in duplicate. One copy is given to the sergeant of the guard as soon as completed, and the other is retained by the corporal of the guard.
- Instructs all the members of the relief regarding their orders and duties.
- Posts the relief as follows:
  - At an appropriate time before sentries are due to go on post, the corporal of the guard assembles them, checks their appearance, fitness for duty, condition of arms if carried, issues ammunition if required, and assures that they understand their general and special orders and any special instructions. When the relief is large, it may be more convenient to form the relief, call the roll, and inspect the sentries in ranks. The corporal of the guard then reports to the sergeant of the guard that the relief is ready to be posted or, if directed, posts the sentries without so reporting. The corporal of the guard will personally supervise the posting of each sentry of a new relief. The corporal of the guard moves the relief to the posts by marching or by vehicle. When movement is by truck, the relief will embark in the inverse order from which the sentries will debark at their respective posts.
  - Where there are few posts, or the posts are only a short distance from the guardhouse, the corporal of the guard may send sentries to their posts by direct order. Thus, "Private A, Private B, take your posts," or if the roll has been called, "Take your posts." Each sentry will then proceed directly to a post. Where sentries are sent to their posts by direct order, one sentry relieves another by meeting at a particular point at a prearranged time. The sentry on post at the expiration of their tour will remain on post within view of the prearranged relieving point, and when relieved by the new sentry, will proceed directly to the guardhouse and report to the corporal of the guard of the old relief. When reliefs are posted in this manner, the last sentry on duty on a night post will proceed directly to the guardhouse at the designated time, and will report to the corporal of the guard that the post has been secured.
  - The corporal of the guard writes down the names of the sentries, the number of each post, the time and date posted, or directed to the posts, and the time to report back to the guardhouse upon being relieved.
  - If the relief was posted with arms loaded, the corporal of the guard of the old relief will see that no cartridges are left in the chambers or magazines before dismissing the members of the old relief.
- Is acquainted thoroughly with all orders of every sentry on the relief. Sees that each sentry understands, carries out, and correctly transmits such orders in detail to one's successor.
- If the guard should need to be activated, the corporal of the guard will ensure the guard members are promptly formed. Tents or bunks are designated in the same vicinity for the reliefs so that all members of each relief may be found and turned out in the shortest time and with the least confusion.
- When the relief is on post, the corporal takes the post in the guardhouse. The corporal does not fall in with the guard when it is formed. There is at least on Marine constantly on the alert at the guardhouse. This is the corporal of the guard whose relief is on post.
- Reports at once to the sergeant of the guard or commander of the guard any violation of regula-

tions or any unusual occurrence which is reported or which comes to their notice.

- Has a rifle or other prescribed arm with them constantly.
- Wakes the corporal of the guard whose relief is next on post in time for the latter to verify prisoners, form the relief, and post it at the proper hour.
- Notifies the sergeant of the guard whenever it becomes necessary to leave the post.
- After notifying the sergeant of the guard, the corporal goes at once to any sentry who may call "CORPORAL OF THE GUARD, Post Number –."
- Promptly notifies the commander of the guard and sergeant of the guard if a sentry calls "The guard" or "Fire."
- If a sentry calls "RELIEF," the corporal relieves them with a supernumerary. If the sentry is relieved for a short time only, the corporal posts again as soon as the necessity for relief ceases.
- Examines the persons or parties detained by a sentry. If there is reason to believe that they have no authority to cross the sentry's post, the corporal of the guard conducts them to the sergeant of the guard or to the commander of the guard.
- Takes custody of all suspicions and disorderly persons and those taken in the act of committing crimes. All such persons are conducted at once to the sergeant of the guard or to the commander of the guard.
- Sees that no persons or parties enter the guardhouse or cross the posts of sentries posted there except by proper authority.
- Challenges all suspicious persons or parties observed during the times for challenging.

Non-rated Marines of the Guard

When you are a private, PFC, or a lance corporal member of the guard, you normally are assigned to a relief by the sergeant of the guard. The corporal of the guard for your relief usually assigns you to your post. You cannot be changed from one relief to another during the same tour of guard duty except by proper authority. Rules which govern your conduct while serving as a member of the guard are:

- All members of the guard will memorize, understand, and comply with the general orders for sentries. In addition, they will understand and comply with special orders applying to their particular posts and the regulations relating to general orders.

- Supernumeraries will understand the special orders for all posts on which they could be posted and comply with those for the particular post if posted thereon as a sentry.
- Members of the guard not on post will remain in the immediate vicinity of the guardhouse except when granted permission to leave by the commander of the guard. Permission to leave will be granted only in case of necessity.

Orders for Sentries

When you go on a tour of interior guard duty, your orders as a sentry will fall into two classes: general orders and special orders.

General Orders

The general orders do not change. There are 11 general orders, and they are the same wherever and whenever you are on interior guard duty. You are required to know and memorize these general orders and be able to recite them whenever you are called upon to do so.

The 11 general orders are listed below with explanations of those which are necessary. The orders themselves are in bold face type.

1. To take charge of this post and all government property in view.

- The number, type (fixed or patrol), and limits of a sentry's post constitute part of the special orders. The post's limits are defined to include every place to which the sentry must go to execute the special orders. Within these limits, the sentry has authority over all persons on the post (see Navy Regulations).
- A sentry reports immediately to the corporal of the guard every unusual or suspicious occurrence noted.
- A sentry halts and detains all persons on or near the post whose presence or actions are subject to suspicion. Apprehends all persons involved in a disorder occurring on or near the post and all persons discovered or suspected of committing a crime or violating regulations. All persons apprehended or detained are turned over to the corporal of the guard.
- The firing of a weapon at another person by an armed sentry is considered justified under certain conditions only. (See the section in this chapter titled "Use of Deadly Force.")

2. To walk my post in a military manner, keeping always on the alert and observing everything that takes place within sight or hearing.

Special orders will prescribe the manner in which a sentry shall walk (stand, ride or sit) the post and carry a weapon. Such manner is dependent upon the type of post (fixed or patrol) and the specific duties involved, but sentries will always conduct themselves in a military manner and remain vigilant and attentive to their duties.

3. To report all violations of orders I am instructed to enforce.

A sentry reports a violation of orders to the corporal of the guard at the first opportunity and to any officer or noncommissioned officer of the guard inspecting them. The sentry apprehends the offender if necessary.

4. To repeat all calls from posts more distant from the guardhouse than my own.

To call the corporal of the guard for any purpose other than relief, fire, or disorder, a sentry will call, "Corporal of the guard, Post Number…." When sentry posts are located within hearing distance of each other, a sentry receiving a call from a post more distant from the guardhouse than one's own, repeats the call to the next post loudly, distinctly, and exactly as received.

5. To quit my post only when properly relieved.

- If a sentry requires relief because of sickness or other reason, the Marine calls, "Corporal of the guard, Post Number…, relief."
- If a sentry is not relieved at the expiration of the tour or at mealtime, the Marine does not abandon the post, but calls the corporal of the guard for instructions.
- When so ordered, a sentry on the last relief of a post leaves at the proper time, returns to the guardhouse, and reports to the corporal of the guard.
- A sentry may leave the prescribed limits of a fixed or patrol post to protect government property in view or to apprehend an offender, but only if these duties cannot be accomplished within the prescribed limits of the post. A sentry must inform the corporal of the guard before leaving the post under these circumstances, unless immediate action is essential.

6. To receive, obey, and pass on to the sentry who relieves me, all orders from the commanding officer, officer of the day, and officers and noncommissioned officers of the guard only.

- During their tour of duty, a sentry is subject to the orders of the commanding officer, field officer of the day, and officers and noncommissioned officers of the guard only. In emergencies, however, the senior line officer present may give orders to sentries. In addition, any officer or noncommissioned officer is authorized to report violations of regulations by members of the guard.
- A sentry will give up a weapon only when ordered by a person from whom they lawfully receive orders while on post. Unless necessity thereof exists, no person will require a sentry to surrender a weapon while that sentry is on post.

7. To talk to no one except in the line of duty.

When persons make proper inquires of a sentry, courteous but brief answers will be given. Long conversations will be discouraged. When challenging or holding conversations with a person, a sentry armed with a rifle will take the position of port arms. If armed with a pistol, the sentry will take the position of raise pistol when challenging and will remain at raise pistol while conversing.

8. To give the alarm in case of fire or disorder.

- In case of fire, the sentry calls immediately, "Fire, Post Number…," and sounds the alarm if one is available. If possible, without endangering anyone or the performance of the duties, the sentry extinguishes the fire. If not, the sentry directs the responding fire personnel to the fire. The sentry notifies the guardhouse of this action as soon as possible.
- In case of disorder, the sentry notifies the corporal of the guard immediately and then takes proper corrective action. If the assistance of the guard is required, the sentry calls, "The guard, Post Number…"
- When authorized by the commanding officer and if the danger is great, the sentry discharges a weapon three times in rapid succession into the air before calling. In time of war, sentries give warning of enemy attacks as directed by the commanding officer.

9. To call the corporal of the guard in any case not covered by instructions.

Whenever a sentry encounters a situation not covered by general or special orders, or about which the sentry is in doubt, the sentry will call the corporal of the guard for instructions.

10. To salute all officers and all colors and standards not cased.

Sentries render salutes as prescribed in Navy Regulations and other portions of this manual with the following exceptions:

- No salute is rendered by a member of the guard who is engaged in the performance of a specific duty, the proper execution of which would prevent saluting.

- A sentry armed with a pistol does not salute after challenging. The sentry stands at raise pistol until the challenged person has passed. While at raise pistol and holding a conversation, the sentry does not salute but remains at raise pistol until the person has passed.
- A sentry armed with a rifle at sling arms does not salute after challenging or when holding a conversation. The sentry stands at port arms until the person has passed.
- A sentry in conversation with an officer will not interrupt the conversation to salute unless the officer salutes a senior, in which case the sentry will also salute.
- A sentry armed with a rifle (except at sling arms) salutes by presenting arms. Present arms is only executed when halted. If armed with a rifle at sling arms or pistol (except after challenging), the sentry halts and renders the appropriate salute. (Colors and standards are cased when furled and enclosed in a protective covering.)

11. To be especially watchful at night and, during the time for challenging, to challenge all persons on or near my post and to allow no one to pass without proper authority.

- If a sentry observes a person approaching the post during the time for challenging, they call, "HALT: Who goes there?" while the person is still far enough away for the sentry to take effective measures should the person rush the sentry after being challenged. Before challenging, the sentry places oneself in the most advantageous covered and/or concealed position from which to identify, detain, or apprehend the person or party. In effecting identification, the sentry may require the challenged person or one of a party to move as necessary to effect positive and prompt recognition. Normally upon receiving an answer to the challenge, the sentry will command, "Advance, (repeats the answer to the challenge, such as 'officer of the day') to be recognized." The sentry halts the person advanced again at a point where recognition can be effected.
- Positive recognition of all persons claiming authority to pass is the sentry's main consideration. The sentry must ascertain that those challenged are, in fact, the persons they represent themselves to be and have authority to be there before permitting them to pass. If the sentry is not satisfied as to their identity, the sentry will detain the person or party and call the corporal of the guard.

- The sentry will permit only one of a party to approach for the purpose of recognition. On receiving an answer that indicates the party is friendly and may be authorized to pass, the sentry will command, "Advance one to be recognized." When that one has been recognized, the sentry directs them to bring up the rest of the party and to identify each individual as they pass.
- If two or more persons or parties approach the sentry's post from different directions at the same time, they will be challenged in turn and required to halt and remain halted until advanced. A sentry never permits more than one person to advance at the same time. The senior person or party is the first advanced.
- If a person or party is already advanced and in conversation with a sentry, the latter will challenge any other person or party that may approach. If the new person or party challenged is senior to the one already on the post, the sentry will advance the new person; otherwise, the sentry will advance no one until the first person or party leaves.
- Answers to a sentry's challenge intended to confuse or mislead the sentry are prohibited, but the use of an answer as "Friend" is not to be construed as misleading. It is the usual answer made by officers or patrols when the purpose of their visit makes it desirable that their official capacity should not be announced.

Special Orders

Your special orders will be those required at a particular post or those required for unusual duties which you are assigned for a single tour of guard duty.

Reporting Posts

A sentry reports the post to an officer as follows: "Sir, Private – reporting post number – all secure. My post and orders remain the same; there have been no unusual occurrences during my watch" (or anything that has to be reported.)

Use of Weapons While Assigned to Interior Guard

It is possible that sometime during your assigned tour of interior guard duty, it will be necessary for you to use the weapon with which you are armed.

The following instructions will govern your actions in the use of your particular weapon.

Nightsticks

A sentry equipped with a nightstick shall confine the use of the nightstick to that portion of the body below the shoulders. The head will not be struck except as a last resort to protect human life.

Firearms

Armed personnel on duty will be governed by command restrictions as specified in their special orders.

Firearms will be used to protect human life, to prevent the destruction or theft of valuable government property, and to give an emergency alarm when there is no other method of giving an immediate alarm.

Use of Deadly Force

Application of deadly force is justified only under conditions of extreme necessity and only as a last resort when all lesser means have failed or cannot reasonably be employed. Deadly force is that force which is used for the purpose of causing or which is known or should be reasonably known to constitute substantial likelihood of causing death or serious bodily harm.

The firing of weapons at another person by military law enforcement and security personnel is considered justified only under one or more of the following circumstances:

- When deadly force reasonably appears to be necessary to protect military law enforcement or security personnel who reasonably believe themselves to be in imminent danger of death or serious bodily harm.
- When deadly force reasonably appears necessary:
  - To prevent the threatened theft of, damage to, or espionage aimed at property or information specifically designated by the commanding officer or other competent authority as vital to the national security.
  - To prevent the actual theft of, damage to, or espionage aimed at property or information which, though not vital to the national security, is of substantial importance to the national security.
- When deadly force reasonably appears to be necessary to prevent the actual theft or sabotage of property, such as operable weapons or ammunition, which is inherently dangerous to others; i.e., property which, in the hands of an unauthorized individual, presents a substantial potential danger of death or serious bodily harm to others.
- When deadly force reasonably appears to be necessary to prevent the commission of a serious offense involving violence and threatening death or serious bodily harm to other persons such as arson, armed robbery, aggravated assault or rape.
- When deadly force reasonably appears to be necessary to apprehend or prevent the escape of a person reasonably believed to have committed an offense of the nature specified in the paragraphs above.
- When deadly force reasonably appears to be necessary to apprehend or prevent the escape of an individual whose unauthorized presence in the vicinity of property or information vital to the national security reasonably appears to present a threat of theft, damage, or espionage. Property shall be specifically designated as vital to the national security only when its loss, damage, or compromise would seriously prejudice the national security or jeopardize the fulfillment of an essential national defense mission.

Guard Aboard Ship

General

The same general regulations and routine for performing guard duty and guard mounting ashore are carried out aboard naval vessels, but with such modifications as may be necessary to conform to service afloat.

Marines normally perform all guard duty on ships having permanent marine detachments. In the event there is no permanent Marine detachment, guard duty is performed by such personnel as the commanding officer of the ship may direct.

The commanding officer of the ship operates in a manner similar to the commanding officers of shore stations with respect to the establishing and functioning of interior guard afloat.

The officer of the deck on a naval vessel performs duties with respect to the guard which are similar to those of the officer of the day ashore. The ship's guard of the day functions under and is responsible to the officer of the deck.

The commanding officer of the ship prescribes such sentry posts as they deem necessary to the safe operation of the ship.

The officer of the deck, when necessary, gives special orders to sentries and, when such orders are of an important nature, informs the executive officer of the ship.

Sentries at the gangways salute all officers going on or coming off the ship, and all sentries salute when passing or being passed by officers close aboard in boats.

Challenging by sentries at gangways or on board ship is dispensed with at the discretion of the commanding officer of the ship.

Reliefs are posted informally by direct order for the individual to take an assigned post.

Troop Units Embarked Aboard Naval Vessels

The senior commander of troop organizations embarked on the ship is designated by higher troop authority as "commanding officer of troops."

The commanding officer of troops is responsible for the management of discipline and efficiency of the command. The officer establishes guard details necessary for the control of Marines and equipment. These details must be in accordance with the policy of the ship and approved by the ship's commanding officer.

All orders to troop organizations embarked aboard ship are, insofar as practicable, given through the commanding officer of troops (see Navy Regulations).

The commanding officer of troops details an officer of the day as a direct representative. The officer of the day supervises the guard, and is responsible to see that interior guard regulations are carried out, ship regulations are enforced, and that special instructions and orders of the ship's commanding officer are obeyed. The officer of the day may also detail officers of the guard when necessary.

Countersigns

The commanding officer directs the use of the countersign. It may be used by sentries of an interior guard, but it is primarily intended for use by sentries or persons defending tactical areas.

By Whom Authorized

If a countersign is prescribed, it is devised by the highest headquarters within a zone or area. The authority to designate a countersign may be delegated to subordinate units when necessary for their immediate use. However, these units notify higher headquarters of such action without delay. Only one countersign will be in effect within a command during a specified period.

Selecting the Countersign

The choice of words or sounds for the countersign is made with care. If possible, words are selected which are difficult for the enemy to pronounce. To minimize the possibility of an unauthorized person guessing the password, the word selected for the secret challenge must not suggest the word selected for the password (e.g., the secret challenge, ATOMIC, suggests the password, BOMB).

Using the Countersign

The initiative for use of the countersign rests with the challenging sentry. Positive recognition of all persons claiming authority to pass is the sentry's main consideration. If the sentry does not visually recognize the challenged person or party, the countersign is used to effect positive recognition. If there is any doubt of the challenged person's authority to pass, even if the password is given, the individual is detained for further action by the corporal of the guard. If the sentry recognizes the challenged person or party prior to using the countersign and there is no doubt that the person or party has authority to pass, the sentry will not use the countersign.

Mutual identification is essential. If the person challenged does not recognize the secret challenge, the password should not be given.

When a secret challenge and password are prescribed, the secret challenge is given by the sentry after the person is advanced to be recognized. The person challenged should then give the password. Both the secret challenge and the password are given in a low tone to prevent them from being heard by others. For example, a sentry observes a person approaching the post during the time for challenging. When the person is still far enough away for the sentry to take effective measures should the person rush the sentry after being challenged, the sentry commands, "HALT! WHO GOES THERE?" After receiving an answer (such as "Captain Jones, Company B, 6th Marines") indicating the person is friendly and may be authorized to pass, and the person having reached a point where the secret challenge spoken in a low tone can only be heard by the person, the sentry again commands, "HALT!" Then the sentry gives the secret challenge in a low tone (e.g., "SNOWFLAKE"). After receiving the correct password from Captain Jones (e.g., "ROOSTER") and otherwise satisfying oneself that the Captain is authorized to pass, the sentry says "Advance, Captain Jones," and salutes if appropriate. If Captain Jones is one of a party challenged and is the person advanced according to established procedures, the sentry then tells Captain Jones to bring up the Marines and identify each individual before passing.

Terrorism Awareness and Counteraction

Terrorism

Terrorism is the calculated use of violence or threat of violence to attain goals which are political, religious or ideological in nature. It involves a criminal act that is often symbolic in nature and intended to influence an audience beyond the immediate victims. Therefore, terrorists want publicity and want to take credit for their crimes.

Types of Attack

Terrorist attacks take many different forms. These include:
- Bombings
- Arson
- Hijacking/Vehicle thefts
- Skyjacking/Aircraft thefts
- Ambushes
- Kidnappings
- Hostage-taking
- Robberies and Expropriations
- Psychological Terror
- Biological and Chemical Attack
- Assassination

Terrorism Counteraction

There are no purely preventative measures that can insure 100 percent protection against terrorism. However, as Marines we must apply all known measures to protect ourselves from attack. Some common rules to follow in order to protect yourself from terrorist attack are:
- Vary transportation methods, routes, and times.
- Park in well-lighted areas with multiple exits.
- Lock unattended vehicles.

- Report unusual activities to local security officials.
- Avoid traveling alone.
- Travel only on busy, well-traveled thoroughfares whenever possible.
- Take proper security precautions at home during travel.
- Attend periodic threat awareness briefings and hostage survival training.
- Avoid establishing a pattern of attendance at certain events, locations, etc.
- Keep a low profile, avoid calling attention to yourself.
- Seek knowledge of the local situation and be aware of your surroundings.
- Be sensitive to the possibility of surveillance.

Force Protection for Marines

What is Force Protection? Active and passive measures taken to deter and defeat threats to Marines, their family members, DOD civilians and facilities and equipment. The following list gives a good checklist for keeping yourself and your family members safe, both in the US and overseas.

Anti-Terrorism/Force Protection Individual Protective Measures

At All Times

Vary eating establishments.
Alternate shopping locations.
Do not establish any sort of pattern!
Avoid crowded areas.
Be especially alert exiting bars, restaurants, etc.
Know how to use the local phone system and carry "telephone change".
Know emergency phone numbers for police, ambulance, and hospital.
Know location of the US Embassy and other safe locations where you can find refuge or assistance.

Bomb Incidents

Be suspicious of objects found around the house, office or auto.

Check mail and packages for -
- Unusual odors.
- Too much wrapping.
- Bulges, bumps, or odd shapes.
- No return or unfamiliar return address.
- Incorrect spelling or poor typing.
- Items sent "registered" or marked "personal".
- Protruding wires or strings.
- Unusually light or heavy packages.

Isolate suspect letters or packages. Do not immerse them in water. Doing so may cause them to explode.

Clear the area immediately.

Notify your chain of command.

Security While Traveling

At Airport Terminal

Use concealed bag tags.
Spend as little time as possible in airports.
Pass through the airport security checks quickly.
Once through security, proceed to a lounge or other open area away from baggage lockers.
If possible, sit with your back against a wall.
Remain alert. Be a "people watcher."

At Hotels

Do not give room number to strangers.
Choose an inside hotel room.
Sleep away from street side windows.
Leave lights on when room is vacant.
Pull curtains.
Arrange knock signals.
Answer telephone "hello". Do not use name and rank.
Look before you exit.
If confronted, have a plan of action ready.
Occasionally exit/enter through the rear entrance.
Keep your room key in your possession at all times.

From Domicile to Duty

Alternate parking places.
Lock car when unattended.
Look for tampering.
Look under your auto.
Be alert when opening door.
Keep gas tank at least half full.
If possible, alter routes and avoid choke points.
Plan "escape" route as you drive.
Watch mopeds/cycles.
Do not pick up hitchhikers.
Drive with windows up and doors locked.
Remember: REMAIN ALERT.

Chapter Ten

Drill

General Rules for Drill

While marching, the guide and alignment is maintained to the right except:

- Upon command GUIDE LEFT or GUIDE CENTER, guide is maintained toward the left or center, as the case may be, until GUIDE RIGHT is given.
- Regardless of the direction in which alignment is established, at the command of execution for a drill movement involving marching, the direction toward which alignment is obtained is the flank toward which the movement is made. Upon completion of the drill movement, alignment will be in the direction established before commencing the movement.
  - Slight changes in direction are made by adding, "Half" to the preparatory command for turning or column movements; for example, Column Half Right (Left) changes direction 45 degrees. When given the command INCLINE TO THE RIGHT (LEFT), the guide changes direction of march slightly to the right (left).
  - Platoons in a company and Marines in a squad are numbered from right to left (the company's or squad's own right) in line by squad and from front to rear by squad in column. Squads in a platoon are numbered from front to rear in line and from left to right in column.
  - Whenever drill movements are executed while troops are marching, the command of execution (MARCH), is given as the left foot strikes the ground if the movement is to the left, and as the right foot strikes the ground if the movement is to the right. The only exception to this rule is that, when moving from port arms to left shoulder arms while marching, the command of execution is given as the right foot strikes the ground in order to take advantage of the natural swing of the arms.
  - Drill movements may be divided into individual motions for instruction. When drills are executed by the numbers, the first motion is made on

the command of execution. Subsequent motions are made in proper order on the commands (TWO), (THREE), (FOUR); the number of counts depending upon the number of motions in the movement. To use this method, the command By The Numbers precedes the preparatory command. All movements are then executed by the numbers until the command Without Numbers is given.

Purposes of Drill

Drill for foot troops accustoms the individual to working as a member of a team – a team moving confidently together in unison and to a measured cadence. Marines are famous for their ability to march in step, keep straight lines and perform the Manual of Arms with precision.

The purposes of drill are to:

- Move a unit from one place to another in a standard, orderly manner.
- Provide simple formations from which combat formations may be readily assumed.
- Teach discipline by instilling habits of precision and automatic response to orders.
- Improve morale by developing team spirit.
- Give troops an opportunity to handle individual weapons.
- Give junior officers and noncommissioned officers the confidence of command and experience in giving proper commands.

Close Order Drill Definitions

The terms defined herein are used in drill for foot troops. Definitions of other military terms are included in Chapter 33.

ALIGNMENT – A straight line on which several elements are formed.

BASE – The element on which a movement is regulated.

CADENCE – The uniform step and rhythm in marching.

CENTER – The middle point or element of a unit or left-center element for an even number of elements.

COLUMN – A formation in which the elements are placed one behind the other.

DEPTH – Space from head to rear of a formation or position. It includes the leading and rear elements. The depth of a person is accepted as 12 inches.

DISTANCE – Space between elements in the direction of depth. Between individuals, the space between the chest and the back of the person to the front. Between vehicles, the space between the front end of the vehicle and the rear of the vehicle to its front. Between troops in formation (either on foot, mounted, or in vehicles), the space from the front of the rear unit to the rear of the unit in front.

DOUBLE TIME – Cadence at 180 steps a minute.

ELEMENT – An individual, squad, section, platoon, company, or other unit which is part of a larger unit.

EXTENDED MASS FORMATION – The arrangement of a company or larger unit in which elements in column are abreast and at a specified interval "greater than normal interval".

FILE – A column of individuals or vehicles one behind the other (Fig. 10-1).

FLANK – The right or left extremity of a unit, either in line or in column. The element on the extreme right or left of the line.

FORMATION – Arrangement of elements of a unit in line, in column, or in any other prescribed manner.

FRONT – The space occupied by an element measured from one flank to the other. The front of a person is accepted as 22 inches.

GUIDE – The individual (base) upon whom a formation or elements thereof regulates its march. To guide: to regulate interval, direction, or alignment; to regulate cadence on a base file (right, left, or center).

INTERVAL – The lateral space between elements on the same line. Interval is measured between individuals from shoulder to shoulder. It is measured between elements other than individuals and between formations from flank to flank. Normal interval between individuals is one arm's length. Close interval is the horizontal distance between shoulder and elbow when the left hand is placed on the left hip and is considered to be four inches (Fig. 10-2).

Fig. 10-1. *Distance and file.*

LINE – A formation in which the elements are abreast except that a section or platoon is on line when its squads are in line and one behind the other.

MASS FORMATION – The arrangement of a company or larger unit in which its elements are in column and abreast at close interval.

PACE – The length of a full step in quick time, 30 inches.

POINT OF REST – The point toward which all elements of a unit establish their dress or alignment.

QUICK TIME – Cadence of 120 steps a minute.

RANK – A line of Marines or vehicles side by side (Fig. 10-2).

SLOW TIME – Cadence at 60 steps a minute; used for funerals only.

SNAP – In commands or signals, the quality that inspires immediate response. In drill, the immediate and smart execution of movement.

STEP – The distance from heel to heel between the feet of a marching Marine. The half step and back step are 15 inches. The right and left steps are 12 inches. The steps in quick and double time are 30 and 36 inches, respectively.

Commands

A drill command is the direction of the commander given orally and in standard wording. In drill for foot troops, the commander is at attention when giving commands. Commands must be delivered in a loud, clear voice. All officers and Marines in the unit must be ready to take heed of the first word of a command.

There are four types of commands: preparatory commands, commands of execution, combined commands and supplementary commands.

- *Preparatory command.* Indicates the movement to be executed and or the direction of the movement, such as Forward, To the Rear etc. Preparatory commands are given in cadence with rise and inflection in the voice. The only commands which use a unit designation such as Squad or Platoon as a preparatory command are HALT and ATTENTION.

- *Command of execution.* Causes the desired movement to be executed, such as MARCH, HALT, FACE etc. Commands of execution are

Fig. 10-2. Interval and rank.

given in a sharp clear manner with force and enthusiasm.

- **_Combined commands_**. These commands, as the name indicates, combine the preparatory command and the command of execution, such as AT EASE, REST, FALL OUT, etc. These commands are given without cadence, rise or inflection in the voice and are delivered the same as the command of execution.
- **_Supplemental commands._** These commands cause a component unit to act individually as part of a larger unit. An example would be the commands the squad leaders would give to their squads following the platoon commanders preparatory command of Column of Files from the Right, and before the command of execution MARCH.

Preparatory commands are indicated in this chapter by small letters; those of execution by CAPITAL LETTERS.

The command AS YOU WERE is given to recall a command or to start over on a command given incorrectly. On this command, Marines should return to the position held before the improper command was given.

Positions

The correct positions to be taken upon receiving various commands are given in detail here.

Attention

- The left heel is brought to the right heel so the heels are on line and touching (Fig. 10-3(a)).
- The feet are turned out equally, forming an angle of 45 degrees.
- The knees are straight without stiffness.
- The hips are level and drawn back slightly; the body is erect and resting equally on the hips; the chest is lifted and arched; the shoulders are held square and level.
- The arms are hanging straight down without stiffness so that the thumbs are along the seams of the trousers; backs of the hands out; fingers held with a natural curl.
- The head is erect and squarely to the front; the chin is drawn in so that the axis of the head and neck is vertical; the eyes are straight to the front.
- The weight of the body rests equally on the heels and the balls of the feet.
- In assuming the position of attention, the heels are brought together smartly.

Rests

All rests are executed from the halt. The commands are: FALL OUT; REST; AT EASE; and Parade, REST. All are executed from the position of attention.

- At the command FALL OUT, Marines leave the ranks but are required to remain in the immediate vicinity. They resume their former places at attention when given the command FALL IN.
- At the command REST, the right foot is kept in place. Talking is permitted.
- At the command AT EASE, the right foot is kept in place. Silence is required. Movement to the extent possible with the right foot kept in place is allowed.
- At the command of execution REST of Parade, REST, the left foot is moved smartly 12 inches to the left of the right foot, and the legs are kept straight so that the weight of the body rests equally on both feet. At the same time, the hands are clasped behind the back, palms to the rear, thumb and fingers of the right hand holding the left thumb without constraint. Fingers are extended and joined. Head and eyes are kept to the front as in the position of attention. Silence is required, and no further movement is permitted. The command is executed from the position of attention only.

The only command that may be given from AT EASE, REST, or Parade REST is ATTENTION. If AT EASE or REST, on the preparatory command of Squad/Platoon, assume the position of Parade REST. On the command of execution ATTENTION assume the position of attention.

Eyes Right or Left

The commands are: Eyes, RIGHT (LEFT); Ready, FRONT. At the command RIGHT (LEFT), the head and eyes are turned smartly to the right (left). On the command FRONT, turn your head and eyes back smartly to the front. During reviews at which the reviewing officer troops the line, Ready, FRONT will not be given after eyes right. At such ceremonies, turn your head and eyes smartly toward the reviewing officer upon the command RIGHT. As the reviewing officer passes to the left, follow the officer with your head and eyes until you are looking directly to the front.

When marching in review the Marines in the right (left) file do not turn their head and eyes on the command of Eyes RIGHT (LEFT).

Facing

All facings are executed from the halt and in the cadence of quick time.

To The Flank. The commands are: Right (Left), FACE. At the command FACE, the left heel and the right toe are slightly raised; face to the right is made turning on the right heel, assisted by a slight pressure on the ball of the left foot. The left leg is held straight without stiffness. The left foot is then placed smartly beside the right. (See Figs. 10-3(a-c).) Left, FACE is executed by turning on the left heel and the ball of the right foot in a corresponding manner.

To The Rear. The commands are: About, FACE. At the command FACE, the toe of the right foot is carried to a position touching the ground a half-foot length to the rear and slightly to the left of the left heel without changing the position of the left foot; the weight of the body is mainly on the heel of the left foot; the right leg is straight without stiffness. Then face to the rear is executed by turning to the right on the left heel and on the ball of the right foot. (See Figs. 10-4 (a-d).)

Hand Salute. The commands are: Hand, SALUTE. At the command SALUTE, the right hand is raised smartly until the tip of the forefinger touches the lower part of the headdress or forehead above and slightly to the right of the right eye, thumb and fingers extended and joined, palm down, upper arm horizontal, forearm inclined at 45-degrees, hand and wrist straight. The hand is then returned smartly in one motion to its normal position by the side, at the same time the head and eyes are turned to the front unless facing that direction.

Saluting distance is the distance at which recognition is easy. Usually it does not exceed 30 paces. The salute is rendered when the person to be saluted is six paces distant, or at the nearest point of approach if it is apparent that the individual is not going to approach within six paces. The first position of the salute is held until the person saluted has passed or the salute is returned. The second movement of the salute is then executed.

Steps and Marching

As a general rule, all steps and marching beginning from a halt start with the left foot. The instructor indicates the proper rhythm by counting cadence,

Fig. 10-3(a). *Attention, as "Right FACE" is given.*

Fig. 10-3(b). *At command "FACE," face to the right.*

Fig. 10-3(c). *Bring left foot up beside the right foot.*

and will do so only when necessary. To change direction on the march, the command of execution is given as the foot on the side of the desired direction of the movement strikes the deck.

Quick Time

If at a halt, the command to march forward at quick time is: Forward, MARCH.

- At the command Forward, the weight of the body is shifted to the right leg without noticeable movement.
- At the command MARCH, the individual steps off smartly, left foot first, and marches straight ahead with 30-inch steps. Arms are swung easily in natural arcs, six inches straight to the front and three inches to the rear. Movements are not exaggerated nor made in a stiff way.

Double Time

The commands are: Double Time, MARCH. It can be executed as either foot strikes the deck.

- If at a halt, at the command Double Time, the weight of the body is shifted to the right leg without noticeable movement. At the command MARCH, the forearms are raised, fingers closed, knuckles out, to a horizontal position along the waistline, and an easy run is started with the step and cadence of double time. The arms are moved in a natural swinging motion across the front of the body. The cadence and step at double time are 180 36-inch steps a minute.
- If marching in quick time, at the command MARCH, one more step in quick time is taken before stepping off in double time.
- To resume the quick time from double time, the commands are: Quick Time, MARCH. At the

Fig. 10-4(a). From left to right, movements of "About FACE" are shown. First stand at attention as command is given.

Fig. 10-4(b). Second, at command "FACE", carry the toe of the right foot to a position touching the ground a half-foot length to the rear and slightly to the left of the left heel.

Fig. 10-4(c). Third, face to the rear, turning to the right on the left heel and on the ball of the right foot.

Fig. 10-4(d). Fourth, place the right heel beside the left.

command MARCH, given as either foot strikes the ground, the other foot is advanced and lowered in double time; quick time is resumed; the hands are dropped by the sides.

Mark Time

The commands are: Mark Time, MARCH.
- Being in march, at the command MARCH, given as either foot strikes the ground, the other foot is advanced and lowered; the foot in the rear is brought up so that both heels are on line, and the cadence is continued by alternately raising and planting each foot. When feet are raised, the balls of the feet are two inches from the ground.
- Being at a halt, at the command MARCH, the left foot is raised and lowered, then the right as described above.
- Mark time may be executed in either quick time or double time.
- The halt is executed from mark time as from quick time or double time by taking two-inch vertical steps in place of 30-inch horizontal steps. Forward march, halt, and mark time may be executed one from the other in quick or double time.

Half Step

The commands are: Half Step, MARCH.
- At the command MARCH, steps of 15 inches are taken in quick time. The half step is executed in quick time only. The half step may be executed from the halt or marching.
- To resume the full step from half step or mark time, the commands are: Forward, MARCH.

Side Step

The commands are: Right (Left) Step, MARCH. At the command MARCH, the right foot is moved 12 inches to the right; then the left foot is placed beside the right, the left knee straight. The cadence is continued in quick time. The side step is executed in quick time from a halt for short distances only. The arms do not swing during the side step.

Back Step

The commands are: Backward, MARCH. At the command MARCH, steps of 15 inches are taken straight to the rear. The back step is executed in quick time from a halt for short distances only. The arms swing naturally during the back step.

To Face in Marching

This is an important part of the movements in Column Right (Left), Close, Take Interval and Extend. For instructional purposes at the halt, the command is: By the Right (Left) Flank, MARCH. At the command MARCH a 90 degree pivot to the right (left) is made on the ball of the right foot and a 30-inch step is taken in the new direction with the left foot.

To March by the Flank

Being in march, the commands are: By the Right (Left) Flank, MARCH. At the command MARCH, given as the right (left) foot strikes the ground, the left (right) foot is advanced and planted; a pivot to the right (left) is made; and a 30-inch step is taken with the right (left) foot in the new direction. This command is not given from the halt.

To March To The Rear

Being at march, the command is: To The Rear, MARCH. It is given when the right foot strikes the deck. At the command MARCH, the left foot is advanced a normal 30-inch step; a pivot to the right is made on the balls of both feet; and immediately another 30-inch step is taken with the left foot in the new direction. Being at the halt, on the command of execution MARCH take one step forward with the left foot, a pivot to the right is made on the balls of both feet; and take a 30-inch step in the new direction with the left foot.

To March Other Than At Attention

Being in march, the commands are: Route Step, MARCH, or At Ease, MARCH.
- Route Step, MARCH. At the command MARCH, Marines are not required to maintain silence or to march in cadence at attention.
- At Ease, MARCH. At the command MARCH, Marines are not required to march in cadence at attention, but are required to maintain silence.
- To resume marching at attention the command is Squad ATTENTION. Members of the squad immediately pick up the step and cadence.

To Change Step

The command is: Change Step, MARCH. It may be given while marching or marking, quick or double time. The command of execution is given as the right foot strikes the deck.

- While marching at quick or double time, at the command MARCH, one more step is taken. As the right foot comes forward to the next step, place the toe near the left heel and step out again with the left foot. This changes the cadence count but not the rhythm.
- While marking time, at the command MARCH, the left foot is raised and lowered twice in succession. The second time it touches the deck, raise the right foot and continue marking time.
- While marking time at double time, at the command MARCH, a hop is repeated on the left foot before continuing marking double time.

Manual of Arms with the M16A2

The following information describes each individual movement for the manual of arms with the M16A2 rifle.

Sling Position

Prior to commencement of the manual of arms for honors and ceremonies, the magazine is removed and the sling is prepared.

The sling is positioned on the left side of the rifle. It is drawn tight with the keeper lying flat at the top of the pistol grip just below the selector lever. This configuration facilitates execution of the manual of arms (Fig. 10-5).

Order Arms

Order arms is the position of the Marine at attention with the rifle. The rifle butt is placed on the ground along side the right shoe, toe of the weapon on the line with the toe of the shoe. The junction of the rifle's front sight assembly and barrel rests in a "V" formed by the thumb and forefinger. All fingers are straight and together; the right hand and arm are behind the rifle. This position may cause a slight bend in the elbow. The tips of the thumb and forefinger are kept in line with the barrel. The right thumb is along the trouser seam (Fig. 10-6).

Trail Arms from Order Arms

Trail arms is assumed without command when executing a command that causes the unit to move a short distance, face a new direction, dress right, etc. At the completion of the movement, the weapon is returned to the order without command.

For training purposes, the command Trail ARMS may be given. The movement is executed in one count.

On ARMS, close fingers and thumb of the right hand around the barrel between the flash compensator and the front sight assembly. At the same time, raise the rifle butt three inches straight up. This will cause a bend in the elbow. In the proper position, the rifle will be in line with the right leg along the trouser seam (Figs. 10-7 and 10-8).

Order Arms from Trail Arms

On ARMS, lower the rifle to the position of order. As the butt touches the deck, move the right hand so that the junction of the rifle's front sight assembly and barrel rests in a "V" formed by the thumb and forefinger. All fingers are straight and together. The right hand and arm are behind the rifle. The tips of the thumb and forefinger are kept on line with the barrel. The right thumb is along the trouser seam (Fig. 10-9).

Port Arms from Order Arms

The command Port, ARMS is executed in two counts.

(1) On ARMS, slide the right hand to the barrel (fingers joined and wrapped around), and without

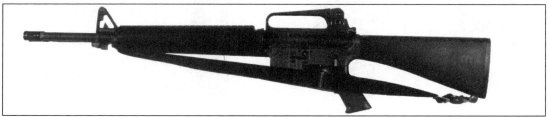

Fig. 10-5. M16A2 prepared for drill.

loss of motion, raise and carry the rifle diagonally across the front of your body until the right hand is in front of and slightly to the left of your face. The right forearm is held down without strain. At the same time, smartly grasp the hand guard (including the sling) with your left hand, fingers joined and wrapped around the hand guard, little finger just above the slip ring. The thumb of the left hand is centered on the chest and the rifle is 4 inches from the body. The left wrist and forearm are straight and the left elbow is held in against the body.

(2) Release the grasp of the right hand from the barrel and grasp the small of the stock with the right hand with the right thumb wrapped around the inboard portion. The right wrist and forearm are straight and parallel to the ground. The right elbow is held in against the body.

Order Arms from Port Arms

The command Order, ARMS is executed in three counts.

(1) On ARMS move the right hand smartly from the stock to the barrel. The rifle does not move on the first count.

(2) Release the hand guard with the left hand and lower the rifle to a position with the butt three inches off the deck, slightly to the right of the right toe, and with the muzzle pointing straight up. The rifle has been rotated one quarter-turn clockwise to a straight fore and aft position. While lowering the rifle, move the left hand, thumb and fingers straight and joined, to a point near the flash suppressor. Keep the palm facing to the rear so it will not resemble a rifle salute. The forearm and wrist are straight.

(3) Lower the butt gently to the deck and at the same time move the left hand smartly back to the left side.

Present Arms from Order Arms

The command Present, ARMS is executed in two counts.

(1) Slide the right hand to the barrel, fingers joined and wrapped around, raising the rifle to a vertical position centered on your body, magazine well to the front. Right wrist and forearm are straight, elbow down without strain. At the same time, smartly grasp rifle at the hand guard with the left hand just above the slip ring, four inches from the body. Left wrist and forearm are straight and parallel to the ground, with the elbow held

Fig. 10-6.

Fig. 10-7.

Fig. 10-8.

Fig. 10-9.

in to the side and the upper arm in line with the back.

(2) Release grasp of the right hand from the barrel and grasp the small of the stock, fingers extended and joined with charging handle resting in the "V" formed by the thumb and fingers, elbow held against the body.

Present Arms from Port, Left or Right Shoulder Arms

When a member of a color guard or when posted as a sentry Present ARMS may be executed from Port, Left or Right Shoulder Arms. The movement may be executed on the command of Present, ARMS or in the case of a sentry, without command.

If at port arms, present arms is executed in one count. The rifle is rotated clockwise with the right hand, the muzzle moves to the right, and the rifle is regrasped above the slip ring with the left hand so that the position of present arms is assumed. To return to port arms the rifle is rotated counterclockwise to the position of port arms.

If at left or right shoulder arms, present arms is executed in three counts. For the first two counts the rifle is first brought to port arms as described elsewhere in this chapter. For the third count the rifle is moved to present arms as described above. To return to the left or right shoulder, the rifle is brought to port arms then to left or right shoulder arms as described elsewhere in this chapter.

Order Arms from Present Arms

The command Order, ARMS is executed in three counts.

(1) On ARMS, release the grip with the right hand and regrasp the rifle at the juncture of the front sight assembly and barrel.

(2) Release the hand guard with the left hand and lower the rifle to a point where the butt is three inches from the ground, slightly to the right of the right toe, and the muzzle pointing straight up. While lowering the rifle, move the left hand, thumb and fingers straight and joined, to a point near the flash compensator. Keep the palm facing to the rear so it will not resemble a rifle salute. The forearm and wrist are straight.

(3) Lower the butt gently to the deck and move the left hand smartly back to the left side.

Right Shoulder Arms from Order Arms

The command is Right Shoulder, ARMS. This is a four-count movement.

(1) At the command ARMS, the right hand should grasp the barrel just above the front sight assembly.

The rifle is raised diagonally across the body; the left hand grasps the hand guard just above the slip ring.

(2) The rifle is regrasped at the butt with the right hand, the heel of the butt between the first two fingers and the thumb and fingers closed around the butt.

(3) Place the rifle into the shoulder with the pistol grip in the armpit. At the same time the left hand is allowed to slide to the junction of the stock and receiver just below the charging handle where it is used to guide the rifle into the shoulder. The thumb and fingers of the left hand are extended and joined with the first joint of the forefinger touching the charging handle and the palm turned toward the body. The left wrist and forearm are straight and held against the body. The weapon is tilted at an angle of 60 degrees to the deck, toe of the weapon pointed to the front. The right wrist and forearm are straight and parallel to the ground with the elbow held against the body.

(4) On the fourth count, the left hand is cut smartly back to the left side. The right forearm is horizontal with the right elbow against the side.

Order Arms from Right Shoulder Arms

The return to order arms is a four-count movement. The command is Order, ARMS.

(1) On the command ARMS, the rifle butt is pulled quickly toward the body with the right hand. As the rifle clears the shoulder, the right hand twists the stock 90 degrees in a clockwise direction, causing the rifle to fall diagonally across the body. At the same time, the left hand is raised smartly to catch the rifle at the hand guard.

(2) The right hand is moved to grasp the front sight assembly.

(3) Release the rifle with the left hand and with the right hand, lower it directly to the side, three inches from the deck and with the muzzle pointing straight up. While lowering the rifle, the left hand is moved, with fingers extended and joined, to a point near the flash compensator. The wrist is kept straight with the palm to the rear.

(4) On the fourth count, the butt is gently lowered to the deck, and the left hand is moved smartly to the side.

Port Arms from Right Shoulder Arms

The command Port, ARMS is executed in two counts.

(1) On ARMS, jerk the butt down so the rifle will spring from the shoulder. As it leaves the the shoulder twist the butt clockwise one-quarter turn so the

rifle will fall in front of the chest, barrel up. Keep a tight grip on the butt. Raise the left hand smartly to catch the hand guard four inches in front of the center of the chest.

(2) Move the right hand to the junction of the stock and receiver just below the charging handle.

Right Shoulder Arms from Port Arms

The command Right Shoulder, ARMS is executed in three counts.

(1) On ARMS, release the stock and grip the heel of the butt between the first two fingers of the right hand. Close the thumb and fingers around the stock. The thumb and forefinger touch.

(2) Place the rifle into the shoulder with the pistol grip in the armpit. At the same time the left hand is allowed to slide to the junction of the stock and receiver just below the charging handle where it is used to guide the rifle into the shoulder. The thumb and fingers of the left hand are extended and joined with the first joint of the forefinger touching the charging handle and the palm turned toward the body. The left wrist and forearm are straight and held against the body. The weapon is tilted at an angle of 60 degrees to the deck, toe of the weapon pointed to the front. The right wrist and forearm are straight and parallel to the ground with the elbow held against the body.

(3) On the third count, move the left hand smartly back to the left side.

Left Shoulder Arms from Order Arms

The command Left Shoulder, ARMS is executed in four counts.

(1) On the command of ARMS, and for the first two counts the rifle is brought to port arms.

(2) For the third count place the rifle into the shoulder with the pistol grip in the armpit. The fingers of the right hand remain wrapped around the small of the stock and the right arm is held against the body. At the same time release the hand guard with the left hand and regrasp the butt of the rifle. The heel of the butt is between the first two fingers of the left hand, the remaining fingers closed around the butt of the rifle. The thumb and forefinger touch. The weapon is tilted at an angle of 60 degrees to the deck, toe of the weapon pointed to the front. The left wrist and forearm are straight and parallel to the ground with the elbow held against the body.

(3) For the fourth count, release the right hand and move it smartly back to the side.

Port Arms from Left Shoulder Arms

The command Port, ARMS is executed in two counts.

(1) On ARMS, grip the stock with the right hand.

(2) Release the butt with the left hand. At the same time, move the rifle across the body with the right hand and grip the hand guard just above the slip ring with the left hand. The right forearm is parallel to the ground. The front sight assembly is at the same level as the eyes. Both elbows are at the sides.

Order Arms from Left Shoulder Arms

The command Order, ARMS is executed in five counts.

(1) On ARMS, grip the stock with the right hand with the right thumb along the receiver in line with the barrel.

(2) Release the butt with the left hand. At the same time, move the rifle across the body with the right hand and grip the hand guard with the left hand.

(3) Move the right hand smartly from the stock to the barrel with the left hand on the hand guard.

(4) Release the hand guard with the left hand and lower the rifle to a point where the butt is three inches off the ground, slightly to the right of the right toe, and the muzzle pointing straight up. The rifle has been rotated one-quarter turn clockwise to a straight fore and aft position. While lowering the rifle, move the left hand (thumb and fingers straight and joined) to a point near the flash compensator. Keep the left palm facing to the rear so it will not resemble a rifle salute. The forearm and wrist are straight.

(5) Lower the butt gently to the ground and move the left hand smartly back to the left side.

Left Shoulder Arms from Port Arms

The command Left Shoulder, ARMS is executed in two counts.

(1) On ARMS, release the hand guard with the left hand and place the rifle on the left shoulder with the right hand. At the same time, take the heel of the butt between the first two fingers of the left hand. Close the left thumb and fingers around the stock. The thumb and forefinger touch. The rifle is at an angle of 60 degrees to the ground and held so it points directly fore and aft. The pistol grip fits snugly into the armpit. The left elbow is against the side, and the left forearm is parallel to the ground.

(2) Move the right hand smartly back to the side.

Parade Rest from Order Arms

The command Parade, REST is executed in one count.

On REST, move the left foot smartly 12 inches to the left. Keep legs straight so the weight rests equally on both feet. Keep the butt of the rifle on the ground on line with the front of the right shoe. Slide the right hand upward grasping the barrel just below the flash compensator, fingers joined and curled around, touching the thumb. Straighten the right arm directly to the front so that the muzzle points forward and up. Place the left hand behind the back, just on the belt. Fingers should be straight and joined, the palm flat and facing rear.

Rifle Salute at Right or Left Shoulder Arms

This is a one-count movement executed on each of two set of commands – Rifle, SALUTE and Ready, TWO.

On SALUTE, move the left (right) hand smartly to the receiver just below the charging handle. Keep the forearm level with the ground, palm down, thumb and fingers joined and straight. The first joint of the forefinger touches the charging handle. When not in ranks, turn head and eyes toward the person or colors saluted.

On TWO, move left (right) hand smartly back to the side.

Rifle Salute at Order or Trail Arms

These are one-count movements executed on each of two sets of commands – Rifle, SALUTE, and Ready, TWO.

On SALUTE, move the left hand smartly to the right side, palm down, thumb and fingers straight and joined. The first joint of the forefinger touches the flash compensator. When not in ranks, turn head and eyes toward the person or colors saluted.

On TWO, move left hand smartly back to the left side.

Facings

All facing movements will be made on their respective command in three counts. When armed with the rifle, all facing movements are executed while at order arms only.

(1) On FACE, tighten the grasp, without moving fingers of the right hand, around the barrel between the flash compensator and front sight assembly, rais-ing the rifle butt three inches straight up. At the same time, execute the first count of the facing movement.

(2) Execute the second count of the facing movement.

(3) Lower the butt gently to the ground and move the right hand back to the order arms position.

Note: Should the manual of arms be done at fix bayonet, all movements would be the same except that the hand grip would include the bayonet and barrel whenever a grip on the barrel is part of the execution as described in this manual.

Inspection Arms from Order Arms

Inspection arms from order arms with the M16A2 rifle is a seven-count movement. The command is Inspection, ARMS.

(1/2) On the command ARMS, execute port arms in two counts. (See Fig. 10-10(a).)

(3) On count three, release the hand guard with the left hand and grasp the pistol grip with the left hand, thumb over the lower portion of the bolt catch. (See Fig. 10-10(b).)

(4) Release the grasp of the right hand, unlock the charging handle with the thumb and forefinger, and sharply pull it to the rear with the thumb and forefinger. At the same time, apply pressure on the bolt catch, locking the bolt to the rear. (See Fig. 10-10(c).)

(5) Push the charging handle until it is locked in its foremost position (Fig. 10-10(d)) and regrasp the small of the stock with the right hand.

(6) On count six, with both hands, (Fig. 10-10(e)) elevate the rifle up and to the left at the same time rotating it so that the chamber is visible, inspecting the chamber to see that it is clear.

(7) Resume the position of port arms. (See Fig 10-10(f).)

Note: Port arms is the only command given from inspection arms. On the command, PORT, move the left hand and regrasp the weapon with the thumb and fingers forming a "V" at the magazine well and trigger guard. Press the bolt catch, allowing the bolt to go forward. With the fingertips, push upward and close the dust cover. Slide the left hand toward the pistol grip and place the thumb on the trigger. On the command ARMS, pull the trigger and resume port arms.

Sling Arms from Order Arms

This is not a precision movement; therefore, there are no counts. From the order arms position (with a parade sling) the command for sling arms is Sling, ARMS.

Fig. 10-10(a).

Fig. 10-10(b).

Fig. 10-10(c).

Fig. 10-10(d).

Fig. 10-10(e).

Fig. 10-10(f).

(1) On the command of ARMS, slide the right hand up and grasp the barrel near the flash compensator. Without loss of motion, raise the rifle to a vertical position where the butt is in front of the right hip with the muzzle pointing up and the pistol grip to the left. At the same time, grasp the rifle at the hand guard just above the slip ring with the left hand. The sling is included in the grasp. The fingers are joined. Place the butt on the right hip. If the rifle belt is worn, the butt will rest just above the belt. Release the grasp of the right hand and with the left hand move the rifle so that it will rest on the inside of the right elbow and cradle it there. The muzzle points slightly to the right. Release the grasp of the left hand from the hand guard and with both hands loosen the sling. After the sling has been loosened, grasp the sling with your left hand and sling the rifle on the right shoulder in the most direct manner. Regrasp the

sling with the right hand. With the exception of the right arm, return to the position of attention. The palm of the right hand is toward the sling. The fingers are joined. The fingers and thumb are wrapped around the sling with the knuckles forward. The wrist and forearm are straight and parallel to the deck. The elbow is holding the rifle in a vertical position and against the body.

Sling Arms from Unsling Arms

This movement is to sling the rifle on the right shoulder when the sling has already been loosened. This is not a precision movement; therefore, there are no counts. From the unsling arms position (order arms with loosened sling), the command for sling arms is Sling, ARMS.

(1) On the command ARMS, slide the right hand up and grasp the barrel near the flash compensator.

The fingers are joined and wrapped around the barrel with the thumb wrapped around the inboard portion. Without loss of motion, raise the rifle and grasp the sling with the left hand near the upper sling swivel. Release the grasp of the right hand and, with the left hand, sling the rifle over the right shoulder in the most convenient manner. Regrasp the sling with the right hand. With the exception of the right arm, return to the position of attention. The palm of the right hand is toward the sling. The fingers are joined. The fingers and thumb of the right hand are wrapped around the the sling with the knuckles forward. The wrist and forearm are straight and parallel to the deck. The elbow is holding the rifle in a vertical position and against the body.

Unsling Arms from Sling Arms

This is not a precision movement; therefore, there are no counts. It is executed when halted at sling arms. The command is Unsling, ARMS.

(1) On the command ARMS, grasp the sling with the left hand in front of the armpit and unsling the rifle from the right shoulder in the most convenient manner. Grasp the rifle at the junction of the barrel and the front sight assembly. Release the grasp of the left hand from the sling and, with the right hand, carry the weapon to the right side until the butt is 3 inches from the deck. The barrel is in a vertical position. At the same time, guide the weapon with the left hand until the right thumb is on the trouser seam. The fingers of the left hand are extended and joined and touching the rifle near the flash compensator. The palm of the left hand is toward the rear. The left wrist and forearm are straight and the left elbow is in against the body. Quietly lower the rifle to the deck with the right hand and at the same time return the left hand to the left side at the position of attention.

To Adjust Sling

This is not a precision movement; therefore, there are no counts. The command is Adjust, SLINGS.

(1) From unsling arms (order arms), on the command of execution, the rifle is brought to a cradle position inside the right elbow as in the movement from order arms to sling arms. While in this position, the sling is tightened to parade sling. The rifle is then returned to order arms.

(2) From sling arms, on the command of execution, grasp the sling with the left hand in front of the armpit and unsling the rifle from the right shoulder in the most convenient manner. Then place the butt on the right hip and cradle the rifle inside the right elbow. Tighten the sling to the parade sling position and automatically assume the position of order arms.

Saluting at Sling Arms

This is a two-count movement and is executed when halted at sling arms. The command is Present, ARMS, however the movement may be executed without command.

(1) On the command of execution and for the count of one, reach across the body with the left hand and grasp the sling just above the right hand. On the second count, release the right hand and execute the hand salute.

(2) To resume order arms, the command is Order, ARMS. On the command of execution ARMS, lower the right hand smartly to the right side and regrasp the sling at the original position. After grasping the sling with the right hand, release the sling with the left hand and return it smartly to the position of attention.

Manual of Arms with the M203 (Not in NAVMC)

This section contains the procedures for executing manual of arms movements with the M203 Grenade Launcher. When it is necessary to conduct a drill or ceremony involving troops armed with the M203, they will carry the weapon at sling arms. The M203 will always be rigged with a loosened sling. Troops armed with the M203 will fall in at sling arms and execute all individual drill movements from that position. The only manual of arms movements they will execute are present arms (hand salute) and inspection arms. If stack arms is to be given, troops armed with the M203 will be positioned in ranks so that their weapons are treated as extras on the stacks. When armed with the M203, present arms will be executed in the same manner as the salute while at sling arms with the M16. Sling arms will be resumed when order arms is given.

Inspection Arms with the M203

This is not a precision movement; therefore, there are no counts. It is executed when halted at sling arms. The command is Inspection, ARMS.

(1) On the command ARMS, the initial movements bring the weapon from sling arms to port arms, then execute counts 3-6 of inspection arms as with the M-16.

(2) When at the inspection arms position as with the M-16, continue with the M203 by pressing the barrel latch and sliding the barrel up to the barrel stop. Elevate the M203 again, turning the head and eyes, visually inspect the chamber of the barrel. Return to a modified port arms position with the left hand holding the barrel at its full forward position.

Returning to Sling Arms from Inspection Arms with the M203

The command to return to the sling arms position from inspection arms is Port, ARMS.

(1) On the preparatory command Port, slide the barrel down to its closed and latched position. Then continue to close the bolt and dust cover of the rifle, and slide the left hand down to grasp the pistol grip and place the thumb on the rifle trigger as with the M-16.

(2) On the command of execution ARMS, pull the rifle trigger with the thumb of the left hand and then move it to the trigger of the grenade launcher and pull that trigger. Return to sling arms.

Manual of the Pistol (Not in NAVMC)

When in ranks and armed with the pistol, facings, rests, open and close ranks, and alignments are executed as if unarmed. The pistol manual of arms is not executed in cadence. It is a simple, quick and safe method of handling the pistol. The pistol manual of arms with the 9mm Service Pistol may be executed with the weapon holstered on either the right or left side. When in formation, remain at attention during all rifle manual movements except those listed below.

Present Arms from Attention (Pistol in Holster)

When the command of Present ARMS is given to the formation, those Marines armed with the pistol execute a hand salute. On the command of Order Arms the hand salute is terminated.

Inspection Arms from Attention (Pistol in Holster)

(1) The command is Inspection, ARMS. It involves several movements which are executed rapidly and smartly without count. It may be executed only when halted at attention with pistol in holster. Inspection arms is not executed with the pistol as part of the rifle manual except when the unit is formed and dismissed. If the pistol is holstered on the left side, the opposite hands are used from those described below.

(2) On ARMS, with the right thumb, unfasten the holster flap, grasp the grip and pull the pistol from the holster. Raise the right hand to a position level with and 6 inches in front of the right shoulder. The grip should be held between the thumb and last three fingers, forefinger extended and outside the trigger guard. The muzzle points forward and up at an angle of 30 degrees.

(3) Without lowering the muzzle or the right hand, turn the pistol handle to the left, look at the pistol, press the magazine catch with the right thumb and remove the magazine with the left hand. Turn the handle back to the right so that the bottom of the magazine well is to the front. Place the magazine between the pistol belt and outer garment.

(4) Without lowering the muzzle or the right hand, grasp the slide with the thumb and fingers of the left hand, thumb on the left side of the slide and pointing downward. Keep the left forearm parallel with the deck. Push the slide all the way to the rear and engage the slide stop in its notch with the right thumb. Look into the chamber; if it is not empty, empty it. Take the magazine from under the belt with the left hand. Raise the left hand to the height of the belt, forearm parallel to the deck, elbow at the side, palm up, fingers extended and joined. Hold the magazine in the open hand, follower toward the left wrist.

Attention (Pistol in Holster) from Inspection Arms

(1) The command is Port, ARMS. It is the only command which may be executed from inspection arms. If the pistol is holstered on the left side, the opposite hands are used from those described below.

(2) On ARMS, return the magazine to a position between the belt and outer garment. With the thumb of the left hand, release the slide stop. Keep the muzzle up and squeeze the trigger. Remove the magazine from the belt with the left hand and insert it into the pistol. Return the pistol to the holster and fasten the flap with the right thumb.

Squad Drill

The basic drill unit is the platoon. However, there will be many times when you drill as a member of a separate squad or detail. The snap and precision which you use in execution of the drill commands will readily show in the performance of the squad, detail or platoon as a whole. This section describes the various movements used in squad drill. A well drilled squad is one which can execute all these movements alone or as part of a platoon. Every Marine in the squad should be able to drill in any position within the squad. For this reason the movements are described in detail.

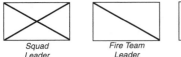 

| Squad Leader | Fire Team Leader | Rifleman or Other |

Fig. 10-11. Symbols indicating squad members.

Figure 10-11 shows the symbols used to indicate the positions of the squad leader, fire team leaders and riflemen or other members of the squad.

Squads are formed for the purpose of instruction, discipline, control and for becoming part of the platoon.

Squad members take post, move and execute the manual of arms as described in the first portion of this chapter. All members execute movements at the same time except where otherwise described.

The integrity of the squad should be retained whenever possible. Normal formation for the squad is a single rank or file. This permits variation in the number of Marines composing the squad, since all squads are not alike. The squad always forms on line, but may assume a column formation on command. A squad may be formed in two lines or two columns except when drilling as part of the platoon. (See Fig. 10-12.)

The squad marches in line for minor changes in position only.

When the squad is armed with rifles, it is brought to right or left shoulder or port or sling arms before being marched in column. However, the squad may be moved short distances at trail arms. In this latter case, the squad may assume the position of trail arms automatically and will, upon being halted, automatically resume the position of order arms.

To Form the Squad

The squad forms at normal or, when directed to do so, at close interval. The command is FALL IN.

The squad forms in line and to the left of the squad leader. Each Marine in the squad, except the individual on the extreme left flank, raises the left arm shoulder high in line with the body and with fin-

gers extended and joined, palm down. All except the squad leader turn their heads and eyes to the right and place themselves on line with the squad leader so that each Marine's shoulder touches the fingertips of the person on the right. (See Fig. 10-13.) As soon as each Marine is in line with the person on the right, and the person on the left has obtained the proper interval, the individual returns smartly and quickly to the position of attention.

To form at close interval, the command is At Close Interval, FALL IN.

The squad forms as described above except that each Marine (except the extreme left flank person) places the left hand on the hip, elbow in line with the body, fingers of the left hand extended and joined, heel of the palm resting on the hip. (See Fig. 10-14.)

When the squad is armed, it falls in at the position of order arms. Weapons are inspected immediately after the squad is formed.

To Dismiss the Squad

The squad is dismissed only from line formation and when at the position of attention.

When armed, the squad is always given commands required to inspect weapons prior to being dismissed. These commands are: Inspection, ARMS; Port, ARMS; DISMISSED.

Unarmed squads are dismissed with the command DISMISSED.

To Count Off

Counting off is done in the cadence of quick time. The squad in line, the command is Count OFF.

At the command, all Marines except the person on the right flank turn their heads smartly and look to the right. The right flank person shouts ONE. The remaining members of the squad, in sequence, call ascending numbers proceeding down the squad to the left. As each Marine shouts a number, the individual turns the head smartly back to the front.

When the squad is in column, the command is From Front To Rear, Count OFF. Each Marine, starting with the front person, turns the head to the right and smartly shouts the number while turning the head back to the front.

To Align the Squad

The squad in line, the commands are Dress Right (Left), DRESS; Ready, FRONT. It may be desired to align the squad at close interval. If so, the commands then become At Close Interval, Dress Right (Left), DRESS; Ready, FRONT.

At the command of execution, DRESS, all members of the squad except the right flank person turn their heads smartly, look, and align themselves to the right. At the same time all except the left flank person extend their left arms shoulder high (or, if forming at close interval, place their hands on hips). All Marines except the right flank person position themselves by short side steps until they are on line and their shoulders are touching the fingertips of the person on the right. (If at close interval, then elbows will be touching the elbow of the person on the right.) (See Figs. 10-13 and 10-14.) This position is held until the command Ready, FRONT is given. On the command FRONT, all Marines resume the position of attention by placing arms at their sides and smartly turning their heads and eyes to the front.

The left arm is used to obtain the proper interval whether dressing to the right or to the left.

To Obtain Close Interval from Normal Interval when in Line

The command is Close, MARCH.

At the command MARCH, all members except the person on the right flank face to the right as in marching. The right flank person places the left hand on the hip. Others march toward the right flank person until approximately a four-inch interval is obtained. They then halt, face to the left, and place left hands on hips as when dressing at close interval. As each Marine feels the person on the left assume the proper interval, the individual lowers the left hand smartly and turns head to the front.

To Obtain Normal Interval from Close Interval when in Line

The command is Extend, MARCH.

At the command MARCH, all Marines except the right flank person face to the left and march away from the person on the right, until approximate normal interval has been obtained. They then halt and face to the right. They form at normal interval by extending the left arm at shoulder height and dressing to the right. Each Marine lowers the left arm smartly and turns the head to the front when the person on the left has assumed the proper interval.

To Obtain Double-Arm Interval when in Line

From either close or normal interval, the command is Take Interval To The Left (Right), MARCH.

At the command, MARCH, squad members move as when extending from close to normal interval except that double-arm interval is obtained by each Marine raising both arms and touching the fingertips of the person on either side. The right flank person raises only the left arm. Each Marine lowers the right arm when at the proper interval and lowers the left arm when the person on the left lowers the right arm. Each Marine turns the head smartly to the front as each lowers the right arm. Armed troops are given this command only when at sling arms.

To obtain normal interval from double-arm interval, the command is Assemble To The Right (Left), MARCH. This movement is executed in the same manner as Close, MARCH except that normal interval is obtained.

To March to the Flank from in Line

The squad must be at normal interval. The commands are Right (Left), FACE; Forward, MARCH.

Each Marine executes the movements simultaneously with other squad members, and as explained further in "Steps and Marching" elsewhere in this chapter.

When the squad is under arms, the commands are: Right (Left), FACE, Right (Left) Shoulder, ARMS; Forward, MARCH.

To March to the Oblique

When marching in any formation, the command is Right (Left) Oblique, MARCH.

At the command MARCH, which is given as the foot in the direction of the turn strikes the deck, each Marine takes one more step forward, then faces to the half right (left) in marching, and steps off at a 45-degree angle from the original direction of march (Fig. 10-15 (a and b)).

The command, Forward, MARCH is given to resume the original direction of march. It is given as the foot toward the original front strikes the deck. At the command, MARCH each Marine takes one more step in the oblique, then faces half right or left (as required) in marching, and then steps off to the original front.

The command Squad, HALT is given on the left foot when halting from the right oblique and on the

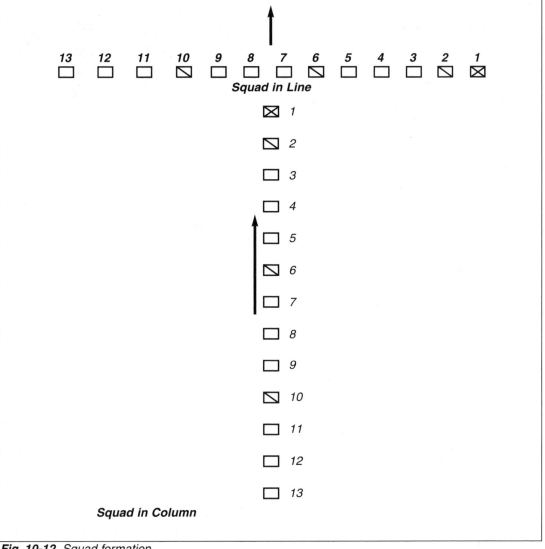

13 12 11 10 9 8 7 6 5 4 3 2 1

Squad in Line

1
2
3
4
5
6
7
8
9
10
11
12
13

Squad in Column

Fig. 10-12. Squad formation.

Fig. 10-13. Fall in.

Fig. 10-14. At close interval, fall in.

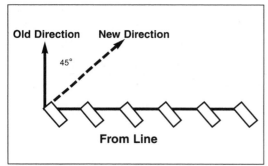

Fig. 10-15(a). Marching to the oblique, from line.

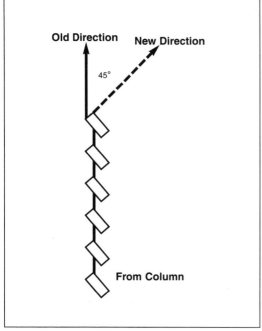

Fig. 10-15(b). Marching to the oblique, from column.

right foot when halting from the left oblique. At the command HALT, each Marine takes one more step in the oblique direction, then turns to the original front on the toe of the right (left) foot, and places the left (right) foot beside the right (left) foot.

The command In Place, HALT, is given as either foot hits the deck. At the command HALT, each Marine halts in two counts but remains facing in the oblique direction (Fig. 10-16). The only command that can be given after halting in place is Resume,

Fig. 10-16. In place, Halt.

MARCH. At the command MARCH, movement continues in the oblique direction.

At half step or mark time while obliquing, resume the full step to the oblique on the command Resume, MARCH.

The word oblique is pronounced to rhyme with strike.

To March to the Flank

To move the squad a short distance to the right or left while marching in column, the command is By The Right (Left) Flank, MARCH. The command MARCH is given as the foot in the direction of the turn strikes the deck.

At the command MARCH, each Marine takes one more step, then faces to the right (left) in marching and steps out in the new direction. This command will not be given while the squad is at a halt.

To Change the Direction of a Column

The command is Column Right (Left), or Column Half Right (Left), MARCH.

The command MARCH is given as the foot in the direction of turn strikes the deck.

At the command MARCH, the front person faces to the right (left) in marching and steps out in in the new direction of march. Other Marines in the column continue the march to the point where the front person pivoted. Upon reaching this point, they successively execute the pivot and march out in the new direction.

When the squad is halted, at the command MARCH, the front person faces to the right (left) in marching by turning to the right (left) on his right toe and steps out with the left foot in the new direction. Other members of the squad march forward to the pivot point. They then face to the right (left) successively in marching and step out in the new direction.

For slight changes in direction, the command INCLINE TO THE RIGHT (LEFT) may be given. At the command, the front person changes direction as commanded. All other Marines march forward to the pivot point so as to follow the line of march established by the front person. This is not a precision movement. It is executed only when marching in a column.

To Form Column of Twos from Single File

When the squad is halted in column, the command is Column of Twos To The Left (Right), MARCH.

On the command MARCH, the front person stands fast. Even-numbered Marines (counting from front to rear) face half left (right) in marching, take two steps, face half right (left) in marching, and move forward until they are beside and at normal interval from the odd-numbered Marines who were in front of them. Each odd-numbered Marine, except the front person, marches forward and halts as each

reaches normal distance from the odd-numbered Marine in front. All Marines required to move do so at the same time.

To Form Single File from Column of Twos

When the squad is halted in column of twos the command is Column of Files From The Right (Left), MARCH.

At the command MARCH, the number one and two person (counting from front to rear) step off at the same time. The number one person moves straight to the front, and the number two person faces to the half right (left) in marching. The number two person takes two steps, then faces to the half left (right) in marching, and follows the number one person at normal distance. The remaining odd-and even-numbered Marines step off in pairs, execute the same movements as numbers one and two, and follow in file of normal distance. This movement is done only from a halt (Fig. 10-18).

Platoon Drill

The movements of the individual Marine with and without arms and the movements of squad drill have already been described. This section sets forth instructions for the conduct of platoon drill.

A platoon consists of two or more squads, a platoon commander and one or more assistants, plus messengers. Some units are organized as sections. A section which has two squads will form and drill as a platoon. Small sections not subdivided into squads will form and drill as one squad.

Squads in a platoon are numbered from front to rear when in line and from left to right when in column.

The platoon forms on line in two or more ranks with 40 inches distance between ranks. The platoon may move in a column of twos, threes or fours. Movements in this section are described for such columns, though the column of threes is normal for most platoons.

When in line, the platoon changes interval, counts off, dresses right (left), and stacks arms in the same manner as the squad, except each squad executes the movements simultaneously with the other squads.

Squad leaders are normally the base for all movements, though, when required, the platoon may be directed to dress or to guide on another base. Each Marine in rear of the front rank covers the corresponding number in the front rank.

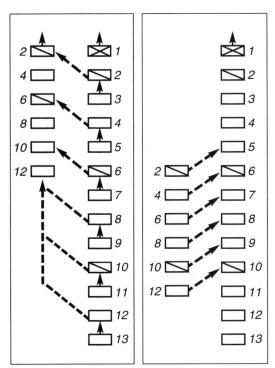

Fig. 10-17. Forming column of twos from single file.

Fig. 10-18. Forming single file from column of twos.

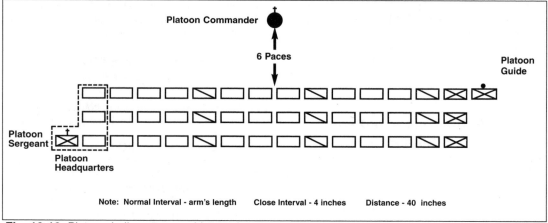

Fig. 10-19. Platoon in line at normal interval.

The platoon guide moves to the right when the platoon takes interval to the left, and does not count off.

Formations

The two formations for the platoon are column and line. (See Figs. 10-19 and 10-20.)

The platoon forms in line with the squad leaders on the right. The platoon is marched in line for short distances only.

Posts of Individuals

In line, the platoon commander takes post six paces in front of the center of the platoon. In column, the platoon commander marches at the head of the platoon and in front of the first squad leader. (See Figs. 10-19 and 10-20.)

When the platoon is in line, the platoon sergeant takes post to the left of the left flank person of the rear rank. In column, the platoon sergeant marches behind the rear Marine of the right squad.

The platoon guide takes post on the right of the first squad leader when the platoon is in line. When the platoon is in column the platoon guide marches in front of the squad leader of the right squad.

Extra Marines may be attached to platoons without changing permanent squad organization. These Marines fall in on the left when the platoon is in line in such a fashion as to even up the squads or ranks.

Rules for the Guide

Except when the platoon commander directs otherwise, guide is to the right, and the guide takes post

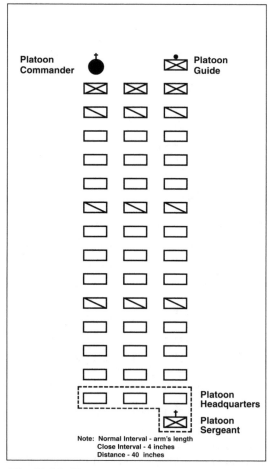

Fig. 10-20. Platoon in column at normal intervals.

on the right. With the platoon in line, the guide takes post on the right of the first squad leader. In column, the guide takes post in front of the squad leader of the right squad. (See Figs. 10-19 and 10-20.)

In column, when it is desired to guide left, the command GUIDE LEFT is given. At this command, the guide and the platoon commander exchange positions if the platoon is in column. The guide crosses between the platoon commander and the body of the platoon. To return the guide to normal position, GUIDE RIGHT is commanded. The platoon commander and the guide again change positions, with the guide passing between the platoon commander and the body of the platoon. This movement may be made at a halt or on the march. The base squad or base file is the one behind the guide.

The guide does not change position when the platoon is commanded to Dress Right (Left), DRESS.

When a platoon in line is commanded to execute right face, the guide executes the movement with the platoon and then immediately faces to the right as in marching and marches to a position in front of the right squad leader, halts, and executes left face. When the platoon is commanded to face to the left from in line, the guide executes movement with the platoon but does not change position.

When a platoon in column is given the command Column Of Files From The Left, MARCH, the guide, on the preparatory command, takes the position in front of the left squad leader and is at the head of the column.

When a platoon in column is given the command of Column Of Twos From The Left, MARCH, the guide, on the preparatory command, takes the position in front of the second file from the left, and heads the right column to be formed.

When reforming in a column of threes or fours from a file or columns of twos, the guide posts in the normal position when the movement is completed.

The guide sets direction and cadence of the march. The leading Marine in each file establishes interval.

When a platoon is marching in column and the command to march by a flank or to the rear is given, the guide executes the movement with the platoon but does not change position within the platoon.

The guide does not count off.

To Form the Platoon

Unless otherwise directed, the platoon forms at normal interval. At the command FALL IN given by the platoon sergeant, the guide takes post so as to center the platoon on the platoon sergeant and three paces away. The squad leader of the first squad takes post to the left of the guide. Other squad leaders fall in directly behind the first squad leader with 40 inches distance between them. Marines in the first squad fall in as prescribed in the squad drill. After obtaining proper interval, members of the squads behind the first squad cover the corresponding number in the front rank.

To form at close interval, the command At Close Interval, FALL IN is given. The formation is executed as described previously except that close interval is obtained.

If the platoon is armed, Marines fall in at the position of order arms, and the commands to inspect weapons are given as soon as each Marine is in position.

To Dismiss the Platoon

The platoon is dismissed only from a line and at the position of attention.

When armed, the platoon is dismissed with the commands: Inspection, ARMS; Port, ARMS; DISMISSED.

Unarmed platoons are dismissed with the command DISMISSED.

The platoon sergeant is usually called forward by the platoon commander to dismiss the platoon.

To Align the Platoon

The platoon obtains proper interval and alignment as prescribed for the squad, except that the guide raises the left arm to obtain proper interval and the first squad leader turns the head to the right and aligns with the guide. Other squad leaders cover on the first squad leader and obtain proper distance.

As soon as the command Dress Right, DRESS, is given, the platoon commander verifies the alignment of each rank. To do this, the platoon commander moves by the most direct route to a point one pace to the guide's right (or to the right of the first squad leader if there is no guide). The platoon commander faces down the line and aligns the front rank by directing Marines to move up or back as required. When the front rank is aligned, the platoon commander faces to the left in marching and dresses succeeding ranks in like manner, maintaining the one-pace distance from the guide, until all ranks are properly dressed. After verifying the alignment of the last rank, the platoon commander faces to the right in marching and marches straight to a point three paces beyond and one pace to the right of the guide. The platoon commander then halts, faces to the left, and commands Ready, FRONT; COVER. The squads then return to the position of attention and rear squads cover their corresponding number in the front rank.

When the platoon is well drilled or when there is not enough time to verify alignment, the platoon commander may command Ready, FRONT; COVER from the normal post without verifying the alignment of the ranks.

When marching in column, the platoon is aligned by the command COVER. The base squad leader obtains 40 inches distance from the guide. Without turning the head other squad leaders obtain proper interval and dress on the base squad leader. Without turning the head other Marines in the base squad obtain proper distance and cover the squad leader. The remaining members of the platoon cover their squad leaders and dress on the base squad.

To March to the Right (Left)

The platoon being in line, to march to the right (left), the commands are Right (Left), FACE; Forward, MARCH. The platoon executes the movements as in squad drill.

The platoon marches in a column of two or more files to the right (left).

Supplementary Commands

When the platoon commander gives a command which all squads are not to execute simultaneously, the squad leaders must give appropriate supplementary commands.

To Obtain Close Interval from Normal Interval, in Column

When the platoon is in a column at normal interval either at a halt or on the march, the command is Close, MARCH.

When at a halt, on the command MARCH, members of the base squad stand fast. Other squads obtain close interval by executing right step until proper interval is obtained.

When marching, the command, MARCH, is given on the right foot. On the command of execution, the base squad takes up the half step, and other squads oblique toward the base squad until close interval is obtained. They then oblique toward the front and take up the half step. The platoon commander then commands Forward, MARCH, and all squads resume the 30-inch step.

To Obtain Normal Interval from Close Interval, in Column

When in column at close interval and at a halt, or in march to obtain normal interval between files, the command is Extend, MARCH.

At a halt, on the command MARCH, members of the base squad stand fast. Other squads obtain normal interval by doing left step.

When marching, the command MARCH, is given on the left foot, the base squad is always on the right. At the command MARCH, the base squad takes up the half step. Other squads oblique away from the base squad until normal interval is obtained. When squad members are abreast of corresponding members of the base squad, they oblique to the front and take up the half step. At the command, Forward, MARCH, all squads resume the 30-inch step.

When the platoon executes flanking movements from a column at close interval, squads in rear of the squad which becomes the leading squad take up the half step after doing the flank movement until 40 inches distance is obtained between ranks. After such a movement, the platoon maintains normal interval and distance until it is again directed to close march.

To Change the Direction of March

The command is Column Right (Left), MARCH (or Column Half Right (Left), MARCH). The base squad for this movement is always the squad on the flank in the direction of the turn. The pivot person is the Marine in lead of the base squad, exluding the platoon commander or the guide.

When marching, the command of execution is given on the foot in the direction of the turn. On the command MARCH, the pivot person faces to the right (left) in marching, steps out with one full 30-inch step, and then takes up the half step. When the other Marines in rank are abreast, the pivot person resumes the full step. Other Marines of the leading rank oblique twice to the right (left) without changing interval and place themselves abreast of the pivot person, conforming to the pivot person's step. They execute the first oblique at the command of execution and the second oblique when opposite their new line of march. Ranks in rear of the leading rank execute the movement in the same manner and on the same ground as the leading rank.

When halted, at the command of execution, the pivot person faces to the right (left) in marching by turning to the right (left) on the right toe and stepping out with the left foot in the new direction. The pivot person then takes up the half step as described above. Other Marines of the leading rank oblique twice to the right (left) in marching without changing interval and place themselves abreast of the pivot person and conform to the pivot person's step. They execute the two oblique movements as when the platoon is commanded to execute column right while marching. Other Marines march forward and execute the movement on the same ground and in the same manner as the leading rank.

During column movements, the platoon commander and the guide oblique smartly in the direction of the turn, half step, and resume full step in a manner that places them in their proper positions in the formation for march in the new direction.

For slight changes of direction, the command INCLINE TO THE RIGHT (LEFT) may be given. The guide then changes direction as commanded, and the rest of the platoon obtains proper interval, distance and direction of march on the guide. This is not a precise movement, and is executed only on the march.

To Form Line from Column

To form a line from a column, the formation must be halted at order arms. The command Left, FACE is then given to place the unit on line.

To March Toward a Flank

The command is By The Right (Left) Flank, MARCH. It may be given from any marching formation, but it is never given at a halt. The command of execution is always given on the foot in the direction of the turn.

At the command MARCH, each Marine takes one more step, faces to the right (left) in marching and steps out in the new direction at full 30-inch steps.

This movement is used to move a column for short distances to the right or left.

After execution of a flanking movement, dress is always to the right, regardless of the direction of the turn unless commanded otherwise.

To Stack Arms

The command is Stack, ARMS; however, this command must be preceded by preliminary commands in order to prepare the platoon to stack arms. Assuming the platoon is halted in line at normal interval, the sequence of commands will be: Count, OFF; NUMBERS 3, 7 AND 11 ARE STACKERS;

Prepare, SLINGS; Open Ranks, MARCH; Ready, FRONT; COVER; and then Stack, ARMS.

The numbers 3, 7, and 11 for stackers is for a rifle squad so that fire team weapons are stacked together. In units where there are no fire teams the numbers 2, 5, 8, and 11 may be used.

Those Marines designated as stackers prepare slings by placing the butt of their rifles on their right hip and cradling them in the crook of their right arm. They then adjust their slings to form a 4-inch loop next to the upper sling swivel. As soon as they have prepared the loop, they return to order arms.

Ranks are then opened as described elsewhere in this chapter.

The command Stack, ARMS is then given. This is a non-precision movement, therefore there are no counts. The stackers, and Marines on their right and left execute the following movements on ARMS.

(1) The designated stackers place their weapons directly in front of and centered on their bodies with the sights to the rear. The heel of the rifle butt is placed on the ground on line with the toes of their shoes. Each stacker grasps the rifle at the upper portion of the hand guard with the left hand, keeping the rifle vertical. The first two fingers of the left hand hold the inner part of the loop against the rifle. The stacker reaches across the front of the rifle with the right hand, grasps the outer part of the loop and holds it open for insertion of the rifles. At the same time, the individuals to the left and right of the stackers perform the following movements simultaneously:

(2) The individuals on the stackers' right raise and center their weapons by bringing their right wrists to shoulder height and centered on their bodies, magazine wells face the front. They then grasp the hand guards (midway) with their left hands, release their right hand and regrasp the weapon at the small of the stock. Arms are then lowered to a dead hang, so that the weapons are held in a horizontal position with the muzzles to the left and magazine wells still to the front.

(3) The individuals on the stackers' left raise and center their weapons by bringing their right wrists to shoulder height and centered on their bodies, magazine wells face the front. They then grasp their weapons at the small of the stock with their left hands, release their right hands and regrasp the hand guards (midway). Arms are lowered to a dead hang so that the weapons are held in a horizontal position with the muzzles to the right and the magazine wells still to the front.

(4) As soon as the stackers have placed their rifles in position, both the individuals to the right and left

move their feet nearest the stackers 18-inches in the oblique toward the stackers. The individuals on the stacker's left insert the muzzles of their rifles into the loops to a point approximately halfway between the compensator and the front sight. They hold their weapons in this position until the individuals on the stackers' right insert the muzzles of their rifles in a similar manner but above the other rifle in each loop.

(5) The butts of the rifles inserted into the loops are swung outward and down to the ground until the stacks are tight with the rifle butts on line and approximately 2 feet forward of the stackers' rifles. The rifles rest on the side of the butts with the pistol grips pointing inboard toward each other. As each stack is completed, all three individuals stand up at the same time and resume the position of attention.

(6) Extra rifles are passed to the nearest stacks on the right. Individuals holding extra rifles grasp the barrels of their rifles, raise them vertically and then extend their right arms horizontally to the right front. The persons to the right grasp the weapons at the hand guard, center them on their bodies, grasp the barrels with their right hands and extend their right arms horizontally to the right front. This action is repeated until the rifles reach the stackers. The stackers lean the rifles against the stacks in such a manner as to prevent them from falling or knocking the stacks over.

(7) If the numbers 3, 7 and 11 were stackers, the squad leaders would then pass their rifles to the stacker. The squad leaders pass their rifles to the first stack on the left by raising the weapon with the right hand to a position centered on the body. They then grasp the weapon with the left hand at the hand guard and pass the weapon to the left by extending the left arm horizontally to the left front. The individual to the squad leader's left then grasps the rifle at the barrel with the right hand, centers it on the body, grasps the hand guard with the left hand and passes it to the stacker.

(8) After the squad leader of the front rank has passed his/her weapon, the guide would then pass his/her weapon to the stacker in the same manner as the squad leaders.

To Take Arms

The purpose of this movement is to recover arms that have been stacked. It may be executed only when the platoon has fallen back in on the weapons stacks. The command is Take, ARMS.

(1) On the command ARMS if there are extra arms they are passed back in a reverse order and

manner of the way they were passed to the stacks. When extra arms have been passed back, or if there were no extra arms, the stackers grasp their rifles and hold the loops in the same manner as was done for stacking arms. The individuals to the left and right step in the oblique, reach down and regrasp their weapons and bring them to a horizontal position. Weapons are freed from the loops, persons' on the right first, and order or unsling arms is assumed. Stackers cradle their rifles and adjust slings to their original position and then assume the order or unsling arms position.

(2) Once everyone is at the position of order or unsling arms, the command Close Ranks, MARCH is given.

To Open Ranks

The commands are: Open Ranks, MARCH; Ready, FRONT; COVER. They are given only when the platoon is HALTED in line. At the command MARCH, the front rank takes two paces to the front, halts, and executes dress right. The second rank takes one pace to the front, halts, and executes dress right. The third rank, if present, stands fast and executes dress right. Remaining ranks take two, four, or six steps backward, as appropriate, halt, and execute dress right. The platoon commander verifies alignment of the squads or ranks and then commands Ready, FRONT; COVER.

To Close Ranks

The command is Close Ranks, MARCH. It is given only from open ranks.

At the command MARCH, the front rank stands fast. The second rank takes one pace forward and halts. Succeeding ranks take two, three, four, or five paces forward and halt. Each Marine covers the corresponding number in the front squad. The platoon commander normally gives the command to close ranks from the same position from which the command Ready, FRONT was given. After ranks are closed, the platoon commander moves by the most direct route to the post six paces in front of and centered on the platoon.

To Form for Shelter Tents

The purpose of this movement is to pitch shelter tents in line and in formation. It is used for the purpose of instruction and formal field inspections only. Normally in bivouac, full use will be made of available cover and concealment and straight lines will be avoided. The movement may be executed when the platoon is halted in line at attention. The platoon then forms into one line to pitch shelter tents. If sufficient space is not available, squad lines may be used. If armed, rifles will be at sling arms.

Arms are slung prior to forming to pitch shelter tents and are grounded when pitching tents.

The platoon in line, commands are: Form For Shelter Tents To The Left, MARCH; Take Interval To The Left, MARCH; Count, OFF.

At the command Form For Shelter Tents To The Left, the platoon sergeant moves to a position on the right of the right flank person of the front rank. Messengers, if any, take post to the left of the left Marine at the rear rank. The squad leader of the first squad commands STAND FAST, and other squad leaders command By The Left Flank. (NOTE: This is the one time when a flanking movement is commanded from a halt.)

At the command MARCH, all squads except the first face to the left as in marching and step off. Squad leaders move their squads into line abreast of the squad(s) already on line by giving the commands By The Right Flank, MARCH; Squad, HALT.

At the command Take Interval To The Left, MARCH, the entire platoon of one rank takes interval as prescribed in "Squad Drill".

At the command count OFF, the entire rank counts off as prescribed in "Squad Drill."

When directed by the platoon commander, the odd-numbered Marines will draw bayonets and thrust them into the ground alongside the outside of their left heel near the instep. The bayonet indicates the position of the front tent pole. Odd-numbered Marines without bayonets mark the spot with their left heel. After positions are marked shelter tents are pitched or equipment is laid out for inspection. Odd- and even-numbered Marines pitch their shelter halves into one tent. ·

To assemble, the commands are: Assemble To The Right, MARCH; Right, FACE; Column Of Twos (Threes, Fours) To The Right, MARCH. At the command MARCH, the platoon sergeant and messengers resume their normal posts. The squads other than the

first squad march to their proper positions abreast of the first squad as described earlier.

To Form Columns of Twos and Single File and Reform

The platoon may be marched in column of twos or single file by the procedures described in this section. The change in column is always given from a halt.

Being in column of threes, to form column of twos, the commands are as follows: The platoon commander commands Column of Twos From The Right (Left), MARCH. After the preparatory command, but before the command of execution MARCH, the squad leaders would give the appropriate supplemental commands to form the column of twos (e.g. Stand Fast; Column of Twos to the Left; Forward; etc.). After the command of execution MARCH, the squad leaders would give the appropriate commands to their squads to form the column of twos. At the command MARCH, the left (right) squad forms a column of twos to the left (right) as prescribed in "Squad Drill" then executes column half right (left) and column half left (right) so as to follow the leading squads in column. Normal distance is maintained. (See Fig. 10-21.)

Being in column of twos, to reform into column of threes, the command is Column Of Threes To The Right (Left), MARCH. After the preparatory command, but before the command of execution MARCH, the squad leaders give the appropriate supplemental commands to form the column of threes/fours (e.g. Stand Fast; Column of Files from the Right, Column Half Left; etc.). After the command of execution MARCH the squad leaders would give the appropriate commands to reform into a column of threes/fours. At the command MARCH, the leading two squads stand fast. The rear squad forms a single file from the right (left), moving to its normal position beside the leading squads by executing column half left (right) and then column half right (left). The squad leader gives the commands for these movements and halts the squad when the lead-

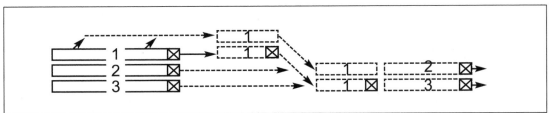

Fig. 10-21. *Column of twos from column of threes.*

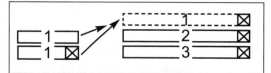

Fig. 10-22. *Reforming column of threes*

ing file is on line with the leading rank of the platoon (Fig. 10-22).

Whenever there are more than three squads to a platoon, variations in the aforementioned procedure are authorized. For instance, if there were four squads in a platoon, and it was desired to march in a column of twos, the two remaining squads would simply execute half column movements and march behind the leading squads.

To march in single file, the command is Column Of Files From The Right (Left), MARCH. After the preparatory command, but before the command of execution MARCH, the squad leaders would give the appropriate supplemental commands to form the column of files (e.g. Forward, Stand Fast; etc.). After the command of execution MARCH, the squad lead-ers would give the appropriate commands to their squads to form the column of twos. The right (left) squad then marches forward, and the remaining squads follow in trace by executing half column movements. To reform after marching in single file, the command is Column Of Twos (Threes, Fours) To The Left (Right), MARCH. After the preparatory command, but before the command of execution MARCH, the squad leaders give the appropriate sup-plemental commands to form the column of threes/fours (e.g. Stand Fast; Column Half Left; Forward; etc.). After the command of execution MARCH the squad leaders would give the appropri-ate commands to reform into a column of threes/fours. At the command MARCH, the right (left) squad stands fast, and the remaining squads execute the necessary column half right (left) move-ments to march forward to a position abreast of the leading squad. When abreast, the squads are halted.

(Editorial assistance and information provided by Sergeant Major T. Chapman, Marine Corps Combat Development Command, Quantico, Virginia.)

Chapter Eleven

First Aid

First aid is the immediate treatment administered to a victim of injury or illness before the services of a doctor or corpsman can be obtained.

Although the medical department has the finest equipment and its personnel have been trained in the most modern methods of saving life and easing pain, there may be a time when your life or that of a friend will depend on your knowledge of first aid. You can save a life if you know what to do and what not to do, and if you act quickly and calmly. If you are injured, you can save your own life by caring for your own injuries or by directing others toward proper care. Remember, where medical help is not readily available, apply self-aid and then seek professional help or care. The basic rules for first aid given in this chapter are to help you to help yourself and your fellow Marines when it is necessary.

Your primary responsibility when in battle is to continue fighting when someone is wounded. Do not jeopardize the mission, your life or that of others by stopping to aid a wounded Marine. By continuing to fight, you will make it possible for the corpsmen to advance with the troops and give emergency treatment. Your first job when you are on the battlefield is to fight.

You have been issued a first aid kit containing simple, but effective, medical items. Learn the contents and use of each item in your kit, and keep it with you at all times.

In addition, always be ready to improvise first aid materials and equipment. There is always the possibility that supplies will not be immediately available or will run out.

Wounds are the most common conditions requiring first aid. Before you treat a wound you have to see all of it so that you can tell exactly where it is, how large it is and how much it is bleeding. Usually it is better to cut or tear the clothing rather than to try removing it. Removing clothing over the wound increases the danger of infection. Moving the wounded parts may make the wound worse and cause needless pain. Look for the place where the bullet or other object that caused the wound came out because that wound may be larger than the entering one.

The Four Life-Saving Steps

The four life-saving steps in first aid are:
* restore breathing,
* stop bleeding,
* prevent or treat shock,
* protect the wound.

Every Marine should memorize these four steps and learn the simple methods for carrying them out. Prompt and correct first aid for wounds will not only speed healing, but will often save a life – and that life may be yours!

Restore Breathing

If a casualty stops breathing, you must give artificial respiration immediately. The sooner you begin artificial respiration, the more likely you are to succeed in restoring breathing. There are two primary methods for administering artificial respiration: the mouth-to-mouth method and the chest-pressure arm-lift method. The mouth-to-mouth method is preferred, however it cannot be used if the casualty has a crushed face or is in a toxic environment.

Mouth-to-mouth (nose) method

Evaluate casualty. Check for a response then call for help. Check the mouth for objects. Turn the head up and open the mouth by placing your thumb on the tongue and pulling the jaw out and downward. Clear the casualty's upper airway by turning the head to one side. Using the finger sweep quickly remove from the mouth any vomitus, mucus or debris by running a hooked finger behind the lower teeth and over the back of the tongue. If the Marine is wearing removable dentures, put them into his or her pocket.

Airway Obstruction. Open the airway, as described below, and attempt artificial respiration. If the chest does not move give 6 to 10 abdominal thrusts (do this only if the victim is not pregnant, obese or wounded in the abdomen). Straddle the casualty's thighs and place the heel of one hand on the abdomen in the middle just above the navel. Place the hand well below the last rib at the bottom center of the rib cage. Place the second hand directly on top of the first hand. Press into the abdomen with quick thrusts angled upward toward the lungs. Apply each thrust with the intent of freeing the obstruction. Continually check for success.

For chest thrusts, use the same hand position as for external chest compressions in CPR (Cardiopulmonary Resuscitation). Exert a quick, downward thrust. (See Fig. 11-8.)

Apply finger sweep as necessary.

Attempt to get the casualty air. Check the pulse and either do external chest compressions (CPR) or continue artificial respiration.

Note: Repeat all steps in rapid order until you clear the airway. As the casualty becomes more deprived of oxygen, muscles relax and thrusts may be more effective.

Open the airway. Position the casualty on his or her back. Place the casualty face up and put a rolled blanket or similar object under the shoulders so that the head will drop back as in Figure 11-1. If such an object is not immediately available, tilt the head back so that the neck is extended and the head is in a chin-up position.

Adjust the casualty's lower jaw to a jutting-out position. This moves the base of the tongue farther away from the back of the throat, thus enlarging the airway passage to the lungs.

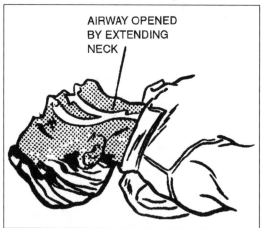

AIRWAY OPENED BY EXTENDING NECK

Fig. 11-1. Shoulder raised and head tilted back in chin-up position.

Head Tilt/Chin Lift. Kneel beside the casualty's head and place one hand on the forehead. Place the fingertips of the other hand under the chin.

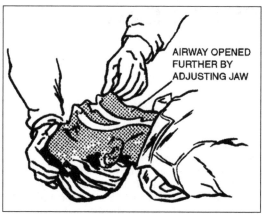

AIRWAY OPENED FURTHER BY ADJUSTING JAW

Fig. 11-2. Head Tilt/Chin Lift.

While pressing on the forehead to tilt the head back, lift the chin forward to open the airway. Do not press on soft tissues under the chin; pressing may obstruct the airway. Bring the teeth together, but do not close the mouth completely. (See Fig. 11-2.)

Jaw Thrust Technique. In case the casualty's jaws are so tightly closed that the thumb cannot be inserted into the mouth, the jaw thrust technique is used. Grasping the angles of the lower jaw with both hands just below the ear lobes, lift the jaw forcibly forward; then open the lips by pushing the lower lip toward the chin with the thumbs. (See Fig. 11-3.)

Continuing to hold the casualty's jaw forward, seal the airway opening (nose or mouth) which is not to be used when inflating the lungs. The seal must be secured to prevent leakage of air. If the nose is to be sealed, pinch it shut with your free hand or press your cheek firmly against it. If the mouth is to be sealed, firmly close the lips with two fingers placed lengthwise.

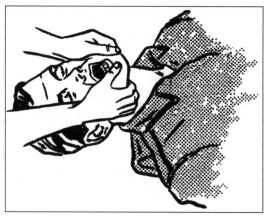

Fig. 11-3. Jaw thrust technique.

Administer artificial respiration as follows:

1. Place one of your hands on the casualty's forehead and pinch the nostrils together with your thumb and index fingers, using the same hand. (See Fig. 11-4.) Let this hand exert pressure on the forehead to maintain the backwards head tilt and to maintain an open airway. With the other hand, keep the fingertips on the chin (or your hand under the neck) to hold it upwards. Take a deep breath and place your mouth (forming an airtight seal) around the casualty's mouth.

Note: If the injured person is small, cover both the nose and mouth with your mouth, sealing your lips against the skin of his face.

2. Within 3 to 5 seconds, blow four quick full breaths into the casualty's mouth, taking a breath of fresh air each time before you blow. (Into infants and small children, blow small puffs of air from your cheeks rather than deep breaths from

Fig. 11-4. *Nose sealed with thumb.*

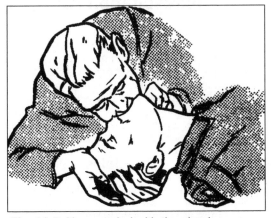

Fig. 11-5. *Nose sealed with the cheek.*

your lungs.) Watch from the corner of your eye for the casualty's chest to rise. Release the casualty's nose after the final breath.

If the chest rises, sufficient air is getting into the casualty's lungs. In this case the procedure is continued (steps 3 and 4). If the chest does not rise, reestablish the airway and ensure that air is not leaking from around the mouth or from the causualty's pinched nose. Attempt to ventilate again. If the chest does not rise, corrective action must be taken. Reposition the head and look for foreign material in the casualty's mouth. If any is observed, carefully remove it. If no foreign material is observed, insert the index finger into the throat and feel for an object. Once the airway is cleared, inflate the lungs with a single breath.

3. Remove your mouth from the casualty's airway opening, and listen for the return of air from the lungs. If the casualty's exhalation is noisy, elevate the jaw more.

4. After each exhalation of air from the casualty's lungs, blow another deep breath into the airway. Make the first five or ten breaths deep (except for infants and small children) and give at a rapid rate in order to provide fast reoxygenation. Thereafter give the breaths at a rate of 12 to 20 per minute or one breath every 5 seconds until the casualty is able to breathe satisfactorily or until you are positive life is gone. A smooth rhythm is desired , but split-second timing is not essential. As the casualty attempts to breathe, adjust the timing of your efforts to assist the person.

After a period of resuscitation the casualty's abdomen may bulge. This indicates that some of the air is going into the stomach. Since inflation of the stomach makes it more difficult to inflate the lungs, apply gentle pressure to the abdomen with the hand.

If your breathing at the start has been very deep and rapid, you may become faint, tingle or even lose consciousness if you persist. After administering the first five or ten deep, rapid breaths, you should adjust your breathing to a rate of 12 to 20 times a minute with only moderate increase in normal volume so that you will be able to continue to give artificial respiration for a long period without temporary ill effects.

Chest-pressure arm-lift method

Use this method only if mouth to mouth breathing cannot be performed, such as if the casualty has severe facial injuries or is in a contaminated area, as this method is not nearly as effective in providing respiration. (See Fig. 11-6.)

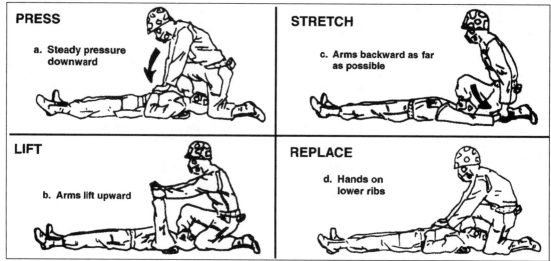

PRESS	STRETCH
a. Steady pressure downward	c. Arms backward as far as possible
LIFT	REPLACE
b. Arms lift upward	d. Hands on lower ribs

Fig. 11-6. Chest-pressure arm-lift method of artificial respiration.

- Clear the casualty's upper airway (as described earlier). If the patient is wearing a protective mask, quickly lift the mask, clear the upper airway and the mask with your fingers and replace the mask. Maintain a clear airway by repeating this procedure later, if necessary. If the casualty should be masked, then do so.
- Position the casualty on his or her back.
- Position the casualty's head in the same manner as for mouth-to-mouth resuscitation.
- Position yourself: Stand at the casualty's head and face the feet; then kneel on one knee and place your opposite foot to the other side of the head and against the shoulder to steady it. If you become uncomfortable after a period of time, quickly switch to the other knee.

Administer artificial respiration as follows:

1. Grasping the casualty's hands and holding them over their lower ribs, rock forward and exert steady, uniform pressure almost directly downward until you meet firm resistance. This pressure forces air out of the lungs.
2. Lift the arms vertically upward above the head; then stretch them backward as far as possible. This process of lifting and stretching the arms increases the size of the chest and draws air into the lungs.
3. Replace the hands on the chest and repeat the cycle: Press—Lift—Stretch—Replace. Give 10 or 12 cycles per minute at a steady uniform rate. Give counts of equal length to the first three steps. The fourth or "replace" step should be performed as quickly as possible.

4. Continue artificial respiration until the casualty can breathe satisfactorily or until you are positive life is gone. As the casualty attempts to breathe, adjust the timing of your efforts to assist the person.

When you become tired, release your position to another person, if available, with no break in rhythm. Continuing to administer artificial respiration, move to one side while the replacement takes their position from the other side. During the "stretch" step, the replacement grasps the casualty's wrists and continues artificial respiration in the same rhythm, shifting the grip to the casualty's hands during the "replace" step.

Cardio Pulmonary Resuscitation (CPR)

If a casualty's heart stops beating, you must administer CPR as well as artificial respiration immediately. When a victim's heart stops beating, breathing will almost immediately stop. To determine if the casualty's heart is beating, check the pulse by placing the tips of your fingers on the neck to the side of the windpipe as shown in Figure 11-7. If you do not detect a pulse immediately, don't waste time checking further; start CPR at once.

Principles

CPR provides artificial circulation to keep blood flowing until the heart begins to beat normally. The heart is located between the breastbone and the spine. Pressure on the breastbone pushes the heart against

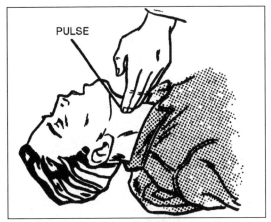

Fig. 11-7. Placement of the fingers to detect pulse.

the spine forcing blood out of the heart into the arteries. Release of pressure allows the heart to refill with blood.

Procedure

If another person is available to help, one of you should do compressions while the other gives artificial respiration (Fig. 11-8, Example a). Perform five chest compressions to one breath. You should coordinate your efforts so that one is not blowing into the casualty's airway at the same time the other is pressing on the breastbone. If you must administer first aid alone, alternate between the two procedures by performing 15 chest compressions followed by two breaths. (See Fig. 11-8, Example b.)

• Prepare the casualty for mouth-to-mouth artificial respiration. The surface on which the casualty is placed must be solid.
• Position yourself.
   1. Kneel at a right angle to the casualty's chest so that you can use your weight to apply pressure on their breastbone.
   2. Place the heel of your hand on the lower half of the breastbone and the heel of the other hand on top of it. (If the casualty is a child, omit placing the second hand over the first. If the casualty is an infant, place only the fingertips of one hand on the breastbone.) Spread and raise your fingers so that you can apply pressure without pressing the ribs (Fig. 11-9).

Administer CPR as follows:
1. With your hand in position and your arms straight and locked, lean forward to bring your shoulders directly above the casualty's breastbone; then press straight downward (Fig 11-9). Apply enough pressure to push the breastbone down 1 ½ to 2 inches. Too much pressure may fracture the

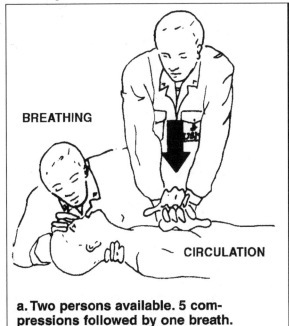

BREATHING

CIRCULATION

a. Two persons available. 5 compressions followed by one breath.

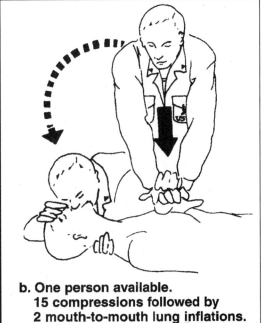

b. One person available. 15 compressions followed by 2 mouth-to-mouth lung inflations.

Fig. 11-8. CPR and mouth-to-mouth resuscitation.

casualty's ribs; therefore do not push the breast-bone down more than 2 inches. If the casualty is a child, press the breastbone with only one hand. If the casualty is an infant press the breastbone lightly with your fingertips.

2. Release the pressure immediately, lifting the hands slightly (Fig 11-10).

3. Repeat the press-release cycle 60 to 80 times per minute. After a few minutes, check for a pulse by placing your fingers on the casualty's neck. If only a feeble, irregular pulse or no pulse can be detected, elevate the casualty's legs about 6 inches above the level of the head to help the blood return to the heart. Continue CPR and the mouth-to-mouth resuscitation until the casualty is able to function without assistance, until you are relieved or until you are positive life is gone.

4. If you are performing alone, you will have to administer both mouth-to-mouth resuscitation and CPR. In this case, you should compress the chest 15 times and then follow this by two mouth-to-mouth lung inflations. Continue to repeat this cycle as depicted in Figure 11-8, Example b.

Stop the Bleeding

Uncontrolled bleeding causes shock and finally death. The use of pressure dressing is the best method for the control of bleeding in an emergency situation. The application of a tourniquet is another method to control bleeding, but it should not be used unless the pressure dressing fails to stop the bleeding.

Pressure dressings

The application of a sterile dressing with pressure to a bleeding wound helps clot formation, compresses the open blood vessels and protects the wound from further invasion of germs. The following procedure should be used when a person is wounded:

- Look for more than one wound. For example, a projectile may have come out at another point. The wound where a projectile comes out is usually larger than the one where it enters.

- Cut the clothing and lift it away from the wound to avoid further contamination. Tearing the clothing might result in rough handling of the injured part. Do no touch the wound; keep it as clean as possible. If it is already dirty, leave it that way. Do not try to clean it in any way.

- Cover the wound with a first aid dressing and apply pressure to the wound by use of the band-

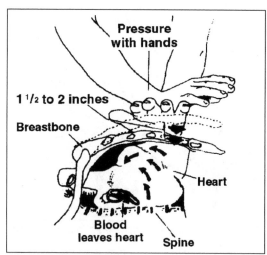

Fig. 11-9. Blood forced out of the heart into the arteries by application of pressure on the breastbone.

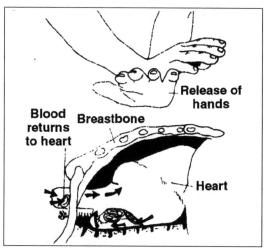

Fig. 11-10. Release of pressure to allow the heart to refill with blood.

ages attached to the dressing. If additional pressure is required to stop the bleeding, apply another pressure dressing or place your hand over the dressing and press hard. Pressure from your hand may be required for 5 to 10 minutes, thus allowing the clot to form with sufficient strength to hold with the help of only the dressing and bandages when your hand is removed.

- Frequently, bleeding can be lessened by raising the injured part above the level of the heart. Elevation is not used if there is a broken bone in the injured part. Moving an unsplinted fracture

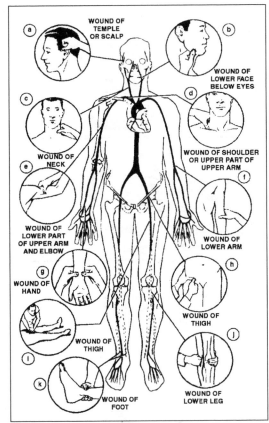

Fig. 11-11 *Pressure points.*

causes pain, can increase shock and may further damage nerves, muscles and blood vessels.

Pressure Points

Bleeding from a cut artery or vein may often be controlled by applying pressure to the appropriate pressure points shown in Figure 11-11. A pressure point is a place where the main artery to the injured part lies near the skin surface and over a bone. Pressure at such a point is applied with the fingers or with the hand; no first aid materials are required. The object of the pressure is to compress the artery against the bone, thus shutting off the flow of blood from the heart to the wound.

There are 11 principal points on each side of the body where hand or finger pressure can be used to stop bleeding.

You should memorize these pressure points so that you will know immediately which point to use

for controlling hemorrhage from a particular part of the body. The correct pressure point is that which is: (1) nearest the wound, and (2) between the wound and the main part of the body.

It is very tiring to apply digital pressure, and it can seldom be maintained for more than 15 minutes. Pressure points are recommended for use while direct pressure is being applied to a serious wound.

If bleeding continues to be severe even after direct pressure and pressure points have been used, you may have to apply a tourniquet.

Use of a Tourniquet

Only when direct pressure, elevation and pressure points fail to stop bleeding from a limb, or when blood is gushing from a major wound such as a limb amputation, should a tourniquet be applied. (See Fig 11-12.) The use of a tourniquet can cause the loss of a limb below the band, hence, it must be used as a last-resort measure.

Tourniquet application

- Place the tourniquet around the limb and between the wound and the heart. Never place it directly over a wound or fracture.
- For amputation or partial amputation of the foot, leg, hand or arm and for bleeding from the upper arm or thigh, place the tourniquet just above the wound or amputation.
- For hemorrhage from the hand or forearm with no associated amputation, place the tourniquet immediately above the elbow.
- For hemorrhage from the foot or lower leg with no associated amputation, place the tourniquet immediately above the knee.
- When possible, place the tourniquet over the smoothed sleeve or trouser leg to prevent skin from being twisted or pinched.
- Once a tourniquet has been applied, inspect it and the dressing frequently to see if the tourniquet has slipped and if any sign of further bleeding is present. If necessary, tighten the tourniquet, but under no circumstances loosen it. It should only be loosened by medical personnel.
- If the condition of the casualty or the weather make it necessary to cover the casualty, leave the tourniquet exposed so that it can be readily seen. If possible, mark the casualty with a "T" on the forehead and indicate the time the tourniquet was applied.
- Note: avoid using a narrow constriction band that would cut the tissue when applying a tourniquet.

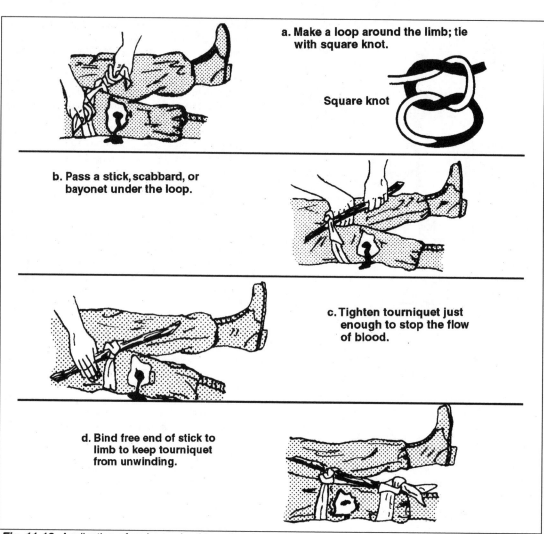

a. Make a loop around the limb; tie with square knot.

Square knot

b. Pass a stick, scabbard, or bayonet under the loop.

c. Tighten tourniquet just enough to stop the flow of blood.

d. Bind free end of stick to limb to keep tourniquet from unwinding.

Fig. 11-12. Application of an improvised tourniquet.

Shock Control

Shock may result from any type of injury. The more severe the injury, the more likely shock is to develop. The early signs of shock are restlessness, thirst, paleness of the skin and a rapid heartbeat. A casualty in shock may be excited or may be calm and appear very tired. The casualty may be sweating even though the skin feels cool and clammy. As shock becomes worse, a casualty may breathe in small, fast breaths or gasps even when the airway is clear, and may stare vacantly into space. The skin may have a blotchy or bluish appearance, especially around the lips.

Maintain adequate respiration and heartbeat. To maintain adequate respiration and heartbeat, you may need to do nothing more than clear the casualty's upper airway, position the body to ensure adequate drainage of any fluid obstructing the airway and observe to ensure that the airway remains unobstructed. You may need to administer CPR.

Control bleeding. Control bleeding by application of pressure dressing, by elevation of part and by use of pressure points as appropriate. Apply tourniquet if necessary.

120

Loosen constrictive clothing. Loosen clothing at the neck and waist and at other areas where it tends to bind the casualty. Loosen but do not remove shoes.

Reassure the casualty. Take charge. Show the casualty by your calm self-confidence and gentle yet firm actions that you know what you are doing and initiate conversation only to give instructions or warnings or to obtain necessary information. If the casualty asks questions regarding the seriousness of the injury, explain that a medical officer will have to do an examination in order to determine the extent of injury. Remember, ill-timed or erroneous information can increase a casualty's anxiety.

Splint fractures. If the casualty has a fracture, apply a splint.

Position the casualty. The position in which the casualty should be placed varies, depending upon the type of wound or injury and whether the casualty is conscious or unconscious. Unless the casualty has an injury for which a special position is prescribed, gently place the individual on a blanket or another suitable protective item in one of the following positions:

- If conscious, place the casualty on his back on a level surface with the lower extremities elevated 6 to 8 inches to increase the flow of blood to the heart. This may be accomplished by placing a pack or other suitable object under the feet. Remember, however, do not move a casualty who has a fracture until it has been properly splinted.
- If unconscious, place the casualty on his side or on the abdomen with the head turned to one side to prevent chocking on vomitus, blood or other fluid.

Keep the casualty comfortably warm. Do not overheat the casualty. If possible place a blanket, a poncho, a shelter half or another suitable material underneath. The casualty may not need a blanket overtop, depending upon the weather. If the weather permits, remove any wet clothing, except shoes, before covering the casualty.

Relieve pain. Proper dressing and bandaging of a wound, splinting of a fracture and positioning of a casualty are the best first aid measures for relieving pain.

Special First Aid Measures

The four life-saving rules, which you have just learned, apply to the treatment of all wounds. However, there are certain types of injuries which require special first aid measures. These are chest wounds, belly wounds, jaw and face wounds, burns and fractures (broken bones).

Chest wounds. Chest wounds through which air is sucking in and blowing out are particularly dangerous. The chest wound itself isn't as dangerous as the air which travels through it into the chest cavity. This air squeezes and compresses the lungs and prevents proper breathing.

The life of the person may depend upon quickly making the wound air-tight. As the victim inhales, place a piece of plastic (such as an I.D. card) over the wound site and immediately place a dressing firmly over the plastic. The plastic and dressing must be large enough to cover the entire wound, if the flow of air is to be stopped. Bind this covering securely with belts or even strips of torn clothing. Encourage the person to lie on the injured side. This may ease their breathing.

Belly wound. For a belly wound, give no food or water because anything taken orally will pass out from the the intestine and spread germs through the belly.

Do not try to replace protruding organs. Cover the protruding organs with a loose clean wet bandage. Pour clean water from a canteen on the bandage prior to applying it. Cover the wound with a sterile dressing and fasten securely. Treat for shock.

Jaw wounds. Wounds of the face and neck need special treatment to avoid choking on blood. Bleeding from the face and neck is usually severe because of the many blood vessels. First, stop the bleeding by exerting pressure with a sterile dressing. Then bind the bandage so as to protect the wound. If the jaw is broken, tie the bandage around it and up over the head so as to give support. Make sure you don't prevent the blood from draining out of the mouth.

To prevent choking on the blood, the person may sit up with his head held forward and down, or he may lie on his back with the head turned to one side, or on his side. These positions will allow the blood to drain out of the mouth instead of going down the windpipe. Treat for shock.

Burns. Burns are just as likely to cause shock as any other severe wound. There is also a great danger of infection. Do not pull clothes away from the burned area; instead, cut or tear the clothes and gently lift them off. Do not try to remove pieces of cloth that stick to the skin. Carefully cover the burned area with sterile dressings. Never break blisters or touch the burn.

It is especially important to treat for shock. The victim should drink plenty of water, because burns result in a great loss of body fluids. They also cause loss of body salts. Therefore, if possible, add one teaspoon of loose salt to each canteen (liter) of water. Three or more canteens should be drunk in 24 hours.

Fractures. A fracture is a broken bone. One or more of the following signs may be present:
• tenderness over the injury,
• pain with movement,
• inability to move injured part,
• deformed shape,
• swelling and discoloration.

A fracture may or may not have all these signs. If you aren't sure, give the wounded victim the benefit of the doubt and treat the injury as a fracture.

Fractures are to be immobilized to prevent further injury, to reduce pain and to help reduce shock. Do not attempt to reset a fracture yourself. This is done at the medical facility. All fractures of long bones should be splinted "where they lie" before movement or transportation of any kind is attempted.

There are two kinds of fractures: a closed break in the bone, and a broken bone with a wound adjacent to the fractured site.

The second type, open fracture, can be caused by a broken bone piercing the skin or by a bullet which pierces the flesh and breaks the bone. (See Figs. 11-13 and 11-14.)

Standard leg and arm splints are the most desirable forms of splints when available and when trained personnel are available for their application. However, first aid in the field may require you to improvise with splints from any material that is handy. The following paragraphs tell how to improvise when it is necessary. Figure 11-15 shows how various broken bones are splinted.

Be careful. If you suspect a broken bone, handle the person's body with the greatest care. Rough or careless handling causes pain and increases the likelihood of shock. Furthermore, the cracked ends of the bone are razor-sharp and can cut through muscle, blood vessels, nerves and skin. So don't move a person with a fracture unless you have to. If you must, be gentle and keep the fractured part from moving. If there is a wound with a fracture, treat it as any other wound by applying pressure and a clean dressing.

Broken leg or hip. The quickest way to splint a broken leg is to tie it to the uninjured leg. Tie the legs together in at least two places, above and below the break. You can use a belt, cartridge belt, strips of cloth or handkerchiefs tied together. Don't move a person with a broken leg unless it is necessary to get the casualty off a road or away from enemy fire. Then grasp the casualty by the shoulders and pull in

Fig. 11-13. *Simple fracture.*

Fig. 11-14. *Compound fracture.*

Fig. 11-15. *Splint for broken leg or thigh (upper left); splint for arm fracture where elbow can't be bent (upper right); splint for fracture of lower arm (lower left); splint for fracture of upper arm (lower right).*

a straight line. Do not roll or move the body sideways.

Splints for broken leg, thigh or hip. If you have time, you can make a good splint for the lower limb by using two long sticks or poles. Roll the sticks into a folded blanket from both sides. This forms a trough in which the leg rests. Bind the splints firmly at several places. For fractures of the lower leg, splints should extend from above the knee to below the foot. If the thigh or hip is broken, the inside splint should extend to the crotch and the outside splint should extend to the armpit. Always be sure that the ends of the sticks are well padded.

To support an injured arm or shoulder. A sling is the quickest way to support a fractured arm or

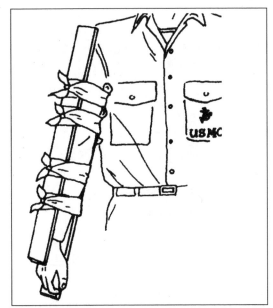

Fig. 11-16. Board splints applied to fractured arm or elbow when elbow is not bent.

Fig. 11-17. Protection for broken neck.

shoulder, a sprained arm, or an arm with a painful injury. Use a sling only after any fracture has been splinted.

Splint for a broken arm. When possible, keep a broken arm from moving by support with splints. Splints should extend from the joint below to the joint above the fracture. Temporary splints are made from boards, branches, bayonets, scabbards, etc. Splints should always be padded with some soft material to protect the limb from pressure and rubbing. Bind splints securely at several places above and below the fracture, but not so tightly as to stop the flow of blood. It is well to apply two splints, one on either side of the limb. (See Fig. 11-16.) If an injured elbow is bent, do not try to straighten it; if straight, do not bend it.

Broken back. It is often impossible to be sure a person has a broken back. Be suspicious of any injury, especially if the back has been sharply struck or bent, or the person has fallen. The sharp bone fragments will cut the spinal cord if they are moved. This would cause permanent paralysis of the body and the legs, and possibly death.

For a broken back, don't move the victim except in extreme emergency and then only by hard board, door or stretcher. Don't raise the head. Don't twist the neck or back.

Broken neck. Handling a broken neck is extremely dangerous. Bone fragments may cut the

spinal cord just as in a broken back. Keep the head straight and still. Moving may cause death. Keep the head and neck motionless by placing large stones or packs on each side of the head to support it. (See Fig. 11-17.) Place a rolled blanket around the head and neck for support and padding but do not place anything under the neck. If the victim must be moved, get help. One person supports the victim's head and keep it straight while others lift. Put the victim on a hard stretcher or board. Keep the victim face up.

Remember. It is always better to be on the safe side and splint an unbroken bone if there is any question about it being broken.

Other First Aid Measures

Electrical shock. Electrical shock is a frequent accident resulting from contact with a "live" wire. Being struck by lightning is not so common. If a person comes in contact with an electrical current, turn off the switch if it is nearby, but do not waste time looking for it. Use a dry wooden pole, dry clothing, dry rope, or some other material which will not conduct electricity, to remove the person from the wire or the wire from the person. If a pole is not handy, simply drag the patient off the wire by means of a loop of dry clothing. Do NOT touch the wire or the person with your bare hands or you will get a shock too. (See Fig. 11-18.)

Note: Excitement is a frequent side effect of electrical shock as is cardiac (heart) irregularity. It is important to have the patient seen by a doctor or medical department personnel. Until you can get medical aid, keep the patient quiet and calm. Be prepared to start CPR if required.

Fig. 11-18. *Removing an electrical wire from electric shock victim.*

Carbon monoxide poisoning. Carbon monoxide has no odor and kills without warning. Symptoms include: dizziness, headache, ringing (noise) in ears, throbbing in temples. Skin, lips and nail beds are often bright red. These symptoms occur rapidly and in quick succession. Poisoning from this gas occurs most often from breathing motor vehicle exhaust gas. This happens frequently from running an engine with the garage doors closed. It happens from sitting in a vehicle with the windows closed and the motor running. Faulty mufflers are also a major cause of carbon monoxide poisoning. The same gas is formed by stoves in poorly ventilated shelters, where it is equally dangerous. If overcome with carbon monoxide, get the victim into fresh air immediately. Commence mouth-to-mouth resuscitation efforts, if indicated, and keep the person quiet.

Transportation of the Sick and Wounded

Knowing how to move seriously injured persons is one of the most important parts of first aid. Careless or rough handling not only may increase the seriousness of an injury, but may even result in death. Unless there is a good reason for moving an injured person immediately, do not transport until a litter or ambulance is available. Sometimes, when the situation is urgent, and you know that no medical facilities are available, you will have to move the victim yourself. That is why you should know the different ways of carrying casualties. Always give necessary first aid before attempting to move a person who is wounded.

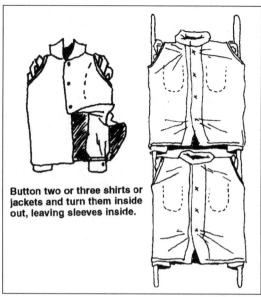

Button two or three shirts or jackets and turn them inside out, leaving sleeves inside.

Fig. 11-19. *Litter made with poles and jackets.*

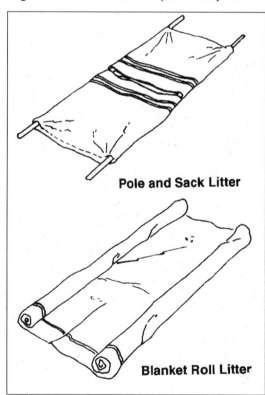

Pole and Sack Litter

Blanket Roll Litter

Fig. 11-20.

Fig. 11-21. Fireman's drag.

Fig. 11-22. Poncho drag.

Fig. 11-23(a). *Fireman's carry, first step.*

Fig. 11-23(b). *Fireman's carry, second step.*

Fig. 11-23(c). *Fireman's carry, third step.*

Fig. 11-23(d). *Fireman's carry, fourth step.*

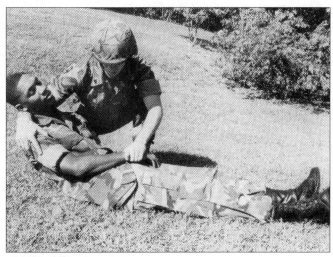

Fig. 11-23(f). Fireman's carry, sixth step.

Fig. 11-23(e). Fireman's carry, fifth step.

Fig. 11-24. Chair carry.

Fig. 11-25. The back lift.

Fig. 11-26. Pack strap carry.

Fig. 11-27. Arm carry.

Fig. 11-28. D carry.

Fig. 11-29(a). Link two pistol belts together into a continuous belt. Place it under the person's thighs and hips so that a loop extends from each side. Lie between the person's outstretched legs, thrusting arms through belt loops. Grasp the right hand with your right hand.

Fig. 11-29(c). First, rise to your knees, then stand, as shown. This carry leaves your hands free to help you over obstacles.

Fig. 11-29(b). Roll toward the side, turning your face downward. Carry the wounded person onto your back.

Fig. 11-30. *Arms carry.*

Fig. 11-31. *Supporting carry.*

If the casualty has a broken bone, never attempt to move until you have splinted it.

Improvised litters. Using a litter not only makes it easier to carry the casualty but also makes the journey safer and more comfortable.

If the distance is long, or if the person has a fractured leg, hip, back or skull, the casualty must not be moved except on a litter. A litter can be improvised from many different things. A blanket, shelter half, tarpaulin, or other material may be used for the litter bed. The poles may be made from strong branches, tent poles, rifles, skis, etc. (See Figs. 11-19 and 11-20.)

Carries. There are several ways by which a casualty may be moved without using a litter. Use the carry which is easiest for you and which is best fitted to the situation.

Figures 11-21 through 11-31 illustrate some of the carries.

Common Emergencies

In addition to the first aid kit which every Marine carries, special first aid kits are often available. These are for use in common emergencies such as cuts, burns and eye injuries. First aid kits found in many motor vehicles contain tourniquets, swabs, adhesive tape, and dressings of several sizes. Familiarize yourself with them. Directions are included with each kit.

Minor wounds. Small wounds, such as cuts, usually do not bleed very much and will stop bleeding

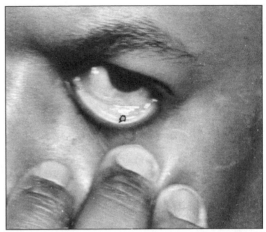

Fig. 11-32. *To remove an object from the lower lid or eyeball, have someone pull down the lower lid and remove the object with a clean handkerchief.*

once a dressing has been applied. Infection is the principal danger, and any break in the skin should be protected. Do not touch a wound with the fingers or allow clothes to touch it. Keep it clean.

Apply a dressing over the wound. There are various sized dressings in the motor vehicle and other first aid kits. Pick out a size which is large enough to cover the wound adequately. Be careful not to touch the inside of the dressing with the fingers.

Burns. Small burns frequently occur and, unless properly protected, can become infected. Large

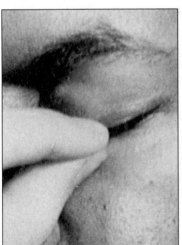 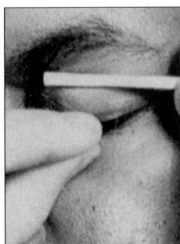 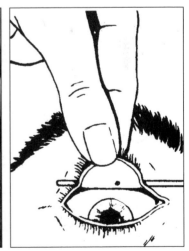

Fig. 11-33. *To remove foreign body from the upper lid, have someone pull down the upper lid (left picture). Next, have the person place a matchstick on the upper lid (middle photograph). Then roll the upper lid back (right illustration), while another person removes the object with a clean handkerchief.*

burns must be treated by a medical officer, but small burns can be handled at the first aid level. Severe sunburn requires similar first aid measures. Cover the burned area with a sterile or clean dressing of suitable size. If no burn ointment is available, at least cover the burn with the dressing from your first aid kit.

Foreign body in eye. If a particle gets in your eye, do not rub the eye. Close it for a few minutes and tears may wash away the object. If tears have not washed away the particle, try flushing it out with canteen water. Your eyelids must be held open widely with your fingers while flushing. If this does not work, have someone treat the eye as shown in Figures 11-32 and 11-33.

When a foreign body cannot be dislodged or the eyeball is scratched, obtain medical attention at once. When an acidic or caustic solution enters the eye, immediately flush with a large volume of water.

Foreign bodies in ear, nose and throat. Never probe into the ear with a pin, wire or stick if an object is in the ear. Let the medical officer get it out. An insect in the ear may be killed with a few drops of oil or water. Other objects also may be flushed out this way. However, if the object is something which swells when wet (such as a bean), do not put water into the ear.

Probing into the nose will merely jam the foreign body tighter. Try to loosen it by gently blowing the nose. If this doesn't work, wait until you see a medical officer. Objects in the nose are usually not dangerous.

When a foreign body becomes lodged in the throat, try to cough it up. Coughing takes precedence over removal by fingers, because the latter method can result in the item being pushed farther down the throat. To remove a foreign object from the throat of another person, strike sharply between the shoulder blades with one hand, while you support the chest with the other. If this does not work, stand behind the victim and wrap your arms around the waist. Grasp your wrist and place the thumb side of your fists against the victim's abdomen, above the navel and just below the rib cage. Give a quick thrust to the victim. The obstruction should pop out like a champagne cork. Repeat the procedure if necessary. This procedure is called Abdominal Thrust and is illustrated in Figure 11-34.

Care of the feet. Marines have to use their feet constantly. Prevention of foot trouble is the best first aid for feet. Keep feet clean. Drying the feet thoroughly after bathing, especially between toes, helps prevent athlete's foot. For itching or redness between the toes, apply foot powder twice daily. If it does not improve, see your medical officer. Don't try to treat it yourself. Don't cut a callus or corn unless you want to risk a serious infection. Report to your medical officer instead. To avoid ingrown toenails, keep toenails clean and short, and cut them straight across.

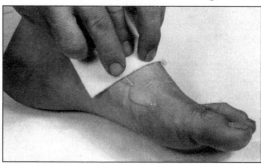

Fig. 11-35(a). *Open blister at the lower edge with a needle which has been cooled after having been heated red hot with a match. Opening must be large enough to allow the fluid to escape. Leave the loose skin on as a cover.*

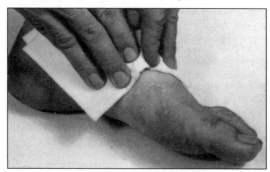

Fig. 11-35(b). *Apply a sterile gauze pad.*

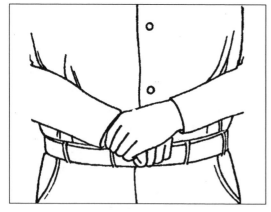

Fig. 11-34. *Abdominal thrust.*

Dust feet with foot powder after bathing and before a march. Foot powder absorbs perspiration and prevents chafing. Put on clean socks every day if possible. Don't wear socks that have holes, are poorly darned or don't fit properly. Break in shoes before wearing them on a march. If a blister develops and a medical officer is not available, use the treatment shown in figures 11-35(a) and (b).

Poison plants. Poison ivy, poison oak, and poison sumac cause skin irritation. The faster you give first aid after exposure, the milder the effects will be. Learn to recognize the plants so you will know when you have touched them and can start first aid before a rash appears. Poison ivy is a creeper having three leaves on each stem. The leaves are shiny, pointed and have prominent veins. Poison oak and poison sumac are shrubs or small trees. If you discover that you have been exposed to a poison plant, wash the parts of the body affected promptly and thoroughly, using cold water and strong soap. The rash starts with redness and intense itching. Later, little blisters appear. If a rash has already developed, do not wash it. Avoid scratching, for it will make the condition worse by spreading it to other areas of the body. These areas can become easily infected. Seek medical attention.

Unconsciousness. It is often impossible to find the cause of unconsciousness. Bleeding, heat stroke or head injury may have been the cause. If you can't fine the cause, keep the victim lying down. Do not move the victim unless absolutely necessary, and then do so very carefully. If cold, make the victim warm. If the casualty has suffered the effects of excessive heat, give first aid accordingly. Do not pour liquids into the mouth of an unconscious person, because you may cause choking. If vomiting occurs, turn the patient over onto the stomach (if not contraindicated by injuries) and turn the head to one side. Check to make sure the patient does not inhale the vomitus. Take off equipment. Loosen clothing. Get a medical officer.

If the victim has merely fainted, consciousness will be regained in a few minutes. Let the victim lie quietly. Loosen the clothing. Apply a wet, cold cloth to the face. If the victim is about to faint or has actually fainted while sitting up, lower the head between the knees so that the blood can flow to the head. Hold the victim carefully so that a fall does not occur and cause injury.

Snake Bites

Poisonous snakes are found throughout the world, primarily in the tropics and temperate regions. Within the United States there are four kinds: rattlesnakes, copperheads, moccasins and coral snakes.

Poison is injected from the venom sacs through grooved or hollow fangs which, depending on the species, are either long or short.

The venoms of different snakes cause different effects. Pit viper venom destroys the tissues into which it is injected and destroys blood cells. The cobra, adder and coral snakes inject powerful venoms which affect the central nervous system (neurotoxins) causing respiratory paralysis. Sea snakes have venom that has both effects.

The identification of poisonous snakes is imperative since the antivenom and course of treatment will be different for each type of venom. The snake should be killed and saved if possible. When this is not done, the identification may be difficult because many venomous snakes resemble harmless varieties. When dealing with snake-bite problems in foreign countries, seek native advice, professional or otherwise.

Treatment: In treating snakebites, the aim is to reduce circulation of blood through the bite area, delay absorption of venom, prevent aggravation of the local wound, maintain vital signs and transport as soon as possible to medical personnel. First aid in most instances will be mainly supportive.

- Wrap a constricting band (rubber tubing, belt, necktie, stocking, etc.) 2-4 inches above the fang marks. It should be tight enough to stop the flow of blood in the veins but not tight enough to shut off the arterial blood supply. The victim's pulse below the band should be countable. If swelling should get beyond the band, put another one just above it and remove the first.
- Check the pulse and respiration frequently. Give artificial ventilation if necessary.
- Calm and reassure the victim, who will often be excited or hysterical. Keep the victim lying down, quiet and warm. The victim should not be given alcohol or any other stimulant to drink.
- Treat for shock.
- Use a splint to immobilize the victim's affected extremity, keeping the involved area below the level of the heart.
- Cleanse the bite with soap and water or an antiseptic solution. Flush the area well with water.
- Apply an ice bag or chemical coolant bag, if a physician so directs. Under no circumstances should the limb be packed in ice!
- Telephone ahead to the nearest medical help so that the proper antivenom can be made available. Administration of antivenom is not a first aid procedure. It requires preliminary testing of the vic-

tim for sensitivity to horse serum. Only a person with medical training should attempt to give the antivenom.
• Transport immediately.

If the victim is reached within 20 to 30 minutes of the time bitten, *if* the victim already shows definite signs of poisoning and *if* a physician concurs, a sterile knife blade may be used to make an incision about one-half inch long by one-forth inch deep lengthwise over each fang mark. Suction by mouth is not recommended, because the human mouth contains so many different bacteria that the bite could become infected. Incision and suction later than 30 minutes from the time of the bite are not recommended.

Pit Vipers

The rattlesnakes, copperheads and moccasins (cottonmouths) are called pit vipers. The victim's condition provides the best information as to the seriousness of the solution. The bite of the pit viper is extremely painful and is characterized by immediate swelling around the fang marks, usually within 5 to 10 minutes. If only minimal swelling occurs within 30 minutes, the bite will almost certainly have been from a poisonous snake which did not inject venom.

When the venom is absorbed, there is general discoloration of the skin due to destruction of blood cells. This reaction is followed by blisters and numbness in the affected area. Other signs which can occur are weakness, rapid pulse, nausea, shortness of breath, vomiting and shock.

Corals, Cobras, Kraits and Mambas

Corals, cobras, kraits and mambas all belong to the same group even though they are found in different parts of the world. All four inject their venom through short grooved fangs.

The small coral snake, found in the Southeastern United States is brightly colored with bands of red, black and yellow (or almost white). Other nonpoisonous snakes have the same coloring, but in the coral snake the red ring always touches the yellow ring.

The venom of corals, cobras, kraits and mambas produces symptoms different than that of the pit vipers. Because there is only minimal pain and swelling, many people are led to believe that the bite is not serious. Delayed reactions in the nervous system normally occur after 1 to 7 hours.

Symptoms include blurred vision, drooping eyelids, slurred speech, drowsiness, and increased salivation and sweating. Nausea and vomiting, shock,

respiratory difficulty, paralysis, convulsions and coma will probably develop if the bite is not treated promptly.

Treatment: Due to the delayed reaction of the venom, all bites should receive prompt attention regardless of the victim's seemingly favorable condition. Identify the snake, if possible, so that the proper antivenom treatment may be started at the hospital. Emergency care is the same as that described earlier, with the exception that incision and suction are not recommended since there is little local effect from the bite. The danger is to the nervous system.

Sea animals

A number of sea animals are capable of inflicting very painful wounds by biting, stinging or puncturing. Except under rare circumstances, stings and puncture wounds are not fatal. Major wounds from sharks, barracuda, moray eels and alligators can be treated by controlling the bleeding.

Heat Casualties

Heat exhaustion

Heat exhaustion is caused by excessive body heat which overloads the body control mechanisms, and results in excessive loss of body water and salt through prolonged sweating.

Symptoms include: headache, excessive sweating, dizziness, muscle cramps. The skin is pale, cool, moist and clammy.

Treatment:
• Lay the casualty on his or her back in a cool shaded area and loosen the clothing.
• If conscious, give the casualty cool water to sip.
• Handle as litter case and evacuate to medical facility as soon as possible.

Heatstroke

Heatstroke is caused by a failure of the body's heat regulating mechanism which causes the body to become overheated. Sometimes called "sunstroke."

Symptoms include: stoppage of sweating, hot and dry skin, headache, dizziness, fast pulse, mental confusion and collapse and unconsciousness. The face may appear flushed or red.

Treatment:
• Immerse casualty in coldest water available. Add ice if available.

- If a cold water bath is not possible, get the casualty into the shade, remove clothing and keep the entire body wet by pouring water over top. Cool further by fanning the wet body.
- Transport the casualty to the nearest medical facility at once and continue to cool the body on the way. Handle as a litter case.
- If conscious, give the casualty cool water to sip.

Heat Cramps

Heat cramps are caused by loss of salt.

Symptoms include: painful spasms of muscles (legs, arms, abdomen).

Treatment:
- Give casualty salt water to drink. Dissolve two crushed salt tablets (one-quarter teaspoon of table salt) in a canteen (liter) of cool water. The casualty should drink 3 to 5 canteens during a period of 12 hours.
- If cramps are severe, take casualty to medical facility.

Cold Injuries

When the body is subject to severely cold temperatures, blood vessels constrict and body heat is gradually lost. As body temperature drops, tissues are easily damaged or destroyed.

All cold injuries are similar, varying only in degree of tissue injury. The extent of injury depends on such factors as wind speed, temperature, type and duration of exposure and humidity. Tissue freezing is speeded by wind, humidity or a combination of the two.

In general, the effects of cold are broken down into two types: general cooling of the entire body and local cooling of parts of the body.

General cooling

General cooling of the entire body is caused by continued exposure to low or rapidly dropping temperatures, cold moisture, snow or ice.

The first symptom is shivering, followed by a feeling of listlessness, indifference and drowsiness. Unconsciousness can follow. Shock becomes evident as the victim's eyes become a glassy stare, respiration becomes slow and shallow, and the pulse weak or absent.

Treatment:
- Observe breathing and heartbeat. CPR may have to be provided during the rewarming process.

- Rewarm the victim as soon as possible. It may be necessary to treat other injuries before the victim can be moved to a warmer place.
- Replace wet or frozen clothing.

If the victim is in a warm place and is conscious, the most effective method of warming is immersion in a tub of warm water.

If a tub is not available, apply external heat. Body heat from the rescuers, called "buddy warming" is also effective. Placing the victim under a blanket or in a sleeping bag is *not sufficient.* (Do not place artificial heat next to bare skin.)

If the victim is conscious, give warm liquids to drink. (NEVER give alcoholic beverages or allow the victim to smoke.)

Dry thoroughly if water is used to rewarm the victim.

As soon as possible, transfer the victim to a medical facility, keeping the body warm en route.

Local cooling

Local cooling injuries affecting parts of the body fall into two categories: freezing and nonfreezing. In order of increasing seriousness, they include chilblain, immersion foot, superficial frostbite and deep frostbite. The areas most commonly affected are the face and extremities.

Chilblains. Chilblains are a mild cold injury caused by prolonged and repeated exposure for several hours to air temperatures from above freezing to as high as 60 degrees. Chilblains are characterized by redness, swelling, tingling and pain of the skin area. Injuries of this nature require no specific treatment except to warm the affected part, keep it dry and prevent further exposure.

Immersion foot. Immersion foot, which also may occur in the hands, results from prolonged exposure to wet and cold at temperatures ranging from just above freezing to 50 degrees, and usually in connection with limited motion of the extremities and water-soaked protective clothing.

Signs and symptoms of immersion foot are tingling and numbness of the affected areas; swelling of the legs, feet or hands; bluish discoloration of the skin; blisters and pain. Gangrene may occur.

Treatment:
- Get the victim off his or her feet.
- Remove wet shoes, socks and gloves.
- Expose the affected area to warm dry air.
- Keep the victim warm.
- Do no rupture blisters or apply salves and ointments.

If the skin is not broken or loose, the injured part may be left exposed. If it is necessary to transport the victim, the injured area should be covered with loosely wrapped fluff bandages or sterile gauze.

If the skin is broken, gently wrap with a sterile sheet to protect the sensitive tissue from pressure and additional injury.

Transport to a medical facility as soon as possible.

Frostbite

Frostbite occurs when ice crystals form in the skin or deeper tissues after exposure to a temperature of 32 degrees or lower. Depending upon the temperature, altitude and wind speed, the exposure time necessary to produce frostbite varies from a few minutes to several hours. The areas commonly affected are the face and extremities.

The symptoms of frostbite are progressive. Victims generally incur this injury without being acutely aware of it. The affected skin reddens and there is an uncomfortable coldness. With continued exposure, the affected area becomes numb. As ice crystals form, the frozen extremity appears white, yellow-white, or mottled blue-white and is cold, hard and insensitive to the touch or pressure.

Frostbite is classified as superficial or deep, depending on the extent of tissue involvement.

Superficial frostbite

In superficial frostbite, the surface of the skin will feel hard, but the underlying tissue will be soft, allowing it to move over bony areas. Only the skin and the region just below it are involved.

Treatment:
- Bring the victim indoors.
- Rewarm hands by placing them under the arm pit, against the abdomen or between the legs.
- Warm feet by placing in the arm pit or against the abdomen of a buddy.
- Gradually rewarm the affected area by warm water immersion, or skin to skin contact.
- Never rub a frostbite area.

Deep frostbite

In deep frostbite, the freezing reaches into the deep tissue layers. There are ice crystals in the entire thickness of the limb. The skin will not move over bony ridges and feels hard and solid.

The objectives of treatment are to protect the frozen area from further injury, to rapidly thaw the affected area and to be prepared to respond to circulatory or respiratory difficulties.

Treatment:
- Treat other injuries first. Constantly monitor the victim's pulse and breathing. Respiratory and heart problems can develop rapidly. Be ready to administer CPR.
- Make no attempt to thaw the frostbitten area if there is a possibility of refreezing. It is better to leave the part frozen until the victim arrives at a medical facility equipped for long-term care. (Refreezing of a thawed extremity causes severe and disabling damage.)

Treat all victims with injuries to feet or legs as litter cases. However, if this is not possible, walking will not lessen the chances of successful treatment as long as the limb has not been thawed.

When protection from further exposure is available, remove victim's gloves, boots and socks. Boots and clothing frozen on the body should be thawed by immersing them in warm water before removal.

Rapidly rewarm frozen areas by immersion in water at 100 degrees to 105 degrees. Keep the water warm by adding fresh hot water, but do not pour it directly on the injured area. The frozen area must be completely surrounded by water. Do not let it rest on the side or bottom of the tub.

After rewarming has been completed, pat dry the area with a soft towel.

Protect tissues from additional injury and keep clean. (Sterile dressings and linen should be used.)

Victim may be given hot, stimulating fluids, such as tea or coffee. (Do NOT allow the victim to smoke or drink alcoholic beverages.)

Transport the victim to a medical facility as soon as possible. During transportation, slightly elevate the frostbitten area, keep the victim and the injured area warm and do not allow the injured areas to be exposed to the cold.

Chapter Twelve

Sanitation and Hygiene

If a unit suffers a breakdown in sanitation, it is because one or more members of the unit have become careless. As a result, Marines get sick. The fighting efficiency of the unit falls off. Its members are less alert, and Marines' lives may be lost because of it. Disease and sickness help only the enemy.

The rules of sanitation and hygiene are simple but must be followed daily. By employing them, a Marine will increase the fighting efficiency of the unit and its ability to win.

Personal Hygiene Measures

Personal hygiene is the practice of health rules by each individual to safeguard their own health and that of their comrades. Rules of personal hygiene include:

- Wash your body frequently from head to foot at regular intervals at least once a week. While washing, pay particular attention to body creases. If bathing facilities are not available, scrub your body frequently with a wet cloth.
- Wash your hands with soap and water after working, before eating and particularly after each visit to the head. Disease germs on your hands from such activities can get into the food you eat and infect your body.
- Change underclothing daily if possible. Outer clothing should be cleaned when it becomes soiled. If water is not available, crumple up your clothing, shake it well and hang it in the sunlight for at least two hours.
- Inspect your body and clothing frequently for body lice or fleas. If you find any of these vermin, report to sick call at once.
- Change clothing or shoes as soon as possible after they get wet. Try to keep your feet dry in order to avoid colds, immersion foot or other serious illness.
- Brush your teeth at least twice a day; one brushing should be before going to bed. If a toothbrush is not available, use dental floss or a toothpick to remove food from the teeth, then rinse your mouth with water. Brush your teeth on the inside and outside, keeping the bristles at a 45-degree angle against the gumline. If your teeth are bad or ache, report to a dental officer. After brushing your teeth, never eat anything before going to bed.
- Get into the habit of having your bowels move regularly. Always go to the toilet to urinate or to move your bowels. Using the ground for this purpose is a source of great danger to everyone. Insects, especially flies, alight and feed where you have relieved yourself, pick up your germs and later transfer them to your food where they also eat and relieve themselves. These germs can also be carried to streams or wells which serve as water supply areas.
- When adequate supplies are available, drink plenty of water at intervals during the day.
- Use only your own eating and drinking utensils. You may contract disease germs from another's mess gear. For the same reason, don't exchange cigarettes, cigars, towels, combs or shaving outfits.
- Be sure to use mosquito repellent and a net when mosquitoes are present. Make sure the net is well tucked in and that no holes are in it. Take all prescribed medication designed to protect you from malaria and other diseases.
- Keep your hair cut short and your fingernails clean. This is especially important if you are detailed as a cook or in other positions in which you handle food.
- Do not bite your fingernails, pick your nose or scratch your body.
- Exercise muscles and joints regularly to maintain physical stamina and good health. Exercise should be suited to the age and physical condition of the Marine and should stop short of extreme fatigue and exhaustion. Obtain rest and sleep, 6-8 hours uninterrupted each day is desirable.
- Avoid sexually transmitted diseases (STDs). These diseases are caught through unprotected sexual intercourse with an infected person. If you have sexual intercourse, follow the medical

advice you have received for taking precautionary measures. Remember, the only sure way to avoid STDs is by abstinence.

- If you think that you have caught a STD, report to a medical officer at once and follow their directions. Any STDs can be cured much more quickly if treatment is begun early. Do not try to treat yourself or go to an unqualified doctor. Either may result in permanent damage to your body.

Sanitation in the Field

While all of the foregoing rules are as important in the field as they are in the barracks, the following are of special significance while in the field:

Never *drink any water from an untreated source until it has been declared pure by a medical officer and a sign posted that it is safe to drink. Tap water in many areas is unsafe.*

When orders have been issued that all drinking water must be boiled, be sure that the water you drink has actually boiled for 20 minutes.

Sometimes water will be provided for drinking which has been purified in a sterilizing bag known as a Lyster bag. These bags are usually placed in your company area. When this is done, drink only the water from the bag. Do not mind the taste. It will not hurt you. It comes from a chemical issued for the purpose of purifying the water. Let the water run from the faucet of the bag into your own cup. The bag should remain well covered at all times. Do not dip a cup into the bag, and do not drink by putting your lips to the faucet. Keep the Lyster bag clean inside.

Use water purification tablets to make water safe for drinking when no treated water is available. Follow the procedures shown in Figure 12-1.

Be sure that your mess kit, knife, fork and spoon are washed in hot, soapy water and rinsed in boiling water before and after use. Unless facilities are available for you to take these sterilization precautions in the field, mess gear should not be used. At the completion of the meal, scrape the food remnants from your mess gear into the designated pit or garbage can. Then proceed to the area which contains three or four cans of boiling water. The first and second cans (if provided) have soap added and the last two contain boiling water only. Dipping your utensils into each of these cans will thoroughly clean them. Don't use a cloth to dry them. The heat of the metal will cause them to dry quickly in the air. Unless the washing is done in boiling water, your mess gear may pick up disease germs. Dysentery can result from unclean, greasy mess gear.

The eating utensil washing facility is set up as shown in Figure 12-2.

- SCRAPE FOOD particles from eating utensils into a garbage can and attach the canteen cup, mess kit pan cover, knife, fork and spoon to the handle of the mess kit pan.
- Using the long-handled brush provided, WASH the eating utensils in the FIRST CONTAINER of hot soapy water.
- Using the long-handled brush provided, WASH the eating utensils in the SECOND CONTAINER of hot soapy water (if provided).
- IMMERSE the eating utensils in the FIRST CONTAINER of clean boiling water for approximately 30 seconds.

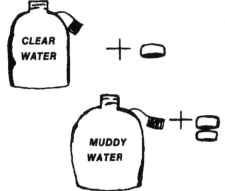

Add one iodine tablet to a quart canteen of clear water. Use two iodine tablets if the water is muddy. Iodine tablets must be checked before use. If not steel-grey in color or if stuck together or crumbled, do not use. Place cap on canteen loosely.

CLEAR WATER

MUDDY WATER

NOTE: Double the amount if you have a 2-quart canteen.
- Replace cap and wait 5 minutes.
- Shake the canteen.
- Loosen the cap and tip the canteen over to allow leakage around the canteen threads.
- Tighten the cap and wait another 25 minutes before drinking (total of 30 minutes).

Fig. 12-1. Use of water purification tablets.

- IMMERSE the eating utensils in the SECOND CONTAINER of clean boiling water for approximately 30 seconds.
- SHAKE the eating utensils to remove excess water. Check to insure that the eating utensils are clean. If not, repeat the washing cycle.

....

- Use a mosquito net and repellent whenever mosquitoes or other flying insects are in the area. The repellent should be replaced more frequently if you are sweating profusely, but at least every six hours. Properly worn clothing, netting and repellents are your primary defense against insect-

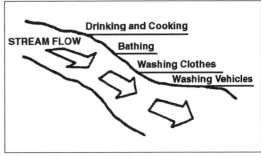

Draw water upstream from other activities.

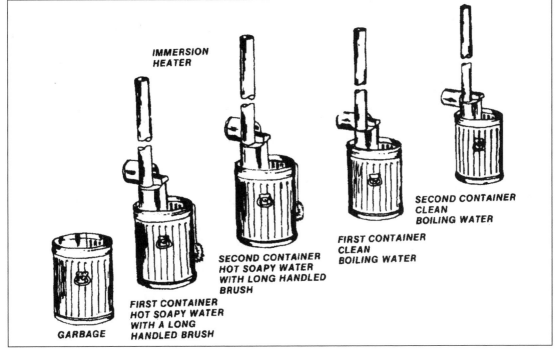

Fig. 12-2. Utensil washing facility.

borne diseases. Malaria pills are a secondary means of protection against one form of insect-borne disease, malaria. Take the malaria pills your corpsman gives you.

- Watch for lice or other vermin on your body and clothing. If you find them, report to a medical officer immediately.
- Wear clothing that is suitable to the weather conditions, temperature and your activities. Stay as dry as possible in order to avoid pneumonia or other illnesses.

- If conditions allow, shake your bedding well and lay it in the sun to air.
- Wash your shirts, underwear and socks frequently. Whenever possible, open your tent so the air can circulate through it.
- Dig a drainage ditch around your tent immediately after putting it up. This precaution will prevent rain water from washing through the tent.
- If possible, prepare your sleeping areas before dark. If you have no cot or air mattress, level the ground and scrape a hollow area out for your hips. Use straw, leaves, dry grass or small branches for

a mattress. Sleep on your poncho. This keeps dampness from coming up from the ground.

- Bury empty ration cans. They provide breeding places for disease-carrying insects and rodents. (See Fig. 12-3.)
- If you choose a camp site, there are some definite

Fig. 12-3. *Marking field garbage pit.*

sanitary advantages you should try to obtain: (a) a site with a stream nearby, (b) an elevated site to allow drainage and some freedom from insects, (c) an area large enough to allow living quarters to be 100 yards from heads and latrines, (d) a prevailing wind blowing towards heads away from camp, and (e) a site free from swamps and low water where various harmful insects might breed.

- In a short bivouac situation where time does not allow for digging deep pit trenches used in more permanent camp sites, straddle trench sites should be constructed immediately after arriving on location. A straddle trench latrine is dug one foot wide, two and a half feet deep and four feet long. It will accommodate two Marines at a time. The number of trenches provided should be sufficient to serve eight percent of the unit's strength at one time. The earth removed in digging is piled at the end of the trenches with a can or shovel so that Marines can cover their waste after using the trench. This continues until the unit leaves or the straddle trenches are filled to within one foot of the surface. Before breaking camp, all heads, including straddle trenches, must be filled, mounded over, and marked with the date they were closed. Dispose of waste while on the march by using a cathole. This is a hole dug approximately one foot deep and one foot wide. Catholes must be covered and packed down after use.
- The proper use of heads cannot be stressed too greatly. Desirable camp sites are few, and a careless unit may so contaminate a camp site that it will be unfit for further use for months.

Chapter Thirteen

Physical Fitness

"Nations have passed away and left no trace, and history gives the naked cause of it; one simple reason in all cases; they fell because their people were not fit."

Rudyard Kipling

The price of freedom is not cheap. As United States Marines, we historically have been the "first to fight" to protect American freedom. When crises occur, regardless of the clime and place, we've responded to the call to arms. In a sense, Marines have a two-fold responsibility to remain fit; first a responsibility to our society to remain healthy and alert, in all ways to be contributing members; and second, a responsibility to the American people to be an effective, powerful combat force-in-readiness prepared to take whatever military action is necessary to accomplish our assigned mission.

Why You Need to Know about Physical Fitness

The rigors of Marine Corps recruit training and the mention of "boot camp" bring to mind the legend and the image of the highly motivated, physically fit and well-trained Marine. But the high level of physical fitness which you enjoyed as a "basic Marine" only lasts for a short time unless regular physical fitness training becomes one of your personal habits. Here we will give you the knowledge necessary to achieve a high level of personal fitness and to enable you to plan and conduct physical training programs suited to help you develop the Marines whom you lead.

Physical fitness for a Marine means the maintenance of a healthy body, the endurance to withstand the stress of prolonged activity and adverse environment, the capacity to endure the discomforts that accompany fatigue and the maintenance of combat effectiveness. Physical fitness is also a part of a Marine's professional qualifications. Responsibility for a Marine's physical fitness is shared jointly by the Marine and the commander.

If you are physically fit you'll look better, feel better and perform better. In other words, you'll be a happier and more effective person and Marine. What better motivation could you have?

Components of Physical Conditioning

1. **Components of Physical Conditioning.** To capitalize on those components that can benefit training efforts, the following categories of exercises should be included in both individual and unit Physical Conditioning Programs (PCP):

a. Strength. Muscular strength refers to the ability of the muscular system to move the body through resistance. Many associate strength training with progressive resistive exercises using weights and machines. However, the ability of a Marine to effectively handle their own body weight should be a prerequisite before integrating strength training with machines into their program. This can be accomplished through the Daily 16 Program described in paragraph 3a, and applying the principles listed in section 2.

Strength training can be broadly separated into two categories, general and specific.

(1) General strength training. This type of training strengthens the muscular system by focusing on a full body workout for strength and size. In this type of training, the major muscle groups are exercised without a specific task or functional goal in mind. This type of strength training contributes to overall health.

(2) Specific strength training. This type of strength training is task specific. For example, Marines desiring to climb a rope better would do rope climb training wearing body armor, and focus their training on muscles involved in rope climbing. A company of Marines expecting to operate in hilly terrain would focus their strength training on lower body strength.

b. **Endurance.** Two types of endurance training are needed for a Marine to meet the physical demands of combat, aerobic and anaerobic.

    (1) Aerobic endurance. Aerobic activity, meaning "in the presence of oxygen", is categorized by physical demands that are sub-maximal (not "all out") and involve activity that is continuous in nature (lasting more than 3-5 minutes). Two examples are road marching and long distance running.

    (2) Anaerobic endurance. Anaerobic activity, meaning "without oxygen", is categorized by physical demands that are high intensity and of shorter (less than 2-3 minutes) duration. Examples are rope climbing, most forms of weight lifting and running short, quick distances.

c. **Mobility.** Mobility training is geared towards improving quality of movement. Quality of movement depends on the following:

    (1) Posture
    (2) Balance and stability
    (3) Agility
    (4) Coordination
    (5) Power
    (6) Speed
    (7) Flexibility

2. **Principles of Physical Conditioning.** There are several different principles to consider when developing an effective PCP:

a. **Progression:** Training programs must incorporate a systematic means to increase training load.

b. **Regularity:** To realize a training effect, training programs must be conducted at least 3-4 times per week.

c. **Overload:** Only when the various systems of the body are overloaded will they become able to handle greater load.

d. **Variety:** Varying a program from time to time maintains interest and prevents staleness.

e. **Recovery:** Essential for allowing the systems overloaded during training to adapt and become stronger.

f. **Balance:** Balanced training programs ensure that all the components of physical fitness conditioning (strength, endurance, mobility) are properly addressed.

g. **Specificity:** Training that is specific in nature yields specific gains. For example, stationary bike riding is of little value in improving running.

3. **Specific Physical Conditioning Programs.** Commanding Officers who strive to augment their unit's PCP should use innovative combinations of the types of exercise defined below:

a. **"Daily 16" Program.** The "Daily 16" Program is a comprehensive series of warm-up, conditioning, and cool-down exercises replacing the former Daily 7 Program. This all-encompassing program can be incorporated into any unit aerobic or anaerobic training session, or can be used as a conditioning session in and of itself.

    (1) The "Daily 16" warm-up exercises facilitate gradual distribution of blood flow to the muscles, preparing both the cardiovascular and musculoskeletal systems for the exercise session, by effectively targeting both the upper and lower body. The increased blood flow to the muscles produces a warming effect, increasing the elasticity of the muscles and connective tissue, which is believed to reduce injury.

    (2) The "Daily 16" conditioning exercises provide a total body workout through the proper execution of traditional calisthenics.

Conditioning exercises can be used as a workout session in and of themselves, or to augment the main fitness event (e.g., squad ability run or obstacle course).

    (3) The "Daily 16" cool-down exercises (which are basically the same as the warm-up exercises) allow the body to gradually return to the pre-exercise state.

b. **Occupational Conditioning.** This training is comprised of general physical conditioning exercises that will develop and maintain strength, endurance, and the physical skills necessary to sustain a Marine during combat. Good examples of occupational conditioning that prepares Marines to successfully handle the demands of their particular billet are: Physical Readiness Training (PRT), progressive load-bearing marches, martial arts training, dry net training, Military Operation in Urban Terrain (MOUT) training, combat water survival training, obstacle course and confidence course.

c. **Competitive Conditioning.** Competitive conditioning activities consist of teams or individuals competing against an opponent to win. This includes a combination of sports and military skills designed to foster the unit's combat readiness, competitive spirit and esprit de corps, (e.g., speed-march reaction courses, orienteering, and water-can re-supply/stretcher/fireman carry relays).

d. **Alternate Aerobic Conditioning.** In cases of lower limb injury or related physical/medical conditions, which often result in light/limited duty that prevents running or hiking, Marines may opt to perform other low impact activities to supplement the requirement for cardiovascular training.

Swimming, cycling, cross-country skiing, stair stepping, and rowing are excellent examples of low impact, endurance exercises that provide good augmentation or substitution to running/hiking regimens. For example, the advantages of swimming include the use of all major muscle groups during exercise, reduced lower body stress due to partial body weight being supported by the water, and the absence of impact on bones and joints.

Additionally, the body's position in the water increases the efficiency of the circulation back to the heart during exercise. Although these types of aerobic training alternatives may not improve overall running ability (e.g., speed and endurance), it can enhance a current running/hiking regimen, while minimizing related injuries.

EXECUTION OF THE PFT. The standard PFT consists of three events that measure cardiovascular endurance, and muscular strength and endurance. Male Marines will perform dead-hang pull-ups, abdominal crunches and a 3.0-mile run. Female Marines will perform the flexed-arm hang, abdominal crunches, and a 3.0-mile run.

1. Individual performance on each PFT event will be executed as follows:

a. Dead Hang Pull-up/Chin-up. The goal of the pull-up event is for the Marine to execute as many accurate and complete pull-ups as possible before dropping off the bar. The procedures are:

(1) This is not a timed event.

(2) Sweatshirts will be removed during the conduct of the pull-up event in order to observe the lockout of the elbows with each repetition.

(3) Assistance to the bar with a step up, being lifted up, or jumping up is authorized. Any assistance up to the bar will not be used to continue into the first pull-up.

(4) Grasp the bar with both palms facing either forward or to the rear.

(5) The correct "starting position" begins when the Marine's arms are fully extended beneath the bar, feet are free from touching the ground or any bar mounting assist, and the body is motionless.

(6) Marine's legs may be positioned in a straight or bent position, but may not be raised above the waist.

(7) One repetition consists of raising the body with the arms until the chin is above the bar, and then lowering the body until the arms are fully extended; repeat the exercise. At no time during the execution of this event can a Marine rest his chin on the bar.

(8) The intent is to execute a vertical dead hang pull-up. A certain amount of inherent body movement will occur as the pull-up is executed. However, the intent is to avoid a pendulum-like motion that enhances ones ability to execute the dead-hang pull-up. Whipping, kicking, kipping of the body or legs, or any leg movement used to assist in the vertical progression of the pull-up is not authorized. If observed, the repetition will not count for score.

(9) A repetition will be counted when an accurate, complete pull-up is performed.

b. Flexed-Arm Hang. The goal of the flexed-arm hang event is for a Marine to hang (maintain elbow flexion) for as long as possible.

(1) This is a timed event.

(2) Sweatshirts will be removed during the conduct of the flexed-arm hang event in order to observe when the Marine has completely locked-out the elbows.

(3) Assistance to the bar with a step up, being lifted up, or jumping up to the start position is authorized.

(4) The bar must be grasped with both palms facing either forward or to the rear.

(5) The correct starting position begins when the Marine's arms are flexed at the elbow, the chin is held above the bar and not touching it, and the body is motionless. At no time during the execution of this event can a Marine rest her chin on the bar.

(6) Marines are authorized to drop down below the bar, however, some degree of elbow flexion must be maintained. Once a Marine's arms are fully extended or the Marine drops off the bar, the clock will stop.

c. Abdominal Crunch. The goal of the abdominal crunch event is for a Marine to execute as many proper and complete crunches as possible within the prescribed time limit.

(1) Two-minute time limit.

(2) On a flat surface Marines will lie flat on their back with shoulder blades touching the deck, knees will be bent and both feet will be flat on the deck.

(3) The arms will be folded across the chest or ribcage with no gap existing between the arms and chest or ribcage. The arms must remain in constant contact with chest or ribcage, when raising the upper body from the starting posi-

tion until the forearms or elbows touch the thighs and then returning to the starting position with the shoulder blades touching the deck.

(4) The buttocks will remain in constant contact with the deck throughout the event. No arching of the lower back or lifting the buttocks is permitted.

(5) An assistant may be used to hold the Marine's legs or feet, below the knees in whatever manner that is most comfortable for the Marine. Kneeling or sitting on the Marine's feet is permitted.

(6) A single repetition consists of raising the upper body from the start position until the forearms or elbows touch the thighs, then returning to the starting position touching the shoulder blades to the deck. When an accurate and complete abdominal crunch is performed, a repetition will be counted.

d. 3.0 Mile Run. The goal is for a Marine to complete the measured course as quickly as possible.

(1) This is a timed event.

(2) Marines will run three (3) miles over a reasonably level surface.

(3) The two (2) Marines monitoring the run portion of the PFT will synchronize their watches in advance. On the command to start, both Marines will start their watches simultaneously when the last Marine passes the starting point. One Marine will remain at the start/finish and the second Marine will go to the halfway point (1.5 mile mark). Both Marines will call out the split or finishing time as appropriate, as each Marine passes.

(4) An indoor or outdoor track is permissible for the conduct of the 3.0-mile run.

DAILY 16 PROGRAM

1. Background

The Daily 16 Program is a comprehensive series of warm-up, conditioning, and cool-down exercises; it replaces the former Daily 7. The Daily 16 warm-up exercises facilitate gradual distribution of blood flow to the muscles, preparing both the cardiovascular and musculoskeletal systems for the exercise session, by effectively targeting both the upper and lower body. The increased blood flow to the muscles produces a warming effect, increasing the elasticity of the muscles and connective tissues, which is believed to reduce injury risks. The Daily 16 condi-

tioning exercises include traditional calisthenics that are safe in providing a total body workout, which can vary in duration, degree of difficulty and level of intensity. The Daily 16 cool-down exercises (the same exercises used in the warm-up) allow the body to gradually return to the pre-exercise state.

There are three different ways the Daily 16 Program can be used during physical training:

Daily 16 Warm-Up (D16WU). A series of warm-up and dynamic stretching exercises that should be conducted prior to the main activity (e.g., formation run, obstacle course, circuit course, etc.), of every physical training session.

Daily 16 Workout (D16WO). A series of conditioning exercises that can be used as augmentation to another conditioning activity (circuit course, PFT, etc.), or can be used as a conditioning activity in and of itself by simply increasing the number of repetitions or by slowing down the execution of the repetition.

Daily 16 Cool-Down (D16CD). A series of cool-down exercises that should be used as the final activity of a physical training session.

2. Daily 16 Warm Up and Dynamic Stretching Descriptions

A. Warm Up Exercises:

(1) Heel to Toe Rocking. Starting position is standing with feet together and hands on hips.

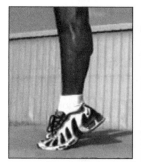

Photo Courtesy of Mr. Timothy L. Bockelman

Rock back onto the heels, pause, then rock forward onto the toes and pause. Repeat ten to fifteen repetitions.

(2) Partial Squats. Starting position is standing with feet shoulder width apart, arms at the

sides (1). Keeping the heels on the deck, partially squat until hands are near mid-calf. The knees should only bend to about 60 degrees, just short of a sitting position (2). Return to the starting position (3). Repeat ten to fifteen repetitions.

1/3   2

Photo Courtesy of Mr. Timothy L. Bockelman

(3) <u>Butt Kicks.</u> Starting position is standing with feet shoulder width apart, hands on hips. Shift weight onto the right foot and quickly bend the left knee five times, bringing the left heel toward the buttocks. Switch legs and repeat. Repeat the whole cycle two or three times, until a total of fifteen to twenty repetitions with are done on each leg.

Photo Courtesy of Mr. Timothy L. Bockelman

(4) <u>Double Time in Place.</u> Starting position is standing with arms at the sides. Slowly begin to run in place and gradually increase speed. While double-timing, conduct "punches to the front (1)" (throw easy punches to the front of the body). Switch to "punches to the sky (2)" (throw easy punches straight up to the sky). Finish with "arm circles (3)" (begin small then transition to large arm circles; repeat in other direction).

1   2

3

Photo Courtesy of Mr. Timothy L. Bockelman

(5) <u>Neck Flexion and Extension.</u> Starting position is standing with feet shoulder width apart, hands on hips. Flex the neck forward bringing the chin toward the chest, pause. Extend the head back and pause. Repeat for five to ten repetitions.

Photo Courtesy of Mr. Timothy L. Bockelman

(6) <u>Neck Lateral Flexion.</u> Starting position is standing with feet shoulder width apart, hands on hips. Tilt the head to the left side, bringing the left ear toward the left shoulder, pause. Switch sides and repeat. Repeat for five to ten repetitions.

Photo Courtesy of Mr. Timothy L. Bockelman

(7) <u>Trunk Flexion and Extension.</u> Starting position is standing with feet shoulder width apart, hands on hips. Flex the trunk forward to about a forty-five degree angle and pause (1). Extend the trunk backward bringing a slight hyperextension of the trunk and pause (2). Repeat for five to ten repetitions.

1   2

Photo Courtesy of Mr. Timothy L. Bockelman

(8) <u>Trunk Lateral Flexion.</u> Starting position is standing with feet shoulder width apart, hands on hips. Bend the trunk to the left side (1), pause, then switch to the right side (2) and pause. Repeat for five to ten repetitions. Proceed to the Stretching Exercises.

1   2

b. Dynamic Stretching Exercises:

(1) <u>Upper Back Stretch.</u> Starting position is standing with feet shoulder width apart. Extend the arms and clasp the hands in front of the chest. Push the arms forward, rounding the shoulders and upper back. Hold the position for 10 seconds and breath naturally. The stretch should be felt over the upper back.

Photo Courtesy of Mr. Timothy L. Bockelman

(2) <u>Chest Stretch.</u> Starting position is standing with feet shoulder width apart. Clasp hands together behind the lower back, palms up. Pull the arms up toward the head. Hold the position for 10 seconds and breath naturally. The stretch should be felt in the front of the chest and shoulders.

Photo Courtesy of Mr. Timothy L. Bockelman

(3) <u>Modified Hurdler Stretch.</u> Starting position is in the sitting position. Extend the left leg out while tucking the right leg in front of the hips with the knee pointing outward. Bend the torso forward toward the left knee. The stretching should be felt over the back of the left thigh. Hold the position for 10 seconds and breath naturally. Switch sides and repeat.

Photo Courtesy of Mr. Timothy L. Bockelman

(4) <u>Hip and Back Stretch.</u> Starting position is in the sitting position. Extend the right leg straight out and cross the left leg over the right leg by bending the left knee and placing the left foot on the deck next to the right knee. Turn the upper torso to the left pushing the left knee to the right with the right elbow. Hold the position for 10 seconds and breath naturally. The stretch should be felt over the lower back and left hip. Switch sides and repeat.

Photo Courtesy of Mr. Timothy L. Bockelman

(5) <u>Groin Stretch.</u> Starting position is in the sitting position with both knees bent and the bottoms of the feet together. Grasp the feet and gently push the knees with the elbows toward the deck. Hold the position for 10 seconds and breath naturally. The stretch should be felt over the inside of both thighs.

Photo Courtesy of Mr. Timothy L. Bockelman

(6) <u>Calf Stretch.</u> Starting position is standing with arms at the sides. Place the left foot approximately two feet forward and slightly bend the right knee. Lean forward toward the left foot pointing the left toes up to the sky. Hold the position for 10 seconds and breath naturally. Grabbing the left foot and gently pulling it towards you can increase the level of intensity. The stretch should be felt over the left calf. Switch sides and repeat.

Photo Courtesy of Mr. Timothy L. Bockelman

(7) <u>Iliotibial Band (ITB) Stretch.</u> Starting position is standing with arms at the sides. Place the left foot behind and a few inches to the right of the right foot. Bring the left arm over the head. Place your body weight on the left leg and bend at the waist to the right. Hold the position for 10 seconds and breath naturally. The stretch should be felt over the left hip. Switch sides and repeat.

Photo Courtesy of Mr. Timothy L. Bockelman

(8) <u>Hamstring Stretch.</u> Starting position is lying down with the back flat against the deck. Bring the left knee toward the chest grasping the left leg just below the knee. Gently straighten the left knee and hold for the count.

The right leg should remain on the deck. Hold the position for 10 seconds and breath naturally. The stretch should be felt on the back of the left thigh. Switch sides and repeat.

Photo Courtesy of Mr. Timothy L. Bockelman

(9) <u>Shoulder and Neck Stretch.</u> Starting position is standing with feet shoulder width apart. Move both arms behind the back and grasp the left wrist with the right hand. Tilt the head to the right and pull the left arm to the right. Hold the position for 10 seconds and breath naturally. The stretch should be felt over the left shoulder and left side of the neck. Switch sides and repeat.

Photo Courtesy of Mr. Timothy L. Bockelman

(10) <u>Triceps Stretch.</u> Starting position is standing, arms at the sides. Bend the left elbow and bring the left arm up and back placing the left hand between the shoulder blades. Gently pull the left elbow with the right hand behind the head. Hold the position for 10 seconds and breath naturally. The stretch should be felt over the back of the upper arm. Switch sides and repeat.

Photo Courtesy of Mr. Timothy L. Bockelman

(11) <u>Quadriceps Stretch.</u> Starting position is lying down on the left side. Bend the left hip and knee to 90 degrees. Grasp the right ankle with the right hand and pull the right knee straight back. Do not hyperextend the lower back. Hold the position for 10 seconds and breath naturally. The stretch should be felt over the front of the right thigh. Switch sides and repeat.

(12) <u>Lying Down ITB Stretch.</u> Starting position is lying down on the deck. Bring the left leg with the knee straight across the body (1). Hold the position for 10 seconds and breath naturally. The stretch should be felt over the left hip. Switch sides and repeat (2).

1

Photo Courtesy of Mr. Timothy L. Bockelman

2

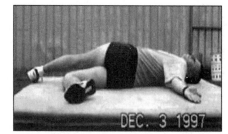

Photo Courtesy of Mr. Timothy L. Bockelman

(13) <u>Posterior Shoulder Stretch.</u> Starting position is standing with feet shoulder width apart, arms at the sides. Bend the left elbow and bring the left arm across the chest. Give a gentle pull with the right hand. Hold the position for 10 seconds and breath naturally. The stretch should be felt over the posterior left shoulder. Switch sides and repeat.

Photo Courtesy of Mr. Timothy L. Bockelman

(14) <u>Hip Flexor Stretch.</u> Starting position is standing, hands on hips. Step the left foot forwards three to four feet. Place the right knee on the deck. Gently move the left knee forward. Hold the position for 10 seconds and breath naturally. The stretch should be felt over the front of the right thigh and hip. Switch sides and repeat.

Photo Courtesy of Mr. Timothy L. Bockelman

(15) <u>Single-Leg Low Back Stretch.</u> Starting position is lying with the back flat against the deck. Bring the right knee toward the chest grasping the right knee. Gently pull the knee tight into the chest. The left leg should remain on the deck. Hold the position for 10 seconds and breath naturally. The stretch should be felt along the low back to the right buttock. Switch sides and repeat.

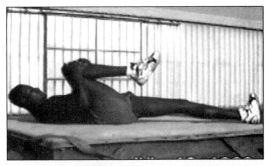

Photo Courtesy of Mr. Timothy L. Bockelman

(16) <u>Prone Abdominal Stretch.</u> Starting position is lying on the stomach with the hands placed near the shoulders as if in the down position of a push-up. Slowly raise the upper body up, keeping the waist on the deck. Hold the position for 10 seconds and breath naturally. The stretch should be felt over the abdomen.

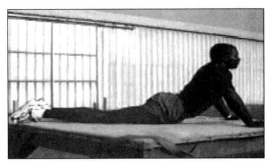

Photo Courtesy of Mr. Timothy L. Bockelman

3. <u>Daily 16 Conditioning Exercise Descriptions</u>

(1) <u>Pushups.</u> Starting position is lying on your stomach with hands shoulder width apart, toes on the deck, and elbows, back, and knees straight. On the first and third count, lower the chest to the deck; bend the elbows to at least 90 degrees (1/3). On the second and fourth count, extend the arms back to the starting position (2/4). This exercise conditions the chest, primarily in the anterior shoulder region, and secondarily, the triceps.

Photo Courtesy of Mr. Timothy L. Bockelman

(2) <u>Crunches.</u> Starting position is lying on the back with the hips bent to 90 degrees and the knees bent, feet off the deck. Bend the elbows to 90 degrees and fold the arms across the chest or ribcage. On the first and third count raise the upper torso off the deck touching the thighs with the forearms (1/3). On the second and fourth count, return to the starting position (2/4). The arms must remain in constant contact with the chest/ribcage when executing the crunch. This should be done in a slow and controlled manner. This exercise conditions the abdominal muscles.

(3) <u>Dirty Dogs.</u> Starting position is on the hands and knees. On the first and third count raise the left leg to the side, while keeping the knee bent (1/3). On the second and fourth count return the leg to the starting position (2/4). Switch sides and repeat. This exercise conditions the hip abductors.

Photo Courtesy of Mr. Timothy L. Bockelman

(4) <u>Wide Pushups.</u> Starting position is lying on the stomach with hands beyond shoulder width apart, toes on the ground, and elbows, back, and knees straight. On the first and third count, lower the chest to the deck, bending the elbows to at least 90 degrees (1/3). On the second and fourth count, extend the

arms back to the starting position (2/4). This exercise conditions the chest, primarily in the anterior shoulder region, and secondarily, the triceps. With the wider hand position, the chest muscles increase their workload.

1/3

2/4

Photo Courtesy of Mr. Timothy L. Bockelman

(5) <u>Dive Bomber Pushups.</u> Starting position is lying on the stomach with hands and toes on the deck, and elbows and knees straight. The hands will be slightly beyond shoulder width apart. The hips will be raised up and the shoulders will be behind the hands. On the first count, lower the chest down and forward to the deck, the shoulders will be even with the hands (1). On the second count, continue forward extending the elbows where now the shoulders are in front of the hands (2). On the third count, reverse the direction lowering the chest down and back to the deck, the shoulders will be even with hands (3). On the fourth count, continue back and up to the starting position (4). This exercise is done in a smooth, continuous motion. This exercise conditions the chest and anterior shoulder primarily, and secondarily, the triceps through a greater ranger of motion.

1

2

3

4

Photo Courtesy of Mr. Timothy L. Bockelman

(6) <u>Elbow to Knee Crunches.</u> Starting position is lying on the back with the right foot flat on the deck and the left foot crossed over the right knee, and the arms crossed over the chest. On the first and third count, raise the upper torso off the deck rotating to the left touching the right elbow to the left thigh (1/3). On the second and fourth count, return to the starting position (2/4). This exercise should be done in a slow and controlled manner. Switch sides and repeat. This exercise conditions the abdominal muscles with more emphasis on the oblique.

1/3

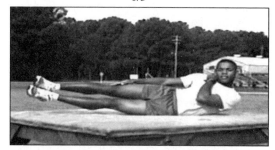

1/3

2/4

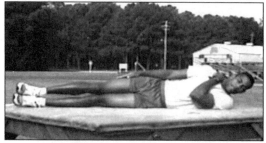

2/4

Photo Courtesy of Mr. Timothy L. Bockelman

Photo Courtesy of Mr. Timothy L. Bockelman

(7) <u>Side Crunches.</u> Starting position is lying on the left side with the left arm across the chest and right arm along the side of the body. On the first and third count, raise the upper torso and feet off the deck sliding the right hand down the thigh (1/3). On the second and fourth count, return to the starting position (2/4). Switch sides and repeat. This exercise conditions the abdominal muscles with emphasis on the internal oblique and external oblique.

(8) <u>Prone Flutter Kicks.</u> Starting position is lying on the stomach. On the first count raise the left leg off the deck while the right leg remains on the deck (1). On the second count, lower the left leg to the starting position (2). On the third count, raise the right leg off the deck while the left leg remains on the deck (3). On the fourth count, lower the right leg to the starting position (4). This exercise conditions the muscles that extend the hip and back.

1

2

1/3

3

2/4

Photo Courtesy of Mr. Timothy L. Bockelman

4

Photo Courtesy of Mr. Timothy L. Bockelman

(9) <u>Back Extension.</u> Starting position is lying on the stomach with hands behind the head. On the first and third count, raise the upper torso and legs off the deck (1/3). On the second and fourth count, lower the upper torso and legs to the starting position (2/4). This exercise conditions the muscles that extend the back.

(10) <u>Donkey Kicks.</u> Starting position is on the hands and knees. On the first and third count, kick the left leg back and up straightening the knee (1/3). On the second and fourth count, bend the knee and hip bringing the left knee into the chest (2/4). The back should not hyperextend during this exercise. Switch sides and repeat. This exercise conditions the muscles that extend the hip.

1/3

Photo Courtesy of Mr. Timothy L. Bockelman

(11) <u>Hip Abduction.</u> Staring position is lying on the left side with the right leg bent setting the right foot in front of the left knee. On the first and third count, raise the straight left leg off the deck squeezing the thighs together (1/3). On the second and fourth count, lower the left leg to the starting position (2/4). The left toes should be pointing straight forward, not to the sky. Switch sides and repeat. This exercise conditions the muscles on the inner thigh.

1/3

2/4

Photo Courtesy of Mr. Timothy L. Bockelman

(12) <u>Side Leg Raises.</u> Starting position is lying on the left side with the left knee bent, the hip vertical and the toes on the right foot pointing forward, not to the sky. On the first and third count, raise the right leg approximately 18 inches leading with the heel (1/3). The toes will still point forward, not to the sky. On the second and fourth count, lower the right leg to the starting position (2/4). Switch sides and repeat. This exercise conditions the muscles on the side of the hip and thigh.

1/3

2/4

Photo Courtesy of Mr. Timothy L. Bockelman

(13) <u>Steam Engines.</u> Starting position is standing with the feet shoulder width apart and hands behind the head. On the first count, touch the right elbow to the left knee by bending and raising the left knee and twisting and bending the upper torso to the left (1). On the second count, return to the starting position (2). On the third count, touch the left elbow to the right knee by bending and raising the right knee and twisting and bending the upper torso to the right (3). On the fourth count, return to the starting position (4).

1

2

3

4

Photo Courtesy of Mr. Timothy L. Bockelman

(14) <u>Lunges.</u> Staring position is standing with the feet shoulder width apart and hands on the hips. On the first count, touch the right knee to the deck by stepping forward with the left foot and bending both knees (1). On the second count, return to the starting position (2). On the third count, touch the left knee to the deck by stepping forward with the right foot and bending both knees (3). On the fourth count, return to the starting position (4). Do not bend the forward knee more than 90 degrees. This exercise should be done in a slow and controlled cadence. This exercise conditions the muscles that extend the hip and knee of the forward leg.

1

2

3

4

(15) <u>Side Straddle Hops.</u> Starting position is standing with the feet together and arms at the sides. On the first and third count, jump and land with both feet just beyond shoulder width apart while bringing the hands together overhead (1/3). On the second and fourth count, jump back to the starting position (2/4).

1/3

2/4

(16) <u>Diamond Pushups.</u> Starting position is lying on the stomach with hands under the chest, palms flat on the deck, thumb and index finger of each

hand touching each other. The hands should form a diamond between them. Legs are spread slightly more than shoulder-width apart, toes on the ground, and elbows, back, and knees straight. On the first and third count, lower the chest to the deck, trying to touch the chest to the hands, bending the elbows to at least 90 degrees. On the second and fourth count, extend the arms back to the starting position. This exercise conditions the chest, primarily in the pectoral region, and secondarily, the triceps. With the close hand position, the chest muscles increase their workout.

Daily 16 Warm-up/Cool-down, Stretching and Exercise Cards

STRETCHING CARD A

Chest Stretch
Triceps Stretch
Posterior Shoulder Stretch
Iliotibial Band (ITB) Stretch
Modified Hurdler Stretch
Hip and Back Stretch
Quadriceps Stretch
Low Back Stretch
Abdominal Stretch

STRETCHING CARD B

Upper Back Stretch
Chest Stretch
Shoulder and Neck Stretch
Triceps Stretch
Posterior Shoulder Stretch
Lying Down (ITB) Stretch
Modified Hurdler Stretch
Groin Stretch
Calf Stretch

STRETCHING CARD C

Active Hamstring Stretch
Groin Stretch
Hip Flexor Stretch
Low Back Stretch
(ITB) Stretch
Calf Stretch
Neck Stretch
Upper Back Stretch
Chest Stretch

EXERCISE CARD 1

Wide Pushups
Donkey Kicks
Crunches
Dive Bomber Pushups
Dirty Dogs
Side Crunches
Back Extensions
Lunges
Side Straddle Hops

EXERCISE CARD 2

Pushups
Crunches
Side Leg Raises
Diamond Pushups
Elbow-to-Knee Crunches
Prone Flutter Kicks
Hip Abduction
Lunges
Steam Engines

WARM-UP/COOL DOWN CARD

Toe-Heel Rocking
Partial Squats
Butt Kicks
Trunk Bends
Neck Bends
Run in Place
Punch to the Front
Punch to the Sky
Arm Circles
* Stretch Card (10 Seconds)

Running

In order to improve your running you must *run, run, run.* Surveys indicate that millions of Americans either jog or run regularly. While a small percentage of these people race competitively, this vast majority run in order to enhance their personal fitness or their health. The Marine Corps recognizes the importance of running, and each Marine is required to exercise a minimum of three hours weekly, with the intent being that all Marines run regularly. Do you have any idea why regular running is so important to fitness? The answers are not all readily apparent, but this much we know.

Running stresses many of the major bodily systems. As these systems adjust to stress they become more efficient, capable and physiologically stronger.

One such system is the circular-respiratory system. Running forces the heart to pump blood throughout the body at a much faster pace than is necessary when the body is at rest. The blood carries much needed oxygen to the body's cells and washes away carbon dioxide and cellular waste products which accumulate during activity. The need for oxygen forces the lungs to increase their capacity by opening previously dormant air sacs. The increased stress on the heart causes it to grow in strength and in ability to pump large quantities of blood. All these changes result in increased circular-respiratory endurance (wind).

The continuous motion of running strengthens the muscles of the trunk and legs and helps control weight and maintain appearance.

Regular strenuous running is an effective way to control nervous tensions or anxiety. A hard run requires a great deal of effort and concentration, which takes the mind off everyday problems.

Running which is rigorous enough to pump blood throughout the body aids in the nourishment of the body tissues by the circulatory system and aids in the proper regulation of the body's chemical makeup by stimulating the endocrine (glandular) system.

Proper running form. A good form is just as important to the Marine who runs as the offhand, kneeling, sitting and prone positions are for the Marine shooter. Figure 13-7 shows ideal form: the head and torso are erect, the arms swing loosely from front to rear in a relaxed manner, and the fists should be loose or open. Clenched or tight fists can cause cramps. The hips should rotate slightly with each stride following the direction of the lead knee forward and upward. The feet should land heels first followed by the rest of the foot as the center of the body weight passes over the foot. The toes should always point straight ahead. The planting of the foot upon impact should naturally be centered under the body. Although the type of run (sprint, uphill, jog, etc.) or individual build and style may require slight modification of these general principles, certain rules should never be broken:

- Carry the body in a relaxed fashion, loose and natural. Over or under striding can cause unnatural fatigue, poor performance, and even injury.
- Breathing should be as relaxed as possible. Never force your breathing. This will cause cramping. Breathe through the mouth and nose naturally.

Running should be frequent, with approximately three to five workouts a week best for most young Marines. Not every Marine's body is structurally suited for running, so for some, too much running in a Physical Fitness Program may lead to injuries, illness, and loss of interest until such time as each individual Marine is proficient enough to handle the added miles. Too little running, however, will not help you improve at all. Two or three good runs a week will sustain an acceptable level of fitness for all but the serious competitors; however, each individual should already be at a level of proficiency in their running to benefit from these few runs. Marines who have difficulty in their runs will benefit little to nothing from only two to three runs a week.

How far? The key to success is to gauge your present ability and determine what you would reasonably like to accomplish. A self-inventory of your running ability may be made by looking at your last PFT three-mile run. If you ran slower than 26 minutes, you should start a moderate running program of two to four miles, three to five times a week. If you ran between 20 and 26 minutes, you may start with three to fives miles, four to six times a week. If you ran in less than 20 minutes, you're a good runner and may train harder (e.g., four to eight miles daily up to six times a week). But keep in mind, these figures are guidelines and do not apply to everyone equally. Also the length and duration of a run is only one of the training variables involved. Other important considerations include how you feel when you start, the environment you're running in and the intensity (speed, pace) of the run.

Training variations. The following methods may be used to increase speed and endurance and to decrease the time needed to recover (useful in many team sports). The type of training you choose should be as close as possible to the type you have to perform in your sport or activity.

Wind sprints. These build speed and leg power. Distances should range from 30 to 50 yards. Start with 4-14 repetitions with at least 10 and no more than 30 seconds between sprints. Effort should be high but just under maximum in order to avoid injury. Remember, *the aim is to train, not strain.*

Fartlek. This is a Swedish word meaning "speed play." Usually performed on a forest path or trail, the runner varies his pace spontaneously by setting immediate goals of running at three-quarter speed to the top of a hill or sprinting to a target tree in a meadow or running backwards to the next bend in the trail. This form of training increases stamina and should cover a middle distance of one and a half to four miles. For variety and additional conditioning, perform five repetitions of pushups, situps and bends and thrusts every so often (from 3 to 12 sets on runs ranging from 20 to 45 minutes). This program will develop your ability to recover quickly and keep going strong.

Interval running. This is much the same as fartlek running except that the variations in pace are preplanned and are usually run around a track or a marked field. This form of running is more complex and is done in sets. For example, on a field you might walk 20 yards, jog 20 yards, run 40 yards at half speed and then sprint the last 20 yards of a 100-yard distance. Then you'd turn around and start the next repetition of a six-repetition set. Or if a track is available, you might just run the straightaways at three-quarter speed and jog the turns. Whatever your method, it should match up with what you ultimately hope to be able to perform.

Speed. This is running at greater than 80 percent of your maximum effort for a very short period of time. This form of training will help you increase your speed and will also help you to maintain a moderate effort and good form over a long distance.

Resistance. The most popular forms of resistance running are up hills or across sandy beaches. The distance should be kept short (60-70 yards) and the effort maintained (50-80 percent of maximum). Four to eight repetitions make up the first set as you begin to develop power. Work up to 12 repetitions. Running with weights is another option to consider; however, never use leg (ankle) weights as they can injure the legs, ankles and feet.

Cross-Country. This run is laid out on a course over natural terrain including fields, hills and woods. It may be used for conditioning or competition and has been a Marine favorite for many years. Comfortable distances range from 5-10 miles. Although training should be often (three to five times weekly), competition should never be more than biweekly, because the body needs time to recover following a peak effort. These runs strengthen leg muscles, develop circular-respiratory endurance, and enhance agility and coordination.

Fig.13-7. Proper Running Form.

Negative Effects of Physical Training

Fatigue

In addition to muscular soreness and stiffness, the Marine who exercises for fitness will experience fatigue as a result of exertions. Fatigue is a feeling of tiredness which results from prolonged or intense physical or mental activity. Fatigue is a regulator in that it prevents us from damaging our body's systems by overexertion (too much work). Fatigue may be neuromuscular, organic or mental.

Neuromuscular fatigue is indicated by cramps, heaviness in the limbs and failure of the muscular system to perform. It is temporary and normally not dangerous. Examples of neuromuscular fatigue would be the cramps in the stomach muscles when you've done just about your maximum in situps or the heaviness felt in your legs at the end of a long run.

Organic fatigue is normally felt in the inner organs and is indicated by hyperventilation (uncontrollably high rate of breathing), heat illness (the failure of the body's cooling system to maintain the normal temperature range), and nausea or other illness.

Mental fatigue may be brought on by nervousness, low morale, depression and lack of rest. Energy is spent on worry and through muscular tension. Chronic mental fatigue contributes to an inability to exert maximum physical effort. This lack of tolerance for effort is called the *effort syndrome*.

Fatigue is natural and normal. Everyone experiences it in one of its forms. It is important to be able to recognize fatigue, because unchecked fatigue will lead to exhaustion and collapse. An example of exhaustion is the case of a runner who has gone far past the point of a good maximum effort, is starting to experience severe muscular pain and an inability to focus vision, nausea, a very high body temperature (104 degrees F or higher) and an uncontrollable shortness of breath. If that person continues to run, one or more body systems will fail and cause collapse. A good warning sign of overexertion is a strong pounding sensation in the temples of the individual with each pulse.

Sleep and Rest

Nature's way of eliminating fatigue is through sleep and rest. Our need for sleep and rest is obvious, and the Marine Corps plans accordingly. Even during basic training, which may be the most demanding experience a Marine faces, each recruit normally receives a full eight hours of sleep. The sleep is necessary in order for a recruit's body to recover from one training day and build its reserves of energy for the next.

Sleep. Sleep is a state of unconsciousness produced by the body's central nervous system for the purposes of restoring and rebuilding its capabilities. The characteristics of sleep are relaxation of the muscles and of the mind. While all people do not require the same amount of sleep, eight hours are recommended for most young adults. Getting the proper amount of sleep is important. Too much sleep can cause you to be lazy. Too little sleep causes irritability and a reduction in the mental powers of reasoning and learning.

Rest. Rest is a relaxation of the mind and body. The characteristics of rest are a lessening of physical and mental activities. The amount of time required for rest depends upon a person's age, level of fatigue and overall physical condition. An example of rest is the 10-minute break given during each hour of a forced march. Resting regularly during the day will increase both your effectiveness on the job and your enjoyment of your daily pursuits.

The Rewards of Physical Fitness

Physical fitness of a Marine is not a gift. Like the respect of your fellow Marines, it must be earned again and again. You must do it yourself. No one can do it for you. Self-improvement requires a hard, determined effort. But the reward is a strong, healthy body. You have all the information that you need. The rest is up to you.

Chapter Fourteen

Clothing & Equipment

CLOTHING

During combat operations, or in peacetime, it is important to properly maintain the clothing and equipment issued to you. To be prepared to deploy on short notice to a combat area, you must always have the required amount of clothing and equipment in your possession and it must be in serviceable condition.

In combat, supplying the individual with his or her needs is a critical problem. It is easy to see the problem when you consider that every pound of supplies used for the Vietnam War or Desert Storm, including heavy items such as ammunition and gasoline, had to be shipped halfway around the world.

Material will be expended in combat. However, it is not expected that equipment will be carelessly lost or destroyed. There are numerous examples where discarded equipment has cost lives in battle!

Minimum Clothing Allowance, Care, and Marking

When you entered the Marine Corps, you were issued certain items of clothing. It is your responsibility to maintain those items. If they become lost or unserviceable you have to replace them. (The only exception is in a combat zone where clothing is replaced at no cost when it becomes unserviceable or lost through no fault of your own.)

Minimum Allowance. The clothing you were issued at the recruit depot was the minimum allowance. It is the minimum amount that you are required to have at all times. A list of current allowances can be found in the Marine Corps 1020 Bulletin series; these allowances will change periodically. In addition to minimum clothing allowance, special issues are made to individuals assigned to certain types of duty such as recruiting, embassy duty, drill instructors, etc.

Annually, on your active duty base date, you receive an annual clothing allowance to assist you in maintaining your clothing. This money is included in your paycheck and is intended to be used to replace unserviceable clothing and to repair or alter serviceable clothing.

Care. No matter how well a uniform fits when it is new, it will not continue to look its best or keep its shape unless it is given proper care. The following hints may assist you in maintaining your uniforms:

- Coats should always be kept buttoned and large or heavy objects should never be carried in the pockets.
- When storing uniforms for a long time, remember that some of the items are wool and should be safeguarded against moths, mildew and unpleasant odors. Clean and mothproof your uniforms before putting them in storage.
- Spots and stains should be removed from uniforms as soon as possible. Dry cleaning establishments are best qualified to do this. Be sure to tell them what caused the spot in order to facilitate its removal. Specific guidance is contained in the Marine Corps Uniform Regulations, available in your company office.

Marking. Every article of uniform clothing in your possession except those issued on temporary loan (field jackets, cold weather clothing, etc.), shall be plainly and indelibly marked with your name. Marks shall be of a size appropriate to the article of clothing and the space available for marking. Letters will be not more than one-half inch in size. Marking machines, stencils, name tapes, or stamps may be used. Names are marked in black on light-colored material and utilities and in white on dark material. Marks will be placed so that they do not show when the clothing is worn. The precise location for marking is not specified except:

- *Bag, Duffel.* On the outside on the bottom of the bag.
- *Belts (Except Trouser Belts).* On the underside, near the buckle end.
- *Belts, Trouser, Web.* On one side only, as near the buckle end as possible.

- *Caps.* Inside on the sweatband.
- *Coats, Outercoats.* Inside the neckband.
- *Cover, Cap.* Inside the band.
- *Drawers.* On the plain waistband, near the front. Immediately below the stretch waistband, near the front.
- *Footwear.* Inside near the top.
- *Gloves*. Inside at the wrist.
- *Handbag.* Stenciled on the space provided.
- *Neckties (Male Marines).* On the inside of the neck-loop. (Hook-on ties: On the inside, near the top.)
- *Neckties/Necktabs (Women Marines).* On the underside of the left strap.
- *Shirts.* Inside the neckband.
- *Trousers, Skirts, Slacks.* Inside the waistband.
- *Undershirts.* On the inside back, near the neckband.

Designation of Uniform (Men)

Authorized uniforms for enlisted men are designated as blue dress "A," "B," "C" and "D;" service "A," "B," "C," "D" and blue-white dress uniform.

Except for those commands authorized the blue uniform, the uniform of the day will be the service uniform. For commands authorized the blue uniform supplementary allowance, the uniform of the day will be service or blue dress "B" or "C" at the discretion of the commander. The service uniform and the blue dress "B" uniform may be prescribed for leave or liberty.

Except for individuals assigned to the Department of State, commanders will prescribe the duty, liberty and leave uniform for Marines stationed outside the United States. All uniforms will conform with these regulations. Uniform regulations for Marines serving with the Department of State will be prescribed by Headquarters Marine Corps.

The wearing of blue uniforms of mixed materials by enlisted men is authorized. Gabardine coats and kersey trousers or vice versa may be worn on all occasions including formations.

Dress Uniforms

The blue dress "A" uniform shall be prescribed for parades, ceremonies, reviews and official social functions when the commander considers it desirable to pay special honors to the occasion. The uniform includes medals and may include breast insignia if prescribed by the commanding officer.

The blue-white dress "A" or "B" uniforms are the prescribed uniforms for the summer season, but are not authorized for leave and liberty. They consist of the same items as blue dress "A" and "B" except that the trousers shall be the standard white trousers as issued by the Marine Corps supply system. Black shoes are worn with this uniform.

The blue dress "B" uniform shall be prescribed for enlisted personnel when reporting for sea duty and for parades, ceremonies, and reviews, as determined by the commander. The dress "B" uniforms shall consist of the same items as the corresponding dress "A" uniforms except that ribbons shall be worn in lieu of medals.

The blue dress uniform without coat is designated as blue dress "C." The long sleeve khaki shirt, insignia of grade, ribbons, and service necktie with necktie clasp may be prescribed in lieu of the blue coat. In commands authorized the blue uniform, commanders may prescribe the blue dress "C" or "D" as the uniform of the day. These uniforms are authorized to be worn on leave or liberty. The uniform may be worn for honors and ceremonies where climate conditions preclude the comfortable wearing of the blue dress "A" or "B" uniforms.

Service Uniforms

The service uniform "A" appropriate to the season shall be prescribed for the following official military occasions:
- When reporting for duty on shore.
- When assigned duty as a member of a court-martial.

The designated service uniforms for male enlisted personnel shall be worn in accordance with the following:
- The service "A" uniform shall include the appropriate service coat. When service "A" uniforms are prescribed as the uniform of the day, it is considered appropriate to dispense with the wearing of the coat in office buildings within the confines of a military activity or establishment.
- The service "B" uniform shall consist of the same items of uniform as the service "A" uniform except that the service coat is not worn. When the coat is not deemed appropriate, commanders may, at their discretion, authorize the wearing of the service "B" uniform on base and in the immediate vicinity thereof, and for commuting to and from work.
- The quarter-length sleeve shirt with appropriate service trousers is designated as the service "C" uniform. During the winter season, commanders

may, at their discretion, when the weather requires, authorize the wearing of the service "C" uniform. This uniform may be worn as the uniform of the day, and for leave or liberty, unless otherwise prescribed by the commander, and may be prescribed for wear in formation at ceremonies on and off the military activity. This uniform shall not be worn for formal or semiformal social events.

• For regulations regarding the wearing of ribbons on shirts worn as outer garments, see subparagraph 5301, MCO P1020.34.

The summer weight polyester/wool service uniform may be worn interchangeably with the winter weight service uniform of poly/wool gabardine on a year-round basis at the option of the individual. Individuals are not authorized to mix service items of different materials.

Individuals may wear either the polyester/wool green or the poly/wool gabardine uniform on a year-round basis, for all formations, unless otherwise prescribed by the commander. These uniforms are being phased out and replaced with an all season green uniform.

Staff noncommissioned officers who elect to purchase officer-type uniforms may wear these uniforms at all times, including formations, in lieu of the comparable seasonal enlisted uniform.

Utility Uniform

The camouflage utility uniform is not authorized for wear except when in the field, for field type exercises, or for those work conditions wherein it is not practical to wear the service uniform. An exception to this is within the Fleet Marine Forces wherein the wear of the utility uniform by designated units is an enhancement of readiness.

The wearing of the utility uniform shall be as prescribed in paragraph 3037, MCO P1020.34.

Service Sweater

The green crew neck sweater may be worn in lieu of the service coat when the service uniform is prescribed, including leave and liberty. The sweater may be worn with either the long or quarter-length shirt (whichever is prescribed as the seasonal uniform shirt). When the sweater is worn with the long sleeve shirt, the necktie will not be worn, except when wearing the V-neck sweater. The top button of the shirt will be unbuttoned and the collar will be worn outside the sweater with the appropriate grade insignia. The sleeves of the sweater may be turned up; however, the sleeves should be of sufficient length to conceal the shirt cuff. The waistband of the sweater may be turned under; however, the length of the sweater should be sufficient to cover the belt.

The sweater may be worn with the camouflage utility uniform. When the sweater is worn with the camouflage utility uniform, it will be worn under the utility coat.

The sweater is not authorized for wear in formal formations and ceremonies, or parades on or off the military activity. It may be worn underneath the over-coat, raincoat, or field coat or windbreaker and can be worn during inspections at the commander's discretion.

When wearing the V-neck sweater, the tie will be worn and the appropriate grade insignia will be worn on the epaulet in accordance with regulations.

Wearing the Uniform (Men)

Long sleeve cuff. (See Fig. 14-1.) The long sleeve shall cover the wrist bone and extend to a point 7/8 inch from the thumb. A plus tolerance of ¼ inch is acceptable.

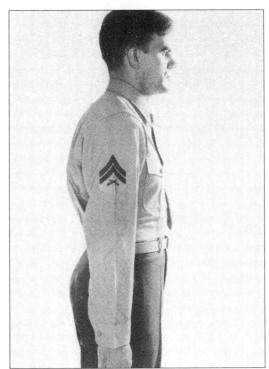

Fig. 14-1.

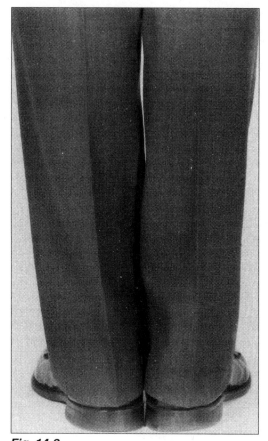

Fig. 14-2.

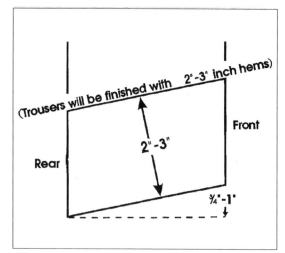

Fig. 14-3.

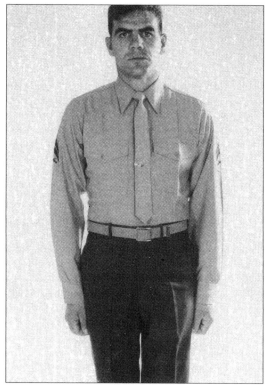

Fig. 14-4.

Trouser length (rear). (See Fig. 14-2.) The trousers shall be of sufficient length to reach the top of the heel of the shoe in the rear. A variation of ¼ inch above or below the top of the heel is acceptable.

Trouser length and hem. (See Fig. 14-3.) When the legs of the trousers have been hemmed, they will be ¾ to 1 inch shorter in the front than in the back in order to present a slight "break" at the lower front above the shoe top. The sharpness of the "break" will vary, depending on the size of shoes being worn, the height of the individual's instep, and the width of the legs of the trousers. Trousers shall be finished with a 2-3 inch hem.

Trouser fit. (See Fig. 14-4.) Trousers shall be of sufficient looseness around the hips and buttocks to prevent gapping of the front pockets and visible horizontal wrinkles across the front.

The fly of the trousers shall hang in a vertical line without gapping when unzipped.

The tip end of the web belt will pass through the buckle to wearer's left and will extend not less than two inches nor more than four inches beyond the buckle. The right edge of the buckle is centered on line with the edge of the fly front or coat flap.

Fig. 14-5.

Fig. 14-6. *Wearing the Garrison cap.*

Green service coat. (See Fig. 14-5.) The left side of the front closure should overlap the right side by not less than three inches or more than four inches. When body conformation precludes obtaining the minimum, less than three inches is permissible provided the front does not gap open and is parallel to the pocket edges. The front closure of the coat will not form a vertical line with the crotch, but will offset it by ¾ inch to the wearer's right. The horizontal edges of the front panels shall be even, plus or minus 1/8 inch.

Garrison cap. (See Fig. 14-6.) The fit around the head shall be adequate to place the cap on the head, but will not cause the top or front/rear contour of the cap to "break."

Wearing Ribbons and Badges

- Bottom edge of rifle bar 1/8 inch above the edge of pocket.
- Top of the pistol bar is even with the top of the rifle bar; therefore, the bottom of the pistol bar will be more than 1/8 inch above the highest point of the pocket, not 1/8 inch above the top edge of the pocket.
- The first row of ribbons will be 1/8 inch above the top edge of the shooting badges. The second and succeeding row(s) of ribbons will either be worn 1/8 inch apart or flush, with each row touching the row above and below.
- Whether or not ribbons are worn, badges will be spaced so that outboard ends would be even with the end of a ribbon bar, which is 4-1/8 inch long. The center of this ribbon bar (whether real or imaginary) should coincide with the center of the pocket as shown.
- Ribbons must be worn in proper order of seniority.
- Stars will be worn with single ray up.
- Ribbons must be clean, not faded or frayed.

Proper wearing of ribbons and badges (male Marines). (See Fig. 14-7.)

Wearing insignia of grade (male Marines). (See Fig. 14-8.)

Designation of Uniforms (Women)

Authorized uniforms for women enlisted personnel are designated as blue dress, service (summer/winter) and utility.

The uniform of the day should normally be the service "A" uniform. When seasonal or climatic conditions make it impractical to wear the service "A" uniform, the service "C" uniform may be prescribed. For those commands wherein the blue uniform is authorized for enlisted personnel under a supplementary clothing allowance, the uniform of the day will be the service or blue dress uniform, at the discretion of the commander. The service uniforms and the blue dress "B" uniform may be prescribed for leave and liberty within the United States.

Dress "A" Uniforms. The blue dress "A" uniform shall be prescribed for parades, ceremonies,

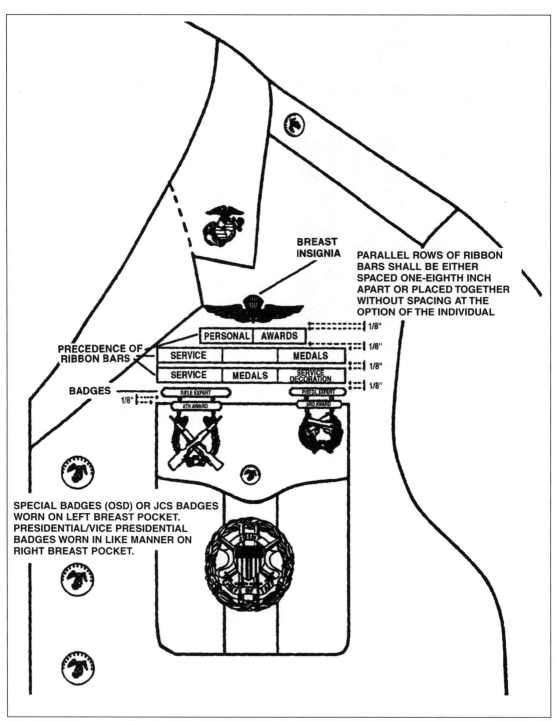

Fig. 14-7. *Proper wearing of ribbons and badges (male Marines).*

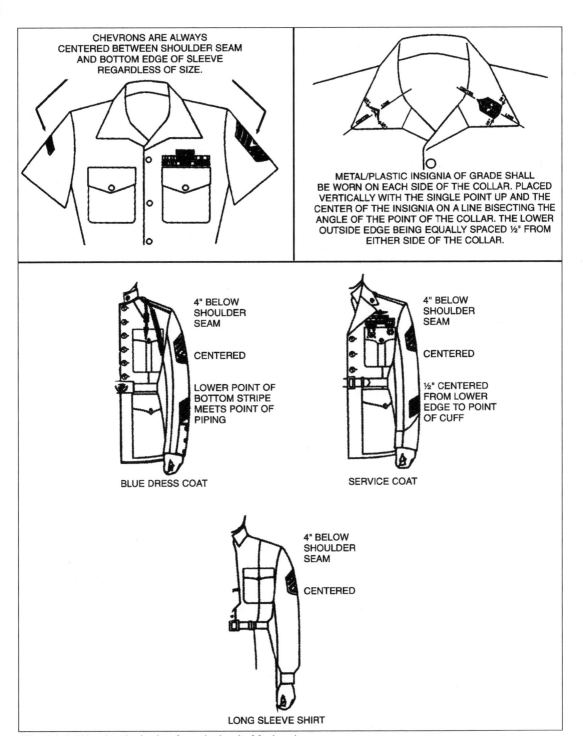

Fig. 14-8. *Wearing insignia of grade (male Marines).*

reviews and official social occasions when the commander considers it desirable to pay special honors to the occasion.

Dress "B" Uniforms. The blue dress "B" uniform shall be prescribed for enlisted personnel for parades, ceremonies, reviews, and at such other solemnities or entertainment as determined by the commander.

The blue dress "B" uniform is authorized for leave or liberty.

The blue dress "B" uniform shall consist of the same items as the blue dress "A" uniform, except that ribbons shall be worn in lieu of medals.

Dress "C" Uniforms. The new blue dress uniform with long sleeve khaki shirt is designated as blue dress "C." The khaki shirt and black necktab may be prescribed in lieu of the blue coat. In those commands authorized the blue uniform, commanders may prescribe blue dress "C" as the uniform of the day; however, this uniform will not be worn in ceremonies, parades, on liberty, leave, or other functions for which the coat would be appropriate.

Dress "D" Uniforms. The blue dress uniform with short sleeve khaki shirt is designated as blue dress "D." In those commands authorized the blue uniform, commanders may prescribe the blue dress "D" as the uniform of the day. During the period winter uniforms are prescribed, commanders may, at their discretion, when weather requires, authorize the wearing of the blue dress "D" as the uniform of the day. Commanders may prescribe the wearing of this uniform for honors and ceremonies where climatic conditions preclude the comfortable wearing of the blue dress "A" or "B" uniforms. This uniform will not be worn on leave or liberty.

Service uniforms. The service "A" uniform appropriate to the season shall be prescribed for the following military occasions:

When reporting for duty.

When assigned duty as a member of a court-martial.

The designated service uniforms of women enlisted personnel shall be worn in accordance with the following:

The service "A" uniform shall include the appropriate service coat. Either the long or short sleeve khaki shirt and green necktab may be worn with this uniform. When service "A" uniforms are prescribed as the uniform of the day, it is considered appropriate to dispense with the wearing of the coat in office buildings within the confines of a military activity or establishment.

The service "B" uniform shall consist of the long sleeve khaki shirt and green necktab with appropriate green skirt. When the coat is not deemed appropri-

ate, commanders may, at their discretion, authorize the wearing of the service "B" uniform. Service "B" can be worn on liberty.

The short sleeve khaki shirt with appropriate green skirt is designated as the service "C" uniform. No necktab will be worn with this uniform. During the winter season, commanders may, at their discretion, when the weather requires, authorize the wearing of the service "C" uniform. This uniform may be worn as a uniform of the day, and for leave and liberty, unless otherwise prescribed by the commander, and may be prescribed for wear in formation at ceremonies on and off the military activity. This uniform shall not be worn for formal or semiformal social events.

The wearing of slacks as part of the service "A," "B," or "C," uniforms is authorized.

The summer weight polyester/wool service uniform may be worn interchangeably with the winter weight service uniforms of gabardine or serge on a year-round basis at the option of the individual. Individuals are not authorized to mix service items of different materials, except that the green serge or gabardine service cap is authorized to be worn with the polyester/wool uniform.

Individuals may wear either the polyester/wool green or the winter weight service uniforms of approved materials on a year-round basis for all formations, unless otherwise prescribed by the commander. The new seasonal uniform is being phased in.

Utility Uniform. The camouflage utility uniform is not authorized for wear except when in the field, for field type exercises, or for those work conditions wherein it is not practical to wear the service uniform. An exception to this is within the Fleet Marine Forces wherein the wear of the utility uniform by designated units is an enhancement of readiness.

Wearing the Uniform (Women)

Dress and service caps. (See Fig. 14-9.) Dress and service caps are centered and worn straight with the tip of the visor in line with the eyebrows. The dress and service cap insignia are worn on the appropriate cap in the eyelet provided with the wing tips parallel to the ground.

Garrison cap. (See Fig. 14-10.) Garrison caps are centered and worn straight or slightly tilted to the right, with the base of the sweatband approximately one inch above the eyebrows. The left service collar insignia is worn on the green garrison cap. The

Fig. 14-9. Wearing of the dress and service caps.

Fig. 14-10. Wearing of the garrison cap.

Fig. 14-11. Coat length and fit.

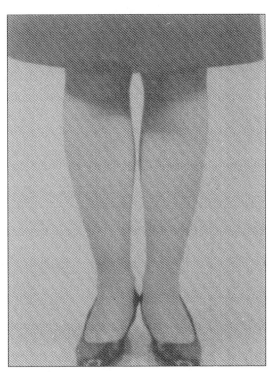

Fig. 14-12. Skirt hems.

insignia are worn centered vertically in the eyelets provided.

Dress and service coats. (See Fig. 14-11.) The coat should fit easily through the waist, extending to a smooth flare over the hips and allowing a two inch overlap in the center front to hang evenly. The proper length of the coat is approximately seven inches below the natural waistline.

Skirt hems. (See Fig. 14-12.) Skirts are of a conventional length and sweep appropriate for the appearance of the uniform and the individual. They will have a hem or facing of not less than two inches or more than three inches. Skirts will be knee length (not more than one inch above the top of the kneecap nor more than one inch below the bottom of the kneecap).

Shirts. Shirt wear is authorized as indicated:

• The long sleeve shirt may be worn as part of the winter/summer green service "A" and "B" uniforms in accordance with the regulations for wearing the khaki shirtwaist except as otherwise indicated herein.

• The short sleeve shirt may be worn with the appropriate green service skirt or slacks and cap when the winter/summer service "C" uniform is prescribed for wear by male Marines. It may be worn as a uniform of the day and on leave or liberty, unless otherwise prescribed by the commander.

- The short sleeve shirt may be worn with the blue dress skirt or slacks and cap when the blue dress "D" uniform is prescribed for wear by male Marines; however, this uniform will not be worn on leave or liberty. Khaki shirts will never be worn with the blue dress coat.
- The khaki shirts will not be tucked in, but will be worn outside the skirt at all times, except by women who are required to wear a duty belt.
- The green necktabs will be worn in accordance with the following instructions:
  - The necktab will be worn at all times when the long sleeve shirt is worn, both with and without the service coat.
  - When the necktabs are worn, the outer edge of the tabs should be parallel to the outer edge of the collar. Green necktabs will vary in width according to the size of the Marine and manufacture of necktab. An equal amount of necktab should show on each side of the shirt collar.
- Insignia of grade will be worn on the long sleeve shirt centered 4 inches below the shoulder seam.
- On the short sleeve shirt, enlisted insignia of grade (green on khaki) will be worn centered on the outer half of each sleeve, midway between the shoulder seam and peak of the cuff.
- When the khaki shirts are worn as outer garments, the wearing of ribbons and badges shall be at the option of the individual unless otherwise prescribed by the commander. Either all ribbons should be worn or decorations should be limited to personal U.S. decorations, U.S. unit awards and the Good Conduct Medal only. If worn, ribbons/badges will be placed on the shirt 1-2 inches above the first visible button and centered so that they are in the same approximate position as ribbons/badges worn on the service coat.
- Either the long or short sleeve shirt (whichever is authorized as the seasonal uniform shirt for male Marines) may be worn with the green service sweater.

Wearing of the Service Sweater by Women Marines

The green sweater may be worn in lieu of the service coat when the service uniform is prescribed, including leave and liberty. When the crew neck sweater with the green/white shirtwaist is worn the

necktie will not be worn, the top button of the shirtwaist will be unbuttoned, and the collar will be worn outside the sweater. The necktie is required with the V-neck sweater.

The sleeves of the sweater may be turned up; however, the sleeves should be of sufficient length to cover the shirt cuff. The waistband of the sweater may be turned up, but should be of sufficient length to cover the waistband of the skirt.

When the green sweater is worn with the camouflage utility uniform, it will be worn under the utility coat.

Wearing insignia of grade (women). (See Fig. 14-13.)

Wearing Medals and Decorations

As explained earlier in this chapter, certain uniform combinations require the individual Marine to wear appropriate ribbons and badges. Other uniform combinations allow for the optional wear of ribbons. In both cases, it is your responsibility to wear the ribbons authorized and to wear them properly.

Placement of ribbons (and the devices mounted on the ribbons) can be somewhat confusing. However, by following some basic rules you will be assured that you are in proper uniform.

First, your administrative office can tell you exactly what ribbons and devices you are authorized to wear. The PX sells the ribbons, devices and a ribbon holder. You don't have to buy all new ribbons, but if the old ones are looking ragged, new ones should be purchased.

Devices

The most common types of devices used are stars. There are large (5/16 inch) and small (3/16 inch) stars and bronze, gold and silver stars.

Small stars. The small stars come in bronze and silver. They usually represent subsequent awards of the ribbon to which they are attached, one bronze star for each subsequent award. When you receive your fifth identical award you put on a single silver star in lieu of the five bronze stars. If you have six or more additional awards you add one bronze star for each award over five. For example, for six subsequent awards, you have one silver star and one bronze star; for seven additional awards you have one silver star and two bronze stars, etc.

A service medal is different; each star stands for a campaign. Thus if you rate the ribbon, you normally

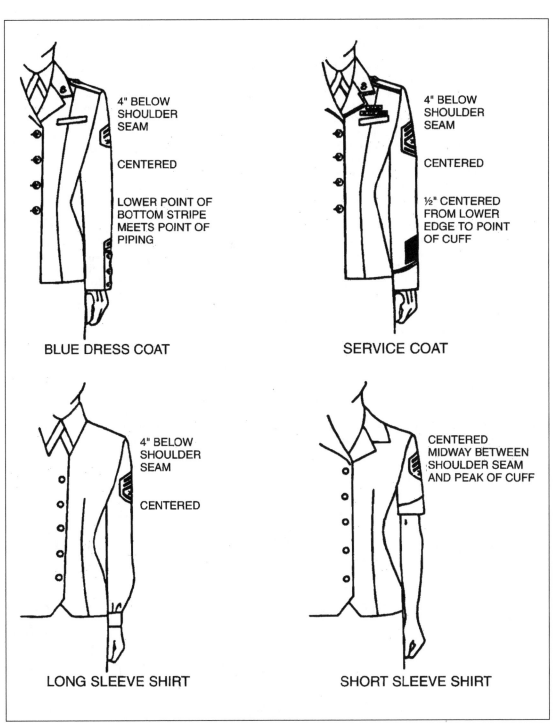

BLUE DRESS COAT

4" BELOW SHOULDER SEAM

CENTERED

LOWER POINT OF BOTTOM STRIPE MEETS POINT OF PIPING

SERVICE COAT

4" BELOW SHOULDER SEAM

CENTERED

½" CENTERED FROM LOWER EDGE TO POINT OF CUFF

LONG SLEEVE SHIRT

4" BELOW SHOULDER SEAM

CENTERED

SHORT SLEEVE SHIRT

CENTERED MIDWAY BETWEEN SHOULDER SEAM AND PEAK OF CUFF

Fig. 14-13. Wearing insignia of grade (women).

rate at least one star with it. Your administrative office will confirm how many campaigns you've been in.

Large stars. Large stars represent subsequent awards of a personal decoration. They come in two colors – gold and silver. The gold ones are to show subsequent awards up to five. The silver star is used in lieu of the five gold stars, and if you rate more than five subsequent awards, you use a silver star with an additional gold star for each award over five. The sliver star is senior and goes to the right side of the ribbon, or it is flanked by the gold ones, depending upon how many you are authorized.

Combat "V." Another common device is the "V." The only color you should wear is brushed bronze. If you have stars to go with the "V," the "V" is always in the middle of the ribbon and the stars are attached on either side. The first star goes on the right side of the ribbon, the second on the left, etc. If you have more than five stars with a "V," the silver star goes to the right side of the ribbon. (See Fig. 14-14.) Note: One ray of the star must point straight up.

Star Placement

If you rate a ribbon and one star, you attach the star in the middle; if you rate two stars, you divide the ribbon in thirds and attach the stars to the two lines that make the divisions; if you rate three stars, you divide the ribbon into fourths and attach the stars on the three dividing lines; and if you rate four stars, you divide the ribbon into fifths and the stars go on the four dividing lines. (See Fig. 14-15.) A good idea is to make a template of cardboard. Trace the drawing in Figure 14-15 and you'll know where to attach the stars.

Precedence

Ribbons are designated as to precedence (established rank) and must be arranged according to this rank. Figure 14-16 is a list of most ribbons worn by Marines. They are numbered as to precedence. Ribbon precedence is established from right to left.

Blue is the key color in figuring out which way a ribbon goes. On the Presidential Unit Citation (PUC), the blue goes up; on the Combat Action Ribbon, the big blue end goes to the right. Keep this in mind when attaching stars to your PUC.

The Air Medal is a tricky ribbon to wear properly. Numerals may be substituted for strike flight awards on the decoration. The numerals indicate the total number of awards received after April 9, 1962. The numbers are positioned on the ribbon as far to the left as possible without overlapping the edge of the ribbon. Stars worn in combination with numbers are spaced evenly between the edge of the numerals and the opposite end of the ribbon. Stars worn alone on the ribbon are subject to the same rules discussed earlier.

Ribbon Holders

Ribbon holders take care of most problems concerning spacing of separate rows of ribbons, but the rule is: Rows may consist of three or four ribbons, but the lapel on the service "A" uniform should not cover more than one-third of any ribbon. To avoid this, ribbons will be graduated, keeping a flush edge to the left; the top row may be evenly spaced from side to side.

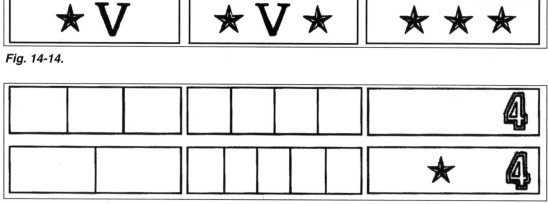

Fig. 14-14.

Fig. 14-15.

PRECEDENCE OF MEDALS

1. Medal of Honor
2. Navy Cross
3. Defense Distinguished Service Medal
4. Navy Distinguished Service Medal
5. Silver Star
6. Defense Superior Service Medal
7. Legion of Merit
8. Distinguished Flying Cross
9. Navy and Marine Corps Medal
10. Bronze Star
11. Purple Heart
12 Defense Meritorious Service Medal
13. Meritorious Service Medal
14. Air Medal
15. Joint Service Commendation Medal
16. Navy & Marine Corps Commendation Medal
17. Joint Service Achievement Medal
18. Navy & Marine Corps Achievement Medal
19. Combat Action Ribbon
20. Presidential Unit Citation
21. Joint Meritorious Unit Award
22. Navy Unit Commendation
23. Meritorious Unit Commendation
24. Navy "E" Ribbon
25. Non-Military U.S. Decorations (Note 1)
26. Prisoner of War Medal
27. Marine Corps Good Conduct Medal
28. Selected Marine Corps Reserve Medal
29. Marine Corps Expeditionary Medal
30. China Service Medal
31. American Defense Service Medal
32. American Campaign Medal
33. European-African-Middle Eastern Campaign Medal
34. Asiatic-Pacific Campaign Medal
35. World War II Victory Medal
36. Navy Occupation Service Medal
37. Medal For Humane Action
38. National Defense Service Medal
39. Korean Service Medal
40. Antarctic Service Medal
41. Armed Forces Expeditionary Medal
42. Republic of Vietnam Service Medal
43. Southwest Asia Service Medal
44. Kosovo Campaign Medal
45. Armed Forces Service Medal
46. Humanitarian Service Medal
47. Military Outstanding Volunteer Service Medal
48. Sea Service Deployment Ribbon
49. Navy Arctic Service Ribbon
50. Navy & Marine Corps Overseas Ribbon
51. Marine Corps Recruiting Ribbon
52. Drill Instructor Ribbon
53. Marine Security Guard Ribbon
54. Armed Forces Reserve Medal
55. Marine Corps Reserve Ribbon
56. Philippine Presidential Unit Citation (Note 2)
57. Korean Presidential Unit Citation
58. Vietnam Presidential Unit Citation
59. Republic of Vietnam Meritorious Unit Citation (Gallantry Cross Medal with Palm and Frame)
60. Republic of Vietnam Meritorious Unit Citation (Civil Actions Medal First Class with Palm and Frame)
61. Philippine Defense Ribbon
62. Philippine Liberation Ribbon
63. Philippine Independence Ribbon
64. United Nations Service Medal – Korea
65. United Nations Medal
66. North Atlantic Treaty Organization Medal – Yugoslavia
67. Multinational Force and Observers Medal
68. Inter-American Defense Board Medal
69. Republic of Vietnam Campaign Medal
70. Kuwaiti Liberation Medal – Saudi Arabia
71. Kuwaiti Liberation Medal – Kuwait
72. Republic of Korea Service Medal

Note 1: These are awards by Federal Agencies, such as NASA, and the Public Health Service.

Note 2: No medal authorized for Philippines, Korea, RVN PUCs and RVN MUCs

Fig. 14-16.

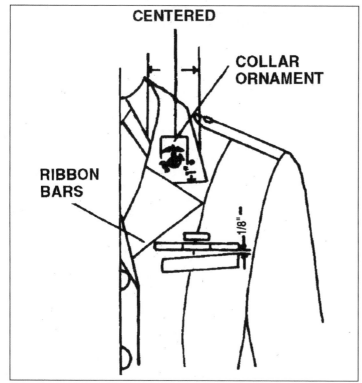

CENTERED

COLLAR ORNAMENT

RIBBON BARS

1/8"

Fig. 14-17. Wearing of ribbons (women)

Marksmanship Badges

After all of your ribbons are properly assembled, you'll have to attach your shooting badges to your uniform. Remember, your rifle badge is senior to the pistol badge and goes to the right. The top edge of all badges will be on line. There will be a 1/8 inch space between the lower edge of the rifle badge bar and the top of the pocket and a 1/8 inch space between the upper edge of the badge bar and the first row of ribbons. If you have both a rifle and pistol badge they are worn in the following manner. The outside edge of the pocket is your guide. They should line up with the outside edge with a minimum of ¼ inch between the rifle and pistol badges. If ¼ inch isn't possible with the outer edge flush with the outside of the pocket, they can be moved so ¼ inch is achieved.

Note: The terms "left" and "right" refer to the wearer's left or right.

Various foreign awards are worn in manners which differ from the rules outlined above, and numerous awards of any one decoration will cause differences. If you have any questions, ask one of your SNCO's.

Wearing of Ribbons (Women)

The first row of ribbons will be 1/8 inch above the top edge of the pocket. The second and succeeding row(s) of ribbons will be worn either 1/8 inch apart or flush, with each row touching the row above and below. In determining the proper location for attaching ribbons on women's coats with slanted pockets, a horizontal line tangent to the highest point of the slanted pocket is considered as the top of the pocket. (See Fig. 14-17.)

Ribbons must be worn in proper order of seniority. Stars are worn with single ray up and horizontally spaced. Ribbons must be clean, not faded or frayed.

EQUIPMENT

Whether you are an infantryman, a truck driver or a cook, you may be issued a set of field equipment. You are responsible for these items just as you are for your individual clothing. The following basic equipment is issued to all Marines:

- *Pack.*
- *Rifle belt.*
- *Bayonet with scabbard.*
- *Rifle* with the gear needed to keep the weapon in proper working condition, including a cleaning rod case (swab holder, rifle bore brush and sectional cleaning rod), combination tool, and oil and grease container.
- *Canteen, cup and cover* (two canteens with covers may be issued).
- *First aid packet and pouch.*
- *Poncho.*
- *Shelter half* with a three-section pole, five pins and a guy line.
- *Entrenching tool.*

Individuals armed with a pistol will have a pistol belt in lieu of the rifle belt. Special equipment may also be issued in certain areas or to specific individuals. Examples of special equipment would be protective masks, cold weather clothing, field glasses, wire cutters and compass.

MOLLE – MOdular Lightweight Load-carrying Equipment

MOLLE is a modular Load-Bearing system designed to enhance the survivability and lethality of the modern Marine. MOLLE is a replacement for the current ALICE system and components of the Integrated Individual Fighting System including the Enhanced Tactical Load-Bearing Vest. Your Unit Supply should issue a complete MOLLE set with the appropriate pockets to match your squad position.

The MOLLE system consists of the fighting load vest, the main rucksack, the sleep system carrier, the patrol pack, the frame, sustainment pockets, six foot lashing straps, hydration bladder, repair kit, and additional pockets. A common **vest** is provided for all Soldiers and Marines with specialized **removable pockets** for Rifleman, Pistol, SAW Gunner, Grenadier and Corpsman configurations.

Every vest regardless of duty position also comes with a **utility pouch** attached to the belt. The **rucksack** and **shoulder straps** come pre-assembled to the **frame**. The other components are provided as add-ons that can be attached by the individual Marine as needed. The MOLLE system provides far more load carrying capabilities than the ALICE and other fielded systems. However, proper new equipment training is required in order for the system to be used to its maximum capabilities. These capabilities are illustrated to assist Marines with familiarization of the system. The **vest modularity** allows for commanders to tailor the loads to meet mission needs without unnecessary extra pockets and gear. The vest is designed to reduce heat build up on the back with minimum area of coverage with the **H-Harness design**. The **wide shoulder straps** of the vest help distribute the load without the need for excessive padding that can hinder mobility and sighting a weapon.

The **Rifleman configuration (below left)** is designed to hold two 30 round magazines in the double pockets and one magazine in the single pockets. Two fragmentation grenade pockets are also worn by the rifleman along with a utility pouch.

The **Rifleman - Pistol configuration (below)** holds four single 9mm magazine pockets and two fragmentation grenades as shown. In addition to the configuration shown, you will receive two single 30 round magazine pockets and two double 30 round magazine pockets.

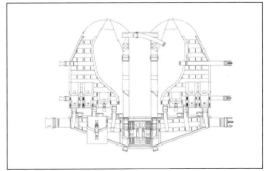

Fig. 14-19. Rifleman - Pistol configuration.

The **Rifleman - SAW Gunner configuration (below)** accommodates two 200 round magazine pockets and three 100 round magazine pockets (one of which is the utility pocket), and two single 30 round magazine pockets as shown. In addition to the configuration shown, you will also receive two double 30 round magazine pockets and two fragmentation grenade pockets. Twelve five-round shotgun pouches are also available to fit mission needs.

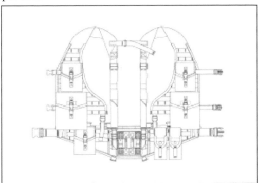

Fig. 14-20. Rifleman - SAW Gunner configuration.

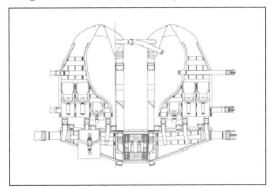

Fig. 14-18. Rifleman configuration.

The **Rifleman - Grenadier configuration (below)** consists of fourteen single high explosive grenade pockets and two double illumination round pockets. Also included are two double 30 round magazine pockets and a utility pouch as shown. In addition to the configuration shown, you will receive two single 30 round magazine pockets and two fragmentation grenade pockets.

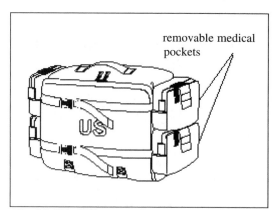

removable medical pockets

Fig 14-22b. Rifleman - Corpsman configuration.

The **ruck attachment straps** are attached at the top slot on the frame with a three bar buckle and webbing. The sides of the ruck are attached to the frame by using the buckles as toggles through the vertical openings. The belt comes in three sizes: small, medium, and large. The small belt fits waists 28" to 35", the medium fits 35" to 40", and the large fits 40" and larger. A properly fit belt should not be able to touch at the ends when fully tightened around the waist, yet the ends should extend beyond the prominence of the hipbone towards the center of the body.

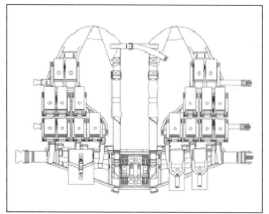

Fig. 14-21. Rifleman - Grenadier configuration.

The **Rifleman – Corpsman configuration (below)** will receive four zippered medical pockets for the vest and two double 30 round magazine pockets as shown below. In addition to the configuration shown, you will also receive two single 30 round magazine pockets and two fragmentation grenade pockets. There will also be a specialized panel loading medical bag that has an additional four removable medical pockets attached to it.

It is important to have a belt that fits properly in order for the system to shift some of the rucksack load off of the shoulders and onto the hips.

Get to know your MOLLE system and experiment with different load configurations. Get used to removing items that are not needed so the load is as clean and streamlined as possible.

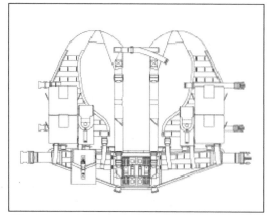

Fig 14-22a. Rifleman - Corpsman configuration.

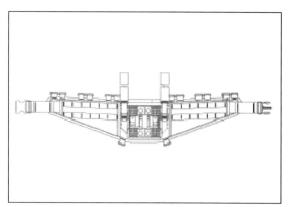

Fig 14-23. Ruck attachment straps.

Cleaning and Maintenance

Scrape dirt and dust from the item using a brush that will not cut into the fabric.

Hose or wash the item in a pail of water using mild detergent or soap. Rinse thoroughly with clean water.

Do not use chlorine bleach, yellow soap, cleaning fluids, or solvents that will discolor or deteriorate the item.

Dry the item in shade or indoors. Do not dry in direct sunlight, direct heat or open flame.

Do not launder or dry item in fixed commercial home type laundry equipment. Do not attempt to dye or repair.

Turn in for repair or replacement.

Remember, extremely dirty or damaged equipment can eventually fail to perform its intended function.

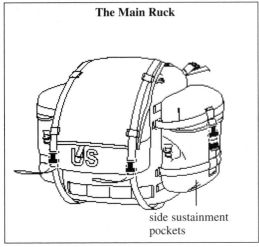

The Main Ruck

side sustainment pockets

Fig 14-24a. The Main Ruck.

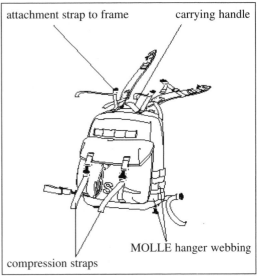

attachment strap to frame   carrying handle

MOLLE hanger webbing

compression straps

Fig 14-25a. The Patrol Pack.

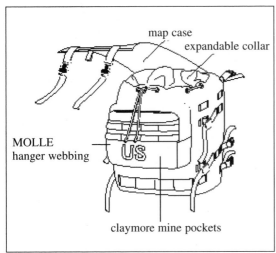

map case
expandable collar

MOLLE hanger webbing

US

claymore mine pockets

Fig 14-24b. The Main Ruck.

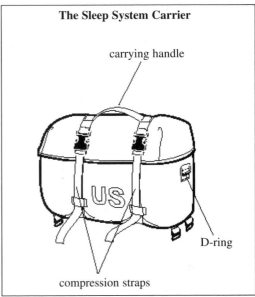

The Sleep System Carrier

carrying handle

D-ring

compression straps

Fig 14-25b. The Sleep System Carrier.

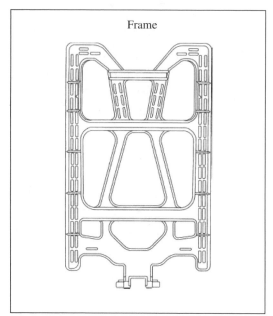

Fig 14-25c. Frame.

All-Purpose Lightweight Individual Carrying Equipment (ALICE)

The medium pack, designed to carry up to 50 pounds, is generally used by most combat troops. Figures 14-26 and 14-27 show front and back views. The pack is water repellent but not waterproof. Four waterproof liners are issued with each pack, one large one for the main compartment and three small ones for each of the three pockets. Equipment should be inserted first in the waterproof liners, then into the main compartment and pockets. Instructions for making a water-tight closure are printed on the outside of each liner.

The small pocket in the main compartment can be used to carry a radio.

The main flap for covering the loaded pack can be opened by pulling apart the two tabs. The camouflage cover or other small flat objects can be stored in it. Simply pressing the flap together seals it.

Equipment hangers (webbed loops and webbing with eyelets for use with slidekeepers and/or hooks) are provided on the sides of the pack and above the pockets for carrying equipment on the outside of the pack.

For carrying equipment such as a bayonet scabbard or machete sheath, pockets are tunneled between the pockets and main compartment. By sliding the piece down through the tunnel, it can be fastened to the hanger above it with slidekeepers or hooks.

The medium pack is most commonly carried using the shoulder straps without the frame. When required, the pack can be attached to the frame and shoulder straps.

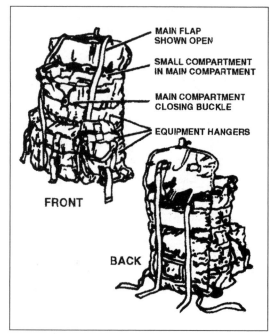

Fig 14-26. Front and back views of medium pack.

Cleaning and Maintenance

Water-repellent-treated nylon duck and webbing were used to fabricate all of the fabric items of equipment. The entrenching tool carrier is molded of ethylene-vinyl acetate. The pack frame and cargo shelf are fabricated from aluminum with solid steel rivets in certain high stress areas.

The equipment is cleaned by removing mud or other foreign matter with a brush, damp or dry cloth, or by scrubbing the exceedingly dirty areas using the following procedure:

• Scrape dirt or mud from the equipment using a flat stick or a dull instrument which will not cut the fabric or webbing.

1. The Light Fighting Load which consists of the Load-Bearing Vest and Butt Pack.

3. The Light Rucksack Load consists of the four items from the Assault Pack Load plus the Rucksack and Frame.

2. The Assault Pack Load consists of the Load-Bearing Vest, Butt Pack and Patrol Pack.

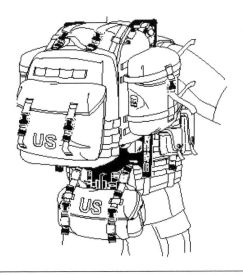

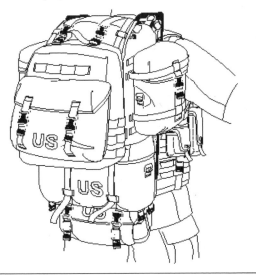

Attach Butt Pack loosely to make sure socket is exposed when the pack frame will be worn.

4. The Intermediate Rucksack Load consists of items from the Light Rucksack Load plus the side sustainment pockets on the ruck.

5. The Full Rucksack Load consists of the items from the Intermediate Rucksack Load plus the Sleep System Carrier.

 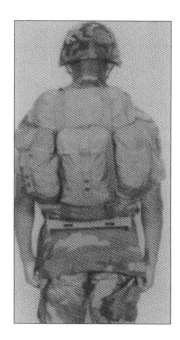 

Fig 14-27. *ALICE with frame.*

- Remove loose dirt from soiled surfaces using a cloth or soft brush.
- Wet the surface and apply a warm solution of detergent. Scrub with a soft brush, cloth or sponge.
- Flush the item thoroughly with clean, warm water until all the cleaning solution has been rinsed away.
- Dry the item or equipment away from direct sunlight, direct heat, and open flames.

"Field expedient" maintenance is limited to the repair of damaged or loose stitching by hand sewing or taping and replacement of damaged or missing keepers on suspenders, small arms ammunition case, field first aid dressing case, entrenching tool carrier, and water canteen cover.

Clothing and Equipment Displays

Commanding officers are required to conduct frequent inspections of clothing and equipment. These inspections are designed to see that you have all the prescribed equipment, that you have no one else's equipment, and that your equipment is in good condition.

In order to assist inspecting officers in quickly examining your equipment, standard layouts for both clothing and equipment have been prescribed for displays inside on your bunk or outdoors in ranks. These displays are designed for a Marine who is issued the standard equipment and minimum clothing allowance. If you are issued special equipment or items not part of the minimum clothing allowance, appropriate modifications will be required.

The correct arrangement for the displays of clothing and equipment on the bunks are shown in Figures 14-28 through 14-41.

All articles of uniform clothing possessed by an individual will be displayed regardless of current allowances. Items not displayed will be those worn by the individual at the time of the inspection and those accounted for by an itemized laundry, dry cleaning, tailor or cobbler slip.

Individuals required to wear a medical warning tag in accordance with the BUMED Instructions will display this tag next to their identification tags.

Display of Equipment in Ranks

Equipment can also be displayed outdoors. To accomplish this, the unit is formed for inspection with Marines displaying their equipment.

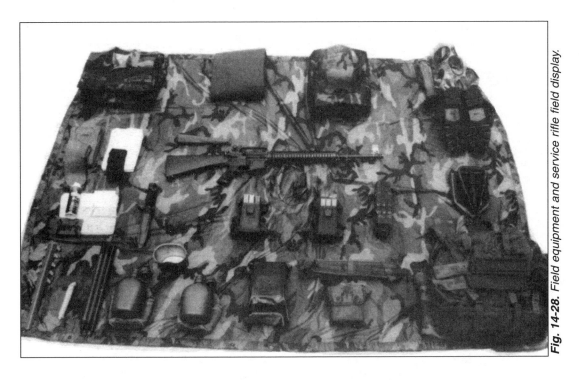

Fig. 14-28. Field equipment and service rifle field display.

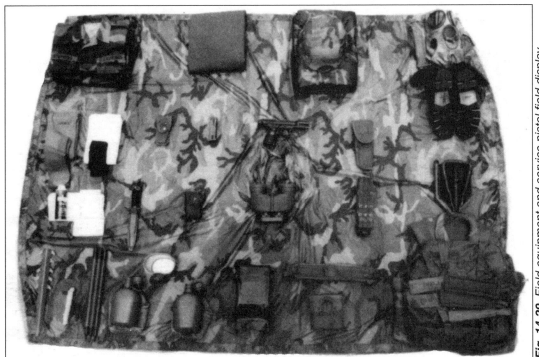

Fig. 14-29. Field equipment and service pistol field display.

181

Fig. 14-30. *Field equipment and service rifle bunk display.*

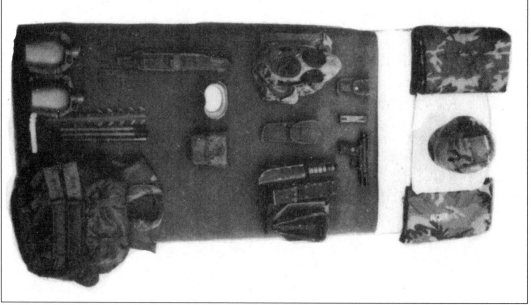

Fig. 14-31. *Field equipment and service pistol bunk display.*

182

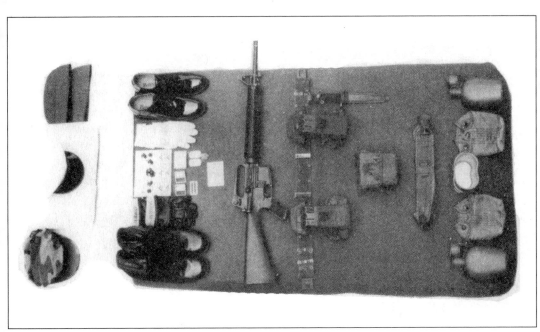

Fig. **14-32.** *Garrison equipment and service rifle bunk display (male).*

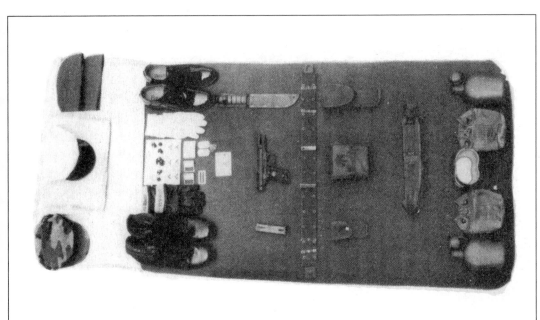

Fig. **14-33.** *Garrison equipment and service pistol bunk display (male).*

Fig. 14-34. Field equipment, partial uniform clothing and service rifle bunk display (male).

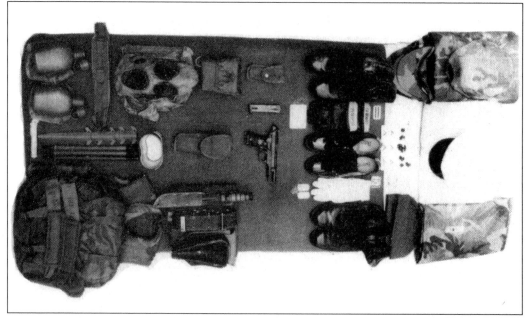

Fig. 14-35. Field equipment, partial uniform clothing and service pistol bunk display (male).

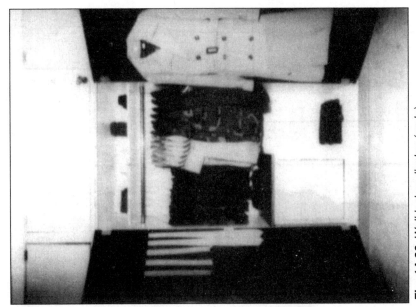

Fig. 14-36. Wall locker display (male).

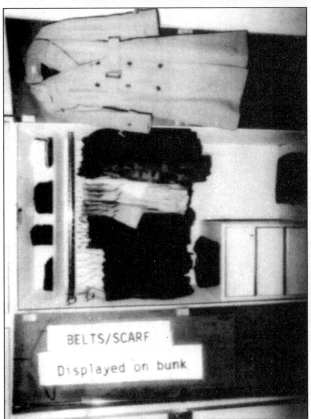

BELTS/SCARF

Displayed on bunk

Fig. 14-37. Wall locker display (female).

185

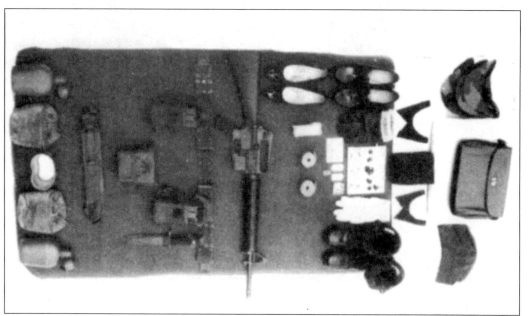

Fig. 14-38. Garrison equipment and service rifle bunk display (female).

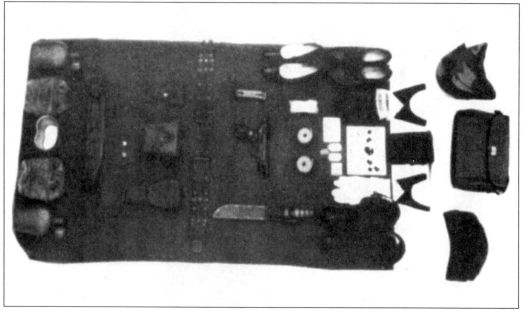

Fig. 14-39. Garrison equipment and service pistol bunk display (female).

Fig. 14-40. Field equipment, partial uniform clothing and service rifle bunk display (female).

Fig. 14-41. Field equipment, partial uniform clothing and service pistol bunk display (female).

Chapter Fifteen

Small Arms

The discussion in this chapter relates to general characteristics and principles of small arms.

A small arm is defined as a weapon which discharges small antipersonnel projectiles over relatively short ranges. Currently, weapons with a bore diameter of 1.181 inches (30mm) or less are classified as small arms. The size or bore diameter of some weapons is expressed in millimeters.

For example, the M16A2 rifle is a 5.56mm weapon and the M60 is referred to as a 7.62mm weapon. Small arms are also classified into three main groups. These are hand guns, shoulder weapons and machine guns.

Component Parts of Small Arms

Every small arm has four basic components which are barrel, breech mechanism (bolt), firing mechanism and receiver.

Barrel

The barrel is a straight metal tube with the primary purpose of directing the projectile toward the target. The breech end is the end into which the cartridge is inserted. The part of the tube through which the projectile is pushed by the propelling gases is called the bore. The bore may contain rifling which is a system of lands and grooves. Lands are ridges between grooves which give the projectile a stablizing spin to provide for greater accuracy.

The chamber is located just behind the bore and is shaped for a cartidge to fit snugly. When a high pressure cartridge is fired, the cartridge case expands against the inner wall of the chamber forming a gas tight seal. This action is known as obturation. It is important because it prevents the escape of gases around the bolt. This protects the shooter and ensures accuracy of the weapon.

Breech Mechanism (bolt)

The breech mechanism is a device which keeps the cartridge case in the chamber while obturation provides the gas tight seal. (See Fig. 15-1(a).) The following parts may be added to the basic bolt:

- A portion of the firing device such as the firing pin.
- An extractor for removing the expended cartridge case from the chamber.
- An ejector for throwing the expended cartridge case from the weapon.
- A locking device for locking the bolt to the barrel. Three common locking methods are the following:
  - The rotating bolt (Fig. 15-1(b)) has locking lugs which are rotated into locking recesses in the receiver or barrel to positively lock the weapon. The M16A2 rifle and the M60 machine gun have this type of breech mechanism.
  - The interrupted screw-horizontal swinging breech (Fig. 15-1(c)) is constructed so that the entire bolt swings into a locking recess.
  - The locking block breech mechanism (Fig. 15-1(d)) has a block that swings or is cammed into position in a locking recess in the bolt.

Types of Bolts

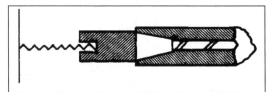

Fig. 15-1(a). Inertia.

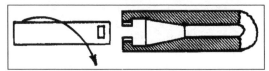

Fig. 15-1(b). Rotating.

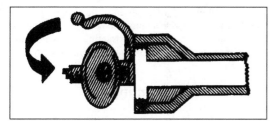

Fig. 15-1(c). *Swinging.*

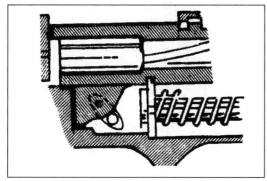

Fig. 15-1(d). *Locking.*

Firing Device

This is a device which causes ignition of the cartridge in the chamber. The firing mechanism normally includes a firing pin, hammer, sear and trigger.

The firing pin strikes the primer of the cartridge causing ignition. There are two types of firing pins, moveable and fixed.

- A moveable firing pin is a steel rod that runs longitudinally through the bolt and is driven forward either by spring expansion or hammer action, or a combination of both. The three types of movable firing pins are free-floating, inertia and percussion.
  - *Free-floating* – is driven forward by a sharp blow of a hammer and is retracted by a cam action (the M16A2). No spring force is used on either forward or rearward movement of the pin.
  - *Inertia* – is shorter than the total distance it must travel to strike the primer of a cartridge. It is driven forward by a hammer. A spring, which is compressed on the forward movement, retracts the pin.
  - *Percussion* – is driven forward by the force of a compressed spring and is retracted by the camming action that cocks the weapon (M60 machine gun).

- No small arms employed by the Marine Corps use a fixed firing pin.

Receiver

The receiver is a device secured to the barrel to contain certain other parts of the weapon. The receiver may fulfill any or all of the following purposes. It may house a bolt, a source of ammunition (such as a clip or magazine) or a major portion of the firing mechanism. Further, it may provide a base for a rear sight or provide a means of securing a stock to the weapon.

Additional Parts

In addition to the basic components, small arms normally have other parts which are added for safety, accuracy and convenience, such as the following examples:
- Safety devices to prevent premature or accidental firing.
- Sights used to aim the weapons.
- A means for holding ammunition in position ready for use, such as a clip, magazine or belt.

A clip is a device that secures a number of rounds together and is placed completely inside the receiver.

A magazine is a container that holds a number of rounds and fits into the receiver. A built-in spring in the magazine pushes the round into position to permit chambering.

A belt is used in rapid fire automatic weapons like the machine gun. The rounds are held together in flexible cloth or metal link belts. Once the first round is fired, the belt is automatically fed into the weapon, placing each round in such a position that it may be rapidly chambered and fired.

Cycle of functioning

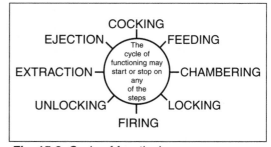

Fig. 15-2. *Cycle of functioning.*

Every small arm has a specific cycle of functioning (Fig. 15-2). This cycle refers to the actions that occur each time a round is fired. The sequence or manner of accomplishing them may vary in weapons of different design. However, the following steps are normally performed:

Feeding

This action places a round in the receiver ready for chambering. In its simplest form, it is the insertion of a cartridge by hand. Feeding is usually accomplished by a spring in a magazine, a mechanism in the receiver or a series of cams and pawls.

Chambering

This is the action required to place the new round in the chamber. Again, in its simplest form, the shooter places the round into the chamber by hand. In some weapons, it takes place as the bolt strips the new round from the feed mechanism and forces it into the chamber.

Locking

This action secures the bolt to the barrel, preventing the loss of gas pressure until after the bullet has left the muzzle. It is accomplished manually by the shooter or automatically by mechanical action of various parts.

Firing

This is accomplished when the primer of the cartridge is struck by the firing pin. The explosive composition in the primer is crushed and ignites the propellant in the cartridge case, forcing the bullet out of the barrel.

Unlocking

The bolt is unlocked so that it may move. Weapons using high pressure cartridges combine slow initial extraction with the unlocking of the bolt to overcome the effects of obturation. The cartridge case head could be torn off if it was not loosened in the chamber before extraction.

Extracting

This action is the removal of the empty cartridge case from the chamber. This step must be timed to prevent a blowback of gases into the shooter's face. The extractor may be a small hooked piece of metal in the bolt, which grips the extracting groove or rim of the cartridge case and pulls the empty case to the rear.

Ejecting

This action is the removal of the expended cartridge case from the receiver. This step can be accomplished by placing an ejector in the receiver. The case is carried to the rear by the extractor until it strikes the ejector. The ejector causes the case to be removed from the receiver. Another way of accomplishing this step is to use a spring-loaded ejector in the face of the bolt. When the case clears the chamber the spring expands throwing the case from the weapon.

Cocking

Cocking is the positioning of the operating parts in readiness to fire another round. The hammer or firing pin is moved to the rear and held there until released.

Types of Operating Systems

The cycle of functioning is accomplished by one of three types of operating systems. They are classified according to their source of power.

Manual Operation

In manual operation, the source of power is the shooter. An example is the bolt action rifle. The shooter chambers the round by pushing the bolt forward. After the round is fired, the shooter unlocks the bolt and pulls it to the rear. This causes extracting, ejecting and cocking. Bolt action rifles, most revolvers and some shotguns, are manually operated weapons.

Gas Operation

In gas operated weapons, a portion of the expanding gas is tapped off through a port in the barrel. The gas is vented into a gas cylinder or into a tube as with the M16A2. The gases moving rearward act against the operating parts, which causes unlocking, extracting and cocking. A feed mechanism then feeds the new round. The forward motion of the bolt chambers the round and locks the breech.

Recoil Operation

This system uses the rearward thrust (recoil) of the weapon to drive the barrel, bolt and other operating parts to the rear. The bolt is locked to the barrel at the time of firing and remains locked, recoiling rearward with the barrel, until the bullet has left the muzzle and the gas pressure is reduced. After the bullet has left the muzzle, the bolt is unlocked from the barrel and continues to the rear. Various methods are used to unlock the bolt and actuate the other operating parts. The 9mm pistol has this type of operation.

Automatic and Semiautomatic Firing Systems

A weapon that functions automatically utilizes gas, blowback or recoil operation. *Automatic functioning does not mean that a weapon that functions automatically also fires automatically.*

Semiautomatic Fire

This is the firing of one round each time pressure is applied to the trigger. The cycle of functioning is completed automatically, however the trigger must be released and pressure reapplied to fire a subsequent round. The 9mm pistol is a weapon that is capable only of semiautomatic fire.

Automatic Fire

This is the continuous operation of a weapon while the trigger is held to the rear. It ceases to operate when the trigger is released, all ammunition is expended or a stoppage occurs. The M60 machine gun is an example of a weapon that is capable only of automatic fire.

Combination of Automatic and Semiautomatic Fire

Some weapons are designed to fire automatically or semiautomatically. These weapons have a selector which permits the shooter to choose the type of fire. The M16A2 is an example of this type of weapon.

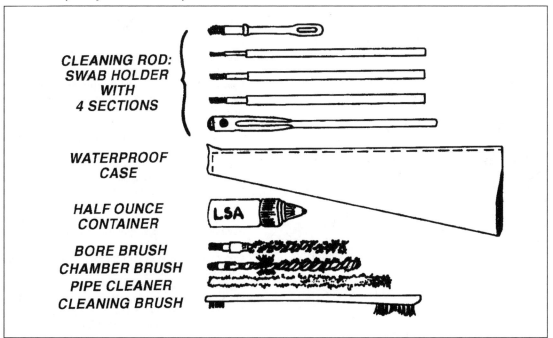

CLEANING ROD:
SWAB HOLDER
WITH
4 SECTIONS

WATERPROOF
CASE

HALF OUNCE
CONTAINER

LSA

BORE BRUSH
CHAMBER BRUSH
PIPE CLEANER
CLEANING BRUSH

Fig. 15-3. *M-16 cleaning and lubrication accessories*

General Care and Cleaning

(Specific care and cleaning of the M16A2 and M60 can be found in the chapters dealing with those weapons.)

The Marine today is armed with the finest infantry weapons devised by man, but unless given the proper care, they are no better than the clubs carried by cave men. Seventy-five percent of the stoppages that occur in a modern automatic or semiautomatic weapon can be traced back to improper care and cleaning.

In general, the care and cleaning of your weapon is a simple job, but here are a few things to remember under unusual conditions. Let us first take a look at some of the tools (Fig. 15-3) that you use to care for your weapons:

1. Bore Cleaner – This fluid dissolves corrosive primer salts left in the bore of weapons after firing.
2. Oil – Used for day by day protection of weapons at all temperatures down to –65 degrees F.
3. Cleaning Rod – A steel or brass rod with a swivel handle on one end and provisions for holding a cleaning swab or cleaning brush on the other, used to clean the bore of a weapon. Some rods may be taken apart making them compact for carrying.
4. Swab (patch) – A one-inch or 2 ½-inch square piece of cloth used with the cleaning rod to clean the bore of a weapon. Swabs are packed in a plastic bag or cardboard box.
5. Bore Brush – A brush having brass bristles used with a cleaning rod and rifle bore cleaner to clean the bore of a weapon after firing.
6. Cleaning Brush – Used to clean out corners and crevices.

Cleaning of Weapons in Garrison

The daily care of your weapon is a small job requiring only a few minutes of your time. Then you will have a weapon that will pass inspections and stand by you when you need it. Here is all there is to it:

1. Inspect your weapon. Be sure the weapon is in Condition 4.
2. Field strip it.
3. With a dry rag, wipe off all old oil and dirt.
4. Use your small arms cleaning brush to clean the corners, screw heads, etc.
5. Run a dry swab through the bore to remove old oil and dirt. Repeat this process until several swabs

come out clean. If the bore is still dirty, proceed as you would to clean the weapon after firing.
6. Run a lightly oiled swab through the bore. Don't forget the chamber.
7. Put a light coat of oil over all metal parts on your weapon, being careful not to trap perspiration off your fingers under the oil, where it can start rust.
8. If your weapon is magazine fed, inspect the interior of the magazine by depressing the follower. If the interior is dirty or rusted, disassemble, clean and oil lightly. You can avoid many stoppages by always handling your magazines so that they will not become dirty or dented.
9. Assemble your weapon and store it in a dust free place.

REMEMBER:

DO

1. Clean your weapon at least once a day.
2. Clean the chamber with the same care as the bore.
3. Use a cleaning brush to clean the small, hard-to-reach parts. Your squad leader may miss it, but will your weapon forget it?
4. Run the swab or brush all the way through the bore before you try to pull the rod back out.

DON'T

1. Don't use unauthorized cleaning materials. They will damage your weapon.
2. Don't handle parts carelessly after you have oiled them. Perspiration from your hands will cause rust.
3. Don't place a swab or plug in the muzzle of your weapon. The barrel will rust due to moisture trapped by the swab. Serious injury may result if you should forget to remove the swab or plug and attempt to fire the weapon.
4. Don't wrap your weapon. The wrapping will hold moisture and rust your weapon.
5. Don't attempt to disassemble your weapon beyond authorized stripping. You may damage certain parts beyond repair.
6. Don't damage the face of the bolt with a cleaning rod that is too long. The rod should be long enough to pass through the bore and chamber but not so long that it strikes the face of the bolt. If a long rod is used, remove the bolt or cover the face of the bolt with a cloth stuffed into the receiver.

Cleaning Weapons Before Firing

Before you fire your weapon you should do the following:
1. Clean your weapon as you would in garrison but DO NOT put oil in the bore, chamber or on parts of the weapon that will come in contact with the ammunition.
2. In the field, make sure there is no dust, dirt, mud or snow in the bore. Failure to observe this precaution may result in serious injury.
3. If your weapon is magazine fed, check to see that magazines are clean and operative.

Cleaning Weapons After Firing

After your weapon has been fired, the task of cleaning it is even more important than the everyday care you give it in the barracks. When the primer of a military cartridge explodes, it covers the bore with potassium chloride, a substance like table salt.

This salt in the bore holds moisture and starts rust. As rusting progresses, it eats into the metal in the bore, leaving a hole or pit. Pits not only weaken the metal but allow gas to escape around the bullet, cutting down muzzle velocity and accuracy. Therefore, barrels that are badly pitted must be replaced.

If properly cared for, a weapon may be fired for years without pitting. Here is how it's done:
1. Follow steps 1 to 4 as you would when cleaning your weapon in garrison.
2. Run a swab soaked with rifle bore cleaner through the bore, following this with a wire brush, then by several dry swabs. Repeat this process until the dry swabs come out clean. Clean the chamber the same way.
3. Clean the face of the bolt, piston and cylinder (on gas operated weapons), and inside of receiver with a swab soaked in bore cleaner. Clean the bore cleaner off with several dry swabs. Repeat this process until all traces of carbon are removed. (Cleaning of piston and gas cylinder will be accomplished only when inspections reveal that the piston cannot travel under its own weight in the gas cylinder.)
4. Follow steps 6 to 8 as you would when cleaning your weapon in garrison.
5. *Important. Repeat this entire process daily for at least three days after the weapon has been fired.*

REMEMBER:

DO

1. Clean your weapon as soon as possible after firing.
2. Clean your weapon daily for the next three days.
3. Run the wire brush all the way through the bore. Pumping it back and forth in the barrel will ruin the brush.
4. Clean the chamber, face of bolt and other places where carbon has accumulated with rifle bore cleaner.

DON'T

Don't use commercial type bore cleaner.

Care of Weapons in Arctic Climates

In the cooler regions of the earth, grease and oil thicken and cause much trouble. These materials, while fluid at normal temperatures, usually become thick or almost solid as the temperature drops below freezing. Consequently, they can slow down or stop the operation of weapons. For this reason, the proper type of lubricants must be used and then only in small quantities.

Much difficulty is caused by bringing cold weapons into a warm room or tent. When the cold metal of the weapon comes in contact with the warm moist air, condensation takes place, leaving drops of moisture on the weapon. These drops of moisture will cause rust, or will freeze when the weapon is taken out-of-doors. If possible, weapons should be stored in unheated sheds. Snow, blown or drifted into the weapon, will cause no harm as long as the temperature is below freezing. But when the weapon becomes heated by firing, the snow melts and the moisture spreads to other surfaces. When the weapon cools, the moisture will freeze and lock the mechanism tightly, preventing further operation. Occasional operation of the weapon by hand may keep its parts from freezing together.

Care of Weapons in Tropical Climates

In those tropical parts of the world where large water areas exist, there is a large amount of moisture in the air and extra precautions must be taken to prevent your weapon from rusting. At all times it will be necessary to clean your weapons more than once a day.

Care of Weapons in Desert Climates

Due to the fact that there is little moisture in the air, rust is a small problem in the desert, but where vegetation does not cover the earth, a large quantity of dirt, dust and sand is constantly swept through the air by wind. This material sticks to exposed oil and grease on your weapon. Grit of this nature caught between moving parts increases friction. A large amount will jam the moving parts and prevent their functioning. If the weapon does function under these conditions, the parts will almost certainly become worn, resulting in stoppage and requiring frequent replacement. Remember, in desert climates, use as little oil as possible and clean your weapons often.

Repairs

When you find a part broken or missing on your weapon, report it at once. Your weapon will be repaired by a qualified ordnance repairman. Above all, do not attempt to detail strip or repair your weapon yourself. Modern military weapons are expensive and made by precision methods. Without the proper skill and tools, attempts by you to repair your own weapon can be damaging to the weapon and dangerous to you.

Special Instructions

Due to the difference in operation and construction of some weapons, additional steps and precautions are required for their care that are not covered by this chapter. These special instructions are covered in the chapter on the particular weapon.

Chapter Sixteen

Service Pistol

The Marine Corps is currently using the 9mm, M9, which came into service in 1986.

The 9mm service pistol, M9, is a semiautomatic, recoil operated, double action pistol. It fires the 9mm round from a 15 round staggered magazine.

Cycle of Operation

There are eight steps in the cycle of operation for the M9 service pistol:

Feeding: The slide starts forward, pushed by the recoil spring. The face of the slide makes contact with the cartridge at the top of the magazine, stripping it from the magazine and pushing it toward the chamber.

Chambering: As the slide continues forward, it pushes the cartridge into the chamber.

Locking: As the slide assembly continues to move forward, the locking block lugs move into the locking block recesses on the right and left sides of the slide.

Firing: Once the thumb safety is off and the trigger is pulled to the rear, the hammer falls on the firing pin, which strikes and ignites the round.

Unlocking: As the slide assembly moves to the rear, the locking block rotates out of the notches in the slide and begins its movements rearward.

Extracting: As the slide moves rearward, the extractor withdraws the cartridge case out of the chamber.

Ejecting: As the face of the slide passes over the ejector, the case strikes the ejector and is knocked upward and outward through the ejection port.

Cocking: As the slide moves rearward, the hammer is pushed back allowing the sear to engage the hammer hooks.

Equipment Description

Principles of Operation

The M9 pistol has a short recoil system utilizing a falling locking block.

Upon firing, the pressure developed by the combustion gases recoils the slide-barrel assembly. After a short run, the locking block will stop the rearward movement of the barrel and release the slide which will continue its rearward movement. The slide will then extract and eject the fired cartridge case, cock the hammer and compress the recoil spring. The slide moves forward feeding the next cartridge from the magazine into the chamber.

The slide and barrel assembly remains open after the last cartridge has been fired and ejected.

Major Components

The five major components of the M9 service pistol are shown in Figure 16-1.

Slide and Barrel Assembly (1). Houses the bolt, firing pin, striker, and extractor, and cocks the hammer during recoil cycle.

Recoil Spring and Recoil Spring Guide (2). Absorbs recoil and returns the slide assembly to its forward position.

Barrel and Locking Block Assembly (3). Houses cartridge for firing, directs projectile and locks barrel in position during firing.

Receiver (4). Serves as a support for all major components. Houses action of pistol through four

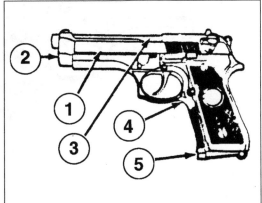

Fig. 16-1. *Major Components.*

major components.   Controls functioning of pistol. Magazine holds cartridge in place for stripping and chambering.

Magazine (5). Holds 15 cartridges in place for feeding and chambering.

The 9mm pistol has the following characteristics:
Caliber 9x19mm (9mmNATO)
System of Operation..Short recoil, semiautomatic
Locking System ....Oscillating block
Length ....217mm (8.54 in.)
Width ....38mm (1.50 in.)
Height..140mm (5.51 in.)
Weight (w/empty magazine ....960 gr (33.86 oz.)
Weight (w/15 round magazine) 1145 gr (40.89 oz.)
Barrel Length ....125mm (4.92 in.)
Rifling…R.H. 6 groove [pitch 250mm (about 10 in.)]
Front Sight ....Blade, integral with slide
Rear Sight ....Notched bar, dovetailed to slide
Slide Stop..........Holds slide open after last round

Safety Features

The 9mm pistol incorporates several valuable safety features. These include:
- Manual safety, located on the slide, which separates the firing pin from the hammer, lowers the hammer when cocked and interrupts the connection between the trigger and sear.
- Firing pin block, prevents any motion of the firing pin and is overcome only by pulling on the trigger.
- Half cock position hammer.

Operating

Operations and Characteristics

Double Action. When a cartridge is in the chamber with the safety on and the hammer down, double action allows the pistol to fire by placing the safety in the fire position and pulling the trigger.

Magazine. Has a 15 cartridge capacity (Fig. 16-2, Number 1.)

In non-tactical situations, visual inspection of the chamber is recommended.

Extractor/Loaded Chamber Indicator. When there is a cartridge in the chamber, the upper surface of the extractor protrudes from the right side of the slide. In the dark, the protrusion can be felt by touch. The loaded chamber indicator should be used in tactical situations (combat environment) where visual

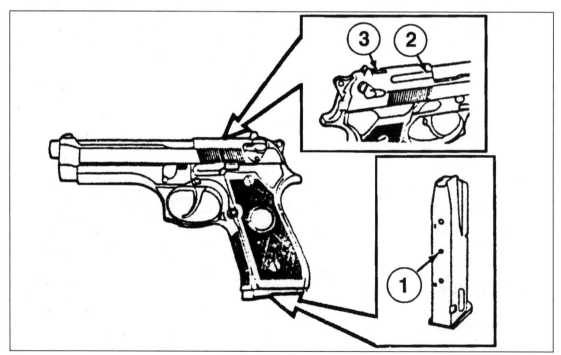

Fig. 16-2.

inspection of the chamber is not desirable and stealth must be maintained. (Fig. 16-2, Number 2.)

Warning: A potential safety hazard exists if the firing pin block is missing or does not return flush with the slide surface after firing.

Firing Pin Block. When the trigger is not pulled, the firing pin block secures the firing pin and prevents it from moving forward, even if the pistol is dropped. (Fig. 16-2, Number 3.)

Ambidextrous Safety. Allows safe operation of the pistol by both right and left handed users, and lowers the hammer without causing an accidental discharge. Pistol is shown with safety in the fire (up) position. When hammer is cocked, it may be safely lowered by moving the safety to the safe (down) position. (Fig. 16-3, Number 4.)

Lanyard Loop. Compatible with standard lanyards. (Fig. 16-3, Number 5.)

Receiver. The front and back straps of the grip are vertically grooved (Fig. 16-3, Number 6) to ensure a firm grip even with wet hands or under conditions of rapid combat fire. The trigger guard (Fig. 16-3, Number 7) is extended and the concave forward portion is grooved for a firm grip when using two hands or gloves.

Disassembly Lever and Disassembly Button. Allows for quick field stripping and, at the same time, prevents accidental assembly. (Fig. 16-3, Numbers 8 and 9.)

Slide Stop. Holds the slide to the rear after the last cartridge is fired. It can also be manually operated. (Fig. 16-3, Number 10.)

Weapons Handling

Safety Rules

These four rules must be repetitive to ensure adherence will be automatic when in possession of or in proximity to weapons.

Rule 1: Treat every weapon as if it were loaded.

Rule 2: Never point a weapon at anything you do not intend to shoot.

Rule 3: Keep finger straight and off the trigger until you are ready to fire.

Rule 4: Keep weapon on safe until you intend to fire.

Weapons Conditions

Condition 1: Magazine inserted, slide forward, round in chamber, hammer down and safety on.

Condition 2: Does not apply to the M9 service pistol.

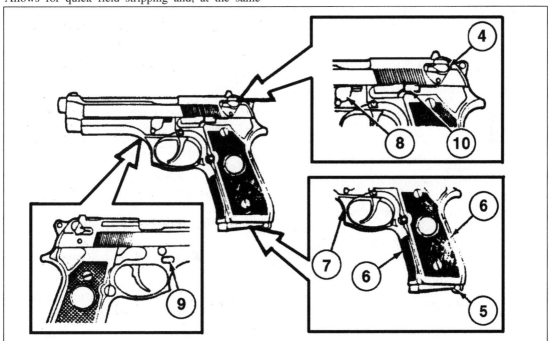

Fig. 16-3.

Condition 3: Magazine inserted, slide forward, chamber empty and safety on.

Condition 4: Magazine removed, slide forward, chamber empty and safety on.

Commands

"**LOAD**" is the command to take a weapon from condition 4 to condition 3.

A. Ensure the pistol is in condition 4.

B. Raise the muzzle of the pistol to eye level and turn the magazine well inboard at a 45 degree angle.

C. Remove a magazine from the ammunition pocket.

D. Index the magazine with the left hand by sliding the index finger along the forward edge of the magazine until the finger is touching the tip of the round to ensure the magazine is filled.

E. Insert the filled magazine into the magazine well by guiding it with the index finger. Ensure it is fully inserted.

"**MAKE READY**" is the command to take a weapon from condition 3 to condition 1.

A. Grasp the serrated sides of the slide with the fingers and thumb of the left hand.

B. Pull the slide to its rearmost position and release.

"**UNLOAD**" is the command to take a weapon from any condition to condition 4.

A. Place the decocking/safety lever in the "safe" position.

B. Remove the magazine from the M9 and retain.

C. Pull the slide to the rear.

D. Ensure the chamber is empty and no ammunition is present.

E. Release the slide allowing it to go forward on an empty chamber.

F. Place the M9 in holster.

G. Recover, inspect and insert any ejected ammunition into magazine.

H. Return magazine to ammunition pocket and close pocket.

"**UNLOAD SHOW CLEAR**" is the command used that will allow the chamber to be checked by a second individual prior to going to condition 4.

A. Place the decocking/safety lever in the "safe" position.

B. Remove the magazine from the M9 and retain.

C. Lock the slide to the rear.

D. Ensure the chamber is empty and no ammunition is present.

E. Have a second party inspect the chamber to ensure no ammunition is present.

F. Release the slide allowing it to go forward on an empty chamber.

G. Place the M9 in the holster.

H. Recover, inspect and insert any ejected ammunition into the magazine.

I. Return magazine to ammunition pocket and close pocket.

Immediate Action

An unintentional interruption in the cycle of operation is a stoppage. Applying immediate action can correct a stoppage. Immediate action is an essential subject for all Marines.

To clear an interruption in the cycle of operation, perform the following steps:

• TAP: Tap the bottom of the magazine to ensure it is seated.

• RACK: Rack the slide to the rear and release.

• BANG: Aim the pistol and fire.

Immediate action is performed without investigating the cause of interruption.

Remedial Action

Remedial action is performed when a stoppage cannot be cleared by immediate action. Remedial action requires investigating the cause of the stoppage, clearing the stoppage and returning the weapon to operation. To perform remedial action, use the procedures outlined in the acronym "SPORS." SPORS is divided into two phases:

Phase 1.

S – Seek cover.

P – Pull the slide all the way to the rear and attempt to lock the slide to the rear.

O – Observe for a round or brass to be ejected and take appropriate action to clear the stoppage.

Phase 2.

R – Release the slide by depressing the slide stop.

S – Sight and attempt to fire.

Weapons Transports

Holster Transport: Pistol is transported in the M12 holster when no immediate threat is present.

Administrative Transport: The pistol is carried at raised pistol, in condition 4, for administrative purpose, and only when the Marine does not have a holster.

Weapons Carries

Tactical Carry: This carry is used when enemy contact is likely. The arms are extended down at a 45 degree angle to the body while holding the pistol firmly with both hands. The decocking/safety lever is in the safe position. The trigger finger is straight along the receiver .

Ready: This carry is used when contact with the enemy is imminent. The arms are extended toward the target, just below eye level, while holding pistol firmly with both hands. The decocking/safety lever is in the safe position. The trigger finger is straight along the receiver.

Preventative Maintenance Checks and Services (PMCS)

Preventative Maintenance Checks and Services (PMCS) are performed before, during and after operation of the M9 pistol. The PMCS consist of eleven items which are listed in the following PMCS table.

Note: Always keep in mind the WARNINGS and CAUTIONS.

Preventative Maintenance Checks and Services (PMCS)

B-Before Operation   **D-During Operation**   **A-After Operation**

Item NO.	Interval B	D	A	ITEM TO BE INSPECTED Procedure	Equipment is NOT READY/AVAILABLE IF:
1	•			**Equipment.** Check the additional authorized equipment for completeness and serviceability.	
2	•			**9mm Pistol.** Visually inspect the entire pistol for damaged or missing components. 	There are damaged or missing components.
3	•			**AMBIDEXTROUS SAFETY.** a. Place safety in safe position, pull trigger. Hammer should not move.	Hammer moves to the rear.
				b. Place safety in fire position (shown). Pull trigger fully to the rear. Hammer should cycle.	Hammer does not move to the rear.
				c. Manually cock hammer. Place safety in safe position. Hammer should not fall. — SAFETY	Hammer remains cocked.

Preventative Maintenance Checks and Services (PMCS)

	B-Before Operation	D-During Operation	A-After Operation

Item NO.	B	D	A	ITEM TO BE INSPECTED Procedure	Equipment is NOT READY/AVAILABLE IF:
4	•			**SLIDE STOP.** Place safety in fire position. Pull slide fully to rear while pushing up on slide stop. Slide should lock to the rear. **SLIDE STOP**	Slide stop does not lock and slide returns to forward position. ←
5	•			**MAGAZINE CATCH ASSEMBLY.** **MAGAZINE RELEASE BUTTON**	a. Insert an empty magazine into the magazine well until fully seated in place. Hold pistol in an upright position. Magazine should remain seated. Magazine falls free. ← b. Prepare to catch magazine. Depress magazine release button. Magazine should fall free. Magazine does not fall free. ←
6	•			**MAGAZINE ASSEMBLY.** a. Visually inspect for missing or damaged parts. Magazine should be free of damage. **FOLLOWER** **MAGAZINE ASSEMBLY** **WARNING** - Be sure to clear weapon before performing PMCS.	There are missing or damaged parts. ← b. Depress follower with finger and release. Follower should move freely. Follower does not return to uppermost position. ← c. Insert empty magazine into the magazine well until fully seated in place. Hold pistol in an upright position. Magazine should remain seated. Magazine falls free. ←
7	•	•		**PERIODIC INSPECTION OF PISTOL AND MAGAZINE.** a. Periodically inspect pistol and magazine to ensure that they are clean. b. Clean and lubricate pistol and magazine daily, when in use.	

Preventative Maintenance Checks and Services (PMCS)

B-Before Operation			**D-During Operation**	**A-After Operation**

Item NO.	Interval B	D	A	ITEM TO BE INSPECTED Procedure	Equipment is NOT READY/AVAILABLE IF:
8			•	**9mm PISTOL.** Disassemble pistol. Clean and lubricate according to instructions. Inspect all parts for serviceability.	Any parts require replacement.
9			•	**MAGAZINE ASSEMBLY.** Disassemble magazine. Clean and lubricate according to instructions. Inspect all parts for serviceability.	Any parts require replacement.
10	•		•	Perform Safety/Function Check.	
11	•	•	•	Report all damaged or missing parts to organizational maintenance/next authorized repair level.	

Before you operate. Perform your before (B) PMCS.
During operation. Perform during your (D) PMCS.
After operation. Perform after your (A) PMCS.
Warning: Before starting an inspection procedure ensure the pistol is in condition 4. Do not keep live ammunition near work/maintenance area.

Warning: Always keep a straight trigger finger unless you intend to fire. Make sure the pistol is not already in condition 1.

Preparation for firing

Perform your Before Operation (B) PMCS.

Filling the Magazine

Hold the magazine (Fig. 16-4, Number 1) in one hand. With the other hand place a cartridge (2) on the follower (3) in front of the lips (4). Press down and slide the cartridge completely back under the lips.

Repeat until the magazine is completely filled (15 cartridges). Holes (5) on the back side of the magazine allow for visual counting of cartridges.

Loading the Pistol

Warning: The M9 pistol incorporates single and double action modes of fire. With the safety in the fire position in the double action mode, squeezing the trigger will automatically cock and fire the pistol. Always keep your finger away from the trigger unless you intend to fire.

Note: Always ensure that the pistol is in condition 4 before loading.

Insert the filled magazine (Fig. 16-5, Number 1) into the magazine well (2) of the pistol until a click of the magazine catch is heard. This will ensure proper catch engagement.

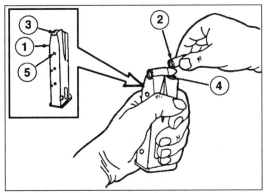

Fig. 16-4. *Filling the magazine.*

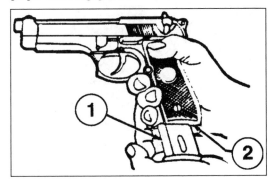

Fig. 16-5. *Loading the pistol.*

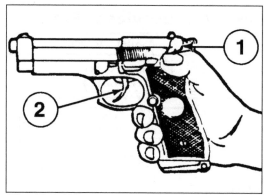

Fig. 16-6. *When ready to fire.*

With the pistol pointed in a safe direction, grasp the serrated portion of the slide and retract the slide to the rear. Releasing the slide will strip a cartridge from the magazine and chamber it.

Warning: The pistol is now in condition 1.

Release the manual safety by rotating the safety lever (Fig. 16-6, Number 1) to the fully upward position with the thumb.

Warning: The pistol is now ready to fire. Aim the pistol at the target. Fire by squeezing the trigger (2).

Note: For double action firing, the hammer must be in the forward or half cocked position. Squeezing the trigger will cock and release the hammer, firing the pistol.

After the first shot the pistol will continually fire in the single action mode.

When the hammer is in the down position, the single action firing mode can be accomplished by manually cocking the hammer with the thumb.

When the last round in the magazine has been fired, the slide will remain to the rear.

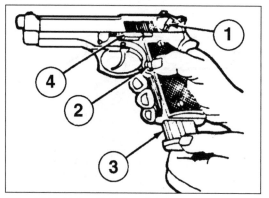

Fig. 16-7. *Unloading the pistol.*

Unloading the pistol

- Place safety (Fig 16-7, Number 1) in "safe" position.
- Depress the magazine release button (2) to remove the magazine (3) from the pistol.
- With the pistol pointing in a safe direction, grasp the slide serrations and fully retract the slide to remove any chambered cartridge.
- Lock the slide to the rear using the slide stop (4) and visually inspect the chamber to ensure that it is empty. Depress the slide stop and watch the slide go forward on an empty chamber. You are now in condition 4.

Emptying the Magazine

With one hand, hold magazine upright with front end forward. With the thumb firmly press down on the cartridge rim and push forward. As the cartridge moves forward, tip it upward and out with the index finger.

Repeat the above step until the magazine is empty.

Maintenance Procedures

Disassembly (Field Stripping)

Caution: Dry firing of the pistol is only to be done in conjunction with the function checks in PMCS and/or during training.

Do not allow the hammer to fall with full force by pulling the trigger when the slide is removed as damage to the receiver will occur. If necessary, the hammer should be manually lowered.

Step 1. Ensure the pistol is in condition 4. (See Fig. 16-8, Number 1.)

Step 2. Allow slide (2) to return fully forward.

Step 3. Hold pistol in the right hand with muzzle slightly elevated. With the forefinger press disassembly lever release button (3) and with thumb rotate disassembly lever (4) downward until it stops.

Step 4. Pull the slide and barrel assembly (5) forward and remove.

Step 5. Slightly compress recoil spring (Fig. 16-9, Number 6) and spring guide (7), while at the same time lifting and removing recoil spring (6) and spring guide (7). Allow the recoil spring to stretch slowly.

Warning: Use care when removing recoil spring and spring guide. Due to the amount of compression, assembly will be released under spring tension and

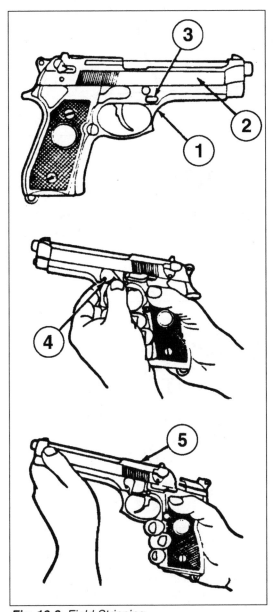

Fig. 16-8. Field Stripping.

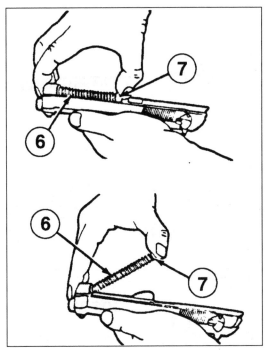

Fig. 16-9.

rel assembly (11) from slide (12).

Note: Use the following steps to disassemble the magazine.

Step 8. Ensure there is no ammunition present in the magazine.

Step 9. Grasp the magazine firmly with the floor-plate (Fig. 16-12, Number 1) up and back of the magazine tube (2) against the palm of the hand.

Note: To remove the floorplate use the barrel locking block plunger. By depressing the locking block, the locking block plunger will protrude and can be used to assist in removal of the floorplate.

Step 10. Release the floorplate (Fig. 16-13, Number 1) by pushing down on the floorplate retainer stud (2) in the center of the floorplate (1). At the same time, slide the floorplate (1) forward for a short distance using the thumb.

Caution: Magazine spring is under slight tension. Use care when removing magazine floorplate.

Step 11. While maintaining the magazine spring pressure with the thumb, remove the floorplate (Fig. 16-14, Number 1) from the magazine.

Step 12. Remove the floorplate retainer and magazine spring (3) and follower (4) from the magazine tube (5). Remove the floorplate retainer (6) from magazine spring (3).

could cause possible injury to personnel or become damaged or lost.

Step 6. Separate recoil spring (Fig. 16-10, Number 6) from spring guide (7).

Step 7. Push in on locking block plunger (Fig. 16-11, Number 8) while pushing barrel (9) forward slightly. Lift and remove locking block (10) and bar-

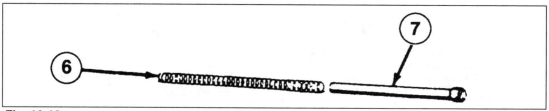

Fig. 16-10.

Fig. 16-11.

Fig. 16-12.

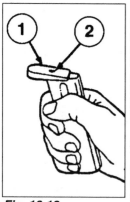

Fig. 16-13.

Inspection

Note: If faults are found during inspection that cannot be corrected, evacuate pistol to organizational maintenance/next authorized repair level.

Slide Assembly (Fig. 16-15, Example A). Check for free movement of ambidextrous safety (1) and push on firing pin block (2). Check for rear sight (3) looseness.

Barrel Assembly (Fig. 16-15, Example B). Inspect bore and chamber (4) for pitting or obstructions. Check locking block plunger (5) for free movement of locking block (6). Inspect locking lugs (7) for cracks and burrs.

Recoil Spring and Recoil Spring Guide (Fig. 16-16, Example C). Check recoil spring (1) for damage. Check that it is not bent. Check recoil spring guide (2) for

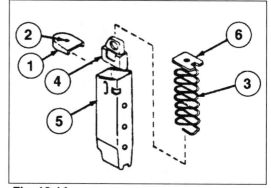

Fig. 16-14.

straightness and smoothness. Check to be sure that it is free of cracks and burrs.

Receiver Assembly (Fig. 16-17, Example D). Check for bends, chips and cracks. Check for free movement of slide stop (1) and magazine catch assembly (2). Check guide rails (3) for excessive wear, burrs, cracks or chips.

Magazine Assembly (Fig. 16-18). Check for spring (1) and follower (2) damage. Ensure that the lips (3) of the magazine are not excessively bent and are free of cracks and burrs. The magazine tube (4) should not be bent or dirty.

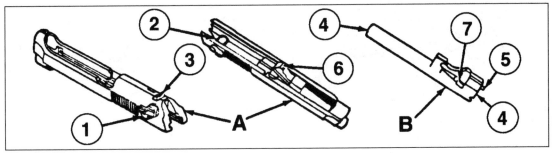

Fig. 16-15.

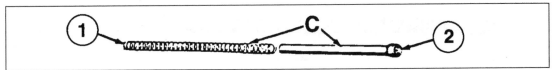

Fig. 16-16.

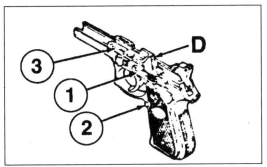

Fig. 16-17.

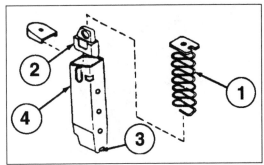

Fig. 16-18.

Cleaning and Lubrication

Note: When cleaning, be careful not to lose component parts.

Caution: Bore brush is for cleaning bore only. Use of bore brush on any other part of the pistol will cause damage.

Slide Assembly (Fig. 16-19). Clean slide assembly with cloth. A soft brush and CLP (cleaner-lubricant-preservative) can assist in removal of excess dirt and carbon buildup. Ensure the safety (1), bolt face (2), slide guides (3) and extractor (4) are free of excess dirt and residue.

Wipe dry with a cloth and apply a light coat of CLP.

Barrel Assembly (Fig. 16-20). Insert bore brush into chamber end (1) of barrel, making sure it completely clears the muzzle (2) before it is pulled back through the bore. Repeat several times to loosen carbon deposits.

Dry the barrel by pushing a swab through the bore. Repeat as necessary until a clean swab can be observed. Clean locking block (3) with a soft brush.

Apply a light coat of CLP to the barrel bore and chamber area. Also, lubricate the exterior surfaces of the barrel and locking block.

Recoil Spring and Recoil Spring Guide (Fig. 16-21). Clean recoil spring (1) and recoil spring guide (2) using CLP and soft brush or cloth. After wiping the recoil spring (1) and recoil spring guide (2), apply a light coat of CLP/LSA.

Receiver Assembly (Fig. 16-22). Wipe receiver assembly clean with cloth. Use a soft brush for hard to clean areas. Pay special attention to disassembly lever (1), trigger (2), slide stop (3), hammer (4) and magazine release button (5). Apply a light coat of CLP/LSA.

Magazine (Fig. 16-23). Wipe magazine tube (1) and follower (2) with a cloth. Clean the magazine tube and follower with CLP and a soft brush.

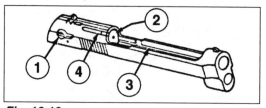

Fig. 16-19.

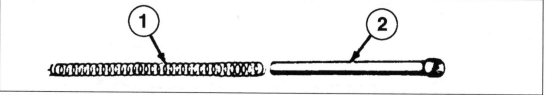

Fig. 16-20.

Fig. 16-21.

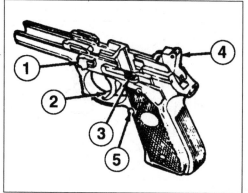

Fig. 16-22.

With a cloth, wipe the magazine spring (3), floorplate retainer (4) and floorplate (5) clean. Apply a light coat of CLP/LSA.

Reassembly. To reassemble the pistol and magazine follow the twelve steps described below:

Step 1. Grasp the slide (Fig. 16-24, Number 1) with the bottom facing up. With the other hand grasp the barrel assembly (2) with the locking block (3) facing up.

Step 2. Insert muzzle of the barrel (2) into the forward open end of the slide (1). At the same time lower the rear of the barrel assembly by slightly moving the barrel downward with light thumb pressure. The barrel will fall into place.

Step 3. Insert recoil spring (Fig. 16-25, Number 4) onto recoil spring guide (5).

Caution: During spring insertion, spring tension must be maintained until spring guide is fully seated onto the cutaway on the locking block.

Step 4. Insert end of recoil spring (Fig. 16-26, Number 4) and recoil spring guide (5) into slide recoil spring housing (6). At the same time, compress the recoil spring and lower the spring guide until fully seated onto the locking block cutaway (7).

Caution: Be sure hammer is uncocked and firing pin block lever is in the down position. If the hammer is cocked, carefully and manually lower the hammer. Do not pull the trigger while placing the slide onto the receiver.

Step 5. Push firing pin block lever (Fig. 16-27, Number 8), opposite ejector (9) down. Grasp the slide and barrel assembly, sights (10) up and align the slide (11) onto the receiver assembly guide rails (12).

Step 6. Push until the rear of the slide (11) is a short distance beyond the rear of the receiver assem-

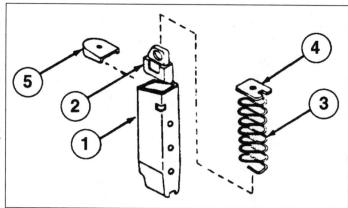

Fig. 16-23.

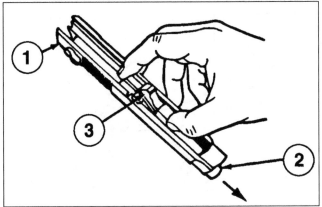

Fig. 16-24.

bly (13) and hold. At the same time, rotate the disassembly latch lever (14) upward. A click indicates a positive lock.

Note: Use the following steps to reassemble the magazine.

Step 7. Insert the follower (Fig. 16-28, Number 1) into the top coil (2) of the magazine spring. The top coil has an upward and forward pointing end.

Ensure that the notches (3) on the follower and magazine tube are on the same side.

Step 8. Insert the magazine spring with the follower into the magazine tube.

Step 9. Turn the magazine bottom up with the back side against the palm of the hand.

Step 10. Attach and center the floorplate retainer (4) to bottom spring coil.

Caution: After insertion, spring tension must be maintained using the thumb.

Do not place lips of magazine tube on a hard surface during reassembly.

Step 11. Push and hold the magazine spring (5) and floorplate retainer (4) down. At the same time, slide floorplate (6) over the side walls until fully seated. This will be indicated by a click.

Step 12. Insert the magazine into the magazine well of the pistol carefully. A click indicates the locked position.

Warning: Make sure pistol is in condition 4.

Safety/Function Check. Now check the pistol using the following seven steps:

Step 1. Insure the pistol is in condition 4.

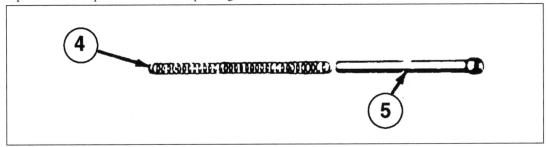

Fig. 16-25.

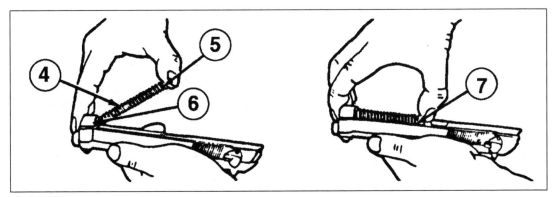

Fig. 16-26.

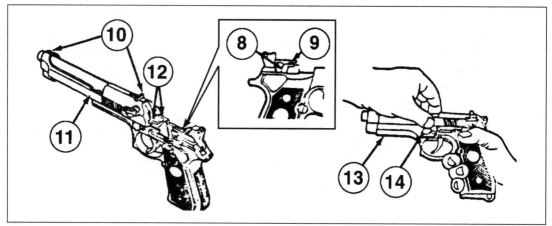

Fig. 16-27.

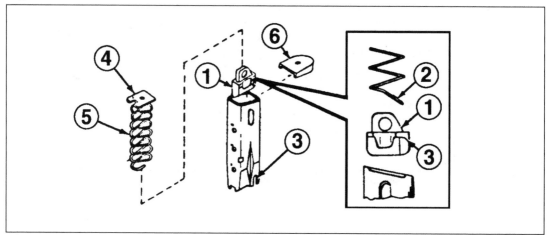

Fig. 16-28.

Step 2. Squeeze and release trigger. Firing pin block should move up and down. Hammer should not move.

Step 3. Place safety in fire position.

Step 4. Squeeze trigger to check double action. Hammer should cock and fall.

Step 5. Squeeze trigger again and hold to rear. Manually retract and release slide while holding trigger to the rear. Release trigger, click should be heard, hammer should not fall.

Step 6. Squeeze trigger to check single action. Hammer should fall.

Step 7. If the above safety/function checks perform as indicated, pistol is mission ready. If the checks do not perform as indicated, evacuate to organizational maintenance/next authorized repair level.

Qualification Firing

With the adoption of the 9mm pistol the Marine Corps has instituted a new, more realistic pistol qualification firing course. This course consists of 15 rounds slow fire at 25 yards, fired single action; 5 rounds quick fire at 25 yards, fired double action; two 6-round strings fired double action at 15 yards and four 2-round strings in quick reaction drill firing at 7 yards. Additionally, a 40-round Close Combat Pistol Course is also used.

The firing positions for the service pistol are shown in Figures 16-29 through 16-40.

Fig. 16-29. Open holster.

Fig. 16-30. Withdraw pistol.

Fig. 16-31. Insert magazine.

Fig. 16-32. Tap to seat magazine.

Fig. 16-33. Pull slide to rear.

Fig. 16-34. Correct hand position to pull slide to rear.

Fig. 16-35. Release slide using slingshot method.

Fig. 16-36. Ready position.

Fig. 16-37. Correct position of hands in ready position.

Fig. 16-38. Firing position.

Fig. 16-39. Firing position (note position of feet).

Fig. 16-40. *Firing position (note pistol alignment).*

Chapter Seventeen

M16A2

During your early training you learned the Creed of the United States Marine, *My Rifle*. In that Creed is included a solemn promise to hit, for it is only the hits that count. Every Marine has made the same pledge. Every Marine has been trained as a rifleman, for it is the rifleman who must close with and destroy the enemy.

Each item of equipment in the modern amphibious assault force – from the multimillion-dollar aircraft carrier to the least expensive radio battery; every highly skilled Marine – from a jet pilot to the operator of a small, portable radio – exists to get the Marine rifleman in position to close with and destroy the enemy. Once there, the job done will depend on how well you know your rifle, the care you give it and the manner in which you use it.

This chapter tells you the names and parts of your rifle, the way to strip it and put it back together, the proper care to keep it operating and how to reduce common stoppages.

Rifles used to be made one at a time, of carefully selected hardwoods and machined steel. However, science has enabled us to mass produce rifles from lightweight alloys and plastics. But the basic weapon of a Marine is still the rifle, regardless of the model, the type or the manner in which it's made. This fact will never change. The present rifle used by Marines is the M16A2, which is an improved model of the M16A1 adopted by the Marine Corps during the Vietnam War.

Become thoroughly acquainted with your rifle and treat it well. The success of your mission, your life and the lives of your buddies, may someday depend on you and your rifle.

Description

Description. The M16A2 rifle is a 5.56mm, magazine-fed, gas-operated, air-cooled, shoulder-fired weapon. It is designed for either semiautomatic or three-round burst-control fire through the use of a selector lever. The barrel is surrounded by two aluminum-lined fiberglass hand guards which are notched to permit air to circulate around the barrel

and further serve to protect the gas tube. A super nylon butt plate is attached to the rear of the stock to partially reduce the effects of recoil. A forward assist assembly located on the right rear of the upper receiver permits manual locking of the bolt when this is not done by the force of the action spring. A spring-loaded retaining pin can be depressed with the nose of a cartridge to allow the trigger guard to be rotated down against the pistol grip to permit the firer ready access to the trigger when wearing gloves. A dust cover is provided to prevent dirt and sand from getting into the rifle through the ejection port. The dust cover should be kept closed at all times when the rifle is not being fired. It is opened automatically by the forward or rearward movement of the bolt carrier. (See Fig. 17-1.)

General Data

Weight	Kilograms	(Pounds)
Rifle without magazine	3.50	(7.78)
Empty magazine		
(20 rounds)	0.09	(.20)
(30 rounds)	0.11	(.25)
Full magazine		
(20 rounds)	0.32	(.70)
(30 rounds)	0.46	(1.01)
Rifle with 30-round magazine	3.99	(8.79)
Bipods, M3	0.27	(.60)
Bayonet-knife, M7	0.27	(.60)

Length

	Centimeters	(Inches)
Rifle with bayonet knife, M7	114.0	(44.87)
Rifle overall with flash compensator	100.6	(39.62)
Barrel (with flash compensator)	53.34	(21.00)
Barrel (without flash compensator)	50.8	(20.00)

Ammunition

Ball (standard)
Tracer (standard)
Blank (standard)

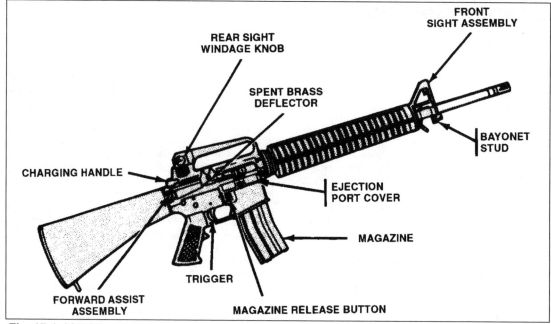

Fig. 17-1. *M16A2.*

Operational Capabilities

Cyclic Rate of Fire ....800 rds/min
Average Rate of Fire ....10-12 rds/min
Sustained Rate of Fire..............12-15 rds/min
Maximum Range......................3,534 m
Maximum Effective Range ......550 m (pt target)
....800 m (area target)
Muzzle Velocity ....3,100 fps
Chamber Pressure ....52,000 psi

Disassembly and Assembly

Disassembly of the M16 Rifle

Individual Marines are authorized only to field strip the M16A2. This is done for cleaning or instruction only. No force should be used in disassembling or assembling the rifle. When disassembling the M16 rifle the parts should be laid out left to right in the order they are taken out of the rifle and put back in the reverse order.

Clearing the M16 Rifle

The first consideration in handling any weapon is to ensure that the weapon is clear. To clear the M16 rifle:

- Attempt to point the selector lever to SAFE. If the weapon is not cocked, the selector lever cannot be pointed to SAFE. In either case go on to the next step.
- Remove the magazine by grasping it with the right hand and depress the magazine release button with the thumb. Pull the magazine straight down to remove it from the weapon.
- Lock the bolt carrier to the rear by grasping the charging handle and depressing the charging handle latch and pulling the charging handle all the way to the rear; press in on the bottom of the bolt catch with the thumb or forefinger. Allow the bolt carrier to move slowly forward until the bolt engages the bolt catch. Return the charging handle to its forward position.
- Inspect the receiver and chamber by looking through the ejection port to ensure that these areas do not contain any ammunition.
- Check the selector lever to ensure that it points toward SAFE. (See Fig. 17-2.)
- *Note:* The rifle is clear only where there is no round in the chamber, the magazine is out, bolt carrier is

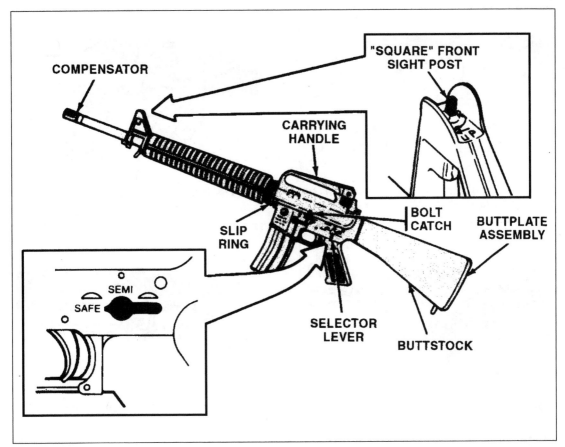

COMPENSATOR

"SQUARE" FRONT SIGHT POST

CARRYING HANDLE

SLIP RING

BOLT CATCH

BUTTPLATE ASSEMBLY

SEMI

SAFE

SELECTOR LEVER

BUTTSTOCK

Fig. 17-2.

locked to the rear, and the selector is in the "safe" position.

Field Stripping

- Ensure the weapon is in condition 4 (magazine removed, chamber empty, bolt forward, safety on, ejection port cover closed). Allow the bolt carrier to go forward by depressing the upper portion of the bolt catch.
- Remove the sling and place the rifle on a table or flat surface, muzzle to the left, weapon on its right side.
- *Caution:* During the next step the selector must be in the SAFE position to prevent damage to the automatic sear.
- Use the nose of a cartridge to press the take down pin out from the left to the right until the upper

receiver swings free of the lower receiver. (See Figures 17-3 and 17-4.)
- *Caution:* The takedown pin does not come completely out of the receiver.
- Again using the nose of a cartridge, press out the receiver pivot pin. Separate the upper and lower receiver groups and place the lower receiver group on the table. (See Fig. 17-5.)
- *Caution:* The receiver pivot point pin does not come completely out of the receiver.
- Hold the upper receiver group with the muzzle to the left and the carrying handle up. Grasp the charging handle, depress the charging handle about 3 inches to the rear to withdraw the bolt carrier from the receiver. Grasp the bolt carrier and pull it from the receiver. When the bolt carrier is removed, the charging handle can be removed from its groove in the receiver. Place the upper receiver on the table. (See Figures 17-6 and 17-7.)

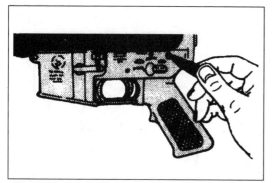

Fig. 17-3. *Push takedown pin as far as it will go. Pivot upper receiver from lower receiver.*

Fig. 17-4. *Push receiver pivot pin.*

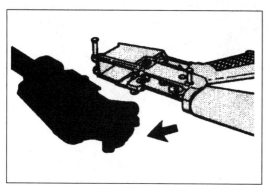

Fig. 17-5(a). *Separate upper and lower receivers.*

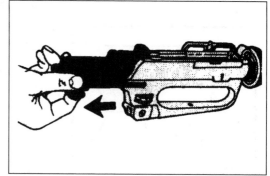

Fig. 17-5(b). *Pull back charging handle and bolt carrier.*

Fig. 17-6. *Remove bolt carrier and bolt.*

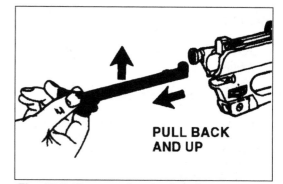

PULL BACK AND UP

Fig. 17-7. *Remove charging handle.*

- To disassemble the bolt carrier group, press out the firing pin retaining pin from right to left using the nose of a cartridge.
- Elevate the front of the bolt carrier and allow the firing pin to drop from its recess in the bolt. Rotate the bolt until the cam pin is clear of the bolt carrier key and remove the cam pin by rotat-

ing the head 90 degrees (1/4 turn) in either direction and lifting it out of the well in the bolt and bolt carrier.
- After the cam pin is removed, the bolt can be easily removed from its recess in the bolt carrier. (See Figures 17-8 through 17-14.)

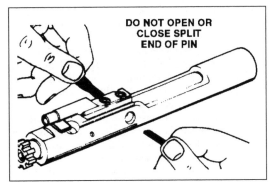

Fig. 17-8. Remove firing pin retaining pin.

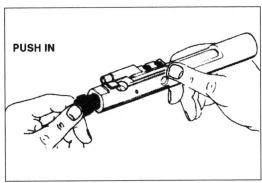

Fig. 17-9. Put bolt assembly in locked position.

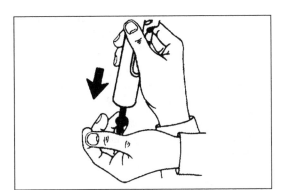

Fig. 17-10. Drop firing pin out rear of bolt carrier.

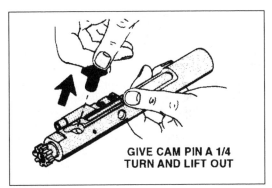

Fig. 17-11. Remove bolt cam pin.

Fig. 17-12. Remove bolt assembly from carrier.

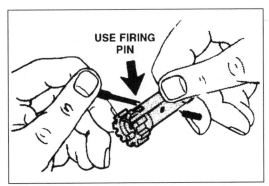

Fig. 17-13.

- Remove the extractor pin from the extractor by applying pressure on the extractor body just behind the pin (this compresses the extractor spring and reduces pressure on the pin). With a small pointed object push the extractor pin from the extractor body. This completes disassembly of the bolt carrier group. Only qualified ordnance personnel can further disassemble the bolt and bolt carrier.
- *Note:* Press rear of extractor to check spring function.
- *Caution:* The next two steps, removal of the buffer and action spring and of the hand guards, are described below but should be performed only

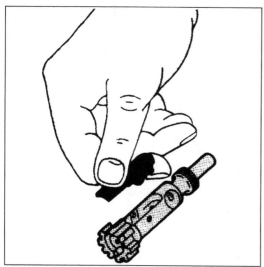

Fig. 17-14. Remove extractor and spring.

when absolutely necessary for care and cleaning.
- With the nose of a cartridge or the tip of the firing pin, push down on the buffer retainer. Allow the buffer assembly to move forward slowly until it is clear of the buffer retainer. Depress the hammer to the rear (downward) enough to allow the buffer assembly to clear the hammer. Remove the buffer assembly and the action spring.
- The last parts authorized to be removed by the individual Marine are the hand guards. To remove the hand guards, place the butt of the stock against a flat surface and pull down on the slip ring until the lower lip of one hand guard is clear; pull out and down on the hand guard until the upper lip is free of the hand guard cap. Repeat the same operation to remove the second hand guard. Considerable pressure is required to pull the slip ring down.
- This completes field stripping. The individual Marine ordinarily has no need to disassemble the weapon further. The lower receiver will not be disassembled by the individual rifleman without special authorization from one's superiors.

Assembly of the M16 Rifle

To reassemble the rifle, reverse the procedures of disassembly.

Assembly of the Lower Receiver. Place the trigger and disconnectors in position in the lower receiver. The trigger spring has to be forward. Press down on top of the disconnector until the holes in the trig-

ger and disconnector are aligned. Insert pin from right to left. Once pin is inserted, check trigger and disconnector for freedom of movement.
- Place the selector lever into the receiver from the left. Use the nose of a cartridge to depress the selector lever detent plunger. The selector lever is properly seated when the plunger snaps into a notch on the selector lever shaft.
- The selector lever must be in the BURST position before the sear is inserted. The tang of the sear fits in the left rear slot of the selector lever shaft. The long end of the sear spring fits in the groove on the left front of the selector lever shaft. Insert and seat the sear pin. Ensure that the sear moves into the proper position when the selector lever is rotated.
- Rotate the selector lever to the SEMI position. Press the hammer down into position, ensuring that the tails of the hammer spring are to the rear and on top of the trigger pin. Push down and forward on the hammer until the holes are aligned. Insert the pin from right to left. Ensure that the cam and clutch spring are connected to the right side of the hammer shaft.
- Insert the action spring and buffer assembly into the stock and push the open end of the spring into the receiver extension until the buffer retainer snaps into position. This completes assembly of the lower receiver.

Assembly of the Upper Receiver. When assembling the bolt carrier group, hold it in the right hand with the key up and to the left. Insert the bolt into the front of the bolt carrier; the ejector has to be down and to the left. Place the cam pin in its well and rotate it ¼ turn in either direction. Insert the firing pin through the open end of the bolt carrier and seat fully. Replace the firing pin retaining pin from left to right.

Note: Elevate the front end of the bolt carrier group to ensure that the firing pin is properly seated.
- Place the charging handle into the groove in the top of the receiver. The lugs on the charging handle must be seated in their grooves in the receiver. Slide the charging handle halfway forward. Insert the bolt carrier group with the bolt in the unlocked position. The carrier key must be in the slot on the underside of the charging handle. Push forward on the charging handle and the bolt carrier group until both are fully seated.
- Place the upper receiver group and lower receiver group together and reseat the receiver pivot pin.

Function Check – A function check of the rifle consists of checking the operation of the rifle while the selector lever is in each position; SAFE, SEMI and BURST. The rifle should be broken down into its three main groups to do this.

- To check the safety, the rifle has to be cocked. With the selector lever on SAFE, squeeze the trigger; the hammer should not fall.
- With the selector lever in the SEMI position, squeeze the trigger. The hammer should fall. Hold the trigger to the rear and recock the hammer. Still holding the trigger to the rear, push forward on the top of the automatic sear; the hammer should not fall.
- With the selector in the BURST position pull the hammer to the rear and release it. Pull the trigger and hold it to the rear. The hammer should fall. With the trigger held to the rear, pull the hammer to the rear and push forward on the top of the sear. The hammer should fall. Do this four times. On the fourth attempt the hammer should not fall. Release the trigger and pull again; press the sear and the hammer should fall.
- Cock the hammer and rotate the selector lever to the SAFE position. Withdraw the takedown pin and close the weapon. Fully seat the takedown pin and replace the sling. Caution: Before securing the upper and lower receiver the selector lever must be in the SAFE position to prevent damage to the automatic sear.

Introduction to the M16A2 Sights

Sight Adjustment

The sight system of the M16A2 rifle consists of a square front sight post and an aperture type rear sight. The front sight is adjustable for elevation and the rear sight is adjustable for both windage and elevation. The rear sight must be kept lubricated and extra clean. (See Fig. 17-15.)

Rear Sight. The rear sight consists of two flip type apertures, a windage knob and an elevation adjustment knob with scale. The aperture marked 0-2 is for ranges of 200 m or less. The smaller aperture is used to engage targets at ranges greater than 200 m. (See Fig. 17-16.) To adjust the windage simply turn the windage knob located on the right of the rear sight. To move the strike of the round to the right turn the windage knob clockwise. Turning the windage knob one click will move the strike of the round 1/2–inch (1.2 cm) for every 100 m of range. To adjust the sight for elevation, turn the horizontal elevation knob located under the sight. Read the scale on the left side of the elevation knob to determine the range setting. The setting of 8/3 may indicate a range setting of either 300 m or 800 m. If there is a noticeable gap between the rear sight base and the receiver

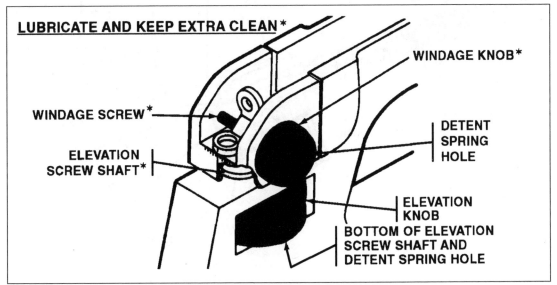

LUBRICATE AND KEEP EXTRA CLEAN *

WINDAGE KNOB *

WINDAGE SCREW *

ELEVATION SCREW SHAFT *

DETENT SPRING HOLE

ELEVATION KNOB

BOTTOM OF ELEVATION SCREW SHAFT AND DETENT SPRING HOLE

Fig. 17-15. Rear Sight.

SHORT RANGE (0-200 METERS)

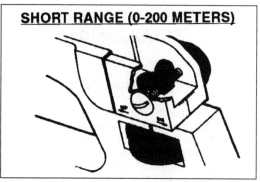

Fig. 17-16(a). Short Range - This "larger" aperture is used for 0-200 meters range. As shown above, the sight is set for 0-200 meters. This larger aperture is only used when the rear sight is all the way down. In other words, the 300-meter mark is aligned with the mark on the left side of the receiver.

NORMAL RANGE (300-800 METERS)

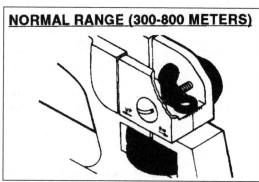

Fig. 17-16(b). Normal Range - This aperture is unmarked and used for most firing situations. It is used in conjunction with the elevation knob for 300, 400, 500, 600, 700, and 800 meter targets.

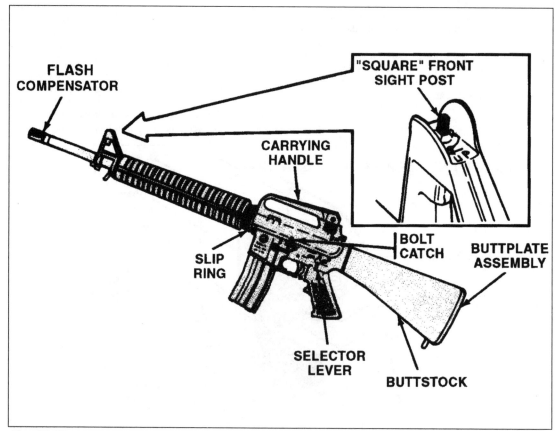

FLASH COMPENSATOR

"SQUARE" FRONT SIGHT POST

CARRYING HANDLE

SLIP RING

BOLT CATCH

BUTTPLATE ASSEMBLY

SELECTOR LEVER

BUTTSTOCK

Fig. 17-17.

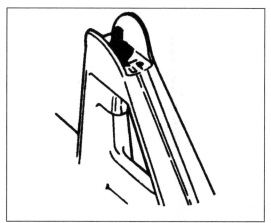

Fig. 17-18. The front sight post is moved up or down when zeroing the rear sight. Once the rear sight is zeroed, the front sight post should not be moved.

and the 8/3 setting is on the elevation scale then the sights are set for a range of 800 m. If no gap is visible the elevation is set for 300 m. One click on the elevation adjustment knob will move the strike of the round 1.5 inches (3.6 cm) for every 100 m of range.

Front Sight. The front sight consists of a rotating, square sight post with a spring-loaded detent. (See Fig. 17-17.) The front sight is used only when battlesighting the weapon. To move the strike of the round up, turn the front sight post clockwise. (See Fig. 17-18.) To lower the strike of the round, turn the front sight post counterclockwise. A sharp instrument such as the tip of a round will be necessary to press the detent down when turning the sight. Turning the front sight post one click will move the strike of the round 2.8 centimeters or approximately 1 inch for every 100 m of range.

Functioning

The cycle of functioning consists of eight basic steps: feeding, chambering, locking, firing, unlocking, extracting, ejecting and cocking. More than one of these steps can take place at the same time. Functioning in the rifle may be either burst-controlled or semiautomatic through the use of the selector lever.

Cycle of Operation

There are eight steps in the cycle of operation for the M16A2 service rifle:

Feeding: Feeding is the stripping of a round from the magazine by the bolt.

Chambering: Chambering is the pushing of the round into the chamber by the bolt.

Locking: Locking is the alignment of the locking lugs on the bolt with the lugs on the barrel extension.

Firing: Firing is the ignition of the propellant within the cartridge case forcing the projectile out of the barrel.

Unlocking: Unlocking is the rotation of the bolt until the locking lugs no longer align with the lugs on the barrel extension.

Extracting: Extracting is the withdrawal of the cartridge case from the chamber by the extractor claw.

Ejecting: Ejecting is the expulsion of the cartridge case by the ejector and spring.

Cocking: Cocking is the resetting of the chamber.

Burst Control Fire

With the selector lever set in the BURST position, the rifle will fire 3-round bursts.

• As the trigger is squeezed, the cycle of functioning begins. The hammer is cocked as the bolt carrier recoils, but the center cam holds the disconnector down preventing it from engaging the lower hammer hook.

• The automatic sear, the bottom of which is now moved forward, catches the upper hammer hook and holds it until the bolt carrier moves forward. As the bolt carrier moves forward the rear portion strikes the top of the sear, releasing the hammer and causing the rifle to fire.

• The rifle will fire a 3-round burst using the cycle of function described. On the fourth round the burst control cam on the hammer retention pin causes the secondary disconnector to move upward and engage the lower hammer hook and thus interrupt the cycle of functioning.

• If the trigger is released the hammer moves forward and is caught by the nose of the trigger. This will end the burst-control automatic cycle until the trigger is again squeezed.

• All other portions of the cycle of functioning remain the same.

Action of the Magazine. The cycle of functioning stops when the trigger is released or when the magazine is empty.

• As the last round is fired, the magazine follower pushes up on the bottom of the bolt catch forcing it into the path of the bolt. This holds the bolt carrier to the rear.

- To chamber a round, first press in on the upper portion of the bolt catch to release the bolt carrier. *Caution:* If a new magazine has been inserted and the bolt carrier goes forward, the weapon is charged and ready to fire.

Weapons Handling

Purpose: Weapons handling prepares a Marine to employ individual weapons safely and confidently, standardizes procedures used during training and combat to enhance safety, and ensures consistency for loading, unloading and employing individual small arms.

Safety Rules

These safety rules apply to all weapons at all times and must never be violated.

Rule 1: Treat every weapon as if it were loaded.

Rule 2: Never point a weapon at anything you do not intend to shoot.

Rule 3: Keep finger straight and off the trigger until you are ready to fire.

Rule 4: Keep weapon on safe until you intend to fire.

Weapons Conditions

A weapon's readiness/safety status is described by one of four conditions. The steps in the loading and unloading process take the weapon through four specific conditions which indicate the weapon's readiness for live fire.

Condition 1: Magazine inserted, round in chamber, bolt forward, safety on, ejection port cover closed.

Condition 2: Not applicable to M16A2 service rifle.

Condition 3: Magazine inserted, chamber empty, bolt forward, safety on, ejection port cover closed.

Condition 4: Magazine removed, chamber empty, bolt forward, safety on, ejection port cover closed.

Commands

"UNLOAD" is the command used to take a weapon from any condition to condition 4.

A. Attempt to put the weapon on safe.

B. Remove the magazine from the weapon and retain it on your person.

C. Rotate weapon with ejection port down.

D. Pull the bolt to the rear.

E. Ensure the chamber is empty and no ammunition is present.

F. Release the charging handle and observe the bolt going forward on an empty chamber. *Note:* Put the weapon on safe now if it would not go on safe earlier.

G. Close ejection port cover.

H. Check sights.

I. Recover, inspect and insert any ejected ammunition into magazine.

J. Return magazine to magazine pouch and close pouch.

"LOAD" is the command that takes a weapon from condition 4 to condition 3.

A. Ensure the weapon is in condition 4.

B. Withdraw the magazine from the magazine pouch.

C. Ensure the magazine is filled.

D. Fully insert magazine in the magazine well.

E. Tug downward on the magazine to ensure that it is held into the rifle by the magazine catch.

F. Close the magazine pouch.

G. Close the ejection port cover.

"MAKE READY" is the command to take a weapon from condition 3 to condition 1.

A. Pull the charging handle fully to the rear and release.

B. Check sights.

C. Close ejection cover (if time and situation permit). *Note:* To ensure that ammunition has been chambered, pull the charging handle slightly to the rear and visually inspect the chamber. (You may tap the forward assist to ensure the bolt closes after inspecting the chamber.) *Caution:* Pulling the charging handle too far to the rear when inspecting the chamber may cause a double feed or ejection of one round of ammunition.

"FIRE" is the command used to specify when Marines may engage targets.

A. Take weapon off safe and place finger on trigger.

B. Engage target.

"UNLOAD, SHOW CLEAR" is the command used that will allow the chamber to be checked by a second individual prior to going to condition 4.

A. Attempt to put the weapon on safe.

B. Remove the magazine from weapon and retain it on your person.

C. Rotate weapon until ejection port is down.

D. Lock the bolt to the rear

E. Ensure chamber is empty and no ammunition is present.

Note: Put weapon on safe now if it would not go on safe earlier.

F. Have a second party inspect weapon to ensure no ammunition is present.
G. Release bolt catch and observe bolt going forward on an empty chamber.
H. Close ejection port cover.
I. Check sights.
J. Recover, inspect and insert any ejected ammunition into magazine (omit this step at night).
K. Return magazine to magazine pouch and close pouch.

Weapons Carries

Tactical Carry: Used when no immediate threat is present. Locate the buttstock of the weapon to the side of your body at approximately hip level with the muzzle angled up at approximately eye level and in the direction of the enemy.

Alert: Used when enemy contact is likely. Place the buttstock of the weapon in the pocket of your shoulder with the muzzle angled down at approximately 45 degrees in the direction of the enemy.

Ready: Used when enemy contact is imminent. Place the buttstock of the weapon in the pocket of your shoulder with the muzzle pointed in the direction of likely enemy contact. A clear field of view is maintained over the weapon sights until the target has been identified.

Immediate Action

An unintentional interruption in the cycle of operation is a stoppage. Applying immediate action can correct a stoppage. Immediate action is an essential for all Marines.

To clear an interruption in the cycle of operation, perform the following steps:
• TAP: Slap the bottom of the magazine.
• RACK: Pull the charging handle to the rear and release.
• BANG: Sight and attempt to fire.

Remedial Action

Remedial action is performed if immediate action fails to clear an interruption. During remedial action, Marines must investigate the cause of the interruption in order to return the weapon to a usable state.

If the weapon fails to fire after performing immediate action, apply remedial action as follows:
• S – Seek cover.
• P – Pull the charging handle to the rear and attempt to lock the bolt to the rear.

• O – Observe for a round or brass to be ejected and take appropriate action to clear the stoppage.
• R – Release the bolt.
• T – Tap the forward assist.
• S – Sight and attempt to fire.

Function Check

The function check is performed to ensure the rifle works properly.

A. Ensure the weapon is in condition 4.
B. Pull the charging handle to the rear and release, ensure the selector lever is on safe and pull the trigger. The hammer should not fall.
C. Place the selector lever on semi. Pull the trigger and hold it to the rear. The hammer should fall. Pull the charging handle to the rear and release. Release the trigger and pull again. The hammer should fall.
D. Pull the charging handle to the rear and release. Place the selector lever on burst. Pull the trigger, hold it to the rear. The hammer should fall. Pull the charging handle to the rear three times and release. Release the trigger and pull again. The hammer should fall.
E. Pull the charging handle to the rear and release. Place the selector lever on the safe.

Marine Corps Rifle Marksmanship Program

Marine Corps rifle marksmanship is taught sequentially in three basic phases: Preparatory Marksmanship Training (phase I), Known Distance Firing (phase II) and Field Firing (phase III). These basic phases teach the shooter the application of marksmanship fundamentals to function as an individual or part of a unit engaged in combat, and train individual skills and knowledge needed by a Marine rifleman.

Phase I: Preparatory Marksmanship Training. During this phase, students will develop a sound foundation of marksmanship knowledge and will practice skills under close supervision.

Phase II: Known Distance Firing. During phase II, the knowledge and firing techniques learned in phase I will be applied on a known distance (KD) range.

Phase III: Field Firing. In phase III, the shooter will apply the firing techniques taught in the first two phases to field firing (combat-type) situations. Phase III training will help refine these techniques until they become instinctive.

Care and Cleaning
of the M16A2

Normal care and cleaning will result in proper functioning of all parts of the weapon. Improper maintenance causes stoppages and malfunctions. Only issue type cleaning materials are carried by the rifleman in the compartment provided in the stock of the weapon. Do not use any abrasive material to clean the rifle. CLP is the preferred lubricant for the M16A2 rifle.

Cleaning and Lubricating the Barrel

- Attach a bore brush to the cleaning rod, dip it in cleaning compound solvent (bore cleaner) and brush the bore thoroughly. Brush from the chamber to the muzzle using straight-through strokes. Push the brush through the bore until it extends beyond the flash compensator. Continue this process until the bore is free of carbon and fouling. (Never reverse the direction of the brush while in the bore.) Remove the brush from the cleaning rod and dry the bore with clean M16 patches. No more than one patch should be used at a time in the bore. Do not attempt to retract the patch until it has been pushed all the way out of the flash compensator. Caution: The cleaning rod is to be supported by hand, one section at a time, to prevent flexing and damage to the bore.
- Attach the chamber-cleaning brush to a section of the cleaning rod. Dip it in bore cleaner and insert it in the chamber. Use five or six plunging strokes and three or four rotations (360 degrees) of the brush to clean the chamber. Then remove the brush and dry the chamber thoroughly with clean patches.
- Clean the locking lugs in the barrel extension, using a small bristle brush dipped in bore cleaner to remove all carbon deposits. A toothbrush is good for this operation.
- Clean the protruding exterior of the gas tube in the receiver with the bore brush attached to a section of the cleaning rod. The top of the gas tube can be cleaned by inserting the rod and brush in the back of the receiver. The sides and bottom of the gas tube can be cleaned from the bottom of the receiver.
- After cleaning, lubricate the bore and locking lugs in the barrel extension by applying a light coat of CLP to prevent corrosion and pitting. If the hand guards have been removed, rub a light coat of CLP on the surface of the barrel enclosed by the hand guards.

- Place one or two drops of CLP on the front sight post and exercise it.

Cleaning and Lubrication
of the Bolt Carrier Group

- Remove the bolt carrier group from the upper receiver and disassemble it. Thoroughly clean all parts with a patch or bristle brush dipped in cleaning compound solvent (bore cleaner) or CLP.
- Clean the locking lugs of the bolt, using a small bristle brush and cleaning solvent. Insure that all carbon and metal filings are removed; then wipe it clean with dry patches and oil lightly.
- Use a small bristle brush dipped in bore cleaner or CLP to scrub the extractor and extractor well to remove carbon and metal filings. Also clean the firing pin recess and the firing pin.
- When dry and before final assembly, apply a coat of CLP to the bolt body, rings and carrier key. When the bolt carrier group is reassembled apply a liberal amount of CLP to all exterior surfaces with particular emphasis to the friction points (i.e., rails and cam area). Put one drop cleaning solvent or CLP in the cam pin track and two drops in the gas ports.

Cleaning and Lubrication
of the Upper Receiver

- Clean the upper receiver until free of powder fouling with cleaning compound solvent or CLP.
- After cleaning, coat the interior surfaces of the upper receiver with CLP. Pay particular attention to shiny surfaces which indicate areas of friction.

Cleaning and Lubrication
of the Lower Receiver Group

- Wipe any particles of dirt from the trigger mechanism with a clean patch or brush. Place a drop of CLP on each of the pins for lubrication.
- Components of the lower receiver group can be cleaned with cleaning compound solvent or CLP and an artist's brush or similar brush. Use a scrubbing action to remove all carbon residue and foreign material. Drain solvent cleaner from the lower receiver and wipe dry. Use the opposite end of the brush with a piece of cloth to clean the hard-to-get places. After the lower receiver has been dried, a generous coat of CLP should be applied to the interior of all components.

Cleaning and Lubrication of the Magazine

- Disassemble the magazine, being careful not to stretch or bend the magazine spring. Scrub the inside of the magazine with a bristle brush dipped in bore cleaner or CLP. Wipe it dry. Caution: The magazine is made of aluminum. It does not need any lubrication.
- Scrub the spring clean of any foreign material using a bristle brush dipped in bore cleaner. Wipe dry and apply a very light coat of CLP to the spring.

Chapter Eighteen

Marksmanship

The fundamentals that the rifleman must learn in progressive marksmanship training are broken down into three phases: preparatory marksmanship training, known-distance range firing and field range firing. These phases are a steady progression that must be followed, in that order, if the objectives of the Marine marksmanship training are to be satisfied.

Preparatory marksmanship training. This is training a shooter must learn before firing a range course. The degree of proficiency obtained by the shooter will depend on the foundation of good shooting principles built during the preparatory phase.

Known-distance range firing. It is during this phase that the shooter applies the fundamentals of marksmanship. Known-distance firing serves three purposes.

- To give the shooter the ability to hit a selected spot with one shot, using marksmanship fundamentals.
- To build the shooter's confidence in the ability to kill with one well aimed round.
- To enable the Marine to obtain battle sights.

Field range firing. There are many necessary prerequisites for engaging the enemy that are not, and should not be, taught on the known-distance range. The combat application of fundamentals learned on the known-distance range is accomplished during this phase of progressive marksmanship training.

Preparatory Marksmanship Training

Preparatory marksmanship training is taught in eight steps. To complete the training, it is essential that the basic steps be taught in the following sequence:

1. Sighting and Aiming
2. Positions
3. Trigger Control
4. Rapid Fire
5. Sight Adjustments
6. Effects of Weather
7. Zeroing
8. Data Book

Sighting and Aiming

In sighting and aiming, the shooter is concerned with correctly pointing the rifle so the bullet will hit the target when fired. To do this, the shooter must have the rear sight, the front sight blade and the target or aiming point in their proper relationship. This relationship is known as sight picture. Sight picture involves two elements: sight alignment and aiming point.

Sight alignment. Figure 18-1 illustrates correct sight alignment. The top center of the front sight blade is exactly in the center of the rear sight aperture. If an imaginary horizontal line is drawn through the center of the rear sight aperture, the top of the front sight blade will appear to touch the line. If an imaginary vertical line is drawn through the center of the rear aperture, the line will appear to bisect the front sight blade.

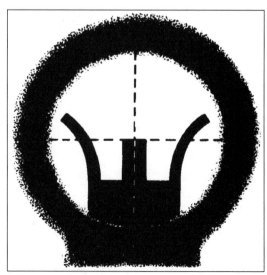

Fig. 18-1. *Sight alignment.*

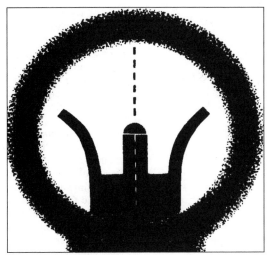

Fig. 18-2. Aiming point.

Fig. 18-3. Sight picture.

Aiming point. The aiming point is correctly placed when it is centered on top of the front sight blade. An imaginary vertical line drawn through the center of the front sight blade will appear to cut the target in half. (See Fig. 18-2.) An imaginary horizontal line drawn across the top of the front sight blade will appear to cut the target in half. This is commonly called "center hold" or "center mass."

Sight picture. The correct sight picture is obtained when the sights are properly aligned and the aiming point is in the correct relationship to the front sight blade. (See Fig. 18-3.)

Method of sight alignment. To ensure the correctness of the sight alignment, the eye must be focused on the front sight blade at the instant the rifle fires. However, the target cannot be ignored. The shooter must alternate the focus of the eye between the target and the front sight blade. Initially, the shooter should focus on the front sight blade and properly align the sights. The shooter then shifts focus to the target and completes the sight picture. Finally, as the trigger is squeezed, the shooter again shifts the focus of the eye to the front sight blade to ensure correct sight alignment as the rifle fires. At this moment, the sight picture should be similar to that shown on the left in Figure 18-4. Notice that the front sight blade is distinct while the target and rear aperture appear to be slightly blurred.

Eye relief. Eye relief is that distance from the rear sight aperture to the eye (Fig. 18-5). The shooter should keep the eye between two to three inches away from the rear sight aperture. The closer the eye is to the aperture, the more target area will be visible. It is important to attempt the same eye relief for all

shots fired from a particular position. This is done by using the stock weld, which is the point of firm contact between the rifleman's cheek and the stock. The stock weld will be discussed more in the explanation of positions later in this chapter.

Hasty Sling

Forming the hasty sling:

A. Hold the rifle vertical with the barrel pointing upward and unhook the j-hook from the lower sling swivel.

B. Loosen the sling keeper and adjust the sling until the j-hook hangs approximately ten inches below the butt of the rifle.

C. Turn the sling a half turn outboard.

D. Attach the j-hook to the lower sling swivel. The open end of the j-hook should face away from the rifle.

E. While holding the rifle with the right hand, insert the left arm between the sling and the rifle to a point midway between the elbow and shoulder.

F. Rotate the left hand outboard, placing the back of the hand flush against the sling.

G. Place the left hand under the rifle so the hand guard rests in the "V" formed by the thumb and forefinger.

H. Move the left hand as required to level the rifle with the line of sight.

I. Move the feed end of the sling in or out of the sling keeper to adjust the hasty sling.

J. Position the sling keeper near the feed end of the sling and secure.

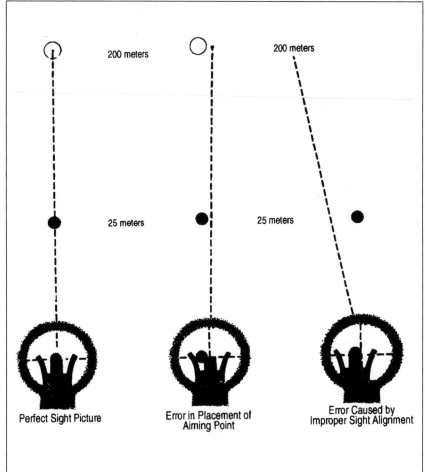

Fig 18-4. *Importance of correct sight picture.*

Positions

The four basic shooting positions used in the Marine Corps are prone, sitting, kneeling and standing. These positions may be modified to fit the individual. On the battlefield, a Marine rifleman must use the steadiest possible position which can provide observation of the target area and cover and/or concealment. Considering the many variables of terrain, vegetation and combat situations, there are numerous possible positions that may be used. However, in most instances, these positions are variations of those listed above. Some Marines have more difficulty in assuming a particular position than do others. If you apply the fundamentals of maximum support for your rifle and relaxation, then your position can be adjust-

ed to fit your own body conformations. Throughout position training, Marines should be continually checked on the proper application of the principles on which positions are based.

Factors common to all positions. There are seven factors which affect holding the rifle steady while aligning the sights and firing the rifle. These factors are the same for all firing positions; however, the precise manner in which they apply differs slightly with the various positions.

- *Left hand.* In all positions it is desirable that the hand guard of the rifle rest in the "V" formed by the thumb and index finger of the left hand. The left wrist is straight with the rifle resting across the heel of the hand. The left elbow should be positioned under the weapon to create bone support and a consistent resistance to recoil. The fingers can curl around the hand guard, but should apply only the minimum amount of pressure to prevent the hand from slipping on the hand guard. The configuration of the body in different positions will affect the placement of the left hand along the hand guard.

- *Rifle butt in the pocket of the shoulder.* The shooter places the rifle butt firmly into the pocket formed in the right shoulder. The proper placement of the butt lessens the effect of recoil, helps steady the rifle and prevents the rifle butt from slipping on the shoulder during firing.

- *Grip of the right hand.* The pistol grip is grasped firmly with the right hand and the forefinger is placed on the trigger with the thumb and remaining fingers wrapped around the pistol grip. Firm rearward pressure should be exerted to help keep

Fig. 18-5. *Eye relief/stock weld.*

the rifle butt firmly in the shoulder, reducing the effects of recoil. The trigger finger should be placed naturally on the trigger and care should be taken to ensure that the trigger finger can move independently without dragging on the side of the receiver. A proper grip allows the trigger to be moved straight to the rear without disturbing sight alignment.

- **Right elbow.** The placement of the right elbow provides balance to the shooter's position. Correctly positioned, the elbow helps form a pocket in the shoulder for the rifle butt. The exact location of the right elbow varies in each position.
- **Stock weld.** The stock weld is the point of firm contact between the rifleman's cheek and the stock. It is obtained by lowering the cheek to the stock. This enables the head and the weapon to recoil as one unit, thereby allowing rapid recovery between rounds. The stock weld also enables the eye to be positioned at the same distance behind the rear sight aperture each time the rifle is fired.
- **Breathing.** Breathing causes movement of the chest and a corresponding movement in the rifle and its sights. To minimize this movement and the effect it has on your aim, learn to control your breathing and extend your natural respiratory pause for a few seconds during the final aiming and firing process. When firing rapid fire shots, it may be necessary to take small short breaths to produce respiratory pause between each shot. The respiratory pauses help to maintain natural point of aim, however, holding your breath too long may lessen your ability to maintain focus on the sights.
- **Relaxation.** Relaxation prevents undue muscle strain and reduces excessive movement. If proper relaxation is achieved, natural point of aim and

sight alignment are more easily maintained.

Trigger Control

Trigger control is the skillful manipulation of the trigger causing the rifle to fire without disturbing the alignment of the rifle with respect to the target.

Technique of trigger control. During the firing process, gradual increase of pressure should be applied straight to the rear of the trigger as long as the sight alignment and sight picture remain good. Trigger control is very important, since the sight picture cannot be in alignment continuously. The shooter must be able to stop pressure on the trigger when the sight picture is not good. The shooter applies pressure to a point when it is known that only a small additional pressure on the trigger will cause the hammer to fall. The shooter then applies additional pressure, when the sights are aligned, without causing movement in the weapon.

Follow-through. Follow-through is the continued application of fundamentals after each shot has been fired. That is, the shooter does not shift position, move the head or let the muzzle of the rifle drop until a few seconds after the rifle has been fired.

Rapid Fire

There is no basic difference between rapid and slow fire. Accuracy in both requires each shot to be properly aimed, held steady and squeezed through. Rapid fire is only a series of slow-fire shots fired with a short time allowance for each. Time is saved and speed is gained by blending the elements of good position, sighting and aiming, trigger control, controlled breathing, and reloading into a smoothly coordinated rhythm or cadence.

Rapid-fire exercises. Rapid fire is taught by using three exercises: the one-shot exercise, reloading exercise and the 10-shot exercise.

- **One-shot exercise.** In the one-shot exercise, the shooter must be able to assume a position rapidly and fire the first shot. The shooter first assumes a regular position and adjusts the natural point of aim onto the target. When satisfied with a position, the shooter marks the position of the crotch or buttock (sitting) or the left elbow (prone) to facilitate retaking the position. The shooter then rises; on command, retakes position rapidly. Using the marks as a guide, the shooter readjusts the natural point of aim if necessary and applies the correct trigger control to fire the shot within the specified time limit (generally 11 seconds for sitting and 12 seconds for prone).

Prone Position

Fig. 18-6(a). *Stand at ready, loop sling high on arm.*

- **Reloading exercises.** Reloading with the M16A2 is time consuming. However, with practice, reloading can be done smoothly and with a minimum of wasted time and motion. The loaded magazine should always be placed in the pouch, ammunition down, bullet forward. When the shooter completes firing the first magazine, the butt of the rifle is dropped to the thigh (sitting) or the ground (prone). The shooter reaches forward and with the right hand grasps the magazine. With the thumb releasing the magazine catch, the shooter pulls downward and forward and retains the unloaded magazine on his person. Reaching to the rear, the shooter removes the loaded magazine from the pouch and inserts it into the magazine well. The shooter then pulls the charging handle to the rear and releases it to go forward to chamber the top round, then strikes the forward assist forward.

- **10-shot exercise.** In the 10-shot exercise, the shooter quickly assumes a good position, perfects aim and applies the proper trigger control in firing the initial five rounds. The shooter then reloads, reassumes position, aims and fires the remaining rounds within the specified time limit.

Fig. 18-6(c). *Place butt of rifle well forward. Pivot down to right side.*

Fig. 18-6(b). *Drop to knees holding rifle securely.*

Fig 18-6(d). *Place left elbow right and forward so it will be directly under the rifle.*

Fig 18-6(e). *Force butt of rifle into right shoulder.*

Fig 18-6(f). *Relax into the sling and obtain your stock weld.*

Fig 18-6(g). *Feet apart, heels down; back straight, shoulders level with the ground.*

Fig 18-6(h). *Reloading -- press magazine release button.*

Fig 18-6(i). *Place magazine in feedway and push up.*

Fig 18-6(j). *Press bolt catch allowing bolt carrier to go forward.*

Steps in assuming the sitting position

Fig 18-7(a). Stand cross legged at the ready, loop sling high on arm.

Fig 18-7(b). Drop to the ground breaking fall with right hand.

Fig 18-7(c). Place upper left arm inside left knee (crossed-leg position).

Fig 18-7(d). *Force the butt of the rifle into the right shoulder.*

Fig 18-7(e). *Lower right arm until it rests inside right knee. Relax forward into sling and obtain stock weld. (Open-leg position shown with upper left arm down along left shin. Either crossed-leg or open-leg positions allowed.)*

Fig 18-7(f). *Reloading - press magazine release button.*

Fig 18-7(g). *Place magazine into feedway and push up.*

Fig 18-7(h). *Press bolt catch allowing the bolt carrier to go forward.*

Steps in assuming the kneeling position

Fig 18-8(a). *Drop to right knee, right leg parallel to target, left foot toward target, lower left leg approximately vertical.*

Fig 18-8(b). *Lower buttock to foot, upper arm on top of knee. Force rifle into shoulder.*

Fig 18-8(c). *Relax forward into sling and obtain stock weld (high position shown).*

Fig 18-8(d). *Right foot in low kneeling position.*

238

Fig 18-8(e). Right foot in medium kneeling position.

Fig 18-8(f). Optional kneeling position.

Standing Position

Fig 18-9(a). *Spread feet a comfortable distance.*

Fig 18-9(b). *Using a modified parade sling (not used for support), put left hand under rifle to best support it.*

Fig 18-9(c). Grasp the pistol grip and place rifle into right shoulder. Obtain stock weld.

Fig 18-9(d). Body erect and balanced.

Fig 18-9(e). High elbow forms pocket for butt.

Initial Sight Setting

The Initial Sight Setting is the position at which the front and rear sights are adjusted to begin the zeroing process with the M16A2 rifle at 300 yards/meters.

Front Sight Elevation Initial Sight Setting. On the M16A2 rifle, the Front Sight Elevation Initial Sight Setting is when the base of the Front Sight Post is "flush" with the Front Sight Housing. To achieve this, depress the front sight detent and rotate the front sight post either clockwise or counterclockwise until the base of the front sight post is flush with the front sight housing.

Rear Sight Elevation Initial Sight Setting. Rear Sight Elevation Initial Sight Setting is established by first rotating the Rear Sight Knob counterclockwise until the rear sight assembly is bottomed out on the upper receiver. Now rotate the rear sight elevation knob clockwise to bring the setting back to 8/3 (or 3) position.

Note: The rear sight elevation knob should move 3 distinct clicks counterclockwise from the 8/3 setting. If the rifle sight moves other than 3 distinct clicks below 8/3, the sight must be recalibrated by an armorer.

Rear Sight Windage Initial Setting. Locate the windage index scale on the rifle rear sight assembly. Rotate the windage knob until the index line located on top of the larger rear sight aperture (which is in the down position) aligns with the center line on the windage index scale located on the moveable base of the rear sight assembly.

Using the Short Range Aperture for Low Light Conditions and Moving Targets. The Short Range Aperture (marked 0-2, large hole) is only used to engage stationary and moving combat targets in low light conditions and at a range of 183 meters (200 yards) or less. To fire at combat targets under these conditions, raise the Short Range Aperture (marked 0-2, large hole) to its "UP" position. Then, add three clicks of rear sight elevation to the 274 meter (300 yard) True Battlesight Zero, by turning the Rear Sight Elevation Knob three clicks in a clockwise direction. The three clicks of elevation must be added because the center of the aperture hole on the Short Range Aperture is located about .0057 inch lower than the Long Range Aperture (unmarked, small hole). Unless three clicks are added, the bullet will impact three minutes of angle (about six inches) too low at 200 yards. Figure 18-11 (a) shows the Short Range Aperture (marked 0-2, large hole) in its "UP" position. Since the Short Range Aperture hole

Fig. 18-11(a). *Short Range Aperture (large hole, marked 0-2) set in the "UP" position and centered on the Windage Index Scale.*

is so large, much more careful attention must be paid to precise Sight Alignment. Many riflemen have some difficulty in obtaining precise alignment of the Front Sight Post tip in the exact center of the Short Range Aperture. Precise Sight Alignment is critical to accuracy of fire.

Using Painted Sight Markings to Verify Precise Sight Settings and Adjustments. The importance of accurately marking the sights with a bright paint or fingernail polish cannot be over emphasized. The precise realignment of these marks verifies that the sight is precisely located at the original position it was located at when the sight was originally marked. If by some chance the sight adjustment knob has slipped out of its original position on its shaft, the marks will no longer align when an attempt is made to bring the sight back to the position it was in when the marking took place. If a sight has slipped for some reason, the painted marks will allow the sight to be slipped by a qualified armorer and repositioned to its original position at the time of marking. The painted marks also allow the rifleman to count down the zero back to the initial sight setting position and verify actual zero in "clicks" at the time of firing. In addition, the movements on sights with ½ Minute of Angle (MOA) adjustments are so small that many times they are difficult to pick up with the human eye. The separation of the painted marks gives telltale evidence that a small sight movement of 1-2 clicks has occurred. (See Fig. 18-11(b) and 18-11(c).)

Fig. 18-11(b). *Rear sight with 2 Clicks of Right Windage on the Windage Index Scale.*

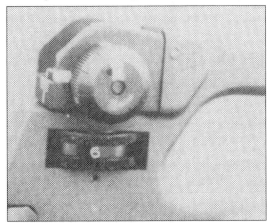

Fig. 18-11(c). *Rear Sight Windage Knob with 2 Clicks of Right Windage Viewed from the Right Side.*

Effects of Weather

Wind constantly presents the greatest problem to the shooter. Wind has a considerable effect on the bullet which increases with range. Wind also affects the shooter, particularly in the standing position. The stronger the wind, the more difficult it is to hold the rifle steady. The effect can be partially offset with good training and conditioning.

Classification of winds. Winds are classified according to the direction from which they are blowing in relation to the direction of fire. The "clock system" (See Fig. 18-12) is used to indicate direction. A wind blowing from right to left directly across the shooter's front is called a "3 o'clock wind." A wind

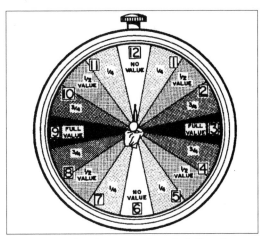

Fig. 18-12. *Clock system for wind direction.*

blowing toward the shooter from the left front is called an "11 o'clock wind." The direction from which the wind is blowing also denotes the value of the wind.

Winds from either flank are "full value winds," those from the oblique are "half value winds." Winds blowing from either the front or rear are "no-value winds." A half-value wind will affect a bullet approximately half as much as a full value wind. A 1:30 wind having a velocity of 10 miles per hour is equivalent to a five mile per hour, 3 o'clock wind. For basic firing, the effect of a no-value wind on a bullet is negligible and may be discounted.

Wind velocity. There are three common field expedient methods of determining velocities. Since the tactical situation may limit the use of some methods, Marines must be thoroughly familiar with all techniques.

• *Flag method.* (See Fig. 18-13.) If a flag (or any cloth-like material similar to a flag) can be observed hanging from a pole, the shooter should estimate the angle (in degrees) formed at the junction of the flag and the pole. Dividing this angle by the constant number "4" will give the wind velocity in miles per hour.

• *Pointing method.* (See Fig. 18-14.) If no flag is visible, a piece of paper or other light material may be dropped from the shoulder. By pointing directly at the spot where it lands, the angle (in degrees) can be estimated. This figure is also divided by the number "4" to determine the approximate wind velocity in miles per hour.

• *Observation method.* If the tactical situation prevents the use of the above two methods, shooters

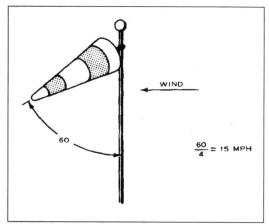

Fig. 18-13. *Flag method for determining wind velocity.*

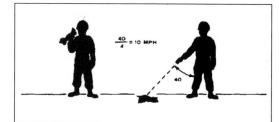

Fig. 18-14. *Pointing method for wind speed.*

can use the following information in determining wind velocities:
- Under three miles an hour, winds can hardly be felt, but the presence of slight wind can be determined by drifting smoke.
- A three to five mile an hour wind can be felt lightly on the face.
- Winds of five to eight miles an hour keep tree leaves in constant motion.
- At eight to 12 miles an hour, winds will raise dust and loose paper.
- A 12 to 15 mile an hour wind will cause small trees to sway.

Determination of windage adjustment. After finding the wind direction and velocity, necessary windage correction is determined using the formula RxV/Range Constant = number of clicks of windage to be placed on the rear windage sight on the M16A2, for a full value wind. R = range in hundreds of yards/meters, V = velocity in miles per hour, and the range constant is explained below.

Note: The range constant will depend on the type of ammunition. The range constant for M855 ammunition is as follows: If the range to the target is 200-400 yards, the range constant is 5. If the range to the target is 500-700 yards, the range constant is 4.

A working example of this formula is: A 10 mph wind is blowing from 9 o'clock. The range to the target is 500 yards. Therefore, Range (R) = 5, Velocity (V) = 10 mph, 500 yard Range Constant = 4.

$$\frac{RxV}{4} = \frac{5x10}{4} = \frac{50}{4} = 12.5 \text{ or } 13 \text{ clicks left on the windage knob.}$$

Note: In adjusting the windage on the rifle, the rear sight aperture must always be moved in the direction from which the wind is blowing. For example, if the wind is blowing form the right, the rear sight aperture must be moved right.

Zeroing

To understand the principles of zeroing, the Marine should have a basic knowledge of the relationship between the path of the bullet in flight and the line of sight. In flight, a bullet does not follow a straight line but travels in a curve or arc which is called its trajectory. The maximum height of a bullet's trajectory depends on the range to the target. The greater the distance a bullet travels before impact, the higher it must travel in its trajectory.

On the other hand, the line of sight is a straight line from the eye through the rear sight aperture, across the front sight, to the aiming point or target. After the bullet leaves the rifle, it is initially moving in an upward path, intersecting the line of sight. As the bullet travels farther, it begins to drop and will eventually again intersect the line of sight. The range at which this intersection occurs is the zero for that sight setting.

Elements of Zeroing. To accurately engage targets, the strike of the bullet must coincide with your point of aim on the target. This must be done while compensating for the effects of weather and the range to the target. This is accomplished by adjusting the sights on your rifle to achieve point of aim/point of impact. This process is called zeroing and it is critical for accurate target engagement.

- ***Line of Sight:*** Line of sight is a straight line beginning at the center of the eye, passing through the center of the rear sight aperture, and then across the tip of the front sight post to the exact point of aim on the target.
- ***Point of Aim:*** The point of aim is the precise point where the tip of the front sight post is placed on the target while maintaining sight alignment.
- ***Centerline of Bore:*** Centerline of the bore is an imaginary straight line beginning at the chamber end of the barrel, proceeding out of the muzzle and continuing indefinitely.

- *Trajectory:* A bullet does not follow a straight line to the target. Instead, a bullet travels in a curved path, or arc, which is called bullet trajectory.
- *Range:* Range is the known distance from the rifle to the target.

Types of Zeros

Zero: A zero is the elevation and windage settings required to place a single shot, or the center of a shot group, in a predesignated location on a target at a specific range, from a specific firing position, under specific weather conditions.

True Zero: A true zero is the elevation and windage settings required to place a single shot, or the center of a shot group, in a predesignated location on a target at a specific range, from a specific firing position, under ideal weather conditions.

Battlesight Zero: A battlesight zero, or BZO, is the elevation and windage settings required to engage point targets from 0-300 yards under ideal weather conditions. This means the sights of the rifle are adjusted so the trajectory of the bullet and the line of sight intersect at a range of 300 yards in a no wind condition. BZO is the sight setting placed on the rifle when going into combat.

Temporary Sight Setting. A temporary sight setting is the elevation and windage settings required to engage point targets from 0-300 yards/meters in a given weather condition. It also provides grazing fire from 0-300 yards/meters.

Note: Apply hasty sight settings for ranges of 400-800 yards/meters by rotating the elevation knob to the number that corresponds with the engagement distance of the enemy.

Hasty Sight Setting for Extended Ranges. To achieve a hasty sight setting for extended ranges (in excess of 300 yards/meters), apply the windage or elevation required to cause a single shot or the center of a shot group to impact the desired aiming point in a given wind condition.

Note: Upon completion of firing with a hasty sight setting for extended ranges, return the sights to the BZO setting.

Method of Zeroing: The initial zeroing phase should start at the 200-yard line (183 meters) with the sights set at the Initial Sight Setting described earlier in this chapter. To determine the 200-yard zero quickly, rounds should be fired slow fire in the sitting position. When the slow fire shots are striking near the center of the target, three 3-round shot groups are fired in rapid-fire cadence; followed by a rapid-fire string of 10. During this firing, sight changes are made to bring the group into the center of the target.

Often, the rapid-fire zero will be different from the slow-fire zero. This is due to a difference in position and trigger control. Therefore, it is necessary to establish a slow-fire zero. To do this, simply fire several rounds slow-fire from the appropriate position and call each shot accurately. When the shots appear on the target "on call," then the slow-fire zero is obtained.

300-Yard (274-meter) and 500-Yard (475-meter) Lines. The 300-yard slow-fire and rapid-fire zero are determined by firing the same exercises as were fired at the 200-yard line: while at 300 yards, single shots are fired until the group is centered in the target. The normal sight change is up three clicks on long range sights from 200 to 300 yards and up seven clicks from 300 to 500 yards. These changes are subject to variations in shooters, light and temperature.

Field Expedient Battlesight Zeroing. Because the line of sight and trajectory of a bullet intersect twice if a rifle is properly zeroed, field expedient battlesight zeroing must be performed if a range is not available to conduct zeroing at 300 yards. To establish a BZO for 300 yards, complete the following steps:

Note: M855 62-grain ammunition does not stabilize for the first 27 yards after it leaves the barrel. Therefore, zeroing at 25 yards is not recommended if the M16A2 is firing M855 ammunition.

- Place a target 36 yards from the muzzle of the rifle.
- Set rear sight elevation at 8/3.
- Fire a three-shot group at the sustained rate of fire (12-15 rounds per minute).
- Make required elevation and windage adjustments to center the shot group on the point of aim (use the front sight post to make all elevation adjustments).
- Confirm zero by firing an additional three-shot group.

Data Book

The data book is used to record every shot fired by the shooter. It is also used to record weather conditions and their effects on the shooter. If used properly, it will provide necessary information for initial sight settings at each range. It provides a basis for analyzing the performance of the shooter and the rifle, and is a valuable aid in making bold and accurate sight changes.

Use (slow fire). The following procedure should be used for maintaining the data book in slow fire:
- *Before firing.* Before firing, the date, hour, rifle number, target number, wind (word description

and direction), light (word description and direction), windage zero, elevation used and any other appropriate remarks to aid the shooter are entered in the spaces provided or under remarks.

- **During firing.** The following strict sequence of recording data during firing must be followed:
  - If a wind is blowing, the value is determined and set on the sights and entered in the data book.
  - After firing each round, the call is plotted.
  - When the target is marked, the location of the hit is plotted with a number and the call is compared to the hit.
  - The correct sight setting (determined from analyzing the group) is then recorded.
  - During a slow fire, a good rule to follow is: "SHOOT WHEN THE TARGET IS UP – RECORD INFORMATION IN THE BOOK DURING TIME TARGET IS BEING MARKED."
- **After firing.** Upon completion of firing, the results should be analyzed and studied carefully.

Use (rapid fire). The following procedure should be used for filling out and maintaining the scorebook in rapid fire:

- **Before firing.** Before firing, the shooter records the same information as was done for slow fire.
- **During firing.** In rapid fire, the sequence to be followed during firing is different than that of slow fire:
  - The final windage correction, if needed, is made shortly before the targets appear, and this is applied to the sights. While firing, a mental note is made of any shots called out of the group.
  - The calls are plotted immediately after firing. This is done by placing small circles for any erratic shots on the call target.
  - When the target is marked, all visible hits are plotted with an "X" and compared to the calls.
  - The correct sight setting determined from analyzing the group is then recorded.
- **After firing.** Upon completion of firing, the results should be analyzed and studied very carefully.

Known-Distance Range Firing

The known-distance range is an extremely important phase in the building of a sound foundation of marksmanship principles. It would be impossible to eliminate this second phase of marksmanship training and still expect the training to produce a rifleman with the degree of proficiency required of a Marine. During this phase the rifleman acquires the elementary skills necessary to perform well on any firing range. After thorough instruction in the fundamentals of marksmanship, the Marine is given the opportunity to apply those principles under close supervision.

Course of Fire

Firing courses are established to provide standardized rifle training throughout the Marine Corps and to provide for evaluating the capabilities of riflemen. Therefore, there are certain criteria that must be met for a course to be effective.

Several distances. The rifleman fires at several different ranges up to the maximum effective range of the rifle. This is necessary to teach the shooter the effects of wind on a bullet at various ranges and how to manipulate the rear sight in moving from one distance to another. It also builds the rifleman's knowledge and reinforces confidence to engage targets at great distances.

Basic position. The course of fire requires the rifleman to use all four of the basic positions (prone, sitting, kneeling and standing or offhand positions). All combat or field positions are variations of these basic positions.

Slow and rapid fire. The rifleman fires both slow and rapid fire stages. The slow-fire stages allow both the coach and the rifleman to analyze each round to determine the reason for each hit or miss. It is necessary to learn to fire one well-aimed round, since rapid fire is nothing more than a sequence of individual well-aimed rounds. During rapid fire, the rifleman fires an accurate volume of fire at specific targets. The rifleman must also be able to reload his rifle during the string of fire.

Field Range Firing Techniques

Field range firing is the third phase of progressive marksmanship training. During this phase, the rifleman is provided with practical experience in firing at realistic targets in battlefield-like surroundings. The rifleman also receives instruction in basic field firing techniques.

Although field firing is primarily designed to teach skills which cannot be effectively conducted on the known-distance range, the fundamentals learned during earlier training phases continue to be important.

Target Location

Success in locating combat targets depends upon the observer's position, skill in searching an area, maintaining observation over the area and the ability to recognize indicators presented by the target.

Observer's position. Depending upon the situation, the individual rifleman may or may not select a position. In most defensive situations, the rifleman is told where to prepare a position. However, there are situations such as the attack and reorganization on the objective, which require the individual to select a position.

A good position is one that offers maximum visibility of the area while affording cover and/or concealment. "Position" is both the observer's location on the ground and the position of the body.

Searching an area. Searching is done using two methods:

- ***Hasty search.*** When a Marine moves into a new area, it must be quickly checked for enemy activity or immediate danger. This search is conducted by making quick glances at various specific points throughout the area rather than sweeping the eyes across the terrain in one continuous panoramic view. It is effective, because the eyes are sensitive to any slight movements occurring within a wide arc of the object on which they are

focused (commonly called "side vision" or "seeing out of the corner of the eye"). However, the eyes MUST be focused on a SPECIFIC POINT to have this sensitivity.

- ***Detailed search.*** If the Marine fails to locate the enemy during the hasty search, a systematic examination known as the 50-meter overlapping strip method of search is begun. (See Fig. 18-15.) Normally, the area nearest the Marine offers the greatest potential danger. Beginning at either flank, the Marine systematically searches the terrain to his front in a 180-degree arc, 50 meters in depth. After reaching the opposite flank, the Marine searches the next area nearest his position. This search should cover the terrain located between approximately 40 to 90 meters of his position. The second search of the terrain includes about 10 meters of the area examined during the first search. This technique ensures complete coverage of the area. The Marine continues searching from one flank to the other in 50-meter overlapping strips as far as can be seen.

Fig. 18-16(a). 100-meter method (up to 500m).

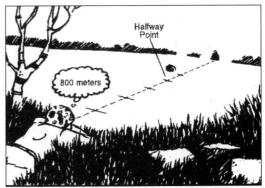
Fig. 18-16(b). 100-meter method (over 500m).

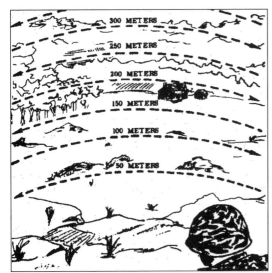
Fig. 18-15. Detailed search.

247

Range Estimation

Range estimation is determining the distance between two points. In most situations, one of these points will be the observer's own position. The other point may be a target or prominent feature.

100-meter unit of measure method. The Marine must be able to visualize a distance of 100 meters on the ground. For ranges up to 500 meters, the individual determines the number of 100-meter increments between the two points to be measured. (See Figures 18-16(a) and 18-16(b).) Beyond 500 meters, the Marine selects a point halfway to the target, determines the number of 100-meter increments to the halfway point and then doubles it to find the range to the target.

Appearance of Objects method. This method is a means of determining range by the size and other characteristic details of the object in question. This technique is used by a rifleman to determine ranges

Fig. 18-17. Range card method.

on the battlefield. If the characteristic size and detail of people and equipment at known ranges is known, then the rifleman can compare these characteristics to similar objects at unknown ranges. When the characteristics match, so does the range.

Range card method. A range card is a rough sketch made of an observer's area of responsibility. (See Fig. 18-17.) It shows the range and direction from the observer's position to easily recognizable objects, terrain features, avenues of approach and possible enemy positions. If practical, the observer should pace the distance between his position and reference points in order to minimize range errors. By referring to the range card, the observer can quickly estimate the range to a target appearing in the vicinity of a reference point.

Stationary targets. In combat, targets will seldom be large or clearly outlined. Generally, they will be partially or completely concealed, such as as enemy peering around a bush. The enemy's head will offer a very small target. By firing into the part of the bush that the enemy's body is behind, the rifleman has a larger target and a better chance of obtaining a hit.

Moving targets. There are less detection problems involved in locating moving targets than in locating stationary targets. However, the movement itself complicates the selection of an accurate aiming point. Unless completely unaware of the rifleman's presence, the enemy will normally move by rushes from one covered and concealed position to another. While making the rush, the enemy presents a rapidly moving target. For a brief moment as the enemy begins and ends the rush, the movement is usually slow. It is at these two moments that a moving target is most vulnerable. For a target moving directly toward or away from you, aim the same as at a stationary target. To hit a target moving laterally across

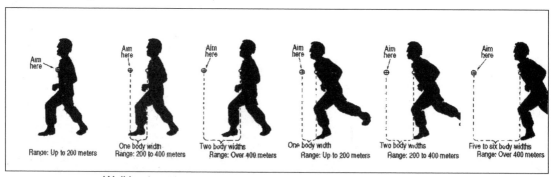

Walking target.   *Running target.*

Fig. 18-18. Aiming at moving targets is called "leading."

your front, aim far enough in advance of the target so the bullet will meet the target. (See Fig. 18-18.)

Field Firing Positions

During training in fundamentals, positions are taught as a step-by-step process. In combat the Marine must be able to assume positions rapidly. There are any number of intermediate positions a combat rifleman might use before assuming a final firing position. To assume any field firing positions, the rifleman should:

- Use available support.
- Use the hasty sling when time permits.
- Avoid touching any part of the support with the rifle. This reduces control of the rifle and hinders rapid recovery between shots.
- Adjust the position to fit the available support.

Common field firing positions. Some of the field firing positions the Marine is likely to use in combat are:

- ***Fighting hole.*** The Marine enters the fighting hole; adds or removes dirt, sandbags or other supports to best fit height; and assumes a comfortable firing position. The firing position is obtained by placing the right foot to the rear as a brace and leaning forward until the chest is against the forward wall of the fighting hole. Extend the left arm and elbow over the forward side of the fighting hole, thus supporting the left forearm with the parapet or sandbags. Place the rifle into the pocket formed in the right shoulder and grasp the pistol grip with the right hand. Place the right elbow

on solid support using the parapet of the fighting hole or sandbags placed beside the foxhole.

- ***Rubble pile.*** The rifleman must present the lowest possible silhouette behind the rubble, but at the same time use the rubble to achieve maximum support. (See Fig. 18-19.)
- ***Kneeling supported.*** Assume the kneeling position. Shift weight forward until the left shoulder, left arm and left leg come in contact with the support. The rifle must not touch or rest on the support. The friction of the rifle against the support would slow recovery between shots and limit the rifleman's ability to rapidly shift his point of aim. (See Fig. 18-20.)
- ***Log.*** Right-handed shooters fire from the right end of the log and left-handed shooters from the left end of the log. This ensures a comfortable position while making maximum use of the cover provided by the log. (See Fig. 18-21.)
- ***Prone supported.*** Assume the prone position as shown earlier. Adjust the position to fit the available support. Place the left forearm against the support. It is not necessary to position the left elbow directly under the rifle in this position, because the support sustains the weight of the rifle rather than the arm. (See Fig. 18-22.)
- ***Barricade.*** Assume a position which permits firing over the barricade or wall while presenting a low silhouette. The height of the position will depend on the shooter's height in relation to the height of the wall. (See Fig. 18-23.)
- ***Forward slope.*** Adapt the standard sitting position. (See Fig. 18-24.)

Fig 18-19. *Firing from a pile of rubble or rocks.*

- **Rooftop.** Place the left arm over the apex of the roof in such a manner that will hold the weight of the body but not expose too much of the head and shoulders. (See Fig. 18-25.)
- **Bunker.** When firing from a bunker, the same technique is used as in the fighting hole position.
- **Window position.** When firing from a window, where possible, the rifleman should remain well back from the opening of the window so the rifle will not protrude. The rifleman should take position to the right or left of the window (depending whether the individual is shooting right- or left-handed), concealing the major portion of the body from the enemy's view, while retaining good observation of the target area. (See Fig. 18-26.)

Assault Fire

Successful advance by fire and maneuver leads naturally to an assault of the target area or objective. Assault fire is fire delivered by a unit during its assault on an enemy position.

Technique. The rifleman fires well-directed shots from either the offhand or "pointing" position. The pointing position is similar to "pointing" a shotgun. It is assumed from a standing or crouch position by rapidly placing the rifle in the vicinity of the shoulder. With both eyes open and focused upon the target, the rifleman "points" the rifle at the target.

Fig. 18-20. Firing from a supported kneeling position.

Fig. 18-21. Firing from behind a log.

Fig. 18-22. *How to fire from a prone supported position.*

Fig. 18-23. *Barricade position.*

Fig. 18-24. *Forward slope position.*

Fig. 18-25. *Rooftop position.*

Fig. 18-26. Window position.

Chapter Nineteen

M240G Machine Gun

The M240G machine gun is a belt fed, aircooled, gas operated, fully automatic machine gun. It is able to provide a heavy, controlled volume of accurate, long range fire that is far beyond the capabilities of individual small arms. The weapon fires from the open-bolt position and is fed by a disintegrating belt of metal links. The gas from firing one round provides the energy for firing the next. Thus, the gun functions automatically as long as it is supplied with ammunition and the trigger is held to the rear. It can be fired utilizing either the attached bipod mount or by mounting the M240G on the M122 tripod with flex mount. When mounted on the tripod it enables the gunner to deliver a high degree of accurate fire from a stable base. The traversing and elevating mechanism permits controlled manipulation in both direction and elevation, and makes it possible to engage predetermined targets during darkness or periods of reduced visibility. (See Figure 19-1.)

Characteristics

Ammunition ....7.6mm + 51
    ball, tracer, blank, dummy, armorpiercing
Length..49 inches
Weight ....24.2 lbs
Weight of spare barrel......................6.6 lbs
Weight of M122 tripod,
felt mount, T and E ....19.5 lbs
Rates of fire
    Sustained ....100 rpm
    Rapid ....200 rpm
    Cyclic............................650-950 rpm
Maximum range ....3,725 meters
Maximum effective range ......1,800 meters
Muzzle velocity...........................2,800 fps
Grazing fire ....600 rpm

Fig. 19-1. M240G on the M122 tripod with flex mount.

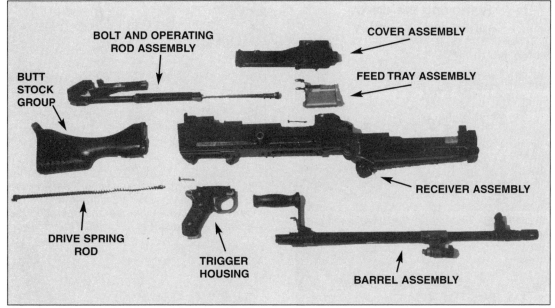

Fig. 19-2. Eight major groups (disassembled).

Condition Codes

The weapon conditions for the M240 Family of Machine Guns Are:
- Condition 1: The bolt is locked to the rear. The safety is on. The source of ammunition is in position on the feed tray or in the magazine well. The cover is closed.
- Condition 2: Not Applicable.
- Condition 3: The bolt is forward. The chamber is empty. The safety is off. The source of ammunition is in position on the feed tray or in the magazine well. The cover is closed.
- Condition 4: The bolt is forward. The chamber is empty. The safety is off. The feed tray is clear of ammunition and/or no magazine is inserted. The cover is closed.

General Disassembly

The M240G is designed for easy disassembly and assembly. The use of force is not necessary, and no special tools are required. As the weapon is disassembled, place the parts (in the order in which they are removed) on a clean, flat surface. This reduces the possibility of losing a part and aids in assembly, as all parts are replaced in reverse order. To prevent unnecessary wear, disassembly should be kept to a

Removing the butt stock and buffer assembly

Fig. 19-3(a). Press the backplate latch.

Fig. 19-3(b). Slide the butt stock upward and remove from the receiver.

255

Removing the drive spring rod assembly

Fig. 19-4(a). To remove the drive spring rod assembly first push against its base.

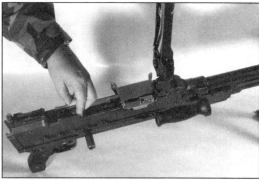

Fig. 19-5(b). With the index finger, reach inside the top of the receiver and pull rearward on the face of the bolt until the bolt and operating rod assembly is exposed at the rear of the receiver.

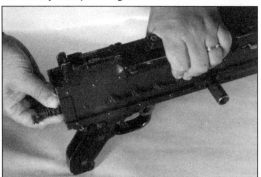

Fig. 19-4(b). Lift up and outward so that it clears its retaining studs inside the receiver. Remove it from the rear of the receiver.

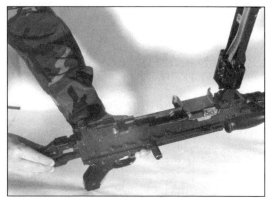

Fig. 19-5(c). Grasp the bolt and operating rod assembly and remove it from the rear of the receiver.

Removing the bolt and operating rod assembly

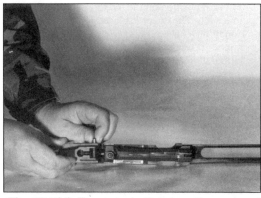

Fig. 19-5(a). Pull the cocking handle to the rear to start the rearward movement of the bolt and operating assembly inside the receiver.

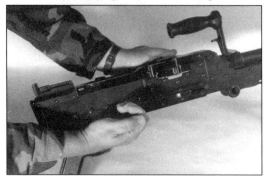

Fig. 19-5(d). To separate the operating rod and bolt remove the spring-loaded pin that holds them together.

Removing the barrel assembly

Fig. 19-7(a). Press the barrel locking lever.

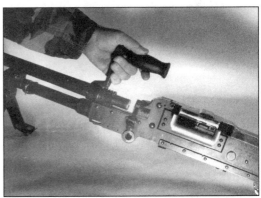

Fig. 19-5(e). Then pull the bolt forward until it is clear of the firing pin, thus disengaging the bolt from the operating rod.

Removing the trigger housing assembly

Fig. 19-6(a). Remove the trigger housing assembly spring pin.

Fig. 19-6(b). Rotate the rear of the trigger housing assembly down, disengage the holding notch at the front of the assembly from its recess on the bottom of the receiver and remove the assembly from the receiver.

Fig. 19-7(b). Rotate the charging handle to the upright position.

Fig. 19-7(c). Push forward separating the barrel from the receiver.

Fig. 19-7(d). *Grasp and rotate the gas collar clockwise until it releases from the gas plug.*

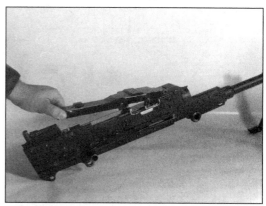

Fig. 19-8(b). *Remove the cover assembly.*

Fig. 19-7(e). *Slide the gas regulator plug to the rear out of gas regulator.*

Fig. 19-8(c). *Remove the feed tray. Lift off the receiver assembly.* **This will make the receiver assembly the eighth assembly.**

Removing the cover assembly

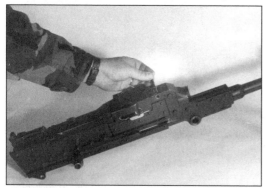

Fig. 19-8(a). *Remove the hinge pin spring.*

minimum consistent with maintenance and training requirements.

Disassembly and assembly may be divided into two categories - general and detailed. General disassembly involves separation into the eight main assemblies. Detailed disassembly involves the removal of the component parts of the main assemblies. Detailed disassembly will not be covered in this chapter.

General disassembly (field stripping) is the separation of the M240G into the eight main assemblies. They are the butt stock and buffer assembly, drive spring rod, bolt and operating rod assembly, trigger housing, barrel assembly, cover assembly, feed tray assembly and receiver assembly. Before the weapon is disassembled, it must be cleared. General disassembly begins with the bolt forward, the cover raised and the safety on safe. Figure 19-2 shows the eight major groups. Figures 19-3 through 19-8 demonstrate general disassembly of the M240G.

General Assembly

General assembly is replacing the other main assemblies on the receiver group. It is accomplished in reverse order of disassembly.

1. Replace the feed tray.
   (a) Place the cover onto the receiver aligning its guides with the receiver bracket.
2. Replace the cover assembly.
   (a) Place the cover on the receiver, aligning its hole with the mounting bracket.
   (b) Close the cover.
   (c) Insert the hinge pin spring.
   (d) Open the cover.
3. Replace the barrel assembly.
   (a) Insert the gas regulator and set it to number one.
   (b) Place the collar over the forward end of gas regulator plug, rotate it counter-clockwise until it locks into place.
   (c) Place the barrel in the receiver.

(d) Rotate the charging handle down.
(e) While rotating count and listen to the clicks. If there are less than two or more than seven, then the head space is incorrectly set. Notify the armorer.

4. Replace the trigger housing assembly.
   (a) Insert the forward notch of the trigger housing into the recess of the receiver.
   (b) Rotate the trigger housing up to the rear mounting lug.
   (c) Insert the trigger housing spring pin.
5. Replace the bolt and operating rod assembly.
   (a) Slide the bolt over the firing pin.
   (b) Insert the spring loaded pin.
   (c) Replace the bolt and operating rod assembly back into the receiver.
6. Replace the drive spring rod assembly.
   (a) Insert it in the back of the receiver.
   (b) Push it in and down.
   (c) Align the retaining stud up with the receiver bottom.
7. Replace the butt stock and buffer assembly.
   (a) Align the butt stock with the receiver.
   (b) Press on the back plate latch.
   (c) Push down to seat it on the receiver.

Chapter Twenty

M249 Squad Automatic Weapon (SAW)

The SAW is a 5.56mm light, automatic weapon which supplements the firepower of the 5.56mm M16A2 rifle. It is used by all types of FMF units and by Marine Barracks. In the Marine Infantry Battalion the SAW is found in each fire team and is manned by the automatic rifleman. Therefore you will find nine SAW's in each Marine rifle platoon.

The SAW performs the mission of the automatic rifle in the fire team. The Marine Fire Team and the Marine thirteen man rifle squad were developed in World War II to exploit the firepower of the automatic rifle. At the time the Marine Corps was equipped with the famous Browning Automatic Rifle (BAR) which was used in World War I, World War II and Korea. The BAR was one of the most effective infantry weapons in the world for more than forty years. Today's recently developed SAW provides a lighter weight, modern counterpart for this vital mission of providing combat units with an automatic weapon of extended range and greater accuracy.

Description

The SAW is a gas-operated, belt/magazine fed, air-cooled, automatic, shoulder-fired weapon. The SAW is designed to be operated by one Marine which increases the agility and mobility of the automatic rifleman in consonance with other members of the fire team. Like the M60 machine gun, the SAW fires from the open-bolt position but can fire ammunition from an M16 magazine as well as from a linked belt. Utilizing the M855 or SS109 ammunition the SAW provides the Marine Corps with a light, automatic weapon capable of providing firepower and much greater effective ranges over Warsaw Pact weapons of similar caliber.

General Data

Ammunition can be fired from both a linked belt and an M16 magazine.

Weight

	Kilograms	Pounds
SAW (with bipod and tools)	6.88	15.16
200 rd box ammo	3.14	6.92
SAW and 200 rds	10.02	22.08

Length

	mm	Inches
Overall	1, 038	40.87
Rifling Twist	1 turn in 7 inches	

Rates of Fire

Cyclic	725 rds/min (normal)
	1000 rds/min (max)
Sustained	85 rds/min
Rapid Rate	100 rds/min

Sights

Front Sight. The front sight post is the fixed type. It is adjusted at the time of manufacture and should not be adjusted by using units. It is encircled by a metal hood to protect it from breakage or marring.

Rear sight. The rear sight is adjustable for both elevation and windage by means of two adjustment knobs on the left side of the weapon (loading port side). The front knob is used to adjust windage and the rear knob is used to adjust elevation. One click of either windage or elevation will move the strike of the round two inches for every 100m of range. Therefore, one click will move the strike of the round two inches at 100m, four inches at 200m, six inches at 300m, etc. In addition to the elevation adjustment knob, the rear sight aperture may be used to adjust elevation when battlesighting the weapon. To lower the strike of the round with the sight aperture, turn the aperture clockwise, and to raise the strike of the round, turn the aperture counterclockwise. Each full rotation of the rear sight aperture will move the strike

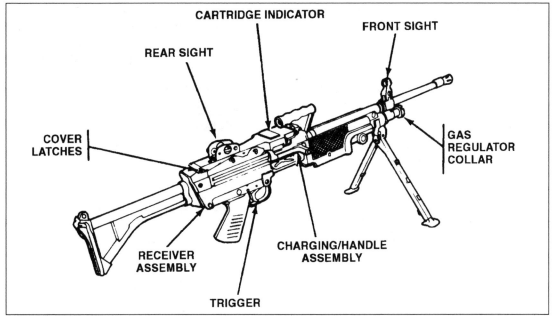

Fig. 20-1. SAW.

of the round two inches for every 100m of range. The use of this aperture to battlesight the weapon will be explained later in the section on Field Zeroing Procedures.

Disassembly and Assembly

Disassembly

Disassembly for the SAW consists only of field stripping for first echelon (operator) maintenance. Operators are not authorized to use any tools, other than cleaning gear and/or a cartridge to disassemble the weapon. When disassembling the SAW, parts should be laid out from left to right or right to left in the order disassembled so the weapon can be easily reassembled in reverse order.

Clearing the SAW

Prior to handling any weapon ensure that it is not loaded. To do this, execute the following clearing procedures:

Pull the charging handle (Fig. 20-2) to the rear and lock the bolt open. Push the charging handle forward until it clicks.

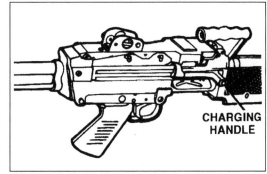

Fig. 20-2. Charging Handle.

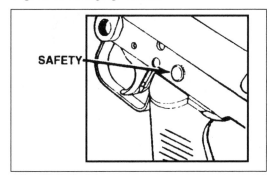

Fig. 20-3. Safety.

Push the safety (Fig. 20-3) from left (loading side) to right (ejection side). Red should NOT be visible on safety!

If the weapon has been firing belted ammunition, open the cover assembly (Fig. 20-4) and remove the ammunition. If the weapon has been firing from a magazine, depress the magazine release tab and remove the magazine; then raise the cover assembly (Fig. 20-5(a)).

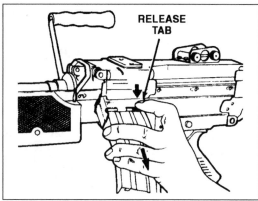

Fig. 20-5(a). *Magazine Release Tab.*

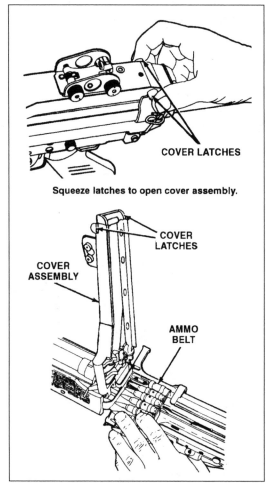

Squeeze latches to open cover assembly.

Fig. 20-4. *Cover Assembly.*

Raise the feed tray and inspect the chamber to ensure that all ammunition has been ejected (Fig. 20-5(b)).

If the chamber is clear, close the cover assembly and lock it.

Push the safety from right to left (red now visible).

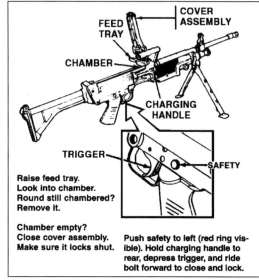

Raise feed tray.
Look into chamber.
Round still chambered?
Remove it.

Chamber empty?
Close cover assembly. Push safety to left (red ring vis-
Make sure it locks shut. ible). Hold charging handle to
rear, depress trigger, and ride
bolt forward to close and lock.

Fig. 20-5(b). *Clear, Close and Lock SAW.*

Hold the charging handle to the rear, squeeze the trigger and ride the bolt home. The weapon is now clear.

Field Stripping

Field stripping is accomplished to break down the SAW into its major components. These major components are illustrated in Figure 20-6. The specific steps to be followed in field stripping the SAW are shown in Figures 20-6(a-1).

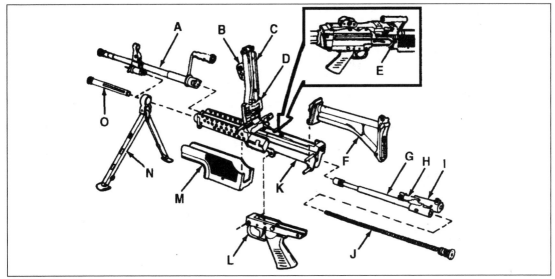

Fig. 20-6. *Major Components of SAW.*

LOCATION OF MAJOR COMPONENTS

A – BARREL ASSEMBLY
B – REAR SIGHT ASSEMBLY
C – COVER AND FEED MECHANISM ASSEMBLY
D – FEED PAWL ASSEMBLY
E – CHARGING HANDLE ASSEMBLY
F – BUTT STOCK AND SHOULDER ASSEMBLY
G – PISTON ASSEMBLY
H – BOLT ASSEMBLY

I – SLIDE ASSEMBLY
J – OPERATING ROD ASSEMBLY
K – RECEIVER ASSEMBLY
L – TRIGGER MECHANISM ASSEMBLY
M – HAND GUARD ASSEMBLY
N – BIPOD
O – GAS CYLINDER ASSEMBLY

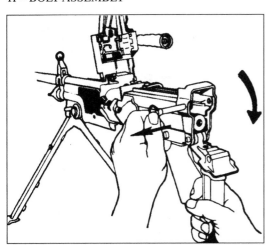

Fig. 20-6(a). *After ensuring that a weapon is clear, pull the upper retaining pin at the rear of the receiver to the left and let the stock pivot downward.*

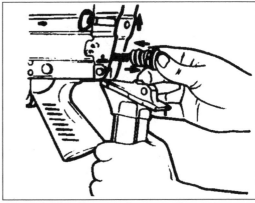

Fig. 20-6(b). *Remove the operating rod assembly from the receiver by pressing inward and up on the rear of the return spring with both thumbs. Slowly let the return spring expand and remove it from the receiver (separate the return spring and operating rod).*

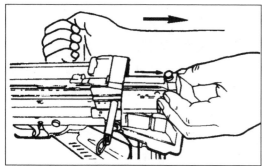

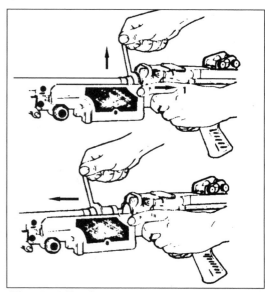

Fig. 20-6(c). *To remove the piston assembly, take the weapon off safe, squeeze the trigger and pull the charging handle to the rear so that the bolt clears the trigger. Finish pulling the piston assembly to the rear with finger pressure and pull it from the rear of the receiver.*

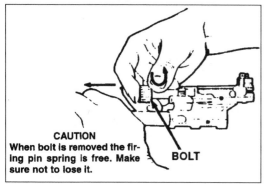

CAUTION
When bolt is removed the firing pin spring is free. Make sure not to lose it.

BOLT

Fig. 20-6(d). *Separate the bolt from the slide assembly by rotating it counterclockwise (looking at the face of the bolt) and pulling it forward.*

Fig. 20-6(f). *Close the cover assembly and depress the barrel locking lever on the left side of the weapon (loading side). While the locking lever is held to the rear grasp the barrel handle and lift upward at the same time. The barrel should separate easily.*

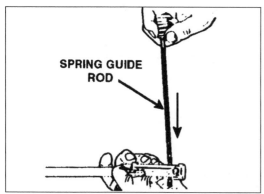

SPRING GUIDE ROD

Fig. 20-6(e). *To separate the slide assembly from the piston, press the retaining pin from the right to the left. Once the pin is shifted, lift the slide assembly upward from the piston.*

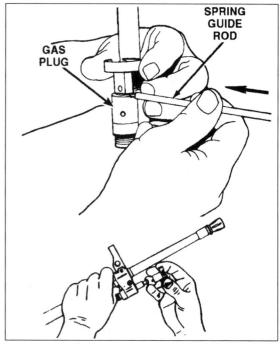

SPRING GUIDE ROD

GAS PLUG

Fig. 20-6(g-1).

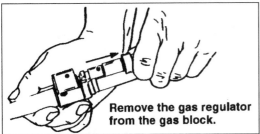

Remove the gas regulator from the gas block.

Fig. 20-6(g-2). Remove the gas regulator from the barrel by positioning the regulator lever between normal and maximum (lever pointing downward away from barrel). Place the tip of the scraping tool in the notch in the front left of the gas block. Holding the tip of the operating rod in this position, rotate the regulator detent up and over the tip and onto the top of the gas block. Pull forward on the gas collar and separate it from the gas block.

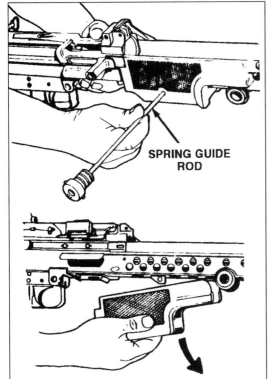

SPRING GUIDE ROD

Fig. 20-6(h). Remove the barrel hand guard by pressing the retaining pin from right to left (the pin will not separate completely from the hand guard). Pull down on the rear of the hand guard and separate it from the receiver.

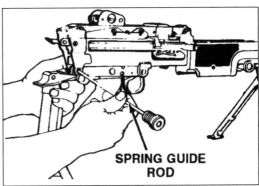

SPRING GUIDE ROD

Fig. 20-6(i). Remove the stock from the receiver by pressing the lower retaining pin from the right to the left. Notice that the pin can be pressed outward far enough to let the stock fall free but can still hold the trigger assembly in place (this is important for assembly).

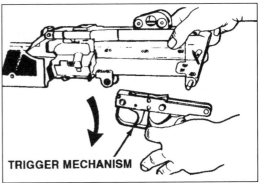

TRIGGER MECHANISM

Fig. 20-6(j). Pull the lower stock retaining pin to the left as far as possible (pin will not completely clear the receiver), and remove the trigger assembly by pulling downward and to the rear on the handgrip.

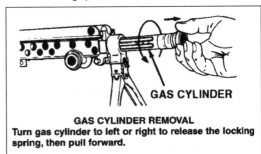

GAS CYLINDER

GAS CYLINDER REMOVAL
Turn gas cylinder to left or right to release the locking spring, then pull forward.

Fig. 20-6(k). Remove the bipod and gas cylinder by turning the gas cylinder to the left or right until you hear a click.

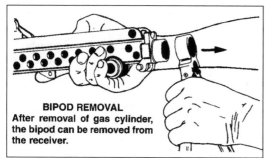

BIPOD REMOVAL
After removal of gas cylinder, the bipod can be removed from the receiver.

Fig. 20-6(I). Pull the gas cylinder forward and separate it from the bipod.

ASSEMBLY

To reassemble the SAW, reverse the above procedures. The following details are important in reassembling the weapon.

Ensure that the bipod yoke is placed on the gas cylinder small opening first.

When replacing the gas cylinder into the receiver, some manipulation will be required with the fingers of the free hand to get the base of the cylinder to line up with the receiver. Be sure to turn the gas cylinder until it clicks and is locked into place.

When replacing the trigger assembly, push the retaining pin inboard just far enough to catch and hold the trigger assembly in place. If you push it too far you will block the stock recess and you cannot put the stock in place until the pin is pulled outward.

When reassembling the gas regulator, ensure that the lug on the rear of the regulator lines up with the lug on the rear of the gas block. Place the gas regulator collar over the front of the gas regulator and align the tapered lug of the regulator with the tapered recess of the collar. Hold the rear of the regulator, press down on the regulator collar, and rotate the collar clockwise and lock it in place.

When placing the piston assembly in the receiver make sure that the slide recesses on the sides of the slide assembly are aligned with the slide rails of the receiver.

FUNCTION CHECK

After assembly has been completed it will be necessary to perform a functional check. Remember that functional checks are only to check reassembly procedures. Functional checks are not meant to take the place of actual live fire operational tests to be done before movement to contact if the tactical situation

permits. Functional checks for the SAW consist of the following:

With the weapon off safe, hold the charging handle, depress the trigger, and ride the bolt back and forth several times. The bolt should lock to the rear when the trigger is released.

With the bolt to the rear and weapon on safe, squeeze the trigger. The bolt should not go home.

OPERATION, SIGHT ADJUSTMENT, BATTLESIGHTS

OPERATION

Loading (belt). To load the SAW attach a 200 round box of ammunition to the underside of the receiver. Note that the underside of the receiver has a dovetail locking recess that will accept the dovetail lug on the ammo box. Align the recess and lugs and push them together until they lock.

Pull outward on the ammo box to ensure that it is, in fact, locked in place. Locate the green belt tab on the top of the ammo box and pull up on it (the belted ammo is affixed to this tab and will be pulled from the ammo box). Open the cover assembly and place the belt of ammunition on top of the feed tray with the open side of the links facing downward. The first round should be placed against the cartridge stop and the belt tab should be placed to the right of the cartridge stop. Hold the belt in place and shut the cover assembly, making sure that it locks in place. If the bolt is forward, pull it to the rear (weapon can be loaded with the bolt closed or open) and push the charging handle forward until it clicks. Check the cartridge indicator to ensure that it is in the up position indicating that the belt is loaded properly. Place the weapon on safe. To fire, take weapon off safe and squeeze the trigger.

Loading (magazine). To load the SAW using an M16 magazine, insert the magazine into the magazine well and push inward until the magazine latch clicks. If the bolt is not already to the rear, pull it rearward and lock it open, push the charging handle forward and put the weapon on safe. The weapon will fire when taken off safe and the trigger is squeezed.

Unloading the SAW. To unload the SAW the operator follows the same procedures for clearing. Pull the charging handle to the rear and lock the bolt open, place the weapon on safe, open cover assembly, remove ammo, raise the feed tray and inspect the chamber, close the cover assembly, take the weapon off safe, squeeze the trigger and ride the bolt home.

CHANGE BARREL PROCEDURES

The barrel of the M249 SAW should be changed after firing at the rapid rate (100 rds/min) for five minutes. To change barrels, first make sure that the bolt is not forward (the locking lugs will be engaged in the locking recesses of the chamber, making removal/installation impossible). Clear the weapon but leave the bolt locked to the rear; weapon on safe. Depress the barrel locking lever, grasp the barrel handle with the other hand and pull forward and up on the barrel to remove it from the receiver (Fig. 20-

7(a)). Handle the barrel carefully and avoid touching it. Install the cool barrel in the reverse order (Fig. 20-7(b)) making sure it is locked in place before attempting to fire.

USE OF GAS REGULATOR

The SAW is equipped with a gas regulator that can decrease or increase the pressure of the expanding gases that is applied against the face of the piston. The gas regulator has two different settings (Fig. 20-8). This is made possible by the use of two gas ports of different sizes in the regulator. The normal setting (smaller gas port) is attained by turning the gas regulator so that it is pointing to the left (loading port side). If the functioning of the weapon should

Fig. 20-7(a). Removal. Clear weapon. Depress the locking lever of the barrel with left hand. Hold the carrying handle with the right hand, lift it up and push the barrel forward. If the barrel is hot, handle carefully.

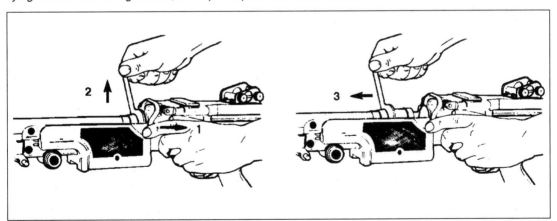

Fig. 20-7(b). Installation. Depress the locking lever of the barrel backwards with left hand. Holding the carrying handle with the right hand, pull the barrel rearward, push downward and lock by releasing locking lever. Reload.

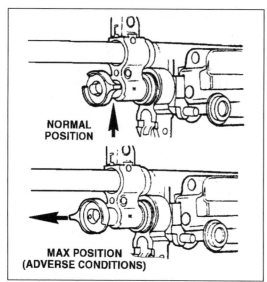

NORMAL
POSITION

MAX POSITION
(ADVERSE CONDITIONS)

Fig. 20-8. Gas Regulator.

become sluggish due to freezing temperatures or dirt and carbon build up, the gas regulator should be turned to the maximum setting. In this position the gas regulator is turned to the right (pointing toward the ejection port side). This allows more gas to escape through the gas port and the result is greater pressure being applied to the face of the piston, which, in turn, drives the operating parts at a much greater operating speed.

MAX position is to be used ONLY when weapon will not function properly in NORMAL position.

FIELD ZEROING PROCEDURES

Prior to field zeroing it will be necessary to set mechanical zero on the sights of the weapon. To do this rotate the windage knob (front knob) until the sight aperture is all the way to the left or right (Fig. 20-9). Then rotate the knob all the way back until the sight aperture is on the other side; at the same time

WINDAGE
KNOB

ELEVATION
KNOB

Fig. 20-9. Windage and Elevation Knobs.

count the number of clicks and divide this number of clicks by 2. Example: 24 clicks from full right windage to full left windage (24 ÷ 2 = 12). Mechanical zero is 12, so count back 12 clicks from full left windage. Rotate the rear sight aperture clockwise until it will not turn any farther. Rotate the aperture counterclockwise and count the number of rotations until it stops; divide this number by two and rotate the aperture clockwise this number rotations. Mechanical zero is now set for both windage and elevation.

Place a range setting of 300m on the rear sight elevation scale. With mechanical zero set, fire a 3-5-round burst at a target 300m away. Adjust the rear sight for windage and elevation until the impact of the burst is centered on the target. Do not use the elevation adjustment knob to correct elevation. To do this rotate the rear sight aperture in the desired direction. Rotating the rear sight aperture clockwise will lower the impact of the burst; rotating it counterclockwise will raise the impact of the burst.

NOTE: The weapon can be zeroed at any range so long as the range set on the rear sight elevation scale corresponds with the actual range to the target.

FUNCTIONING

The cycle of functioning of the M249 SAW occurs in the following sequence:

Feeding. This step takes place as the operator places a belt of ammunition on the feed tray or inserts a loaded magazine in the magazine well. Whichever method is used, the results are the same. A cartridge is placed in the path of the bolt so that as the bolt is driven forward from the force of the expanding operating spring, the face of the bolt makes contact with the rim of the first cartridge and strips it from the links or magazine.

As the bolt continues forward, the cam roller on top of the bolt forces the feed cam, in the cover assembly, to the left. This positions the feed pawl over the next cartridge to be chambered. When the burning gases of the fired cartridge cause the bolt to move to the rear, the feed cam lever and feed pawl are forced to the right. This causes the next round in the feed tray to be pulled to the right and placed in the feed tray groove ready for chambering.

Chambering. This action occurs as the bolt continues to move forward and forces the cartridge into the barrel chamber.

Locking. This occurs as chambering takes place. The locking lugs of the bolt pass through the locking recesses cut into the chamber. When the locking lugs and bolt face make contact with the rear of the chamber, the forward movement of the bolt stops. The slide assembly pushes the rotating lug of the bolt to the right. This rotation of the bolt causes the locking lugs to disalign with the locking recesses and locking takes place.

Firing. After locking has occurred, the piston and slide assembly continue forward slightly. This forward movement ends when the slide assembly forces the firing pin through the face of the bolt. The firing pin then strikes the primer of the cartridge and firing takes place.

Unlocking. Unlocking begins when expanding gases from the ignited propellant are vented off through the gas port in the gas regulator. The pressure of the expanding gases is directed rearward through the gas cylinder and forces the piston, piston assembly, slide assembly and bolt to the rear. As the slide assembly moves to the rear, the camming recess forces the camming lug of the bolt to the left. This causes the locking lugs on the bolt to align with the locking recesses in the chamber. The slide assembly continues to move to the rear and the bolt is withdrawn from the chamber.

Extracting. The extraction claw on the face of the bolt grips the cartridge case tightly by engaging the extraction groove. Thus as the bolt moves rearward the cartridge case is pulled from the chamber.

Ejecting. The extractor claw grips the lower right portion of the cartridge rim, and as the spent casing or cartridge is pulled to the rear, the ejector strikes the upper left of the base of the cartridge just as the bolt face clears the rear of the ejection port. This causes the cartridge case to pivot over the extraction claw and to be thrown clear of the receiver through the ejection port.

Cocking. As the bolt continues its movement to the rear, the piston assembly causes the operating spring to be compressed. Cocking is completed when the spring is fully compressed just before it begins to expand and drive the operating parts forward again.

CONDITION CODES

The weapon conditions for the M249 SAW are:
- Condition 1: The bolt is locked to the rear. The safety is on. The source of ammunition is in position on the feed tray or in the magazine well. The cover is closed.
- Condition 2: Not applicable.
- Condition 3: The bolt is forward. The chamber is empty. The safety is off. The source of ammunition is in position on the feed tray or in the magazine well. The cover is closed.
- Condition 4: The bolt is forward. The chamber is

empty. The safety is off. The feed tray is clear of ammunition and/or no magazine is inserted. The cover is closed.

IMMEDIATE ACTION

Should stoppage of the M249 SAW occur immediate action consists of the following steps:
- Pull the cocking handle to the rear, palms up, observing the ejection port to ensure ammunition is ejected.
- Push the cocking handle fully forward to the locked position.
- Sight and fire.

WARNING: If a round is not ejected and the barrel is hot (200 rounds fired in a two minute period), DO NOT open the feed tray cover. Put the weapon on safe and allow 15 minutes for cooling. After 15 minutes, unload the weapon.

NOTE: *During combat, the pace of the battle will dictate how long you will be able to wait until attempts are made to clear the round.*

RUNAWAY GUN PROCEDURES

A runaway gun is a weapon that continues to fire when the trigger is released. This is normally caused by a worn trigger sear but can also be a result of a dirty or worn gas system. To stop a runaway gun follow the procedures listed below:
- KEEP THE WEAPON POINTED DOWNRANGE!
- If firing from a magazine or if near the end of a 200 round belt, let the weapon continue to fire until the ammunition is expended.
- If you are not near the end of the ammunition belt execute the following steps:
  - Grab charging handle (palm up), pull it all the way back and hold.
  - Push the safety to the right (red not visible).
  - Clear the weapon (raise cover, remove ammunition, inspect chamber, ride bolt home).

CARE AND CLEANING

GENERAL

Like any other weapon the M249 SAW requires proper maintenance in order to operate properly. This maintenance can be conducted by the operator utilizing authorized cleaning agents and equipment. Each M249 is equipped with cleaning tools located in

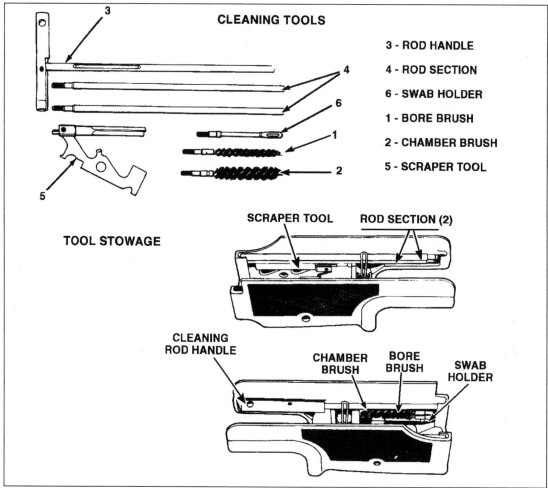

Fig. 20-10. Cleaning Tools and Stowage.

the hand guard (Fig. 20-10). This section covers the use of these tools in order to conduct first echelon care and cleaning. Prior to cleaning, the weapon should be field stripped and laid out in order of disassembly.

CLEANING AND MAINTENANCE OF THE BARRELS

To clean the barrels of the M249 SAW, follow the same barrel cleaning procedures for the M16A2. Do NOT attempt to exercise the front sight. Adjustment of the front sight is not operator authorized.

Each M249 will have one spare barrel. The barrels will not have serial numbers or any identifying marks. Each unit should have both barrels for each M249 marked in such a manner that they can be readily "married" to the M249 with which originally issued.

Barrels should not be switched among other M249's. The wear on the barrel extension of each M249 will be slightly different and switching barrels from another weapon will cause the weapon to function with a different head space*. Under these conditions a stoppage or malfunction will be likely.

Efforts should be made to ensure that both barrels receive the same amount of use. This will cause the wear of both barrels to remain uniform and the head space will not change.

*HEAD SPACE is the distance between the face of the bolt, when locked, and the rear of the chamber.

Head space is normally very small and usually measured in thousandths of an inch.

Place a light coat of CLP on the rear sight and exercise the windage and elevation knobs.

CLEANING THE RECEIVER AND FEED COVER ASSEMBLY

To clean the receiver and cover assembly use CLP, general purpose brush (toothbrush) and M60 machine gun receiver brush (if available). Wipe the receiver clean and leave a light coat of CLP on the surface. Leave a moderate coat of CLP on the slide rails and the moving parts of the cover assembly.

CLEANING THE GAS SYSTEM

To clean the gas system (regulator, cylinder, gas block and piston) use CLP or cleaning solvents such as RBC (rifle bore cleaner). Do not use any type of oil to clean or lubricate the gas system. Wipe the gas system dry. To clean the gas system utilizing the scraper tool follow the diagrams in Figures 20-11(a-g).

REGULATOR

The regulator must be cleaned with the special tool (scraper). Clean the gas vent hole of the regulator body as indicated.

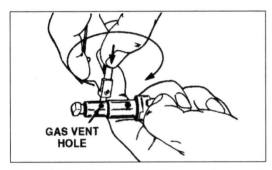

GAS VENT HOLE

Fig. 20-11(a). The regulator body can be heavily fouled and will require more thorough cleaning.

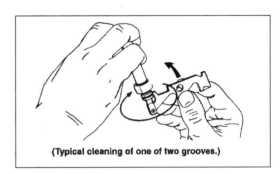

(Typical cleaning of one of two grooves.)

Fig. 20-11(c). Use the protruding tips of the scraper to clean the two groves of the regulator body. The regulator sleeve is generally not heavily fouled and can be easily cleaned with a rag.

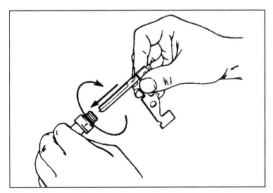

Fig. 20-11(b). Clean the central hole of the regulator (port) with the appropriate part of the scraper by turning it clockwise and pushing it inward to the bottom of the housing.

Fig. 20-11(d). GAS CYLINDER AND PISTON. Clean the front of the gas cylinder (internal diameter) by inserting and turning the flat side of the scraper in the hole.

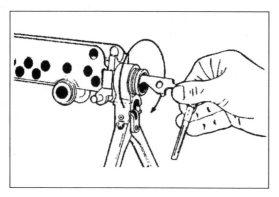

Fig. 20-11(e). *Clean the internal groves of the front side of the gas cylinder using the flat side of the scraper.*

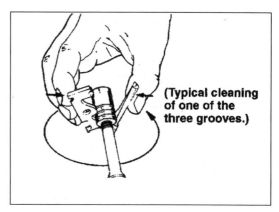

(Typical cleaning of one of the three grooves.)

Fig. 20-11(f). *The groves of the piston will be cleaned as shown.*

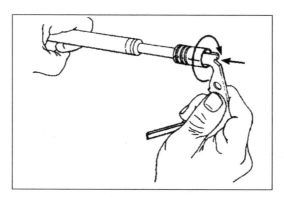

Fig. 20-11(g). *Clean the hole of the front of piston with the same scraper part as the front hole of the gas cylinder.*

Chapter Twenty-One

Bayonet

The modern amphibious assault requires a closely coordinated, well equipped, highly skilled team. The most important member of this team is the individual Marine. Other members of the team transport the Marine to the target area, prepare the objective and give support in the attack with a powerful array of modern weapons. But in the final assault, it is the individual Marine, with a rifle and bayonet, who closes with and destroys the enemy.

The rifle and bayonet, in the hands of a Marine, become a deadly combination of spear, sword, club and shield. At night, this combination weapon can kill silently and with surprise. In hand-to-hand fighting, when the rifle cannot be reloaded and the use of grenades would be impractical, it is the decisive weapon. At these times, the aggressive bayonet fighter will win.

The assault is the critical moment of any battle. A vigorous bayonet assault, executed by Marines eager to drive home cold steel, can strike terror into the ranks of the enemy. Skill and confidence in the ability to use the bayonet give a Marine the fortitude to make a bayonet assault. With such courage, the Marine truly becomes the spearhead and the most important member of the amphibious assault team.

In developing your skill with the rifle and bayonet, you must master the principles and movements described and illustrated in this chapter. They are not difficult. The Marine Corps system of bayonet fighting is based on natural movements. It can be compared with boxing, since the hands move in the same pattern as a boxer's fists. But as a bayonet fighter, your reach is greater than a boxer's. In one hand you have a pointed blade for slashing and stabbing. In the other hand is a weighted club for pounding and

smashing. These weapons must be driven at the enemy in a fast, relentless attack until destroyed. Hesitation will give the enemy a chance to recover and make you the object of the attack.

Principles

Get the blade into the enemy. This is the main principle in bayonet fighting. Parrying the enemy's attack, smashing with the butt of your rifle and using proper form and footwork are all important. But they are actions taken to enable you to sink the blade. It is usually the blade that kills.

Be ruthless, vicious and fast in your attack. Never pause until you have won. Follow each movement with another in a constant, aggressive cycle.

Seek vital areas, but don't wait for an opening. Make one. The throat is the best target. The belly is good too. Your enemy will instinctively protect those areas. When they cover one, attack the other. If the enemy succeeds in protecting both, go for the face, hands or side with the hacking, slashing blade and cut your way to a vital area. A solid butt stroke in the groin will open the enemy's guard. Deliver it hard and close in for the kill.

Protect yourself. You can dodge and parry. Your rifle and bayonet make a good shield. But remember that the best protection you have is to strike the first blow and then follow through.

Bayonet Fighting

This chapter describes all techniques for a right-handed person. However, all techniques can be executed from either side.

In drawings, the Marine is depicted in woodland camouflage utilities; the opponent is depicted without camouflage. In photographs, the Marine is depicted in woodland camouflage utilities; the opponent is depicted in desert camouflage utilities.

Bayonet Techniques

All Marines armed with a rifle carry a bayonet. The bayonet is an effective weapon if Marines are properly trained in offensive and defensive bayonet techniques. An offensive attack, such as a thrust, is a devastating attack that can quickly end a fight. Defensive techniques, such as the block and parry, can deter the opponent's attack and allow Marines to regain the initiative. Through proper training, Marines develop the courage and confidence required to effectively use a bayonet to protect themselves and destroy the enemy. In situations where friendly and enemy troops are closely mingled and rifle fire and grenades are impractical, the bayonet becomes the weapon of choice.

Holding the Rifle

To execute bayonet techniques, Marines hold the rifle in a modified basic warrior stance. All movement begins and ends with the basic warrior stance. To hold the rifle, Marines—

Use an overhanded grasp to grab the small of the rifle's stock. Use an underhanded grasp to grab the handguard of the rifle.

Lock the buttstock of the rifle against the hip with the right forearm.

Orient the blade end of the rifle toward the opponent.

Offensive Bayonet Techniques

Straight thrust. Marines use the straight thrust to disable or kill an opponent. It is the most deadly offensive technique because it causes the most trauma to an opponent. Target areas are the opponent's throat, groin, or face. The opponent's chest and stomach are also excellent target areas if not protected by body armor or combat equipment. To execute the straight thrust, Marines—

Lift the left leg and lunge forward off the ball of the right foot while thrusting the blade end of the weapon forward, directly toward the opponent.

Retract the weapon and return to the basic warrior stance.

Slash. Marines use the slash to kill an opponent or to create an opening in his defenses. The target area is the opponent's neck. To execute the slash, Marines—

Extend the left hand back toward the left shoulder.

Thrust the left hand forward and swing it to the right, bring the right hand back toward the hip, and turn the cutting edge of the blade toward the opponent's neck. The movement is a slashing motion so the blade cuts across the opponent's neck.

Horizontal Buttstroke. Marines use the horizontal buttstroke to weaken an opponent's defenses, to cause serious injury, or to set him up for a killing blow. Target areas are the opponent's head, neck, and legs. To execute the horizontal buttstroke, Marines—

Step forward with the right foot and drive the right hand forward. Rotate the hips and shoulders into the strike. Move the left hand back toward the left shoulder.

Strike the opponent with the butt of the weapon.

Vertical Buttstroke. Marines use the vertical buttstroke to weaken an opponent's defenses, to cause serious injury, or to set him up for a killing blow. Target areas are the opponent's groin and face. To execute the vertical buttstroke, Marines—

Step forward with the right foot and drive the right hand straight up.

Pull the left hand back over the left shoulder.

Strike the opponent with the butt of the weapon.

Smash. Marines use the smash as a follow-up technique to the horizontal or vertical buttstroke, particularly if they missed the target. The target area is the opponent's head. To execute the smash following a buttstroke, Marines—

Step forward with the right foot and place the blade end of the weapon over the left shoulder and elevate the right elbow above the shoulders.

Drive the arms straight forward, striking the opponent with the butt of the weapon.

Defensive Bayonet Techniques

Parry. Marines use a parry as a defensive technique to redirect or deflect an attack. A parry is a slight redirection of a linear thrust or a smash. To execute the parry, Marines—

Use the bayonet end of the rifle to redirect the barrel or bayonet of the opponent's weapon.

Lock the weapon against the hip with the right forearm.

Rotate to the right or left, moving the bayonet end of the rifle to parry the opponent's attack. Rotation is generated from the hips.

Redirect or guide the opponent's weapon away from the body by exerting pressure against the opponent's weapon.

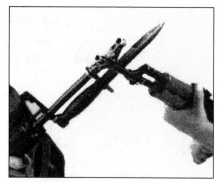

High Block. Marines execute a high block against a vertical attack coming from high to low. To execute the high block, Marines—

Thrust the arms up forcefully at approximately a 45-degree angle from the body. The weapon should be over the top of the head and parallel to the ground. The elbows are bent, but there is enough muscular tension in the arms to absorb the impact and deter the attack.

Low Block. Marines execute the low block against a vertical attack coming from low to high. To execute the low block, Marines—

Thrust the arms down forcefully at approximately a 45-degree angle from the body. The weapon should

be at or below the waist and parallel to the ground. The elbows are bent, but there is enough muscular tension in the arms to absorb the impact and deter the attack.

Left and Right Block. Marines execute a left or right block against a horizontal buttstroke or a slash. To execute the left or right block, Marines—

Thrust arms forcefully to the right or left, holding the rifle vertically in the direction of the attack. The elbows are bent, but there is enough muscular tension in the arms to absorb the impact and deter the attack.

Counter Action Following the Block. After deflecting an opponent's attack with a block, Marines counter with a slash or a horizontal buttstroke to regain initiative. However, the objective in any bayonet fight is to thrust forward with the blade end of the weapon to immediately end the fight.

Group Strategy

On occasion, Marines may engage an opponent as a member of a group or numerous opponents by one's self or as a member of a group. By combining bayonet fighting movements and simple strategies, Marines can effectively overcome their opponent or opponents.

Offensive Strategy: Two Against One. If two bayonet fighters engage one opponent, the fighters advance together.

Fighter 1 engages the opponent while fighter 2 swiftly and aggressively attacks the opponent's exposed flank and destroys the opponent.

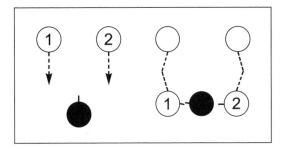

Offensive Strategy: Three Against Two. If three bayonet fighters engage two opponents, the fighters advance together keeping their opponents to the inside.

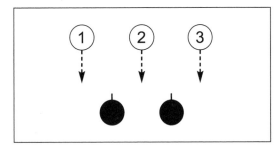

Fighters 1 and 3 engage opponents. Fighter 2 attacks the opponent's exposed flank engaged by fighter 1 and destroys the opponent.

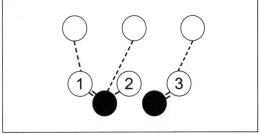

Fighters 1 and 2 turn and attack the exposed flank of the opponent engaged by fighter 3 and destroy the opponent.

Defensive Strategy: One Against Two. If a fighter is attacked by two opponents, the fighter immediately positions himself at the flank of the nearest opponent and keeps that opponent between himself and the other opponent.

Using the first opponent's body as a shield against the second opponent, the fighter destroys the first opponent quickly before the second opponent moves to assist.

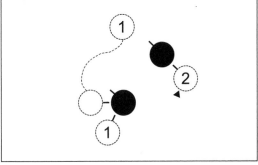

Then, the fighter engages and destroys the second opponent.

Defensive Strategy: Two Against Three. If two fighters are attacked by three opponents, the fighters immediately move to the opponent's flanks.

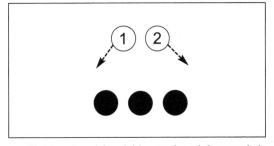

Fighters 1 and 2 quickly attack and destroy their opponents before the third opponent closes in.

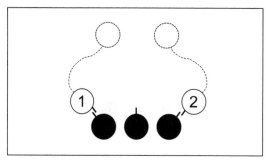

Fighter 1 engages the third opponent while fighter 2 attacks the opponent's exposed flank and destroys the opponent.

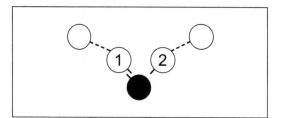

Training

Train yourself as a bayonet fighter by developing skill in all the movements. Concentrate on being aggressive. Shout and yell as you close with your opponent. This will unnerve the enemy and make you more eager to "close for the kill." Remember to keep your balance and to move with speed. Good timing and judgment of distance will come with practice.

Learning the movements. Go through each movement step by step, until you have learned it thoroughly. Then execute the entire movement slowly and smoothly. After you do it properly, start speeding up your action. When you have mastered all the movements, start combining them in sequence. Learn a series of movements that follow one another naturally. Always start the series from the guard and return to the position after you complete your combined series of attacks.

Coach and pupil. Get another Marine to watch you and correct any wrong move you make. Then do the same as the Marine goes through the movements. Use pugil sticks while practicing against one another. Practice teamwork against another "enemy." Learn to work in pairs and threes as a smoothly operating team.

Chapter Twenty-Two

M203, 40mm Grenade Launcher

Fig. 22-1. *The 40mm grenade launcher, M203, attached to the M16A2 rifle.*

General Description

The 40mm Grenade Launcher, M203, is a light-weight, single-shot, breech-loaded, pump action (sliding barrel), shoulder-fired weapon attached to the M16A2 rifle. It consists of a handguard and sight assembly group, receiver assembly, quadrant sight assembly and barrel assembly (Fig. 22-1).

Data and Capabilities

Length of rifle and grenade
    Launcher (overall)............90 cm(39 in.)
Length of barrel only ....30.5 cm(12 in.)
Weight of launcher unloaded ......1.4 kg(3.0 lbs.)
Weight of launcher loaded ....1.6 kg(3.5 lbs.)
Weight of rifle and grenade launcher
    with both fully loaded...5.0 kg(11.0 lbs.)
Action ....Single Shot
Maximum range ....400 meters (1,312 ft.)
....(approximately)

Maximum effective range:
Fire-team sized area target..................350 meters
....(1,148 ft.)
Vehicle or weapon point target ....150 meters
....(492 ft.)
Minimum safe firing range (HE):
Training ....165 meters (541 ft.)
Combat ....31 meters (102 ft.)
Minimum arming range ....14 to 38 meters
....(46 to 125 ft.)
....(approximately)

Nomenclature

Safety

The safety is located forward of the trigger, inside the trigger guard. To fire the launcher the safety must be in the forward position. (See Fig. 22-2.) To place the launcher on *safe* the safety must be in the most rearward position. (See Fig. 22-3.) The safety must be manually placed in the *safe* or *fire* position.

279

Fig. 22-2. Location of the safety in the firing position.

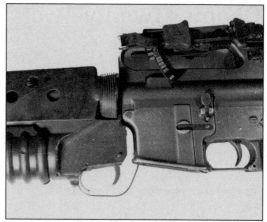

Fig. 22-4. Trigger and trigger guard.

Fig. 22-3. Location of the safety in the safe position.

Fig. 22-5. Trigger guard rotated down.

Trigger and Trigger Guard

The position of the trigger and trigger guard is shown in Figure 22-4. The trigger guard protects the trigger. Depressing the rear portion of the trigger guard allows the trigger guard to rotate down and away from the magazine well on the rifle thus allowing the grenadier to fire the weapon while wearing gloves or mittens. (See Fig. 22-5.)

Barrel Latch

The barrel latch is on the left side of the barrel (Fig. 22-6). This latch locks the barrel and receiver together. To open the barrel depress the barrel latch and slide the barrel forward.

Quadrant Sight

The quadrant sight assembly mounts on the left side of the carrying handle of the M16A2 rifle. The quadrant sight assembly consists of a mounting screw, quadrant sight assembly clamp, sight bracket assembly, sight latch, rear sight aperture, sight aperture arm, front sight post and sight post arm.

Quadrant sight assembly clamp, sight bracket assembly and mounting screw. The quadrant sight assembly clamp and sight bracket assembly (Fig. 22-7) hold the quadrant sight assembly to the carrying handle of the M16A2 rifle and are secured by a mounting screw inserted through the right side of the quadrant sight assembly clamp into the sight bracket assembly.

Quadrant sight arm and range quadrant. The quadrant sight arm serves a dual purpose. It mounts

Fig. 22-6. *Operating the barrel latch.*

Fig. 22-8. *Controls.*

Fig. 22-7. *Quadrant sight assembly.*

the sight aperture arm (which holds the sight aperture) and the sight post arm (which holds the front sight post) as shown in Figure 22-8. This permits the sight to pivot on the range quadrant to the desired range setting. The range quadrant is graduated in 25-meter increments from 50 to 400 meters. To move the quadrant sight arm along the range quadrant, move the sight latch rearward. This rearward pressure unlocks the quadrant sight arm, allowing it to move along the range quadrant so that the desired range number can be centered in the window on the quadrant sight arm. To lock the sight in position, release the sight latch.

Front sight post. The front sight post mounts on the quadrant sight arm by means of a pivot bracket that can be opened when the sights are in use or closed when not in use, to prevent damage to the sights. The sight post can be used to make minor adjustments in elevation when zeroing the launcher. For elevation adjustments, turn the elevation adjustment screw on the sight post to the right to decrease

elevation and to the left to increase elevation. One full turn on the elevation adjustment screw will move the impact of the projectile five meters at a range of 200 meters.

Rear sight aperture. The rear sight aperture (Fig. 22-8) connects to the sight aperture arm, which is attached to the rear portion of the quadrant sight arm. The sight aperture arm serves the same purpose as the sight post arm. The rear sight aperture can be adjusted for minor changes in deflection when zeroing the launcher. For windage adjustment, press the rear sight retainer and move the aperture away from the barrel to move impact to the left. One notch on the rear sight aperture will move the impact of the projectile one and one-half meters at a range of 200 meters.

Sight Leaf Assembly

The sight leaf base is part of the handguard and sight assembly group. It is located on top of the handguard and consists of a sight leaf, sight leaf base, sight leaf mount, elevation adjustment machine screw and a sight windage screw. The elevation and windage scales are marked on the sight leaf mount. The sight leaf is a folding, adjustable open ladder design that permits rapid firing without sight manipulation. The sight leaf uses the front sight post of the M16A2 rifle as the front aiming post.

Sight leaf base. The sight leaf base is permanently attached to the rifle handguard by two mounting screws. The sight leaf base serves to protect the sight leaf from damage when the leaf is not being used and in the down position.

Sight leaf mount and sight leaf. The mount is attached to the sight base and is used to raise or lower the sight leaf blade. The sight leaf is graduated in 50-meter increments from 50 to 250 meters and numbered at 100 and 200 meters. (Fig. 22-9.)

Elevation adjustment screw and elevation scale. The screw attaches the sight leaf to the sight mount. To make minor adjustments in elevation when zeroing the launcher, the sight leaf can be moved up or down by loosening the screw. The rim of a 40mm cartridge case may be used to turn the elevation adjustment screw. Raising the sight leaf increases the range, and lowering it decreases the range. The elevation scale consists of five lines spaced equally apart on the sight leaf. The index line is on the left of the sight leaf. One increment will move the impact of the projectile 10 meters in elevation at a range of 200 meters.

Windage screw and windage scale. The left end of the screw consists of a knob which is used to turn the sight windage screw to adjust for deflection. The windage scale consists of a zero line in the center of the scale and two lines spaced equally on each side of the zero line. When making minor adjustments in deflection while zeroing the launcher, one increment on the windage scale will move the impact of the projectile one and one-half meters at a range of 200 meters.

Condition Codes

Condition 1 Round in chamber, action closed, safety engaged.
Condition 2 Not applicable to M203.
Condition 3 Not applicable to M203.

Condition 4 Chamber empty, action closed, safety engaged.

Types of Stoppages

The two most common types of stoppages with the M203 are hangfires and misfires.
- **Hangfire:** A hangfire is a delay in the functioning of a propelling-charge-explosive-train at the time of firing.
- **Misfire:** A misfire is a complete failure to fire.
- **Failure to Fire:** Each shooter should know what to do the moment the weapon fails to fire. To clear a failure to fire, the shooter should:
  Shout "misfire" (training only). Keep the weapon pointed downrange and maintain muzzle awareness.

Immediate Action

Definition: an unhesitating response to a stoppage without investigating the cause.
- Wait 30 seconds.
- Depress the barrel latch and push barrel assembly all the way forward.
- Clear obstructions in the chamber.
- Insert round into chamber.
- Pull barrel assembly to the rear until the barrel latch locks.
- Sight and fire.

Fig. 22-9. *Grenade launcher, sight leaf and front sight post of the M16A2 rifle.*

Ammunition

The M203 is a versatile weapon. It has more types of rounds available than any other fixed-type ammunition weapon. There are eight types of rounds we will discuss in this chapter and many new types under development. The 40mm cartridge is a fixed-type ammunition. Fixed-type means that the ammunition has two major assemblies, projectile and cartridge case, and both are "fixed" together into one round. Characteristics of the different types of rounds vary greatly.

High-explosive dual purpose (HEDP) round. This round has an olive drab aluminum skirt with a steel cup attached, white markings and a gold ogive; it penetrates at least 5 cm (2 inches) when fired straight at steel armor. It arms between 14 and 27 meters, and it causes casualties within a 5-meter radius (Fig. 22-10).

High-explosive (HE) round. This round has an olive drab aluminum skirt with a steel projectile attached, gold markings and a yellow ogive. It arms between 14 and 27 meters, and it produces a ground burst that causes casualties within a 5-meter radius (Fig. 22-10).

Star parachute round. This round is white impact or bar alloy aluminum with black markings. It is used for illumination and signals and is lighter and more accurate than comparable hand-held signal rounds (Fig. 22-10). The parachute attached to the round deploys upon ejection to lower the candle at 7 feet per second. The candle burns for about 40 seconds.

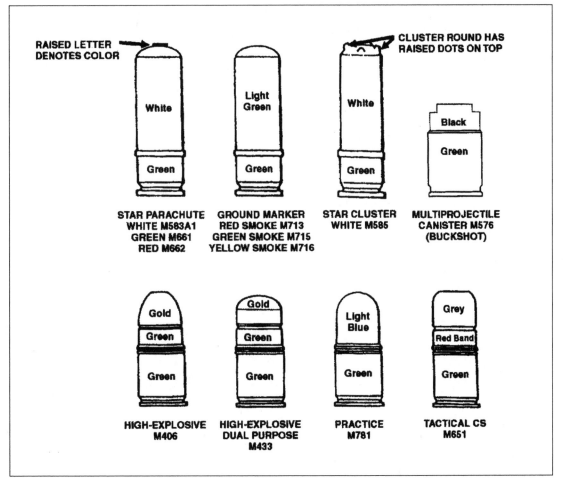

Fig. 22-10. Ammunition.

White star cluster round. This round is white impact or bar aluminum alloy with black markings. The attached plastic ogive has a raised "W" for night identification. The round is used for illumination or signals (Fig. 22-10). It is lighter and more accurate than comparable hand-held signal rounds. The individual stars burn for about 7 seconds during free fall.

Ground marker round. This round is light green impact aluminum with black markings. It is used for aerial identification and for marking the location of personnel on the ground (Fig. 22-10). It arms between 15 and 45 meters. If a fuze fails to function on impact, the output mixture provided in the front end of the delay casing backs up the impact feature.

Practice round. This round is blue zinc or aluminum with white markings. It is used for practice and produces a yellow or orange signature on impact (Fig. 22-10).

CS round. This round body is grey aluminum; its casing is green with black markings. Though it is a multipurpose round, it is most effective for riot control and in Military Operations in Urban Terrain (MOUT). It produces a white cloud of CS gas on impact (Fig. 22-10).

Multiprojectile Canister M576 (Buckshot). This round has a short, black projectile and provides the grenadier with effective fire power for close enemy engagements (Fig. 22-10). The effective range of the multiprojectile round is up to 30 meters. It can be used in jungle environments, built-up areas and during hours of poor visibility when targets are at close ranges. Due to its high muzzle velocity and flatter trajectory, the grenadier should aim at the base of the target when using the multiprojectile round.

Storage of Ammunition

Ammunition should be stored under cover. If this is not possible, it must be stored at least 15 centimeters (6 inches) above the ground and covered with a double layer of tarpaulins. These should be placed so that they protect the ammunition, allowing for ventilation. Trenches must be dug to prevent water from flowing under the ammunition.

Care, Handling and Preservation

Ammunition containers should not be opened until ammunition is to be used. Ammunition removed from the airtight containers is likely to corrode, particularly in damp climates. Marines must take the following precautions:

- *Protect ammunition from mud, dirt and water.* If it gets wet or dirty, wipe it off before using it. Also, wipe off lightly corroded cartridges as soon as the corrosion is discovered. Heavily corroded or dented projectiles and those with loose parts or particles should *not* be fired.
- *Avoid exposing ammunition to the direct rays of the sun.* Hot powder can cause excessive pressure when the round is fired.
- *Do not lubricate ammunition.* This can cause dust and other abrasives to collect on it and damage the operating parts of the weapon.
- M203 ammunition *cannot* be used in the MK19 heavy machine gun.

Chapter Twenty-Three

Infantry Battalion Weapons

The Marine Corps has many different types of organizations. Among these are recruit depots, formal schools, bases and stations. The main fighting strength of the Corps, however, is in its Fleet Marine Force.

The Fleet Marine Force is an organization made up of ground and air units. It is designed to serve with the fleet for seizing and defending advanced naval bases and for conducting such land operations as may be essential in the prosecution of a naval campaign.

The key fighting organization of the Fleet Marine Force is the infantry battalion. All of the many other types of units within the Fleet Marine Force such as artillery, aviation, communication, tank, engineer, motor transport, supply, maintenance and medical units are included to help the infantry carry out its mission. Supporting fires to supplement those of the infantry are provided by artillery, aviation and naval gunfire units. In combat, these supporting fires can usually be delivered within minutes.

The infantry battalion is the basic tactical unit of the Marine Division. The mission of the infantry battalion in the attack is to close with the enemy and destroy or capture them by fire and movement; and in the defense, to repel their assault by fire and close combat.

Elsewhere in the Guidebook are the descriptions of the weapons most frequently available to support the Marine rifleman, the SAW and the M240G machine gun. Within the infantry battalion, other weapons are available to help carry out an assigned mission. The remainder of this chapter will describe briefly those weapons which are usually found within the infantry battalion.

JAVELIN

Javelin is a portable antitank weapon. It is shoulder-fired and can also be installed on tracked, wheeled or amphibious vehicles.

In 1989, the US Army awarded a contract for the development of Javelin as a replacement for the M47 Dragon antitank missile.

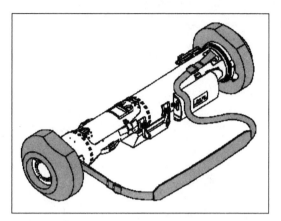

MISSILE

The Javelin system consists of the Command Launch Unit (CLU) and the round. The CLU, with a carry weight of 6.4 kg, incorporates a passive target acquisition and fire control unit with an integrated day sight and a thermal imaging sight. The gunner's controls for the missile system are on the CLU. The

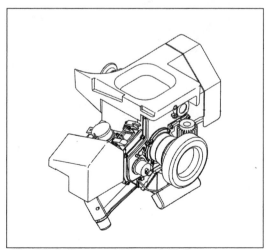

Fig. 23-1. Command Launch Unit.

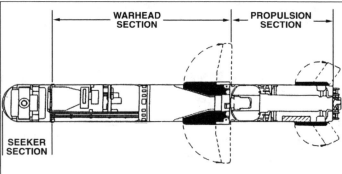

Fig. 23-2. *The gunner engages the target using the sight on the Command Launch Unit (CLU).*

Fig. 23-4.

day sight is equipped with x 4 magnification and the night sight with x 4 and x 9-magnification optics.

The round consists of the Javelin missile and the Launch Tube Assembly. The range of the missile is

Fig. 23-3. *The Command Launch Unit offers stand-alone surveillance to observe opposing forces.*

2500 m. Javelin is a fire-and-forget missile with lock-on before launch and automatic self-guidance. The missile is equipped with an imaging infrared seeker. The tandem warhead is fitted with two shaped charges: a precursor warhead to initiate explosive reactive armor and a main warhead to penetrate

Fig. 23-5. *Javelin is a man portable anti-tank weapon with a carry-weight of 22.3 kg.*

Fig. 23-6. *The Command Launch Unit attaches to the missile and launch tube assembly.*

base armor. The propulsion system is a two-stage solid propellant design, which provides a minimum smoke soft launch.

Fig. 23-7. *Javelin automatically guides itself to the target after launch.*

OPERATION

The system is deployed and ready to fire in less than 30 seconds and the reload time is less than 20 seconds. The missile is mounted on the Command Launch Unit and the gunner engages the target using the sight on the CLU, by placing a curser box over the image of the target. The gunner locks on the automatic target tracker in the missile by sending a lock-on-before-launch command to the missile. When the system is locked-on, the missile is ready to fire and the gunner does not carry out post launch tracking or missile guidance. Unlike conventional wire guided, fibre-optic cable guided, or laser beam riding missiles, Javelin is autonomously guided to the target after launch, leaving the gunner free to reposition or reload immediately after launch.

A soft launch ejects the missile from the launch tube to give a low-recoil shoulder launch. The soft launch enables firing from inside buildings or covered positions. Once the missile is clear, the larger propellant in the second stage is ignited and the missile is propelled towards the target. The weapon has two attack modes, direct or top attack. The gunner selects direct attack mode to engage covered targets, bunkers, buildings and helicopters. The top attack mode is selected against tanks, in which case the Javelin climbs above and strikes down on the target to penetrate the roof of the tank where there is the least armor protection. The missile is launched at an 18-degree elevation angle to reach a peak altitude of 150 m in top attack mode and 50 m in direct fire mode.

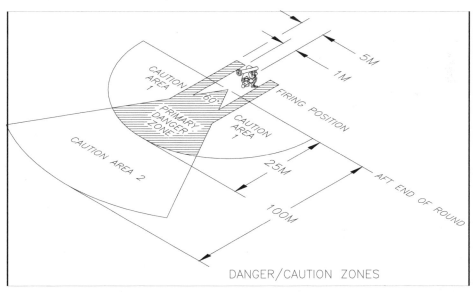

Fig. 23-8. *Javelin back blast danger diagram.*

Total weight	22.3 kg
Missile	
Weight	11.8 kg
Length	1.08 m
Diameter	126 mm
Range	2,000-2,500 m
Seeker	Imaging infra-red, CMT, 64 x 64 staring focal plane array, 8 - 12 micron
Guidance	Lock-on before launch, automatic self-guidance
Warhead	Tandem shaped charge
Propulsion	2-stage solid propellant
Command Launch Unit	
Weight	6.4 kg
Day sight magnification	X 4
Night sight magnification	X 4, x 9

Specifications	JAVELIN	DRAGON
Type System:	Fire and Forget	Wire Guided
Total Carry Weight:	49.5 Lbs.	33.9 Lbs. (Day)
		48.7 Lbs. (Night)
Command Launch Unit:	14.5 Lbs.	21.65 Lbs. (Night w/1 bottle and battery)
		6.75 Lbs. (Day)
Missile (w/Launch Tube):	35 Lbs.	28.89 Lbs.
Crew:	Man Portable (2 Man Team)	Man Portable (2 Man Team)
Ready to Fire:	Less than 30 seconds	Less than 30 seconds
Reload Time:	Less than 20 seconds	Time of Flight + 20 seconds
System Components:	Command Launch Unit	Day Sight
	Round of Ammunition	Thermal Sight
		Round of Ammunition
Method of Attack:	Gunner Selectable	Direct Fire only
	Top Attack or Direct Fire	
Range:	Top Attack: Min 150 meters	
	Max: 2000+ meters	Min: 65 meters
	Direct Attack: Min: 65 meters	Max: 1,000 meters
	Max: 2,000+ meters	
Firing Position Restrictions:	When firing from an enclosed area:	Firing from an enclosed area is possible
	1m x 2m ventilation recommended.	but not recommended except in a
		life or death combat situation.
Guidance System:	Imaging Infrared	Optically Controlled/Wire Guided
Sights:	Integrated Day/Night sight unit	Separate Day and Night Sights
Time of Flight:	1,000 m = approx. 4.6 sec.	
	2,000 m = approx. 14.5 sec.	1,000 m = approx. 11.2 sec.
Sight Magnification:	4X Day, 4X and 9X Night	6X Day, 4X Night

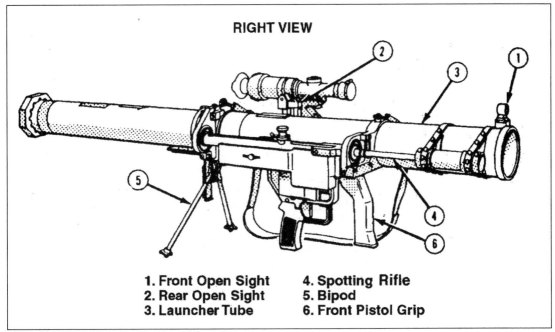

RIGHT VIEW

1. Front Open Sight
2. Rear Open Sight
3. Launcher Tube
4. Spotting Rifle
5. Bipod
6. Front Pistol Grip

Fig. 23-9. *Right side view of the SMAW.*

Shoulder Launched Multi-Purpose Assault Weapon

Another missile firing weapon available within the infantry battalion is the Shoulder Launched Multi-Purpose Assault Weapon or SMAW. It is designed for use by Marine Corps Assault Teams against buildings, bunkers, field fortifications and other hard targets. The SMAW consists of the launcher, sight, firing mechanism and attached spotting rifle. It fires an 83mm dual mode encased rocket which detonates in either a fast mode against a hard target or a slow mode against a soft target. The encased rocket attaches to the rear of the launcher and forms an extension of the launcher to become a shoulder fired weapon system.

The major components are shown in Figures 23-9 and 10 for the weapon in the "Ready to Fire" condition, with an encased rocket fitted to the rear of the launcher.

General Data

Launcher
 Length: 29.92 in.
 Weight: 16.92 lb.

Encased Rocket
 Length: 29.40 in.
 Weight: 12.74 lb.
Weapon Ready to Fire
 Length: 53.10 in.
 Weight: 29.01 lb.
 Range, Optimum: 250 meters.
 Range, Maximum: 400 meters.
 Muzzle Velocity: 725 fps.

Component Operation

The launcher, firing mechanism, sights and spotting rifle (Fig. 23-11) are operated as described below.

The launcher is a smooth bore fiber glass tube. For structural support and protection from rough handling, the launch tube has protective metal rings on each end. Attachments to the launch tube are as follows:

The Cheek Pad is attached to the launcher to provide facial support when using the open sights.

The Front Pistol Grip is a hollow plastic handle attached to the launch tube. It is used for supporting the tube with the left hand and aids the gunner in stabilizing the weapon during aiming and firing.

289

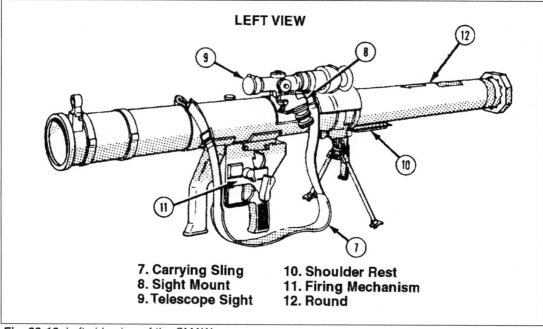

LEFT VIEW

7. Carrying Sling
8. Sight Mount
9. Telescope Sight

10. Shoulder Rest
11. Firing Mechanism
12. Round

Fig. 23-10. Left side view of the SMAW.

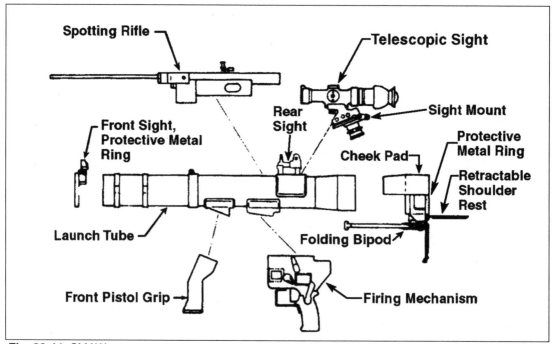

Spotting Rifle

Telescopic Sight

Front Sight, Protective Metal Ring

Rear Sight

Sight Mount

Cheek Pad

Protective Metal Ring

Retractable Shoulder Rest

Launch Tube

Folding Bipod

Front Pistol Grip

Firing Mechanism

Fig. 23-11. SMAW.

The Shoulder Rest is mounted on the underside of the launch tube as part of the rear reinforcing metal ring. It is a retractable shoulder rest consisting of a folding, square metal bracket with two rubber pads which opens at a 90 degree angle when pulled rearward. When retracted, it folds into a channel flush with the underside of the launcher.

The Bipod has two folding legs that are also mounted to the rear reinforcing ring on the underside of the shoulder rest mount. These legs fold along the underside of the launch tube and rotate rearward and spread 60 degrees apart when unfolded to support the center of gravity of the loaded weapon. The gunner uses the bipod only when firing from the prone position.

The Carrying Strap is an adjustable strap and is attached to both the forward and rear spotting rifle attachment rings. The strap permits the gunner to carry the SMAW.

The Firing Mechanism (Fig. 23-12) is operated by the right hand and contains the rocket firing mech-

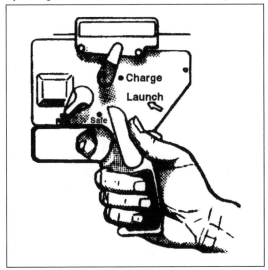

Fig. 23-12. Firing Mechanism.

anism and mechanical firing interface for the spotting rifle. The firing mechanism contains three control levers and a trigger.

The Safety Lever is a two position lever located above and just forward of the trigger. It is marked SAFE and FIRE. In the SAFE position, it mechanically locks the trigger preventing the firing of either the spotting rifle or the rocket. In the FIRE position it releases the trigger for normal operation.

The Charging Lever is a two position lever located near the top center of the firing mechanism. It is

marked only for the CHARGE position. When the spotting rifle is cocked and the lever is placed in the CHARGE position, it remains there until the rocket is launched. Once charged, the charging lever is locked in place by a mechanical sear. It cannot be returned to its "at rest" position by hand. When the charging lever is in the "at rest" position, neither the spotting rifle or rocket can be fired.

The Launcher Lever is a spring loaded lever marked only for the LAUNCH position. It is easily operated by the gunner's thumb. When the launch lever is in its "at rest" position, the trigger will operate the spotting rifle. When the launch lever is depressed and the trigger squeezed, an electrical firing pulse is sent to the rocket.

The Trigger is located above and in front of the hand grip. Depending on the positions of the three control levers, the trigger will either be locked, fire the spotting rifle or launch the rocket.

The Front Open Sight (Fig. 23-13) is mounted on the front protective ring. It consists of a post pro-

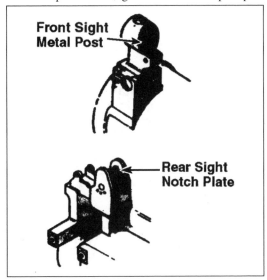

Fig. 23-13. Open Sights.

tected by a metal guard. It is only adjusted by an armorer using a special tool.

The Rear Open Sight (Fig. 23-13) consists of a metal "U" shaped notch through with the front post is aligned with the target. It is not adjustable.

Sight Mount

The Sight Mount is designed to accommodate either the optical sight or the AN/PVS4 night vision

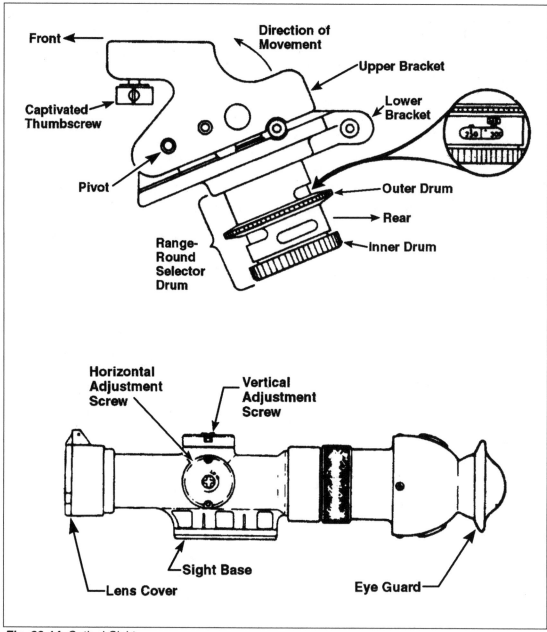

Fig. 23-14. *Optical Sight.*

sight. It has two adjustable drums. The outer drum selects the type of warhead, and is spring loaded so it cannot be accidentally turned while adjusting the range. The sight mount has been designed to accommodate the trajectory of up to four ballistically different rockets when they are fielded. The inner drum can be turned to put the proper superelevation on the sight for a target at a determined range.

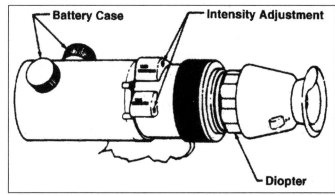

Fig. 23-15. Night Vision Sight.

The Optical Sight (Fig. 23-14) is a 3.8 power sight with a 6 degree field of view used for day and low level light operation. The eyeguard can be turned to fit the gunner's face. Vertical and horizontal adjustment are done by an armorer. The Sight Base has two holes in it for mounting on the Sight Mount. The aft hole is used when firing the SMAW with a gas mask.

The AN/PVS4 Night Vision Sight (Fig. 23-15) fastens to the sight mount in place of the optical sight. This scope is a lightweight, optical sight which functions on the image intensifier principle; its range depends on the amount of light available. It is a 4 power scope, it weighs 3.7 pounds and is battery operated.

Both sights must be boresighted to a given launcher and they become a set with that launcher.

They can be removed and remounted without loss of boresight.

The Spotting Rifle (Fig. 23-16) is attached to the right side of the launcher by two mounting rings which permit it to be boresighted to the launch tube and help it withstand rough handling. The spotting rifle has a semi-automatic, closed bolt, magazine-fed action and fires a 9mm tracer round that is ballistically matched to the rocket. The magazine holds six rounds and locks in place like a magazine locks in place for an M16. It is released by the magazine release lever. The rifle is equipped with a cocking lever to initially cock the firing pin and to help clear or chamber rounds. A loaded magazine is stored inside the front end cap of each encased rocket to insure its availability. The Spotting Rifle can be field stripped by the gunner for cleaning. The Spotting Rifle will NOT be removed from the launcher by the gunner.

Loading and Unloading

Loading

While loading or unloading the launcher, always keep the muzzle pointed down range. To load the SMAW, the gunner will do the following:

Drop to a comfortable position with the rocket launcher across your left leg and firing mechanism pointed up.

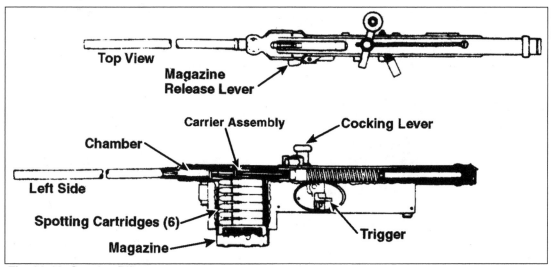

Fig. 23-16. Spotting Rifle.

Insure that the weapon is on safe and the charging lever is not in the CHARGE position.

Remove the front end cap from the encased rocket.
Insert the encased rocket into the aft end of the launcher and rotate clockwise until it firmly locks in place.
Remove the spotting rifle magazine from the forward end cap and insert the magazine into the magazine well of the spotting rifle.

Cock and load the spotting rifle by pulling the cocking lever to the rear and releasing it.

Loading the Assault Rocket Trainer

To load the Assault Rocket Trainer with the noise cartridge, insert the noise cartridge into the rear end of the Assault Rocket Trainer.

Remove the shunt from the noise cartridge and connect the electrical connector to the electrical connection in the Assault Rocket Trainer.
Remove the forward end cap from the Assault Rocket Trainer and mate the trainer in the same manner as you load an encased rocket.

Unloading

To unload the SMAW, the gunner will do the following:
Place the safety lever in the SAFE position.
Remove the magazine from the spotting rifle by pushing the magazine release.
Pull the cocking lever to the rear to eject any cartridge that may be in the spotting rifle chamber.
Check the charging lever to be sure it is in the "at rest" position.
Remove the encasement from the launcher by rotating it counter-clockwise.
Re-install the forward end cap on the encasement if not fired or dispose of expended encasement.

Ammunition

Ammunition for the SMAW includes the 9mm Spotting Round and the Rocket (SMAW), Assault, encased, 83mm Dual Mode MK 3, with a warhead containing a 2.4 pound high explosive charge. There is also a practice round and a trainer device containing a noise cartridge.

Safety - Training and Combat

Range Safety

Down Range Safety Zones. The calculated maximum safety areas extend 2,000 meters down range from the firing point at an angle of 10 degrees left or right of the aim direction. This is the impact zone. The warhead fragmentation zone is 500 meters beyond the impact zone, in all directions. No personnel should be allowed in these areas.

Firing Line Safety

Danger Area - No personnel allowed in this area; severe injury may be sustained from blast and flying debris.

Ear Protection Caution Area - Personnel must wear protection devices. Sound pressure levels may exceed 140 dB.

Caution Area - Personnel should remain clear of this area. Injury may be sustained from flying debris and excessive sound pressure levels (140 dB or more).

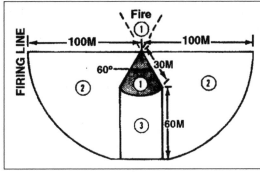

Fig. 23-17. *Firing Line Safety Zones.*

Firing Line Safety Zones. (See Fig. 23-17.) The backblast area of the SMAW extends 90 meters to the rear of the launcher and is broken into two zones. The Danger Zone extends 30 meters to the rear of the launcher at an angle of 60 degrees. No personnel are allowed in this area because severe injury would be sustained. The Caution Zone extends 60 meters beyond the Danger Zone. No personnel should be allowed in this area because of possible injury from flying debris. Ear protection must be worn by personnel within 100 meters on either side of the launcher. During training, the gunner is allowed to fire *only* five rockets per day, because the sound pressure levels will cause hearing loss.

Minimum Safe Engagement Ranges

The following are the minimum ranges that a gunner can safely engage a target:

Tactical Round
 Brick/Cement/Sandbag
 Combat: 50 meters.
 Training: 100 meters.
 Steel/Metal
 Combat: 80 meters.
 Training: 150 meters.
Tracer Cartridge
 Brick/Cement/Sandbag: 50 meters for both Combat and Training.
 Steel/Metal: 50 meters for both Combat and Training
Practice Round
 The Practice Round should not be fired at targets less than 50 meters away.

Targets may be engaged at shorter ranges if the gunner fires from a protected position. Other personnel on or close to the firing line should also be in a defilade position. The minimum target range is 10 meters.

Technique of Fire

Weapon Zeroing

The Optical Sight and Open Sights. When using either the telescopic or open sights, the first thing the gunner does is estimate the range to the target.

Optical Sight. Once the range has been estimated using the optical sight (Fig. 23-18), the gunner will then:
- ***Set*** the estimated range on the sight range selector drum.
- ***Aim*** by placing the cross hairs center mass on the target. Do *not* aim for doors or windows!
- ***Observe*** the impact of the spotting rounds: whether they went over the target or were short, or were to the right or the left.
- ***Adjust*** the aimpoint. With the optical sight, this can be done two ways.
  - If the over/short area was large, make a 50 meter adjustment to the sight range selector drum and fire another spotting round.
  - If the over/short area was small, the gunner can use "Kentucky Windage." If the gunner's first two rounds were a good tight group, the crosshairs of the optical sight can be used to help correct the aimpoint. Looking at the sight picture, we see that the rounds are impacting three lines high and two lines to the left. To

correct this aimpoint, using "Kentucky Windage" and the optical sight, the gunner would aim down three lines and two lines to the right to bring the rounds on target.

- *Fire* the rocket and observe impact.

Open Sight. The open sights are provided in case the optical sight becomes lost or damaged. Since this sight does not have a range adjustment feature, the gunner must remember it is boresighted to 250 meters. The only time the gunner will hold sights at center mass is when the target is actually 250 meters away. If the target is closer than 250 meters, the gunner will aim below or short of the target. If it is further away than 250 meters, the gunner will aim above or over the target. Again, you have six spotting rounds to get on target with. As you can see, the principle of the open sight is the same as that on the M16 when aiming for your sight alignment and sight picture. Once you are on target with your spotting rounds, engage the target with the rocket.

Firing Positions

There are four firing positions (Fig. 23-19) utilized with the SMAW, they are:

- **Standing Position**
- **Kneeling Position**
- **Sitting Position**
- **Prone Position**

When using the standing, kneeling and sitting position, the shoulder stop is used. When in the standing or kneeling position, the gunner should use some kind of firing support, such as a wall, tree or building, to help stabilize the firing position. While in the sitting and kneeling position, bone-to-bone contact should be avoided; i.e. elbows to knees.

When in the prone position, because of the back blast, the gunner's body should be as close to a 90 degree angle, but not less than a 45 degree angle, from the weapon as possible. The bipod is used when in the prone position to help support the launcher. All slack must be taken out of the bipod so as not to interfere with the observation of the spotting round. (If your arm is too short to reach around the rear of the bipod, you may put your arm through or between the bipod legs.) Also, the gunner will have at least six inches of clearance all around the muzzle to allow the rocket stabilizing fins room to extend when launched.

Weapon Deployment

The SMAW is employed against fixed field fortification and other man-made structures. It is capable of destroying sandbagged bunkers or concrete rein-

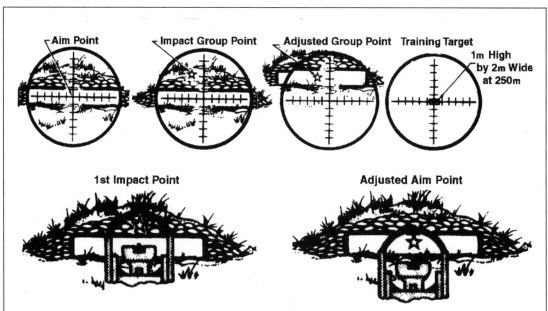

Fig. 23-18. Using the Optical Sight.

STANDING POSITION

KNEELING POSITION

SITTING POSITION

PRONE POSITION

Fig. 23-19. *Firing Positions.*

forced gun emplacements and eliminating any enemy troops inside the enclosure.

A rule for sighting and aiming is to fire at a wall of the structure you want to destroy. Aim at the base of the target about one meter in from the corner or near the center. Do not shoot into gun ports, windows or doors; the warhead might pass through the structure before detonating.

For the selection of a firing position, the gunner must take into consideration the following:

• The backblast area must be clear of obstructions and loose objects for at least 30 meters. Solid obstructions can deflect shock waves and loose objects back toward the gunner.

• Ensure friendly troops are clear of the backblast area.

• The field of fire, down range, should be clear of obstructions such as trees, heavy brush or power lines; they may deflect the rocket, damage the fins or cause premature detonation of the warhead.

It is not recommended that the SMAW be fired from inside any enclosure. The blast, concussion, noise, toxic fumes and fire would be dangerous to the gunner and anyone else inside the enclosure. The structure could also be weakened to the point where it collapses on the personnel inside.

Fig. 23-20. *M2 HB Caliber .50 Machine Gun.*

Heavy Machine Guns

There are two types of heavy machine gun available within the infantry battalion, the caliber .50 and the 40mm. The machine gunners in the Heavy Machine Gun Platoon are equipped with and trained to use both of these and will employ the one which is most suitable for the tactical situation.

M2 HB Caliber .50 Machine Gun

The M2 caliber .50 machine gun can provide close and continuous fire support to the infantry in both offense and defense (Fig. 23-20). It can also provide defense against low-flying aircraft, destroy Light Armored Vehicles and provide protective fires during motor movements.

The M2 HB weapon is a recoil-operated, belt-fed, air-cooled machine gun capable of sustained automatic or single-shot fire. The gun can be fired from the closed bolt position with a very high accuracy in the single shot mode.

General Data

Weight
Receiver	60 lbs.
Barrel	24 lbs.
M-3 tripod,	
with T&E and pintle	44 lbs.
Gun on tripod	128 lbs.

Length
Gun, overall	65 in.
Barrel	45 in.

Range
Maximum (M2ball)	7,400 meters.
Max. effective	1,830 meters.
Muzzle velocity	3,050 feet per second.

Rate of Fire
Sustained	40 rds or less per min.
Rapid	more than 40 rds per min.
Cyclic	450-500 rds per min.

MK 19 Mod 3 40mm Machine Gun

The MK 19 Mod 3 is an air-cooled, blow back operated, belt fed heavy machine gun (Fig. 23-21). It fires a high velocity 40mm grenade out to a range of 2,200 meters. The High Explosive Dual Purpose Round (HEDP) can penetrate 2 inches of armor plate and has a 5 meter casualty radius against personnel. It can be mounted on a vehicle or fired from a ground mount.

General Data

Weight
Gun	75.6 lbs.
Cradle (MK64 mod 4)	21 lbs.
M3 w/T&E mech	44 lbs.

Length
Gun, overall	43.1 in.

Range
Max range	2,212 meters.
Max effect range	1,500 meters.

Rate of fire
Sustained	40 rds per min.
Rapid	60 rds per min.
Cyclic	325-375 rds per min.

Fig. 23-21. *MK 19 Mod 3 40mm Machine Gun.*

Elevation, tripod	100 mils.
Depression, tripod	250 mils.
Traverse, tripod	800 mils. (400 L and 400 R).
Basic load of ammo/gun	400 round for HMMWV and all others prescribed by local commander
Wt/40 rds in container	62 lbs.
Muzzle velocity	790 feet per second.

Mortars

One of the most responsive and effective weapons available to support the Marine rifleman is the mortar. There are two types of mortars found in the infantry battalion, the 60 mm mortars in each rifle company and the heavier 81 mm mortar in the Weapons Company. Both mortars are used to supply high angle fire support to front line troops. They are especially effective against enemy under cover from other weapons, such as when they are in defilade behind a hill or in a ravine.

Fig. 23-22. *60mm Mortar, M224.*

60mm Mortar, M224

The M224 mortar is a muzzle loaded, smooth bore, high-angle-of-fire weapon (Fig. 23-22). It may be drop-fired or trigger-fired. In addition to the conventional mode, it can be fired in the handheld mode. The M224 consists of the M225 Cannon, the M170 Bipod, the M64 Sight and two types of baseplate: the larger, circular M7 and the smaller, rectangular M8 (Fig. 23-23). The M7 baseplate is used when the mortar is fired in the conventional mode and the M8 is used when it is fired handheld. The components and their parts are shown in the following figures:

General Data

Cannon
Length	40 in.
Weight	14.1 lbs.
Rate of fire (sust.)	20 rds per min.

Baseplates
Size, M7	19 3/8 in diameter.
Size, M8	8 in x 10 in.
Weight, M7	14.4 lbs.
Weight, M8	3.6 lbs.

Socket rotation
M7	360 degrees (6,400 mils).
M8	90 degrees (1,600 mils).

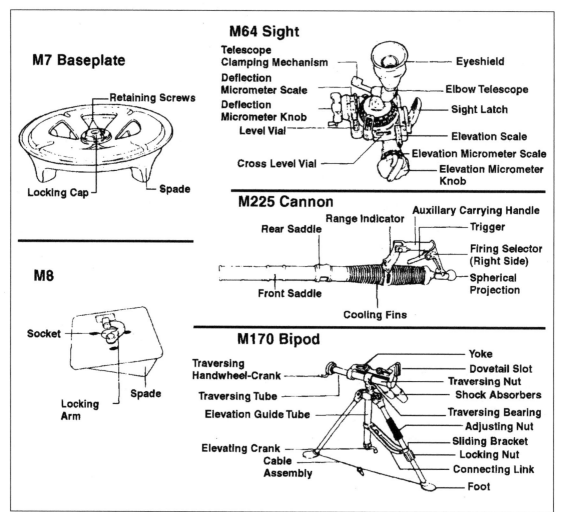

Fig. 23-23. M224 Mortar Components.

Bipod

Weight	15.2 lbs.
Traverse	0250 mils.
Elevation	0800-1511 mils.

Sight

Weight	2.5 lbs.
Field of view	17 degrees.
Magnification	1.5 power.

Ammunition

The ammunition for the M224 60mm mortar is classified as semi-fixed, because the propellant increments can be varied in number to change the range of the projectile. A complete cartridge consists of a fused projectile with a fin assembly and propellant charge.

High Explosive (HE)M888/M720.
Range: 70 meters (min), 3,490 meters (max).
Fuse: M734 multioption w/M720; M935 point-detonating w/M888
Color coding: Olive drab with yellow markings.

Illumination M83A3.
Range: 725 meters (min), 951 meters (max).
Color coding: White with black markings.

Smoke Screen M302A1.
Range: 33 meters (min), 1,630 meters (max).
Color coding: light green, yellow band with red markings.

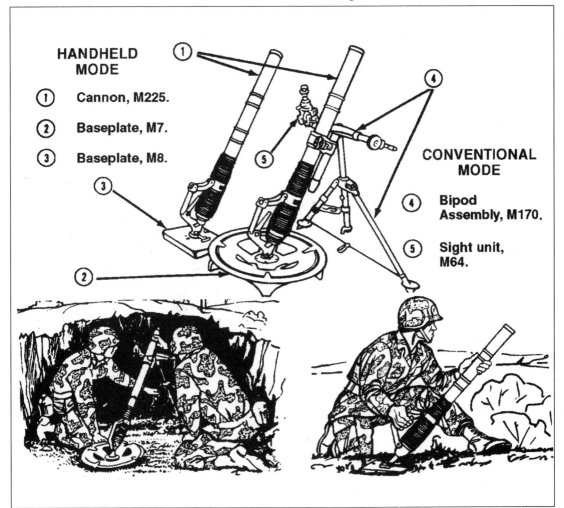

HANDHELD MODE

① **Cannon, M225.**

② **Baseplate, M7.**

③ **Baseplate, M8.**

CONVENTIONAL MODE

④ **Bipod Assembly, M170.**

⑤ **Sight unit, M64.**

***Fig. 23-24.** Modes of fire for M224 Mortar.*

Modes of Fire

The M224 Mortar components are utilized in accordance with the desired mode of fire, as illustrated in Figure 23-24.

In the conventional mode of fire, the mortar is set up and fired by the two man crew.

In the handheld mode, one Marine sets up and fires the mortar.

81mm Mortar, M252

The 81mm Mortar, M252 is a smooth-bore, muzzle-loaded, high-angle-of-fire weapon (Fig. 23-25). The components of the mortar consist of a cannon, mount and baseplate.

General Data

Weight
Barrel (with blast attenuator device),
M253   35 lbs.
Mount, M177   27 lbs.
M3A1 Baseplate   29 lbs.
M64A1 Sight Unit   2.5 lbs.
System Weight   121 lbs.
                                total in three loads

Elevation
Elevation (approximate)   800 to 1511 mils.
For each turn of elevation
drum (approximate)   10 mils.

Traverse
Right or left from center
(approximate)   100 mils.
                                (10 turns)

Range
Minimum   83 meters
Maximum   5,608 meters

Rate of fire
Sustained   15 rounds per minute indefinitely
Maximum   30 rounds per minute for 2 minutes

Ammunition

The ammunition for the M252 81mm mortar is classified as semi-fixed, because the propellant increments can be varied in number to change the range of the projectile. A complete cartridge consists of a fused projectile with a fin assembly and propellant charge.

High Explosive (HE) M821/M889.
Range: 83 meters (min), 5, 608 meters (max).
Bursting area: 40 meter diameter.
Fuse: M734 multioption w/M821; M935 point-detonating w/M889.
Color coding: olive drab with yellow markings.

Illumination M853A1.
Range: 300 meters (min), 5,100 meters (max).
Bursting area: 1,200 meter diameter.
Fuse: M772/M768
Color coding: White with black markings.

Smoke Screen M819.
Range: 300 meters (min), 4,875 meters (max).
Bursting area: 90 to 150 by 30 to 40 meters for 2.5-3 min.
Fuse: M772.
Color coding: light green, brown band with black markings.

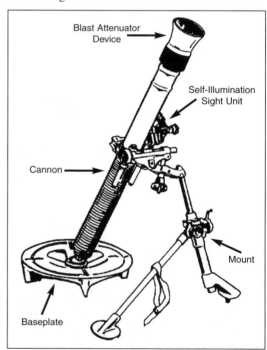

Fig. 23-25. *81mm Mortar, M252.*

Chapter Twenty-Four

Grenades and Accessories

Hand Grenades

History

There are several types of hand grenades. Each has different characteristics and each provides the Marine with a variety of capabilities. Hand grenades give the Marine the ability to kill enemy soldiers, destroy enemy equipment, give signals and control riots. Historically, the most important hand grenade is the fragmentation grenade. It is the Marine's personal indirect fire weapon system.

It was not until the Revolutionary War that we have the first account of hand grenades being used. Continental Marines, under cover of accurate musket fire, threw hand grenades from the riggings onto the decks of British ships, setting them afire and exploding their powder magazines.

During the Civil War, the Union Army used the first grenade that consisted of a fixed-powder train delay fuse. The Confederate Army modified dud artillery and mortar shells to make rampart grenades.

During WWII, the U.S. developed the MK2 fragmentation hand grenade. During the Korean and Vietnam conflicts, the United States' standard offensive/defensive hand grenade was the M26. The standard hand grenade now in use is the M67 with the M213 fuse.

Common Characteristics

All hand grenades share three common characteristics:

Range. The range of any hand grenade depends entirely on the throwing ability of the individual Marine.

Effective Casualty Radius (ECR). Effective casualty radius is defined as the radius of an area around the point of detonation within which at least 50 percent of the exposed personnel will become casualties. The ECR of a grenade is relatively small when compared to that of other bursting weapons. However, casualties occur at distances much greater than the effective casualty radius.

Time Delay Fuse. All standard grenades have a time delay element in the fuse:
- The time delay element permits the safe throwing of the hand grenade.
- All casualty producing hand grenades (frag and WP) have a 4-5 second time delay.
- Burning chemical hand grenades have a 2 second time delay fuse.
- One burning chemical grenade has a 1.4-3 second time delay fuse (M25A2 riot control hand grenade).
- The illumination hand grenade has a 7 second delay.

Main Parts

Although hand grenades vary, they all have three main parts: body, filler and fuse assembly.

Body. The body is the container which holds the filler. It is usually made of metal and it may provide fragments. Grenade bodies are hollow (to contain a filler) and they have an opening into which the fuse is inserted. The body is colored and marked to identify the type of grenade. Basic body colors are:
- High Explosive – Olive drab with yellow markings.
- Chemical – Gray with markings indicating the filler type (old). Green with black markings indicating filler (new).
- Practice – Blue with white markings (old). Blue with white markings and brown band (new).
- Dummy (inert/training) – Black with white markings.

Filler. The filler is the substance with which the grenade body is filled. This filler may be any of the following:
• TNT,
• Composition B,
• Various chemical compounds.

Fuse Assembly. The fuse assembly is a mechanical and chemical device that causes the filler to detonate or burn. It is classified as either a detonating or an igniting type fuse. Most of our grenades are now provided with a silent, sparkless, smokeless fuse. The fuse assembly consists of:
• Safety lever,
• Safety pin pull ring,
• Safety pin,
• Striker,
• Striker spring,
• Primer,
• Delay element,
• Detonator or igniter.

Functions of the Fuse Parts

Fuse Body. Holds the other parts of the fuse. It is screwed into the body of the grenade.

Safety Lever. Holds down the striker arm after the safety pin is removed. One end of the safety lever is under the T-lug on the fuse body.

Safety Pin. Holds the safety lever to the fuse body. When the pin is withdrawn, the grenade is armed. At this time, only the pressure of the thumb on the safety lever holds the safety lever and prevents the fuse from functioning.

Striker. Acts like a firing pin. When the safety lever is released, the striker spring forces the striker to pivot in an arc, throwing off the safety lever and continuing until it strikes the primer. If the grip is loosened on the safety lever, the striker may be released and strike the primer without the lever flying off. It is important that a firm grip be kept on the safety lever at all times after the safety pin has been removed.

Primer. Contains a sensitive chemical which burns when it is struck by the striker. The primer ignites the delay element.

Delay Element. A train of powder enclosed in a small tube. It burns at a controlled rate and prevents the filler from exploding or burning immediately after the striker hits the primer. When the delay element has completed burning, it sets off the igniter or detonator.

Detonator. Similar to a small blasting cap and detonates high explosive or white phosphorous type fillers. An igniter is used in place of a detonator in a grenade with a chemical filler.

Steps in Functioning

When the safety pin is pulled, the safety lever is held down firmly by the thrower's thumb. When the safety lever is released it is thrown free from the grenade, allowing the striker to hit the primer. The primer sets off the delay element, which burns into the detonator or igniter. This chain reaction is ended by the bursting or burning of the filler in the grenade body. The entire action requires only a few seconds.

Types of Hand Grenades

There are four types of combat hand grenades and one type of practice hand grenade. The four combat types are: fragmentation, chemical smoke, riot control and special purpose. This section will look at each type of grenade in detail.

Practice Hand Grenade (See Fig. 24-1.) The M69 practice hand grenade simulates the M67-series of fragmentation hand grenades for training purposes. The grenade provides realistic training and familiarizes the Marine with the functioning and characteristics of the fragmentation hand grenade.

General information on the practice grenade includes:
• Body – Steel.
• Fuse – M228, inserted into grenade body.
• Weight – 14 ounces.
• Safety clip – Yes.
• Capabilities – Can be thrown 40 meters by an average Marine. The M69 grenade emits a small puff of white smoke after a delay of 4 to 5 seconds

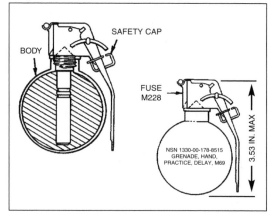

Fig. 24-1. *M69 Practice Grenade.*

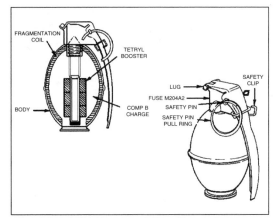

Fig. 24-2. *M61 Fragmentation Grenade.*

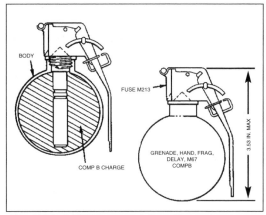

Fig. 24-3. *M67 Fragmentation Grenade.*

and makes a loud popping noise. The grenade body can be used repeatedly by replacing the fuse assembly.
- Color/markings – Light blue with white markings. The safety lever of the fuse is light blue with black markings and a brown tip.
- Warning: Fuse fragments may exit the hole in the base of the grenade body causing injuries.

Fragmentation Hand Grenades. There are two types of fragmentation hand grenades, the M61 and M67.

    A. M61 (See Fig. 24-2.)
- Body – Thin sheet metal. Fragments are produced by a serrated wire coil fitted to the inside of the grenade body.
- Filler – 5.5 ounces of Composition B.
- Fuse – M204A1 or M204A2
- Weight – 16 ounces.
- Safety clip – Yes.
- Capabilities – Can be thrown 40 meters by an average Marine. The effective killing radius is 5 meters and the effective casualty-producing radius is 15 meters.
- Color/markings – Olive drab body with a single yellow band at the top. Nomenclature and or lot number markings are in yellow.
- Warning: Although the killing radius is 5 meters and the casualty-producing radius is 15 meters, fragments can disperse as far away as 230 meters.

    B. M67 (See Fig. 24-3.)
- Body – Steel sphere.
- Filler – 6.5 ounces of Composition B.
- Fuse – M213.
- Weight – 14 ounces.
- Safety Clip – Yes.
- Capabilities – Can be thrown 40 meters by an average Marine. The effective casualty-produc-

ing radius is 15 meters.
- Color/markings – Olive drab body with a single yellow band at the top. Nomenclature and or lot number markings are in yellow.
- Warning: Although the killing radius is 5 meters and the casualty-producing radius of this grenade is 15 meters, fragments can disperse as far away as 230 meters.

Chemical Smoke Hand Grenades

    A. M15 White Phosphorous. The M15 grenade (See Fig. 24-4) is a bursting type grenade used for signaling, screening and incendiary purposes.
- Body – Sheet metal.
- Filler – 15 ounces of white phosphorus.
- Fuse – M206A2.
- Weight – 31 ounces.
- Capabilities – The average Marine can throw the grenade 30 meters. The grenade has a bursting radius of 17 meters. All friendly personnel within this 17-meter area should be in a covered posi-

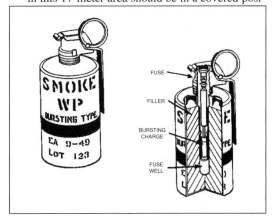

Fig. 24-4. *M15 Smoke Hand Grenade.*

tion to avoid being struck by burning particles. The WP filler burns for about 60 seconds at a temperature of 5,000 degrees Fahrenheit. This intense heat causes the smoke produced by the grenade to rise quite rapidly, especially in cool climates. This makes the M15 grenade less desirable for use as a screening agent.

- Color/markings – Gray with one yellow band and yellow markings.
- First aid – Treat burns caused by white phosphorus (WP) in the same way as ordinary burns. If particles of the WP are embedded in the flesh, immerse the wound in water or pack with wet cloths to halt combustion. Then pick out or squeeze out the WP. The particles will reignite spontaneously if allowed to dry. Apply copper sulphate solution to halt combustion of the WP particles. This permits them to be removed without igniting.

B. AN-M8 HC White Smoke (See Fig. 24-5.) This grenade is used to produce dense clouds of white smoke for signaling and screening.

- Body – Sheet steel cylinder.
- Filler – 19 ounces of Type C, HC smoke mixture.
- Fuse – M201A1.
- Weight – 24 ounces.
- Safety clip – No.
- Capabilities – Can be thrown 30 meters by an average Marine. The grenade emits a dense cloud of white smoke for 105 to 150 seconds.
- Color/Markings - Light green body with black markings and a white top.
- Warning: Any damaged AN-M8 HC grenades that expose the filler are hazardous. Exposure of the filler to moisture and air could result in a chemical reaction that will ignite the grenade.
- Warning: The AN-M8 hand grenade produces

harmful hydrochloric fumes that irritate the eyes, throat and lungs. It should not be used in closed-in areas unless Marines are wearing protective masks.

C. M18 Colored Smoke (See Fig. 24-6.) This grenade is used as a ground-to-ground or ground-to-air signaling device, a target or landing zone marking device, or a screening device for unit movements.

- Body – Sheet steel cylinder with four emission holes at the top and one at the bottom to allow smoke release when the grenade is ignited.
- Filler – 11.5 ounces of colored smoke mixture (red, green, yellow and violet).
- Fuse – M201A1.
- Weight – 19 ounces.
- Safety clip – No.
- Capabilities – Can be thrown 35 meters by an average Marine. The grenade produces a cloud of colored smoke for 50 to 90 seconds.
- Color/markings – Olive drab body with the top indicating the smoke color.
- Field expedient – When employing the M18 or AN-M8 HC hand grenade, it may be desirable to use one of these grenades without the fuse. To do this, the following procedure should be used in combat only:
  - Remove the tape from grenade bottom to expose the filler.
  - Remove the fuse by unscrewing it from the grenade.
  - Ignite starter mixture with open flame.
  - Immediately throw the grenade to avoid burn injury.
- Warning: With both the AN-M8 and M18, there is danger of starting a fire if used in a dry area.

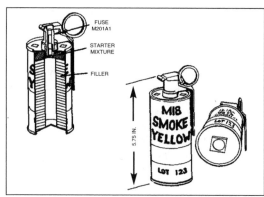

Fig. 24-6. *M18 Colored Smoke Grenade.*

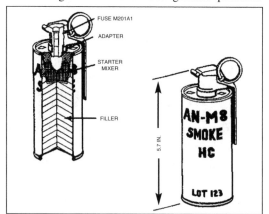

Fig. 24-5. *AN-M8 HC White Smoke Grenade.*

Riot Control Hand Grenades
A. ABC-M7A2 and ABC-M7A3 CS (See Fig.

24-7.) The ABC-M7A2 and the ABC-M7A3 riot control hand grenades contain only CS as a filler. They differ only in the amount of filler and the form of the CS they contain.
- Body – The bodies of both grenades are sheet metal with four emission holes at the top and one at the bottom.
- Filler – 5.5 ounces of burning mixture and 3.5 ounces of CS in gelatin capsules in the ABC-M7A2 grenade, and 7.5 ounces of burning mixture and 4.5 ounces of pelletized CS agent in the ABC-M7A3 grenade.
- Fuse – M201A1.
- Weight – Approximately 15.5 ounces.
- Safety clip – No.
- Capabilities – Can be thrown 40 meters by an average Marine. Both grenades produce a cloud of irritant agent for 15 to 35 seconds.
- Color/markings – Gray body with a red band and red markings.
- Warning: Friendly forces should put on protective masks before throwing these grenades.

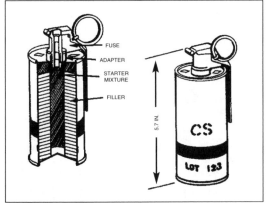

Fig. 24-7. *ABC-M7A2 and ABC-M7A3 Riot Control Grenade.*

B. ABC-M25A2 (See Fig. 24-8.) The ABC-M25A2 riot control hand grenade is a bursting munition with an integral fuse. The M25A2 grenade is an improved version of the M25A1 grenade. The two grenades differ primarily in body construction.
- Body – Compressed fiber or plastic.
- Filler – CS1 varies in weight and composition according to the type of agent contained in the grenade. All fillers are mixed with silica aerogel for increased dissemination efficiency.
- Fuse – Integral.
- Weight – 8 ounces.
- Safety clip – No.

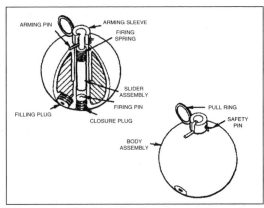

Fig. 24-8. *ABC-M25A2 Riot Control Grenade.*

- Capabilities – Can be thrown 50 meters by an average Marine. The radius of burst (visible cloud agent) is about 5 meters, but grenade fragments may project as far as 25 meters.
- Color/markings – Gray body with a red band and red markings.
- Warning: Friendly forces should put on protective masks before throwing these grenades.

Special-Purpose Hand Grenades

A. Incendiary (See Fig. 24-9.) The AN-M14 TH3 incendiary hand grenade is used to destroy equipment. It can damage, immobilize, or destroy vehicles, weapons systems, shelters or munitions. The grenade may also be used to start fires in areas containing flammable materials.
- Body – Sheet metal.
- Filler – 26.5 ounces of thermate (TH3) mixture.
- Fuse – M201A1.
- Weight – 32 ounces.
- Safety clip – No.

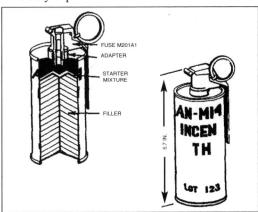

Fig. 24-9. *AN-M14 TH3 Incendiary Grenade.*

- Capabilities – Can be thrown 25 meters by an average Marine. A portion of the thermate mixture is converted to molten iron, which burns at 4,000 degrees Fahrenheit. It will fuse together the metallic parts of any object that it contacts. Thermate is an improved version of thermite, the incendiary agent used in hand grenades during World War II. The thermate filler of the AN-M14 grenade burns for 40 seconds and can burn through a ½-inch homogenous steel plate. It produces its own oxygen and will burn under water.
- Color/markings – Gray with purple markings and a single purple band (current grenades). Under the standard color-coding system, incendiary grenades are light red with black markings.
- Warning: Avoid looking directly at the incendiary grenade as it burns; the intensity of the light is potentially hazardous to the retina.

B. Offensive (See Fig. 24-10.) The MK3A2 offensive hand grenade, commonly referred to as the concussion grenade, is designed to produce casualties during close combat while minimizing danger to friendly personnel. The grenade is also used for concussion effects in enclosed areas, for blasting or for demolition tasks. The shock waves (overpressure) produced by this grenade when used in enclosed areas are greater than those produced by the fragmentation grenade. It is, therefore, very effective against enemy soldiers located in bunkers, buildings and fortified areas.
- Body – Fiber (similar to the packing container for the fragmentation grenade).
- Filler – 8 ounces of TNT.
- Fuse – M206A1 or M206A2.
- Weight – 15.6 ounces.
- Safety clip – Yes.

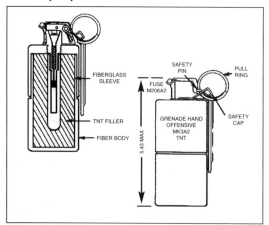

Fig. 24-10. MK3A2 Offensive Grenade.

- Capabilities – Can be thrown 40 meters by an average Marine. The MK3A2 has an effective casualty radius in open areas of 2 meters. Secondary missiles and bits of fuse may be projected as far as 200 meters from the detonation point.
- Color/markings – Black with yellow markings around its middle.
- Warning: Do not use in a closed-in area.

Grenade Throwing

Holding the Grenade

As shown in Figure 24-11, grip the grenade firmly in the fingers of the throwing hand. Left-handed throwers need to ensure the top of the fuse points downward. Hold the safety lever firmly under the thumb. Next, place the forefinger of the throwing hand near the top of the grenade body. Remove the thumb safety clip, still firmly grasping the grenade. Hook the forefinger of the other hand through the safety ring attached to the end of the safety pin. From here, throw the grenade using one of the appropriate techniques mentioned next.

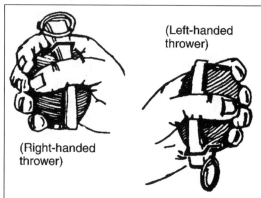

(Left-handed thrower)

(Right-handed thrower)

Fig. 24-11. Proper Grip of the Grenade.

Throwing Techniques

The grenade should be thrown like a baseball, using the throwing motion most natural to the individual. The grenade is given a spin in flight by allowing it to roll off the tips of the fingers and releasing it with a snap of the wrist. The individual Marine should not radically alter throwing style, although minor corrections may be necessary to improve throwing skill.

Throwing Positions

Fig. 24-12(a). Pull pin firmly.

Fig. 24-12(b). Cock arm.

Standing. Half face the target with the weight of the body balanced evenly on both feet. (See Fig. 24-12 (a-c).) Hold the grenade in front of the body, chest high, and remove the safety pin with a pulling, twisting motion. As the grenade leaves the hand, take an additional step forward and follow through, falling forward face down onto the ground. When possible, keep your eyes on the target to observe the strike of the grenade as you fall to the prone position. Errors can be detected and necessary corrections can be made on the next throw.

Kneeling. Half face the target and kneel on the knee nearest to the target. When the grenade leaves the hand, continue the throwing motion so the thrower will fall forward, breaking the fall with the arms. Watch the strike so as to make corrections, if necessary, in the next throw.

Kneeling from Prone. Being in the prone position, hold the grenade in front of the body and pull the pin. (See Fig. 24-13 (a-c).) Move the hands along both sides to the shoulders and raise the body quickly, pushing upward and to the rear. Do not rest the weight of the body on the grenade. The left knee (if throwing right handed) remains on the ground. The right leg is slightly bent so that the body can twist, getting more power while preparing to throw. As the grenade leaves the hand, follow through and fall to the ground, breaking the fall with the arms. Watch the strike.

Fig. 24-12(c). Follow through.

Prone. This position is an extremely awkward one and limits both range and accuracy. It is used when pinned down with little or no cover and the grenade cannot be thrown from any other position. Throwing from this position varies among individuals, so no set manner for it is prescribed. (See Fig. 24-14 (a-d).) Lie on the back, hold the grenade across the chest and pull the pin. When throwing, hold onto any substantial object with the free hand in order to improve both range and accuracy. As the grenade is released, roll on the stomach to complete the follow-through.

Underhand. This throw is used in built-up areas, woods or jungle where a high degree of accuracy is necessary. It will give good control of aim for short throws under low hanging tree limbs or into pillbox embrasures and other openings close to the ground. When releasing the grenade, let it roll off the fingertips in the same manner as when pitching a softball. The underhand throw may be employed from the standing or kneeling position.

Fig. 24-13(a). Pull pin while prone.

Fig. 24-13(b). Rise to knees.

Fig. 24-13(c). Follow through and fall to ground.

Fig. 24-14(a). *Pull pin while lying on back.*

Fig. 24-14(b). *Brace back leg and grab a solid object with free hand.*

Fig. 24-14(c). *Push off, roll and throw.*

Fig. 24-14(d). *End up face down and prone.*

Chapter Twenty-Five

Demolitions and Mine Warfare

Demolitions are not the weapons of the specialist only. All recent conflicts have shown the need for these weapons in the hands of all units. The infantry must do the job of knocking out pillboxes, bunkers and cave positions. In addition, infantrymen must be able to lay and breach minefields.

This chapter deals with the demolitions and mines normally available to the infantry battalion, standard U.S. firing devices and booby traps.

DEMOLITIONS

Types of Explosives

You will need a basic knowledge of the explosives used for demolition charges. The most common explosives you will encounter are TNT, composition C-4 and detonating cord.

TNT

Trinitrotoluene is commonly known as TNT. It is a powerful high explosive used throughout the Marine Corps for general demolition work. Because it is insensitive, stable in any climate and not affected by moisture, TNT is one of the most desirable explosives for underwater use and is ideal for combat.

TNT is pale yellow in color. It is issued in a solid block form, either cylindrical (one-quarter pound) or rectangular (one pound) in an olive drab cardboard container with metal ends (Fig. 25-1). One end of each block is provided with a threaded cap well to receive either an electrical or nonelectrical blasting cap. The one-quarter-pound blocks are normally used for training, and the one-pound blocks are used for cutting and breaching projects. TNT is used as a standard against which all other military high explosives are rated.

Composition C-4

More commonly known as just C-4, it is a white, putty-like odorless plastic explosive more powerful than TNT. It is packed in one and a quarter-pound blocks designated, M112 Demolition Block. Each block is covered by clear plastic and protected by a peelable paper cover. C-4 will normally be encountered by a Marine in the field in the form of the M-183 Demolition Kit (Fig. 25-2). The kit contains 16

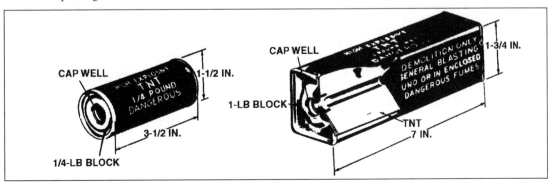

CAP WELL
TNT
1/4 POUND
DANGEROUS
1-1/2 IN.
3-1/2 IN.
1/4-LB BLOCK

CAP WELL
1-3/4 IN.
DEMOLITION ONLY
GENERAL BLASTING
UND OR IN ENCLOSED
DANGEROUS FUMES
1-LB BLOCK
TNT
7 IN.

Fig. 25-1. TNT blocks.

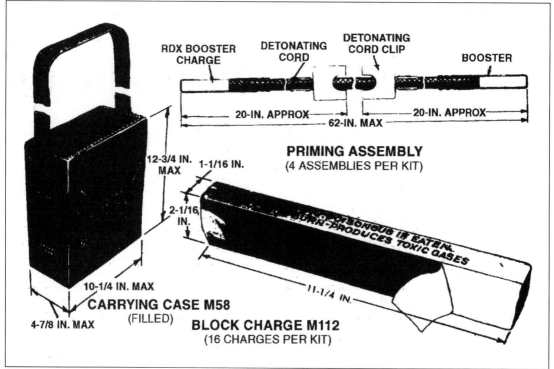

Fig. 25-2. C-4 M-183 demolition kit.

M112 demolition blocks and four priming assemblies. The demolition blocks are packed in two bags of eight blocks each and placed in the M58 Canvas Carrying Case. Each priming assembly consists of a five-foot length of detonating cord with an RDX booster crimped to each end and a pair of M1 detonating cord clips for attaching the priming assembly to a detonating cord main line.

C-4 has many significant characteristics as a military explosive. It remains plastic and pliable over a wide range of temperatures (-70°F to + 170°F/-57°C to + 77°C). It can be molded to fit irregular-shaped objects (the colder the temperature the harder C-4 is to mold until warmed by the heat of your hands.) It may also be used under water in block form as long as it is not removed from its plastic wrapping.

Detonating Cord

Detonating cord (det cord) contains Pentaerythrite Tetranitrate more commonly known as PETN. (See Figs. 25-3 (a) and (b).) This explosive is contained inside either a white, yellow and black or a green flexible waterproof textile, or plastic-covered tube.

PETN is almost insoluble in water and will detonate even when the cord is water soaked, provided the detonation is started from a dry end. Therefore it may be used for underwater demolition. It can be detonated by electric or nonelectric blasting caps.

Detonating cord explodes at a high rate of speed (20,000 to 24,000 feet per second). It has sufficient force to detonate other explosives to which it has been properly attached or it can be detonated by other high explosives to which it is connected. Detonating cord is used to prime a single charge or to explode simultaneously any number of separate charges. It can also be used as an explosive charge itself.

Det cord is issued in 500- and 1,000-foot spools.

Blasting Caps and Fuses

Blasting Caps

A blasting cap, used for priming explosives, consists of a thin, tubular metallic shell of noncorrosive material about two and a half inches long and one-quarter inch in diameter. It contains an initiating

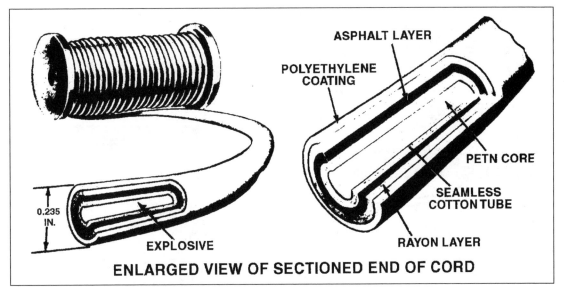

ENLARGED VIEW OF SECTIONED END OF CORD

Fig. 25-3(a). Detonating cord.

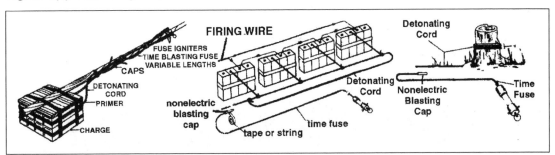

Fig. 25-3(b). Uses of detonating cord.

composition and charge of RDX *(a very sensitive high explosive)*. Blasting caps must be handled very carefully. Blasting caps are used for initiating high explosives such as TNT or C-4 and as the detonating element for certain types of land mine fuses.

An electric blasting cap has two lead wires which may be attached to a firing device, which in turn, is attached to a blasting machine. A nonelectric blasting cap may be crimped to any standard firing device or to a time blasting fuse (safety fuse) fitted with a fuse lighter (Fig. 25-4).

Storage and handling. Blasting caps are extremely sensitive and may explode unless handled carefully. They must be protected from shock and extreme heat and must not be tampered with. Never store them with any other explosive. Nonelectric blasting caps are shipped by the manufacturer in boxes or cans of 50 per package, which are suitable

for storage or commercial shipment ONLY. Use the 10-Cap Box found in the demolition set for transporting nonelectric blasting caps to and from a blasting site.

Electric blasting caps are shipped by manufacturers in a cardboard shipping tube or spool which provides sufficient protection for transporting them to and from a blasting site if handled properly.

Nonelectric blasting caps. There are two types of nonelectric blasting caps used in the Marine Corps. The standard issue is the M-7. However, the older J1 will be used until existing stocks are depleted. The noticeable difference between the two is that the M-7 is flared at the open end for easy insertion of a time fuse or det cord.

Electric blasting caps. The electric blasting cap (M-6) is issued in packages of six by the manufacturer. The lead wires have a short-circuiting device

315

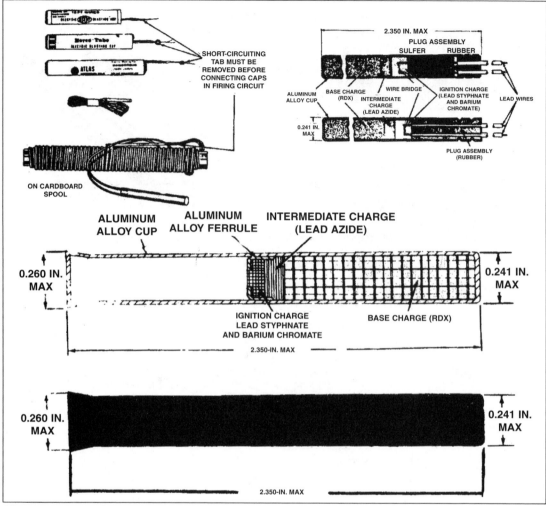

Fig. 25-4. Electric/Nonelectric blasting caps.

called a shunt to prevent accidental detonation by extraneous electricity. This shunt must be removed before the cap can be used. Once the shunt is removed, it cannot be reused. If the cap is not used after the shunt has been removed, or you find a cap without a shunt, twist the bare ends of the wires together to provide the shunting action. When two or more caps are to be used in an electrical firing circuit, they should be from the same manufacturer.

Fuse Blasting, Time, M700

The time blasting fuse M700 (Fig. 25-5) more commonly known as "time fuse" is orange and black

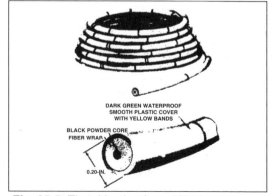

Fig. 25-5. Time blasting fuse, M700.

316

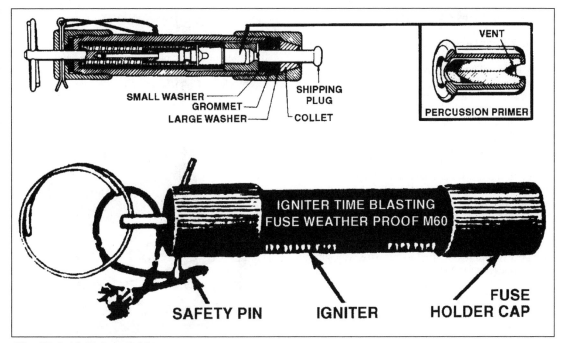

Fig. 25-6. M-60 fuse lighter.

or green with a single yellow band spaced at 12 or 18 inches and a double yellow band spaced at 72 or 90 inches along the length of each roll. These bands are provided for easy measuring purposes. A time fuse contains black powder and has a waterproof covering which permits use underwater for short periods of time. When a time fuse is lighted, it transmits a flame from the lighted end to a nonelectric/electric blasting cap or other explosive charge at a uniform rate of 40 seconds a foot. When measured and cut to proper length, this will allow a person conducting the blasting time to move to a safe place before the explosion. If a time fuse burns at a rate of 30 seconds a foot or faster, DO NOT USE.

Weatherproof Fuse Lighter M-60

The M-60 fuse lighter (Fig. 25-6) is designed to ignite time blasting fuse (M700) in all types of weather conditions and underwater if waterproofed. A fuse lighter is usually more reliable than matches and is ideal for use in windy, rainy weather. It is a weatherproof, pull-type fuse lighter that forms a watertight seal when attached to the smooth surfaced M700 time blasting fuse by using the friction seal washer and the rubber grommet.

Tools

Like for any trade, specialized tools make your job easier when working with military explosives.

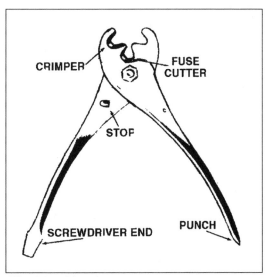

Fig. 25-7. M2 crimper.

M2 Crimper

The M2 crimper (Fig. 25-7) has two primary uses. First, it is used to cut time fuse, safety fuse and detonating cord. The cutting part of the crimper jaws is designed to give a clean, square cut which is important for seating a piece of fuse or detonating cord into a nonelectric blastic cap. Second, the crimper is used to squeeze (crimp) a nonelectric cap onto a piece of fuse or detonating cord. This part of the crimper jaws is designed to squeeze the open end of the cap that receives the piece of fuse or detonating cord just enough to make a water resistant seal and to prevent the cap from being easily pulled off without interfering with the powder train. The end of one handle is shaped into a screwdriver; the other handle end is formed into a punch. The crimper is made of a soft nonsparking metal and will conduct electricity. Crimpers should not be used to cut wire, as a substitute for pliers or for heavy prying.

Wirecutters

Wirecutters (Fig. 25-8) should be used for cutting wire only. Do not use them for cutting fuse or detonating cord.

Fig. 25-8. Wirecutters.

Pocket Knife

The pocket knife (Fig. 25-9) has a one and three-quarter inch cutting blade, a can opener, a punch, a combination bottle opener and screwdriver, and a clevis on one end. This piece of equipment is hard to keep in a demolition set. It has many uses and is an important item of equipment in demolitions. *Do not remove it from a set.* Do not use the knife for cutting fuse or detonating cord.

Fig. 25-9. Pocketknife.

10-Cap Box

The 10-Cap Box (Fig. 25-10) is a rectangular fiberglass or plastic block with 10 holes and a cover. The holes in the block-like interior of the box are receptacles for nonelectric blasting caps. When this cap box is stored in a demolition set, *it must be empty.*

Fig. 25-10. 10-Cap Box.

M51 Blasting Cap Test Set

The M51 Blasting Cap Test Set (Fig. 25-11) was developed to replace the blasting galvanometer for continuity testing of electrical firing circuits. The test set is a self-contained unit with a magnetotype impulse generator, an indicator lamp, a handle to activate the generator, and two binding points for attachment of firing leads. The test set is waterproof and can be used at temperatures as low as –40° Fahrenheit. The M51 is used to complete the continuity testing by connecting the firing circuit to the test set binding posts and then depressing the handle sharply. If there is a continuous (intact) circuit, even one created by a short, the indicator lamp will flash. Handle the test set with care and keep it dry to assure optimum use.

M32 10-Cap Blasting Machine

This small, lightweight blasting machine (Fig. 25-12) produces adequate current (1.5 amperes) to initiate 10 electrical caps connected in series. Use the blasting machine to provide the electric impulse needed in electric blasting operation. The M32 derives its power from an alternator and uses a capacitor discharge output circuit.

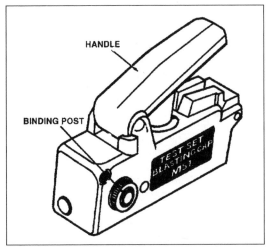

Fig. 25-11. *M51 Blasting Cap Test Set.*

M34 50-Cap Blasting Machine

This small, lightweight machine (Fig. 25-12) produces adequate current to initiate 50 electrical caps connected in series. It looks like the M32 blasting machine except for a black band around the base and a steel-reinforced actuating handle. The testing and operation of the M34 is done the same way as the M32.

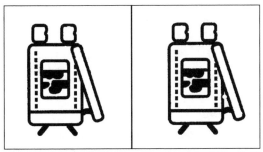

Fig. 25-12. *M32-10-Cap Blasting Machine (left) M34 50-Cap Blasting Machine (right).*

Firing Wire and Reel

Firing wire and reel (Fig. 25-13), used for the electric firing of charges, is issued in 500-foot lengths. It is plastic- or rubber-coated copper wire mounted on a metal firing reel nine inches in diameter, about eight inches wide. Approximately two to three feet of one end of the wire is inserted through a hole near the center of the reel to allow some slack so that it will not be jerked loose when the machine is operated vigorously. The other end of the wire is unwound from the reel for connection to the charge. When not in use, the ends of the wire should be twisted together to short out any stray currents.

Friction Tape and Twine

These two items, included in demolition sets, are used to fasten caps to detonating cord, to insulate electrical connections and to tie or tape blocks of explosive together into a compact package.

Preparing Charges

A basic charge consists of four components: explosive (TNT/C-4), detonator (blasting cap), fuse and igniter (M60 fuse lighter). The type of charge used depends upon the materials available and the object you wish to destroy.

Fig. 25-13. *Firing wire and reel.*

Nonelectric Firing System

A nonelectric firing system (Fig. 25-14) is one in which the explosive charge is detonated by nonelectric means. In this system, a slow-burning time fuse fires a nonelectric blasting cap which, in turn, detonates the charge or length of detonating cord leading to the charge. The success of a nonelectric firing system requires that the primer be made carefully. A nonelectric primer consists of a nonelectric cap and a

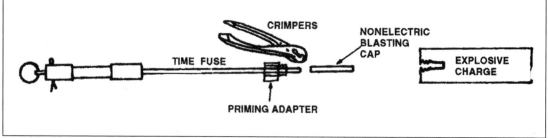

Fig. 25-14. Nonelectric firing system.

length of fuse together with whatever accessories (such as a priming adapter) may be necessary to join these items to the charge. A nonelectric primer does not include a device for creating the spark to set off the charge. A fuse lighter or a match, which will create the spark, is not considered a part of the primer.

Priming Nonelectric Charges

TNT. The best way of priming TNT is with the priming adapter. It is a six-sided hexagonal plastic device used for both electric and nonelectric blasting caps. It has a slot for passing through the electrical wires of the electrical blasting cap. Screw adapter into the cap well (Fig. 25-15).

TNT may be primed by inserting a cap with a fuse/det cord attached into the fuse well. It is secured by either tape or twine (Fig. 25-16).

TNT can also be primed by tying detonation cord securely around the explosive charge with a clove hitch with an extra turn (Fig. 25-17). At least three complete turns are required against the block of explosive, and the loops must be pushed closely together to insure detonation.

C-4. C-4 can be primed either in its original form as an M-112 demolition block or molded to fit the object for demolition (Fig. 25-18).

C-4 can also be primed by tying detonating cord around it the same way as the TNT block. Det cord can also be primed with C-4 molded around it, using either of the two knots shown in Figure 25-19. When inserting either of the knots into the molded piece of explosive, ensure that there is at least one-half inch of explosive on all sides of the knot.

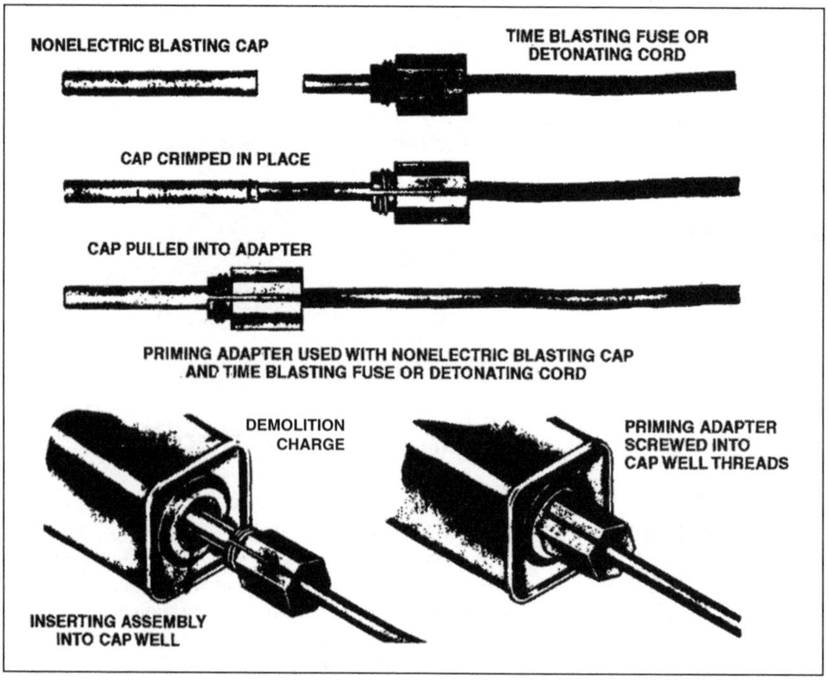

Firing Nonelectric Charges

When the primer has been attached to the explosive charge, the M-60 fuse lighter is attached to the free end of the M700 time blasting fuse (Fig. 25-20) in the following manner:

• Remove the fuse lighter from its carrying box and unscrew the fuse holder cap two or three

NONELECTRIC BLASTING CAP

TIME BLASTING FUSE OR DETONATING CORD

CAP CRIMPED IN PLACE

CAP PULLED INTO ADAPTER

PRIMING ADAPTER USED WITH NONELECTRIC BLASTING CAP AND TIME BLASTING FUSE OR DETONATING CORD

DEMOLITION CHARGE

PRIMING ADAPTER SCREWED INTO CAP WELL THREADS

INSERTING ASSEMBLY INTO CAP WELL

Fig. 25-15. Priming TNT block with priming adapter (nonelectric).

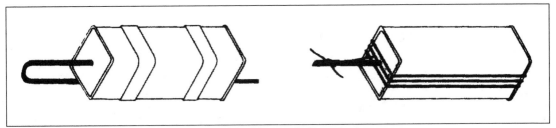

Fig. 25-16. *Priming TNT block (nonelectric) without priming adapter.*

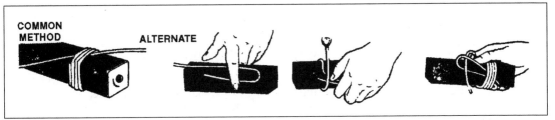

Fig. 25-17. *Priming TNT block with detonating cord.*

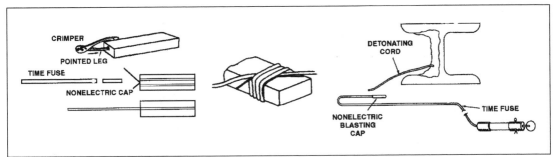

Fig. 25-18. *Priming C-4 (nonelectric).*

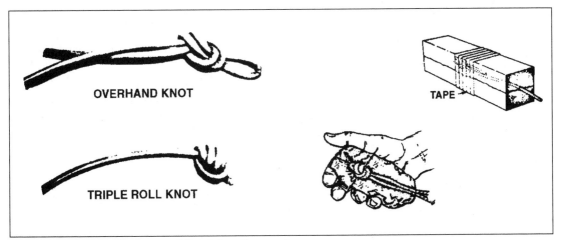

Fig. 25-19. *Molding C-4 around the detonating cord.*

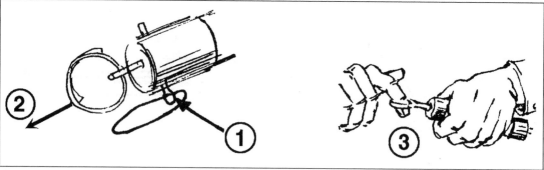

Fig. 25-20. Arming the M-60 fuse lighter.

turns. (Care must be taken not to unscrew the cap completely.)

- Push the shipping plug in and then work the plug from side to side while withdrawing it from the igniter. (Retain the shipping plug and all other parts in case the igniter is not used.)
- Insert the freshly square-cut end of the time blasting fuse (M700) into the igniter as far as possible. (When doing this, a small amount of resistance is offered when the fuse passes through the rubber grommet.) Hand tighten the fuse holder cap sufficiently to insure proper holding and sealing. *The charge is now fully primed and ready to be fired.*
- Now pick up the M-60 fuse lighter, firmly grasp it with one hand and remove the safety pin by pulling the safety pin cord. The igniter is now fully armed.
- Yell *"FIRE IN THE HOLE"* three times to notify everyone that you're preparing to explode your explosive charge and for them to seek safety. Make sure there's no one near your explosive charge.
- To fire – pull outward on the pull ring. Make sure the fuse is burning. (You can see and feel the time fuse burning.) If lit, then walk quickly to your previously selected secure position. *Do not run.*
- If the fuse is not lit (misfire), the M-60 can be reset quickly without disassembly by pushing the plunger all the way in and attempting to fire as before. (It cannot be reset underwater.) If the fuse lighter fails to ignite a second time, cut off the fuse lighter. Put on another fuse lighter or use a match and attempt to relight the fuse.

Safety Precautions

- The M-60 lighter should never be lifted or handled by the pull ring or safety cord.

- The safety pin should not be removed until after the time blasting fuse has been inserted and just prior to use.
- Do not attempt to repair a defective lighter. It should be replaced or a match may be used.

Nonelectric Misfires

Working on or near a misfire is the most hazardous of all blasting operations. If you have a nonelectric misfire:

- Investigation and correction should be undertaken only by the person who placed the charge.
- Delay the investigation for at least 30 minutes after the expected time of detonation.
- If the charge is not tamped (buried or covered), without disturbing it, lay a primed one-pound charge beside it and detonate.
- If the charge has not more than one foot of tamping, attempt to explode with a two-pound charge placed on top.
- If the charge has more than one foot of tamping, carefully remove the tamping to within one foot, place a two-pound charge on top and explode.
- If a nonelectric blasting cap that is used to fire detonating cord fails to detonate, investigation of the misfire should be delayed for at least 30 minutes, after which the detonating cord main line between the blasting cap and the charge should be cut and a new blasting cap fastened to the detonating cord.
- If an exposed electric or nonelectric blasting cap that is used to fire detonating cord explodes but fails to detonate the cord, the failure may be investigated immediately. A new blasting cap should be fastened to the detonating cord with special care taken to fasten it properly.
- If the detonating cord main line detonates but a branch line fails to detonate, a blasting cap should

322

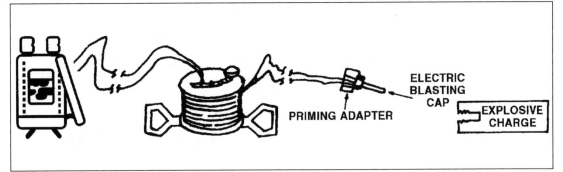

Fig. 25-21. *Electric firing system.*

be fastened to the branch line and the branch line fired separately.

- If the detonating cord leading to a charge detonates, but the charge fails to explode, the failure should not be investigated until it is certain that the charge is not burning. If the charge is still intact, a new primer should be inserted. If the charge is scattered by detonation of the original detonating cord, the explosive, or as much of the original explosive as is practical, should be reassembled, a new charge placed and new primer inserted. Every attempt must be made, particularly in training exercises, to recover all unexploded explosives that are scattered by a misfire.

The person investigating any misfire should be alert to note the probable cause of the misfire. Thus a repetition of the trouble may be avoided.

Electric Firing System

The primary reason for using electrically primed charges is the control exercised over the exact instant of detonation. If, for instance, you desire to destroy a bridge while a train is crossing it or to detonate a demolition ambush during the short time that the enemy is in the killing zone, electrical firing will provide the split-second timing required.

An electric firing system (Fig. 25-21) consists of a block of explosive, an electric blasting cap and whatever accessories (such as a priming adapter) are necessary to join the explosive and cap into a single unit. The electricity-producing device may be a blasting machine or other suitable electricity-producing device such as a generator or battery.

Priming Electric Charges

TNT. Insert the lead wires of the electric cap through the slot of the priming adapter and pull the cap into the adapter (Fig. 25-22). Then insert the cap into the explosive and screw the adapter into the fuse well.

To make certain that these lead wires are not pulled loose from the cap, you should also attach them to the explosive. You should either tie two half hitches around the block of explosive with the cap lead wires or tape the lead wires to the explosive (Fig. 25-23).

C-4. Plastic explosives are primed electrically in the same manner that they are primed nonelectrically except that electric blastic caps are used (Fig. 25-24).

Testing Firing Wire

Preparing. Firing wires that are to be used must have the insulating material stripped from the ends to expose about three inches of bare wire. Remove all enamel as well as any other insulation from these ends before making a connection. Lightly scrape the ends of the wires with the back of a knife blade, exercising care not to nick, cut or weaken the wires.

Testing. Wire may be tested on the reel, but should be retested when unrolled.

- Touch the ends of the wire to the M-51 Blasting Cap Test Set and make sure the wires at the far end are separated. The needle should not move. If it does, the firing wire has a short circuit, and you need a different wire (Fig. 25-25).
- Twist the far ends of the wire together. Retouch those at the M-51 Test Set end to the M-51 Test Set. This should cause a wide deflection of the needle (about 18 units above 0). No movement of the needle indicates a break in the wire. Thus you need a different wire. A slight movement indicates a point of resistance which may be caused by a dirty or loose connection or a wire with several strands broken off at connections. Check the wire and retest.

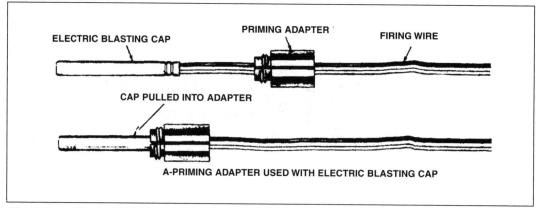

Fig. 25-22. Priming TNT block with priming adapter (electric).

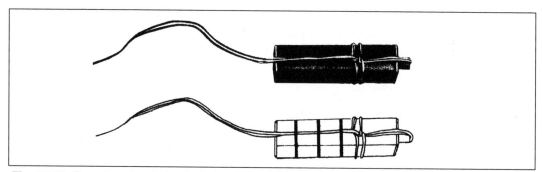

Fig. 25-23. Securing electric lead wires to TNT block.

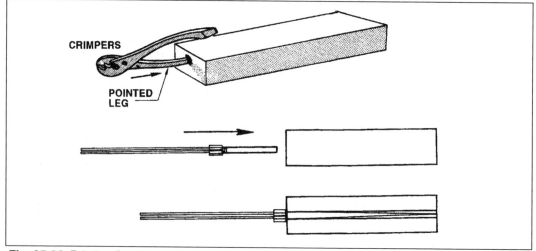

Fig. 25-24. Priming C-4 (electric).

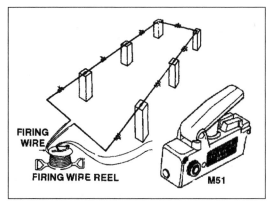
Fig. 25-25. Testing electric firing system.

Connecting the Circuit

Remember, the person who is to do the blasting must keep the blasting machine with them until the charge is set off. (This is to keep them from being blown up).

- Fasten one end of the firing wire to a stake, tree trunk, or piece of equipment so it will not move and shunt the loose ends. Then run the wire to the place of explosion.
- Prime and place the explosive and connect the lead wires to the firing wire. Move back to the firing point.
- Check the circuit with the M-51 Test Set. (If you have a complete circuit, you're ready to explode the electrical charge.)
- Check the 10-cap blasting machine to make sure it works correctly. Connect the firing wires to the terminals on the 10-cap blasting machine.
- Yell "FIRE IN THE HOLE" three times and make sure there is no one around the blasting site.
- Explode the charge.

Electric Misfires

Because of the hazards of burning charges and delayed explosions, extreme care must be exercised in handling electric misfires. A burning charge may result from electric as well as from nonelectric caps. An electric misfire may be investigated immediately provided the cap is above ground and the charge is not also primed with a nonelectric primer. If the system is below ground and primed only electrically proceed to:

- Check the connections of the firing wire to the terminals of the blasting machine to be certain that they make good contacts.

- Make two or three more attempts to fire the circuits.
- Disconnect the firing wire from the machine and allow 30 minutes to elapse before further investigation.
- Check the entire circuit including the firing wire for breaks or short circuits.
- Make no attempt to remove either the primer or the charge.
- If the fault is not located by removing the tamping material to within one foot of the charge, place a new electric primer and two pounds of explosive to this point.
- Disconnect the blasting cap wires of the original primer from the circuit.
- Connect the wires of the new primer in their place.
- Replace the tamping material.
- Explode the charge. Detonation of the new primer will detonate the original charge.

Detonating Cord Firing System

A detonating cord firing system is the most versatile and in many cases the most easily installed of all the firing systems.

Ring Main

The ring main (Fig. 25-26) is made by bringing the main line of det cord back in the form of a loop and attaching it to itself by a girth hitch with an extra turn (Fig. 25-27) or taping the ends together. The ring main makes the detonation of all charges more positive, because the detonating wave approaches from both directions and the charges will detonate even when there is a break in the ring.

Dual Firing Systems

The probability of successful firing is greatly increased by the use of a dual firing system. In combat, misfires may cause the loss of battles. In training, misfires cause the loss of valuable training time and endanger the lives of those who investigate them. Every precaution must be taken to avoid misfires of demolition charges.

Misfires occur most frequently from failure of firing circuits. Whenever time and materials are available, dual firing systems should be used. The firing circuits of the dual firing system must be entirely independent. A dual firing system may consist of two

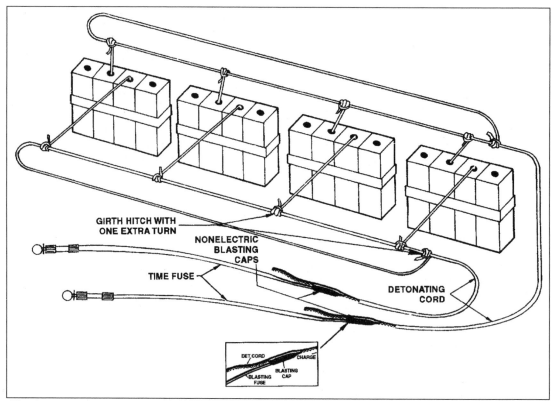

Fig. 25-26. Ring main.

GIRTH HITCH WITH
ONE EXTRA TURN

NONELECTRIC
BLASTING
CAPS

TIME FUSE

DETONATING
CORD

DET CORD
CHARGE
BLASTING
FUSE
BLASTING
CAP

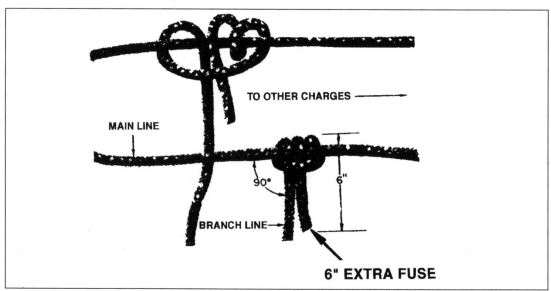

TO OTHER CHARGES

MAIN LINE

90°

6"

BRANCH LINE

6" EXTRA FUSE

Fig. 25-27. Girth hitch with an extra turn.

326

Fig. 25-28. *Nonelectric dual firing system.*

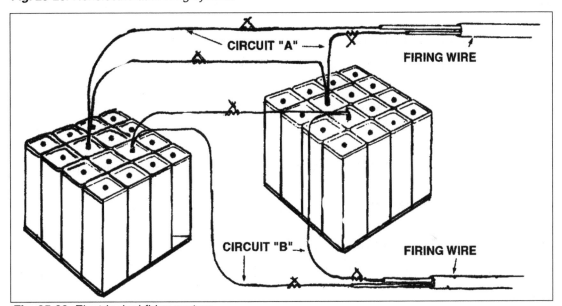

Fig. 25-29. *Electric dual firing system.*

electric circuits, one electric and one nonelectric circuit or two nonelectric circuits.

    Nonelectric dual firing system. A nonelectric dual firing system consists of two independent nonelectric means of firing a single charge or set of charges. Where several charges are to be fired simultaneously, two detonating cord ring mains are laid out, and a branch line from each is run to each charge. Figure 25-28 shows methods of layout for nonelectric dual firing systems.

    Electrical dual firing system. An electric dual firing system consists of two independent electric firing circuits. Each circuit must include an electric

blasting cap in each charge, so that firing either circuit will detonate all charges; thus each charge must contain two electric primers. The correct method of layout for an electric dual firing system is shown in Figure 25-29. The firing wires of the two circuits should be kept separated so that both will not be cut by a single bullet or a single shell fragment.

Prepared Charges

    Special charges for certain types of demolition are sometimes needed. Among these are:

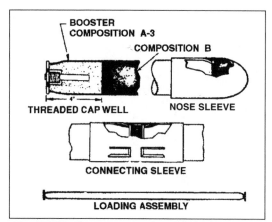

Fig. 25-30. Components of an M1A2 Bangalore Torpedo.

Bangalore Torpedo

The M1A2 Bangalore Torpedo (Fig. 25-30) consists of a series of loading assemblies which are used singly, or in a series, with nose sleeve and connecting sleeves. Each loading assembly is a five-foot length of steel tube, two and an eighth inches in diameter and weighing 15 pounds, of which approximately 11 and a half pounds are explosives. Each loading assembly is equipped with a threaded cap well in each end for priming.

Shaped Charges

Shaped charges are charges shaped to concentrate most of the explosive force in a small area. Standard shaped charges have a cone-shaped top and a conical recess in the bottom. They are provided with supports to hold the charge at the proper distance from the surface of the material to be penetrated. They are used on such objects as concrete bunkers, obstacles and armor plate. The two common shaped charges are the 15-pound M2A3 and the 40-pound M3.

Cratering Charge

A cratering charge is a 40-pound charge packed in a watertight, cylindrical, metal container. A cap well and a detonating cord tunnel are attached to the container to accommodate the primer. To ensure detonation, a booster is provided on top of the container for lowering the charge into a hole. The cleat above and to the side of the cap well is used when the charge is primed either nonelectrically or electrically.

General Safety Precautions

Explosives are dangerous when not handled properly. Carelessness, rough handling and disregard for safety rules cause unnecessary waste, premature explosions, misfires and, in many cases, serious accidents. Demolition explosives and related items are packed to withstand conditions ordinarily encountered in the field, being packed for shipment and storage in moisture-resistant containers and suitable packing boxes. However, containers and boxes must not be handled roughly. When handling or storing explosives, adhere to the following safety precautions at all times:

- Never handle explosives carelessly.
- Never divide the responsibility for the preparation, the placement or the firing of charges. Make one Marine responsible for the supervision of all phases and appoint alternates to take the Marine's place whenever necessary.
- Protect demolition materials from mud, sand, dirt and water. If they become wet or dirty, they should be cleaned at once.
- Do not open explosives in or near a magazine.
- Do not store caps and explosives in the same magazine.
- Do not smoke or permit an open flame near explosives.
- Do not transport explosives and caps in the same vehicle unless absolutely necessary. In an emergency, carry the blasting caps in the cab of the vehicle and the explosives in the cargo compartment.
- Do not leave explosives or caps exposed to direct sunlight or to any other source of heat. Only carry caps in the cap box designed for this purpose.
- Do not carry caps in pockets.
- Do not shoot into explosives with any firearm or allow shooting in the vicinity of an explosives magazine.
- Do not open kegs or wooden cases of explosives with metallic tools. Use a wooden wedge and wooden, rubber or fiber mallet. Metallic slitters may be used for opening fiberboard cases provided the metallic slitter does not come in contact with the metallic fasteners of the case.
- Do not use empty explosives cases for kindling fires, for heating purposes or for cooking.
- Do not permit any paper product used in the packing of explosives to leave your possession. Accumulations of fiberboard cases, paper case liners, cartons or paper should be destroyed by burning after they have been carefully examined to make sure that they are empty.

- Do not use explosives that are obviously deteriorated.
- Do not attempt to reclaim or use fuses, blasting caps or any other explosives that have been water-soaked, even if they have dried out.
- Do not make up primers in a magazine or near large quantities of explosives.
- Do not fire a blast until all persons, vehicles and surplus explosives are in a safe place.

Mines

In the past, land mine warfare has been an engineer specialty. With increased stress being placed on the employment of land mines in recent wars, they no longer can be considered an exclusive engineer responsibility.

In both offensive and defensive operations, obstacles are used to aid you in carrying out your mission. They are used to delay and hamper the enemy, to force the enemy to attack in areas where heavy casualties will be suffered and to provide security. Because land mines are portable, easily and quickly installed and easily removed, they are the best artificial obstacles. Because of their destructive power, mines are also weapons. While mines are a great hazard to the enemy, they are of greater danger to the Marine who does not understand them. Familiarity with mines, fuses and booby traps does not breed contempt but rather a healthy respect.

All Marines are required to know the types and functions of mines. In addition, all Marine infantrymen must be able to lay, arm, disarm and remove mines used for local security of rifle, machine gun and mortar squads.

Mine Components

A land mine consists of a fuse, detonator, booster (absent in some types of mines), main charge and body. A mine is set off when an initiating action causes the fuse to function, resulting in a sequence of actions called the explosive train. The explosive train begins when a small flame or concussion is applied to the detonator. The detonator sets off the booster (if present) or the main charge. If the sequence is broken at any point, the mine may not function. In neutralizing a mine, make sure it is not equipped with more than one explosive train (Fig. 25-31.)

Fuses

Fuses are named according to their initiating action or how they work, or both. Fuses are not issued with mines. Practice fuses are used to arm properly vented, empty practice mines. When set off by an initiating action, a land mine fuse causes a flame or concussion by one of four principal means:

Mechanical. A spring drives a striker against a percussion cap which ignites the detonator.

Chemical. A small vial containing acid is broken by the initiating action. The acid dissolves the striker restraining wire of the fuse striker to fire the detonator, or the acid may cause another chemical to explode to fire the detonator.

Friction. The initiating action causes substances within the fuse to ignite by friction and produce a flame which fires the detonator.

Electrical. The initiating action closes a circuit and fires an electric detonator.

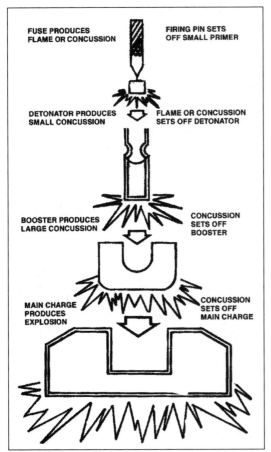

FUSE PRODUCES FLAME OR CONCUSSION

FIRING PIN SETS OFF SMALL PRIMER

DETONATOR PRODUCES SMALL CONCUSSION

FLAME OR CONCUSSION SETS OFF DETONATOR

BOOSTER PRODUCES LARGE CONCUSSION

CONCUSSION SETS OFF BOOSTER

MAIN CHARGE PRODUCES EXPLOSION

CONCUSSION SETS OFF MAIN CHARGE

Fig. 25-31. Explosive train.

Detonator and Booster

A detonator is a sensitive explosive that is set off by the flame or concussion of the fuse to create or transmit a detonation wave to a booster or main charge of high explosives. Some detonators are put into mine explosive trains in the arming procedure while others are integral components of the mine. The booster is a less sensitive but more powerful explosive than a detonator. Some mines do not require a booster. An activator combines a detonator and a booster into one unit and may be used to form an additional firing chain in mines which have activator wells. Such mines contain threaded activator wells to receive the activator. The activator receives a fuse to complete the firing chain. Blasting caps can serve as detonators and may be used in the assembly of additional explosive trains of mines.

Main Charge

This component upon detonation or dispersion accomplishes the purpose of the mine by blast, fragments, projected metal slugs, flame or chemical agents. In addition, some mines may have a burster or propelling charge to disperse or expel the main charge.

STATIC

BOUNDING

HORIZONTAL SPRAY

ANTIPERSONNEL MINE EFFECTS

Fig. 25-32. Antipersonnel mine effects.

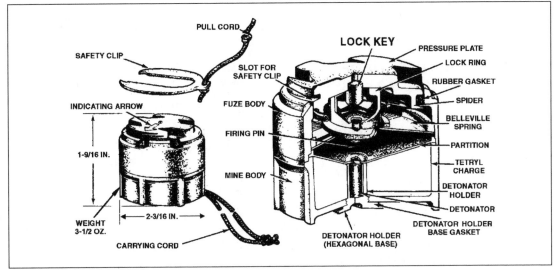

Fig. 25-33. *M-14 APERS.*

Body or Case

The body or case serves as a fuse holder and container for the main charge. Depending on the degree of detection desired and the purpose of the mine, the body may be made of cast or sheet metal, plastic or wood or other materials. Some mines may not have bodies. In these mines, the main charge is exposed, such as in an improvised mine made from demolition material.

Initiating Actions

The types of initiating actions that cause a mine to explode are:
* Pressure from the downward force of a foot or the wheel or track of a vehicle.
* A pull on a wire (called tripwire) attached to the fuse.
* Releasing tension (e.g., cutting a tripwire) which had kept the fuse from functioning.
* Removing a restraining weight (pressure-release) allowing the fuse to function.

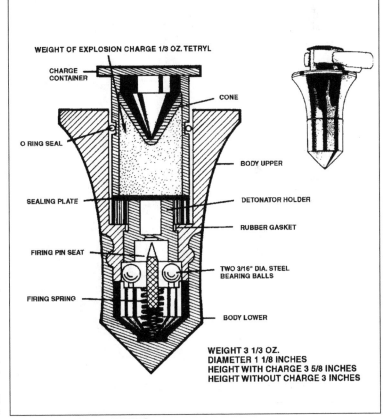

Fig. 25-34. *M-25 APERS.*

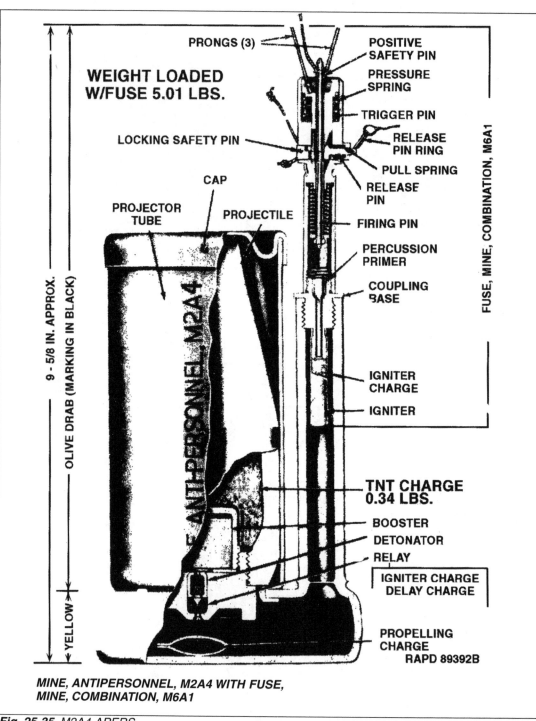

PRONGS (3)

POSITIVE SAFETY PIN

PRESSURE SPRING

WEIGHT LOADED W/FUSE 5.01 LBS.

TRIGGER PIN

LOCKING SAFETY PIN

RELEASE PIN RING

PULL SPRING

CAP

RELEASE PIN

PROJECTOR TUBE

PROJECTILE

FIRING PIN

ANTI-PERSONNEL, M2A4

PERCUSSION PRIMER

COUPLING BASE

9 - 5/8 IN. APPROX.

OLIVE DRAB (MARKING IN BLACK)

FUSE, MINE, COMBINATION, M6A1

IGNITER CHARGE

IGNITER

TNT CHARGE 0.34 LBS.

BOOSTER

DETONATOR

RELAY

IGNITER CHARGE DELAY CHARGE

YELLOW

PROPELLING CHARGE
RAPD 89392B

MINE, ANTIPERSONNEL, M2A4 WITH FUSE, MINE, COMBINATION, M6A1

Fig. 25-35. M2A4 APERS.

- The closing of an electric circuit initiates fuse action.
- Vibrations, magnetic induction, frequency induction and audio frequency.

Types of Mines

Antipersonnel

Antipersonnel mines (APERS) are used primarily to restrict movement of enemy foot troops. These mines are not effective against armored vehicles. Keep in mind that foot troops have a larger field of vision than those in a tank, so when laying APERS mines, special attention should be given to their concealment.

Antipersonnel mines (Fig. 25-32) are designed to disable or kill personnel and are divided into three types of fragmentation mines: static mines, bounding mines and horizontal effect mines.

Static mines: The M-14 and M-25 detonate in place and fire by being stepped on.
- *Mine antipersonnel, nonmetallic M-14 with integral fuse.* The M-14 (Fig. 25-33) takes a force of 20-35 pounds to cause it to detonate and inflict injury at the contact point.
- *M-25 Antipersonnel.* The M-25 Antipersonnel mine (Fig. 25-34) requires 17 to 22 pounds of pressure on the pressure plate to cause it to detonate and inflict injury at point of contact.

Bounding mines: The M2A4, M16A1 and M26 bound into the air and explode several feet above the ground and fire by being stepped on or by tripwire.
- *M2A4 with fuse, combination, M6A1.* The M2A4 (Fig. 25-35) is a highly effective antipersonnel mine with a casualty radius of nine meters and a danger radius of 137 meters. It is used primarily in mine fields to protect antitank mines from breaching parties. However it can be used by itself as a booby trap. It requires 8-20 pounds acting on any of the three prongs of the fuse or 3-10 pounds on a tripwire to detonate.

Horizontal effect mines: The M18A1 expels a spray of shrapnel in one direction and fires by tripwire or as a controlled mine.
- *M16A1 bounding type w/fuse combination M605.* The M16A1 (Fig. 25-36) is a highly effective weapon with a casualty radius of 27 meters and a danger area of 183 meters. Because of its effective area coverage, this mine is primarily employed in mine fields to protect antitank mines

from breaching parties. However, it can be used by itself as a booby trap. Pressure of 8-20 pounds on either of the three fuse prongs or a pull of 3-10 pounds on a tripwire is required to activate.
- *M-26 antipersonnel mine.* The M26 mine (Fig. 25-37) is small, lightweight and relatively easy to arm. It is a bounding antipersonnel mine, which sheds fragments horizontally and toward the ground with a casualty radius of 20 meters. The fragments sent downward are effective against troops lying prone. The M-26 can be used as a pressure mine or a pull mine by using its tripwire lever and a tripwire. Pressure of 14-28 pounds on the pressure plate or a pull of 4-8 pounds on a tripwire is needed to detonate.
- *M18A1 directional mine.* The M18A1, popularly known as the Claymore (Fig. 25-38(a)), is a directional, fixed fragmentation mine which is extremely effective in defense against massed (human wave) infantry attacks. It can be employed as a land mine, controlled weapon or booby trap. The Claymore is generally detonated electrically, but can be rigged to be fired nonelectrically. The casualty radius forward is a horizontal arc of 100 meters to a height of two meters; the forward danger radius is 250 meters. The M18A1 has a backblast area of 16 meters to the rear and sides. In this area, backblast can cause injury by concussion and secondary missiles. Up to 100 meters to the rear and sides, all friendly personnel must be under cover for protection from secondary missiles. (Fig. 25-39.)

The Claymore is the mine that most Marines will come in contact with. It is issued in the M7 bandoleer (Fig. 25-38 (b)), which contains the components for electrical employment. The bandoleer has two pockets; one contains the mine and the other contains an M57 firing device, M40 test set and an electrical blasting cap assembly.

Antitank

The primary use of antitank (AT) mines is to restrict or delay movement of enemy vehicles. An AT mine is so placed in the ground that it will be triggered by movement of enemy tanks or vehicles or by attempted removal by enemy troops.

Friendly troops should avoid all mined areas because of the probability of encountering tripwires and booby traps. Also, antipersonnel mines will almost always be found in conjunction with antitank mines in order to prevent the enemy from removing the antitank mines.

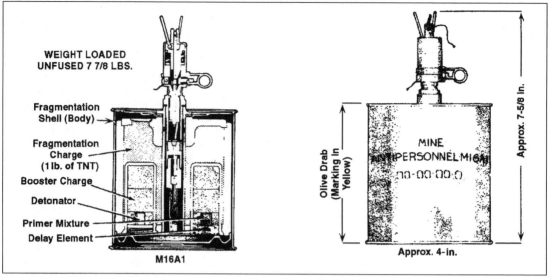

WEIGHT LOADED UNFUSED 7 7/8 LBS.

Fragmentation Shell (Body)
Fragmentation Charge (1 lb. of TNT)
Booster Charge
Detonator
Primer Mixture
Delay Element

M16A1

Olive Drab (Marking In Yellow)

MINE ANTIPERSONNEL M16A1
00-00-00-0

Approx. 7-5/8 in.

Approx. 4-in.

Fig. 25-36. M16A1 APERS.

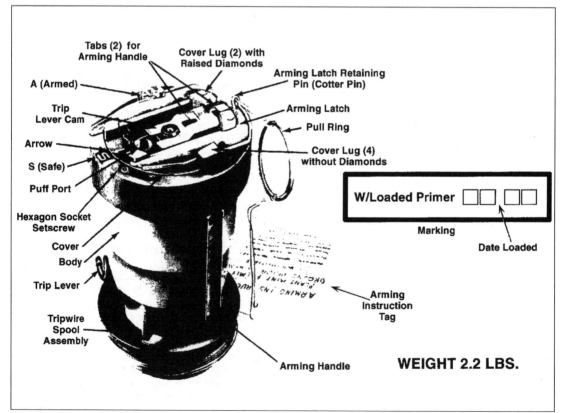

Tabs (2) for Arming Handle
Cover Lug (2) with Raised Diamonds
Arming Latch Retaining Pin (Cotter Pin)
A (Armed)
Trip Lever Cam
Arming Latch
Pull Ring
Arrow
Cover Lug (4) without Diamonds
S (Safe)
Puff Port
Hexagon Socket Setscrew
Cover
Body
Trip Lever
Tripwire Spool Assembly
Arming Handle
Arming Instruction Tag

W/Loaded Primer ☐☐ ☐☐

Marking

Date Loaded

WEIGHT 2.2 LBS.

Fig. 25-37. M-26 APERS.

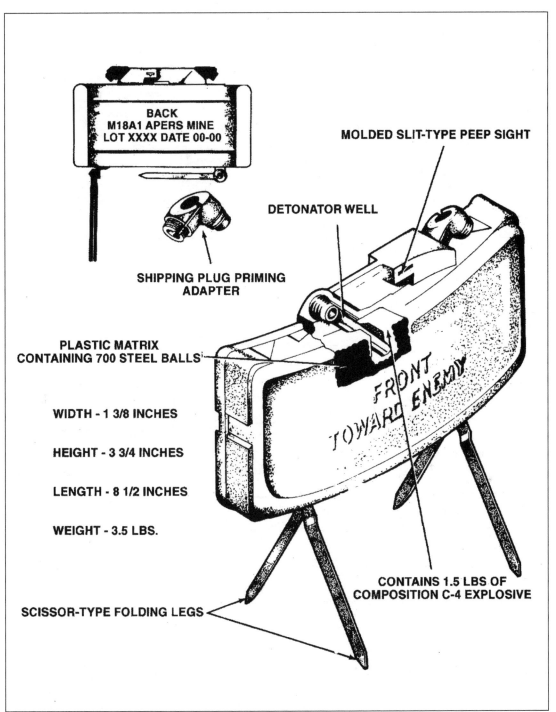

BACK
M18A1 APERS MINE
LOT XXXX DATE 00-00

MOLDED SLIT-TYPE PEEP SIGHT

DETONATOR WELL

SHIPPING PLUG PRIMING
ADAPTER

PLASTIC MATRIX
CONTAINING 700 STEEL BALLS

FRONT
TOWARD ENEMY

WIDTH - 1 3/8 INCHES

HEIGHT - 3 3/4 INCHES

LENGTH - 8 1/2 INCHES

WEIGHT - 3.5 LBS.

CONTAINS 1.5 LBS OF
COMPOSITION C-4 EXPLOSIVE

SCISSOR-TYPE FOLDING LEGS

Fig. 25-38(a). M18A1 APERS.

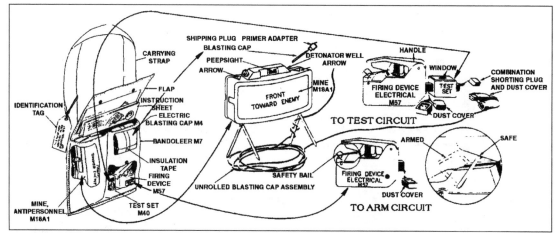

Fig. 25-38(b). *M-18A1 antipersonnel mine and carrying case.*

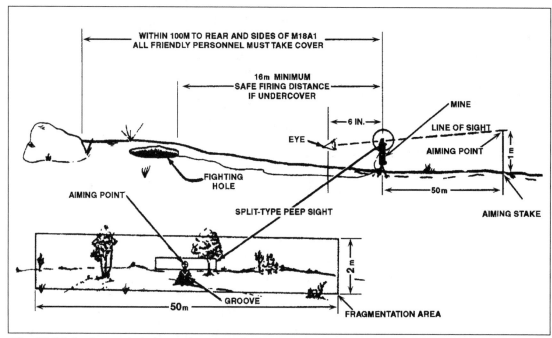

Fig. 25-39. *Laying and aiming antipersonnel mine M18A1.*

Antitank mines are designed to damage or destroy tanks and other vehicles. There are two types in the Marine Corps' inventory: blast mines and vertical penetration mines.

Blast mines (M-15 and M-19) disable the wheels or the tracks of vehicles.

- **M-15 (HE) heavy mine with M603 fuse.** The M-15 is a high-capacity AT mine intended for use

against heavy tanks (Fig. 25-40). It takes a force of 565 pounds plus or minus 174 pounds on the pressure plate to detonate.

- **M-19 AT (HE) heavy mine with M606 fuse.** The M-19 (Fig. 25-41) is used against heavy tanks and other types of heavy-tracked and wheeled vehicles. Of nearly all-plastic construction, the M-19 is undetectable by magnetic mine detectors. A

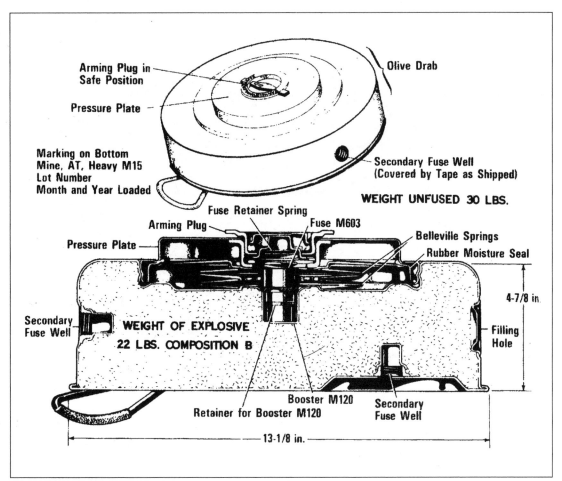

Fig. 25-40. *M-15 (HE) AT mine.*

force of 350-500 pounds on the pressure plate is needed to detonate.

Vertical penetration mines (M-21) penetrate the bottom of a vehicle, wounding or killing its occupants.

- ***M-21 AT (HE) heavy mine with M607 fuse.*** The M-21 (Fig. 25-42) is used primarily for destroying tanks and other types of tracked and wheeled vehicles. The M607 fuse with extension rod attached can be set off by the entire frontal width of a track or the vehicle itself. With the extension rod and adapter removed, the fuse functions conventionally by pressure. Tilting of the tilt rod with a minimum force of 3.75 pounds or a minimum force of 290 pounds on the pressure plate will cause the M-21 to detonate.

Chemical

Chemical mines are used to contaminate an obstacle or area facing the enemy. The United States no longer manufactures or uses chemical mines.

Practice

Practice mines are armed and disarmed in the same manner as the standard mines they replace. They let out a puff of smoke, make a noise or score casualties in some other way when fired. Practice mines normally use specially designed practice fuses and are blue. (Inert mines are black.)

- ***AP M-8 bounding w/fuse combination M-110.*** The AP M-8 is almost identical to the M16A1

337

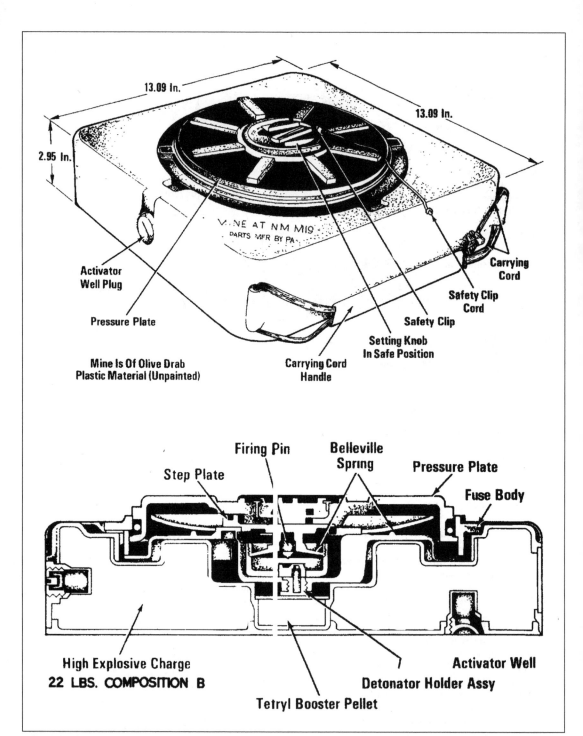

Fig. 25-41. M-19 (HE) AT mine.

338

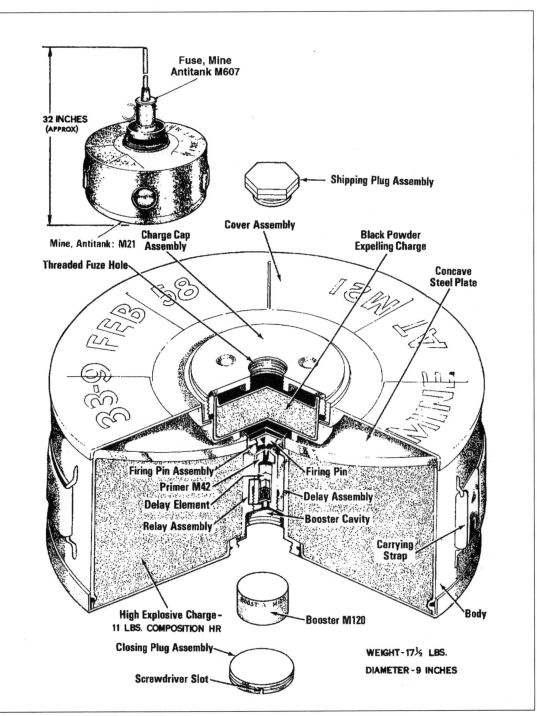

Fig. 25-42. M-21 (HE) AT mine.

339

APERS (Fig. 25-36) without the high explosive charge.

- *AT heavy M-20 w/fuse.* The M-20 is similar to the M-15 (HE) AT mine (Fig. 25-40).
- *AT nonmetallic M-19 (inert).* The M-19 (inert) is an actual M-19 (HE) AT mine (Fig. 25-41) filled with an inert substance.

Explosive Booby Traps

A booby trap is an explosive charge which is set off when an unsuspecting person disturbs an apparently harmless object or performs a presumably safe act. Booby traps usually are made from materials available in a combat area. Normally they are improvised to meet conditions that prevail. An elementary booby trap consists of a small charge of high explosive, a detonator and a firing device.

Bobby Trap Construction

The components of a booby trap must be joined together in a definite and precise arrangement to develop a continuous chain of action until complete detonation of a main explosive charge occurs. The firing device may be attached directly to the detonator or connected to it by means of a detonating cord,

time fuse or electric wires, depending on the type of device. The main charge may be bulk explosive, or it may be a mine, grenade, artillery or mortar shell or other standard charge. Initiating action, usually by personnel disturbing what appears to be a harmless object, acts upon the firing device which sets off the detonator. The detonator detonates the main charge. The main charge provides the striking power of the booby trap.

Firing Devices

There is a wide variety of triggering mechanisms available for use in constructing booby traps. Called fuses, igniters, switches or firing devices, they serve as control mechanisms to hold detonations in check until proper signals are given.

All U.S. standard firing devices use a standard coupling base to facilitate ease of assembly and wide variety in the choice of a base charge. The three types of booby trap firing devices used by the Marine Corps are:

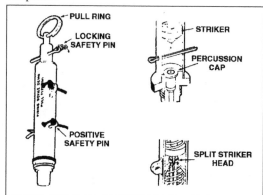

Fig. 25-44. *M1 firing device.*

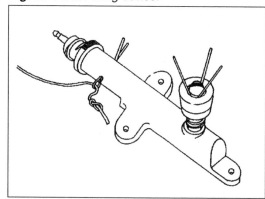

Fig. 25-45. *M1A1 firing device.*

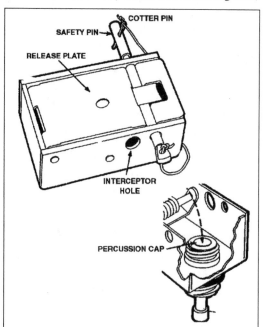

Fig. 25-43. *M5 pressure-release firing device.*

- *Firing device, pressure-release type, M5.* this mechanism consists of a small steel rectangular box with a hinged lid (Fig. 25-43). A spring-loaded striker is held in position by the lid. A special locking safety pin holds the lid in the closed position. This device uses a standard base screwed into an opening in the bottom. A positive safety hole (interceptor hole) is located on the side of the box. The device is adaptable for many kinds of bobby traps. A load of at least five pounds resting on the release plate is required to restrain this device. When the load is removed or allows the striker to raise the release plate at least five-eighths of an inch, the striker, impelled by its spring, rotates about a pivot, strikes the percussion cap and detonates the activator and any charge which may be attached.
- *Firing device, M1.* The M1 firing device (Fig. 25-44) employs a pull device as a trigger designed to fire a percussion cap in a standard coupling base. A pressure of 3-5 pounds on a tripwire anchored and attached to the pull ring of the firing device will release the striker. The striker drives into the percussion cap, detonating the main charge.
- *Firing device, M1A1.* The M1A1 firing device (Fig. 25-45) is similar to the M1 device except it requires pressure of 20 pounds or more on a three-pronged activator to release tension on the firing pin spring.

Individual Countermeasures

Individual countermeasures are those measures each Marine can take to diminish the effectiveness of a mine or booby trap device which has been emplaced and is found or is accidentally detonated. This can be accomplished through physical protective measures, detection and destruction measures, avoidance of explosive devices and through application of immediate action when an explosive device has been accidentally detonated.

Physical Protective Countermeasures

The individual Marine can take these steps to reduce the effectiveness of enemy mines:
- Wear body armor and helmet.
- Sandbag vehicle flooring. When possible, place a heavy rubber mat over sandbags to reduce secondary fragments such as shrapnel, sand, stones and pieces of sandbag.
- Keep arms and legs inside vehicles to achieve maximum protection from sandbags.
- Maintain proper distance from other personnel.
- Don't travel alone.
- Don't pick up or touch what appears to be an attractive "souvenir." That souvenir is most likely a booby trap.

Detection Countermeasures

Once emplaced, a mine or bobby trap must be found before it causes multiple casualties through accidental detonation by a Marine. Unfortunately, too many booby traps are discovered only after they explode. It is imperative that detection techniques be stressed. Detection may be by one of the following methods:

Visual inspection. One of the most effective mine and booby trap detectors in the Marine Corps is an *alert and observant* Marine. Each Marine must know the areas in which booby traps and mines are normally found and be alert for things which "just don't look right." Examples are:
- Mud smears, mudballs, dung or a board on the road.
- Apparent road repair, new fill or paving patches, ditching or culvert work.
- Wires leading away from the side of the road.
- Tripwires across trails; along shoulders of roads at likely ambush sites; across the most accessible route through dense vegetation; and at fords, diches, and across rice paddy dikes.
- Terrain features which do not appear natural. Cut vegetation dries and changes color. Rain may wash away covering material and cause an explosive device to sink, leaving a surface depression. A covered device may appear as a mound.
- Suspicious items in trees, branches or bushes.
- Markings used by the enemy to indicate the location of a mine or booby trap.

Probing. Suspicious spots must be carefully probed with a probe or bayonet.

Mine detectors. Mine detectors are designed to assist the individual Marine in a detailed, deliberate sweep of a specific area, usually a road. Particular attention must be given to the time factors of the individual sweeping situation, since hasty opening of a road can mean an ineffective sweep and quite possibly destruction or injury to vehicular traffic and personnel.

Destruction Countermeasures

Once detected, mines and booby traps must be marked or destroyed in place or both by the discovering person or unit to prevent accidental detonation by a following unit or individual Marines. Considerations for destruction are:

- Mines and booby traps should not be moved unless absolutely necessary and then only by qualified ordnance disposal or engineer personnel. Many booby traps are themselves booby-trapped and, if disturbed, will detonate the associated device.
- Explosive devices should be destroyed by engineers. If engineers are not available, then devices may be destroyed by selected qualified personnel within each unit.
- Mines and booby traps may be destroyed or neutralized by use of grappling hooks, demolitions and artillery fires.

Avoidance Countermeasures

Strict application of training and careful planning of movements through danger areas will reduce casualties by simply avoiding the explosive devices. The unit leader must analyze from the enemy's viewpoint each area through which the leader intends to move Marines. The unit leader must ask the question, "If I were the enemy, where would I put the booby trap?" This question can and should influence both administrative and tactical movements. Some suggested means for avoiding mines and booby traps are:

- Stay off trails, footpaths, cart tracks or other likely routes of travel as much as possible. Vary routes used to villages and key terrain features. Use of the same route twice is an invitation to the enemy to employ booby traps. Keep the enemy guessing as to which route will be used next.
- Move where local inhabitants move. These people generally know the location of the most mines and booby traps and will avoid these areas. In a village, stay near the villagers and watch which buildings they use. Use natives as guides whenever possible.
- Avoid patterns. Constantly change direction of movement.
- Maintain intervals of 15 meters between personnel and 100 meters between Marines and tracked vehicles. In view of the fact that the effective casualty radius of the M67 grenade, for example, is 15 meters, and that two or more casualties are suffered for each booby-trapped grenade accidentally detonated, the maintenance of proper interval is most important.
- Move slowly. Rapid movement generates carelessness. A unit must be allowed sufficient time to move to its objective.
- At times the enemy will appear only when wanting to be seen. When pursuing the enemy, be especially alert for deliberately emplaced booby traps on the axis of advance.
- Artillery and mortar fires near and in the area of operations will not only discourage booby trap emplacement, but will also neutralize devices by sympathetic detonation, overturning and burying emplaced mines and rupturing tripwires. Employment of these fires beside a road, before and during a road sweep, will discourage command detonation of road mines.
- At all times, a lightweight stick or a slender steel rod can be helpful if used to feel for tripwires.
- Mark detected mines and booby traps so those following may avoid them.
- When on roads, stay in the well-used portion and off shoulders.
- Follow the tracks of the vehicle ahead. If there is no vehicle ahead, stay out of the ruts.
- Avoid holes, depressions and objects lying on the road.
- *Remember:* A booby trap too easily detected can be a ruse resulting in detonation of other explosive devices emplaced nearby.

Immediate Action

Little reaction time exists once the detonation chain starts. The maximum delay for the M67 and foreign grenades ranges from four to nine seconds. If the delay element has been modified, the minimum fuse delay can be less than a second. However since the time available cannot be predicted, certain immediate action can assist in reducing casualties and the degree of personal injury.

- Be alert for the "pop" of an exploding cap, the tug of the tripwire or the warning of another Marine.
- Sound a warning such as "hit it," so that others may take cover.
- Drop to the ground immediately.

Immediate action is designed as an instinctive reaction based on minimum fuse delay. When using it also remember:

- Do not attempt to outrun the explosion. The 800 fragments of the M67 grenade have an initial velocity of over 5,000 feet a second. During the available delay, however brief, an individual can best remove oneself from the cone of the explosion by dropping to the ground. The individual must assume a minimum delay in every case.

- If possible, when dropping to the ground, present the smallest target to the force of the explosion by pointing the feet in the direction of the charge.
- All those near should drop to the ground when the warning is sounded.
- Do not immediately rush to the aid of Marines wounded by mines or booby traps. Frequently there is a second booby trap in the vicinity of the first. The Marine nearest each casualty should carefully clear their way to the wounded individual and render first aid. Under no circumstances should others crowd near the wounded Marine.
- Conduct a brief but careful search for other explosive devices in the immediate vicinity before moving on.
- If a device is tripped and does not explode, follow the same immediate action and then blow it in place.

Chapter Twenty-Six

Basic Communications

Throughout the Marine Corps, at all echelons, there is a constant need to exchange information. We often refer to this exchange as "passing the word." Every Marine should know the basic facts concerning the means of communication and communication equipment found in the rifle company. Communications may take the form of radio or written messages, delivered by messenger, telephone conversations, or visual and sound signals.

Radio

Radios are widely used at all echelons of the Marine Corps. Radio communications are flexible. The equipment can go anywhere a Marine can go, and it provides one of the fastest means of communication available. Since ordinary radio communications can be monitored by an enemy, cryptographic devices must be used with tactical radios to achieve security. The length of each transmission should, of course, be made as short as possible, since the enemy is able to determine the location of an active radio set, whether it is used with a cryptographic device or not. The following rules apply to radio transmissions:

1. Always listen before starting to talk so as not to create interference. Know what you are going to say before transmitting.
2. Press the push-to-talk button on the hand set. Do not start talking until the crypto keying tone ceases.
3. Speak distinctly and in a normal tone.
4. Release the push-to-talk button immediately after speaking.
5. In an extreme emergency, the cryptographic device may be switched to the plain (or clear) mode if the radio will otherwise not function.
6. Avoid contact with the antenna while transmitting. Do not allow the antenna to contact power lines while the radio is being transported.

The Marine Corps' primary tactical radio is the AN/PRC-119 SINCGARS (Single Channel Ground and Airborne Radio System) family of radios.

SINCGARS RECEIVER-TRANSMITTERS (RT) (RT-1523, RT-1523A, RT-1523B)

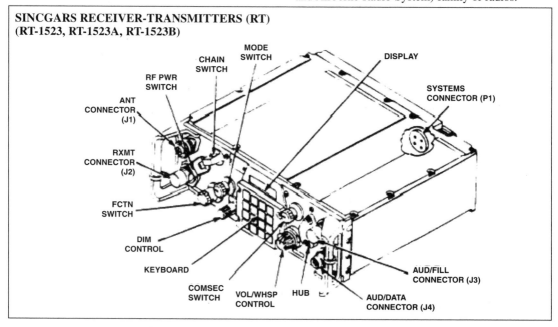

RT Capabilities

SINGLE CHANNEL	Single channel (SC) frequency modulation (FM) operation in very high frequency (VHF) band of 30.000 to 87.975 Megahertz (MHz).
FREQUENCY HOPPING	Frequency hopping (FH) mode for electronic counter counter-measure (ECCM) operation.
DIGITAL TUNING	Quick, silent, precise, digital tuning.
VISUAL DISPLAY	Electronic visual displays provide for quick checks and prompts.
PRESET CHANNELS	Preset channels: eight for SC mode and six for FH mode, each of which may be loaded with COMSEC and used in CT or PT mode.
VOICE-DATA	Voice or digital data communication. Provides data rates of 600, 1200, 2400, 4800, and 16,000 bits per second [BPS]; also provides analog data interface.
FREQUENCIES	More than 2000 SC frequencies.
COMSEC	Provides cipher text (CT) communications with integrated COMSEC (ICOM) feature.
WEIGHT	6.7 kg (14.7 lbs) – RT-1523 only 12.6 kg (27.7 lbs) – manpack radio

Manpack Radio Performance Data

TYPE COMM	RF PWR	RANGE**
VOICE	LOW (LO)	200 M to 400 M
VOICE	MEDIUM (M)	400 M to 5 KM
VOICE	MEDIUM (M)	5 KM to 10 KM
DATA (600-4800 BPS)	HIGH (HI)	3 KM to 5 KM
DATA (16,000 BPS)	HIGH (HI)	1 KM to 3 KM

* Above data apply equally to dismount radios and RCUs.

** Ranges shown are for planning purposes only. They are based upon line of sight and are average for normal conditions. Ranges depend upon location, sighting, weather, and surrounding noise level, among other factors. Use of the OE-254 antenna will increase ranges for both voice and data transmissions. Enemy jamming and mutual interference conditions will degrade ranges. In data transmissions, use of lower baud rate increases the range.

MANPACK COMPONENTS

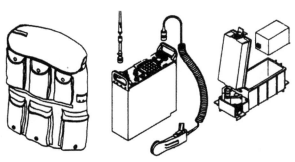
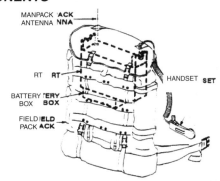
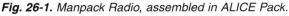

Fig. 26-1. Manpack Radio, assembled in ALICE Pack.

Wire

Wire is the most reliable means of communications, and everyone has had experience in using a telephone. Wire has the inherent characteristics of speed and reliability. Unless appropriate speech security devices are available to the users, however, it should not be assumed that telephone systems can be used to pass classified information. Wire is the primary means of communication in a semi-permanent location or when a unit assumes a defensive position. Learn to recognize the appearance of communication wire, because it is often cut by the movement of our own armored vehicles. When driving a vehicle, try to avoid running over field wire if at all possible. In the event you discover a break in a wire line, report the location of the break to the nearest headquarters. Profanity is prohibited on both radio and telephone sets, and from time to time, transmissions are monitored by higher echelon.

Visual and Sound Communications

In addition to the arm and hand signals depicted in Chapter 28, other visual communications within your platoon or squad are widely used. Some examples are flags, flashing lights, pyrotechnics and aircraft panels. Additionally, sound communications, such as sirens to warn of enemy aircraft or armor, are used.

Messengers

At any time in the field a Marine may be called upon to deliver a message – the most secure means available at the squad and platoon levels. A messenger receiving an oral message repeats it to the sender so that there will be no misunderstanding. Messengers then repeat it to themselves until they have committed it to memory. Messengers must know their principal and alternate routes prior to departure. Cover, concealment, and length and conditions of the various routes available must be taken into account. At all times, additional protection for messengers, in the form of another Marine or a fire team, will have to be provided, dependent on the local combat situation and the time of day the message must be delivered. Sometimes, messengers may follow wire lines to maintain their direction (night or difficult terrain). When delivering messages to a battalion or larger unit, messengers normally deliver the message to the message center. While at the message center, they check for message traffic for their unit.

Messengers should know the names of unit commanders, be able to read a map and know how to use a field Message Book.

The Phonetic Alphabet

When talking over the radio, certain words in the conversation may be misunderstood because of sim-

	PHONETIC ALPHABET		
Letter	*Equivalent Phonetic*	*Letter*	*Equivalent Phonetic*
A	Alfa	N	November
B	Bravo	O	Oscar
C	Charlie	P	Papa
D	Delta	Q	Quebec
E	Echo	R	Romeo
F	Foxtrot	S	Sierra
G	Golf	T	Tango
H	Hotel	U	Uniform
I	India	V	Victor
J	Juliett	W	Whiskey
K	Kilo	X	X-ray
L	Lima	Y	Yankee
M	Mike	Z	Zulu

ilarity in sound to other words. In order to eliminate any misunderstanding by the receiving party, the sender uses the phonetic alphabet to spell out words that might be misunderstood.

Numeral Pronunciation

Numbers are important in military messages and should be spoken clearly in telephone and radio conversations. The pronunciation of numerals should be exaggerated to avoid misunderstanding by the receiving party. Each digit of large numbers is pronounced separately except in the case of even "hundreds" and "thousands."

1 - wun	6 - six
2 - too	7 - seven
3 - tree	8 - ait
4 - fo-wer	9 - nine
5 - fife	0 - zero

Examples

70 - seven zero
84 - ait fo-wer
131 - wun tree wun
500 - fife hun-dred
1,468 - wun fo-wer six ait
7,000 - seven thou-sand

Chapter Twenty-Seven

Land Navigation

In civilian life it is possible for a stranger to find his way around a large city or town by merely asking directions from any policeman or friendly native of the town. He may have to overcome a few wrong directions thrown in with the right ones, but he is sure of finding his way.

In combat, Marines often find themselves in strange surroundings. As a Marine, you will have to ask directions like any other stranger, but you will also get information from your map. Your map has all the answers and you must be able to read it. Reports from Marines in combat show us that every person must know how to read and use a map if the individual wants to stay alive and keep the outfit safe at all times.

Natives of a place can tell us lots of things to help us, but we have to be able to speak their language. We must also learn to read and understand the language of a map. It is a simple and clear language. You will have use for it very often while you are in the Marine Corps, especially when you are in a tight spot. If you learn to use it correctly, it won't let you down.

A map is a picture, a picture of the land and the things people have built on the land. A map is flat, and when we look at a map, we are looking at a picture of the ground from a spot high in the air. That view is different from the one we have looked at all our lives, from one point on the ground to another point on the ground. That is the first thing to remember about maps. *Maps are views of things from directly above.* They give a view as though you were hovering over a football stadium in a helicopter. In map reading we are looking from overhead at something with many more details than a football game, and at an area much larger and not so near to us; the land itself really looks strange.

What Is On A Map?

A map is a picture, but it is not a photographic picture. It is a drawing on paper, and a big difference between a map and a photograph is that the map has signs and symbols instead of photographs of objects. These signs and symbols represent various things on the ground.

To read a map, then, we have to learn what these various signs mean. Map signs and symbols usually look something like the actual things for which they stand. The signs are simple to draw and are easily recognized. In order to better understand the use of signs, look at Figures 27-1 through 27-14.

For example, Figure 27-1 shows a pick crossed with a sledge hammer, the sign for a mine. These two tools are used in mining. Figure 27-2 shows the sign for a schoolhouse, a black block with a flag flying from it. Most schools have a flag on a flagpole, and so the sign gives you the idea of a school.

Let us put these signs on a map and see what they look like. Figure 27-25(b) shows you the mapping signs for the things you see in the photograph of the land in Figure 27-25(a). Identify the signs shown.

The map, however, is still incomplete. So far, we just have our objects on a flat, blank piece of land; but land is not like that. It has much more on it than these signs alone can show us.

On a football field, we see the players not on a blank area, but against a background marked off with lines. These lines mean something to us, and we can tell where the players are by watching how far they are from these lines: the goal lines, the yard lines and the side lines. The lines form a pattern which connects the different objects on the field. On the map on which our signs are placed, there are already certain main lines which make a general pattern. These main lines are also shown by signs, and they stand for such important landmarks as streams, roads, railroads and fences.

We try to make these lines look different from one another, so that we don't get them confused. At the same time, we try to make them resemble the objects they are supposed to represent. Figure 27-15 through 27-24 are examples of these main lines and the signs used to show them on a map.

The heavy line in Figure 27-15 is a primary or first class highway; the second line is a secondary highway; these are sometimes red on your map. The

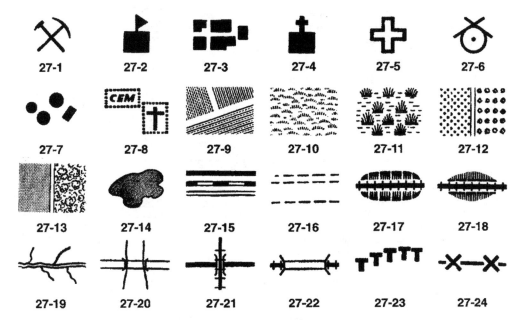

27-1	27-2	27-3	27-4	27-5	27-6
27-7	27-8	27-9	27-10	27-11	27-12
27-13	27-14	27-15	27-16	27-17	27-18
27-19	27-20	27-21	27-22	27-23	27-24

Figures 27-1 through 27-24: 1-Mine, 2-School, 3-Buildings, 4-Church, 5-Hospital, 6-Windmill, 7-Oil Tanks, 8-Cemetery, 9-Cultivated Fields, 10-Grassland, 11-Swamp, 12-Orchard, 13-Woods, 14-Lakes or Ponds, 15-Primary or First Class Highway, 16- Dirt Road and Trail, 17-Cut, 18-Fill, 19-Stream, 20-Bridge, 21-Railroad Underpass, 22-Tunnel, 23-Telegraph, Telephone Wires, 24-Barbed Wire Strand Fence.

Fig. 27-25(a).

Fig. 27-25(b).

solid parallel lines mean other surfaced roads. The two dashed parallel lines in Figure 27-16 mean dirt road, while the single dashed line means a trail or footpath.

Telegraph or telephone wires are often on tall T-shaped poles across the country. The map sign is also T-shaped. (See Fig. 27-23.)

In Figure 27-24, the sign is given for a barbed-wire strand fence, not the kind that is a military entanglement. The sign for a smooth wire fence is a series of small o's connected by dashes. (For example, o-o-o-o-o-o-.)

This covers the signs that are most used in mapping. It is important to remember the colors used with these signs. All water, such as swamps, rivers and lakes, is in blue. Woods and other heavy vegetation are in green. Cuts, fills, some cultivated fields and some roads may be in reddish-brown. Other roads, railroads, buildings, bridges and most man-made objects are printed in black.

If we put all these signs and colors on a map and give them names, we find ourselves with the land picture you see in Figure 27-26. This is more like it! Now we have a pattern of ground on which our signs begin to make sense. This is a simple map, but it tells us much more about the area it represents.

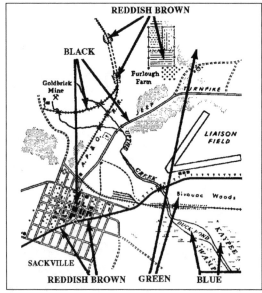

Fig. 27-26.

Elevation and Contour

So far, everything on our map is flat. We must now find a way to learn something about the differ-

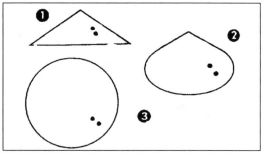

Fig. 27-27.

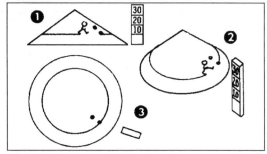

Fig. 27-28.

ent ground levels. It means something to us to know that a hill is in a certain place, but we would further like to know how high it is. A picture of a hill taken from above will not show this, but there is a way for the map to give you this information.

A hill is broader at its base than it is at its top. Let us take an object which is like a hill, a cone, for example, and see what we can do to a picture of it from above to let us know how high it is.

To Judge Height

First, suppose there are two boulders on the side of the cone, as in Figure 27-27, Example 1. When we look at this from above (Examples 2 and 3) we can still tell that there are two boulders there. We would not know which boulder was higher and how high up the cone either boulder was if we had not already seen the cone from the side.

Next, let us suppose that we walk up this cone until we are 10 feet higher than the base (Fig. 27-28). Now let us walk around the cone, staying 10 feet high all the way around. Finally, we will come back to the place we started from. If we had a leaky flour bag with us as we walked, we would have left a mark on the hill which would look like Example 1. From above, this line would look like it does in Examples 2 and 3.

Now what do we know about this mark as we look at it from above? We know that anything on it is 10 feet higher than the base of the cone. Notice that one of the boulders is right on this line; therefore its elevation, or height, is 10 feet. We know that anything between the line and the base of the cone is lower than 10 feet.

Let's move up the cone until we are 10 feet higher and do the same thing again. The result is another flour line (Fig. 27-29). What do we know about this line? We know that everything on it is at an elevation of 20 feet, and that the elevation of everything between it and the first line is somewhere between 10 and 20 feet. Now the second boulder is about halfway between the two lines, so we can judge that its elevation is about 15 feet.

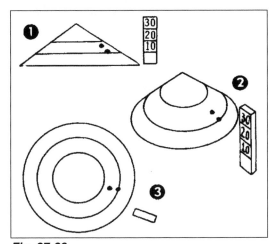

Fig. 27-29.

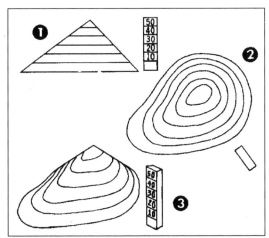

Fig. 27-30.

To Judge Shapes

These lines tell us still more – the shape of objects. They tell us that the cone is round, for example. If the object is not round, an object other than a cone, these lines can tell us that also. Suppose we stretch one side of the cone so that it looks like Figure 27-30, Example 1. If we do our flour bag stunt again, from above the lines look like Examples 2 and 3. We can tell which side it bulges on.

We find, then, that these lines can tell us two things, elevation and shape. Maps have many such lines, and if you understand what they mean, they are easy to read and very helpful. On maps these lines are called *contours* or *contour lines*.

Let us see what happens when we place contour lines on a map. The dashed line in Figure 27-31(a) encloses the hill which overlooks the town of Sackville. In Figure 27-31(b) we have lifted the hill right off the map so we can examine it more closely.

First, let us make flour marks on the hill, just the way we did on the cone. From the side, it looks like Figure 27-32, Example 1. As we rise into the air we can see more of these lines, as Examples 2 and 3.

Finally, we have a view from directly above and we can see that the shape of the hill is shown in Figure 27-33(a) just as the shape of cone was shown in Figure 27-30. if we take these lines out of the photograph and put them on a map, as in Figure 27-33(b), we can tell which parts are high and which low.

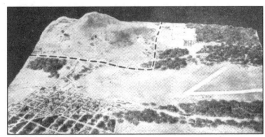

Fig. 27-31(a).

Fig. 27-31(b).

Fig. 27-32.

Fig. 27-33(a).

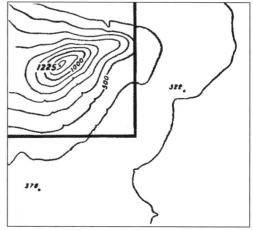

Fig. 27-33(b).

It would clutter up the map too much to have the number showing the elevation of each contour line, so only a few of them are numbered. To make it easy to count these lines, every *fifth* line is heavier than the others. The distance between contour lines on each map is shown by means of a note at the bottom of the map. This note may read, for example: *Contour interval: 10 feet.*

This means that the distance between any two neighboring contour lines on that map is 10 feet in a vertical direction. The contour interval is noted on maps just below the graphic scales. On our map of Sackville, the contour interval is 100 feet.

Since the highest point on the hill in Figure 27-33(b) does not fall exactly on a contour line, this point is labeled with the exact elevation. On maps, such elevation numbers are found often. Some objects take their names from these numbers. If there are a number of road junctions on a part of a map, and we wish to name one of them in a particular way, we may call it RJ 124 (that is, the road junction which is marked as being at an elevation of 124 feet).

Begin at Sea Level

It may be seen, also, that the elevation of the base of a hill in Figure 27-32, Example 1 is 300 feet rather than 0 feet. The reason for this is that elevation is figured from sea level. In other words, we compare the elevation of all land anywhere to the average sea level.

In Figure 27-34, although the hill is far from sea, the base of the hill on the land is 300 feet above sea level. Sea level is zero for all elevation measurements.

Fig. 27-34.

Other Contour Information

It is clear that these contour lines are very helpful things to have and they can help us in other ways. Suppose we have a high spot of ground that breaks off suddenly and becomes a cliff. From the ground, as in Figure 27-35(a), it is easy to tell this is a cliff. It is also easy to tell this by examining the contour lines of the map. When a hill or cliff is steep, the contour lines appear close together as in Figure 27-35(b). This arrangement of contour lines on a map always shows a sharp rise in the ground. If however, the lines are spaced evenly and fairly apart, it means that the hill rises gradually.

If there are two hills with a saddle between them, as in Figure 27-36(a), the contour lines, as in Figure 27-36(b), tell us exactly what they look like.

A special kind of valley is formed by a stream, and contour lines in the area are usually regularly spaced as in Figure 27-37(b). They form "V's" where they cross the stream. It is important to remember that these "V's" all point *uphill or upstream.*

Contours, then, can tell us several things about streams. They can tell us the location of a stream or valley; they can tell us which way the stream is flowing, which shows the slope of the ground; and by the spaces between the contour lines, they can tell us how steep the valley is. Remember, V-shaped contours show valleys or streams.

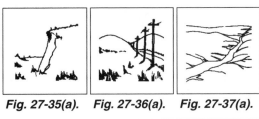

Fig. 27-35(a).   Fig. 27-36(a).   Fig. 27-37(a).

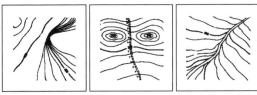

Fig. 27-35(b).   Fig. 27-36(b).   Fig. 27-37(b).

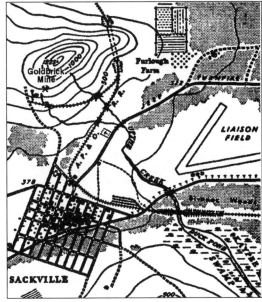

Fig. 27-38.

Figure 27-38 shows the map of Sackville and vicinity with contour lines on it. The map is becoming more complete. The contour lines show the shape of the ground. We can tell now that the land has a hill, with the ground sloping very gradually from its base toward the town and toward the airfield.

Measuring Distance

We have now put a map together and looked at many of its parts, so that at this point we can learn a good deal about a region by reading a map of that same region.

Distances on a map can be measured. The reason for this is that a map is a true picture of the land. Figure 27-39 is a picture of a bayonet, and we want to find out how long the blade is. If we know how much smaller the picture is than the real bayonet blade, we can find out how large the blade is. By measuring the blade on the picture in Figure 27-39, we find that it is two and one-half inches long in the picture.

Now suppose someone tells us that the picture is just one-quarter the size of the real bayonet. We can now figure out how long the blade is. If the picture is one-quarter the size of the real bayonet, the real bayonet is four times as large as the picture.

Let us put these figures to work. The picture of the blade is two and one-half inches long. The real

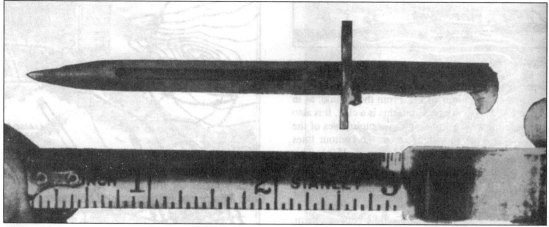

Fig. 27-39.

blade is four times as long; so the real blade is four times two and one-half inches, or ten inches long.

4 x 2 ½" = 10"

In the same way, a map always tells you how much smaller it is than the real land. A map can tell you this in two ways.

By Scale

One way is the same as we have just used on the picture of the bayonet.

A distance is measured on the map. The map tells you how much smaller this distance is than the actual ground by means of a number found in the bottom margin about in the center (Fig. 27-40). This number is called the scale.

The scale number may be shown in two ways, both meaning the same thing. It may be written as a fraction, 1/25,000, or it may be written 1:25,000. In either case, it is the same as saying that 1 inch on the map is equal to 25,000 inches on the ground, just as in our picture of the bayonet, where one inch on the picture was equal to four inches on the real bayonet. The scale of that picture of the bayonet would have been ¼ or 1:4.

Let us try this out on our map. We want to find out how long the right-hand runway of Liaison Field is. First, place an ordinary ruler along the runway, as in Figure 27-41.

It reads one inch. Now our scale reference says 1:25,000, or one inch on the map equals 25,000 inches on the field. So for each inch we have measured on the runway, we must substitute 25,000 inches. That means one times 25,000, or 25,000 inches.

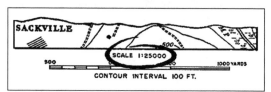

Fig. 27-40.

Fig. 27-41.

Distances on the ground are not usually given in inches. By the equivalents listed below, we can change inches into other units of measure.

Linear Measure:
1 foot (')=12 inches (")
1 yard = 3 feet = 36 inches
1 statute mile = 1,760 yards = 5,280 feet = 63,360 inches
1 meter = 39.37 inches = 1.094 yards
1 kilometer = 1,000 meters = 1,094 yards = .62 miles
1 mile = 1.61 kilometers

For example, let us divide 25,000 inches by 12, 36 and 39.37 and find out the number of feet, yards and meters in the runway.

25,000 divided by 12 equals 2,083 feet.
25,000 divided by 36 equals 694 yards.
25,000 divided by 39.37 equals 635 meters.

By Graphic Scale

Another method for finding distances is by use of the graphic scale. This method is even easier to use than the one we have just discussed. Just below the notation of scale, 1:25,000 are located several objects which look like rulers (Fig. 27-42). They are rulers, special kinds made just for that particular map. These rulers have already done your arithmetic for you.

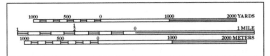

Fig. 27-42.

Let's look at our bayonet picture again with such a ruler and see how it works. The ruler is a special one made just for this particular picture. All we have to do is place this ruler on the picture of the bayonet with the zero at the tip of the blade, as in Figure 27-43. We can see at a glance that the real bayonet blade is ten inches long. The special ruler has shown us the real length of the bayonet.

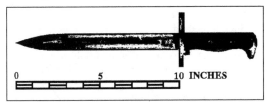

Fig. 27-43.

This special ruler is called a graphic scale and it is used with a map in the following manner:

A straight strip of paper is placed on the map alongside the airfield (Fig. 27-44(a)). We then place marks on the paper at both ends of the field. The paper is then placed beside our graphic scale on the map which shows how long the field really is (Fig. 27-44(b)).

There is another thing to notice about this scale. It has two parts (Fig. 27-45). From the zero mark to the right it reads in large numbers, 500 yards apart (Part A of Fig. 27-45). From the zero mark to the left

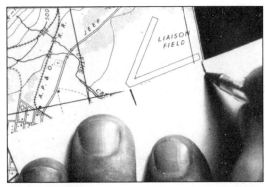

Fig. 27-44(a).

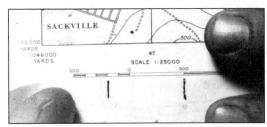

Fig. 27-44(b).

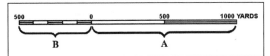

Fig. 27-45.

it breaks down this large distance into smaller distances (Part B of Fig. 27-45), 100 yards apart, so that we can measure more accurately.

For example, in Figure 27-44(b), the marks on our strip of paper are farther apart than the distance between the zero and the 500-yard mark on the graphic scale. If we place the right-hand mark at the 500-yard point on the graphic scale, the left-hand mark overlaps into the "B" part of the graphic scale. We see that it is about at the second mark to the left of the zero, or at the 200-yard mark. By adding 200 yards to the first 500 yards, we can say that the runway is about 700 yards long.

For purposes of allowing different units of measure to be used, three graphic scales are usually found on a map. These scales are usually measured in miles, yards and meters. Refer again to Figure 27-44(b), imagining, this time, that it measures meters, instead of yards. You would follow exactly the same procedure to determine the length of the field in meters that you followed to find its length in yards. The paper strip would be placed along the meter

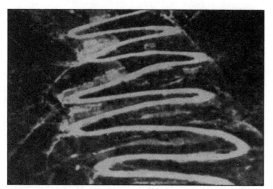

Fig. 27-46(a).

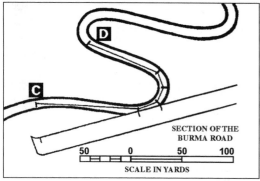

SECTION OF THE
BURMA ROAD

50   0   50   100

SCALE IN YARDS

Fig. 27-46(b).

scale, with the right-hand mark at the 500 meter point. The left-hand mark would again overlap into the "B" area. Add "B" to "A" and you have the total length of the field in meters.

In order to measure a curved or irregular line, for example, a section of the Burma Road (Fig. 27-46(a)), we divide the curved line of the road section, between C and D, into small straight sections (Fig. 27-46(b)). Then we lay the edge of a strip of paper on the tick marks, one after the other, adding each section to what we already have marked. We finish with a straight piece of paper with the total length of the curved road on it. We measure this with the graphic scale, in the same way as we measured the runway.

Watch the Fraction

It is important to be sure which is the larger scale, a 1:25,000 map or a 1:50,000 map. The answer is: the 1:25,000 map. The numbers are fractions and 1:25,000 of something is bigger than 1:50,000, just as ½ is larger than ¼. It is clear enough to us, but

these numbers are a little tricky, and it is easy to make mistakes and forget that the *larger the number* in the lower part of the fraction, the *smaller the scale* of the map. It may be easier to remember that a large scale map covers a small area and a small scale map covers a large area.

Determining Location

In a town or city, it is easy for us to tell someone that the church is at the corner of 6th Avenue and 3rd Street. If you made a date with someone to meet you at the church, you could be pretty sure that both you and your date would be able to find the place.

In the Marine Corps, however, we are faced with a different problem. We must be able to give to someone else the location of a lone tree in the middle of a large field, or a machine gun or sniper in a woods, or a guard along a stream. There are no streets in those places, but our maps have a system of letting us tell someone else where these points are.

The Grid System

This is done by placing on the face of the map a network of lines in the form of squares. These squares are somewhat like the blocks formed by the street system in a city. Any point on the map can be located in relation to these lines or "streets." The method of describing a location is practically the same as we use in town with real streets. The only differences are in the way we name our "streets" and in the way we "spell-out" the description.

Such a method is called a *grid reference system*, and the pattern formed by the lines is called a grid. There are several types of grids used on our maps. The most common is the Universal Transverse

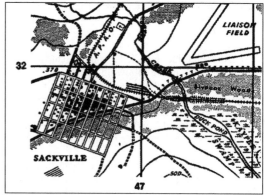

Fig. 27-47(a).

Mercator Grid. You will also find maps bearing British Grids. But don't get confused by this – as far as grid referencing is concerned, all grids look alike in that they are made up of lines forming squares. Figure 27-47(a) shows our map with a military grid on it.

The "streets" in a grid all have very simple names. The names are all *numbers*. When we use these numbers to locate a point on the map, we say we are giving a street address in a town. Before we can use these numbers, however, we must learn a few simple facts and rules.

Every *tenth line* is made heavier in weight. This is to help you find the line you are looking for.

Each grid line on the map has its own number. This number appears in the margin of the map at both ends of the line. It also appears within the map on the line itself.

On some maps, two large figures are used to identify a line; on others only one figure is used; in a few rare cases, three figures are used. The number of large figures depends upon the scale of the map and the grid used on the map. Don't be confused by all this, regardless of what scale map you have in your hands, use only the *large* figures to identify a grid line for referencing purposes, whether the number consists of 1, 2 or 3 large figures. By following this simple rule, you can never make a mistake.

To locate a point by the grid reference system is a simple matter. For example, let us work out, step-by-step, the grid reference for the letter "R" in the word "CREEK" on the map shown in Figure 27-47(a). Four steps are required. First, read the *large* figures labeling the first vertical grid line to the left of the point (47). Second, mentally divide the distance between "line 47" and "line 48" into 10 parts. (Fig. 27-47(b)). Estimate how many tenths (to the nearest tenth) there are between "line 47" and the letter "R,"

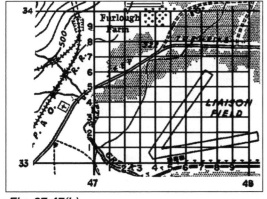

Fig. 27-47(b).

the point being referenced. The estimated tenths is 1. Third, read the *large* figures labeling the first *horizontal* grid line *below* the point (33). Fourth, mentally divide the distance between "line 33" and "line 34" into 10 parts. Estimate the nearest number of tenths between "line 33" and the point being referenced. In this case, the point falls almost on "line 33." The estimated tenths is 0.

The grid reference is written as a continuous number, 471330. Notice that the grid reference always has an even number of digits in it. If there is an uneven number of digits, someone has made an error in copying the grid reference number.

In working this sample grid reference, we were following a simple rule of map reading. The rule is "READ RIGHT UP" and this helps us to remember which number to read first in giving a grid reference or in following out a grid reference.

Suppose your platoon leader tells you to meet a patrol at a point which is referred to as 477336. Mentally break the number down to read 47-7-33-6. You look at the map (Fig. 27-47(b)) and read *right* until you come to the *vertical* grid line which is numbered 47. Still going to the *right* estimate 7 tenths of the distance between "line 47" and the next vertical line to the right, which, of course, is "line 48." Then from this point read *up* until you come to the horizontal line which is numbered 33. Still going *up* estimate 6 tenths of the distance between "line 33" and the next horizontal line above, which, of course, is "line 34." If you've followed these steps correctly, you will find the patrol sitting around waiting for you at the north end of the upper runway of Liaison Field.

If you understand everything that has been explained, you know how to give and you know how to follow a reference given on a map at the scales of 1:50,000, 1:25,000 or larger. Sometimes you can use our street system just to locate quickly a big, easily identified object. Just as you might tell a friend to meet you at the downtown library rather than give an exact address, you can identify a particular thing on a map by a general location. You just use the two streets that form the lower left hand corner of the grid square containing the thing you describe. For example, in Figure 27-47(a), if you say the duck pond (4732), the particular pond you are describing is known. Our READ RIGHT UP rule still applies, for you have moved right to line 47 which is part of the square around the pond, and up to line 32.

On some maps you will find some letters printed on the face of the map at the intersections of heavy grid lines, like in Figure 27-48.

These maps are at the scale of 1:100,000 or 1:250,000. The grid lines on such maps are usually

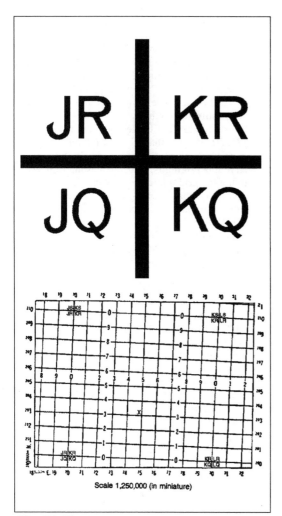

Fig. 27-48.

labeled with only one large number. (See Fig. 27-48.) If you have studied these instructions carefully, you will remember that a reference for a point taken from such a map is made up of four numbers, like 4733. But the reference is not complete until you add, in front of the number, the two letters which label the corners of the heavy lined square in which the point of reference falls. Thus, the grid reference for the point marked "X" in Figure 27-48 would be KR4733.

There are a few more things we should know about this map street system.

The grid lines are sometimes called *easting* lines or *northing*.

Instead of saying that the grid lines are up and down lines or vertical lines; we simply say the are easting grid lines; and instead of saying they are side to side lines or horizontal lines, we simply say they are northing grid lines. The numbers which made up a grid reference are sometimes called *coordinates*. You will also hear them referred to as grid coordinates. A coordinate is made up of an easting ordinate (read first) and a northing ordinate. The easting ordinate is the part of the number of the grid reference (we worked out above) made by reading *right*. It consists of the number in large type labeling the first vertical (easting) grid line to the left of the point and the estimated tenths from that line to the point. The northing ordinate is the part of the reference (the last part) which you made by reading *up*. It consists of the number in large type labeling the first horizontal (northing) grid line below the point of reference and the estimated tenths from that line to the point. In the reference 471330, which we figured out to be the identification of the letter "R" of the word "CREEK" on the map shown in Figure 27-47(a), the easting ordinate is 471 and the northing ordinate is 330. Another point is that the unit of measure and the distance between lines of the grid will not be the same on all military maps. The unit of measure may be either meters or yards, depending upon the grid appearing on the map.

The distance between grid lines, which we call the grid interval, may be either 1,000 units or 10,000 units, depending upon the scale of the map. Maps of the scales of 1:25,000 and 1:50,000 use a grid interval of 1,000 units. Maps at the scales of 1:100,000 and 1:250,000 use a grid interval of 10,000 units. A note appearing in the margin of each map will tell what unit of measure and what interval is used for the grid on the map. Read this note before you use the grid.

For example, Figure 27-47(a) has the 1,000-meter grid on it. We can tell from the map that the circle in town is about 1,000 meters from the first building alongside the airfield runway, because it is about the same distance as that between the two grid lines. This is another way to tell distances on a map, and you can use it instead of the graphic scale.

Use of the Compass

On the ground and on the map, the Marine Corps has an easy way to point out the direction of things. It is easy because the same idea is used wherever we are.

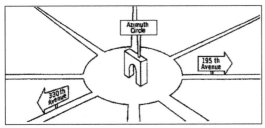

Fig. 27-49.

The idea is simply this: We suppose that wherever we happen to be at any given moment, we are in the center of a circle which has "avenues" running off in all directions, as in Figure 27-49.

What is An Azimuth?

The circle is marked off into 360 avenues. (See Fig. 27-50.) Each of the 360 spaces is called a

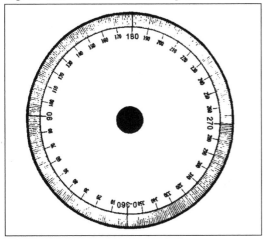

Fig. 27-50.

degree, and each avenue has a name called an azimuth. This azimuth is just a name for a direction line; each of these direction lines has a number, depending upon which of the 360 avenues it is.

We can march off on one of these avenues, or azimuths, starting at the center of the circle. The avenues all start where you are, whether you are in a jungle, on a hill or highway, just as with the man in Figure 27-51. The man has been told to go along the avenue marked "azimuth 60 degrees" (written as 60°) and he is pointing his finger at it. You can think of him in the center of the circle with 360 avenues or azimuths running out from him like the spokes from

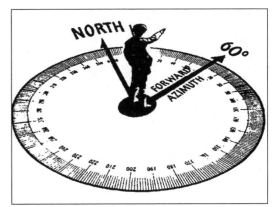

Fig. 27-51.

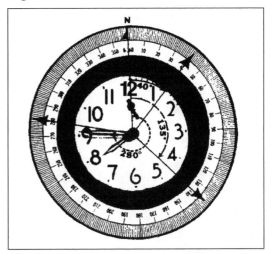

Fig. 27-52.

the hub of a wheel. To make it easier to locate an avenue, every 10th avenue is numbered.

There are two important things to remember about this circle of avenues.

1. The zero – 0 – avenue must always point north. In a moment we will talk about how to find north, but right now don't worry about it.

2. The avenues are numbered *clockwise*. That means we number them in the direction that we number hours on a clock. Figure 27-52 shows what we mean by clockwise direction.

With this knowledge, let's put this circle to work for us. You are told that there is a sniper in a tree in the orchard at Furlough Farm and, if you crawl up the creek to where the railroad crosses it at the foot of the hill, you can see the sniper's tree on an azimuth of exactly 60 degrees (60°). Figure 27-53 shows the situation.

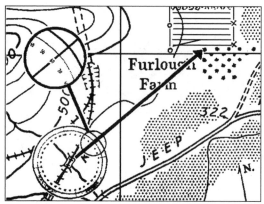

Fig. 27-53.

From the map, you find where the railroad cross-es the creek and go there. You remember that the center of the circle of azimuths is right where you are. The first thing to do is to point the zero mark on the circle at the north. (You will learn later how to do this with your compass). Now it is easy to see which tree is on the avenue or azimuth marked 60° on the circle, using the azimuth system of direction.

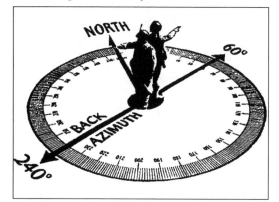

Fig. 27-54.

You take a bead on the sniper and knock him from the tree with your first shot. You move cautiously up to the tree, examine the sniper carefully and find that he is dead. You walk back to the railroad where it crosses the creek. Now what azimuth did you walk back on? Was it 60°? No, it wasn't. Look at Figure 27-54. It shows you that if you face in one direction you have a *forward azimuth*; if you face in the oppo-site direction, you have a *back azimuth*. The back azimuth is a straight line back through the center of the circle from the forward azimuth. Figure 27-55 shows you that at the railroad, with the zero of the

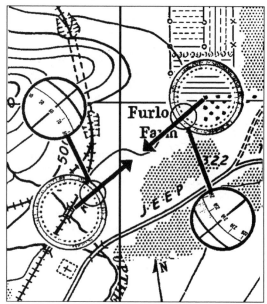

Fig. 27-55.

circle pointing north, the azimuth on the circle reads 60° from there to the tree; and that at the tree, with the zero of the circle still pointing north, the azimuth on the circle reads 240° from the tree to where the railroad crosses the creek.

The back azimuth of a line is its forward azimuth plus 180°, or if this sum is greater than 360°, the back azimuth is the forward azimuth minus 180°. For example, if the forward azimuth of a line is 60° , the back azimuth is 60° + 180° = 240°. If the forward azimuth of a line is 310° the back azimuth is 310° - 180° = 130°.

The back azimuth is an important thing to know about, because if you know how to use it, it will take you back to your starting point. For example, if you are sent on a mission at night to a point in strange country your back azimuth will show you the direc-tion in which you return.

The Lensatic Compass

We come now to the compass, that useful instru-ment which finds north for us and finds our azimuth for us. The compass has on it the circle of numbered avenues or azimuths which we have been talking about in the last few pages. In other words, the com-pass is our direction-finding tool and it has every-thing on it to help us find our way.

There are several types of compasses, but the one which we shall use here is called the *lensatic com-*

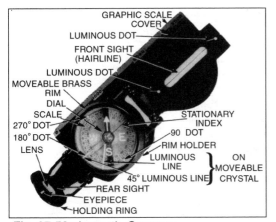

Fig. 27-56. Lensatic Compass.

GRAPHIC SCALE
COVER
LUMINOUS DOT
FRONT SIGHT
(HAIRLINE)
LUMINOUS DOT
MOVEABLE BRASS
RIM
DIAL
SCALE
270° DOT
180° DOT
LENS
STATIONARY
INDEX
90 DOT
RIM HOLDER
LUMINOUS
LINE
45° LUMINOUS LINE
ON
MOVEABLE
CRYSTAL
REAR SIGHT
EYEPIECE
HOLDING RING

pass. There are other types of compasses, but they all work on the same principle. If you understand how to use the lensatic compass, you will find it easy to learn to use the others.

Let us refer now to Figure 27-56 for a good look at the lensatic compass. The most important thing about the compass is that *no matter how you turn it, as long as you hold it level, the arrow always points in the direction of magnetic north.* It won't let you down if you remember one thing, *never use it near any metal object if you can help it.*

To ensure the proper functioning of your compass, keep a safe distance from the following metal objects:

* High-tension power lines ....55 meters
* Field gun, truck, or tank........................10 meters
* Telegraph or telephone
  wires and barbed wire ....10 meters
* Machine gun..2 meters
* Rifle ....1/2 meter
* Steel rim glasses ....1/3 meter

Besides the compass needle which points north, there is another important part of the compass. That is the numbered circle of avenues or azimuths right on the face of the dial. Everything on the compass is designed to help you line up your compass with things on the ground and on your map, and to help you read the azimuth numbers.

Compass Reading

Compass reading is easy, if it is done correctly. It is important to hold the compass correctly. Remember to point the compass in the general direction you want to go before you try to use it, and hold it level. Figure 27-57 shows the compass ready to be

Fig. 27-57.

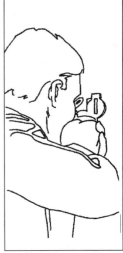

Fig. 27-58.

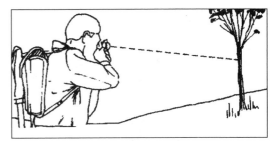

Fig. 27-59.

Fig. 27-60.

used in daytime sighting. Figure 27-58 shows how to hold the compass so that it is steady. Notice that it is held with the eyepiece close to the eye. Figure 27-59 shows how to line up a tree. You look at the tree through the slit in the eyepiece and through the slit in the cover with the hairline in it. The glass eyepiece is used only to read the azimuth numbers on the dial. It is there only so you will be able to glance down and read these numbers at the same time you line up an object with the compass. The view you get when you use the compass correctly is shown in Figure 27-60. The Marine here has lined up the tree in the compass sights and found that the tree is on an azimuth of 60 degrees.

Finding the Back Azimuth

With a compass you can see how easy it is to find a back azimuth. You can do it two ways.

First, read your back azimuth right off the dial by taking the number which is opposite the forward azimuth on a straight line through the center of the dial.

The second way is to sight from the point you have reached, back to the point you started from. The main difference between these two methods is that in the first, you do not have to be able to see your starting point in order to get the back azimuth.

Aligning the Map with the Ground

Before the compass and the map are ready to be used together, the map must be placed in a position so that the directions on the map are lined up with the directions on the ground. There are two ways to do this, one of them without the aid of a compass and the other with the help of a compass or of some other way of finding north. This act is called *orienting the map.*

By Inspection

The first method of lining up your map is called "by inspection," which simply means "looking at the ground with the map in front of you." This can be done when you have found objects on the ground which you recognize on your map and which you can see.

For example, in Figure 27-61(a) you hold your map so that the crossroads on it line up with the crossroads on the ground in front of you. Your map is then oriented.

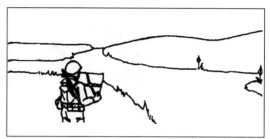

Fig. 27-61(a).

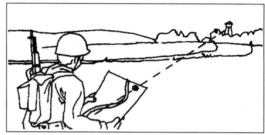

Fig. 27-61(b).

If the objects on the ground are not as simple as crossroads, such as in Figure 27-61(b), you can still line up your map by inspection.

You must know your approximate position on the map, and then turn your map in front of you until the distant object (the tower) on the ground lines up with the same object on the map and with your position on the map. The dashed line in Figure 27-61(b) illustrates this lining-up process. Your map is then oriented.

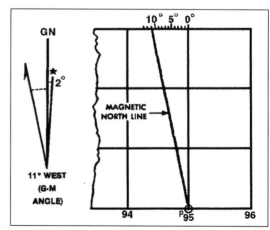

Fig. 27-62(a).   Fig.27-62(b)

By Compass

Another way to line up your map is by using the compass. The compass needle points to magnetic north. The difference between magnetic north, grid north and true north is shown on your map by a declination diagram. (See Fig. 27-62(a).)

The line with the half arrowhead represents *magnetic north*. The "GN" is *grid north*, parallel to the vertical grid lines. (You have probably already noticed that maps such as we have been studying are printed with north toward the top of the sheet.) The third line on the declination diagram represents *true north* and is marked with a star. The three lines are not always in the same position shown in Figure 27-62(a). The position of these three lines, in relation to each other, will vary on maps in different parts of the world.

The angle between grid north and magnetic north is called the G-M (grid-magnetic) angle. The numerical value of this angle is printed with the declination diagram, as in Figure 27-62(a).

There are two ways to use this angle and a compass to orient your map with the ground.

To use the first method, you must draw the magnetic north line on your map. This is easily done with most new maps where you find at the top margin a scale marked off in degrees and at the bottom a circle marked "P" called the pivot point as in Figure 27-62(b). Read the number of degrees of the G-M angle on the declination diagram. Then draw a line from the pivot point to that number of degrees on the scale.

In Figure 27-62(b), the magnetic north line is drawn to the 11° mark, the amount of the G-M angle on the declination diagram shown in Figure 27-62(a).

Before you use a map, ask your platoon leader to see that the magnetic north line you have drawn is correct. Do not try to draw the magnetic north line by extending the magnetic north prong on the declination diagram. The diagram may be exaggerated, especially if the angles are very small. Some maps have a caution printed beside the declination diagram: *Use only to obtain numerical values.*

With the magnetic north line drawn in, lay your map on a flat surface with the top pointing to the general direction of north. Open your compass and place it on the map so the edge of the meter scale lines up with the magnetic north line (Fig. 27-63). Turn the map until the compass needle lies under the stationary index. The map is then oriented.

If your map does not have a pivot point and scale, or if it is folded so as to cover the magnetic north line, you can use the compass another way to orient the map with the ground. Lay your map on a flat surface as in the first method. Place the open compass so that the edge of the meter scale lies on top of a vertical grid line. (See Fig. 27-64.) Read the G-M angle on the declination diagram and note whether magnetic north is right or left of grid north. Turn the map until the compass needle points to the right or left of the stationary index by the amount of the G-M angle.

Fig. 27-63.

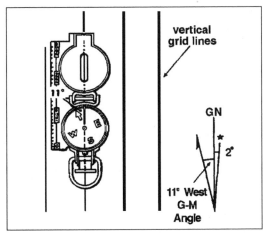

Fig. 27-64.

363

If the declination diagram shows magnetic north right of grid north, then the map should be turned until the compass needle points right of the vertical grid line. In Figure 27-64, the declination diagram shows an 11° G-M angle, with magnetic north left of grid north. The map in the illustration is oriented because the compass needle points 11° to the left of the grid line.

Without a Compass

Even without a compass, however, you can orient your map with a north line. There are ways to find north without a compass.

- During daylight hours you can determine direction without the aid of a compass by the *Shadow Tip Method*. Find a fairly straight stick about three feet long and push it into the ground, as shown in Figure 27-65(a). Mark the tip of the shadow with a small rock. (See Fig. 27-65(b).) then wait 10 to 15 minutes. The shadow will have moved during this time; so you place another rock

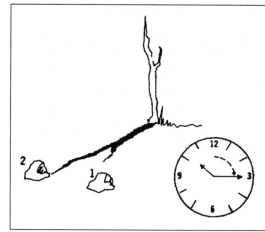

Fig. 27-65(c).

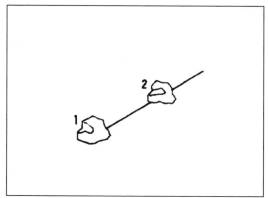

Fig. 27-65(d).

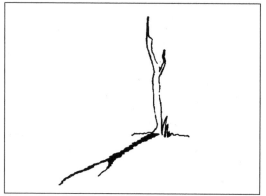

Fig. 27-65(a).

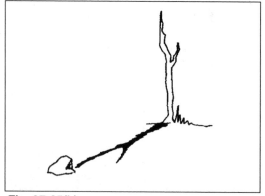

Fig. 27-65(b).

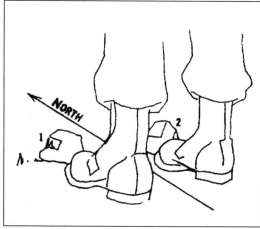

Fig. 27-65(e).

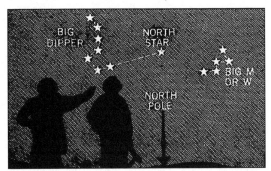

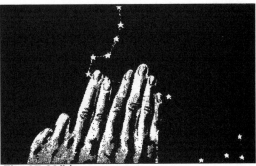

Fig. 27-66(a).

Fig. 27-66(b).

at the tip of the second shadow as shown in Figure 27-65(c). You then draw a line from the first rock to and beyond the second rock. (See Fig. 27-65(d).) Now stand with the toe of your left foot at the first rock and the toe of your right foot at the second rock as shown in Figure 27-65(e). You are now facing north.

- At night, in the Northern Hemisphere, we find north without a compass by means of the stars. In the Northern Hemisphere, one way to use the stars is to find the Big Dipper. The Big Dipper is made up of seven fairly bright stars in the shape of a dipper with a long curved handle, as in Figure 27-66(a). If you can see the Big Dipper, use as pointers the two stars which form the side of the cup farthest from the handle. These point in the direction toward which you would pour from the dipper. These pointers aim at a bright star which is about five times the distance between the two stars of the Dipper cup. This bright star is the North Star and is directly over the North Pole. If you hold a finger away from your eyes so it just fits between the two pointers, and then, keeping your hand the same distance from your eyes, measure five finger-widths from the end pointer, your farthest finger will just touch the north star. (See Fig. 27-66(b).) Sometimes, however, you cannot see the Big Dipper, although you may be able to see other stars. In that case we use a star pattern called the Big "W" or the big "M." Look at it in Figure 27-66(a). Notice that it is on the other side of and about the same distance from the North Star as the Big Dipper. The top of the "W" is open in the direction of the North Star. On a clear night you will always be able to see, in the Northern Hemisphere, either the Big Dipper or

the Big "W." Sometimes you will be able to see both. In either case, you can find the North Star. The Big Dipper and the Big "W" appear to rotate around the North Star during the night. Only occasionally are they in just the positions shown in Figures 27-66(a) and (b). Their position in relation to the North Star and to each other does not change.

- In the Southern Hemisphere you can find true south by relation to the Southern Cross. Two bright pointer stars in the vicinity of the Southern Cross serve as locators to help pick up the right group of stars. (See Fig. 27-67.) There are five stars in the Southern Cross. The outer four are fairly bright and form a cross. Imagine this cross as the frame of a kite. Put a straight tail on the kite four and one-half times as long as the length of the kite itself. Using finger-widths for a measuring stick, as with the Big Dipper in Figure 27-66(b), the end of this tail will be close to a position directly over the South Pole. (See Fig. 27-67.) Usually you won't be able to see a star in that

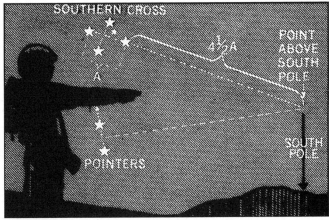

Fig. 27-67.

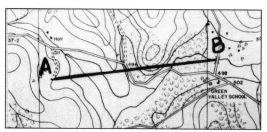

Fig. 27-68(a).

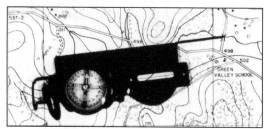

Fig. 27-68(b).

immediate vicinity, because there is no bright star that can be seen directly above the South Pole.

- Another way to find the approximate location of the South Pole without measuring the four and one-half finger-width distance along the kite tail of the Southern Cross is to imagine a straight line perpendicular to the center of a line between the pointers. This perpendicular line intersects the extension of the Southern Cross kite tail. The point of intersection is approximately above the South Pole. This method is shown in Figure 27-67. The Southern Cross and pointers appear to rotate around the South Pole during the night, just as the Big Dipper and the Big "W" do in the northern sky.

The Map and Compass at Work

We know enough now about the compass and the map to start to use them together in a practical way.

Azimuth on the Map

We have learned how to find the azimuth of an objective on the ground by sighting with the compass. Now we come to the problem of learning to find the azimuth of something on a map.

For example, how do you find what the azimuth is from the house (point A) to the bridge (point B) in

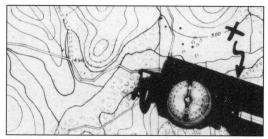

Fig. 27-69.

Figure 27-68(a)? First, you draw a line lightly on your map between the house and the bridge. Next, you orient your map using the magnetic line and your compass as explained earlier in the chapter. Then lay your compass on the map so that the edge of the graphic scale and the pencil line coincide. You read the azimuth 84° on the compass (Fig. 27-68(b)), and you have your answer.

Suppose that you wanted to show on the map that a machine gun was on the path at an azimuth of 105° from the bridge. To find the correct point on the map, you would proceed as follows: First, orient your map; then lay your compass so that the "0" indicator on the graphic scale is directly over the bridge. (See Fig. 27-69.) Pivot the compass, keeping the "0" indicator at the bridge until the stationary index lines up with the 105° on the dial. Draw a line along the edge of the graphic scale from the bridge until it crosses the path. The machine gun is located where the line crosses the path ("X" in Figure 27-69).

Finding Your Location (Resection)

Many times you will need to know accurately your location on a map. If your location is some-

Fig. 27-70(a).

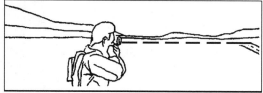

Fig. 27-70(b).

where between the airfield and the creek on the Sackville map, to find your exact location:

- Orient your map with a compass.
- Find two things on the ground in front of you which you can also find on your map.
- With your compass, take an azimuth on a point, for example, the building at the mine. Sight through the compass, line up the building with the hairline in the compass (Fig. 27-70(a)) and read the azimuth through the glass eyepiece (305°).
- Find the back azimuth by subtracting 180° from 305° (305° - 180° = 125°).
- Lay your compass on your map, with the "0" indicator on the graphic scale directly over the building at the mine. (See Fig. 27-71(a).) Then pivot the compass slowly until 125° on the dial lines up with the stationary index. Draw a line along the edge of the graphic scale.
- You are somewhere along this line on your map, but you still need to know exactly where. Repeat the procedure with a second point, for example, the tip of the left-hand runway of the airfield. (See Fig. 27-70(b).) A forward azimuth reading shows it to be 67°. Lay the "0" indicator of the graphic scale directly over the tip of the runway on your oriented map and line up the stationary index with 247° (67° + 180° = 247°).
- Draw your line along the graphic scale until it crosses the first line you drew. The two lines cross at your exact location. (See Fig. 27-71(b).)

Finding an Objective

Suppose you are somewhere southeast of Sackville and your platoon leader tells you to go to a

Fig. 27-71(a).

Fig. 27-71(b).

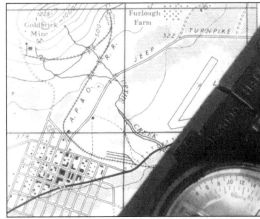

Fig. 27-72.

Fig. 27-73(a).   **Fig. 27-73(b).**

Fig. 27-73(c).

certain bridge, points out the bridge on the map and draws a line on the map from your position to the bridge. By laying your compass on the oriented map, you find that the bridge is on an azimuth of 51° from where you are. (See Fig. 27-72.) Your job is to get to the bridge. That means that you must march along the azimuth.

First you take your compass, sight on an azimuth of 51°, and discover that you cannot see the bridge at all from where you are. You know, however, that it is somewhere up ahead, along that line on which you

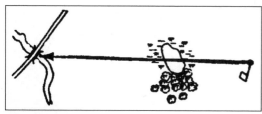

Fig. 27-74(a).

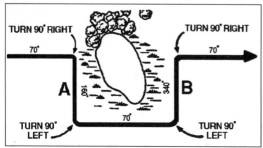

Fig. 27-74(b).

are sighting. You can see the edge of the woods (Fig. 27-73(a)) on your line of sight. So you head for the edge of the woods (Fig. 27-73(b)), and when you get there you find a bridge in front of you. (See Fig. 27-73(c).) If it so happened that you could not see the bridge from the edge of the woods, you would do the same thing again, picking out a tree, fence or other object along your line of march, until you finally reached a point where you could see the bridge.

We cannot always march in a straight line, because we may encounter obstacles such as the pond in Figure 27-74(a). The method for detouring around an obstacle is shown in Figure 27-74(b). A very important rule to remember is that when you make a right turn, you add the number of degrees in the turn to your azimuth. When you make a left turn, you subtract the number of degrees in the turn from your azimuth.

You begin your march on an azimuth of 70°. After making a 90° right turn, you are marching on an azimuth of 160° (70° + 90° = 160°).

You count your paces as you march along line "A" in Figure 27-74(b), because you must march the same distance on line "B" to arrive back on your original line of march. When you have gone far enough along line "A" to clear the pond, you make a 90° left turn and you are again marching on an azimuth of 70° (160° - 90° = 70°). When you have gone far enough to clear the south end of the pond, you make another 90° left turn and you are marching on an azimuth of 340° (70° - 90° = -20°). We do not use negative azimuths in the Marine Corps, so you

must subtract your negative azimuth from the total degrees in a circle to obtain the correct azimuth (360° - 20° = 340°).

You now march on line "B" the same number of paces you marched on line "A," and when you make a 90° right turn, you are on your original line of march on an azimuth of 70° (340° + 90° = 430°). We do not use azimuths larger than 360° in the Marine Corps, so to obtain the correct azimuth, you must subtract the total degrees in a circle from 430° (430° - 360° = 70°).

The Compass at Night

The lensatic compass has two glass faces, one under the other. The top glass face rotates, the under one does not. The top glass rotates with a clicking sound; each click means it has turned 3°. On the top glass are two lines visible at night. One line is about three times as long as the other. These lines are 45° apart.

On the under, or stationary glass face, are three luminous dots and a black line (stationary index). Each of these marks is 90° from the other, or one-quarter of the way around the face of the dial. On the compass dial itself, the letters E, S, W and the arrow for North are luminous. On the inside cover, lined up with the hairline sight, are two more luminous dots. Beneath the dial on the inside of the case is a fixed luminous sector which permits reading azimuths at night.

To follow an azimuth accurately at night, we must be able to pick up aiming points ahead of us, just as we do in the daytime. At night, this is not easy to do. You cannot see very far ahead, therefore, your aiming points will be very near you. If it is so dark that you cannot find an aiming point, send another Marine out a little ahead of you. Direct him to move either to the right or left, until he is in your line of sight. Be sure he does not move until you have reached him. Then do the same thing over again until you find some aiming point in the area ahead or you reach your objective.

Usually, it is not necessary to follow a given azimuth exactly. In combat, the need to move quickly will not always allow the use of this time-consuming method. If it is impractical to use the sights on your compass, we have an easy way to follow an approximate azimuth:

• Turn the movable glass until the long luminous line is directly over the black line (stationary index) on the lower fixed glass, as in Figure 27-75(a).

Fig. 27-75(a).

Fig. 27-75(b).

- Turn the movable glass 17 clicks to the left (counterclockwise). This is a total of 51° (3° per click).
- Rotate the whole compass until the North arrow is directly under the long luminous line on the movable glass, as in Figure 27-75(b). Your compass is now set on an azimuth of 51°.

Now all you have to do to march on this azimuth in the darkness is to keep the North arrow under the long luminous line, and follow the line formed by the stationary index on the lower fixed glass and the two luminous dots on the cover.

Notice the way the compass is held in Figure 27-76. You do not aim through the eyepiece as before. You simply point the compass in the direction you are going by lining up the long luminous line on the upper glass and the North arrow. Then line yourself up with the two luminous dots on the cover and the stationary index and pick out an aiming point that falls on an extension of that line. You walk to your aiming point and repeat the process until you reach your objective.

Because all metal objects exert a magnetic pull on the needle of your compass (causing it to move), carry only essential metallic objects with you on a

Fig. 27-76.

compass march. Keep all metallic objects far enough from the compass so that they will not cause the needle to move from magnetic North.

Use Your Map and Compass

When you are sent out on a reconnaissance or scouting assignment you will find information which must be sent back to your commander. That is your mission. It is necessary, then, to know how to send back this information.

Name Things Exactly

First, you must know the names of things on the land. It is not necessary to know what names things are called by, until you have to tell someone else

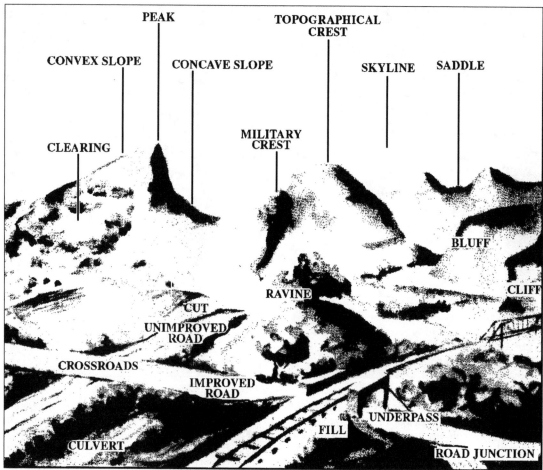

CLEARING **CONVEX SLOPE** **PEAK** **CONCAVE SLOPE** **TOPOGRAPHICAL CREST** **MILITARY CREST** **SKYLINE** **SADDLE** **BLUFF** **RAVINE** **CLIFF** **CUT** **UNIMPROVED ROAD** **CROSSROADS** **IMPROVED ROAD** **UNDERPASS** **FILL** **CULVERT** **ROAD JUNCTION**

Fig. 27-77.

about them. Then it is very important that you know exactly what the names of land forms are. Figure 27-77 is a sketch showing the names of various land forms. Learn these names. It is important that you are able to describe things accurately and in the right words, so that the Marines you work with can understand what you mean.

The Overlay

An overlay is used to send back information obtained by reconnaissance. An overlay is simply a tracing, on a plain piece of transparent paper, of a section of a map. To make an overlay, lay a piece of transparent paper over the section of the map you are interested in and draw on it the corners of the grid

squares, as in Figure 27-78. These crosses are called register marks, and they are put on the overlay to show whoever uses it just where to place it on their map. The register marks should be numbered with the numbers of the grid lines, so that whoever uses the overly will know exactly where to place it.

Once the register marks are on the overlay, you need only to indicate on it the objects you are concerned with. Write your message right on the overlay with the usual information that is commonly put on ordinary written messages.

The person who gets the overlay places it on his map so that the register marks line up on the grid lines, and the message can be read.

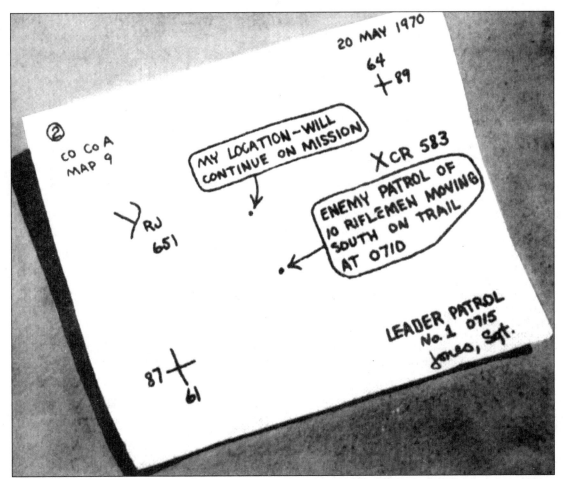

Fig. 27-78.

Fig. 27-79.

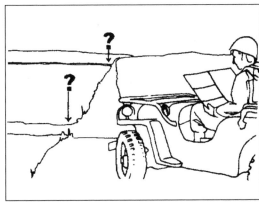

Fig. 27-80.

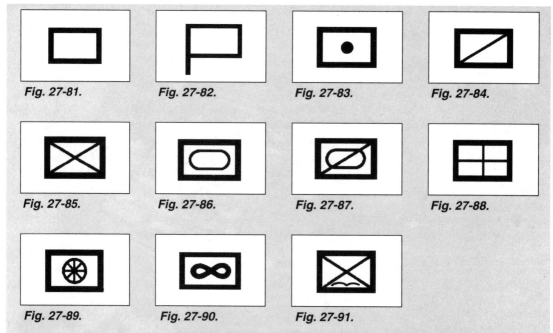

Fig. 27-81. Fig. 27-82. Fig. 27-83. Fig. 27-84.

Fig. 27-85. Fig. 27-86. Fig. 27-87. Fig. 27-88.

Fig. 27-89. Fig. 27-90. Fig. 27-91.

81-Unit; 82-Command Post; 83-Field Artillery; 84-Reconnaissance; 85-Infantry; 86-Armored; 87-Mechanized Infantry; 88-Medical Department; 89-Transportation Corps; 90-Air Forces; 91-Airborne Infantry.

On the Road

It is very easy to get lost when you drive along a highway, even in the United States where there are all kinds of signs and directions for the use of the motorist. It is even easier to lose your way in a strange country and in wartime. Maps and compasses are important instruments to keep you on the right road.

You must keep your map oriented, preferably by inspection, if you are to find the right roads on your map (Fig. 27-79).

The mileage gauge is especially important in a case like Figure 27-80. Here the driver finds two left intersections on the road, a mile apart. The map is out of date and shows just one road. Which one should the driver take? By measuring the distance from the starting point to the junction on the map, the driver can find out how far he should have traveled before taking the turn. Now if he had been careful enough to watch the mileage gauge before starting on the trip, he would be able to figure out how far he had come and he would know which of the two roads was the right one. If he had failed to note the mileage gauge, he would not know which road to take.

Military Symbols on the Map

When a military organization moves onto the land, it also moves onto the map of that land. There are map symbols for military activities. The symbols for different kinds of military units are not only very simple, but they are connected with the nature of the military activity itself.

Unit Symbols

The basic symbol for a military unit is a rectangle (Figure 27-81). We put a little staff on the rectangle (Figure 27-82) and make a flag out of it; that means a command post or headquarters. The flag represents the unit commander's flag. Also see Figures 27-83 through 27-91.

Symbols are also used to show the size of a military unit:

Unit	Symbol
Squad	•
Section	••
Platoon	•••
Detachment	•••
Company, troop, battery or air flight	I
Battalion, calvary squadron or air squadron	II
Regiment, group or air group	III
Brigade, combat command, regimental combat team or air wing	X
Division or Air Division	XX
Corps	XXX
Army or Air Force	XXXX
Army Group or Air Command	XXXXX

Fig. 27-92.   **Fig. 27-93.**

Fig. 27-92 shows a squad while Figure 27-93 shows a company.

Arms Abbreviations

Some arms are shown simply by abbreviation of their full titles

Military Police

Corps of Engineers (Revolved "E")

Using Unit Symbols

We combine symbols and abbreviations to indicate a specific unit. The following diagram shows the method used:

Sub Unit	Type of Unit	Parent Unit

(Caliber) (Type) of weapons

Examples

This is a troop unit

This makes it infantry

This makes it a platoon of infantry

This makes it a platoon in the 1st Marine Regiment

This makes it a platoon in Company A, 1st Marines

This makes it 2d platoon in Company A, 1st Marines

This is an observation post

This makes it artillery

This makes it an observation post of B Battery

Activity Symbols

The symbol for an observation post is a triangle and we indicate whose observation post it is in the same manner we use with the rectangle. For example, the symbol for the observation post of "A" Battery, 2d Artillery Regiment is shown in Figure 27-94. Supply points are indicated by circles. Inside the circles, other symbols show what kind of supplies are there. In Figure 27-95, the crescent (moon shape) means rations, because food and water are usually brought up during the night for the next day; the fun-

Fig. 27-94.

Fig. 27-95.

Fig. 27-96.

Fig. 27-97.

nel stands for gasoline and oil; and the shell stands for ammunition.

Figure 27-96 shows the symbol for areas where chemical agents have been used.

To show a unit defense area, we draw a line around it with the symbol for whatever size unit it is. A squad defense area is shown as a line with the squad symbol in it (Fig. 27-97).

Other Symbols

The following is a selected list of other military symbols:

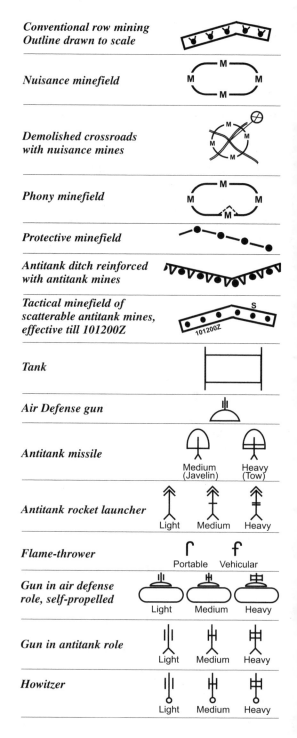

Antitank mine with antihandling device	
Directional mine Arrow points in the direction of main effect	
Mine cluster	
Mine, type unspecified	
A planned minefield Unspecified mines	
Completed minefield Unspecified mines	
Scatterable minefield Date-time groups (DTG) are used for self-destruct mines	
Conventional minefield Thickened with scatterable mines	

Conventional row mining Outline drawn to scale	
Nuisance minefield	
Demolished crossroads with nuisance mines	
Phony minefield	
Protective minefield	
Antitank ditch reinforced with antitank mines	
Tactical minefield of scatterable antitank mines, effective till 101200Z	
Tank	
Air Defense gun	
Antitank missile	Medium (Javelin) / Heavy (Tow)
Antitank rocket launcher	Light / Medium / Heavy
Flame-thrower	Portable / Vehicular
Gun in air defense role, self-propelled	Light / Medium / Heavy
Gun in antitank role	Light / Medium / Heavy
Howitzer	Light / Medium / Heavy

Note: A more accurate method of indicating the size of a known weapon is by writing the caliber of the weapon to the right of the basic symbol.

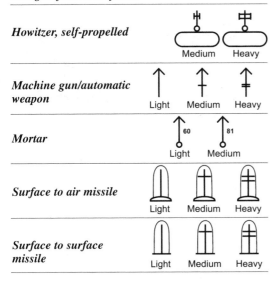

Howitzer, self-propelled	Medium	Heavy
Machine gun/automatic weapon	Light Medium Heavy	
Mortar	Light 60	Medium 81
Surface to air missile	Light Medium Heavy	
Surface to surface missile	Light Medium Heavy	

Color of Symbols

On military situation or operation maps, the enemy troops and installations are shown in red while friendly troops and installations are shown in blue. (Friendly troops may also be indicated by a single black line, with double lines indicating the enemy.)

Take Care of Your Map

In the field, a map is as important as your weapons. Take good care of it. Fold it small enough to slip into your shirt to protect it from rain. Fold it with face outward so that you can read parts of it without unfolding the whole map. The accordion fold (Fig. 27-98) makes it easy to use.

When you mark your map, mark it lightly. It may have to last you a long while. Many marks on it will confuse you. Erasures of heavy lines will smear it and make it difficult to read.

Covering your map with contact paper protects it from water damage. You can also write on it with a grease pencil.

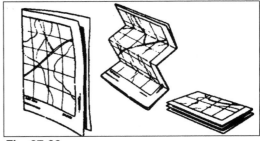

Fig. 27-98.

Chapter Twenty-Eight

Combat Formations and Signals

The close order drill formations that Marines use are not suitable for combat. On the battlefield, troops must move and fight in formations which provide for dispersion, teamwork and the ability to fire at the enemy without hitting other Marines.

Combat formations are designed to group individuals into effective fighting teams that can move up to and assault an enemy position. Both close and extended formations are used, depending upon the situation, terrain and enemy activity. Movement into a formation or from one formation to another is executed on the signals or commands of fire team and squad leaders.

This chapter explains and illustrates the various combat formations used by Marines. Also pictured and explained are the arm and hand signals used in the execution of combat formations.

Fire Team Combat Formations

There are four combat formations for the fire team: COLUMN, WEDGE, SKIRMISHERS RIGHT (LEFT) and ECHELON RIGHT (LEFT).

The Column formation permits rapid, easily controlled movement and permits fire and maneuver to the flanks. It is vulnerable to enemy fire from the front. The ability to fire to the front from the COLUMN formation is limited.

The Wedge formation is easily controlled, provides good all around security and permits fire and maneuver to both the front and the flanks.

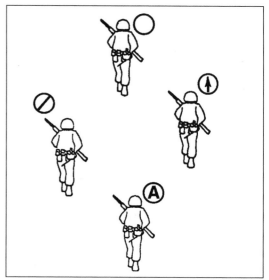

Column

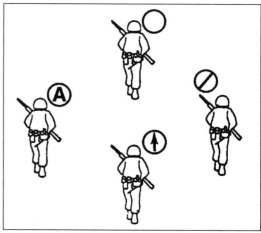

Wedge

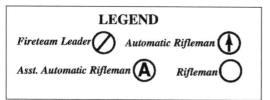

LEGEND

Fireteam Leader ⊘   *Automatic Rifleman* ⬆

Asst. Automatic Rifleman Ⓐ   *Rifleman* ◯

376

Skirmishers (L)

Skirmishers (R)

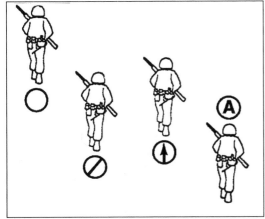
Echelon (R)

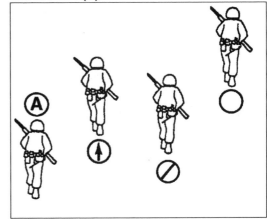
Echelon (L)

Skirmishers Right (Left) permits maximum fire power to the front but is a difficult formation to control. The ability to fire to the flanks is very limited.

Echelon Right (Left) is similar to skirmishers right and left except that one flank is angled to the rear (right or left) permitting fire to the front and one flank. It is a difficult formation to control, and is open to enemy fire from the flank that is not echeloned or angled back.

Squad Combat Formations

There are five combat formations for the squad: SQUAD COLUMN, SQUAD WEDGE, SQUAD LINE, SQUAD ECHELON RIGHT (LEFT) and SQUAD VEE. The characteristics of the first four squad formations correspond generally to those of the fire team. There is no fire team formation similar to those of the SQUAD VEE, which is arranged with two fire teams forward and one fire team back in a "V" formation. The principal difference is that the individual Marine is the maneuver element of the fire team, while the fire team is the maneuver element of the squad.

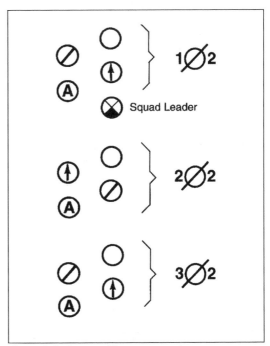
Squad Column - Fire team column

377

Squad Column

The squad column, with fire teams arranged in succession one behind the other, is used to maintain speed and control when moving through thick terrain such as a jungle or woods, during darkness or other periods of reduced visibility and along roads, trails or narrow routes of advance. Although easily controlled, it is open to enemy fire from the front and permits only a limited amount of fire to be returned to the front. The SQUAD COLUMN does favor fire and maneuver to the flanks.

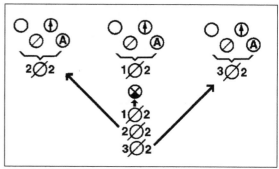

Squad Line - Fire team skirmishers

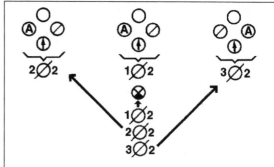

Squad Line - Fire team wedge

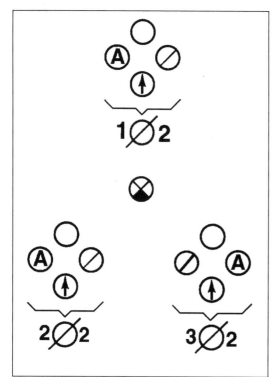

Squad Wedge - Fire team wedge

Squad Wedge

The squad wedge, with one fire team forward and two fire teams back, is normally used when the enemy situation is generally unknown and the terrain and visibility require dispersion. Characteristics of the SQUAD WEDGE are ease of control, all around security and ability to fire and maneuver to both the front and flanks.

Squad Line

The Squad line places all three fire teams abreast or on line and is normally used in the assault or for rapid crossing of an open area exposed to hostile automatic weapons or artillery fire. The SQUAD LINE is difficult to control and maneuver and is open to fire from the flanks. The ability to return fire to the flanks is limited. Maximum fire power is concentrated to the front, and the formation is less vulnerable to enemy fire from that direction.

Squad Echelon Right (Left)

The squad echelon right (left) with fire teams echeloned or angled to the rear (right or left) is used to protect an open or exposed flank. It is a difficult formation to control, and is open to enemy fire from the flank that is not echeloned. This formation can concentrate maximum fire power to the front and the flank that is echeloned or angled to the rear.

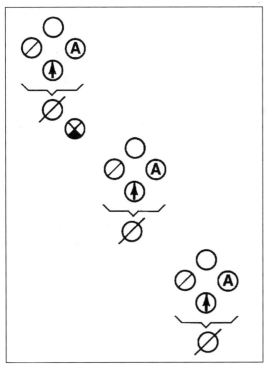

Squad Echelon - Fire team wedge

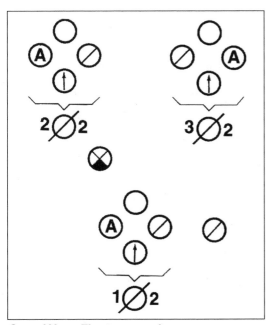

Squad Vee - Fire team wedge

Squad Vee

The squad vee has the same characteristics of control, all around security and ability to fire and maneuver to the front and flanks as the squad wedge. Arranged with two fire teams forward and one back, it is used when the enemy is located to the front and the strength and location are generally known. It may also be used when crossing large open areas. The squad vee facilitates movement into the squad line for the assault.

Positions of Individuals

The accompanying illustrations show the disposition of individuals in all of the basic combat formations.

Squad leaders place themselves within the squad formation where they can best exercise control. The fire team leaders place themselves in the designated formations or as directed by the squad leader. Other members of the squad take their appropriate positions based on the location of the fire team leader or as they direct.

The distance between Marines varies within a formation, depending on visibility and terrain. While maximum dispersion is desirable to reduce vulnerability to direct and indirect fires, effective control must be maintained.

Use of Formations

Initial formations are usually ordered by the platoon commander for the squads and by the squad leader for the fire teams. Thereafter, each leader will normally determine the formation for the unit depending on the mission, situation and terrain. The squad and the fire teams do not have to be in the same formations. For example, the squad may be on LINE with the fire teams in WEDGE formation. Any other combination appropriate to the mission, situation and terrain may be used.

Formations should be changed by the squad leader or fire team leaders as often as necessary to reduce casualties from enemy fire, to present a less vulnerable target, or to cross difficult or exposed terrain.

Normally, all changes in formation are executed on the the double.

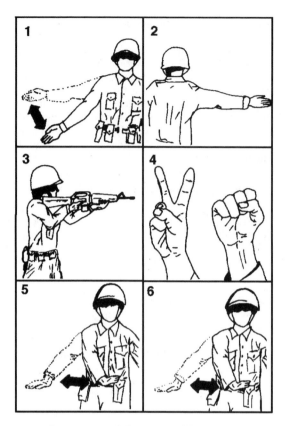

Arm and Hand Signals

Distance and noise on the battlefield often make voice commands completely ineffective. For this reason, visual signals, using the arms and hands are used to enable leaders to give commands to units.

Arm and hand signals are the same as a voice order or command, and leaders must position themselves so the signals can be seen. All arm and hand signals are executed with precision. The arm and hand signals commonly used to control and maneuver a fire team or squad are pictured and explained above and on the following pages.

1. DECREASE SPEED – Extend the arm horizontally sideward, palm to the front, and wave arm downward several times, keeping the arm straight. Arm does not move above the horizontal.

2. CHANGE DIRECTION – or COLUMN (RIGHT/LEFT) – Extend arm horizontally to the side, palm to the front.

3. ENEMY IN SIGHT – Hold the rifle horizontally, with the stock in the shoulder, the muzzle pointing in the direction of the enemy.

4. RANGE – Extend the arm fully toward leader or marine for whom the signal is intended with fist closed. Open the fist exposing one finger for each 100 meters of range.

5. COMMENCE FIRING – Extend the arm in front of the body, hip high, palm down, and move it through a wide horizontal arc several times.

6. FIRE FASTER – Execute rapidly the signal COMMENCE FIRING. For machine guns, a change to the higher rate of fire is prescribed.

7. FIRE SLOWER – Execute slowly the signal COMMENCE FIRING. For machine guns, a change to the next lower rate of fire is required.

8. CEASE FIRING – Raise the hand in front of the forehead, palm to the front, and swing the hand and forearm up and down several times in front of the face.

9. ASSEMBLE – Raise the hand vertically to the full extent of the arm, fingers extended and joined, palm to the front, and wave in large horizontal circles with the arm and hand.

10. FORM COLUMN – Raise either arm to the vertical position. Drop the arm to the rear, describ-

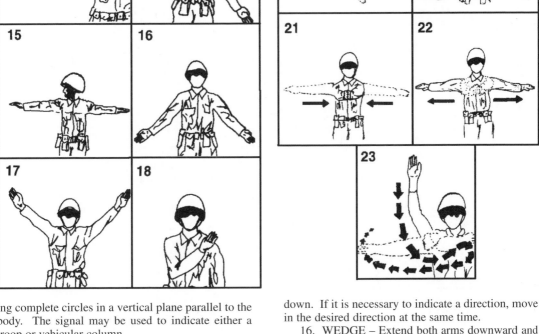

ing complete circles in a vertical plane parallel to the body. The signal may be used to indicate either a troop or vehicular column.

11. ARE YOU READY? – Extend the arm toward the leader for whom the signal is intended, hand raised, fingers extended and joined, then raise arm slightly above horizontal, palm facing outward.

12. I AM READY – Execute the signal ARE YOU READY.

13. SHIFT – Raise the hand that is on the side toward the new direction across the body, palm to the front; then swing the arm in a horizontal arc, extending the arm and hand to the point in the new direction.

14. ECHELON RIGHT (LEFT) – Face the unit being signaled and extend one arm 45° below the horizontal, palm to the front. The lower arm indicates the direction of the echelon. Supplementary commands may be given to ensure prompt and proper execution.

15. AS SKIRMISHERS (FIRE TEAM); LINE FORMATION (SQUAD) – Raise both arms laterally until horizontal, arms and hands extended, palms

down. If it is necessary to indicate a direction, move in the desired direction at the same time.

16. WEDGE – Extend both arms downward and to the side at an angle of 45° below the horizontal, palms to the front.

17. VEE – Extend arms at an angle of 45° above the horizontal forming the letter "V" with arms and torso.

18. FIRE TEAM – The right arm should be placed diagonally across the chest.

19. SQUAD – Extend the hand and arm toward the squad leader, palm of the hand down; distinctly move the hand up and down several times from the wrist, holding the arm steady.

20. PLATOON – Extend both arms forward, palms of the hands down, toward the leader or unit for whom the signal is intended and describe large vertical circles with the hands.

21. CLOSE UP – Start signal with both arms extended sideward, palms forward, and bring palms together in front of the body momentarily. When repetition of the signal is necessary, the arms are returned to the starting position by movement along the front of the body.

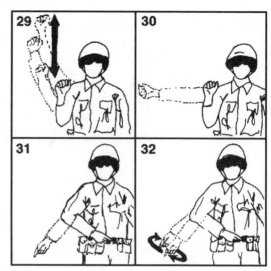

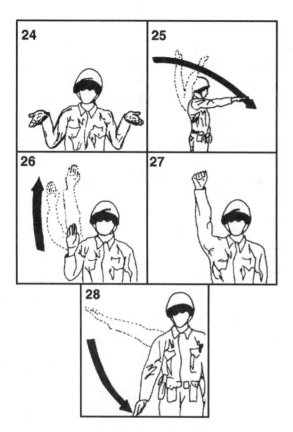

22. OPEN UP; EXTEND – Start signal with arms extended in front of the body, palms together, and bring arms to the horizontal position at the sides, palms forward. When repetition of this signal is necessary, the arms are returned along the front of the body to the starting position and the signal is repeated until understood.

23. DISPERSE – Extend either arm vertically overhead; wave the hand and arms to the front, left, right, and rear, the palm toward the direction of each movement.

24. I DO NOT UNDERSTAND – Face toward source of signal; raise both arms sidewards to the horizontal at hip level, bend both arms at elbows, palms up, and shrug shoulders in the manner of the universal "I dunno."

25. FORWARD; ADVANCE; TO THE RIGHT (LEFT); TO THE REAR (USED WHEN START-

ING FROM A HALT) – Face and move in the desired direction of march; at the same time extend the arm horizontally to the rear; then swing it overhead and forward in the direction of movement until it is horizontal, palm down.

26. HALT – Carry the hand to the shoulder, palm to the front; then thrust the hand upward vertically to the full extent of the arm and hold it in that position until the signal is understood.

27. FREEZE – Make the signal for "HALT" and make a fist with the hand.

28. DOWN; TAKE COVER – Extend arm sideward at an angle of 45° above horizontal, palm down, and lower it to the side. Both arms may be used in giving this signal. Repeat until understood.

29. INCREASE SPEED; DOUBLE TIME – Carry the hand to the shoulder, first closed; rapidly thrust the fist upward vertically to the full extent of the arm and back to the shoulder several times. This signal is also used to increase gait or speed.

30. HASTY AMBUSH RIGHT (LEFT) – Raise fist to shoulder level and thrust it several times in the desired direction.

31. RALLY POINT – Touch the belt buckle with one hand and then point to the ground.

32. OBJECTIVE RALLY POINT – Touch the belt buckle with one hand, point to the ground, and make a circular motion with the hand.

Chapter Twenty-Nine

Protective Measures

There is a Marine Corps rule for fighting which says: "Unit leaders are responsible for the all-around security of their own unit."

This does not mean that just the officer or NCO in charge of your group is the one to see that you and your outfit are protected. It is also your responsibility to take quick measures to protect yourself when your unit may be stopped in a forward movement in battle and at other times when protection is needed. When your outfit cannot advance farther, you usually need protection quickly against the fire of enemy small arms, mortars and artillery. This protection should be simple, available almost at once and should be capable of further improvement as long as you remain in that position.

Entrenchments

Entrenchments are located to cover a selected area with fire and, at the same time, provide concealment from aerial and ground observation and protection from enemy fire. The three most commonly used entrenchments are briefly explained in this section.

The Fighting Hole. Fighting holes are entrenchments normally dug for individual protection when contact with the enemy is imminent or in progress. They provide protection against small arms fire, artillery shell fragments, airplane fire or bombing, and the crushing action of tanks. The one and two-man fighting holes are basic types, the choice of type resting with the squad leader if not prescribed by higher authority. The two-man fighting hole consists essentially of two adjacent one-man fighting holes. It is used when Marines must work in pairs or when, for psychological reasons, battlefield comradeship is desirable. Figures 29-1(a) and (b) show a one-man fighting hole and Figure 29-2 shows a two-man fighting hole.

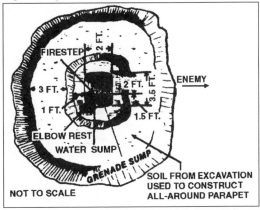

Fig. 29-1(b). One-Man Fighting Hole Dimensions.

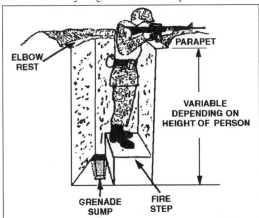

Fig. 29-1(a). One-Man Fighting Hole.

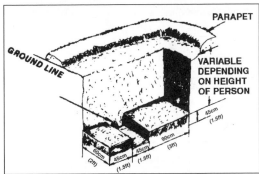

Fig. 29-2. Two-Man Fighting Hole Dimensions.

383

The Individual Prone Shelter. A prone shelter may be dug more quickly than a fighting hole, and it gives considerable protection from small arms fire, artillery and aviation. However, since it is shallow, it does not provide protection against the crushing action of tanks, and it is not suitable as a firing position. Figure 29-3 shows an individual prone shelter.

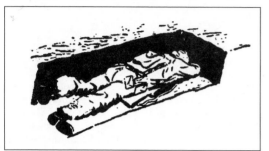

Fig. 29-3. Individual Prone Shelter.

Connecting Trenches. Connecting trenches are conspicuous to aerial observers and on aerial photographs, and thus reveal the defensive dispositions. Continuous connecting trenches are not dug as a normal procedure. When two forces are in contact and dispositions have been revealed beyond any question, a few short trenches may be dug in inconspicuous places to permit necessary daylight movement across exposed areas. Necessary connecting trenches also may be dug in close country, such as jungle, where the position probably will not be disclosed. Further, they may be dug whenever the improved protection, control, communications and supply outweigh the sacrifice of concealment. Figure 29-4 shows a connecting trench.

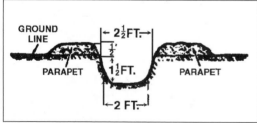

Fig. 29-4. Connecting Trench.

Camouflage

Camouflage has been defined as the science of military deception. It affords protective concealment

for your position so that you can see without being seen. This permits you to strike first, fatally and at no cost to yourself.

Hide, Blend, Deceive. There are three general ways in which you can camouflage yourself. You can hide, you can blend yourself with your surroundings or you can deceive the enemy.

• To hide yourself, use the advantages offered by nature in the terrain. If nature has given you enough camouflage for you and your supplies, let nature do the work unaided.

• Blend with your surroundings so that you match surrounding terrain features and are not conspicuous.

• You can deceive the enemy by using such tricks as making a dummy position with poor camouflage. This may lead the enemy to the dummy position and your range of fire.

Rules of Camouflage. In addition to these general means of camouflaging yourself, there are a number of rules which you need to learn well if you are going to protect yourself successfully.

• Pick out a position which uses as much as possible of the tactical and concealment values of the terrain.

• Practice camouflage discipline by keeping your position free of tell-tale signs of occupancy such as paths, dead leaves on camouflage materials and so on.

• Select your camouflage materials to match the color and texture of the local terrain. If you use natural materials, such as grass or trees, keep them fresh in appearance.

• Avoid over-camouflaging your position. This is just as obvious as no camouflage. Use common sense in covering regular outlines and tell-tale shadows.

• Don't look up from your position. Your face is smooth and light colored, and reflects a great deal of light. Never look up when a plane is overhead, or if you do, break off a branch or bush and look carefully.

• Never throw down a cigarette. Pinch out the fire, split the paper and roll it into a small ball. Scatter the shreds of tobacco around so no clues will be left.

• Some objects shine like mirrors in the sunlight and can be seen for miles. Watch your mess gear and weapons. Keep them under cover or in the shade.

• Tape your dog tags so that they do not clink. Put them together and bind them with a piece of friction tape or adhesive tape.

- Follow the paths laid out for you. The paths may be wired, they may be taped or they may just be blazed. But they were laid out for a purpose. Don't try to take short cuts away from them. You make new tracks.
- Don't cut the brush or limbs you plan to use for camouflage from a bush next to your position. Go some distance for them and don't take them all from the same place.
- Bury all waste material. Fill the dirt back in very carefully and cover the spot with leaves or dry grass. Go as far as to sod the spot if you find it necessary.
- Stay off the horizon. It is important that you know where the horizon is. If the enemy is downhill from you, you usually are on the horizon, and present the enemy with a good target.
- Stay in the shadows and also be sure you have a blending background. You can be seen in silhouette if you are in shadow with a lighted background beyond you.
- Smoke billowing up in a straight column is always bad. Build your fires under trees or put a screen over the fire.

Elementary Obstacles

You can sometimes put out artificial obstacles such as wire, so that the enemy will be channeled into areas where they are covered by your fire. These obstacles are placed in woods, tall grass, brush, or some other place where they can be hidden, if it is possible. They have to be covered by fire at all times to prevent the enemy from removing, destroying or surmounting them.

At all times when wire is used, there should be some alarm system attached to the wire. One of the simplest and most effective alarm systems consists of a few pebbles placed in empty tin cans, which are fastened to the wire.

Tactical Obstacles. Some obstacles are called tactical obstacles. These are obstacles placed to hold the enemy in areas covered by defensive fires, particularly by the final protective fire of machine guns. Such obstacles can be double apron fences, concertinas or a combination of both. Two parallel rows of double apron fences or a pyramid of three concertinas fastened together by strands of barbed wire are common.

Protective Obstacles. Protective obstacles are used to surround a platoon defense area completely. They are set up to hinder a surprise attack by the enemy. They must be placed beyond hand grenade range. A single four-strand barbed wire fence can become a protective obstacle.

The Abatis. An abatis is made by felling dead trees or interlacing live tree branches to form a barrier to enemy infantry. In addition to trees, wires may be intertwined among the branches and booby traps can be placed in an abatis, if ordered.

Chapter Thirty

Squad Tactics

The current Marine Corps rifle squad is the result of many years of development and combat experience. The aggressive, intelligent and effective employment of the rifle squad in combat is the primary basis for success in battle. Before you learn the tactics of a squad in combat, you must know the organization of the squad, its fire teams and the duties of its members.

The rifle squad is made up of 13 Marines: a sergeant (squad leader) and three teams of four Marines each. (See Fig. 30-1.)

Each fire team consists of a corporal (fire team leader), two lance corporals (automatic rifleman and assistant automatic rifleman) and a private first class (rifleman).

Duties of Squad Members

Squad Leader – Sergeant

A squad leader leads the squad and carries out the orders issued by the platoon commander. The squad leader is responsible for the discipline, appearance, training, control, conduct and welfare of the squad at all times and for the condition and care of its weapons and equipment. In combat, the squad leader is responsible for the fire discipline, fire control and maneuver of the squad. A position is taken by the squad leader to best carry out orders as well as observe and control the squad. A squad leader's weapon is fired only in critical situations.

Fire Team Leader – Corporal

A fire team leader leads the fire team and carries out the orders of the squad leader. The fire team

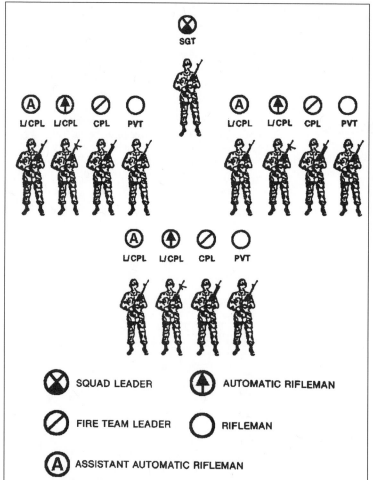

SGT

| A | ↑ | ⊘ | ○ | | A | ↑ | ⊘ | ○ |
| L/CPL | L/CPL | CPL | PVT | | L/CPL | L/CPL | CPL | PVT |

| A | ↑ | ⊘ | ○ |
| L/CPL | L/CPL | CPL | PVT |

⊗ SQUAD LEADER

⊘ FIRE TEAM LEADER

Ⓐ ASSISTANT AUTOMATIC RIFLEMAN

↑ AUTOMATIC RIFLEMAN

○ RIFLEMAN

Fig. 30-1. A rifle squad.

leader is responsible for the effective employment of the fire team, its fire discipline and fire control, as well as the condition and care of its weapons and equipment.

In carrying out orders, the fire team leader takes a position where the fire team can be best observed and controlled. Normally, the fire team leader is close enough to the automatic rifleman to exercise control over the automatic rifle quickly and effectively. In addition to primary duties as a leader, the fire team leader serves as a rifleman and as a grenadier. The fire team leader fires when actions are more or less automatic – that is, during the assault fire portion of closing with the enemy, and when the enemy closes on the squad's position.

The senior fire team leader in the squad serves as assistant squad leader. In the event the squad leader becomes a casualty (or in the squad leader's absence), the senior fire team leader leads the squad.

The Automatic Rifleman – Lance Corporal

The automatic rifleman carries out the orders of the fire team leader, and is also the assistant fire team leader. The automatic rifleman is responsible to the fire team leader for the effective employment of the automatic rifle (SAW) and for the condition and care of one's weapon and equipment. The assistant fire team leader assures leadership for the unit whenever the fire team leader is not present.

Assistant Automatic Rifleman – Lance Corporal

The assistant automatic rifleman carries out the orders of the fire team leader, assists the automatic rifleman in effective employment of that weapon and is responsible for the effective employment of one's rifle. Responsible for the condition and care of one's weapon and equipment, the assistant automatic rifleman is prepared to assume the duties of the automatic rifleman.

Rifleman – Private/PFC

The rifleman in the fire team carries out the orders of the fire team leader and is responsible for the effective employment of one's rifle and for the condition and care of weapons and equipment. The rifleman is also trained as a scout.

Offensive Combat

The purpose of offensive combat is to destroy the enemy and his will to fight.

Offensive action is the only means by which a decision is gained in combat. It is accompanied by fire, maneuver and shock action. Offensive action requires superiority over the enemy, however, superiority in numbers or fire power alone is not necessarily the deciding factor. Superiority is achieved by a combination of higher morale, greater aggressiveness, a higher quality of leadership, and better training and equipment. In short, the Marine's "Esprit de Corps" is a lethal weapon!

Since war is not an exact science, the events of war do not follow a set pattern, and no rule can be offered as the only solution for every combat situation.

The offensive mission of the squad is to attack. The attack is divided into three phases: the preparatory phase, the conduct phase, and the consolidation and reorganization phase. Each of these phases is further subdivided into steps.

Preparatory Phase: Advance to contact, final preparation.

Conduct Phase: Assembly area to line of departure, line of departure to the assault position and assault position through the assigned objective.

Consolidation and Reorganization Phase: Consolidation and Reorganization.

Each step is normally considered during the planning and execution of an attack. This does not mean that in every combat action the squad must go through every step of each phase in sequence. Generally speaking, the squad passes through all phases, even though the time spent in a particular phase may be brief. Often a step within a phase is shortened, omitted or at times even repeated. The discussion that follows explains the three phases (and their component steps) of offensive combat.

Preparatory Phase

Advance to Contact

Advance to contact is a tactical movement to gain or reestablish contact with the enemy. It ends when the unit is forced to open fire upon the enemy in order to advance or when the unit goes into an assembly area to prepare for combat. The route column, tactical column and approach march are troop formations peculiar to advance to contact. An explanation of each follows.

Route Column – When probability of contact with the enemy is remote, the movement is made in route column. Units within the column are administratively grouped for ease of control and speed of movement.

Tactical Column – The tactical column will be employed for greater security when the enemy situation has changed from contact remote to contact probable. The rifle squad may be used as:

- **Part of the Main Body** – When the squad marches as part of the main body, the squad leader's primary duties involve the supervision of march discipline within the squad.

- **Connecting Elements** – Connecting elements are files or groups which are used to maintain contact between the units of the command. Connecting files are individuals who are sent out to maintain contact between units. A connecting group consists of one or more fire teams. They may be classified as either flank or column connecting files or groups, depending upon their mission. (See Fig. 30-2.) The use of connecting files or groups is governed primarily by visibility.

- **Flank Connecting Files or Groups** – Connecting files or groups that maintain contact with units, guards or patrols on the flanks are called flank connecting files or groups. The primary mission is to report the location and situation of the unit with which the file or group is maintaining contact. It may also cover any gaps which exist between units, giving warning of and resisting any hostile penetration.

- **Column Connecting Files or Groups** – Individuals or fire teams used to maintain visual contact among elements in the tactical column are called column connecting files or groups. Contact between the point and the advance party

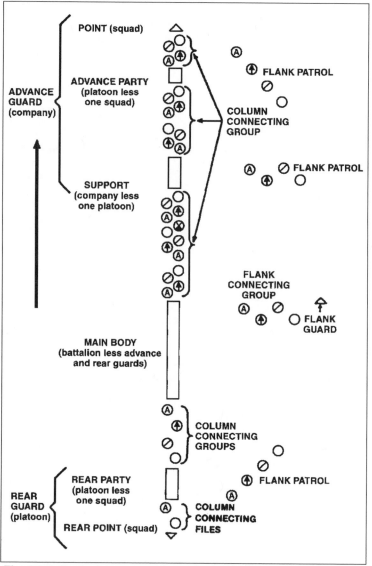

Fig. 30-2. Tactical movement to contact with the enemy.

is provided by either connecting files or a connecting group consisting of one fire team. Between larger units of the advance guard, main body and rear guard, a connecting group may consist of two fire teams or a squad.

- **Point of Advance Guard** – The point precedes the advance party along the axis of advance. The distance between the point and advance party is prescribed by the commander of the advance party.

388

Its mission is to prevent an enemy in the immediate vicinity of the route of march from surprising the troops following and to prevent any undue delay of the column. Possible ambush sites such as stream crossings, road junctions, small villages and defiles are thoroughly probed by the point.

- Formations for the point are prescribed by the squad leader. Generally, the squad uses a wedge formation for all-around protection and ease of deployment. Fire teams within the point usually adopt the wedge or open column formation. (See Fig. 30-3.) The squad leader assigns each fire team a sector of observation,

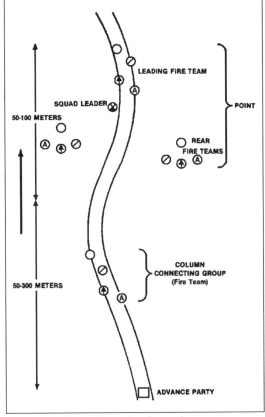

Fig. 30-3. *Point in wedge formation.*

and the fire team leaders assign each individual a sector of observation. (See Fig. 30-4.) This ensures the all-around observation essential for the proper security of the point.

- The squad leader of the point generally moves just to the rear of the leading fire team. From this position, the squad can be most effectively

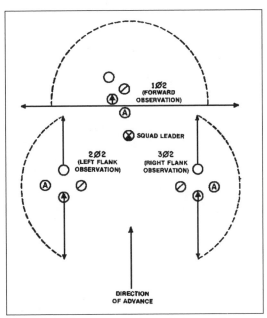

Fig. 30-4. *Fire team sectors of observation.*

controlled. Whenever possible, arm-and-hand signals are used for communications.

- The point engages all enemy elements within effective range. The squad leader reports contacts to the advance party commander who is informed of the enemy situation and the action being taken. If the enemy resistance is weak in comparison to the strength of the point, the squad leader initiates a plan to close immediately with and destroy the enemy. If the enemy resistance is greater than the strength of the point, the squad attacks in a manner that forces the enemy to open fire and disclose disposition and strength.

- • **Rear Point** – In the same manner that the advance party dispatches a point forward, the rear party employs a point to cover its rear. The formation of the squad serving as a rear point is similar to that of the point of the advance guard, but in reverse order. The squad generally uses a vee or a column formation, with the squad leader positioning at the head of the rearmost fire team. (See Fig. 30-5.) The rear point stops to fire only when the enemy action threatens to interfere with the march.

- • **Point of Flank** – The missions, actions and formations of a squad when serving as the point of a flank guard are the same as when the squad is acting as the point of an advance guard.

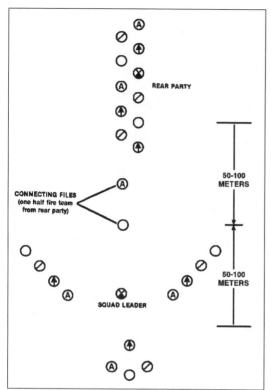

REAR PARTY

CONNECTING FILES
(one half fire team
from rear party)

50-100
METERS

50-100
METERS

SQUAD LEADER

Fig. 30-5. The squad as rear point.

- *Flank Patrol* – Rifle squads are often detailed as flank security patrols. A flank patrol may be ordered to move to and occupy an important terrain feature on the flank of the advance or to move parallel to the column at a prescribed distance from it, the distance depending on the speed of the column and the terrain. When vehicles or helicopters are available, it is highly desirable to provide the patrol with transportation.

  - When moving on foot parallel to the column, the patrol adopts formations based upon consideration of terrain, speed and self protection. In open terrain, a squad wedge formation is usually the best. In heavily wooded terrain, the patrol might use the squad column. The leading fire team serves as the scouting element of the patrol.

  - The patrol moves so as to prevent the enemy from placing effective small arms fire on the column. It investigates areas likely to conceal enemy elements or provide good observation. The patrol moves rapidly from point to point,

keeping between the protected unit and possible enemy locations.

- Enemy patrols moving away from the main body are reported but are not fired upon. All other hostile forces within effective range are engaged immediately by the patrol. If the enemy opens fire on either the patrol or the column, the patrol determines the strength and disposition and reports this information promptly to the unit or column commander.

- *Security of the Halted Column* – Security is established for a halted column by the advance, flank and rear guards. They occupy terrain features controlling the approaches to the halted column. Special attention is given to the flanks.

  - The squad leader positions the fire teams where they can observe and defend all avenues of approach leading into the squad area of responsibility. The squad leader ensures alert observation by detailing observers in pairs and arranging for frequent reliefs.

- *Approach march* – The approach formation is the continuation of the movement when enemy contact is imminent. It is executed with troops fully or partially deployed. Advance is by bounds, stopping on easily recognizable terrain features to coordinate the advance.

- *Initial Formation* – Upon assuming an approach march formation, the platoon commander usually prescribes initial squad formations. As the march progresses, however, the squad leaders order formation changes in accordance with the terrain, the frontages assigned, and the likelihood of enemy contact.

- *Base Squad* – A base squad may be designated by the platoon commander to assist in maintaining direction, position and rate of march. Other squads will guide on the base squad.

- *Duties of the Squad Leader* - The squad leader regulates the squad's advance on the base squad or, if the squad is the base squad, it is advanced as directed by the platoon commander. As the squad leader moves, the ground is studied to the front in order to take advantage of cover and concealment and to control the movement of the fire teams. The squad leader also maintains direction and makes minor detours to take advantage of better terrain.

- *Scouting Fire Teams* – When a rifle platoon in the approach march is not preceded by friendly troops, it uses its own scouting elements. These scouting elements are usually one or two fire teams, however an entire squad may be used. Fire teams used as scouting elements are called scouting or leading fire teams and are controlled by the platoon commander assisted by the squad leader. Scouting fire teams move aggressively to cover the front of the advancing platoon and to force the enemy to disclose positions.

- When a scouting fire team is directed to advance over open ground to an edge of woods, two members of the team, preferably the riflemen, reconnoiter inside the woodline, while the other members of the fire team cover them. When it is determined that the area near the woods is clear, the remainder of the platoon moves up. The scouting fire teams hold a line within the woods until given further instructions.
- When a scouting fire team is fired upon, the individuals immediately take cover. Targets are located and fire returned. The scouting fire team leader then determines:
  Location of enemy (range and reference points).
  Types of positions (fighting holes, bunkers, etc.).
  Number of enemy.
  Nature of terrain.
- The platoon commander contacts the leaders of the scouting fire teams to obtain as much information as possible. The platoon commander then returns the scouting fire teams to the control of the squad leaders.

Final Preparations in the Assembly Area

Final preparations for the attack are normally completed when the squad is in the assembly area. Those not completed may be accomplished in the attack position. These preparations include reconnoitering, formulating plans, and issuing orders, as well as the following six considerations:

1. Additional ammunition is drawn and distributed.
2. Weapons, equipment and personnel are checked for readiness.
3. Equipment not required for the attack is collected and stacked for later pickup.
4. Extra or special equipment needed for the operation is obtained and issued.
5. Personnel are allowed to rest to the maximum extent possible.
6. Communications equipment is checked for serviceability, and frequencies and call signs are promulgated.

Assembly Area – An assembly area is an area where units assemble prior to further tactical action.

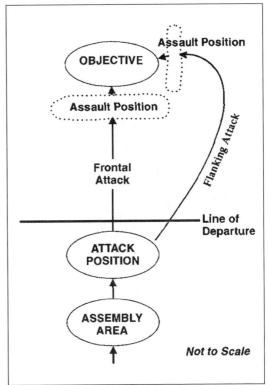

Fig. 30-6. *Typical tactical control measures used by a rifle squad in a dismounted daylight attack (schematic).*

Assembly areas should provide concealment, dispersion, suitable routes forward and security from ground or air attack. When possible, they should be located beyond the effective range of hostile flat trajectory weapons.

Attack Position – The attack position is the last concealed and covered position occupied by assault echelons before crossing the line of departure. It is the location where final coordination, last-minute preparations and deployment into initial attack formations are effected. When all preparations for the attack are completed in the assembly area, there should be no delay when passing through the attack position (See Fig. 30-6.)

Troop Leading Procedure – The troop leading steps are a useful method for assisting the squad leader in preparing for an attack.

Attack Plan – The fourth step of the troop leading procedures requires the squad leader to complete the attack plan. There are two attack plans for a squad: a single envelopment and a frontal attack.

Issue Attack Order – Having completed the plan of attack, the squad leader issues the attack order. An example of the type of information included in a five-paragraph order follows:

Unit: 3d Squad, 2d platoon with assault team attached.

Terrain Orientation (given prior to issuance of the order): "That direction is north (pointing). Notice that ridgeline to our front, generally east and west. Note that line of thick low bushes. Notice the finger ridge running to the north with the trail up its center (pointing)."

Five paragraph order. – (In giving an order, paragraph numbers and titles are not used.)

1. Situation.

Enemy Forces. "The main enemy force is defending along that high ground to the north (pointing). Their automatic weapons are well dug in near the military crest. I observed some riflemen in open fighting holes around automatic weapons. I can't tell exactly how many there are."

Friendly Forces. "Our platoon attacks at 0815 to seize the left half of our company objective. The 2d Squad is on our left. The 1st Platoon attacks on our right to seize the right half of the company objective."

Attachments and Detachments. "An assault team will be attached to us. They're ours at 0745."

2. Mission.

"Our squad attacks at 0815 on a frontage of 125 meters to seize the squad objective."

3. Execution.

Concept of Operation. "We will cross the line of departure in a squad wedge and attack the objective frontally, guiding on that trail up the center of the finger."

Subordinate Mission. "Corporal Jones, I want your team to lead off in the wedge. You will be base fire team for the attack. Guide on that trail going up the center of the finger. We'll go into a squad line at the final coordination line with your fire team in the center. Take the center one-third of the knob from the red dirt slash on the left to the trail on the right.

"Corporal Smith, your fire team will be to the right rear of Corporal Jones' as we move out. Watch for the 1st Platoon on your right. At the assault position, come up abreast of Corporal Jones' fire team. You'll be the right fire team in the assault. Take the right one-third of the knob, from the trail right to the tree line.

"Corporal Webb, keep the 3d Fire Team to the rear of the 1st initially. Watch for the 2d Squad on your left. Come abreast of the 1st Fire Team at the assault position. You'll be the left fire team in the

assault. Assault the left one-third of the knob, left from the red dirt slash to the draw.

"Assault team, general support. Follow in trace of the 1st Fire Team by about 50 meters. Engage targets of opportunity during our movement. Consolidate on the objective with the 1st Fire Team upon completion of the assault."

Coordination Instruction. "Line of departure is that line of thick low bushes. Direction of attack is north. The tentative assault position will be approximately 100 meters short of the objective."

4. Administration and Logistics.

"Corporal Jones, send two men to the platoon guide to draw 10 frag hand grenades. Each fire team will get three. I will carry the other one. A corpsman will be directly to our rear. Rations and ammo will be issued on the objective. Evacuate casualties and EPW's to the immediate rear."

5. Command and Signal.

Communication and Special Signal Instructions. "The red smoke grenades will be used by the assaulting units to signal supporting fires to lift."

Location of the Commander. "I will be with the 1st Fire Team in the assault and when we consolidate on the knob. The lieutenant will be with the 2d Squad. It is now 0709. Any questions?"

Conduct Phase

The conduct phase of the attack begins when one of the following occurs: the squad is forced to fire on the enemy in order to advance; the squad leaves the assembly area; or in the absence of an assembly area or attack position, the leading troops cross the line of departure.

Movement to the Line of Departure

Upon leaving the assembly area, the squad makes a rapid and continuous advance across the line of departure (LD). If necessary, a brief halt to effect last-minute coordination and assume combat formations may be made in the attack position.

If the squad is subjected to artillery or mortar fire along the route, it moves quickly through or around the impact area. (See Fig. 30-6 for tactical control measures used by the squad in an attack.)

Movement Forward of the Line of Departure To the Assault Position

When the squad reaches a point where it can no longer advance without sustaining excessive casualties, the squad leader orders one or more fire teams to fire on the enemy positions. The remainder of the squad moves forward under the protection of this covering fire.

The maneuver used in a particular situation is decided by the squad leader based on the rapid estimate of the situation. When the resistance is isolated and has exposed flanks, the squad leader attempts to maneuver over a covered and concealed route so as to strike the enemy resistance in the flank or rear. When this is not possible, a frontal attack requiring fire and maneuver is executed.

Fire and Maneuver – Fire and maneuver is the process of one or more elements establishing a base of fire to engage the enemy, while the other element or elements maneuver to an advantageous position from which to close with and destroy or capture the enemy. Supporting fires from weapons not organic to the squad may be provided.

Supporting fires should be followed closely by the advancing troops so that the advantage of the shock effect of the fire upon the enemy will not be lost.

Fire and Movement – Once the maneuver element meets enemy opposition and can no longer advance under the cover of the base of fire, it employs fire and movement to continue its forward progress to a position from which it can assault the enemy positions.

In the squad, fire and movement consists of individuals or fire teams providing covering fire while other individuals or fire teams advance toward the enemy or assault the enemy positions.

Squad Teams – The organization of the rifle squad into three fire teams provides the squad leader with three elements to execute fire and movement or fire and maneuver. One or more fire teams are employed either as maneuver elements or base of fire elements.

The role of any fire team may change during the conduct of any particular action. For example, if the maneuver element is prevented by enemy action or terrain from closing with the enemy, it assumes the base of fire role to cover the advance of the other team or teams, which then become the maneuver element.

Base of Fire Element – The base of fire assists the maneuver element in its advance toward the enemy positions by engaging all known or suspected targets. Upon opening fire, the squad seeks to gain fire superiority over the enemy, holding up its advance. Fire superiority is gained by subjecting the enemy to fire of such accuracy and volume that the enemy fire ceases or becomes ineffective.

Maneuver Element – The mission of the maneuver element is to close with and destroy or capture the enemy. It advances and assaults under the close covering fire of the base of fire element.

The maneuver element's principal job is to maintain the advance toward the enemy. It may be the entire squad when the squad acts as a maneuver element for the platoon. It uses available cover and concealment to the maximum.

Depending upon the terrain and effectiveness of the supporting fire, the maneuver element advances by team movement – within the team, by fire and movement, employing rushes, or creeping and crawling as necessary. Regardless of how it moves, it must continue to advance.

If terrain permits, the maneuver element may be able to move forward under cover and concealment to positions within hand grenade range of the enemy.

Control of the Squad – Fire team leaders initiate the action directed by the squad leader. Fire team leaders act as fighter-leaders, controlling their fire teams primarily by example. Fire team members base their actions on their fire team leader.

Throughout the action, fire team leaders exercise such positive control as is necessary to ensure that their fire teams function as directed. Squad leaders locate where they can best control and influence the action.

Use of Maneuver – Once fire superiority has been gained, the squad continues its advance. Fire superiority is maintained throughout the attack in order to ensure the success of any maneuver.

Before advancing any part of the squad, the squad leader should be assured that there is sufficient fire on the enemy positions to render return fire ineffective.

Two forms of maneuver for the rifle squad are the flanking attack and the frontal attack using rushes. In a flanking attack, the maneuver element attacks against the flank or immediate rear of the enemy's positions. The frontal attack exerts pressure against the enemy's front and drives the enemy off the objective.

- *Flanking Attack* – When moving against the enemy's flank, part of the squad provides a base of fire to cover the maneuvering element. This maneuvering element moves toward the flank of the enemy so as to place itself in a position to assault. The maneuvering element takes advantage of all cover and concealment, keeping the enemy unaware of its movements until the assault begins.

  When the assault is commenced by the maneuvering element, the base of fire shifts to another part of the enemy positions or ceases firing entirely. If observation permits, it is desirable to have the base of fire lead the maneuvering element across the objective by fire.

The flanking attack splits the enemy's defensive fires between the supporting attack and the main attack and allows the squad to attack over ground of its choice. However, it increases vulnerability during the attack. If the enemy can defeat the forces that have been divided, they may be able to repel the attack.

• *Frontal Attack* – When there is no opportunity for maneuver to either flank of the enemy, the squad moves directly to the front. The squad leader orders one or more fire teams to advance under cover of the fire of the remaining fire team or a platoon-directed base of fire.

Fire teams advance as rapidly as possible to new firing positions, using the cover and concealment available. When new firing positions have been reached, the maneuver element opens fire. The fire team or teams providing the base of fire ceases fire when the maneuvering element commences firing.

Under cover of this newly established fire, the fire teams which act as the initial base of fire move forward, using the available cover and concealment. This process is continued until the squad is in position to assault the enemy.

The squad leader moves to successive positions to best maintain effective control of the squad. The frontal attack is the most frequently used form of maneuver by the rifle squad. The frontal attack requires less time and coordination and is simpler than the flanking attack. However, the frontal attack has little chance of surprise and moves into the enemy's strength and prepared fires.

Method of Advance – When making either a flanking attack or a frontal attack, a rifle squad has three methods by which it may move. The squad may move as a unit in a series of squad rushes, by fire teams in a series of fire team rushes, or the members of the squad may move forward singly by individual rushes. In all three, the element of speed is necessary.

Movement from the Assault Position through the Objective

As the squad approaches the assault position, supporting fires on the enemy position increase in intensity. The squad completes its deployment so that it crosses the line in its assault formation.

Assault Position – The assault position is used to coordinate the ceasing or shifting of supporting fires and final deployment of the squad in preparation for conducting an assault against an enemy position. It is at the assault position that the leader makes the final decision whether to cease the supporting fires or to shift them.

It is located as close to the enemy positions on the objective as attacking troops can move before becoming exposed to supporting fires (base of fire). The distance from the assault position to the objective varies with the terrain and types of supporting arms employed.

If the squad leader is the assault element leader and determines that fewer casualties will be suffered if the squad moves closer to the enemy positions prior to the assault, the leader may move the assault position closer to the enemy positions than its tentative location.

The assault element then continues to advance to the new location by fire and movement techniques and initiates the assault from there. When the position is changed, the platoon commander and fire support units must be notified.

Squad in the Assault – The assault starts on order or signal from the platoon commander or on the initiative of a squad or fire team leader, depending upon which level is commanding the assault element.

Assault fire techniques are employed when fire superiority is gained. This condition cannot be determined prior to moving out from the assault position, but may occur at any time between the assault position and the enemy positions.

In closing with the enemy, riflemen move rapidly, firing well-directed shots from the pointing position at locations in their zone of advance that could conceivably be occupied by the enemy.

Squad automatic weapons are fired in two- or three-round bursts from the underarm firing position covering as much of the squad front as possible. Riflemen fire well directed rifle fire from either the offhand or underarm position.

Once a hardened or area target presents itself, the fire team leader will commence to fire the grenade launcher until the target is destroyed or neutralized or until fire cannot be placed effectively on the target without endangering friendly troops. Rifle grenades, hand grenades, bayonets and flame weapons are used to overcome pockets of resistance.

The assault element does not stop at the near edge of the objective, but moves far enough through the objective to place fire on enemy withdrawing elements and use fire superiority to protect against a counterattack.

Squad in the Assault without Fire Superiority.

When fire superiority cannot be gained because sufficient supporting fires are not available to neutralize the enemy fires, fire and movement by the maneuver element is the only means by which the attack can proceed.

The maneuver element will take maximum advantage of cover and concealment employing short, frequent individual rushes (creeping and crawling when necessary) and use its own fires to close with the enemy positions.

The first elements to gain a foothold within the enemy positions will support the remainder of the assault to destroy the enemy.

Consolidation And Reorganization Phase

The purpose of consolidation and reorganization is to prepare the squad for future action. It covers the period from the completion of the assault to when further action is taken to exploit success.

Consolidation

Consolidation pertains to all measures taken to organize and strengthen a newly captured position. Immediately upon seizure of the objective, the squad leader will stress security, assign sectors of fire and make a reconnaissance. No action will be taken to slow the momentum of the attack if it is to be continued.

Security Measures – Enemy artillery and mortar fire followed by sharp counterattacks can be expected after capture of an objective. Therefore, the squad leader quickly organizes a defense of the position to repel any enemy counterattacks. The initial defense plans will have been prescribed by the squad leader in the attack order.

A quick visual reconnaissance by the squad leader, a rapid mental estimate of the situation (METT), and brief orders to subordinates are required.

The squad leader gives primary consideration to the positions of the three fire teams, and also gives consideration to the position of the automatic rifle in each fire team. Local security is established to the front. Troops dig in as necessary and reconnoiter to the immediate front.

This position is maintained until orders are received from the platoon commander to continue the advance or until the reorganization of the squad is completed.

Reorganization

Reorganization is a continuous process, but it is given special emphasis upon seizure of the objective. The squad leader accomplishes the following during reorganization:

- Makes spot assignments to replace fire team leaders who become casualties.
- Redistributes ammunition, magazines and grenades.
- Removes casualties to covered positions.
- Notifies the platoon commander of the situation, the position of the squad, the casualties incurred and the status of ammunition supply.
- Disarms enemy prisoners and sends them to the platoon commander. Prisoners and enemy dead are searched for papers, documents and identification. Such material is immediately sent to the platoon commander.
- Ascertains the situation of the units to their flanks.

Exploitation and Pursuit

Exploitation

Exploitation normally occurs after a successful assault and seizure of the objective. It begins immediately after or in conjunction with the consolidation and reorganization phase. It is a continuation of the attack aimed at destroying the enemy's ability to conduct an orderly withdrawal or organize a defense. Pursuit by fire and/or continuation of the attack are methods used to exploit success.

Pursuit By Fire – When the assault through the assigned objective is completed, the squad fires upon the withdrawing enemy forces until they are no longer visible or are beyond effective range.

Continuation of the Attack – The purpose of continuing the attack is to maintain pressure on the retreating enemy and destroy its combat power. When ordered, the rifle squad continues the attack. The squad leader repeats all the steps performed for previous attacks. Frequently, the urgent need of a higher command to maintain momentum requires that these steps be done rapidly so that the attack can be continued with minimum delay.

Pursuit

An exploitation may develop into a pursuit. The primary function of pursuit is to complete the destruction of the enemy force.

It begins when the enemy cannot maintain positions and tries to escape or retreat. The pursuit is continued rapidly with the objective of destroying the enemy's organization and lowering morale.

The squad's participation in a pursuit normally is a continuation of the attack or movement as an element of a tactical or approach march.

Night Attack

A night attack may be made to gain surprise, to maintain pressure, to exploit a success in continuation of daylight operations, to seize terrain for subsequent operations or to avoid heavy losses by using the concealment afforded by darkness.

Characteristics

Night combat is characterized by a decrease in the ability to place aimed fire on the enemy; a corresponding increase in the importance of close combat, volume of fire and the fires of weapons registered during daylight; difficulty in maintaining control, direction and contact.

Despite these difficulties, the night attack gives the attacker a psychological advantage in that it magnifies the defender's doubts, apprehensions and fear of the unknown.

The difficulties mentioned can be overcome by careful planning and preparation for the attack. The demand for time-consuming detailed planning and reconnaissance at all levels normally requires the assignment of night attack missions to units not in physical contact with the enemy.

Control Measures

The degree of visibility will determine the measures necessary to assure tactical control. Terrain features used as tactical control measures, if not easily identifiable at night, may be marked by artificial means. The following tactical control measures will normally be prescribed in a night attack. (See Fig. 30-7.)

- *Assembly Area* – The assembly area may be closer to the line of departure than for a daylight attack.
- *Attack Position* – The attack position should be in defilade, but need not offer as much concealment as in daylight. The area selected should be easy to move into and out of at night.
- *Line of Departure* – The line of departure is a line established to coordinate attacking units when beginning the attack.

- *Release Point (RP)* – Release points are clearly defined points on a route where units are released to the control of their respective leaders.
- *Probable Line of Deployment (PLD)* – The probable line of deployment is an easily recognizable line selected on the ground where attacking units deploy in line formation prior to beginning a night attack.
- *Limit of Advance* – A limit of advance is generally designated beyond the objective to stop the advance of attacking units. It should be easily

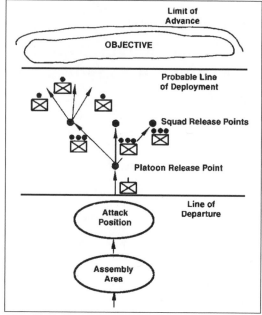

Fig. 30-7. *Control measures for night attacks.*

recognizable in the dark (a stream, road, edge of woods, etc.) and far enough beyond the objective to allow security elements space to operate.

Security Patrols

Members of the squad may be used as security patrols to assist night attacks. These patrols maintain security on the PLD, eliminate enemy security elements and prevent attacking forces from being ambushed while en route to the PLD. They may also act as guides to lead units forward from the release point to the PLD.

Preparation Phase for the Night Attack

Preparation for the night attack is generally the same as for the daylight attack. The squad leader will follow the same format for daylight attack, however, special emphasis is placed on:

- Reconnaissance by squad and fire team leaders to locate assigned control features and terrain features for night orientation. Such reconnaissance should be conducted during three conditions of visibility: daylight, dusk and dark.
- Rehearsals conducted both during daylight and darkness. Rehearsals should include formations, audible and visual signals, and the actions of the squad from the assembly area to the objective.
- Carrying only that equipment absolutely essential for the success of the attack.
- Camouflaging individuals and equipment. Equipment which rattles is padded or tied down.
- Avoiding test firing of weapons and unnecessary movement or doing this in a way which will not prematurely disclose the forthcoming attack.
- Ensuring that the night vision of the squad members is not destroyed prior to the attack.

Conduct Phase of the Night Attack

Movement to the Probable Line of Deployment – Security patrols sent out by higher commanders destroy enemy listening posts and security patrols enabling the unit to move to the PLD undetected.

- The platoons move in column formation from the assembly area to the platoon release point. At the platoon release point, the platoons meet their guides from the security patrol and continue to move along their respective routes to their squad release points.
- Once the squad crosses the line of departure, movement to the PLD is continuous. The rate of advance is slow enough to permit silent movement.
- If flares are fired during the movement forward, all hands quickly assume the prone position until the flares burn out. If a flare is fired after the squad leaves the PLD, the squad ignores the flare and continues the movement toward the assigned objective. Close coordination is required in the use of flares. Indiscriminate use of flares results in loss of surprise. If the attack is to be illuminated, the illumination is started on signal from the attacking elements (usually after reaching the PLD).
- On arrival at the squad release point, the rifle squads are released from the platoon column for-

mation to deploy on line at the probable line of deployment. The squad leader is normally the first member of the squad in the column. When the rifle squad reaches the squad release point, the squad leader leads the column, sets the pace and maintains the direction of movement. Members of the security patrols assist the squad leaders in positioning the squads on the probable line of deployment.

- On order, the squad moves forward silently from the probable line of deployment, maintaining the squad line formation and guiding on the base squad.

Assault – Once the enemy has discovered the attack and firing has commenced, then and only then is the assault commenced. The signal for the assault can take any form, but it must be simple and reliable. The importance of developing a great volume of fire during the assault cannot be overemphasized. It is at this time that fire superiority must be established and maintained.

The assault is conducted aggressively. Tracer fires should be used to increase accuracy of fire and to demoralize the enemy. Preplanned fires are used by higher commanders to isolate the objective.

The assault is conducted in the same manner as discussed earlier under "Movement from the Assault Position through the Objective." The assault is carried forward to the forward military crest of the objective or to some other prescribed limit short of the limit of advance.

Consolidation and Reorganization Phase of the Night Attack

When the objective has been seized, the plans for consolidation and reorganization are carried out as described earlier. The squad does not move or employ security elements forward of the limit of advance. (See Fig. 30-7.)

Infiltration

Tactical infiltration is a form of penetration involving the moving of forces into the enemy's rear by small groups. The infiltrating groups move by stealth, avoid enemy contact and assemble at a concealed rendezvous point.

Planning and Preparation

Organization – The size of the infiltrating group depends primarily on the need for control between infiltrating grips and the number and size of gaps in enemy defenses. Normally, units will be broken down into infiltration groups of platoon or squad size.

Order – A detailed order is issued for the attack. Each infiltrating group is issued the following information as a minimum:

• Release point.
• Time of release.
• Point of departure.
• Time of infiltration.
• Infiltration lane.
• Rendezvous point.
• Alternate rendezvous points.
• Time of rendezvous.
• Routes from rendezvous to attack positions.

Preparation – Upon receipt of the order, the group leaders follow the troop leading procedures as discussed earlier.

The planning, preparation and conduct of each infiltration group is the same as for a separate patrol. (For details on patrolling, see that specific chapter.)

While the group leaders accomplish their troop leading steps, the assistant group leaders prepare their groups for infiltration. Necessary equipment is drawn, checked and secured for silent movement.

Marines prepare themselves and their equipment for the operation. Where possible, each infiltration group should carry the necessary special equipment to accomplish the mission of the major unit. This ensures the accomplishment of the mission in the event all groups do not participate in the attack.

After the group leaders issue their orders, rehearsals covering the passage of lines, actions in danger areas, enemy contact, signals, as well as actions at the rendezvous points and objectives are conducted.

Everyone should be required to memorize the route, azimuths to and the location of rendezvous points.

The accomplishment of the mission rests primarily on the ability of the small-unit leaders. Planning and preparation must be as thorough and as detailed as time and facilities will permit.

Fires are planned by higher commanders to create diversions and to protect and support the unit during the infiltration, at the rendezvous area, and during the attack and consolidation or withdrawal.

Control Measures

Infiltration Lanes – Infiltration lanes extend through known or likely gaps in the enemy's defens-

es and are often located in rough, swampy or heavily forested areas. (See Fig. 30-8.)

Rendezvous Points – Rendezvous points should be concealed from possible enemy detection by observation and patrols. They are secured by the first group into the area. Escape routes should be designated to alternate rendezvous points.

Time of Infiltration – The time of infiltration is selected to take advantage of conditions of reduced visibility such as darkness, rain, snow, fog, etc. it is the time when infiltration groups enter their assigned infiltration lanes.

Routes – Routes to the objective from the rendezvous points should be concealed for surprise and for protection.

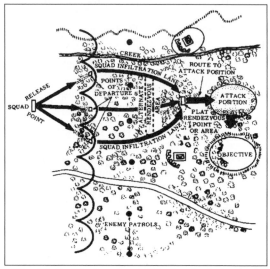

Fig. 30-8. *Attack using infiltration technique.*

Objectives – Objectives may be enemy reserves, artillery units, or command and logistic installations. Infiltrating forces may also seize key terrain or establish roadblocks to restrict enemy movement, isolate the battle area and facilitate the movement of friendly mechanized forces.

Conduct of the Attack by Infiltration

Movement of Groups – The infiltrating groups move by stealth to avoid detection. The major unit will assemble the infiltration groups to the rear of friendly lines. The major unit will then move forward, usually in a column, until it reaches the release point.

At the release point, the infiltration groups are released to their leaders. The infiltration group crosses the line of departure (usually friendly front-lines) at the specified time of infiltration. This is normally during a period of darkness.

Artillery or mortar fires are used as necessary to distract enemy attention. The infiltration groups pass through the gaps in the enemy's lines by using the designated infiltration lanes.

If detected, groups avoid engagement by with-drawing or moving around the enemy. Speed of movement is limited by the requirement for stealth. Groups which are unable to reach their rendezvous point in time follow the previously announced alter-nate plan.

Assembly of Groups – At the rendezvous point, groups assemble and attack preparations are completed. The first infiltration group to reach the rendezvous point secures it. The assembled force leaves the rendezvous point to attack the objective at the designated time. The main body may be preceded by a small security patrol. Its mission is to prevent the main body from being detected or surprised.

Attack – Short of the objective, the force is halted for final reconnaissance and coordination. This attack position should be the last safe, covered and concealed area before reaching the objective.

The attack on the objective is characterized by surprise and maximum firepower at the objective's weakest point to quickly destroy or capture it. The attack may be made by using the raid, daylight attack or night attack technique.

Platoons acting alone use the raid technique. If the objective is retained, it is consolidated against enemy counterattacks.

If plans are to link up with other friendly forces, previously designated visual and sound recognition signals prevent fire fights between friendly units.

If the objective is not retained, the attacking force withdraws to an assembly area for further attacks or withdraws to friendly lines. The withdrawal to friendly lines may be by air or by exfiltration, either as an intact unit or by infiltration groups.

Upon reaching friendly lines, the unit is again reassembled.

Defensive Combat

The purpose of defensive action is to gain time pending the development of more favorable conditions for the offensive or to economize forces on one front for the purpose of concentrating superior forces for an offensive elsewhere.

Definitions

Primary Position – The primary position is the best position from which the squad can carry out its primary mission.

Supplementary Position – A supplementary position is a position from which the squad can fire on targets which cannot be engaged from either the primary or alternate position. The supplementary position is used by the squad to carry out a mission other than its primary mission. For example, firing on enemy troops attacking the flanks or rear of the platoon defense area.

Alternate position – An alternate position is a position given to a weapons unit or individual to be occupied when the primary position becomes untenable or unsuitable for carrying out its task. It is developed in addition to primary and supplementary positions.

The alternate position is so located that the weapon can continue to fulfill its original task. Normally, the rifle squad is not required to prepare alternate positions.

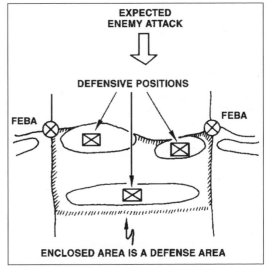

Fig. 30-9. *Defensive positions, defense area and FEBA.*

Defense Area – An area of ground assigned to a unit to defend. The entire defense area is not physically occupied by troops and weapons; unoccupied portions are covered by fire. (See Fig. 30-9.)

Forward Edge of the Battle Area (FEBA) – The FEBA is an imaginary line separating the forward security elements from the forces of the main body.

Defensive Missions of the Squad

The squad will be assigned one of the three types of missions:

Frontline Squad – The squad may be part of a frontline defense platoon. Its mission is to stop the enemy by fire forward of the FEBA and to repel by close combat if the squad position is reached. The mission requires that the squad be assigned a definite position and sector of fire.

The squad holds its position at all cost and withdraws or occupies other positions only on orders from higher authority.

Squad as Part of the Reserves – The squad may be part of the reserve platoon during the defense. As part of the reserve platoon, the squad is normally assigned a position to the rear of the frontline units and supports the frontline units by fire in an assigned sector. The sector of fire is assigned to concentrate fire in the rear or on the flanks of a frontline unit or into a gap between frontline units.

The squad as part of the reserve platoon may also be assigned a defensive position and sector of fire to limit enemy penetrations of the FEBA.

The squad as part of a larger reserve unit may participate in a counterattack or limit large penetrations of the FEBA.

Squad as a Security Element – The squad may serve as part of the security element during the defense, located forward of the FEBA. The squad's mission in this capacity is to gain information about the enemy and to deceive, delay and disorganize the advance.

Preparation for the Defense

Normally, a rifle squad is employed with maximum firepower directed toward the expected direction of enemy attack. Its primary position is located to take maximum advantage of the terrain and fields of fire.

The rifle squad also prepares supplementary positions. These positions are organized the same as the primary positions, but are oriented to cover approaches that cannot be covered by the primary position.

Troop Leading Procedures in the Defense

Upon receiving the platoon defense order, the squad leader will use the troop leading steps to assist in making the best use of time, facilities and personnel. Utilizing these steps and satisfactorily completing an estimate of the situation, the squad leader issues the squad defense order. This follows the standard five-paragraph order format and includes:

- Information about the enemy, the location and identification of adjacent squads and platoons, and the location of supporting weapons within the squad area.
- Mission of the squad.
- Position and sectors of fire for each team leader, rifleman, assistant automatic rifleman and automatic rifleman. Providing for antitank defense by assigning antitank weapons to selected members of the squad. Organization of the ground, including the type of emplacements, priority of work and other instructions.
- Administrative and supply details such as ammunition resupply and the location of the aid station.
- Prearranged signals such as pyrotechnics or audible signals designating when to open fire or deliver final protective fires and the location of the squad leader and platoon commander.

Squad Plan of Defense

After issuing the squad defense order, the squad leader positions the fire teams to cover the front and the flanks of the squad area. Before detailed preparations of positions are begun, the squad leader verifies the observation and sector of fire of each Marine. During a check of positions, the squad leader ensures that sectors of fire overlap and that the desired density of fire can be delivered on avenues of approach. The squad leader's responsibilities during the preparation of the position include:

- In conjunction with fire team leaders, selects firing positions for each rifleman and assigns sectors of fire.
- Selects firing positions and sectors of fire for the squad automatic weapons.
- In conjunction with fire team leaders, selects firing positions and sectors of fire for the assistant automatic rifleman.
- Assigns each automatic rifleman a principal direction of fire (PDF) covering a likely avenue of enemy approach or dead space in the final protective lines of machine guns. The PDF is within the sector of fire assigned to the automatic rifleman or is on one edge of the sector.
- Coordinates with other weapons located in the squad area.
- Supervises the preparation of fighting holes.
- Supervises the clearing of fields of fire.

- Provides squad security through assignment of sentinels or OP's.
- Coordinates all security measures with adjacent units and platoon commander.
- Inspects positions to ensure that camouflage and overhead cover are sufficient.
- Supervises the preparation of supplementary positions.
- Establishes a system of signals for firing.
  - *Signal to Commence Firing.* A forward limit to the assigned sector of fire is established at the range at which the weapon opens fire. For rifles and automatic rifles, this may extend up to their maximum effective range. A terrain feature may be selected to locate the forward limit. As attackers pass this limit, they are brought under fire. This establishes a positive means of fire control to ensure that small arms fire is not premature or withheld too long.
  - *Signal to Commence Final Protective Fires.* Final protective fires consist of the machine gun fires, mortars, artillery, the PDF's of automatic rifles and sectors of fire of individual rifles. The signal to commence these fires (passed by higher echelon) is a prearranged pyrotechnic or audible signal.
  - *Signal to Cease Final Protective Fires.* Predetermined signals are used to cease final protective fires. When the enemy assault is repulsed, the signal to cease fire is given.
- The squad leader prepares a sketch in duplicate of the squad fire plan. One copy of the sketch is given to the platoon commander for approval and one copy is kept. The sketch includes fire team positions and sectors of fire, positions, and principal directions of fire of the automatic rifles, and position of the squad leader. If the squad is providing protection for a crew-served weapon, its position and final protective line or primary direction of fire should be included as part of the sketch. Prominent terrain features and the estimated ranges to them should be so indicated that the sketch of the fire plan can be oriented on the ground.

Squad Security

The rifle squad provides for its security by alertness. Enough squad members are kept on alert to maintain an effective warning system. When a defensive position is being prepared during the hours of daylight and the enemy is not close to the squad's position, a minimum of one sentinel is posted in the squad area.

When contact with the enemy is probable or imminent, or during periods of limited visibility, additional sentinels will be required.

If one-man fighting holes are employed, alternate Marines will be posted. In the case of two-man fighting holes, one Marine from each is normally posted as a sentinel. In either case, those not posted as sentinels will continue preparing the position.

The number of Marines kept on alert during such periods will vary. The frequency of relief for sentinels and listening posts is affected by such considerations as the physical condition of the squad, effects of extreme weather conditions, morale and strength of the squad. As a guide, relief every two hours is desirable.

Organization of the Ground

The organization of the ground begins as soon as individual members of the squad have been assigned defensive positions. It includes the following tasks:
- Posting security (LP's, OP's, patrols).
- Positioning automatic weapons.
- Clearing fields of fire.
- Digging fighting holes.

Posting Security. Security consists of measures taken to prevent surprise and to deny the enemy information concerning the plan of defense. All-around security and protection against surprise are gained by posting a sentinel for surveillance and posting one Marine with each crew-served weapon.

Positioning Automatic Weapons. Automatic weapons are located to cover the most likely avenues of approach into the squad area, to provide mutual fire support for adjacent fire teams and to participate in the delivery of final protective fires.

Clearing Fields of Fire. In clearing fields of fire forward of each fighting hole, the following principles are observed:
- Do not disclose the squad's position by excessive or careless clearing.
- Start clearing near the FEBA and work forward to the limits of effective small arms fire.
- In all cases, leave a thin natural screen of foliage to hide defensive positions.
- In sparsely wooded areas, remove the lower branches of scattered, large trees. It may be desirable to remove entire trees which might be used as reference points for enemy fire.
- In heavy woods, complete clearing of the field of fire is neither possible nor desirable. Restrict work to thinning undergrowth and removing lower branches of large trees. In addition, clear narrow lanes for fire of automatic weapons.

- If practical, demolish other obstructions to fire such as buildings and walls.
- Move cut brush to points where it will not furnish concealment to the enemy or disclose the position.
- Extreme care must be taken by the grenadier/rifleman to ensure that fields of fire are cleared of obstructions which might cause premature detonation of the projectile.

Fighting holes. Fighting holes provide excellent protection against small arms fire, shell fragments, airplane strafing or bombing, effects of nuclear detonations and the crushing action of tanks. The one-man and two-man fighting holes are basic types. The choice rests with the squad leader if not prescribed by higher authority.

The type of fighting hole used is based upon squad strength, fields of fire, size of squad sector and morale. However, the two-man fighting hole permits one Marine to rest while the other maintains security over the assigned frontage.

(Specific information concerning the proper procedures for preparing fighting holes is contained in Chapter 29, "Protective Measures.")

Constructing Obstacles. The squad may be ordered to construct obstacles such as barbed wire, log and brush barriers, ditches and minefields, and may be ordered to improve natural obstacles such as creekbeds and river banks. Usually antitank obstacles and other extensive obstacles are constructed by engineer troops. When obstacles are constructed which affect the squad position, the squad leader ensures that the obstacle is located beyond hand grenade range of the squad position, and that the obstacle is covered by fire from the squad position.

Selecting Supplementary and Alternate Positions. The squad prepares supplementary positions organized the same as the primary positions but oriented in a different direction. If crew-served weapons are employed in the squad, then alternate positions should also be prepared.

Camouflage Measures. Concealment from enemy ground and aerial observation is very important in the selection and organization of each defensive position. Advantage is taken of natural concealment whenever possible. Camouflage measures are strictly carried out from the moment the position is occupied and are continuous.

(Additional camouflage techniques are contained in Chapter 29, "Protective Measures.")

Squad Defense Order

The squad leader follows the standard five-paragraph order format in presenting the squad defense order. An example defense order of a squad leader commencing with a terrain orientation follows:

(Terrain Orientation) "That direction is north (pointing). Notice the stream bed to the front, the road on the left, that destroyed bridge and the woods on the left.

(Par. 1) "An enemy force supported by tanks, artillery and aircraft is expected to attack from that direction (pointing), sometime after midnight tonight.

"Our platoon will defend this high ground from just this side of the road (pointing) 500 meters to the right (pointing). The FEBA runs along the forward slope of the high ground (pointing).

"The 2d squad is on our right and the 2d platoon on our left.

"There is a machine gun squad in the 2d platoon area that fires to the right, across our front, and a machine gun squad in the 1st squad area that fires to the left, across our front. An assault squad is located in our area just to the right of the road and fires down the road. Mortar final protective fires will fall in the bed to our front, and artillery final protective fires will fall in the vicinity of the road.

"Security detachments now in position to our front will withdraw along the road, probably sometime tonight.

(Par. 2) "The mission of our squad is to organize and defend a position on the FEBA from the right side of the road over to and around this knoll, but not including the draw to the right. Our sector of fire includes the area between that bend in the stream on our right (pointing), and the break in the woods on our left (pointing).

(Par. 3) "Our squad will organize our defense with three fire teams on line at H-hour. One fire team's principal direction of fire will be across the front of the 2d squad. The PDF's of the remaining two fire teams will be across the front of our squad with one fire team protecting the assault squad.

"1st fire team, on the right, will defend from the draw (pointing), around the knoll to, and including, that tree stump. Your sector of fire will extend from that bend in the stream (pointing) left to the other side of that large rock (pointing). Your automatic rifleman will fire his principal direction of fire (PDF) across the front of the 2d squad. I want it to be fired with his position (pointing) at that old dead tree there (pointing).

"2d fire team, in the center, will defend from that tree stump to, and including, that bush (pointing). Your sector of fire is from the demolished bridge on the left to that clump of cattails there in the stream bed (pointing). Place your automatic rifleman here and have him fire his principal direction of fire just to the

left of those bushes (pointing). His sector of fire will extend to the right to include that large rock (pointing).

"3d fire team, on the left, will defend from that bush to just this side of the road. Your sector of fire is from that large rock on the right (pointing), left to that small break in the woods (pointing). Place your automatic rifleman over there (pointing) and have him fire his principal direction of fire toward that large maple tree (pointing). The automatic rifle's sector of fire will extend right to include that bush (pointing). You will protect the assault squad located in your area. Your fire team will post one man to act as security for the squad while we are digging in. Have him on this high ground, and have him watch that stream bed in particular. I will have him relieved in one hour.

"I will point out supplementary positions protecting the rear later.

"After I have checked each man's position and sector of fire, clear the fields of fire, dig one-man fighting holes with overhead cover, and camouflage at the same time. Fire team leaders assign tasks.

"Open fire on the enemy when they come out of the woods to our front.

(Par. 4) "Water and rations will be issued before sunset. Make sure all hands have four grenades.

"The battalion aid station is along that road about 800 meters to the rear.

"Send EPW's back to me.

(Par. 5) "The challenge is 'September' and the password is 'Morning.'

"Signal to commence firing the final protective fires is a red star cluster. Signal to cease firing the final protective fires is a green star cluster.

"The platoon commander is in the edge of the woods to our right rear (pointing).

"My position will be here on this knoll just behind the second fire team.

"Any questions?

"It is now 1400.

"Move out!"

Conduct of the Defense

Enemy Preparatory Bombardment – The enemy will normally precede the attack with fire from any or all of the following weapons: artillery, naval gunfire, mortars, machine guns, tanks and aircraft. During this attack, the squad will take cover in its prepared positions maintaining surveillance of the squad's sector to determine if the enemy is advancing closely behind supporting fires.

Opening Fire and Fire Control – Fire is withheld on approaching enemy troops until they come within effective small arms range of the squad's position. Squad members open fire upon the approaching enemy on command of the squad leader or when the enemy reaches a predetermined line. Once fire is opened, direct control passes to the fire team leaders.

The fire team leaders, in accordance with the squad leader's previous plan, designate new targets, change rates of fire when necessary and give the order to cease fire.

Final Protective Fires – If the enemy's attack is not broken and they begin the assault, final protective fires are called. These are fires delivered immediately in front of the defensive lines. When final protective fires are called for, all squad members fire in their individual sectors at a maximum effective rate until told to stop.

Enemy Reaches the Squad Position – Enemy infantry reaching the squad position are driven out by fire, grenades and the bayonet. The success of the defense depends upon each rifle squad defending in place. A stubborn defense by frontline squads breaks up enemy attack formations and makes them vulnerable to counterattack by reserve units.

The squad does not withdraw except when specifically directed by higher authority.

Defense Against Mechanized Attack

When tanks or other armored vehicles support an enemy infantry attack, the primary target of the squad is the hostile infantry. When hostile infantry does not afford a target, the squad directs its small arms fire against the aiming devices and vision slits of enemy armor.

The cumulative effect of armor-piercing ammunition may be effective against tank sprockets, bogie wheels and tank suspension. Under no circumstances will the squad be diverted from its basic mission of engaging and destroying the hostile infantry. Antitank weapons are used against armor.

Every effort is made to separate the tanks and dismounted enemy infantry.

Enemy Penetration of Adjacent and Rear Areas

Enemy Penetrates Adjacent Area – If the position of an adjacent squad is penetrated by the enemy, the squad leader shifts a part of the squad's fire into the penetrated area and, if necessary, moves some Marines to supplementary positions protecting the threatened flank.

Enemy Penetrates Rear Area – If the squad position is threatened by attack from the rear, the squad leader moves some Marines to supplementary positions protecting the rear. In open, flat terrain, the squad leader simply orders Marines to shift fire to the rear.

Movement to Supplementary Positions – Prior to moving Marines to supplementary positions, the squad leader, if possible, requests the approval of the platoon commander. When it is not possible to request permission, the squad leader notifies the platoon commander of the action as soon as possible.

The squad leader avoids moving an entire fire team to supplementary positions, but instead moves one, two or three Marines from each fire team, depending on the number required to protect the flank or rear. In any case, Marines moving to supplementary positions use either the cover provided by the communication trenches or that offered by the terrain.

Local Security for Platoons and Companies

The squad often furnishes local security for platoons and companies. Security posts from two to four Marines are stationed by the platoon or company commander up to 500 meters forward of the platoon position. Small patrols are often used to cover the ground between security posts or as a substitute for security posts.

The platoon or company commander designates the general positions to be occupied by the security posts and the routes to be covered by the patrols.

The squad leader may find the squad divided into small security posts and patrols covering the platoon or company front and flanks. Duties then include:

- Checking to see that the security posts are well concealed and permit observation of the ground over which the enemy is expected to advance.
- Checking to see that patrols are following the prescribed routes.
- Passing on to Marines all available information regarding both friendly and enemy forces.

- Instructing the Marines as to what action to take in case of enemy attack.
- Informing the platoon or company commander immediately of enemy activity.

When the enemy approaches, security posts and patrols take the following action:

- Notify the platoon or company commander immediately of the enemy's strength, actions, direction of advance, and weapons and equipment.
- On order, withdraw along a predetermined route to the FEBA in time to prevent close combat. After reaching the FEBA, report all information regarding the enemy to the commander who originally ordered the patrol or security element.

Forward Local Security

The squad may serve as part of the forward local security which will normally be located from 1,000 to 2,400 meters forward of the FEBA. The exact location and composition of the forward local security is established by higher commanders. Its mission is to give early warning and information of the enemy, and to delay, disorganize and deceive them as to the true location of the battle area.

The forward local security is organized as a series of outguards which vary in strength from a fire team to a reinforced platoon. The outguards organize on terrain which affords observation, long fields of fire and close rifle protection for any supporting weapons. Routes of withdrawal are selected and reconnoitered, and all Marines are fully informed of the withdrawal plan.

When no other friendly troops are forward of the forward local security, contact is maintained with the enemy by patrols. If the enemy approaches, all weapons open fire at long range, and continuous and increasing fire is directed on them. As the enemy advance continues, it is brought under an increasingly heavier volume of fire. The platoon commander is kept informed of the situation.

The decision to withdraw is usually made by either the battalion commander or regimental commander of the frontline units. Routes of withdrawal are used which have been previously determined and reconnoitered. Upon withdrawal and passage through the forward friendly units, the squad will usually resume a role as part of a reserve unit.

Chapter Thirty-One

Individual Movement Techniques and Patrolling

After your unit goes into combat, there will be times when you are sent out as a member of a patrol. Commanders need information about the enemy, the ground you are fighting on and the friendly troops near you. They have to get information that is accurate, detailed and up to the minute, so that they can make plans. When you are appointed to be a patrol member, your commander is going to depend a great deal upon the accurate information you bring back. You are to be the best source of information.

This important job means a lot to your unit. The lives of your entire platoon may depend some day upon your success or failure. The rules of good individual movement and patrolling are given in this chapter.

Individual Movement by Day

When you go out on patrol in daylight, there are several lessons which are important to you. These lessons come under the names of cover, concealment, camouflage and the principles of movement.

Cover

Cover is protection against the fire of the enemy. You are of no use if the enemy sees you and hits you.

Cover can be a natural object like a tree, rock, ditch or an embankment. It also can be a shell hole or a demolished building. It is easy for you to pick out cover such as your surroundings afford.

It is not enough to know this, however. You may be in a place where no such objects are located. You must learn to study the ground and find protection where, at first, there seems to be none. The slightest depression or hump in the ground may give you shelter from the enemy's fire.

Some cover will be good for one purpose and worthless for another. For instance, a reverse slope will give you protection from rifle or machine gun fire, but will not give full protection from the high-angle fire of mortars and howitzers.

This brings up another important part of cover. You must study the ground ahead carefully when you are about to move forward under fire from your position. Select as your next position one that offers cover. Then move to it and move fast.

When you're near the selected position, hit the deck and roll over rapidly a few times. This is done to confuse any of the enemy who may have seen you rush out. When the enemy sees you go down, you are some distance from your selected position and the enemy will not be able to spot your position accurately.

If time permits, artificial means can be used to obtain or improve cover. This means you can dig trenches, erect barricades and so on. Artificial means are always used in a defensive position.

Concealment

Where the word "cover" is used to mean protection from enemy fire, the word "concealment" means protection from observation by the enemy. Concealment may be natural or artificial. Natural concealment is that given by trees, grass, leaves and so on, without any man-made changes. Artificial concealment is that which you construct yourself. You must become an expert in the use of concealment. Here are some rules to help you conceal yourself:

Remain motionless while you are observing. Movement can attract the eye of the enemy and give away your position.

Use all available concealment. Always act as though you were being watched and use the best available concealment.

Observe from the prone position. This position, lying flat on your stomach, gives you a low silhouette and makes it harder for the enemy to see you.

Expose nothing which glistens. Reflection of the sun flashing on bright objects like a wrist watch, knife or bright button will attract the observation of the enemy at once.

Blend with the background. Be sure that the color of you and your clothes does not contrast too much with your surroundings.

Stay in the shade. When you are in the shade, you throw no shadow and you'll be harder to see.

Break regular outline of objects. If you put garlands around your rifle, twigs in your helmet and use other tricks of camouflage, you break the regular shape of objects and make them harder to recognize.

Keep off the skyline. If you outline yourself against the sky at any time, you can be observed from even a great distance.

Observing. When you are observing, look around one of the sides of an object unless you can look through it.

When you fire. You fire around the right side of an object, unless you are left handed.

Never over the top. You never look or fire over the top of concealment or cover unless the outline of the concealment already is broken, or you can otherwise blend in with a suitable background.

Enemy aircraft. When an aircraft approaches, you take a prone position, face down, and remain motionless. If the aircraft comes upon you by surprise, stand still and do not look up.

Good observation points. A small, thin bush in the shadow of a large bush makes a good observation point. Lone trees or rocks, fence corners and other prominent landmarks are easily picked out as targets by enemy observers. Remember this when you are concealing yourself.

Camouflage

You already have seen by reading the above rules on cover and concealment that camouflage will be an important part of your individual movement. There are four things involved in successful individual camouflage. They are: ability to recognize and take advantage of all forms of natural concealment available; knowledge of the proper use of the available vegetation, soil and debris for camouflage purposes; knowledge of the proper use of artificial or issued camouflage materials; and camouflage discipline.

Helmets. Camouflage your helmet with the issue helmet cover or make a cover of cloth or burlap that is colored to blend with the terrain. The cover should fit loosely with the flaps folded under the helmet or left hanging. The hanging flaps may break up the

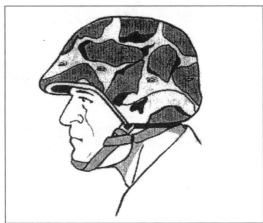

Fig. 31-1(a). Helmet with the issue helmet cover.

Fig. 31-1(b). Camouflage for the helmet.

helmet outline. Leaves, grass or sticks can also be attached to the cover. Use camouflage bands, strings, burlap strips or rubber bands to hold those in place. If there is no material for a helmet cover, disguise and dull the helmet surface with irregular patterns of paint or mud. (See Figures 31-1 (a) and (b).)

Uniforms. Most uniforms come already camouflaged. However, it may be necessary to add more camouflage to make the uniform blend better with the surroundings. To do this, put mud on the uniform or attach leaves, grass or small branches to it. Too much camouflage, however, may draw attention.

When operating on snow-covered ground, wear overwhites (if issued) to help blend with the snow. If overwhites are not issued, use white cloth, such as white bedsheets, to get the same effect. (See Fig. 31-2.)

Sand and light green for desert and dry areas

Loam and white for snow-covered terrain

Loam and light green for vegetated areas

Fig. 31-2. Camouflage uniforms.

	SKIN COLOR	SHINE AREAS	SHADOW AREAS
CAMOUFLAGE MATERIAL	LIGHT OR DARK	FOREHEAD, CHEEKBONES, EARS, NOSE AND CHIN	AROUND EYES, UNDER NOSE, AND UNDER CHIN
LOAM AND LIGHT GREEN STICK	ALL TROOPS USE IN AREAS WITH GREEN VEGETATION	USE LOAM	USE LIGHT GREEN
SAND AND LIGHT GREEN STICK	ALL TROOPS USE IN AREAS WITH GREEN VEGETATION	USE LIGHT GREEN	USE SAND
LOAM AND WHITE	ALL TROOPS USE ONLY IN SNOW-COVERED TERRAIN	USE LOAM	USE WHITE
BURNT CORK, BARK CHARCOAL, OR LAMP BLACK	ALL TROOPS, IF CAMOUFLAGE STICKS NOT AVAILABLE	USE	DO NOT USE
LIGHT-COLOR MUD	ALL TROOPS, IF CAMOUFLAGE STICKS NOT AVAILABLE	DO NOT USE	USE

Fig. 31-3. Application of camouflage materials.

Skin. Exposed skin reflects light and may draw the enemy's attention. Even very dark skin, because of its natural oil, will reflect light. Use the following methods when applying camouflage face paint to camouflage the skin. (See Fig. 31-3.)

When applying camouflage stick to your skin, work with a buddy (in pairs) and help each other.

Apply a two-color combination of camouflage stick in an irregular pattern. Paint shiny areas (forehead, cheekbones, nose, ears and chin) with a dark color. Paint shadow areas (around the eyes, under the nose and under the chin) with a light color. In addition to the face, paint the exposed skin on the back of the neck, arms and hands. Palms of hands are not normally camouflaged if arm-and-hand signals are to be used. Remove all jewelry to further reduce shine or reflection.

When camouflage sticks are not issued, use burnt cork, bark charcoal, lamp black or light-colored mud.

Movement

Some of the principles of movement already have been mentioned. You should plan to move from one concealed location to another and there are rules to help you move around successfully. Some of these rules are as follows:
- Remain motionless when you are not changing your position.
- When you are observing, lift your head slowly but steadily, without making any quick movements.
- Select your next stopping place from each position. Avoid isolated or obvious places of concealment. Before you leave one position, make certain that your next stopping place does not contain an enemy. Hit the deck a few yards from your position and roll to it.
- When you are changing your position by running, spring up and run with your body bent low and drop to the earth quickly. Take advantage of any walls, ditches or similar cover.

Individual Movement by Night

When you go on a night mission, some of your problems, such as cover, concealment, movement and camouflage, are going to be something like a day mission. Night will present special problems, however.

Night Vision

You have to adapt your eyes to seeing at night. This is night vision. The human eye adapts itself for seeing in the dark by enlarging the pupil in order to let in more light. If you are tired or have a vitamin deficiency, your night vision will not be as good as it could be.

You prepare your eyes for a night mission by staying in darkness for about an hour before you go out. If you cannot stay in the dark, keep out of the lights around you as long as possible and avoid looking straight at them. If it is possible, wear red goggles or keep one eye covered.

Appearance and Size

Darkness not only makes it hard or impossible for you to see objects, but it also changes their appearance and apparent size. Details are blotted out. You have to train yourself to identify objects by black outlines at night.
- A tree seen against the night light looks much smaller than it does in the daytime, because the twigs at the tips of the branches cannot be seen at night. For the same reason, an airplane caught in the beam of a searchlight looks larger than the same plane when it is seen as a black mass against a dimly lighted sky.
- Mechanical devices to aid night vision, which may be issued to you, make it possible to see objects or parts of objects that would otherwise be too small to be seen at all, and help to identify objects already spotted.
- Any kind of light is quickly visible at night. Under ordinary conditions, a lighted match can be seen for several miles. Under ideal conditions of darkness and atmosphere, a candle may be visible for 10 miles.

Sounds

At night, the sounds of things will be very important. You depend mostly upon your ears to get information about the enemy, and you have to exercise every care to keep the enemy from hearing you.
- When moving at night, stop frequently to listen. If you are required to wear a helmet, remove it when you stop so that sounds are not distorted by the helmet over your ears.
- By practicing a great deal, you can learn to listen for long periods in perfect silence. This is what you have to remember to do.
- Remember that sounds are transmitted a greater distance in wet weather and at night than in dry weather and in the daytime.
- If you hold your ear close to the ground, you can hear much better such sounds as persons walking and the noise of vehicles.

Smells

Use your nose as well as your ears. Your sense of smell may warn you of enemy fires, cooking, motor parks, gasoline and oil engines, bodies of water and the presence of troops.

Touch

Your sense of touch is going to mean much to you at night. Learn to operate and adjust your equipment by the sense of touch alone. You are also going to have to use your hands instead of your eyes to feel and recognize objects in the dark.

Concealment

Concealment at night is provided by darkness, unless there is bright moonlight. If the moon is giving light, however, you have to use the same methods of concealment that you use in daylight.

Movement

The principles of movement at night are somewhat different from those of daytime. At night, you must be able to move in absolute silence, because your safety depends on your silent movement. The five principles of night movement are:
- Move by bounds you have determined in advance.
- Run at night only in an emergency.
- Stop frequently and listen intently at each stop.
- Take advantage of sounds which may distract the enemy to cover up your own movements.
- If you fall down, don't cry out. Fall as silently as possible.

Other Precautions

In addition to these principles for movement at night, there are other methods which you can use to avoid detection:
- If you feel that you are about to sneeze, press upward on the end of your nose with your fingers. This may stop the sneeze.
- If you feel a cough coming, press lightly on your Adam's apple. This may stop it.
- Sometimes you may have a ringing noise in your head that interferes with your hearing. Try yawning to stop this.
- If it is necessary for you to whisper, expel most of the air from your lungs before you do. This does away with the hissing sound usually made by a whisper.
- If the enemy has been using gas, keep away from depressions in damp and rainy weather. Gas can remain in these places quite a while.
- Whenever you stop, look and listen.
- Do not look at an object too long. This strains your eyes.

- If caught in a flare, drop quickly in the split second that the enemy is blinded after the flare lights. If you hear the flare discharged, drop to the ground before it bursts. Never look at a flare; you will impair your night vision for nearly an hour. Close one eye to preserve your night vision.
- When you come upon patrols or persons, consider all of them to be unfriendly until you identify them. When you meet someone, crouch low in order to get the person silhouetted against the sky and to offer only an indistinct target if the person proves to be an enemy. If you are fired upon, do not return the fire except to avoid capture.
- If you are carrying a luminous compass or watch, be sure that the dial has some covering on it.

Passing Obstacles

The proper passing of obstacles such as wires and trenches is another thing you need to know about night movement. Whenever possible, avoid enemy obstacles, which are frequently covered by their weapons.
- All of your movements near wire must be slow and cautious, because of the danger of booby traps and mines. Walk over low wire at night by grasping the first strand with one hand and reaching forward with the other to feel for a clear spot on the ground. Feel for a spot where you can place your foot without touching another strand, or a mine, booby trap, or any object that might make a noise. When you find such a spot, lift your foot up and over, close to the hand grasping the wire. Place your foot beside your other hand to avoid catching it on another strand. If you are armed, sling your rifle across your back and follow the same procedure.
- You can move under wire on your back by feeling ahead and above for the strands of wire and inching yourself along, holding the wire clear of your body. Be careful not to tug on the wire or jerk it. You might make a noise or set off a booby trap. If you have a rifle with you, you can put it on your stomach, or you can place it between your body and right arm.
- When cutting wire, if you are alone, cut the wire near a picket to avoid having a loose end fly back. When you are operating with another Marine, one of you can hold the wire in both hands while the other cuts the wire between the hands. Then you bend or roll back the wire to make an opening sufficient for passage. When cutting wire, wrap a cloth around it to muffle sound. If a gap is cut in enemy wire, it is best to leave the top wires intact. This lessens chances of discovery.

Fig. 31-4. *How to search terrain.*

- The proper way to cross a narrow trench at night is explained here. You should crawl silently up to the edge of the trench, look into it, and remove all loose dirt and rocks from the edge. Then spring up from the prone position and jump across, sinking quietly to the ground on the other side. Remain there quite still for a moment and listen before you proceed any farther.
- If the trench is too wide for you to jump it in this manner, you must climb into it silently and slowly and then climb out the other side, using the revetment of the trench for support.

Observing

Special actions are needed when your mission is to observe and report. So far, we have studied ways to protect yourself and get around on your job. Now we come to the job itself.

Selecting Observation Posts

When looking for a place from which to observe, study it closely before you occupy it just to be sure it is not already occupied by the enemy.

After you have occupied the position, avoid unnecessary movement. Leave the position by a route different from the one you used to approach it. Be careful not to make paths that would reveal your position.

When you search the ground about your position, there are certain methods you can use to assure that you do a good job.

- In daylight, look first at the ground nearest you. Begin close to your position and search a narrow strip 50 yards or less wide, going from left to right parallel to your front. Then search from right to left a second and similar strip farther away but overlapping the first. You continue in this manner until you have covered your entire field of view.
- At night, you should search the horizon with short, jerky movements and short pauses. Look a little to one side of an object and then to the other side to see it best on a dark night. Low-powered field glasses also increase the range of your vision.
- Look at Figure 31-4, which shows you how terrain is searched. You can see troops as far away as 2,000 meters in the daytime. At 600 meters, you can count the files of a squad, and at 400 meters, the movement of arms and legs can be seen plainly.

Interpretation of Signs

You can tell trained combat Marines by their powers of observation. When they return from a mission, they can describe what sort of country they have passed through, all noticeable landmarks and any indications of the enemy in the vicinity. These Marines have acquired a keen sense of interpretation by constant practice in observing. The ability to do this is valuable. They have learned that the enemy, in its movements, leaves slight indications which show strength, the character and condition of troops, and direction of march.

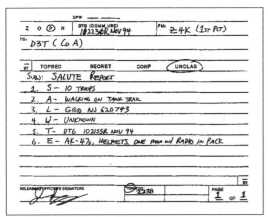

Fig. 31-5. Properly written message.

- The size of a bivouac area usually indicates the number of the enemy there. You can check laundry, ration tins, dumps and so on for clues as to the size of the enemy force.
- Tracks on a road can show you what kinds of troops or vehicles are in the body and their directions of march.
- The state of the bivouac and the amount of abandoned material lying about can reveal the enemy's condition to you. For instance, if you find food left uneaten, you can assume that they are well supplied. If all scraps of food have been eaten, you can assume that they are short on supplies.
- You can check a track for the time it was made. A freshly made track has sharp edges and ordinarily has signs of moisture which disappear in about 15 minutes.
- You can tell whether a footmark was made by a running or walking person. A running person digs the toes into the ground. The walking footprint is fairly even.
- You can easily tell the direction of travel of a car by the way its tracks pass across ruts or splash water from puddles.
- You can estimate the speed of a vehicle by the amount of mud splattered about or the dirt scattered by it. Slow moving vehicles leave shallow, smooth tracks. Faster moving wheels cut deeper.
- You can observe carefully your own unit, when you are on the march, in camp or deployed, in order to develop your power to estimate the size of enemy forces, even at a distance. Here are a few of the things you can learn: If a column is so far away that you cannot count it, you can estimate its size by the length of time it takes the column to pass a given point; infantry on the march usually raises a low, thick cloud of dust; a broken

could indicates artillery on the move; trucks and mechanized vehicles raise a heavy, rapidly moving cloud of dust.

Reporting

You send messages in the field to get information to your commander. A message can be either oral – that is, sent by word of mouth – or can be written. But whether it is spoken or written, you must learn to give accurate, clear and complete information, and you have to get it to your commander in time for them to use it. Figure 31-5 shows a message that is correctly written.

Oral Messages

You send an oral message when it is impractical to write out a message, when the information is just one simple idea or when there is greater danger that the enemy might seize a written one. Oral messages have to be as simple and clear as possible, and you should avoid having a series of numbers or names in them. Always have the person who is delivering an oral message for you repeat it back to you, so that you can be certain they have it correctly memorized.

Written Messages

When you write a message, you should include all information of value about the enemy and about yourself. You should be brief, accurate and clear. Distinguish carefully between facts and opinion. If you send in hearsay information, give the source somewhat in this manner: "Friendly farmer states four-man patrol crossed bridge at 36544273 at 0930 traveling south."

There are six kinds of facts which your commander always wants to know about the enemy. These are: size, activity, location, unit, time and equipment. The key word for remembering what information is needed on the enemy is **SALUTE**.

> **S**ize
> **A**ctivity
> **L**ocation
> **U**nit
> **T**ime
> **E**quipment

Number and place in a separate paragraph each item of information you write. This makes it clearer for your commander when it is read.

If you suspect that your commander did not get a message you sent, include a summary of it in your next message.

You indicate for your commander the place from which the message is being sent. You can do this by reference to an important terrain feature, by map coordinates, by the magnetic azimuth from each of two definitely located points or by the azimuth and distance from one known point. Sometimes you can describe your position best by using a simple sketch or overlay which also makes other information in your message clearer.

Your commander will want to know what you plan to do next, so include in your message your intentions. If you plan to remain in observation, continue your mission or take other action, you must tell your leader. If you think the message might fall into enemy hands, have a messenger give this information orally.

After you have have written your message, reread it carefully. If it is possible, have someone else read it to see that it is complete and easily understood.

Messengers

Information will be valuable to your commander only if it is received in time to act upon it. If you are in doubt about when to send a message, send it at once. This means that a messenger is employed. Here are some suggestions about messengers:

- When you are in friendly territory or close to friendly troops, one messenger is all you need. However, if you are in enemy territory or when it may be necessary to pass through heavy artillery concentrations, you should use two messengers if possible. They should leave at different times and travel by separate routes.
- The messenger must know where the message is to be delivered and the route to take. If there is a map available, the messenger marks a starting point and selects landmarks to help find the way.
- A messenger always travels light and takes only the necessary food and arms.
- If delayed or lost, the messenger should show the message to an officer, if it is possible, and ask the officer's advice. Messengers have the right of way and must be given all practical assistance.
- When there is danger of being captured, the messenger immediately destroys the message. To avoid detection, the messenger uses different routes in entering and leaving a message center or command post.
- If the messenger picks up any information along the route of interest to the commander, it should be reported at the time the message is delivered.

Sketches and Overlays

Sketches are valuable in getting information to your commander. Sometimes your information can be carried in no other manner. You can make two kinds of sketches, panoramic and topographic.

Panoramic Sketches

A panoramic sketch is a picture of the ground (terrain) showing the height and view from your point of observation. A panoramic sketch made by one scout can assist another scout in finding oneself quickly in the same location. Figure 31-6 shows how a panoramic sketch looks.

A panoramic sketch is made as follows:

- You first determine what information you want to give, then draw in the landscape lines that are more or less horizontal.
- Put the prominent points of your area on the sketch, but leave out unimportant details which might be just confusing.
- Do not show the foreground.
- Show on your sketch the location of the information you are sending and place any explanatory notes above the sketch in the margins with arrows pointing to the features explained.
- Select as a reference point the most prominent point in your sketch, and indicate the azimuth to it.
- Then place a title on the sketch, show where it was made, indicate the date and time it was made, and sign it.

Topographic Sketches

A topographic sketch is made so that the person receiving it can plot on a map your scouting position or the information you desire to convey. To make a topographic sketch, you need a map similar to one your commander has. This is the way you make a topographic sketch:

- You find the azimuth from your position to the position of an object you can easily see and describe. Estimate the distance by the most accurate means available.
- Draw the azimuth line from you to the object. Mark the azimuth above this line and the distance below the line.
- At the proper end of the line show the object and, at the other end, indicate your own position.
- Find the azimuth and the distance to some other point on your map or to the position of the com-

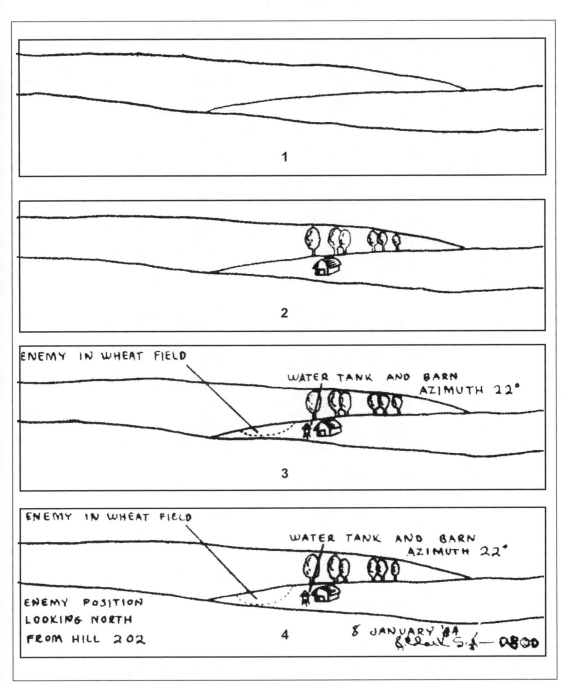

Fig. 31-6. *Method of making a panoramic sketch: (1) Draw the more or less horizontal lines of land-scape; (2) put in the prominent points; (3) put notes above each sketch, give azimuth from position to most prominent point in sketch; (4) give sketch a title and show where made, date and time, sign it.*

413

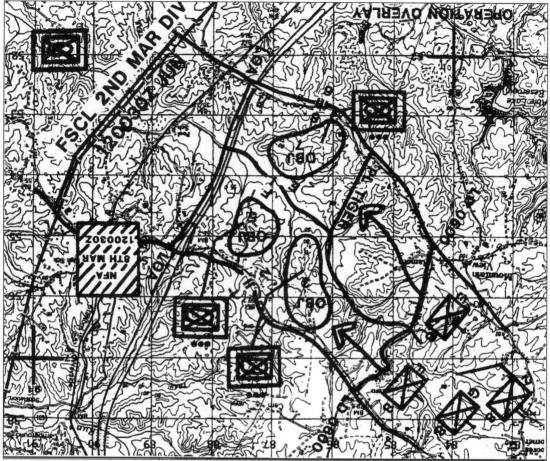

Fig. 31-7. Making an overlay.

mand post. Then draw this line on the sketch and indicate the azimuth, the distance and the object to which it is drawn. Sign the sketch.

Overlays

The topographic sketch is drawn on a piece of transparent paper, which is called an overlay. The overlay can be placed over a map or chart on which locations, such as targets or enemy positions are shown. Your commander can take the overlay you made with your map, place it over the map and see clearly the information you are giving. You can use any kind of thin paper – tracing paper, overlay sheets from a message book or acetate – for your overlay. Figure 31-7 shows you a brief and accurate overlay.

Here is the way to make a simple one:

- Place your map on a hard, flat surface.
- Put the transparent paper over the part of the map you are using and fasten the paper with clips, thumbtacks or pins.
- Next, identify the section that you are reporting on. To do this, trace the intersecting grid lines at two opposite corners of the overlay and give their correct number designations. If there are no grid lines on your map, trace in at least two clearly defined map features, such as road junctions, towns or streams. This lets your commander know the exact area on the map that is covered by your overlay.
- On the overlay, sketch in the object or information you wish to tell your commander about. If some of the information on the map is needed to com-

plete your information, be careful to make your sketches so that the map's information shows through when the overlay is on it.

- Put all your explanatory notes along the margin of the overlay with arrows pointing to the objects mentioned.
- Indicate on your overlay the position on the map from which you saw the object or obtained the information.
- Indicate the title and the scale of the map from which the overlay was made, so that your commander will know to which map the overlay belongs.
- Give the date and hour you obtained the information shown on the overlay.
- Sign the overlay.

Patrolling

When your company is in combat, small groups are sent out from time to time on special missions which are called patrols. A patrol is a detachment of troops sent out from a larger body on a mission of reconnaissance, security or combat.

There are two general classes of patrols, *reconnaissance* and *combat*, either of which might have a mission of security. The classification is derived from the mission assigned a patrol.

Reconnaissance Patrols

Reconnaissance patrols are sent out to gain information about the enemy or the terrain. Such patrols engage in combat only when it becomes necessary to accomplish their assigned mission or in order to protect themselves. In general, they avoid combat and accomplish their missions by stealth.

Reconnaissance patrols have a great variety of tasks, but their primary mission is to obtain and report information in time for it to be of value to the commander who dispatched the patrol.

Some of the tasks that may be assigned to reconnaissance patrols are: (1) to locate and observe the characteristics of a hostile position or installation, (2) to reconnoiter a route of march for a larger force, (3) to reconnoiter a safe and fordable stream crossing for an advancing unit, (4) to reconnoiter a certain terrain feature or the general nature of the terrain in a given locality, (5) to maintain contact with a rapidly withdrawing force. The tasks mentioned are by no means all inclusive but are given as examples.

Combat Patrols

Combat patrols are assigned missions which usually require them to engage actively in combat. They are fighting patrols. Every combat patrol, no matter what its primary mission, has a secondary mission – that of gaining information about the enemy and the terrain.

A combat patrol may be dispatched with the mission of: (1) capturing several prisoners, (2) destroying an enemy installation, (3) protecting an exposed flank of an advancing unit, (4) seizing and holding a piece of commanding ground to prevent enemy occupation of the terrain feature, and (5) ambushing the enemy. Again, the missions mentioned are not all inclusive but are given merely as examples.

Patrol Formations

In Chapter 28, you saw a number of fire team formations. While on patrol as a unit, as part of a squad, or as part of a larger force, the fire team leader may use any or all of these formations from time to time. The factors determining which formation will be used include: mission, terrain, visibility, control and security. The leader must be able to move the team in any direction and to change quickly to another formation by signals. Each member of the patrol is assigned a sector of observation. In order to be sure of security when the patrol halts, each member takes up a firing position from which the sector assigned can be observed.

Duties as a Patrol Member

As a patrol member, you must respond quickly to the decisions and orders of your leader. You must have complete confidence in all members of the patrol and confidence that your team will succeed in its mission.

Your patrol goes in a formation which can be changed to suit conditions you meet. The leader of your patrol tells you by signal where to place yourself in the formation as you proceed.

One member of the patrol remains inside the group where the patrol leader can always be seen. Other members on the points and flanks move in and out to look for any cover which might hold an enemy. They can carefully observe an area up to 100 meters in open terrain to protect the entire patrol.

Members of your patrol automatically move closer together in thick cover, fog and at night. When you are in open country in daylight and the weather is clear, you can move farther apart. However your flank groups usually are not more than 100 meters from the center of the advancing patrol.

Your patrol leader tries to locate so that signals can be seen quickly by all members of the patrol. The leader uses arm-and-hand signals shown in Chapter 28 during the daytime. At night touch and the arm-and-hand signals are used.

Patrol Reports

When your patrol returns, the leader makes a report to cover your activities. This report is written, unless there is not enough time to write it, and the patrol leader must also be prepared to answer questions which the commander or intelligence officer may ask. In case you should be a patrol leader, following is the information you are expected to give either by word of mouth or in writing:

Routine Information. Certain information is gathered as a matter of course and delivered without specific questions being asked:
- The name or number of your patrol, its size and mission, are given first.
- The time the patrol departed and the routes it took are reported.
- You detail the character of the terrain you covered – that is, was it dry, swampy? Could vehicles cross it?
- Tell what you observed. That is, give the number, composition, equipment and attitude of the enemy.

- Where and when the enemy was observed. This includes what the enemy was doing when spotted, the direction of the movement, if the enemy was moving and any changes in dispositions.
- The location and condition of enemy defenses is described.
- If your patrol met any of the enemy, give the results of the encounter.
- The return route and time of the patrol's return are furnished, and the condition of your patrol, including the disposition you made of any dead or wounded, is described.
- Finally, you give your conclusions, including to what extent your mission was accomplished.

Special Information. In addition to this routine information, the patrol leader should be able to answer special questions from the commander or an intelligence officer:
- Your commander might ask you to show on the map just where you went.
- You might be asked to give the routes of approach to your outfit's position.
- You also might be asked if you saw any assembly places close to your front lines from which an enemy assault could be launched.
- Someone might want your opinion as to whether the enemy could use armored vehicles on the ground you covered.
- Other questions could concern whether the security measures taken by your outfit are good or whether there are some particular weaknesses in your unit's positions which you have observed during the patrol.

Chapter Thirty-Two

NBC Defense

Fortunately for mankind in general, nuclear, biological and chemical operations have seldom been a part of either general or limited war. Notwithstanding this fact, many nations have nuclear, biological and chemical weapons in their arsenals which may be used at any time. For this reason, Marines must be familiar with the effects of these weapons and the defensive measures necessary to counter them.

United States policy opposes initiation of NBC attacks, while maintaining a defensive posture sufficient to counterattack, if necessary, with devastating force. In November 1969, the President of the United States announced that this country would no longer maintain an offensive capability with biological weapons because of their epidemic capabilities.

Introduction To Nuclear Defense

The introduction of nuclear weapons in modern warfare has placed greater responsibility on the unit leader.

While nuclear fires produce casualties through blast, heat and radiation, their effect depends upon many variables. Such variables include the size or yield of the weapon, height of burst (subsurface, surface or air burst), distance from ground zero, and the protection afforded Marines by fighting holes or armor.

Marines with a basic knowledge of nuclear weapons and their effects can survive and still function as an effective part of a combat unit.

Tests have proven that troops with adequate protection can operate within a matter of minutes in an area where a nuclear explosion has occurred.

Conventional and Nuclear Explosions

There are several basic differences between a nuclear and a high explosive detonation.

First, a nuclear explosion may be many thousands or millions of times more powerful than that of the largest conventional weapon.

Second, a fairly large portion of the energy of a nuclear explosion is in the form of heat and light or thermal radiation, which is capable of producing injury or starting fires at considerable distances from the point of detonation.

Third, and probably the greatest difference, is the highly penetrating and harmful rays called "initial nuclear radiation."

Finally, the substances left after the explosion are radioactive, giving off harmful radiation over an extended period of time. This is known as the "residual nuclear radiation" or "residual radioactivity."

It is these differences between the conventional and nuclear explosions that require special considerations. (See Fig. 32-1.)

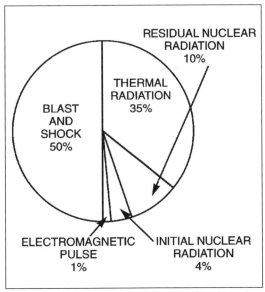

Fig. 32-1. *Energy distribution contained in a low air burst type of nuclear explosion.*

Effects on Individuals

Casualties from nuclear fire result from blast, thermal radiation and nuclear radiation effects. Each is discussed below.

Blast – Injuries are caused by both direct and indirect blast effects. Direct effect injuries such as ruptured eardrums and internal injuries are the result of the very high pressure waves generated by the blast. Indirect effect injuries are caused by falling buildings; flying objects; shattered glass; and fires started from short circuits, overturned stoves and ignited fuels.

The highest percentage of blast injuries will normally be a result of indirect effects.

Thermal Radiation and Other Burns – It has been estimated that approximately 30 percent of the deaths that occurred as a result of nuclear weapons were due to burns of one kind or another.

Persons in the open within two miles of a medium-sized nuclear weapon will receive painful flash burns on exposed skin.

Fires resulting from blast cause other burn injuries. Personnel looking directly at the nuclear explosion may receive eye damage which is usually temporary in nature. Flash and flame burns resulting from nuclear explosions are treated like other burns.

Nuclear Radiation – The damage done by nuclear radiation depends on the dosage received and the time of exposure.

Exposure to nuclear radiation does not necessarily cause radiation sickness. It takes a large amount of nuclear radiation, either initial or residual, to seriously harm an individual. Normally, the effects of nuclear radiation are not noticed during or immediately after exposure.

If a Marine receives an excessive amount of nuclear radiation, such symptoms as nausea, vomiting and a feeling of weakness occur within a few hours. Bear in mind, however, that a person can have nausea, vomiting and weakness and still continue to do duties.

Generally, these immediate effects do not require that the individual be evacuated. Except in cases of extreme overexposure, these effects soon disappear and may not occur again, depending upon the dosage received.

Nuclear bursts are generally described as air, surface and subsurface, depending upon where the explosion occurs in relation to the surface of the earth. The height of the burst is important, because it influences the amount and kind of damage that occurs. (See Figs. 32-2 and 3.)

Air Burst – An air burst is a nuclear explosion in which the fireball does not touch the surface of the earth. The greatest danger from this type of burst is from blast and heat. The primary nuclear radiation hazard is from initial nuclear radiation, but a residual hazard may exist out to several hundred meters from ground zero (GZ) (further with larger yield weapons) and should be avoided or passed through rapidly if attack through or reconnaissance of this area is necessary.

Surface Burst – A surface burst is one in which the fireball touches, but is not beneath, the surface of the earth. Damage from blast is less widespread, and damage from heat is approximately the same as for an air burst of the same size. About the same initial nuclear radiation is present. Residual nuclear radiation is present. Residual nuclear radiation is created in the target area and may occur as fallout in downwind areas.

Subsurface Burst – A subsurface burst is one in which the center of the fireball is beneath the surface of the earth. Most of the blast effect appears as ground or water shock waves. The majority of the heat and initial nuclear radiation is absorbed by the surrounding earth or water. However, considerable residual radiation is produced in the target area and later as fallout.

Individual Protection

The effects of nuclear explosion may be divided into two broad categories, immediate and delayed. The immediate effects are those which occur within a few minutes of detonation and include blast and shock, thermal radiation and initial nuclear radiation. The delayed effects are normally associated with the radioactivity present in fallout and neutron-induced activity. The early fallout from a surface burst will begin to reach the ground within a few minutes after the explosion at close-in locations, and later at greater distances from ground zero.

Protection from Blast

Since the effects of blast are immediate, consider the individual in each of two circumstances: when adequate warning is given prior to the attack and when no warning is forthcoming.

When adequate warning is given, the individual has time to prepare defenses. The fighting hole is good protection. It should be deep and strong with the cover well secured. Bunkers, fortified positions

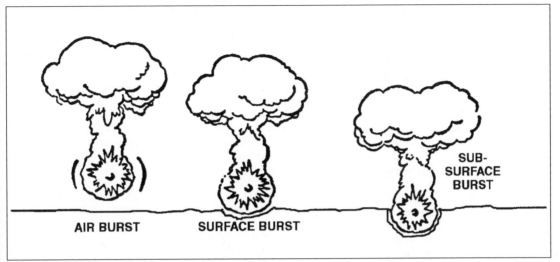

Fig. 32-2. *Three types of nuclear explosions.*

Type of Burst	Initial nuclear radiation	Residual nuclear radiation contamination (target area and/or fallout)	Blast	Heat (thermal radiation)
Air	Extensive and hazardous. Hazard exists, however, only during explosion.	Negligible except as induced radioactivity in soil in target area following low air bursts.	Extensive.	Extensive.
Surface	Generally less extensive than from air burst of the same size, but still hazardous.	Generally extensive. Occurs in target area as induced radioactivity in soil and as fallout in target area and in areas miles downwind of target area. Hazard lasts for long periods of time; fallout may not reach your position until several hours after explosion.	Concentrated in smaller area than in an air burst.	Affects smaller area than does air burst.
Subsurface	So little it is not considered hazardous.	Generally extensive and more dangerous than from a surface burst of the same size. Occurs as induced radioactivity in soil and as fallout, just as from a surface burst. Hazard lasts for long periods of time; fallout may not reach your position until several hours after explosion.	Concentrated in smaller area than in either air or surface bursts.	Negligible because most of it is absorbed or deflected by ground or water.

Fig. 32-3. *Characteristics of nuclear explosions.*

and shelters are excellent protection from all effects of blast.

When there is no prior warning, individual reaction is mandatory. Remember, the flash can be seen a few seconds before the blast wave arrives. In any case, a person should stay down for at least 90 seconds. Ditches, culverts and hills offer good protection, and as the distance from ground zero increases, good protection can be obtained from walls, slight depressions in the ground, or anything that breaks the pattern of the wave.

Protection from Thermal Radiation

Another of the immediate effects that requires reaction on the part of the individual is the thermal radiation that is emitted from the fireball. Thermal radiation has a line of sight effect, so protection from it is the same as for blast. If prior warning of a nuclear attack is received, preparation both for blast and thermal radiation should be complete. If a weapon goes off with no warning, drop flat on the ground or to the bottom of a fighting hole. Keep your eyes closed and protect exposed skin from heat rays as much as possible (keep hands and arms near or under your body and helmet on). This immediate reaction will minimize serious burns.

Protection from Nuclear Radiation

The different effects of nuclear radiation require both immediate and delayed action. Initial nuclear radiation is spent in the first minute or two after the burst, so protection from it is the same as for thermal radiation and blast. Any material will afford some protection from initial radiation, but denser items are better. For example, earth is a better shield than water, and steel is better than concrete.

Residual Radiation – Under conditions where the explosion takes place either on or beneath the surface, the resulting residual radiation hazard is high. Particles of water spray, dust and other debris which become radioactive through contact with the nuclear reaction of the weapon contaminate large areas. Individual protection consists of avoiding the fallout particles. This may be accomplished in the field by covering fighting holes with earth, a shelter half or poncho. Open food and water supplies should be disposed of by burying if contaminated. Personnel and equipment should be checked and decontaminated if necessary.

Nuclear Decontamination

At the small-unit level, decontamination is usually confined to personnel, equipment and food.

Personnel

Personal decontamination should be accomplished as soon as the tactical situation permits.

Normal Procedure – In rear areas, and when permitted in the tactical area, personnel bathe using plenty of soap and water, warm if possible. Particular attention should be given to skin creases, hairy parts of the body and the fingernails (Fig. 32-4).

Field Expedient Procedures – When the tactical situation prohibits normal procedures, field expedient procedures are used. Clothing should be removed and shaken vigorously downwind. Shrubbery can be used to brush radioactive particles from the clothing. Personnel should put on protective masks or cover their noses and mouths with a damp cloth to prevent inhalation of the radioactive dust. Care must be taken to avoid secondary contamination of food or water supplies during the shaking of clothing. Personnel then wipe all exposed skin with a damp cloth and remove as much dust as possible from the hair and from under the fingernails. Personnel should bathe and change clothing when the tactical situation permits.

Equipment

The squad may be required to decontaminate individual items of equipment. The decontamination of equipment may be accomplished by removal (brushing and washing), sealing and aging. In some cases, brushing will reduce dry contamination to a permissible level. In most cases, washing will be adequate even though brushing has not been effective. When speed in the decontamination of equipment is important, brushing is performed first, followed by washing as time and circumstances permit.

Food

Food and water that have become contaminated should be disposed of by burying.

Biological Defense

The individual Marine's primary concern during a biological operation will be that of protection and

Fig. 32-4. *Personal decontamination.*

421

DON'T---

1. Consume native or civilian food or drink of any kind. Eat and drink only approved food and water.
2. Put anything in your mouth unless you are certain it is not contaminated.
3. Bathe in lakes or ponds.
4. Touch animals.
5. Take souvenirs.

DO---

1. Keep immunizations current and use prescribed medications.
2. Be able to recognize the biological contamination marker. Know what it means.

Fig. 32-5. *Precautionary measures for avoiding biological agent contamination.*

continuing the mission. Protection is provided by keeping shots up to date and wearing the protective mask and protective clothing when an attack is suspected (Fig. 32-5). These protective items are described in more detail under the section on Chemical Defense.

Protective Measures to Take Before a Biological Attack

Maintain Natural Body Defenses – A healthy body can better resist disease and infection from any source. Therefore, keep yours in top physical shape. A high standard of personal cleanliness and careful attention to field sanitation is essential. Protection is provided by keeping body, clothes and living area as clean as possible.

Care of minor wounds, cuts and scratches by keeping them clean and using available first-aid supplies is important. Such care speeds healing and reduces the possibility of infection from any source. Soap and water are very effective in keeping cuts and scratches clean.

Biological agents can enter your body through your nose, mouth and skin, depending on the type of agent released. The main danger in a biological agent attack is breathing the agents in an aerosol form. Your protective mask, if properly fitted and worn, will prevent agents from entering your body by inhalation.

Take All Prescribed Immunizations or Other Medication – The Marine Corps has a varied and effective immunization program. In the event of biological weapons employment, additional immunizations may be given or special medications issued.

Immunizations are valuable, because they strengthen the body's defense against certain diseases. If attacked with biological agents, immunizations may prevent diseases and will certainly reduce the severity of the disease.

Train in the Use of the Protective Mask – All Marines must know how to use and care for the protective mask. This mask is so important that it will be dealt with separately.

Detection of a Biological Attack – Detection of a biological warfare attack can be very difficult. Figure 32-6 lists out of the ordinary occurrences that should be reported if observed.

Decontamination and First Aid

The simplest and most effective method of decontaminating the body after a biological agent attack is use of soap and water. There are no first aid measures for biological agents, because there are no immediate effects.

On observing any of the items in Figure 32-6, mask, pass the word and:

- Button cuffs and collar,
- Turn collar up.
- Apply insect repellent if available.

Detection of a Biological Attack

a. Enemy aircraft dropping unidentified material or spraying unidentified substances.
b. New and unusual types of shells and bombs, particularly those which burst with little or no blast.
c. Smoke from an unknown source or of an unknown nature.
d. An increased occurrence of sick or dead animals.
e. Unusual or unexplained increase in the number of insects, such as mosquitoes, ticks, or fleas.
f. Any weapon not seeming to have an immediate casualty effect.

Fig. 32-6. *Early warning signs.*

Chemical Defense

The enemy may use toxic chemical agents at any time, so the field protective mask and protective clothing are very important pieces of equipment.

A chemical attack can be disastrous to those not prepared for it. A properly trained Marine, using the equipment issued, can survive a chemical attack.

Protective Equipment

In addition to the proactive mask which will be discussed in more detail later, you may be issued Chemical Protective Clothing. This consists of the chemical protective suit, glove set, and Green Vinyl Overboots (GVOs) or Black Vinyl Overboots (BVOs), which have been developed to provide the individual Marine with protection against all forms of chemical and biological dissemination.

The suit is a two-layer, two piece overgarment consisting of a coat and a pair of trousers. The outer layer of the coat and trousers is fabricated of nylon-cotton twill fabric which is treated with a water repellent finish. The inner layer is fabricated of charcoal-laminate impregnated polyurethane tricot laminate.

The glove set consists of an outer glove to provide chemical protection and an inner glove to assist in absorption of perspiration. The outer five-fingered glove is fabricated of impermeable black butyl rubber. The inner glove is fabricated of thin white cotton material and can be worn on either hand.

The overboots are green or black rubber that are made to slip over the combat boots.

The suit, glove set and footwear covers, together with the protective mask, provide protection against both biological and chemical agents. However, they can reduce your efficiency and cause heat exhaustion, fatigue or other adverse reaction. The protective equipment will only be worn when the mission and the threat so indicate.

Mission-Oriented Protective Posture (MOPP)

Mission-Oriented Protective Posture levels (MOPP Levels) are established to tell you what level of mission related threat there is against you. Figure 32-7 shows what protective equipment you must use relative to the threat.

The chart at the end of this chapter (Fig. 32-10) depicts some of the chemical agents the enemy may use. Those agents may be disseminated by the enemy in liquid, vapor or aerosol form.

Each Marine, in addition to being equipped with a properly fitting protective mask and protective clothing, must also be equipped with a basic knowledge of toxic chemical agents, their uses and effects.

Types of Chemical Agents

Chemical agents are divided into the following general classifications:

Toxic Chemical Agents – Chemical agents designed to kill or incapacitate are known as toxic agents. They may enter the body through the lungs or by contact with the skin. The current groups of toxic agents are:

- *Nerve Agents* – These agents are quick acting. Entering the body through breathing or by skin

MOPP Levels Before Chemical Attack

MOPP	Overgarment	Overboots	Mask with Hoods	Gloves
0	Available	Available	Available	Available
1	Wear, open or closed based on temperature	Carry	Carry	Carry
2	-Same-	Wear	Carry	Carry
3	-Same-	Wear	Wear, hood open or closed based on temperature	Carry
4	Wear, closed	Wear	Wear, hood closed	Wear

Fig. 32-7. MOPP Levels Before a Chemical Attack.

contact, they are very rapid in action and produce immediate casualties.

- **Blister Agents** – These are delayed action chemicals that produce blisters on exposed skin, in the eyes or in the respiratory system. Symptoms may appear within 4 hours or as long as 36 hours after exposure.
- **Blood Agents** – These are rapid acting agents that deprive the body of oxygen. They must be inhaled to be effective, so the field protective mask affords complete protection.
- **Choking Agents** – These are delayed action casualty producers that are very damaging to the lungs. Low concentrations may be difficult to detect. The protective mask provides adequate defense.
- **Incapacitating Agents** – These chemicals will cause temporary casualties that may be extremely difficult to control. Symptoms of mental confusion may take several hours to appear and may last for several days. Restraint and immediate medical assistance is necessary.
- **Irritant Chemical Agents** – The irritant agents produce temporary irritating or disabling effects if they are inhaled or contact the eyes and skin. The standard agents of this group range from CN (tear agents) through chlorine.

Detection of Chemical Agents

The success of chemical defense depends to a great degree on the thoroughness of the training program conducted by the small-unit leader. This training must consider the various characteristics of the agents as stated above and the three phases of defensive operations: detection, protection and decontamination.

Intelligence Sources – Intelligence sources may warn of expected attacks. These reports are usually based on enemy preparations and capabilities.

Individual Marines – Marines may be able to identify a chemical attack by the use of their physical senses. Agents may have characteristic odors, create a visible cloud, appear as droplets on vegetation or be detectable only by early recognition of symptoms.

Because of this variety and the risk of rapid casualty effects, an automatic masking procedure will be put into effect once chemical operations are initiated.

Any suspicious occurrence (low flying aircraft, smoke screen, unaccountable liquid and unusual physical or mental symptoms) will be considered a potential threat, and all Marines will mask. The situation can then be checked in comparative safety and the decision made to unmask or continue a protected posture as required.

Special Equipment – There are several items of special equipment designed for the identification and detection of chemical agents. The squad should be basically familiar with this equipment and its uses.

- **ABC-M8 Paper, Chemical Agent Detector, VGH** – ABC-M8 chemical agent detector paper is a component of the chemical agent detector kits. The sheets consist of paper impregnated with chemical compounds that vary color when in contact with V- or G-type nerve agents or blister (mustard) agents in liquid form. This paper does not detect vapor and must touch the liquid agent to ensure a positive test.

  Because some solvents cause a change in the color of paper, it is unreliable for determining the completeness of decontamination by the use of solvents. A color chart is included in the kit to aid in interpreting the tests.
- **M9 Paper, Chemical Agent Detector** – M9 paper is issued in a roll with a sticky side and is designed to be worn on the wrist (on which watch is worn), arm (opposite wristwatch arm) and ankle (just above the boot). If it detects chemicals, pink or red spots will appear on the paper. It does not detect the kind of chemicals. Some solvents will cause the pink or red spots to form.
- **M256A1 Kit** – This item is designed for company and larger sized units and provides the means of detecting and identifying vapor concentrations of most chemical agents. Color changes occur in select detector spots and tickets. This device is designed for rapid identification of agents, but cannot be used as a warning device because test reactions may take 15 minutes to complete.
- **M21 Remote Sensing Chemical Agent Automatic Alarm** – When available, this device will detect agents in a unit area. It provides an audible alarm and visual signal when detecting nerve and blister vapors. This is a warning device and further evaluation would be required to actually identify the agent in use.

Protection

Protective Mask – When properly fitted, the protective mask protects against inhalation and facial contamination by toxic agents. This is the primary means of protection in chemical defense.

Protective Clothing – Protective clothing is available for those persons required to enter or remain in a contaminated area for a length of time.

Antidote and Personnel Decontamination Kits – Antidotes for blister and nerve agents are found in the protective mask carrier when issued.

- The Mark I Kit is used as a treatment for any exposure to a nerve agent. It may be given by medical personnel or self-administered by the individual. Effects should be obvious in 15 to 20 minutes.

First Aid and Individual Decontamination

First aid includes the immediate action required to prevent further injury or complications from the effects of chemical agents. This necessarily includes the prompt removal of agents from the eye and decontamination of skin to avoid casualties from lethal liquid agents. Therefore, first aid must include individual decontamination automatically and without orders when it is required, and the use of appropriate medications or actions to reduce the effects of the agent, such as the use of the nerve agent antidote injector for nerve agent poisoning. Each Marine must be thoroughly trained in both first aid and decontamination so that these actions can be performed quickly.

Unidentified Chemical Agents – In most cases the individuals will not be able to immediately identify the chemical agent used in the attack. When exposed to an enemy chemical attack while dressed in chemical protective clothing and equipment, they will not normally be concerned with immediate decontamination. However, if an individual has been contaminated by an unidentified agent, perhaps while unmasked, the following actions are taken:

Decontamination of Eyes and Face – Use the buddy system to decontaminate each other, if alone, proceed as follows. If the eyes and face have been contaminated, the individual must immediately try to get under cover. Shelter is necessary to prevent further contamination during the decontamination process. If no overhead cover is available, throw a poncho or shelter half over the head before beginning decontamination. Then decontaminate the eyes by turning the side of the face upward and, using water from a canteen, repeatedly flush the eyes. The facial skin decontamination should be done by using the components of the M258A1 or M291 skin decontaminating kit.

CAUTION: Do NOT let the solution from the M25A1 or M291 kit get in the eyes!

Nerve Agents – It is imperative that nerve agents in contact with the skin or eyes by neutralized or removed immediately if the individual is to avoid becoming a casualty. These agents are lethal and rapidly absorbed by the eyes and through cuts in the skin. They are absorbed through unbroken skin somewhat more slowly. The most unique symptoms of nerve agent poisoning is pinpointing of the pupils of eyes.

First Aid – The injection of nerve agent antidote and the giving of artificial respiration are first aid measures necessary for individuals showing symptoms of nerve agent poisoning.

Decontamination – The components of the M258A1 or M291 decontamination kit are used to remove contamination from the skin. Plain water only is used to repeatedly flush the eyes. The skin in contact with contaminated clothing should be decontaminated as soon as the clothing can be removed.

Blister Agents – Casualties of blister agents such as HD (distilled mustard) will exhibit redness and inflammation of the eyes. Usually several hours after exposure, reddening of the skin will appear, followed by the appearance of blisters. There is no first aid for blister agents other than decontamination. Blister agent effects will be delayed for several hours to days. To decontaminate the eyes, flush with plain water repeatedly. Any blister agents on the skin and clothing should be removed using the M258A1 or M291 decontamination kits and seek medical care as soon as possible. If evacuation to a medical facility is required, blister agent casualties will receive the same treatment given other burn victims.

Blood Agents – Agents such as AC and CK enter the body by inhalation and produce symptoms ranging from convulsions to coma. They act on the body by interfering with the ability of oxygen carrying cells to transfer oxygen to other body tissue. They may have an irritating effect on nasal passages. First aid includes immediate masking. This may prevent further damage. No specific treatment other than basic first aid is available.

Choking Agents – This agent will produce coughing, choking, nausea and headaches in casualties. Delayed effects include rapid and shallow breathing, painful cough, discomfort, fatigue and shock. First aid includes immediate masking. This may prevent further damage. No specific first aid other than efforts to prevent shock is available.

Decontamination

Decontamination can be accomplished by the removal, neutralization, absorption or weathering of the chemical agent. Decontamination's primary purposes are to prevent casualties and to remove obstacles that may prevent mission accomplishment.

Levels of Decontamination – Individual decontamination is performed by the individual, with material on hand, on the body, clothing and the equipment they use. It is performed as soon as practical and is usually sufficient to allow the individual to carry on the assigned mission. Individuals are issued the M258A1 or M291 decontamination kit which enables one to take care of the body, clothing and equipment. Each tactical vehicle is authorized one M11 portable decontamination apparatus that will hold 1-1/3 quarts of decontamination solution DS-2. It is used to decontaminate parts of the vehicle that must be touched during vehicle operation, such as the controls. It works on the same principle as a fire extinguisher.

A word of caution: DS-2 is very corrosive and flammable, and any metal surface sprayed with DS-2 must be washed to remove it.

Unit decontamination is an organized effort performed by personnel of the unit, with equipment available to the unit, when directed by the commander and under supervision of trained NBC specialists. All officers, NCO's and qualified NBC specialists should be prepared to act as supervisors of decontamination teams, when required.

Decontamination which is beyond the capabilities of the unit is performed by specialized teams equipped with the M17 Light Weight Decontamination System (LWDS). Communication equipment should be decontaminated by using hot air, if available. The next best method is by airing or weathering. The metal parts of field telephones and radios may be decontaminated by the heat given off during operation.

Use and Care of the Protective Mask

The Marine Corps issued M40/A1 field protective mask is the best that modern science can produce.

In the event of an actual chemical or biological attack, commands are not used. The mask is put on and checked as rapidly as possible, because each second can mean the difference between survival and serious injury or death. *Individual proficiency standards call for the Marine to properly put on, seal, clear and check the mask (with hood attached) within nine seconds and complete attachment of the hood under the arms within six seconds (total time 15 seconds).*

Because of the dangers of chemical and biological operations, care of the protective mask is essential. Water damages the filter elements of the mask and destroys efficiency. The waterproof bag issued with the protective mask must be used to protect filter elements against submergence in water. Never sit or lie on the mask. Treat the mask with the same respect shown a weapon, and it will perform properly when needed.

The field protective mask may be carried in one of the following positions: shoulder carry, leg carry, or cartridge belt carry.

M40 PROTECTIVE MASK CHARACTERISTICS AND COMPONENTS

Characteristics:
- Lightweight (3.8 pounds with carrier)
- Transported and stored in carrier
- Facepiece has silicone rubber seal for better fit
- Second skin for additional protection from liquid agents (M40A1 model only)
- Clear and neutral gray eyepiece outserts
- Canister easily replaced
- Side and front voicemitters
- Drinking tube

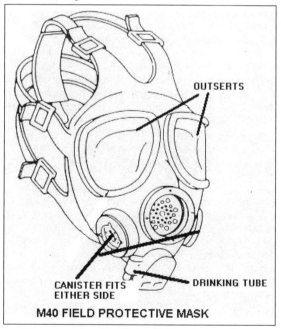

OUTSERTS

CANISTER FITS EITHER SIDE   DRINKING TUBE

M40 FIELD PROTECTIVE MASK

Sighting Rifle While Wearing the Protective Mask

Special procedures are recommended for sighting a rifle while wearing the protective mask. Speed and accuracy in obtaining a proper sight picture may be achieved by repeated sighting of the rifle using the following procedures:

Aim the rifle in the same manner as when unmasked except that the mask should slide up the stock of the rifle to the sighting position.

If a sight picture is not readily obtained, move the rifle butt around (higher or lower, inward or outward) in the shoulder and resight the rifle. Adjust the position. (In some instances a slight canting inward of the weapon will be required.)

Drinking Water While Wearing the Mask in an NBC Area

When the mask is connected to a water canteen with an M1 water canteen cap, a drinking system is formed. The wearer of the mask can then drink safely through the drinking tube inside the mask. When the drinking system is disconnected, self-closing valves seal off both the mask and the water canteen.

Warning: Do not connect the drink tube to your canteen until all mating surfaces are checked and are free of contamination. Chemical agents could be swallowed, resulting in sickness and death.

To use the drink tube, your canteen must be equipped with an M1 canteen cap.

a. Fill your plastic water canteen before entering contaminated area or, if in a contaminated area, work inside a protective shelter.

b. Use M8 chemical agent detector paper to check for contamination before using the drink tube. Warning: Care should be taken not to break the facepiece seal while pressing in on the outlet valve body. Water may leak into facepiece if mouth is taken off internal drink tube.

c. Press in on top of outlet valve until internal drink tube can be grasped between your teeth.

d. Steady facepiece and pull quick disconnect coupling out of outlet valve cover.

e. Remove canteen from canteen carrier.

f. Flip open cover on M1 canteen cap.

g. Push quick disconnect coupling into M1 canteen cap so that pin enters coupling. Warning: If resistance is not felt, your drinking system is leaking. Do not drink. Notify unit maintenance to replace mask as soon as possible.

h. Blow to create positive pressure. You should feel some resistance. Do not tilt head back while drinking.

i. If system does not leak, raise and invert canteen and drink water from canteen.

j. After several swallows, stop sucking and lower canteen. Blow into internal drink tube to prevent canteen from collapsing. Repeat drinking procedure as required.

k. Disconnect drinking system.

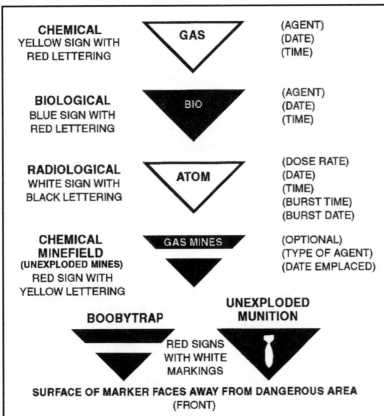

Fig. 32-8. NBC Contaminated Area Marking Signs.

Decontaminating Agents and How They Are Used

STANDARD

SUPER TROPICAL BLEACH

HOW USED: Either in pure form, as dry mix (2 parts bleach to 3 parts earth), or wet mix (slurry; 1 pail water to 6 shovelfuls bleach). If possible, leave on surface 24 hours. One pound of bleach makes enough slurry to cover 1 square yard of average contamination.

ACTION: Reacts with liquid blister agents to form nonvesicant compound, but pure form in direct contact with pools of liquid blister agents reacts violently to cause flame and heavy vapor. Generally used as dry mix or wet mix. Is chemically active, causing vigorous corrosion.

STORAGE: Keep in tightly closed container, away from moisture.

FIELD EXPEDIENTS
BAKING SODA (SODIUM BICARBONATE)

HOW USED: Used with the toothbrush to decontaminate the interior of the mouth.

ACTION: Mild abrasive action on teeth. Physically removing the contaminant from the teeth and gums.

CAUTION: Care must be used to keep exterior contamination out of the mouth.

WASHING SODA (SODIUM CARBONATE)

HOW USED: Add 2 pounds of soda to 2 ½ gallons of very hot water, stir rapidly; apply hot to contaminated surfaces.

ACTION: Destroys blister agents, but much slower than bleach or caustic soda.

CAUSTIC SODA (LYE)

HOW USED: Caustic soda is used in solution with water. Especially effective for destroying lewisite. Decontamination faster with concentrated solutions.

ACTION: Neutralizes chemical agents and biological agents.

CAUTION: Both solid and solution damage skin, eyes and clothing. Do not use for personal decontamination. Caustic soda corrodes surfaces.

WATER OR STREAM

HOW USED: Apply under high pressure; action of hot water is speeded if soap or other detergent is used.

ACTION: Removes dirt or grease containing chemical agents.

FUELS AND SOLVENTS

HOW USED: Spray fuel on contaminated surface and ignite; solvent (like gasoline, kerosene or oil) is applied with swabs. Do not spread contamination.

ACTION: Ignited fuel destroys agents by burning; solvents merely *dilute* them, but if diluted enough, most contamination disappears. Residues remain dangerous.

SKIN DECONTAMINATING PAD

HOW USED: By individual Marine for limited personal decontamination.

ACTION: Absorbs chemical agents from skin.

Fig. 32-9. *Decontaminating agents.*

Protection against the effects of chemical and biological agents and nuclear radiation may depend on avoiding contaminated areas. Figure 32-8 describes the design, lettering and color of the NBC marking signs used to identify contaminated areas. Remember, however, that contaminated areas may not be marked, requiring constant alertness to any signs of possible contamination.

The markers will be placed above the ground suspended from wires, trees or rocks with the right-angled point downward and the front facing away from the contaminated area. When you can see the word GAS, BIO, or ATOM, you are outside the contaminated area. Where more than one kind of contamination is in an area, the appropriate markers will be used near each other.

Decontamination Material and Procedure

In emergencies, Marines may be called upon to accomplish personal decontamination measures. Some will be called upon to act as members of decontamination teams, in which case specially trained personnel will act as supervisors. Figure 32-9 covers simple decontamination agents and procedures. Decontamination of large areas will be accomplished by specially trained units.

M258A1 Decontaminating Kit

The M258A1 kits contain three packs of DECON 1 wipes and three packs of DECON 2 wipes. The wipes are used to decontaminate skin and can decontaminate equipment. If contamination is on the skin, remove decon packet #1, fold at the solid line and tear open quickly. Remove pad and use the pinch blot method on contaminated area for one minute. Then remove decon packet #2, break glass ampoules and tear open quickly. Remove pad, letting screen fall away, and use the pinch blot method on the contaminated area for 2-3 minutes.

Any chemical agent that has not penetrated the skin may be decontaminated with the skin decontaminating pad. The protective mask may also be decontaminated following the procedures for decontaminating the skin.

M291 Decontamination Kit

The M291 kit contains six packs of decontamination resin. The packs are used to decontaminate the skin. If contaminants are on the skin, remove one pack, tear it open, remove applicator pad, slip fingers into handle and scrub exposed skin thoroughly. (Consult the outside package of the M291 kit.)

Self-Aid for Nerve Agents

Mask at once if you notice any of the following symptoms:
- A faint, sweetish, fruity odor.
- The pupils of someone else's eyes shrinking to pinpoint size.
- Your sight blurring or diminishing.
- Running nose.
- Salivation.
- Tightness in your chest and difficulty in breathing.

If you are told that your pupils are getting very small, or if you are having trouble breathing and your chest feels tight, use the Mark I. (*Caution: For use ONLY in NERVE GAS poisoning.*) The injector contains medication to treat the initial symptoms of nerve agent poisoning. But most importantly it will check the more serious effects of nerve agent sickness. The injector is an antidote, not a preventive device – so only use the injector if you actually experience symptoms of nerve agent poisoning.

The directions for use are:
- Pull off the injector's ridged safety cap.
- Place the opposite end of the injector against your thigh.

- Press down hard. Continue to press for at least four seconds to make sure you give yourself the whole injection.
- After you remove the injector, rub the area for a couple of minutes. This will help the antidote to be better absorbed. In about 5 minutes you should feel better. If you don't improve or you feel worse, use a second antidote injector. In time of war, you will be issued three Mark I.

Another type of Mark I may be issued to you. Complete directions for its use will be included with the injector.

Tips on the use of the Mark I:
- Inject the needle into a large muscle in the thigh or upper arm.
- Place the point of the needle against skin, and then with firm pressure force the needle through the skin into the muscle all the way. You will feel little pain, only a slight pricking sensation.
- The needle may be injected through clothing.

Precautions in Applying Self-Aid for Nerve Gases:

DO NOT take an injection of Mark I until you are SURE you NEED it. Pinpointing of they eye pupils or blurred vision along with a tightness in the chest and a hard time breathing are signs that you need it. If you get excited and inject yourself when you have not been exposed to a nerve agent, you will become ill, particularly in hot weather. This would be a real danger in combat. However, if you really do inhale some nerve agent, either injector counteracts it and will make you feel better.

If you have inhaled a really large does of nerve gas vapor, you may need more than one injection of atropine to relieve your symptoms. If nerve agent symptoms persist, you may give yourself two more injections for a total of three. More than three injections may be given under supervision of medical personnel, if available, or under direction of your NCO or officer in charge. If you are issued atropine, you will receive three injectors.

If you get good relief from the atropine and can breathe freely again, carry on with your duties. DRYNESS OF THE MOUTH IS A GOOD SIGN. It means that you have had enough atropine to overcome the dangerous effects of the nerve agent.

If you should get a drop or splash of liquid nerve agent in your eye, INSTANT ACTION is necessary to avoid serious injury. Get some water as fast as possible, tilt your head back so that your eyes look straight upward, and slowly pour water into the contaminated eye to flush it out. Hold the eye open with the fingers if necessary. Pour the water slowly so that the irrigation will last not less than 30 seconds. This irrigation must be done in spite of the danger of breathing nerve gas vapor. Get your mask on quickly after completing the irrigation. Then if symptoms of nerve gas develop, give yourself an injection of the Combo-Pen or atropine.

If liquid nerve gas gets on your skin or clothing, fast action is needed to get rid of it. Immediately use the M258A1 or the M291 decontamination kit. Then carry on with your combat duties. Meanwhile, notice if there is any twitching of the muscles under the contaminated area. If none develops in the next half hour and you have no tightness in your chest, your decontamination was successful.

If twitching of the muscles under the area of contaminated skin does develop, do not wait for the appearance of other symptoms, but give yourself an injection of the Combo-Pen or atropine AT ONCE. If no other symptoms develop, one injection of either is enough. The atropine does not relieve the local twitching of the muscles, but this twitching is not dangerous.

Avoid water and food that may be contaminated with nerve agents. Let the corpsman check food and water for safety before you use them. If you have swallowed contaminated food or water and all of these symptoms occur – increased flow of saliva, nausea, pains in the stomach and a tightness in the chest – give yourself an injection of the Combo-Pen or atropine.

Alarms

Two types of NBC alarm systems may be used to alert Marines in the event of nuclear, biological or chemical attack.

General Alarm – will be spread by normal communication means such as telephone and radio.

Local Alarm – will be initiated within the unit in accordance with the local NBC SOP and may be spread by striking an artillery shell casing, a short length of iron rail, a triangle or a bell. As a supplement to this, certain visual signals, such as putting on the mask, are used to give emergency warning of an attack. In the event of a chemical attack, all Marines should mask immediately to protect themselves from becoming a casualty.

TYPE OF AGENT	HOW NORMALLY DISSEMINATED	MEANS OF DETECTION	SYMPTOMS	EFFECTS	RATE OF ACTION
A. TYPES OF ENEMY CHEMICAL AGENTS					
NERVE	Aerosol or vapor	Automatic chemical agent alarm and chemical agent detector kits to detect vapors and aerosols; chemical agent detector paper to detect liquids.	Difficult breathing, drooling, nausea, vomiting, convulsions and sometimes dim vision.	Incapacitates; kills if high concentration is inhaled.	Very rapid by inhalation; slow through skin.
NERVE	Liquid droplet			Incapacitates; kills if contaminated skin is not decontaminated in time.	Delayed through skin; more rapid through eyes.
BLISTER	Liquid droplet		Mustard; nitrogen mustard - no early symptoms. Lewisite; mustard-lewisite - searing of eyes and stinging of skin. Phosgene oxime - irritation of eyes and nose.	Blisters skin, is destructive to upper respiratory tract; can cause temporary blindness. Some agents sting and form welts on skin, and others sear eyes.	Blistering delayed hours to days; eye effects more rapid. Mustard-lewisite and phosgene oxime very rapid.
BLOOD	Vapor		Convulsions and coma.	Incapacitates; kills if high concentration is inhaled.	Rapid
CHOKING	Vapor		Coughing, choking, nausea and headache.	Damages and floods lungs.	Immediate to 3 hours.
INCAPACITATING	Aerosol	May look like smoke at point of release.	Unpredictable, irrational behavior.	Temporarily incapacitates, mentally and physically.	Delayed
B. TYPES OF ENEMY IRRITANT AGENTS					
VOMITING	Aerosol	May look like smoke at point of release	Coughing, nausea, vomiting and headache.	Irritates and physically incapacitates.	Rapid
IRRITANT	Aerosol	May look like smoke at point of release, turning colorless. Instant eye irritation.	Coughing and copious tears.	Irritates respiratory tract, eyes and skin.	Instantaneous

Fig. 32-10. Characteristics of and defense against types of chemical and irritant agents.

TYPE OF AGENT	INDIVIDUAL		PROTECTION REQUIRED	EQUIVALENT US AGENT	
	First Aid	Decontami-nation		Symbol/Name	Characteristics in the Field
A. TYPES OF ENEMY CHEMICAL AGENTS					
NERVE	Mark I injection. Artificial respiration or resuscitation may be necessary.	None needed	Protective mask and protective clothing	GA—Tabun GB—Sarin GD—Soman	Colorless
		Flush eyes with water; use skin pad from a M258A1, or M291, or wash skin with soap and water.		VX Thickened G-agent	
BLISTER	None	Flush eyes with water; use skin pad from M258A1, or M291, or wash skin with soap and water.	Protective mask and protective clothing	HD—Mustard	-Pale yellow droplets
				HN—Nitrogen mustard	-Dark droplets
				L—Lewisite	-Dark, oily droplets
				HL—Mustard lewisite	-Dark, oily droplets
				CS—Phosgene chloride	-Colorless droplets
BLOOD		None needed	Protective mask		Colorless
CHOKING	For severe symptoms, avoid movement and keep warm.	None needed	Protective mask	CG—Phosgene	Colorless
INCAPACI-TATING	Remove excessive clothing in temperatures above 78° F.	Wash with soap and water.	Protective mask	BZ	White to grayish smoke
B. TYPES OF ENEMY IRRITANT AGENTS					
VOMITING	Move vigorously to lessen duration of effects.	Wash with soap and water.	Protective mask	DM—Adamsite	White to grayish yellow smoke
IRRITANT	Face the wind with eyes open; do not rub eyes.	Flush eyes, face and skin with water.	Protective mask	CS and CN—Riot control agents	White cloud

Fig. 32-10. Continued.

Chapter Thirty-Three

Common Military Terms

ASSIGN
1. The placement of units or personnel in an organization where such placement is relatively permanent and/or such organization controls and administers the units or personnel for the primary function, or greater portion of the functions, of the unit or personnel.
2. The detailing of individuals to specific duties or functions where such duties or functions are primary and/or relatively permanent.

ATTACH
1. The placement of units or personnel in an organization where such placement is relatively temporary. Subject to the limitations of the attachment order, the commander of the formation, unit or organization receiving the attachment will exercise the same degree of command and control as the commander does over units and persons belonging to the command. However, the responsibility for transfer and promotion of personnel will normally be retained by the parent formation, unit or organization.
2. The detailing of individuals to specific functions where such functions are secondary or relatively temporary.

AXIS OF ADVANCE
A line of advance assigned for the purposes of control, often a road or a group of roads, or a designated series of locations, extending in the direction of the enemy.

BARRAGE
A prearranged barrier of fire designed to protect friendly troops and installations by impeding enemy movements across defensive lines or areas.

BATTALION LANDING TEAM (BLT)
In an amphibious operation, an infantry battalion normally reinforced by the necessary combat service and combat service support elements; the basic unit for planning an assault landing.

BATTERY
1. Tactical and administrative artillery unit or sub-unit corresponding to a company or similar unit.
2. All guns, torpedo tubes, searchlights or missile launchers of the same size or caliber or used for the same purpose, either installed on one ship or otherwise operating as an entity.

BEACHHEAD
A designated area on a hostile shore which, when seized and held insures the continuous landing of troops and material, and provides maneuver space requisite for subsequent projected operations ashore. It is the physical objective of an amphibious operation.

BEATEN ZONE
The space on the ground or target on which the shots forming the cone of dispersion strike.

BILLET
1. Shelter for troops.
2. To quarter troops.
3. A personnel position or assignment which may be filled by one person.

BOOBY TRAP
An explosive charge which is exploded when an unsuspecting person disturbs an apparently harmless object or performs a presumably safe act.

BOUND
1. Single movement, usually from cover-to-cover, made by troops often under enemy artillery fire or small arms fire.
2. Distance covered in one movement by a unit which is advancing by bounds.

CHAIN OF COMMAND
The succession of commanding officers from a superior to a subordinate through which command is exercised. Also called command channel.

CHALLENGE
Any process carried out by one unit or person with the object of determining the friendly or hostile character or identity of another.

CLEAR
1. To approve or authorize, or to obtain approval or authorization for:
   a. a person or persons with regard to their actions, movements, duties, etc.;
   b. an object or group of objects, such as equipment or supplies, with regard to quality, quantity, purpose, movement, disposition, etc.;
   c. a request with regard to correctness of form, validity, etc.
2. Specifically, to give one or more aircraft a clearance.
3. To give a person a security clearance.
4. To fly over an obstacle without touching it.
5. To pass a designated point, line or object. The end of a column must pass the designated feature before the latter is cleared.
6. To operate a weapon so as to unload it or make certain no ammunition remains or to free it of a stoppage.

CLOSE AIR SUPPORT (CAS)
Air action against hostile targets which are in close proximity to friendly forces and which require detailed integration of each air mission with the fire and movement of those forces.

COLLECTING POINT
A point designated for the assembly of personnel casualties, prisoners of war, stragglers, disabled materiel or salvage for further movement to collecting stations or rear installations.

COMBAT INTELLIGENCE
That knowledge of the enemy, weather and geographical features required by a commander in the planning and conduct of tactical operations.

COMMAND
1. The authority which a commander in the military service lawfully exercises over subordinates by virtue of rank or assignment. Command includes the authority and responsibility for effectively using available resources and for planning the employment of, organizing, directing, coordinating and controlling military forces for the accomplishment of assigned missions. It also includes responsibility for health, welfare, morale and discipline of assigned personnel.
2. An order given by a commander – that is, the will of the commander expressed for the purpose of bringing about a particular action.
3. A unit or units, an organization or an area under the command of one individual.
4. To dominate by a field of fire or by observation from a superior position.

COMMAND POST
A unit's or subunit's headquarters where the commander and the staff perform their activities.

CONCEALMENT
The protection from observation only.

CONE OF DISPERSION
A conical-shaped pattern formed by the trajectories of a group of shots fired from the same weapon with the same sight setting.

CONTAIN
To stop, hold or surround the forces of the enemy or to cause the enemy to center their activity on a given front and to prevent the withdrawing of any part of the forces for use elsewhere.

CONTOUR INTERVAL
The difference in elevation between two adjacent contour lines.

CONTOUR LINE
A line on a map or chart connecting points of equal elevation.

COUNTERATTACK
Attack by a part or all of a defending force against an enemy attacking force for such specific puposes as regaining ground lost or cutting off or destroying enemy advance units, and with the general objective of denying to the enemy the attainment of the purpose in attacking.

COUNTERGUERRILLA WARFARE
Operations and activities conducted by armed forces, paramilitary forces or nonmilitary agencies of a government against guerrillas.

COVER
1. The action of land, air or sea forces to protect by offense, defense or threat of either or both.
2. Shelter or protection, either natural or artificial.

COUNTERINSURGENCY
Those military, paramilitary, political, economic,

psychological and civic actions taken by a government to defeat subversive insurgency.

CRITICAL POINT
1. A key geographical point or position important to the success of an operation.
2. In point of time, a crisis or a turning point in an operation.
3. A selected point along a line of march used for reference in giving instructions.
4. A point where there is a change of direction or change in slope in a ridge or stream.
5. Any point along a route of march where interference with a troop movement may occur.

D-DAY
1. The unnamed day on which a particular operation commences or is to commence.
2. Time in plans will be indicated by a letter which shows the unit of time employed, and figures, with a minus or plus sign to indicate the amount of time before or after the reference event, e.g., "D" is for a particular day, "H" for an hour. Similarly, D+7 means 7 days after D-day, H+2 means 2 hours after H-hour. If the figure becomes unduly large, for example, D-day plus 90, the designation of D+3 months may be employed.

DEADLINE
To remove a vehicle or piece of equipment from operation or use for one of the following reasons:
a. is inoperative due to damage, malfunctioning or necessary repairs. The term does not include items temporarily removed from use by reason of routine maintenance and repairs which do not affect the combat capability of the item.
b. is unsafe; and
c. would be damaged by further use.

DEAD SPACE
The area within the maximum range of a weapon which cannot be covered by fire from a particular position because of the intervening obstacles or because of the nature of the ground.

DEFILADE
1. Protection from hostile ground observation and fire provided by an obstacle such as a hill, ridge or bank.
2. A vertical distance by which a position is concealed from enemy observation.
3. To shield from enemy fire or observation by using natural or artificial obstacles.

DEMILITARIZED ZONE (DMZ)
A defined area in which the stationing or concentrating of military forces, or the retention or establishment of military installations of any description is prohibited.

DEMOLITION
The destruction of structures, facilities or material by use of fire, water, explosives, mechanical or other means.

DEPLOY
1. In a strategic sense, to relocate forces to desired areas of operations.
2. To extend or widen the front of a military unit, extending from close order to a battle formation.
3. To change from a cruising approach or contact disposition to a disposition for a naval battle.

DIRECT FIRE
Fire in which the gunner aims the weapon by means of a sight directly at the target.

DISPERSION
1. A scattered pattern of hits by bombs dropped under identical conditions or by projectiles fired from the same gun or group of guns with the same firing data.
2. The spreading or separating of troops, material, establishments or activities which are usually concentrated in limited areas to reduce vulnerability to enemy action.

DISPLACEMENT
The movement of supporting weapons from one firing position to another.

DISTANCE
The space between adjacent personnel, vehicles or units in a formation measured from front to rear.

DUMP
A temporary storage area, usually in the open, for bombs, ammunition, equipment or supplies.

ECHELON
1. A subdivision of a headquarters, i.e., forward echelon, rear echelon.
2. Separate level of command. As compared to a regiment, a division is a higher echelon; a battalion is a lower echelon.
3. A fraction of a command in the direction of depth, to which a principal combat mission is assigned, i.e., attack echelon, reserve echelon.

4. A formation in which the subdivisions are placed one behind the other, extending backward either left or right at an angle from the lead element.

ELEVATION
The vertical distance of ground forms, usually measured in feet or meters, above mean sea level (plus elevation) or below mean sea level (minus elevation).

EMPLACEMENT
1. A prepared position for one or more weapons or pieces of equipment, for protection against hostile fire or bombardment, and from which they can execute their tasks.
2. The act of fixing a gun in a prepared position from which it may be fired.

ENFILADE FIRE
Fire delivered on a target so that the beaten zone of the fire coincides with the long axis of the target (fire in the direction of the length of a line or column).

ENVELOPMENT
An attack made on one or both of the enemy's flanks or rear, usually accompanied by an attack in the front.

FIELD OF FIRE
The area which a weapon or group of weapons may cover effectively with fire from a given position.

FINAL PROTECTIVE LINE
A predetermined line along which, in order to stop enemy assaults, interlocking fire is placed from all available flat-trajectory weapons, fixed as to direction and elevation and capable of delivery under any conditions of visibility. Gaps in these interlocking bands of fire are filled in by barrages fired by mortars and artillery.

FIRE DISCIPLINE
A state of order, coolness, efficiency and obedience existing among troops engaged in a fire fight.

FIRE MISSION
1. Specific assignment given to a fire unit as part of a definite plan.
2. Order used to alert the weapon battery and indicate that the message following is a call for fire.

FIXED FIRE
Fire from a weapon or weapons directed at a single point or a small area.

FLANKING FIRE
Fire directed against a target from an area on its flank. Flanking fire may be enfilade or oblique fire.

FLAT TRAJECTORY
A trajectory having little or no curvature.

FLEET MARINE FORCE (FMF)
A balanced force of combined arms comprising land, air and service elements of the U.S. Marine Corps. A Fleet Marine Force is an integral part of a U.S. Fleet and has the status of a type command.

FORWARD AIR CONTROLLER (FAC)
An officer (aviator) member of the tactical air control party/team who, from a forward position, controls aircraft engaged in close air support of ground troops.

FORWARD EDGE OF THE BATTLE AREA (FEBA)
A line at the forward edge of the battle area, designated for the purpose of coordinating the fire of all units and supporting weapons including air and naval gunfire. It defines the forward limits of a series of mutually supporting defensive areas, but does not include the areas occupied or used by covering or screening forces.

FORWARD OBSERVER (FO)
An observer operating with front line troops and trained to adjust ground or naval gunfire and air bombardment and pass battlefield information to the rear.

FRONT
1. The lateral space occupied by an element, measured from the extremity of one flank to the extremity of the other flank.
2. The direction of the enemy.
3. The line of contact of two opposing forces.

GENERAL ORDERS
1. Permanent instructions issued in order form that apply to all members of a command, as compared with special orders which affect only individuals or small groups. General orders are usually concerned with matters of policy or administration.
2. A series of permanent guard orders that govern the duties of a sentry on post.

GRAZING FIRE
Fire which is approximately parallel to the ground and does not rise above the height of a person standing.

GUERRILLA WARFARE
Military and paramilitary operations conducted in enemy-held or hostile territory by irregular, predominantly indigenous forces.

HARASSING FIRE
Fire designed to disturb the rest of the enemy troops, to curtail movement, and, by threat of losses, to lower morale.

HELICOPTER ASSAULT FORCE
A task organization combining helicopters, supporting units and helicopter-borne troop units for use in helicopter-borne assault operations.

HELICOPTER LANDING ZONES
A specified ground area for landing assault helicopters to embark or disembark troops and/or cargo. A landing zone may contain one or more landing sites.

HELICOPTER TEAM
The combat-equipped troops lifted in one helicopter at one time.

H-HOUR
The specified hour on D-Day at which a particular operation commences.

INDIRECT FIRE
Fire delivered at a target that cannot be seen from the gun position.

INFILTRATION
The movement through or into an area or territory occupied by either friendly or enemy troops or organizations. The movement is made by either small groups or by individuals at extended or irregular intervals. When used in connection with the enemy, it implies that contact is avoided.

IN SUPPORT OF
Assisting or protecting another formation, unit or organization while remaining under original control.

INSURGENCY
A condition resulting from a revolt or insurrection against a constituted government which falls short of a civil war.

INTERDICT
To prevent or hinder, by any means, enemy use of an area or route.

KEY POINT
A concentrated site or installation, the destruction or capture of which would seriously affect the war effort or the success of operations.

LINE OF DEPARTURE (LOD)
1. A line designated to coordinate the departure of attack or scouting elements; a jump-off line.
2. A suitably marked offshore coordinating line to assist assault craft to land on designated beaches at scheduled times.

LOCAL SECURITY
A security element independent of any outpost established by a leader to protect the unit against surprise and assure its readiness for action.

LINES OF COMMUNICATION (LOC)
All of the routes, land, water and air, which connect an operating military force with a base of operations, and along which supplies and reinforcements move.

LOGISTICS
The science of planning and carrying out the movement and maintenance of forces. In its most comprehensive sense, those aspects of military operations which deal with:
a. design and development, acquisition, storage, movement, distribution, maintenance, evacuation and disposition of material;
b. movement, evacuation and hospitalization of personnel;
c. acquisition or construction, maintenance, operation and disposition of facilities; and
d. acquisition or furnishing of services.

MAIN ATTACK
The principal attack or effort into which the commander throws the full weight of the offensive power at their disposal. An attack directed against the chief objective of the campaign or battle.

MANEUVER
The operation of a ship, aircraft, vehicle or unit to cause it to perform desired movements.

MARINE AIR-GROUND TASK FORCE (MAGTF)
A Marine Corps air-ground team consisting of one ground combat unit, one air combat unit, one combat support unit and one command unit. Examples of MAGTF are MEU, MEF and SPMAGTF.

MARINE EXPEDITIONARY FORCE (MEF)

A Marine air-ground task force built around a Marine division and a Marine aircraft wing. The Marine expeditionary force normally employs the full combat resources of one Marine division/wing team and a force service support group.

MARINE EXPEDITIONARY UNIT (MEU)

A Marine air-ground task force built around a battalion landing team and a composite squadron (includes two or more types of helicopters and may include VSTOL attack aircraft). The Marine expeditionary unit normally employs about one-ninth of the combat resources of one Marine division/wing team and a logistical support unit.

MASK

Any natural or artificial obstruction which affords shelter or interferes with observation or fire.

MASS

1. The concentration of combat power.
2. To concentrate or bring together, as to mass the fire of all batteries.
3. The military formation in which units are spaced at less than normal distances and intervals.

MILITARY CIVIC ACTION

The use of preponderantly indigenous military forces on projects useful to the local population at all levels in such areas as education, training, public works, agriculture, transportation, and others contributing to economic and social development, which would also serve to improve the standing of the military forces with the population. (U.S. Forces may at times advise or engage in military civic actions in overseas areas.)

MISSION

1. The objective; the task together with the purpose, which clearly indicate the action to be taken and the reason therefor.
2. In common usage, especially when applied to lower military units, a duty assigned to an individual or unit; a task.
3. The dispatching of one or more aircraft to accomplish one particular task.

MUZZLE VELOCITY

The velocity of a projectile at the instant the projectile leaves the muzzle of a weapon.

OBJECTIVE

The physical object of the action taken, e.g., a definite tactical feature, the seizure and/or holding of which is essential to the commander's plan.

OBLIQUE FIRE

Fire placed on a target from a direction that is diagonal to the long dimension of the target or on an enemy from a direction which is between the enemy's front and flank.

OBSERVATION POST (OP)

A position from which military observations are made or fire directed and adjusted, and which possesses appropriate communications; may be airborne.

OBSERVED FIRE

Fire for which the points of impact or burst can be seen by an observer. The fire can be controlled and adjusted on the basis of observation.

OCCUPY

To take possession of or to remain in a place or area.

OPERATION ORDER

A directive, usually formal, issued by a commander to subordinate commanders for the purpose of effecting the coordinated execution of an operation.

ORDER

A communication, written, oral or by signal, which conveys instructions from a superior to a subordinate. In a broad sense, the terms "order" and "command" are synonymous. However, an order implies discretion as to the details of execution whereas a command does not.

ORGANIZE

To prepare a position or terrain for defense.

OUTPOST

A stationary body of troops placed at some distance from the main body, while at the halt or in a defensive position, to protect the main body from surprise, observation, and annoyance from enemy ground troops.

PASSAGE OF LINES

A rearrangement of units in which the rear unit moves forward through the already established line while the replaced unit remains in position or moves to the rear.

PATROL

A detachment of ground, sea or air forces sent by a larger unit for the purpose of gathering information or carrying out a destructive, harassing, mopping-up or security mission.

PENETRATION

A form of offensive maneuver which seeks to break through the enemy's defensive positions, widen the gap created and destroy the continuity of their positions.

PERIMETER DEFENSE

A defense without an exposed flank consisting of forces deployed along the perimeter of the defended area.

PHASE LINE

The line utilized for control and coordination of military operations, usually a terrain feature extending across the zone of action.

POSITION

The area or locality occupied by combat elements, especially for defense.

PREPARATION FIRE

Fire delivered on a target preparatory to an assault.

PRIMARY FIRING POSITION

The best available position from which the primary fire mission of a weapon, individual, unit or units is executed.

RAID

An operation, usually small scale, involving a swift penetration of hostile territory to secure information, confuse the enemy or to destroy installations. It ends with a planned withdrawal upon completion of the assigned mission.

RANGE

1. The distance between any given point and an object or target.
2. Extent or distance limiting the operation or action of something, such as the range of an airplane, vehicle or of a weapon.
3. Area equipped for practice in shooting at targets.

RATE OF FIRE

The number of rounds fired from a weapon in a minute.

REAR GUARD

Security detachment that protects the rear of a column from hostile forces. During a withdrawal, it delays the enemy by armed resistance, destroying bridges and blocking roads.

RECONNAISSANCE

A mission undertaken to obtain, by visual observation or other detection methods, information about the activities and resources of an enemy or potential enemy; or to secure data concerning the meteorological, hydrographic or geographic characteristics of a particular area.

RECONNAISSANCE BY FIRE

A method of reconnaissance in which fire is placed on a suspected enemy position to cause the enemy to disclose a presence by movement or return of fire.

REGISTRATION FIRE

Fire delivered to obtain accurate data for subsequent effective engagement of targets.

REINFORCE

To strengthen by the addition of personnel or military equipment.

RESERVE

A fraction of a unit held initially under the control of a unit leader as a maneuvering element to influence future action.

SEARCHING FIRE

Fire distributed in depth by successive changes in the elevation of the weapon.

SECTOR OF FIRE

An area, limited by boundaries, assigned to a unit or to a weapon to cover by fire.

SECURE

To gain possession of a position or terrain feature with or without force, and to make such disposition as will prevent, as far as possible, its destruction or loss by enemy action.

SECURITY

All measures taken by a unit to protect itself from observation, annoyance or surprise attack by the enemy.

SENSOR

A technical means to extend man's natural senses; equipment which detects and indicates terrain configuration, the presence of military targets, and other natural and man-made objects and activities by means of energy emitted or reflected by such targets or objects.

SITE
The position of anything. For example, the position of a gun emplacement.

SMALL ARMS
All arms including automatic weapons, up to and including caliber .60 and shotguns.

SPECIAL PURPOSE MAGTF
A SPMAGTF is organized to accomplish missions for which the MEF and MEU are not appropriate or are too large to employ. It can be deployed by amphibious or commercial ships, tactical or strategic airlift, or organic Marine Corps aviation.
  a. The Command Element (CE) is structured to conduct command and control of operational functions and is tailored to the mission and task organization of the SPMAGTF.
  b. The Ground Combat Element (GCE) is composed of at least a platoon-sized element.
  c. The Aviation Combat Element (ACE) is a task-organized detachment of aircraft.
  d. The Combat Service Support Element (CSSE) is task-organized to meet the specific service support requirements of the SPMAGTF and is centered on the unit designated to provide most of the service support.

SUPPLEMENTARY FIRING POSITION
A position assigned to a unit or weapon to accomplish fire missions other than those to be accomplished from the primary or alternate positions.

SUPPORT
1. The action of a force which aids, protects, complements or sustains another force in accordance with a directive requiring such action.
2. A unit which helps another unit in battle.
3. A part of any unit held back at the beginning of an attack as a reserve.
4. An element of a command that assists, protects, or supplies other forces in combat.

SUPPORTING FIRE
Fire delivered by supporting units to assist or protect a unit in combat.

TACTICS
1. The employment of units in combat.
2. The ordered arrangement and maneuver of units in relation to each other and/or to the enemy in order to realize the full potentialities.

TARGET OF OPPORTUNITY
A target visible to a surface or air vehicle or observer, which is within range of available weapons and against which fire has not been scheduled or requested.

TERRAIN
An area of ground considered as to its extent and natural features in relation to its use in a particular operation.

TRAJECTORY
The curved path followed by any projectile in its flight through the air.

UNIT
1. Any military element whose structure is prescribed by competent authority, such as a table of organization and equipment; specifically part of an organization.
2. A standard or basic quantity into which an item of supply is divided, issued or used. In this meaning, also called "unit of issue."

ZONE OF ACTION
A tactical subdivision of a larger area, the responsibility for which is assigned to a tactical unit; generally applied to offensive action.

ZONE OF FIRE
An area within which a particular unit delivers, or is prepared to deliver, fire.

Notes:

The Marine Corps Association

Purpose and Aims

- Disseminate knowledge of the military art and science among its members.
- Provide for professional advancement.
- Foster the spirit and preserve the traditions of the United States Marine Corps.
- Increase the efficiency of the United States Marine Corps.
- Further the interest of the military and naval services in all ways not inconsistent with the good of the general government.

MCA Publications

The Marine Corps Association is best known for its publishing activities, including its distinguished monthly magazines, *Marine Corps Gazette* and *Leatherneck*, its special publications, and its book and gift service that provides Marines and members with the U. S. Marine Reading Program and other books of military interest.

Professional Journal of U.S. Marines

The *Marine Corps Gazette* is the professional journal for all Marines, published continuously since 1916. The *Gazette* is written by Marines for Marines, providing a forum for expression and debate on matters that advance knowledge, interest, and esprit within the Corps. Articles include new weapons systems and development; theories and concepts of land, sea (amphibious), and aviation operations; national security issues, insurgencies, and terrorism; physical and mental fitness, discipline and ethics. Manuscript submissions are welcome. To ask the editor for details, call toll-free 1-866-622-1775 ext. 344. *Leatherneck, Magazine of the Marines*, was founded in 1917 as a general interest magazine to inform and entertain Marines, former Marines, their families and friends of the Corps. Its focus is on individual Marines, where they serve, the duties they perform, their fitness and training programs, recreation, schools and equipment. *Leatherneck* also reports on major battles fought throughout the history of the Corps, featuring legendary Marines who will always be respected for their valor. Although *Leatherneck* has its own staff of photo journalists, timely, well-written articles may be accepted. To ask the editor for details, call toll-free 1-866-622-1775 ext. 315. To subscribe to either *Gazette* or *Leatherneck*, call toll-free 1-866-622-1775 or visit the MCA web site at www.mca-marines.org.